Hiking guide to
Poland & Ukraine

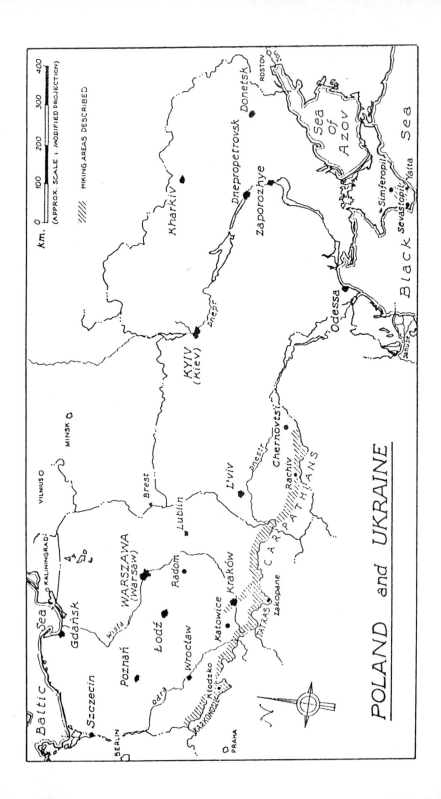

POLAND and UKRAINE

Hiking guide to
Poland & Ukraine

Tim Burford

BRADT PUBLICATIONS

First published in 1994 by Bradt Publications, 41 Nortoft Rd, Chalfont St Peter, Bucks SL9 0LA, England.

British Library Cataloguing in Publication data

A catalogue record for this book is
available from the British Library

ISBN 0 898323 02X

Drawings by Julian Drake
Front cover photo Pieniny massif, Poland, by Liba Taylor, courtesy Panos Pictures
Rear cover photo by Tim Burford: St Andrew's Church, Kyiv
Maps by Hans van Well
Typeset from the author's disc by Patti Taylor, London NW10 1JR
Printed by the Guernsey Press, Channel Islands

What is good? Garlic. A leg of lamb on a spit.
Wine with a view of boats rocking in a cove.
A starry sky in August. A rest on a mountain peak.

Czesław Miłosz
from 'Provinces' (Carcanet 1993)

This book is for Carolyn

Many thanks are due to many people, both in Poland and Ukraine and outside, including Marco Bojcun, Dr Jonathan Aves, Dr Andrew Wilson, Danuta Holata, Radek Truś, Iwone Krasodomska, Margareta Kreisman, Volodya Shooshniak, Yuri Makovirzki, Vika and Tanya in Kherson, Nick Crane, Hol Crane, Mary Hall, Linda Reynolds, Paul Watts, Bernie Gilman, Heather Anderson, Bob Egan, Paul Knott, Stefan Krywawych, Roger Manser, and David Buxton. Thanks also to Hilary Bradt, and Patti Taylor, Hans van Well and Roger Jordan. All errors, of fact or of interpretation, are entirely my own.
    You too, dear reader, can earn everlasting gratitude by sending corrections and updates to me c/o Bradt Publications.

MAPS in this book

adhere, more or less, to the following conventions:-

International Boundary

Provincial or Regional Boundary

National Park, Nature or Game Reserve
    (Entrance also shown)

Motorway, Major Highway
    (Plus Road Reference)

Other Major Road

Secondary Road

Track (may be seasonal)

Path, Bridleway or Trail

Railway & Railway Station

Bridge; Embankment; Viaduct

Cutting; Tunnel

Cable Car, Chairlift

Power Cables; Pipeline

Bus Station; Taxi Rank

Airport or Airstrip

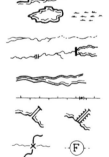

Coast or Shoreline

Lake; Seasonal Lake, Swamp or Marsh

River; Seasonal River

Waterfall or Cataracts; Dam

River (Town Maps)

Canal; Lock

Wharf, Pier or Jetty; Marina or Docks

Ford; Ferry

Spring or Well-head

Travelling Distances - km [hrs] {days}

Recommended Route

MAPS *in this book*

adhere, more or less, to the following conventions:-

Mountain, Peak, Hill or Volcanic Cone   ▲ (or ∧)

Spot Height (m.) ; Contour Line (m.)

Cliff or steep slope;   Ridge

Ravine ;   Crater

Rocks ;   Lava Flow ;   Cave

Cities, Towns, Villages
  (According to Size or Importance)

Chapter Reference; Map Key Reference   5   13

Forest or Woodland; Park or Garden

Plantation or Farm; Cemetery, Burial Gnd.

Oilfield ; Factory or Industrial Area

Market   MKT.

Post Office ; Telephone ; Bank

Hospital, Medical Centre ; Official Building

Sports Centre or Stadium

Hotel, Hostel or Pension   H

Hut, Refuge or Lodge

Campsite   △

Restaurant or Bar   ♀

Educational or Cultural Establishment

Ancient Monument or Historic Site   ▽

Castle, Palace ; Religious Building   ◆

Lighthouse ;   Tower or Mast

Other Buildings

Miscellaneous Features

Mountain Pass   OR

CONTENTS

Introduction

THE CARPATHIAN MOUNTAINS

Although many people would not know quite where or what the Carpathians are, they would probably associate them with that inchoate *terra incognita* behind what was the Iron Curtain. They are in fact a continuation of the Alps, the backbone of that whole area north of the Balkans, starting not far from Vienna and running east into Ukraine before swinging south and west through Romania to finish on the Danube where Romania meets Serbia. This book covers the Carpathians and associated ranges (the Beskids and Karkonosze) in southern Poland and Ukraine, as well as the Crimean mountains; my previous book *Hiking guide to Romania* (Bradt Publications, 1993) dealt with the Romanian Carpathians, of course, and the Slovak Carpathians are covered by Simon Hayman's *Guide to Czechoslovakia* (second edition 1991), also from Bradt Publications.

In the future the Carpathians will increasingly be seen as the lungs of Europe, an area where people can genuinely get away from the concrete that has swallowed up the Alps and similar areas. However if hiking here is not like trekking in Nepal or Peru, where you spend most of your time in cultivated areas going from one village to another and constantly meeting the locals on the trail, neither is it like backpacking in the wilderness areas of Alaska or the Rockies, where you meet nothing but the occasional bear. The Carpathians are not totally untouched by human hands, and in particular you will often meet shepherds, but they do offer a huge expanse of virtually unspoilt mountains where you can indeed see bears and much more.

The people are immensely hospitable and are delighted to welcome Westerners who take an interest in their country. In this book I offer a wide range of routes, some in largely depopulated areas and others in alpine areas with developed tourist facilities.

MITTELEUROPA AND THE DEATH OF COMMUNISM

Much of what we are used to calling Eastern Europe (or Mitteleuropa) is now increasingly known as Central or East-Central Europe as it draws closer to the west; Eastern Europe was always a misnomer, as Norway stretches further east than Poland and Prague is a long way west of Vienna, and Mitteleuropa was more a concept or state of mind than a geographical entity, referring to the spirit of the multi-ethnic hotch-potch of the area, almost all at one time or another under the sway of the Austro-Hungarian Empire of the Hapsburgs; this included much of southeastern Poland and southwestern Ukraine, then known as Galicia, and excluded the Orthodox, Russian-dominated areas, such as the rest of Ukraine, more accurately known as Eastern Europe.

This broke up after the First World War, when there was an eruption of nationalist passions leading to the establishment of new countries such as Czechoslovakia and Yugoslavia. However after 1945 the situation returned more or less to what it had been, with central and eastern Europe under the sway of another empire and its stifling bureaucracy. This has now in its turn collapsed, and all the repressed ethnic tensions and passions are once more being unleashed with their original venom undiluted; we have already had terrible warnings of this in Yugoslavia and in Georgia.

In human terms, this is part of the eastern/central European 'Shatter Zone', the tangled web of overlapping ethnic groups that grew up under the Turkish and Austro-Hungarian empires and is only now slowly disentangling itself. Huge population movements at the end of the Second World War left Poland, and to a lesser extent Ukraine, ethnically virtually homogenous; however the Romanian province of Transylvania remains an intractably complicated patchwork of different cultures that give it much of its fascination. While Romania is largely a Latin country, it is also clearly part of the eastern Orthodox world; Ukraine is also Orthodox but is drawn much more towards Russia and the Slav world; Poland, though Slav, is resolutely western European, and it is only the fervour of its Catholicism that sets it apart from the increasingly secular west. These countries also share the legacies of up to 74 years of communist rule, which they are all disposing of in different ways and at different rates.

In all these countries there is a sense of total economic dislocation and a fear of being overwhelmed by the developed economies of the West, although it was largely a desire for the goodies of the consumer economy that brought about the downfall of the communist system. Marx and Engels described this best in the *Communist Manifesto* (1848): 'The bourgeoisie, by the rapid improvement of all instruments of production, by the immensely facilitated means of communication, draws all, even the most barbarian, nations into civilisation. The cheap prices of its commodities are the heavy artillery with which it batters down all Chinese walls, with which it forces the barbarians' intensely obstinate hatred of foreigners to capitulate. It compels all nations, on pain of extinction, to adopt the bourgeois mode of production; it compels them to introduce what it calls civilisation into their midst, ie to become bourgeois themselves. In one word, it creates a world after its own image'. Ironically, it takes Marx himself to describe the death of Marxism.

In addition to the inherent conservatism of the communist (or more accurately Stalinist) system, there is also (in Ukraine) the spirit of conformism inherent in the Orthodox religious outlook, which stifles the development of private enterprise; people are conditioned in every way to wait for orders rather than to get up and go on their own. As a result many people want to do exactly that — get up and go to western Europe where they hope the system will give them a job and lots of money. There are widespread fears in the West of floods of economic refugees from the east (and from Africa) that will destabilise the whole of Europe (as from South to North America); the Iron Curtain has now been reversed, as the west seeks to invade (commercially) the east and to keep out migrants from the east. People will ask you for help in obtaining a visa, and you must tell them frankly about mass unemployment and immigration laws in the European Union, and that it takes more than consumer goods to make people really happy.

Part One

Chapter 1

Outline

GEOGRAPHY

The Carpathian system is part of the Alpine-Himalayan chain, formed relatively recently in the Tertiary alpine orogeny, but there is as yet no explanation for the formation of the Carpathian-Balkan S-bend. The Carpathian system is as long as the Alps (1,300km, but with its ends on the Danube at Bratislava and the Iron Gates only 500km apart) but only half their height, making them easier to cross. For the most part the Carpathian chain is 35-40km wide, and generally consists of three distinct bands, with Flysch (or turbidite) on the outside, young crystalline massifs in the centre and some volcanic ranges intruding on the inner side. The far older and lower remnants of the Hercynian mountains, granite, limestone and schists dating from the Primary era, lie parallel to the north, running from the Vosges via the Ardennes, the Black Forest, the Erzgebirge, and the Karkonosze in southern Poland to northern Dobrogea on Romania's Black Sea coast. Quarternary glaciation occurred only in the Karkonosze, Tatras, Rodnas and the southern Carpathians.

Starting from the western end the chain is divided into four sections, of which the first and second are partly in Poland and the second and third in Ukraine:

1. The western Carpathians, from Bratislava to the line of the Biała river, the Tylicz pass, and the Topl'a and Hornad rivers near Kosice — the widest, highest and most complex section, above all the High Tatras on the Polish-Slovak border, glaciated granite often covered with limestone.

2. The Central or Forest Carpathians, from the Tylicz pass to the upper Tisa (Tisza) River; lower sedimentary hills providing major routes from Poland to eastern Slovakia and from Ukraine to Hungary.

3. The eastern Carpathians, from the sources of the Tisa almost to Brașov in Romania, consisting of parallel ridges of sedimentary rocks (sandstone and conglomerates) to the east, a central crystalline schist zone with some resistant limestones, and to the west an inner zone of volcanic material.

4. The southern Carpathians, from Braşov to the Iron Gates, are, with the Tatras, the only truly Alpine section of the Carpathians, formed of hard crystalline rocks, with some karstitic limestone. Like the Alps, they underwent intense folding followed by glaciation.

In Poland only the Tatras form part of the Carpathians, with the bulk of the range just over the border in Slovakia, although the border does follow the watershed; the half-buried hills to the north and east, known as the Beskids, are divided into massifs such as the Beskid Sląski, Żywiecki, Wyspowy and Niski (the Silesian, Zywiec, Island, and Low Beskids). East of the Łupków pass these are known as the Bieszczady and soon pass into Ukraine; this is also a major botanical divide. To the west the Hercynian mountains along the Czech border are known as the Sudety, with the main range the Karkonosze, and others such as the Góry Izerskie, Góry Stołowe and Góry Złote; to the east the Hercynian uplands disappear under the later sediments of the Silesian basin.

In Ukraine the Carpathians form three fairly continuous parallel ridges, sedimentary to the north, crystalline in the centre, and volcanic to the south, with two inter-montane basins between them. The central ridge, loosely grouped together as the Polonynian Beskyd, is the highest and most continuous, culminating to the east (beyond the Tisa) in the Chornohora massif and Hoverla (2,061m). In this book I also cover the Crimean mountains, a limestone massif rising from the sea to 1,545m. Although there are minor Hercynian relics in Podolia, the vast bulk of Ukraine is black-earth steppe, immensely fertile plains.

NATURAL HISTORY

Flora

The natural vegetation of the eastern European mountains is forest, in fairly clearly defined zones: below 500-700m altitude there are mainly lowland forests of oak (*Quercus robur* and *Q sessiflora*), lime and beech (*Tilio-Carpinetum* associations), from there to 1,150-1,250m is the Lower Forest Montane Zone of fir and beech forests (*Abies, Luzulo nemorosae-Fagetum* and *Dentario glandulosae-Fagetum*), with some sycamore and spruce, and from there to 1,400-1,550m the Upper Forest Montane Zone, mainly spruce with rowan and sycamore (*Piceetum excelsae carpaticum, Sorbo-Aceretum carpaticum*). Above this is the sub-alpine zone, mainly with dwarf pine, *Juniperus sibirica* and rowan (*Pinetum mughi carpaticum*), and in a few areas there is also an alpine level, with small hardy plants and lichen. Naturally much of the forest has long since been cleared, but in the National Parks and other hiking areas you will still find plenty of it, although now badly scarred by acid rain in places.

Above and amidst the forest are meadows which in springtime can still be full of flowers such as gentians, campanulas, *Crocus scepusiensis* (aconite saffron), *Doronicum austriacum, Arnica montana, Dryas octopetala* (mountain aven), the thistle *Carlina acaulis*, and orchids such as *Listera cordata* and *ovata*; the greatest diversity is at around 1350m altitude. Alpine plants include *Galanthus nivalis, Lycopodium alpinum*, saxifrages, and bushes such as *Rhododendron kotschyi* and *Vaccinium myrtillus* (bilberry).

In the Bieszczady and western Ukraine, west of the Łupków pass, the flora is distinctively east Carpathian, more Eurasian than Atlantic or Mediterranean, and the subalpine meadows, known as *połoninas*, are a unique feature. Running along the long narrow hilltops immediately above the beech trees (here at the eastern limit of their range), with no intervening coniferous level, they are covered with distinctive long grasses such as *Poa chaixii* and *Deschampsia caespitosa* (tufted hairgrass) as well as *Nardus stricta*, the more widespread matgrass, and rowan shrubs (*Sorbus acuparia*); typical *połonina* flowers include *Trollius europaeus* (the globeflower), found as far west as Britain, *Centaurea kotschyana, Veratrum album* (the white false helleborine), *Viola dacica*, *Carex* sedges and reeds such as *Calamagrostis villosa*.

More details are given in sections on specific areas.

Fauna

The birds of the Polish and Ukrainian mountains are less rigidly stratified than the flora, but the same broad divisions apply, with only a few of the hardiest species living at the exposed higher altitudes. Of these the most obvious and impressive is the golden eagle (*Aquila chrysaëtos/orzel przedni*), with also the alpine accentor (*Prunella collaris/płochacz halny*), water pipit (*Anthus spinoletta/siwerniak*), and the ubiquitous raven (*Corvus corax/kruk*). (Names are given here in English, Latin and Polish; see page 264 for some Ukrainian and Russian names.)

In the Upper Forest Montane Zone there are game birds such as the hazel hen (*Tetrastes bonasia/jarząbek*) and the capercaillie (*Tetrao urogallus/głuszec*), as well as nutcrackers (*Nucifraga caryocatactes/orzechowka*) (which drop into the deciduous woods for the winter). Although there is far more to the animal kingdom than the big, dramatic carnivores, it is worth pointing out the great variety of raptors (or birds of prey) in the Carpathians, even though these all look much the same soaring at great heights: mainly the goshawk (*Accipiter gentilis/jastrzab*), sparrowhawk (*A nisus/krogulec*), lesser spotted or Pomeranian eagle (*Aquila pomarina/orlik krzykliwy*), buzzard (*Buteo buteo/myszołow*), hobby (*Falco subbuteo/kobus*), peregrine (*F peregrinus/sokol wędrowny*), and eagle owl (*Bubo bubo/puchacz*). To the east, particularly in the Bieszczady and the Ukrainian Carpathians, there is an even greater variety, including the spotted eagle (*Aquila clanga*), the short-toed eagle (*Circaëtus gallicus*), the hen harrier (*Circus cyaneus*), the booted eagle (*Hieraaetus pennatus*), the tawny and Ural owls (*Strix aluco/puszczyk* and *S uralensis/puszczyk Uralski*), and in

Ukraine Tengmalm's owl (*Aegolius funereus*) and the pygmy owl
(*Glaucidium passerinum*), both in conifer forest. To the north you may
see various types of harrier and kite, the hobby and saker falcons, the
short-toed, white-tailed and booted eagles, and the osprey and honey
buzzard, variously in open woodland, the steppes or marshy terrain.

Equally there seems to be a much greater variety of woodpeckers
(*dzięcioł*) to the east of Poland and in Ukraine, away from acid rain and
such problems; those found only to the east are *Dendrocopus* (or
Dryobates) *leucotus*, the white-backed woodpecker, in montane
deciduous trees, mainly dead ones, and *Picoides tridactylus*, the three-
toed woodpecker, in the higher conifers. The most widespread is
Dryocopus martius, the black woodpecker (with a bright red cap), found
in coniferous forests throughout Poland and Ukraine north of the Black
Sea, and others are *Dendrocopus minor*, the lesser spotted woodpecker,
D medius, the middle spotted woodpecker, mainly in oak and hornbeam,
D major, the great spotted woodpecker, *Picus viridis*, the green
woodpecker, and *P canis*, the grey-headed woodpecker, in deciduous
mountain forest. These are generally much tamer and easier to observe
than those in Britain.

Other less exotic birds include the collared and red-breasted flycatchers
(*Ficedulla albicollis* and *F parva*), mainly in deciduous forests, the rock
thrush (*Monticola saxatilis/Nagórnik skalny*, with a striking orange breast
and blue head), white wagtail (*Motacilla alba/pliszka siwa*), dunnock
(*Prunella modularis/płochacz pokrzywica*), and the ring ouzel (*Turdus
torquatus/drozd obrożny*), on rough moorland. A favourite of mine is the
rockcreeper (or wallcreeper) (*Tichodroma muraria/pomurnik*), which
flutters like a butterfly, on wings like a woodpecker's, along rock faces.
By mountain streams you may find the grey wagtail (*Motacilla
cinerea/pliszka górska*) and the dipper (*Cinclus cinclus/pluszcz*), and by
the slower-moving streams the kingfisher (*Alcedo atthis/zimorodek*);
perhaps the most characteristic of eastern European birds are the white
and black storks (*Ciconia ciconia* and *C nigra/bocian biały* and *czarny*),
both found in marshes although the white stork (which does have black
on its wings) prefers to nest on chimneys and telephone poles in villages.

In Poland there are 220 species of nesting birds and 150 migratory
birds, so I can barely scrape the surface. However the most endangered
of the mountain species are the peregrine and the spotted and golden
eagles, with the lesser spotted eagle and eagle and Ural owls apparently
now stable or increasing their populations. To the north of the hills and
mountains endangered birds include the great bustard (*Otis tarda*) and
the stone curlew (*Burhinus oedicnemus*), with the great and jack snipe
(*Gallinago media* and *Lymnocryptes minimus*), red-breasted merganser
(*Mergus serrator*) and pintail (*Anas acuta*) on the coast and lakes.

With regard to mammals, there are 87 species recorded in Poland;
again there is a tendency to see the big carnivores as the most
glamorous and exciting, in part because they might wish to eat you, but
of course as often as not the lives of the smallest rodents are as
intriguing, while these often play a more crucial rôle in the ecosystem as

a whole. However, starting at the top anyway, the Polish population of brown bear (*Ursus arctos/niedźwiedź*) slumped to about half a dozen after the Second World War, but has been boosted by bears migrating from Slovakia to the Tatras and Bieszczady, although the Ukrainian population has been more stable, with perhaps 20,000 in the European part of the former Soviet Union. Now there are estimated to be about 68 bears in the Polish Bieszczady, about one per 20km², and maybe a dozen or more in the Polish Tatras, as well as the odd one or two in the Gorce and Babia Góra. They live in the more inaccessible parts of the mountain forests, and feed on fruit, beech nuts, maize and other crops (put out by hunters to attract boar), and small mammals, with beechnuts particularly important in the pre-hibernation phase when their energy consumption reaches 20,000kcal per day. A male bear can weigh up to 315kg and can live for up to 25 years; they normally mate every two or three years and have one to three cubs per litter, of which only about a third reach maturity. It's interesting that cubs in eastern Europe weigh about 680g at birth, against only 350g in western Europe. Bear tracks are similar to human footprints, and their legs are further apart than those of any other European animal.

In 1992 there was one case of young bears being fed by tourists, which resulted in their losing their fear of humans and having to be taken to Wrocław zoo, where I gather the mother soon died; however this was an isolated case and in general there is no need to take the kind of precautions so necessary in North America, nor is there the kind of mass ursophobia one finds in Romania. If you do meet a bear it will normally be as alarmed as you, and may leave a steaming pile as evidence.

Wolves (*Canis lupus/wilk*) are more widespread and more mobile, with perhaps 30 in the Bieszczady, a dozen in the Tatras, and about half a dozen each in the Gorce and Babia Góra National Parks (as far west as they go), and a nationwide population estimated at anything up to 800, in packs up to a dozen strong; the charity Earthwatch (Belsyre Court, 57 Woodstock Rd, Oxford OX2 6HU) is working with the Jagiellonian University in Kraków to count the wolf population in the Bieszczady and study their interaction with red deer, now increasingly important in attracting foreign hunters. However the increase in deer numbers means that wolves don't have to go near the villages to feed, so they are less of a problem for the local people and tourists.

Most of the deer are roe deer (*Capreolus capreolus/sarna*), which you are very likely to see when hiking in woodland, especially in the early morning, or to hear feeding around you at night when camping wild; red deer (*Cervus elaphus/jeleń europejski*) are less common; they are protected but require culling, which is a useful source of revenue for the National Parks, as one red deer can be worth US$10,000. These feed mainly on spruce shoots and bark, shedding their antlers in March and April and rutting in September and October, when the hills ring with a mooing roar with a touch of chainsaw. These are found in both the Polish and Ukrainian Carpathians, as is the wild boar (*Sus scrofa/dzik*), although this is more in the open deciduous woods of the foothills than the higher areas; boar are supposedly nocturnal and highly protective of their young, but when I saw one in broad daylight it abandoned its young to fend for themselves.

Other nocturnal mammals that you would be very lucky to see are the lynx (*Lynx lynx/ryś*), living in the steepest and least accessible forests (between three and a dozen in the Bieszczady and in the Tatra, and smaller numbers elsewhere), and the wildcat (*Felis silvestris/żbik*, most now cross-bred with domestic cats); while most European wildcats weigh about 5kg, one Carpathian specimen came in at 15kg. Along the forest edge and in wetlands you may see the polecat (*Mustela putorius/tchórz*), and also the stoat (*M erminea/gronostaj*), smaller than its British cousins, and the weasel (*M nivalis/łasica*). Similar to these are the pine marten (*Martes martes/kuna leśna*) and stone marten (*Martes foina/kuna domowa*); the red squirrel (*Sciurus vulgaris/wiewiórka czarna*) is more distinctive, although often found in a black form here. Other mammals include the otter, badger, fox, and at the smaller end of the scale the common, forest and edible dormice *Muscardinus avellanarius, Dryomys nitedula* and *Glis glis/popielica*, the water shrews *Neomys fodiens* and *N anomalus*, the alpine shrew *Sorex alpinus*, recognisable by a tail as long as its head and body together at 60mm, and *Sicista betulina*, the Northern birch mouse.

One interesting group of mammals are all North American natives, freed from fur farms in the Soviet Union in the 1920s and now naturalised and still spreading westwards, combined with Second World War escapees from Germany; these include muskrat (*Ondatra zibethica/piżmak*), raccoon (*Procyon lotor*), and mink (*Mustela vison/norka*). A 1990s arrival is the raccoon dog (*Nyctereutes procyonoides/jenot*), originally from the forests of Siberia and China and released in European Russia in 1928.

In the High Tatras you may see chamois (*Rupicapra rupicapra/kozica*), the symbol of the National Park, amazingly agile mountain goats that can leap 6m gaps and land on 30cm rockshelves, and marmots (*Marmota marmota/świstak*), apparently cut off from their alpine cousins for 25,000 years now, and now more recently intro-'uced to the eastern Ukrainian Carpathians as well. In the Karkonosze and the Crimean mountains, and southeast of Mukachevo in Ukraine are herds of moufflon (*Ovis musimon*), a reddish brown wild sheep with a white flank patch, and in the case of the male large back-curving horns, introduced from Corsica for shooting.

There are 20 species of bat (*nietoperz*), of which the most common are Schreiber's bat (*Miniopterus schreibersi*), the greater mouse-eared bat (*Myotis myotis*, the second largest in Europe with a body length of up to 82mm), the greater horseshoe bat (*Rhinolophus ferrum equinum*), the whiskered bat (*Myotis mystacinus*), and the Northern bat (*Vespertilio nilssoni*).

There are also 17 species of amphibia in Poland, perhaps most notably the salamander (*Salamandra salamandra*, a beautiful shiney black with orange spots, most often seen after rain), as well as the alpine and

Carpathian newts (*Triturus alpestris* and *T montandoni/traszka karpacka*, smaller and greener). Frogs (*żaba*) include the edible frog (*Rana temporaria*), the tree frog (*Hyla arborea*, green, with a cute baby face), the springing frog (*R dalmatina*), and the water frog (*R esculenta*), together with toads such as the European toad (*Bufo bufo*), the so-called British toad (*B calamita*, found all over central Europe), and the green toad (*B viridis*, similar but found more to the east).

As for reptiles, there are 9 species, including the adder (*Vipera berus/żmija*), which is mobile in temperatures as low as 3°C and thus is found at remarkably high altitudes, the Aesculapius snake (*Elaphe longissima/wąż esculapia*), which is harmless but, as its name suggests, very long, at up to 1.3m, the diced snake (*Natrix tesselata*, in water), the smooth snake (*Coronella austriaca*) which is similar to the adder and so is often killed, although it too is harmless, and the sand lizard (*Lacerta agilis/jaszczurka*).

Most fish species are fairly standard, such as brown trout (*Salmo trutta m fario/pstrąg*), grayling (*Thymallus thymallus/lipien*), minnow (*Phoxinus phoxinus*), and barbel (*Barbus barbus/brzana*), as well as the mountain loach (*Cobitis montana*), Balkan barbel (*Barbus meridionalis*) and the huchen or Danube salmon (*Hucho hucho/głowacia*), trout-shaped but twice the length at 90cm, which is endemic to the Tisa and Cheremosh rivers in Ukraine. Fish in rivers flowing into the Black Sea include gobies (*Gobiidae/vyrezub*), the Ukrainian lamprey (*Lampetra mariae*), various sturgeons, and the sterlet (*Accipenser ruthenus*).

Of the insect species the most attractive are the butterflies (*motyl*); as with meadow flowers, these are still very numerous and diverse due to the lack of pesticides on the higher pastures. The most common are familiar species such as the red admiral (*Vanessa atalanta/Rusałka Admirał*), which migrates from North Africa and can easily fly to the higher parts of the Tatras, the European peacock (*Nymphalis io*, to 1,900m), the Camberwell beauty or mourning cloak (*N antiopa/załobnik*, also to 1,900m), and the European swallowtail (*Papilio machaon/paz królowej*). In the połoninas of the Bieszczady and Ukraine there are rarer species such as *Parnassius mnemosyne/Niepylak mnemozyne*), with a rare black form, *Iphiclides podalirius, Parnassius apollo, Inachis io, Pyramis atalanta, Vanessa cardui* (painted lady) and *Pieris* or cabbage white types. Among the treetops, but rarely at ground level, is the purple emperor (*Apatura iris*), perhaps the most sought-after of all; the female is a dull brown, but the male has wonderful iridescent blue-brown wings. I found no mosquitoes here, but frequently found the most amazing quantities of flies swarming around me; these were generally worst in bramble undergrowth and best in clearer beechwoods.

Finally, there are some truly amazing electric blue, green, and violet slugs to be seen after rain in Ukraine and the San valley, along the border.

If you have a serious interest in wildlife, one place not to be missed is the Białowieża National Park, on Poland's eastern border and reached by bus or train from Białystok. Here there are 11,000 different animal species (including 8,500 insects, 227 birds and 62 mammals), more than in any other single habitat in Europe, in some of Europe's last remaining primeval forest, with oak trees over 400 years old, as well as over 1,000 species of fungi. This is best known for the herd of European bison (or aurochs, *Bison bonasus/zubr*), taken from zoos in the 1920s; there are almost 300 here, perhaps 30% of the world population, and there are now also a couple of dozen in the Bieszczady and 50 in the Ojców Park, as well as 250 across the border in Belarus, and north of Uzhgorod and near Lake Sinevir in Ukraine. There was also a herd in the Tatras, according to Violet Mason, until it made the mistake of charging at a regiment of Austrian cavalry. In addition you can see the żubron (a cross of the bison with the domestic cow), elk (*Alces alces/łos*), the tarpan or Polish wild horse (also the name of the Polish-built four-wheel drive vehicle), beaver, boar, and red and roe deer.

Orbis lay on a 12 day nature tour, from £320 from the UK, taking in Białowieża and many of the northern marshes and lakes, including Lake Łuknajno, home to the greatest concentration of swans in Europe. They also do fishing trips in the Bieszczady, if that's what you're into. In 1993 the PTTK also laid on its first Photo-Safari tour to northeastern Poland, mainly the Masurian lakes, the Biebrza marshes and Białowieża.

Chapter 2

Preparations

WHAT TO TAKE

As Saint-Exupéry said, 'He who would travel happily must travel light'; you should take the standard 20kg airline allowance as your absolute maximum, bearing in mind that you gain a kilogram when you put a litre of water into your bottle, and that food in eastern Europe tends to come in heavy glass jars; dispose of as much packaging as you can before departure, but this may not be possible with what you buy after arrival. I find that a Body Shop plastic bottle carries enough shampoo for several months, and soap can be carried in a film canister. In eastern Europe basins never have plugs, so take a squash ball or universal plug if this is important to you.

Specifically for hiking, you should remember the six essentials of map, compass, matches (and maybe a firelighter) in a waterproof box, first-aid kit, extra food and extra clothing. A knife, spoon and mug or bowl are also pretty important. Wood fires are becoming environmentally unacceptable nowadays, even in the Carpathians where there seems to be no shortage of wood; if you want to cook, take a stove but plan your fuel supplies in advance, as Camping Gaz is hard to find in eastern Europe and cannot be taken by air, and petrol is in short supply. Personally I don't bother for three to five day trips in summer.

With regard to clothing, the key principle is that of layering; in the mountains the weather can change suddenly, or you might finish a long hot climb by reaching a ridge and walking into a cutting cold wind. Modern lightweight breathable materials such as GoreTex make this easier, but you can apply the principle just as well with normal everyday clothes, a T-shirt to soak up sweat, then a shirt and thin pullovers for warmth topped by a cagoule to protect against both wind and rain — in modern terminology wicking, insulation and shell layers. You will need waterproof trousers as well, and the jacket or cagoule should have semi-waterproof pockets sealed by Velcro or a zip under a storm flap. Wear jeans at your peril, as they take days to dry. I find army-surplus fatigue trousers ideal, with a map pocket on the lower thigh, an adjustable waistband to allow me to lose weight on a long trip, and very fast drying properties; you can also buy similar trousers from companies like Rohan, at much higher prices. Shorts are perfectly acceptable except perhaps for visiting churches. A fleece top is wonderful for warmth but is neither wind- nor water-proof. Midges and mosquitoes are not a problem.

Good boots are essential for rough, rocky or wet terrain, or long cross-country routes; light boots or trainers might be acceptable for easy walks without a heavy load, and are kinder to sensitive terrain as well as being useful to change into at the end of the day. Take a spare pair of bootlaces (also useful for drying laundry and so on) if you're likely to need them, as local laces can break on day one.

To carry all this you need a backpack or rucksack — above all make sure you have a padded hip belt, and pity the poor eastern Europeans who have to carry all their load on their shoulders. Ideally you should carry 50% of your load on the hips — any more and you slip out of your shoulder straps, even with a chest strap. Nowadays there are also likely to be straps to adjust the balance of the load for uphill or downhill work, away from the body going uphill, and closer to the body downhill. At airports wrap the hip belt backwards around the pack, do it up in reverse and tuck away or tie up any strap ends, both to stop them getting caught in conveyor belts, and to delay anyone wanting to sneak a look inside; a small padlock is also useful, although more as a deterrent than as a real barrier. No rucksack is really totally waterproof, so you should keep clothes and the like in plastic bags.

You are also likely to need a tent, and again don't wait till you get there before buying one. Unless making a winter trip you won't need an especially warm sleeping bag, but a camping mat is always invaluable.

A camera should be as robust as possible, as I have destroyed several in the past by travelling on rough roads; remember not to sit behind the rear axle of a bus. A telephoto lens renders binoculars or a telescope unnecessary, but otherwise a 35mm compact camera may be ideal. Nowadays some compact cameras incorporate a zoom lens. You will need a spare battery for a long trip, and you should take enough film; ASA 200 and 400 film is not available, and the only slide film is poor quality made by ORWO of East Germany (now taken over by AGFA). There is a lot to be said for the view that if you take photographs you don't really appreciate the scenery.

With all this you should have insurance, available from most travel agents and insurance agents. One policy I have recently spotted is Activcard from General Accident (Pithleavis, Perth PH2 0NH) which covers high risk sports, such as mountaineering, climbing, potholing, hang gliding, parachuting and paragliding, and for Europe premiums are from £18 for five days to £35 for 25-31 days, with extra weeks costing £5 up to a 90 day maximum. West Mercia Insurance Services (High St, Wombourne, near Wolverhampton, WV5 9DD) have cheaper policies excluding climbing. Normal hill-walking should be covered by a standard policy, and if under 35 the cheapest (not necessarily the best) may be from Campus Travel (£8 for a month, or £16 covering personal baggage). Having done this you should remember to carry a pocket diary with a list of numbers of insurance policies, travellers' cheques, passport, credit cards, etc, as well as the addresses to which you intend to send postcards.

HYGIENE AND NUTRITION

For the traveller health is of course closely related to fitness, but you should not let yourself be daunted by this, as most people humping a backpack around Europe are already basically fit. Keep to a good easy rhythm, with reasonably long strides, and remember that hiking is above all a matter of mental discipline; if you want to get up that mountain, you will, although you may not be fit for much the next day. If in a group you may be obliged to keep up with the group and with daily targets, but the independent hiker can go as slowly as he/she desires. In any case some walking or cycling before leaving home will help; although modern boots do not need much breaking in, it is still helpful to wear them for a few days before departure. Contrary to much medical advice, I am a believer in lancing my own blisters before bed, with a needle sterilised in a flame. Keep your feet clean and dry, and your toenails short, and with modern boots you should have few problems.

You should also remember to have your teeth checked and bring your tetanus jab up to date. There is no need for other jabs for travel in eastern Europe, but if in doubt contact your local health centre, MASTA (Medical Advisory Service for Travellers Abroad), at the London School of Hygiene and Tropical Medicine, Keppel St, London WC1E 7HT (tel 071 631 4408), or any of the vaccination services run by British Airways, Thomas Cook, Trailfinders and others.

The United Kingdom still has reciprocal health agreements with Poland and the former Soviet Union entitling British visitors to free basic treatment — an NHS card may be useful, and take an E111 form if travelling overland through EU countries. To call an ambulance dial 061 in Poland or 03 in Ukraine. In any case basic advice can be obtained at a pharmacy (*apteka* in Polish and Ukrainian); a dentist is a *dentysta*.

Prevention is better than cure, but you will need a basic first aid kit: sterile needles are available from that well known high street chemist for about 10p each. Obvious things are sticking plasters and dressings, pain-killers, antiseptic cream and throat lozenges, as well as tubular bandages to support sore ankles and knees.

Tap water is not particularly pure (see pages 19 and 225), but stream water in the hills must be presumed to be dilute sheep urine: use Puritabs or Sterotabs, from high street chemists and camping shops, or boil water for five minutes. Do not throw food scraps, or any other rubbish, into streams; all rubbish should be taken out, or failing that burnt; burying litter is a waste of time as animals will dig it up. Dig a 10cm toilet hole, at least 100m from any water or path, and fill it in afterwards; then wash your hands.

Diarrhoea is the classic traveller's ailment; if it happens, avoid alcohol, fatty and spicy foods, and milk products. Rice and potatoes are helpful.

Replace lost fluids with treated or bottled water, or preferably with a rehydration (electrolyte) formula — one litre of water with three teaspoons of sugar, one of salt, half of baking soda and three-quarters of potassium chloride (or dextrose and salt tablets). Dark orange urine indicates a lack of fluid. Bumblockers such as Lomotil only relieve the symptoms for the duration of a long bus journey, but they will not tackle the causes. Persistent diarrhoea can be treated with antibiotics (available over the counter in eastern Europe) but Hilary Bradt notes that Vibromycin can cause increased sensitivity to the sun, particularly at altitude, which may be an increasing problem if the European ozone hole grows. In general avoid alcohol when hiking, especially during the day. If it really is forced on you, wet your lips to taste it and hand the glass or bottle back. If suffering fron constipation, boost your fibre intake.

Rabies is rare, with 460 cases in Poland, against 1,344 in Germany (mostly in eastern Germany), but with all those sheepdogs, not to mention bats, it can be a worry. It can be transmitted by scratches or even licks where the skin is broken, as well as by bites; get treatment at once, after immediately washing the wound, ideally with alcohol. Vipers can also be a problem, as there is no anti-venom, but in Britain at least more people die of bee stings than of snake bites. (Bees can be irritable in dull or humid weather.) There is no malaria, but even so bites and stings can turn septic, and clouds of flies can be intensely annoying — insect repellant may work, although I have little faith in it. It should contain at least 80% Diethyl Toluamide, but many do not; this is toxic and should not be used for too long.

I always wear a floppy sun-hat and only use sunglasses on snow; 70% of heat loss is from the head, so wearing a hat can stop your toes freezing, and a hat also protects the eyes, ears and the back of the neck from sun and flies. Heat exhaustion is caused by over-exercising when the body cannot dissipate its heat quickly enough: symptoms are nausea, florid complexion, stumbling, lack of alertness, cramp and eventual collapse. Like exposure, it tends to affect those unaccustomed to being outdoors in extreme weather, the old, the unwell and convalescents. Don't wear or carry too much (young people should not carry more than a quarter of their body weight), shelter from the sun, remove excess clothing, apply cold wet towels to the limbs and head, and take salty drinks. Exposure is defined as 'a reduction in body heat usually caused by getting wet in cold or windy weather... Symptoms are unexpected or unreasonable behaviour, stumbling, lack of alertness, complaints of cold and tiredness, pale complexion and shivering which stops as the patient becomes colder' (NB). Again, do not wear or carry too much as this hastens exhaustion, and change wet clothing.

Altitude sickness should not be a problem at under 3,000m, but there is also a greater risk of sunburn and sunstroke even at lower altitudes — take care, wear a hat and don't confuse the symptoms.

Motion sickness could be a problem on Ukrainian roads, although it's less likely in Poland; remember to sit near the centre of any vehicle, ie not behind the rear axle of a bus. Again, avoid alcohol and if necessary take pills 30 minutes before travel.

As for sex, my advice is don't do it; getting involved with alien cultures, which is what these are, is a minefield of potential problems, and many of the best educated women are desperate to get out of the country and settle in the West, by hook or by crook. If you must, bring your own condoms and other contraceptives from western Europe.

Healthy feeding for hiking

Here I give an outline of what you should eat and drink for ideal health and performance; see pages 67 and 271 for what is actually available in Poland and Ukraine, which is not quite the same thing.

Energy comes from four sources: protein, alcohol, fat and carbohydrate. Protein will only be used for energy when other sources are exhausted, therefore you need take in only the body's basic requirement of about 1-1.5g per kilogram bodyweight. Beans, white meats and dairy products are suitable sources. Alcohol is not a suitable energy source either as it is only broken down slowly, by the liver, and it also intoxicates. Generally alcohol and hiking do not mix well — even if you just have a couple of drinks in the evening, the effects on your legs will be obvious in the morning. Only a few hundred grams of fat will be consumed by a hearty day's exercise, and as men have a fat store of 12-15kg, and women of 15-20kg, you need make no particular effort to boost your stocks.

Therefore we are left with carbohydrates as our main energy source, most easily obtained from foods such as cereals, bread, pasta, bananas, potatoes and rice. This can be topped up with refined or sugary carbohydrates such as jam, chocolate or other foods containing sugar; however consuming large amounts of refined sugary carbohydrate just before or during exercise may actually cause fatigue as its rapid absorption can cause insulin to be released into the bloodstream with a consequent drop in blood sugar levels. For sustained hiking you need three times your normal carbohydrate intake.

You also need to replace **fluids** lost through sweating, an inevitable consequence of muscular activity. Make sure you drink at least half a litre (say a pint) at the start of the day, and then keep yourself topped up as you go — don't wait until you're thirsty, and drink more in the evening; in hot weather it's worth having a water bottle by your bed as well. Roughly speaking you should take a pint for every 10°F every 24 hours, if you still know what pints and Fahrenheit are — ie if the temperature is 80°F you should take eight pints of fluid a day. Water is obviously ideal, but you can also add some carbohydrate such as fruit juice. However this will slow the rate of absorption, so keep it dilute.

In addition B vitamins are needed for energy metabolism — these can be obtained from fruit, vegetables (particularly pulses), cereals, nuts, and fish or white meat. Iron is also needed for oxygen transport — best obtained from meat, eggs, pulses and green vegetables, nuts, seeds and cereals. If possible take this with orange juice or some other source of vitamin C to aid uptake.

In the Valley of the Five Lakes,
Tatra Mountains

Part Two

Poland — The Land and the People

16

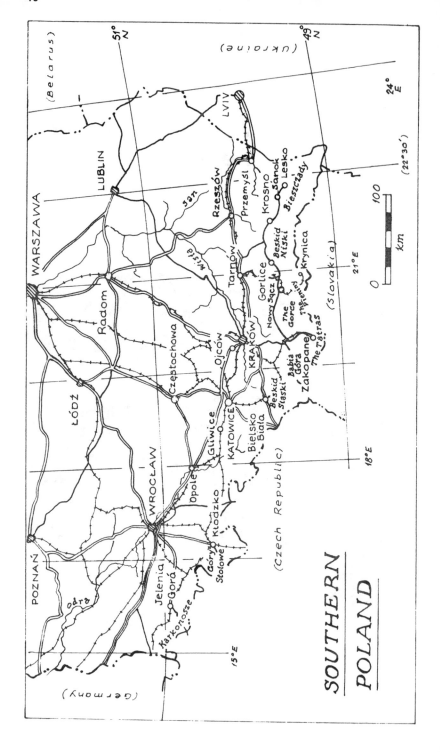

SOUTHERN

POLAND

Chapter 3

The Land

GEOGRAPHY

Most of Poland is more or less flat, being part of the great north European plain linking Germany and Russia; although there are many national parks in central and northern Poland and much good walking, notably in the Mazurian Lakes, this book is unashamedly concerned with the mountains that form the southern fringe of the country. These, with the Baltic Sea to the north, are Poland's only fixed borders; between them the country has slid about alarmingly to east and to west, as detailed in the *History* section, but it is now largely cradled betwen the Wisła (Vistula) and Odra (Oder) rivers, which almost meet up in the Silesian Beskids south of Katowice. The province of Silesia, formerly part of Bohemia and then of Prussia, is Poland's most industrialised and thus most polluted area, with 65.5bn tonnes of coal reserves, 3.4bn tonnes of copper, as well as lead, zinc, and silver; Łódź (pronounced wodge and meaning boat), southwest of Warsaw, is 'the Manchester of Poland', its main textile centre, and there are major shipyards on the Baltic, in the 'Tri-City' area of Gdańsk/Sopot/Gdynia and in Szczecin. Otherwise the bulk of Poland is pleasant farmland, with many woods (covering 28% of the national area) and about 10,000 post-glacial lakes (over 1% of the national area, with the largest, Sniardwy, in Mazuria, covering 114km²).

The best-known and most spectacular mountains are the Tatras, south of Kraków; most of this massif is in fact in Slovakia, and the Polish portion is compact and easily reached from Zakopane; it is truly spectacular and often very busy. However the most developed resort areas are in the Silesian Beskids (Beskid Śląski), southwest of Bielsko-Biała, and the Karkonosze, near the German border and still full of German visitors. In the southeast are largely depopulated hills, the Beskid Niski and Bieszczady, which are more akin to those of Ukraine both in their flora and in their human legacy.

There is a population of 38 million (as many as in Czechoslovakia, Hungary and Bulgaria together) in 49 voivodeships (*Wojewodztwo*) or provinces, in an area of 312,700km² (649km from north to south, 689km from east to west); in 1991 the population was 62% urban, but there were still 2.6 million peasant households. One third of the population is under twenty.

The Polish **climate** is oceanic-continental, similar to that of Britain but less humid in the summer and with long cold winters; in the east winters are Siberian, with three to four months averaging sub-zero temperatures. There are six seasons: winter (mid-December to late February), a changeable pre-spring (*Przedwiośnie,* to early April), spring (to late May), summer (to late August), a sunny autumn (the Polish Golden Autumn, in September and October), and a foggy and drizzly early winter (November to mid-December). Average temperatures in Kraków in July are 19.4°C, and in January –2.8°C, and in Wrocław 18.9°C and –1.1°C; in Białowieza (on the eastern border) temperatures can drop as low as –38°C, and summers can be as warm as 32°C. Annual precipitation is 730mm in Kraków and 574mm in Wrocław, and up to 1,800mm on the peaks. The Tatras are generally under snow from mid-October to late March, making the September full moon and Easter the most popular times to visit them, other than for skiing. After a short wet spring, there is a warm summer in the mountains, with late afternoon thunderstorms; the autumn is also wet, but in winter the mountains are the sunniest part of Poland.

Nature conservation has a long history in Poland, with beavers protected from hunting since the 11th Century, yew trees since the 15th Century, and bison since the 16th Century. Poland now has 17 **National Parks**, covering 177,000ha, and the number is growing steadily. The Biebrza and Góry Stołowe parks are to be created by 1995, and should then be followed by five more, boosting the total protected area to 290,000ha and almost 1% of the national area. Four are on the UNESCO list of Biosphere Reserves: Słowiński (on the coast), Białowieża (on the eastern border), Łuknajno Lake (in the Mazurian lake district) and Babia Góra (west of the Tatras), with more planned in the Tatras, Karkonosze and Bieszczady mountains. Twenty-eight per cent of the parks' area is under strict protection; 68 landscape parks have also been created since 1976, covering 1,215,485ha and 3.9% of the country; these are less strictly protected and walking is not restricted to marked paths as in the National Parks.

In addition, under the 1991 Nature Conservation Law there are 1,062 smaller nature reserves (126,087ha), 160 areas of protected landscape (3.5m hectares, over 11% of the country), and 16,000 nature monuments (individual trees and rocks). In other post-communist states there are fears that protected land is up for grabs for forestry or for reclamation by former owners, but this seems unlikely to be a problem in Poland.

The Karkonosze, Góry Stołowe, Ojców, Babia Góra, Tatra, Gorce, Pieniny and Bieszczady National Parks are all dealt with below in the relevant chapters; of the others the most interesting are Białowieża, dating from 1921 and famous for its herd of bison in virgin forest, and

Święty Krzyż (Holy Cross), east of Kielce, the oldest mountains in Poland. The Kampinos Park is just west of Warsaw, the largest of the National Parks and full of historical associations.

GREEN ISSUES

To put it bluntly, Poland is an environmental disaster on a staggering scale, due to the Stalinist mania for heavy industry and total disregard for efficiency, health or the environment. Various planning and environmental laws were passed in the early 1980s (the State Council for the Conservation of Nature dates back to 1919), but whereas until 1978 the growth in pollution had been less than the rate of economic growth, from 1978 to 1988 GNP fell by 0.7% on average per year while gas emissions rose by 1.6% annually, solid waste rose by 1.4% annually, while sewage output was stable (although only 35% is treated) and only particulate emissions fell, by 2.6% per annum. Particulate emissions in the Comecon bloc were 13 times higher than in the EU (18.3kg per US$1,000 of GDP, as against 1.4kg), gas emissions double (57.2kg/25.5kg), and water consumption double; energy consumption is triple the OECD average. Power station efficiency was just 21-36% (partly due to burning cheaper brown coal or lignite from opencast sites, rather than investing in deep pits), with 11% of power lost in transmission.

Therefore in southern Poland there are excess levels of atmospheric sulphur dioxide (of which Poland is the world's seventh greatest producer, with levels up to 10 times EU limits) at 26% of measuring points, of nitrogen oxides at 62%, and of suspended particulates at 80%, almost entirely from heavy industry rather than from transport. From the 1960s to the 1980s the proportion of Polish surface waters fit for human consumption fell from 33% to 13%, and the proportion unfit even for industrial purposes (largely saline water pumped from coal mines that literally corrodes the machinery) rose from 22.8% to 42.3% (see page 21).

Now a third of all food produced is estimated to be contaminated (and 25% of that produced in Upper Silesia is unfit for human consumption), at least 49% of Poland's forests are affected by acid rain, and quite simply no tree is healthy in Silesia, including most of the mountains west of the Tatras. Life expectancy is actually falling, as in much of eastern Europe, from 67.3 years (for a man) in 1982 to 66.8 years in 1986, and in 1988 there were 27 official areas of ecological hazard, covering 11% of the country's area and 35% of the population. The worst areas are Upper Silesia, Kraków, Rybnik, Legnica-Głogów, and Gdańsk; occupational diseases are most common in Katowice, Kraków, Bielsko-Biała, and Wałbrzych, and smog is worst in Katowice, Kraków and Łódź. In Upper Silesia there are 15% more circulatory diseases than in the rest of Poland, 30% more cancers, 47% more respiratory illnesses. 35% of children show the symptoms of lead or cadmium poisoning (soil lead levels here are the highest in the world), and the numbers born with disabilities has doubled in ten years to about 20%. Groups of 'Katowice kids' are common sights in the mountain resorts, just as 'Chornobyl kids' are in Ukraine. These are long-term problems; anyone visiting for a short period is unlikely to suffer unless abnormally sensitive, and the forests are still standing, by and large. Incidentally, it is also said that Warsaw is the fourth worst city in the world for noise pollution: London is the worst.

The huge funds needed to make any real difference are of course lacking, despite international appeals, and naturally there are many thousands of jobs at stake, particularly in the huge and inefficient steel plants, bastions of Solidarity but mostly doomed by the European steel glut. United States aid of US$35m was supplied under the SEED (Support for Eastern European Democracy) Act to provide for restoration and air quality monitoring in Kraków (where stonework is being eroded by half a centimetre per year) and for fitting sulphur filters to the Skawina power station just to the south. Kraków, being on the UNESCO World Heritage list and a major tourist centre, is receiving more attention than the Katowice conurbation and towns from hell such as Wałbrzych.

The government has established an Institute of Environmental Protection and an Environmental Protection Bank, lending money for ecological projects, in Warsaw, and ecology colleges in Katowice and Wrocław. However it is more likely to be moves such as the wholesale closure of the antiquated Polish, East German and Czech heavy industry (half of the atmospheric pollution is 'imported' — one power station in eastern Germany pumps out 460,000t of sulphur dioxide annually, more than the total for Norway and Denmark), a switch to cleaner coal and gas for power generation, and greater efficiency forced by fuel prices rising to world levels, that will produce improvements. Already there are reports of SO2 levels in Silesia dropping by 30%.

The *Polski Klub Ecologiczney* was founded in 1981 and surviving the martial law period only because of a clause in the constitution stating that 'The citizens of the Polish Peoples' Republic have the right to enjoy the full value of a natural environment and a duty to protect it'. In 1986 it became affiliated to Friends of the Earth, the first body in eastern Europe to do so, and now has 5,000 members and 17 regional offices, running an Air Pollution Information Centre and co-ordinating campaigning with other groups; it calculates that doing nothing about acid rain costs up to 10% of GNP. There are also fringe 'eco-commando' groups that have failed to achieve much against such deeply institutional problems. *The Squandered Dividend* by Roger Manser (Earthscan 1993) gives more information.

As for *our* individual responsibilities, it is important to say that green or eco-tourism is a question not just of using biodegradable sunscreen and not littering, but also of attitude. You should be clear in your own mind just why you are travelling in the first place. You have great economic power which should be used wisely. If you take a package holiday or stay in 'international' hotels, the profits never reach the country you visit, whereas if you travel independently, staying in locally-owned establishments, travelling on public transport, buying food as you go and preferably not changing money on the black market, you are putting funds directly into the economy. The tourist industry currently has plenty of spare capacity, but in general you should consider travelling out of season if possible. Leave all unnecessary packaging at home, and if possible use the local system of returning bottles to shops for a deposit, although this may well disappear as TetraPak and the rest of the Western packaging industry move in. Bottle banks are now appearing in Poland, but reuse is better than recycling.

Remember that you are exploring not just a region but also a culture; try to learn the basic words of greeting at least, and take care not to behave insensitively, in particular by not dressing immodestly or showing physical affection in public, not taking unwanted photographs, and by respecting religious sites and artefacts. Try to repay hospitality fully, but not by showering money around; it is better to offer some reciprocal service, although simply taking photographs of people can be too much of an easy option.

The key advice can be summed up in the slightly hackneyed saying of the Sierra Club: *Take nothing but pictures, kill nothing but time, leave nothing but footprints.*

Footnote

With the decline in industrial production in the 1990s, the situation has improved: although the Wisła is still unfit to drink, the proportion too polluted even to be classified has halved, the proportion suitable only for industrial use has fallen by a third, and parts are even fit for swimming.

Equally, between 1989 and 1991 sulphur dioxide emissions fell by two fifths, and nitrogen oxides and steel industry dust emissions by a third. However the amount of rubbish generated in Poland has increased by 40%, due largely to western concepts of packaging.

Women in Poland

Sexism is deeply entrenched in rural Poland as in all of central and eastern Europe: women work and queue and cook and bring up children, while men work and then drink; although they can be very chivalrous, kissing a lady's hand and so on, they are little use around the house. The woman's rôle as mother and homemaker is deeply engrained due to the influence of the Catholic church. Solidarity extended maternity leave to two years, and day nurseries are provided in most workplaces, but this largely reinforces the present system. Feminism is linked in most people's minds with Soviet propaganda (like the Peace movement); a poll showed a 'feministka' as the least desirable neighbour. It must be said that the Poles are never the most tolerant of neighbours, as 79% wanted nothing to do with gays, 75% with prostitutes, 65% with gypsies, and 62% with alcoholics (many clearly failing to recognise it in themselves or their families): in fact practising Catholics were more tolerant and less inclined to see the world as 'us' against 'them'. The educated classes in major cities also have more liberal attitudes.

Despite the prevalence of Catholic attitudes, there is little support for bans on contraception or abortion, the general view being that people should take control of their lives themselves. Sanitary protection is now available in major towns, but it is safer to bring your own, as well as your contraception. Bars are very male-dominated, but except in parts of Warsaw the streets are generally safe at night. It should also be stressed that there are more women high-achievers than in the rest of central and eastern Europe, notably the former prime minister Hanna Suchocka, the late climber Wanda Rutkiewicz, and the film director Agnieszka Holland.

You may find it useful to contact a group called 'Women Welcome Women' (c/o Frances Alexander, Granta, 8A Chestnut Ave, High Wycombe HP11 1DJ, tel 0494-439 481), which can put women in touch with 1,200 members in over 50 countries.

'The dominant feeling of travelling in Poland was not of being a lone woman but of being a cyclist. For most of the time I didn't feel I attracted any more attention because of my gender, the initial focus always being the bike and luggage followed by gasp! horror! It's a woman! People I stayed with or talked to along the way were absolutely horrified that I was cycling alone and usually tried to stop me from going any further, insisting that I would be murdered in my bed that very night. Their concern was genuine but unfounded; it was often easier for a lone woman to be accepted by local folk, being a lot less intimidating than a lone man and apparently a whole lot more interesting. That isn't to say that hassle is non-existent: as in any country there are a few slimeballs just awaiting a chance to be obnoxious and unpleasant. Fortunately, Polish slimeballs are not too persistent and I only had to enlist another person's help to make them slurp back into the sewers — regardless of the enlisted 'help' helping or not.

I generally used official camp sites and always got to know the 'warden' so he would keep an eye out for me and the bike. It was also more comfortable camping with others rather than out on my own. However camp sites vary in quality and in price: it can be cheaper to stay in a youth hostel or private accommodation. One of my best experiences must have been camping on a farm one night: when I rolled up, the whole male side of the family were out socialising/working, so we women had a fine old time not understanding much of each other but laughing lots. Asking at a farm or large house will invariably mean meeting all the women of the house and having fun. Women certainly seem to stay at home and do all the work, often having very primitive equipment to work with, such as wells and ever-hungry wood stoves.

In southern Poland I came across petty officiousness. There seemed to be an abundance of minor officials who delighted in being unhelpful and rude. The increasing number of tourists to Poland can only highlight the relative poverty of the country, so increasing the frustration of these people.

I met many other women travellers in pairs or alone, and none had had any problems. As I said, in my case the cycling was the focus of attention; I was no doubt usually assumed to be male, always wearing T-shirt and cycling shorts. The next step would be to assume I was Russian (three elderly men on the village bench questioned me closely in Russian before realising, to their delight, that I hadn't the foggiest what they were on about!); and finally horror of horrors a lone Englishwoman, poor defenceless thing!

Most Poles say their country is far too dangerous to do this, but I would have to disagree; after all it's never so much fun travelling in your own country.'
Mary Hall

Chapter 4

The People

HISTORY

The Polish national consciousness has been shaped above all by their history, with pride deriving from the phase when Poland joined with Lithuania to form Europe's largest state and its bastion against the eastern hordes, outweighed by the memory of the times when its neighbours conspired to take over its entire territory and suppress its culture. Poles see their country as 'the Christ of Nations' because of this suffering, and because it is set between two thieves, Russia and Germany, which plotted to wipe Poland off the map.

The Polish plains have been the main highway for tribes moving from Asia into Europe ever since Neolithic times; eventually it was the West Slav tribes who settled in the 6th and 7th Centuries in what they called Polonia or Land of the Fields, near modern Poznań. In 965 Prince Mieszko I adopted Christianity, and this date is generally taken as the foundation of the Polish state under the Piast dynasty, although initially he only ruled Wielkopolska (Great Poland), the area around Poznań. In 1225 the Teutonic Knights, a half-monastic, half-military order, were mistakenly invited into Poland to help establish a bulwark against pagan tribes to the east such as the Prussians; they soon became a state within a state, building some of the most impregnable fortresses in Europe and taking over the port of Gdańsk, and were not crushed until 1525; in addition the Tatars' Golden Horde ravaged the country in 1241-42 and again in 1259. It was not until the reign of Kazimierz III (the Great) from 1333 to 1370 that governmental authority was really established; he also conquered Red Ruthenia and Podolia, now in Ukraine, reformed the currency, codified the laws and encouraged Jews fleeing from persecution elsewhere to settle in Poland, giving vital impetus to the development of trade and crafts.

The succeeding Jagiellonian dynasty came to the throne in 1386 when Queen Jadwiga married Władysław Jagiełło, Grand Duke of Lithuania, Europe's last pagan country, but one that stretched from the Baltic to the Black Sea; the union of these two countries created a state with enough power to defeat the Teutonic Knights at the great battle of

Grunwald in 1410 and confine them to East Prussia, nowadays the Russian enclave of Kaliningrad (or Königsberg), before finally subduing them in 1525. From the late 15th Century Poland was also threatened from the east, by Tatars, Turks and Muscovites; but by the 16th Century Poland was the most powerful nation in Europe, ruling Bohemia and Hungary for a while, and home to many of the scholars and artists of the Renaissance, while itself producing figures such as Nicolas Copernicus (1473-1543).

Lithuania still has a significant place in Poland's soul; the poets Czesław Miłosz and Tadeusz Konwicki, and Generals Józef Piłsudski and Wojciech Jaruzelski came from Lithuania, and many ethnic Poles remained there even after the Second World War; even though there is no claim on the territory, it is significant that Mickiewicz's most famous poem *Pan Tadeusz* opens 'Lithuania, my fatherland! You are like health;/ How much we should value you he alone knows/ Who has lost you'.

Meanwhile the aristocracy, about 10% of the population, gradually increased its power, creating a parliament or *Sejm* with wide powers, which after the death in 1572 of Zygmunt August, last of the Jagiellonians, took up the practice of electing the king. Over the next 223 years of 'Noble Democracy' there were 11 of these elected kings (seven of them foreigners), starting with the French Henri de Valois, and then the Transylvanian (Hungarian) Stefan Batory, who drove back Ivan the Terrible between 1579 and 1582. The Muscovite (or Russian) Czars were growing in power and saw themselves as protectors of the large Orthodox populations in Poland's eastern territories; despite the Reformation Poland remained, then as now, firmly Catholic, and yet managed to remain neutral throughout the Thirty Years' War. However Sweden emerged from this war as the leading military power of Europe and invaded Poland in 1655, almost conquering it and doing great damage in what is remembered as the 'Flood'.

Poland survived and was strong enough for Jan III Sobieski to save Vienna in 1683 and drive the Turks from Hungary by 1686. Internally there was increasing confusion as the *Sejm* argued, having allowed any member the right of veto from 1652, and Russia and Sweden supported rival candidates for the throne, until Frederick the Great of Prussia (known as Brandenburg until it absorbed East Prussia, the former stronghold of the Teutonic Knights) was able to conquer almost all of Silesia between 1740 and 1763.

Stanisław-August Poniatowski was elected Poland's last king (as it turned out) in 1763, thanks to his former lover, Catherine the Great of Russia; in 1772 he was forced to cede 30% of the national territory to Prussia, Russia and Austria in the First Partition of Poland. Russia gained much of what is now Belarus (Byelorussia), Austria gained Ruthenia and Galicia, the strip of territory south of the Wisła reaching east into Ukraine, and the Prussians gained more land to the west. In reaction to this, what was left of Poland undertook a programme of radical reform, adopting the modern world's second written constitution on May 3 1791 and beginning to free the serfs (75% of the population); naturally this enraged the absolute monarchies and led to a Russian invasion in 1792 and a further partition the next year. In 1794 Tadeusz Kościuszko, a hero of the American War of Independence and the war of 1792 (after whom Australia's highest mountain is named), led a heroic but self-defeating revolt against the Russians which could only fail and led to the obliteration of Poland in the Third Partition of 1795. The three partitions were fundamentally driven by the frantic determination of Catherine the Great of Russia to avoid any reform in eastern Europe, while Prussia and Austria simply played the roles of scavengers, seizing what scraps they could. The historian Norman Stone memorably described Stanisław-August as 'all fur coat and no knickers' as after a lavish coronation he found that the nobility, all rich enough to have armies of their own, would not vote him enough funds to have an army or even a cook; then, of course, he was betrayed by Catherine, but was still disowned by his compatriots for not having sought a glorious death.

By now, though, Napoleon's armies were on the march and after defeating Prussia and then Austria, he created the puppet Duchy of Warsaw in 1807. The army of the Duchy included the Polish Legions, raised in Italy from prisoners and deserters in 1797, and were commanded by Prince Józef Poniatowski, Stanisław-August's nephew, who led Napoleon's march on Moscow and the disastrous retreat, before choosing an honourable death in the Polish tradition at the Battle of the Three Emperors in 1813. (The Poniatowski family is still active in French politics.) After the Congress of Vienna in 1814-15 the *status quo ante* was restored with Prussia dominating the Grand Duchy of Posen (Poznań), Russia ruling the 'Congress Kingdom', centred on Warsaw, Austria ruling Galicia from Lemburg (Lviv), and only Kraków surviving as a small 'independent' republic until 1846 when it was swallowed up by Austria.

After relatively liberal beginnings, the Congress Kingdom soon fell into autocracy; there were revolts in 1830-31, 1863-64, and 1905-06, all of which failed and led to repression, massive emigration, and the creation in exile of the myth of the martyred Poland, notably by Adam Mickiewicz, the greatest Polish poet. After 1864 the Congress Kingdom was abolished and the Catholic church repressed, but the serfs were freed, in a case of Divide-and-Rule to alienate them from the nobility. Galicia remained relatively liberal and became the focus of Polish nationalism, but it was also chronically poor and under-developed; during 1911-14, when the average peasant plot would support a family for only a quarter of the year, about 25% of its population emigrated, mainly to America. In the Prussian, later German, sector of Poland, industrialisation proceeded more rapidly, especially in Silesia, and living standards were higher, but the Catholic church was again repressed, this time in the interests of Protestantism rather than Orthodoxy.

During the First World War both sides attempted to buy Polish support with offers of independent statehood, with Woodrow Wilson, President of the United States, most sincerely committed to this; the Germans drove the Russians out and, acting as liberators, set up a Polish administration. Józef Piłsudski and his Polish National Organisation opted to support the Germans and again raised Polish Legions to fight with them against the Russians, while his great rival Roman Dmowski and the Nationalist Committee backed the winning side. Piłsudski was interned by the Germans but then released and installed as head of state in November 1918, with Dmowski's protégé, the great pianist Paderewski, as prime minister. The new country's frontiers were to be defined by the Paris peace conference, and by the war that Piłsudski waged in 1919 and 1920 against the new Bolshevik regime in Russia; he advanced as far as Kyiv (Kiev) before being driven back by Trotsky's Red Army. The Treaty of Riga, on March 18 1921, moved the frontier 150km east of the 'Curzon Line' set by the Paris peacemakers (and even further east of the natural ethnic border), to include most of Galicia and present-day Belarus, as well as Piłsudski's hometown of Vilnius, now capital of Lithuania. Germany was able to retain East Prussia, but it was separated from the rest of Germany by a corridor linking Poland to the Baltic: Danzig, now Gdańsk, but then largely German, became a free city. After insurrection and a referendum in Silesia, this province was split, with Poland gaining the Katowice conurbation to give it a sound industrial base.

The population of this new Poland was 15% Ukrainian (or Ruthenian), 5% Belorussian, 9% Jewish and 2% German; it rose from 26.34m in 1921 to over 35m in 1939. Politically the situation was chaotic, with a constitution modelled on that of the equally chaotic French Third Republic, and an economy sharing the hyperinflation of the German Weimar Republic. The president elected in 1922, Gabriel Narutowicz, was soon assassinated because of his 'non-Polish' (ie Jewish) support; in May 1926 Piłsudski seized power again and instituted the *Sanacja* ('cleansing') regime, which in an increasingly fascist Europe was largely supported by the left and opposed by Dmowski's right-wing nationalists. With Piłsudski ruling largely from behind the scenes, economic development at least advanced; he was one of the first to recognise the threat of Nazism, and was able to sign a non-aggression pact with Hitler in 1934, the year before his death.

Having allowed Hitler to seize Austria and Czechoslovakia, Britain and France finally gave Poland guarantees of security in 1939; when Hitler seized Danzig on September 1 and invaded Poland, he began the Second World War. On September 17 Stalin also invaded and took half the country, as agreed in a secret clause of the Nazi-Soviet Non-Aggression (or Ribbentrop-Molotov) Pact of August 1939; this was the infamous 'stab in the back', in effect a fourth partition.

Hitler had made no secret of his contempt for the Poles, and his Governor-General Hans Frank said 'We do not admit the right of the Poles to exist in any form. Our policy is biological extermination'. (Nevertheless about 200,000 Polish babies were taken and Germanised, purely on aesthetic grounds, such as their having blue eyes: these people are now retracing their families and trying to sort out their mammoth identity crises.) The Nazis killed about 15,000 priests and intellectuals in Dachau and in the Palmiry forest, now in the Kampinos National Park northwest of Warsaw. Meanwhile up to 3m were sent to Germany for slave labour, and from 1940 huge camps were set up on Polish territory to begin the even more urgent business of exterminating the Jews of all Europe. The Warsaw Ghetto was set up in October 1939, enclosing a third of the city's population, and in 1941 alone 11,000 Jews starved to death there, before mass deportations began in July 1942. More harrowing details are given in the section on Auschwitz, but suffice it to record that perhaps 9m Jews, gypsies, communists and others died in the camps, taking as little as 20 minutes from the arrival of the train and the selection of those fit enough for slave labour to sorting out the gold teeth from the ashes of the others.

From the Soviet-occupied territories up to 2m Poles were deported to Siberia, under a half of whom returned, and 15,000 officers and intellectuals were massacred (as finally admitted in 1990), mainly in the forest of Katyń, now in Belarus. After 'Operation Barbarossa', Hitler's invasion of the Soviet Union on June 22 1941, a more generalised mayhem was unleashed on Poland, with reprisals for any resistance, and over 300 villages flattened.

A government in exile was set up in London under General Władysław Sikorski, a pre-Sanacja prime minister, and about 250,000 Poles were able to join the Allied forces in the west, performing notably well in the Battle of Britain (when maybe 20% of Royal Air Force pilots were Poles, perhaps saving Britain from invasion with their desperate nothing-left-to-lose courage: remember this when passing the Polish War Memorial junction on the A40 in Northolt) and at Tobruk and Monte Cassino. The Home Army (*Armia Krajowa* or AK) was the largest resistance movement in occupied Europe, numbering 350,000 and able to make over 1,100 attacks on the railways, to destroy over 4,300 military vehicles, and to mount spectacular coups such as seizing 100 million zloty or the entire core of a V2 rocket. From 1943 an army of 78,000 Poles was also raised in the Soviet Union, rising to 400,000 in 1945 with conscription in the liberated territories and then merged with the relatively few communist partisans of the People's Army, to form the postwar Polish Army.

Sikorski died in July 1943 when his Liberator aircraft crashed off Gibraltar; this remains unexplained, but may not be unconnected with Stalin transferring his support from him to the communist partisans. In April 1943 the Jewish Fighting Organisation had led a desperate uprising in the Warsaw Ghetto, from where 400,000 people had already been taken to the death camps; after three weeks 14,000 had been killed and the last 56,000 inhabitants were taken to Treblinka. On August 1 1944 there was a more general uprising by the Home Army in Warsaw, wishing to free the capital themselves before the advancing Red Army arrived; however the Soviets stopped on the far bank of the Wisła and waited for 63 days (going off to conquer Romania and Hungary instead) until the Nazis had, with appalling brutality, crushed the rising. When they finally sent supplies, it was Soviet ammunition which could not be used in the AK's captured German weapons; RAF and South African planes flew from Italy to parachute in supplies but had to give up after taking 90% losses. As with the Katyń massacre, the aim was to wipe out any possible opposition to a communist take-over; Stalin had already, back in 1938, liquidated the Polish Communist Party, exiled in Moscow, and replaced it with his own men.

Ten per cent of Warsaw's buildings had been damaged in 1939, 15% more during the Ghetto uprising, but after 1944 84% were uninhabitable. In the Warsaw Uprising 200,000 civilians were killed, more than at Hiroshima, and in all Warsaw lost 700,000 of its 1.3m pre-war inhabitants; overall Poland suffered appallingly in the war, losing 6m from a population of 35m (while Britain lost just 245,000 and the USA 310,000), as well as 90% of its industry and 70% of its livestock. In the midst of the final firestorm the world's worst maritime disaster occurred when a Soviet submarine sank the German refugee evacuation ship *Wilhelm Gustloff* off Danzig, but this was hardly noticed.

The Yalta conference (known as 'Yowta' to the Poles) of February 1945, between Stalin, Churchill and Roosevelt, is seen as the great betrayal of eastern Europe, but as the Red Army was already occupying most of it, having begun its last great offensive in January, there was little the free world could have done to prevent Stalin from having his way with it. In fact the principle of 'spheres of influence' had already been conceded at the Teheran conference of November 1943, which also accepted the principle of moving Poland's eastern border west, to the Curzon line suggested after the First World War.

A smaller area was gained from Germany, shifting Poland bodily 200km westwards to the Oder-Neisse line (on the Odra and Nysa rivers); Poland lost its minorities and marshes and gained more industrially developed areas. Three and a half million Germans were expelled, and 4½ m Poles arrived from the lands seized by Stalin, while of the 250,000 in the West only 100,000 chose to return home. Almost all the surviving 70-80,000 Jews (of 3.5m before the war) left for Palestine, and in 1947, 750,000 Ukrainians were deported from the southeastern areas.

Non-communist opposition groups fought against the Soviet occupiers until 1947, in the Święty Krzyż (Holy Cross) and Bieszczady mountains and the Podhale and Lublin/Białystock areas, until finally accepting an amnesty or fighting their way west to safety with US forces in Czechoslovakia. A provisional government was set up in Lublin in July 1944, in opposition to the internationally recognised government in London, and although 'there were hardly enough native Polish communists to run a factory, let alone a country of some 30m people', they were able to seize power, with the help of the Red Army and the NKVD security police (whose predecessor, the Cheka, had, ironically, been set up by the Polish Bolshevik Felix Dzierzynski). Only Stanisław Mikołajczyk (leader of the Peasant Movement) was persuaded to return from London to join the Provisional Government of National Unity (TRJN), which was then recognised by Britain and the United States, before fleeing in January 1947 just in time to avoid arrest. The 'free and unfettered elections' promised at Yalta did not materialise: instead there was a rigged referendum in 1946 and then elections in January 1947 before which 143 candidates were disqualified and one million voters summarily disenfranchised.

Together the communists and socialists won the elections, before the socialists were 'persuaded' to merge with the communists as the Polish United Workers' Party (PZPR); the party leader Władysław Gomułka was forced to resign in late 1948 for alleged Titoism (in reality because he was opposed to forcible collectivisation) and was replaced by the Stalinist stooge Bolesław Bierut, already state president. Industry was nationalised from 1946 and land redistributed to the peasants, but even in the period of full Stalinism (c1949-54) the Polish communists were unable to collectivise agriculture (only 9% of farmland by 1956) or subjugate the church (despite interning the primate Cardinal Wyszynski for three years in a Bieszczady monastery, as well as eight bishops and 900 priests); they were too mild in their approach to break 'civil society' but too harsh to win support, which held the seeds of their eventual failure in the 1980s.

Stalin died in 1953, and in 1955 there was some liberalisation; at the famous 20th Congress of the Soviet Communist Party in 1956 Krushchev denounced Stalin's crimes and Bierut died, apparently of a heart attack. In June 1956, as in Hungary just after, there was a popular revolt against worsening economic conditions, with at least 53 workers killed in Poznań, but the restoration of Gomułka to power in the 'Polish October' was enough to avoid the type of Soviet invasion that followed Imre Nagy's excessive reforms in Hungary. Nevertheless Poland was able to achieve some limited freedom, moving from being a puppet state to being a client state of the Soviet Union. Rokossowski, the Red Army Marshal who had been Bierut's watchdog, returned home, and the peasantry and church were left alone as long as they left the regime alone. However the economy stagnated throughout the 1960s, with no real rise in incomes.

Finally in 1970 the government moved to tackle food shortages (largely caused by its neglect of the largely private agricultural sector) by raising the prices of staple foods by a third, just a fortnight before Christmas; again there were riots, and a total of 300 were killed, this time mainly in Gdańsk. Edward Gierek replaced Gomułka and set off on a policy of raising living standards by borrowing from the West to invest in new industries and then pay off the debts by exporting to the West. However, driven by ideology, the investment was mainly in heavy industry and the West did not want the tatty products of the incompetent Polish system; it would have been far wiser to have boosted the private agricultural sector to buy off the people with food, but Poland, unable to pay the interest on its debts (which doubled in the 1970s to US$20bn, equal to those of the USSR) and overwhelmed by the cost of food subsidies, was doomed to find history repeating itself, in 1976 when 60% rises in staple food prices were again defeated by riots in Radom and Ursus, and again in 1980.

The ensuing story of Solidarity and Poland's present situation can be seen to be determined by its past history, above all the way in which the national identity has long been defined by opposition to Russia, as the easternmost bastion of Catholicism, and then during the two centuries of almost continuous occupation. Thus the Polish instinct, as they see it, is for democracy versus despotism, individualism versus collectivism, and Catholicism versus Orthodoxy (and German Protestantism). The Polish soul is felt to be predestined for martyrdom and vain resistance; although unable to avoid being swallowed by enemies, as Rousseau put it Poland is 'well able to save itself from being digested', and thus must eventually emerge again.

POLITICS

'The end of communism ... is something we have not yet been able to assimilate. It is like suddenly being left without a familiar pain, like the void left by a missing limb ... the conflict with communism has overshadowed our century. It dominated our politics, our hopes and fears, our view of the world. It cost us many lives and much money. We learned to live with a permanent enemy, studied his every trait and listened to his endless dreary polemics (we should not overlook sheer boredom as a factor in communism's fall).' This summary, from *Time* magazine, is apt enough for those of us living outside the communist bloc, but it was even more so for those obliged to live under communism. Now, of course, they are faced with immense problems in adapting from this former life to one of democracy and free-market capitalism, and are finding that this is no easy transition, but one that brings many new problems with it.

Of the eastern European states, Poland has been the most resolute in rejecting communism, for various reasons such as its long history of domination by foreign systems in general and by Russia in particular, the strength of the church, and the massive foreign debt built up under Gierek. Due to the strength of the faction in Solidarity that stands for traditional trade union welfare values, there is a great divide between the extreme free-marketeers and those seeking more restraint and compassion; thus the stakes are now higher in Poland than perhaps anywhere else in the region.

According to Timothy Garton Ash, it all began with the new Pope's first visit in 1979, when he drew massive crowds and 'broke through the barrier of fear'; as Cardinal-Archbishop of Kraków until his election as Pope John Paul II in 1978, Karol Wojtyła had shared his compatriots' conviction of national martyrdom and stood with them against the state. In August 1980 workers in the Lenin shipyard in Gdańsk went on strike (not for the first time) and occupied the yard in protest at 100% rises in food prices and then the sacking of a colleague accused of political agitation, and formed a free trade union called Solidarity (*Solidarność*), led by a charismatic electrician, sacked in 1976, called Lech Wałęsa;

although there were already strikes elsewhere, much underground publishing and an organisation called the Workers' Defence Committee (KOR) involving figures such as Jacek Kuroń and Adam Michnik, later major players in the Solidarity movement, it took this strike in the traditional centre of opposition to draw together all the dissident forces, workers and intellectuals, with the backing of the church, to draw up demands not just for better pay and conditions, but also for political rights such as free unions, the right to strike, and a free press.

Astonishingly, the government gave way, as strikes spread nationwide, in the Gdańsk Agreements of August 31 1980, and Solidarity soon had 9m members. However it was unable to force the government into real reforms (even though a fifth of the delegates at the Party congress were also Solidarity members), and the Soviet Union and Poland's other neighbours understandably felt threatened by this outbreak of liberty; the threat of an invasion, as in Hungary in 1956 and Czechoslovakia in 1968, grew until the Minister of Defence, General Jaruzelski, took control of the government in February 1981 and finally, after playing for time for as long as possible, was forced by the combined threat of renewed strikes and Soviet invasion to impose martial law in the early hours of December 13 1981. At least eight died, but resistance was passive, with factory occupations soon broken up.

Solidarity was banned and all its leaders interned, while hundreds of others went into hiding and set up an amazing network of underground publications and resistance. In June 1982 President Reagan met the Pope in the Vatican and apparently agreed to hasten the collapse of communism by supporting Solidarity, with funds channelled through US trade unions as well as through the church and the CIA; the cause was helped by another visit from the Polish Pope and by the award of the Nobel Peace Prize to Wałęsa in 1983, and in that year martial law was lifted. However Solidarity remained illegal, and while the government again tried desperately to dig the country out of its economic morass, the underground struggle for human rights and reform continued; a martyr was provided in 1984 when the security police murdered the Warsaw priest Jerzy Popiełuszko, although he was only one of at least 78 people killed in this period. By 1985 there were more than 400 underground magazines (mostly short-lived), with circulations of up to 30,000, as well as 'Solidarity lives' banners appearing illegally on TV, most notably at half-time of the soccer cup final.

In 1986 there were some reforms to allow the limited working of market forces, with some incentives and decentralisation, and the release of most political prisoners, and in early 1987 US sanctions were lifted, and Most Favoured Nation status restored, after the Polish government agreed on dialogue with the church. The government foolishly held a referendum on its reforms, which it lost, finally scuppering any hopes of turning around the economy; the Pope also returned in 1987, and in 1988 it was the turn of Soviet President Gorbachev (who had come to power in 1985) who signalled the need to come to an agreement with Solidarity, implicitly lifting the threat of armed intervention. The government again decided to remove food subsidies in 1988, but another wave of strikes, and Gorbachev's hands-off approach, led to the Round Table Talks of February 1989, preceded by the renunciation of the monopoly of power by the Polish communist party (PZPR).

On April 4 1989 Wałęsa and the Interior Minister General Kiszczak agreed that free unions and a free press should be restored and that elections should be held in June, in which 35% of the *Sejm*'s seats and all of those in a restored Senate would be openly contested, with the PZPR and its satellite parties guaranteed the rest and thus a majority in the *Sejm*. In return Solidarity accepted that wages should rise by only 80% of inflation, and that Jaruzelski and Kiszczak, the masterminds of martial law, should continue to rule.

The elections were held as communists were busy killing people in Tiananmen Square and produced a stunning defeat for the government, all but two of whose leading candidates were scratched from the 'National List' of seats reserved for the party. The opposition won all 161 available seats in the *Sejm* and 99 out of 100 Senate seats, which gave them a veto. The new parliament elected Jaruzelski president by one vote in an unspoken quid pro quo, to allow the communist establishment to retain control of the army and police. However the communists' satellite parties, the Democratic and Peasants' Parties, left the sinking ship and joined Solidarity in August to elect the Catholic intellectual Tadeusz Mazowiecki as President of the Council, ie the first non-communist prime minister in eastern Europe since the communist take-over. His 23-member cabinet had 11 Solidarity members, four communists, seven from the satellite parties and one independent.

The problems facing the new government were immense, but there was enough public goodwill to allow it to introduce the austerity measures that had led to strikes against the communist government. It also announced plans for a totally Western democracy and market economy even before the Berlin Wall, and the other communist regimes, crumbled in November 1989. In January 1990 the IMF approved economic shock therapy known as the Balcerowicz plan after the finance minister who master-minded it, which achieved the miracle of stabilising the economy and halting hyperinflation, then heading for 4,000% *per annum*. Income tax was to be introduced (above all to provide a direct link between the individual and the state), state enterprises gradually privatised, and a stock exchange opened, although industrial production fell by 23% in January 1990, and real incomes by 24%, and the cost of living rose by 76.8%.

The communist *apparat* served loyally under its former prisoners, but as communism collapsed all over Europe what had seemed an impossibly radical political arrangement began to be left behind by events, and Wałęsa, feeling increasingly marginalised in Gdańsk, began to agitate for faster reforms and fresh presidential elections. He had always had a slightly tangential relationship to the democratic principles of his intellectual advisers, and Solidarity not surprisingly began to split in mid-

1990 under the pressures of his manoeuvring and the stresses of being in power, as opposed to simply being defined and united by its opposition to 'Them'. Wałęsa's populist faction, the Centre Alliance (*Porozumienie Centrum*), manipulated nationalist emotions and discontent with the austerity programme by blaming it on the IMF, while the faction of prime minister Mazowiecki and other leading intellectuals such as Adam Michnik, Jacek Kuroń and Bronisław Geremek, became first ROAD (Civic Movement-Democratic Action) and then the *Unia Demokratyczna* or Democratic Union.

The former Polish Communist Party transformed itself into the Polish Social Democrats (SdRP), part of the Democratic-Left Alliance (SLD) in the *Sejm*, while many new parties sprang up, the most important of which are the Christian Democrats (ZChN, pronounced ZedHaEn) and the Liberal-Democrats (KLD). There are now 166 parties in all, rather less than in Spain or Italy.

Jaruzelski stepped down to allow presidential elections in November 1990, in which Mazowiecki came a bad third and resigned with his government; in a second round Wałęsa defeated the maverick Polish-Canadian outsider Stanisław Tymiński, largely a protest candidate (whose Party X was later disqualified in the general elections for electoral fraud in 32 regions, and won only three seats). In early 1991 Jan Krzysztof Bielecki of the KLD was appointed prime minister and continued the reform programme, with Balcerowicz remaining finance minister; by May 1991 78% of households were pessimistic about their economic prospects and Solidarity actually organised a day of protest *against* the government. By September the former communists in parliament were blocking over 100 reform bills and all further public spending cuts, although the budget deficit was now three times the IMF targets, leading to the withdrawal of credits; Bielecki and his government resigned, and new parliamentary elections were held in October.

In these, the first fully free elections since 1926, the campaigning seemed more like recruiting than electioneering and there was only a 43% turnout due to general disillusionment. Due to the complex proportional representation system there were 29 parties in the *Sejm* or parliament, 11 with only one member; the UD was the largest party with 12.3% of the vote and 62 out of 460 seats (and 21 of 100 Senate seats), although the seven ex-Solidarity parties took 45% of the vote in all and now began a very gradual process of reconciliation.

Close behind them came the SLD, which has a very solid bedrock of support among former Party members and their families, with 12% and 60 seats, and then the right-wing Catholic Action (49 seats), the PSL, the United Peasants' Party, now a right of centre party (48), the far-right Confederation for an Independent Poland (46), Wałęsa's PC (44), and the more market-orientated KLD (37), while the Polish Beerlovers' Party (*Polska Partia Przyjaciół Piwa* or PPPP) won 16 seats. This party ran a highly entertaining campaign, fronted by the 18-stone Guinness-loving singer and comedian Janusz Rewiński, but did have a serious programme, wanting the taxation of alcohol by volume, to cut vodka consumption and thus alcoholism, and less polluted water supplies. It has now become the Polish Economic Programme (PPG), speaking for the new entrepreneurs, but nevertheless in April 1993 it claimed to have set the record for the world's greatest binge, when 30 drinkers sank 400 litres in 12 hours, 'to show that beer can be enjoyed socially. A spokesman claimed none of the group got drunk during the binge'.

President Wałęsa's rôle and powers were undefined, but increasingly he saw himself as a sort of licensed opposition to his own government, seeming to model himself on Piłsudski; after the UD failed to put together a government, Jan Olszewski of the PC became prime minister with a coalition of five centre-right parties including the Christian Democrats and Peasants. He maintained the reformist economic programme, although accepting the need to ease its harshness, and Wałęsa almost immediately began to cast doubt on his ability to govern. When Olszewski presented his budget in February 1992 his finance minister resigned in protest at plans to increase the money supply and risk increasing inflation, but Poland was able to get more World Bank credits, to have much of its existing foreign debt cancelled, and to become an associate member o the EC, with Hungary and Czechoslovakia, fellow members of the 'Visegrád Group'. Exports to the EC rose by 53% during 1988-90, and imports by 59%, about double the rate in Hungary and Czechoslovakia.

However the *Sejm* refused to accept the budget; the government refused to resign, but Wałęsa and his kitchen cabinet continued to undermine it and to press for more powers to rule by presidential decree. The budget debate continued through April, while Wałęsa attempted to build a new government coalition; the Minister of Defence resigned warning of the risk of a coup and a return to authoritarianism, and finally the Interior Minister resorted to blackmail by threatening to release secret files showing that even Wałęsa had been an informer for the security police.

The farce was finally brought to an end in June 1992 when Olszewski lost a vote of confidence and resigned; at the time this was seen as Wałęsa's finest hour, restoring his reputation for dynamism by cutting through the impasse and appointing as prime minister Waldemar Pawlak of the PSL, who was expected to be more pragmatic and pliable, bringing a younger generation to power. However, he was unable to form a coalition, and in July a workable compromise was finally reached to bring the UD, in many ways the natural party of government and inheritor of what was left of the legacy of Solidarity, back into power under Hanna Suchocka (pronounced Suhotska), backed by almost every major party bar the far-right KPN, the far-left SLD, and Pawlak's PSL. This was seen as the last chance of avoiding direct presidential rule, and stability was only achieved by allowing the president implicit control of foreign, internal and defence affairs, while the prime minister ran the economy. She was competent and hard-working, known as 'Poland's Iron Lady', although reputed to have even less sense of humour than Mrs Thatcher. More strikes in mid-1992 led to a social pact, but the government still struggled to pass its budget, with further welfare cuts, despite threats of early elections. In addition there was a shock defeat in March 1993 for its Mass Privatisation Programme; what had been a seven-party coalition had now become nine parties due to the fragmentation of existing parties.

The reputation of the *Sejm* was so bad, besmirched by sexual and financial scandals, that almost no party wanted elections before absolutely necessary, particularly as changes to the electoral system would see many marginal parties excluded from the *Sejm*; however the SLD and ZChN were seen as clean and could only gain by waiting for more scandals to unfold. Local government is now seen as pragmatic and hard-working (50% of votes in the May 1990 local elections went to independents), but parliament was seen as purely careerist and self-seeking. Nevertheless, the economic shock therapy was now seen to be working, with a stable currency and real growth of about 2% expected in 1993, although the growth of unemployment from virtually zero to 3m is still a problem.

The campaign orchestrated by Olszewski for 'lustration', the opening of security police files on all those suspected of collaboration, continued in spite of police harassment of journalists naming names; however it seems likely that many files, including those on Wałęsa, were shredded and delivered by the truckload to paper factories. There have also been calls for Jaruzelski to be tried for the excesses of martial law, but 52% of the population now feel that it was justified as a way of buying off Soviet intervention.

By April 1993 the social contract was under threat, with threats of a general strike as pay continued to lag behind rising prices; the Non-party Bloc for Reform (BBWR) was, as expected, set up as a political vehicle for Wałęsa (based on the workers in the large state enterprises), and in May 1993 the government lost a confidence debate by one vote, and elections were called for September.

These produced a clear victory for the ex-communists, who doubled their 1991 vote, with the SLD the largest party (with 20% of the vote and 171 out of 460 seats), the PSL second (with 15% and 132 seats), and then the DU third (with 11% and 69 seats). The right-wing Catholic/nationalist parties almost all fell below the new threshold of 5% of the total vote. The result was seen as a reaction against church influence rather than against economic reform; the winners promised 'reform with a human face' and promised to be pragmatic, continuing the process of modernisation, while respecting the views of those who felt that life was 'easier if not better' under communism. The SLD was not keen to work with the PSL, feeling it to be too much of a single-issue party and that the farmers' demands for subsidies and restrictions on western imports would impede reform and integration with the EU; they might even have kept Suchocka in power, but the DU refused to work with them. In the end, after three weeks of negotiation, it was the PSL's Pawlak who emerged as prime minister of a SLD/PSL coalition. He is seen as duller than John Major, but appointed Miss Poland, Ewa

Wachowicz, as his spokesperson in an attempt to lighten his image.

A new constitution is needed to ease the friction between the directly-elected president, the parliament, and the government; large-scale privatisation, seen in the Balcerowicz plan as the only answer to wage-push inflation, has proceeded very slowly, although the retail sector was, fortunately, privatised, and many new shops opened, before prices were freed, thus avoiding the chaos seen in Russia, and the Mass Privatisation Programme was finally approved just a month before the Suchocka government fell. The environmental disasters in so many areas have hardly been tackled yet, due to lack of funds.

In the areas under presidential control there is some confusion: in September 1992 Poland acceded to the Geneva Convention on Refugees and Asylum-Seekers, but in July it had, in return for £48m, agreed to take back potentially huge numbers of unwanted refugees from Germany: in 1992 one million refugees and immigrants arrived in Germany, with about 20 a night illegally fording the Nysa (Neisse) river from Poland. Poland was also undecided about whether it wished to forge closer links with the EU, thus perhaps sacrificing to Brussels some rights only just regained, and whether to be truly neutral or to align itself with NATO; in the end it pushed for full NATO membership, and (with Ukraine) signed up for the 'Partnership for Peace' in February 1994. Already some Euro-Regions are being set up overlapping Poland's frontiers, around Szczecin (Stettin), in Silesia, and in Transcarpathia. Polish troops have also served with the UN in Cambodia.

THE ECONOMY

Poland's communist government avoided every difficult economic decision, and then allowed wages to rise by 200% in the six months before the elections of 1989 (not collecting taxes from businesses so that they could pay workers more); then after the elections subsidised food prices were raised six times, so that in 1989 the cost of living rose 250%. The new government opted for a Big-Bang approach to economic reform, and output plunged as it ceased bailing out technically bankrupt state enterprises, which had yielded 80% of state revenue. Gross National Product (ie total economic activity) fell by 40% and unemployment rose to two million.

However in 1993 (despite the loss of 70% of Poland's export markets with the collapse of the Soviet Union) it seems clear that the Polish economy has turned the corner. GDP, having fallen by 25% since 1990, rose by 0.5% in 1992 (with 3% growth expected in 1993, and 40-55% of economic activity now in the private sector), unemployment is stable at 2.8m (15%), and inflation is down (from 585% in 1990) to 60% pa in 1992, with a rate of 35% expected in 1993. More than US$1bn of foreign capital was invested in Poland in 1992, following an agreement with the IMF restricting the budget deficit to 5% of GNP. The most visible foreign investment has been in the motor industry, with General

Motors taking an 80% stake in FSO (the Passenger Car Factory) to produce Opel Astras, FIAT buying 90% of FSM (the Small Car Factory) to build its new Cinquecento in Tychy, south of Katowice, and Volkswagen buying 91% of FSR (the Agricultural Car Factory) to build pick-ups in Poznań (where Ford is also planning a factory). These changes created 38,000 jobs; although Polish factories annually produced 127 cars per 1,000 workers, against an EU average of 360 (and an eastern European average of 117), wage levels are still so low (US$2.50 per hour, against US$24 in western Germany) that production here is cheaper than in the EU. There is some resentment that of the US$8.7bn foreign aid supplied by late 1992, only US$1.6bn has been cash, with the rest in the form of credits to allow Western companies to dump their products in the Polish market.

However the rushed programme to privatise Poland's existing industry is going less well. Poland avoided the mistakes later made in Russia, and quickly sold 100,000 small and medium-sized shops before freeing prices, to create a free retail market, although there still seems to be no concept of undercutting or competition. Nine private banks were hived off from the National Bank (although seven of these are only surviving with government support) and 80 private banks have now been created. A stock exchange opened in April 1991 (in the former Communist Party Central Committee building; a casino was set up in the former Palace of Culture), but by September 1993 only 19 stocks were quoted, of which the most successful were the Okocim and Żywiec breweries. Plans to transfer 600 state enterprises to twenty management funds, and then to private shareholders, were finally passed by the *Sejm* in April 1993, but only when the government made it a vote of confidence. It was also planned to sell 7,000 smaller firms, 50% of the state sector, between 1989 and 1992, but by June 1992 only 1,714 had been sold. Private savings had been wiped out by inflation, and few Polish businesses were in a state to justify risking private capital in them. As 'selling something without value to people without money' proved difficult, privatisation was effected by giving vouchers to the population; these have not been a great hit, and this technique doesn't deal with the crucial problem of getting private-sector management expertise into state enterprises. In addition capital is needed for new investment.

Nevertheless 1.5m new businesses have been created, most seemingly *Fryzjer* (hairdressers) and *Kwiaty* (flower shops), and the many near-identical grocery shops in the ground floors of houses. These all charge the same corner-shop prices for the same German processed foods. There is also a rash of new video shops, most busily copying Western films without paying copyright fees; the film (and software) companies are using former secret policemen as enforcers, but in a country where underground publishers were so recently heroes there is a reluctance to return to anything like censorship. Agriculture in Poland has always been largely private, but now 44% of non-agricultural employment is also outside the state sector.

There have been far greater social costs here than for example in

Hungary, where a more gradualist approach to reform was possible due to a lesser foreign debt burden; unemployment is something that the communist states never had to face, but equally there was a long tradition of extended families taking the strain and of people finding work in the 'grey' economy. Unemployment benefit has been introduced, initially at 70% of earnings and dropping to 40% or the minimum wage level. There has been an increase in social differentiation, with a 4:1 (and widening) ratio between the incomes of the bottom and top quintiles. More tellingly, suicides, which fell by a third in the glory days of 1980-81, are now rising steadily. Wałęsa, who initially espoused rapid reforms to copy Spain's transition from dictatorship to democracy and EU membership within 10 years, soon changed to a more populist position, demanding an easing of the austerity programme, while Mazowiecki and his left-of-centre supporters later demanded a social contract as the only way of preventing social collapse; but in any case the Poles have proved capable of struggling through the few local difficulties confronting them. Full EU membership should be possible within a decade; however Western business people still find it hard to work with Poles as equals, seeing them either as stuck in a communist mind-set that does not allow them to act on their own initiative, or as infected with a false concept of capitalism that leads them to act cynically for short-term gains rather than building long-term relationships on a basis of trust.

MINORITIES

Betwen the World Wars only 69% of Poland's population was actually Polish, with large numbers of Ukrainians and Byelorussians in the east of the country, and a huge Jewish population. By 1989 only 1.5% of the population was non-Polish, making it to my mind rather too uniform. This was due of course to the elimination of almost all the Jews and to the postwar changes to the borders, with a far more positive approach to mass population movements than has ever been possible before or after. However there are still interesting traces of Jewish, German and Ukrainian (Łemk and Boyk) cultures, as well as some remaining Tatars on the border near Białystok.

Jews apparently first reached Poland in the 10th Century, from the Rhône valley and from the Khazar empire between the Don and Volga rivers. More came from the 12th to the 15th Centuries, driven from western Europe by crusading fervour and then the Inquisition, and were welcomed as much-needed artisans and merchants. In the 18th Century the Hasidic reform movement began in Poland. The Jewish community developed until in the 19th Century they were at the heart of Poland's industrialisation and of its cultural life. A highly urbanised people, they made up over a third of the population of Warsaw (where 60% of doctors were Jewish) and often over half the population of smaller towns, particularly in the east. In the independent Poland of the 1920s Jews, 10% of the population, were excluded from the civil service, and even in the Second World War they were excluded from the Home Army, forming the ZOB, the Fighting Jewish Fighting Organisation, instead.

After this war many of the 300,000 surviving Jews (of 3-3.5m before it) naturally left for Palestine, particularly after pogroms in 1946, and in 1968 more left after an officially condoned anti-Zionist campaign, led by the army magazine. The Chief Rabbi left for Israel in 1973, returning as a temporary visitor in 1988; in early 1989 a second Chief Rabbi was appointed, leading to a bizarre situation as they wrangled over the proceeds from kosher vodka exports.

By 1989 there were just 6-10,000 Jews in Poland, of whom 4,000 were practising their religion. Now these numbers are expected to double as some Polish Jews feel freer to return home, and others still in Poland rediscover their heritage, helped by rabbis sent by US charities. Nevertheless there is still widespread anti-semitism in Poland, which as explained above defines its national character by contrast to what is 'not-Polish' and thus to what is 'not-Catholic'. Poles, like Jews, see themselves as martyrs, but it is hard to accept two competing martyrdom ideologies. In a recent poll 40% of Poles felt Jews played too important a rôle in public life, even though there are virtually none left.

Communism was seen as Jewish; it is still generally assumed by Poles that anyone who seeks political power is somewhere deep down Jewish, and this is a smear hinted at even by Wałęsa and others who should know better. In a nutshell the assumption seems to be that because there are problems there have to be Jews. There has long been controversy about the rôle of ordinary Poles in the Holocaust; it is true that there were many cases of Poles helping Jews to escape deportation to the camps, but there were also many cases of either active or passive anti-semitism, particularly among the peasantry. There was a creeping progression from the early Christian 'You may not live among us as Jews' to the medieval 'You may not live among us' to the Nazi 'You may not live'; thus there were many degrees of complicity in the Final Solution, from those who drove the trains to those who helped pick out Jewish Poles for deportation.

Orbis runs special tours of Poland's Jewish heritage (from £530 for a week), and publishes an excellent free leaflet and a map showing sites of interest from synagogues and cemeteries to ghettos and concentration camps. In particular you will still find many Jewish cemeteries, with their attractive and evocative tombstones. In Warsaw the Social and Cultural Society of Jews in Poland and the State Jewish Theatre are to be found at Plac Grzybowski 12/16, and the Jewish Historical Institute at ul Tłomackie 3/5, with other Jewish bodies mostly at the same addresses. Interesting books that appeared too late for me to use are *Jewish Heritage Travel* by Ruth Gruber (Wiley 1992), which does not include any of the former Soviet republics, and *Poland's Jewish Heritage* by Joram Kagan (Hippocrene 1992).

The entire western part of present-day Poland was part of Germany until 1945, and has almost no Polish history before then. At least 3m **Germans** were deported to Germany from this area after 1945, with many more moving to the DDR in 1956; they were replaced by the Polish population of the areas of Galicia transferred to Ukraine. In particular the inhabitants of Lviv were largely transplanted to Breslau, which became Wrocław. Nevertheless something like 300,000 Germans (estimates range from 100,000 to 1.2m) remain in this area, although they were increasingly driven underground and denied their identity. German language teaching was banned from 1946 to 1951, and many do not now speak German, but particularly since the end of communism German culture has been resurgent, and they had seven deputies in the 1991 *Sejm*. The German villages are easily identified by their manicured lawns and rows of satellite dishes, and often by a new memorial to the German dead of the Second World War; some of the Silesian Germans still talk of having a 'higher culture' than the Poles, and do not understand that these memorials are deeply offensive.

In addition the resorts of the Karkonosze are again full of German visitors popping across the border for the day or the weekend; they fit in very well, as there are many buildings with Teutonic oxeye windows in the roof, and memorials to *Unser Gefallenen* of the First World War.

Gypsies are increasingly to be seen in Poland, simply and blatantly begging far more than they do in Romania, Slovakia and Hungary. They are concentrated in the major towns and resorts such as Zakopane, Kraków, Wrocław, and Katowice, and can be seen with children strategically placed around road junctions with their mother watching and orchestrating things. It is unfortunate that Poles don't distinguish between Romany and Romanian, which has unfortunate consequences for Romania's image. There are however more long-established Polish gypsy communities in the south of the country, in hamlets such as at Łegi Gorzków, south of Nowy Sącz, who may be euphemistically described as a 'Slovak' minority. Although these are discriminated against as gypsies are everywhere (and of course many gypsies lost their lives in the Holocaust), many of them are reasonably integrated into the broader society.

The **Łemks** and **Boyks**, together with the Hutuls living further east in Ukraine and Romania, are usually regarded as Ukrainian (Ruthenian or *Rusyn*) sub-groups, but their origins seem to be more confused. The empty hills of the Bieszczady and the poloninas to the east were inhabited in the middle ages by groups of migrant shepherds from the south known as Croats or Vlachs. They then seem to have expanded westwards into the mountains of eastern Moravia and western Slovakia from the 15th Century. The Bieszczady, south of Lesko and Ustrzyki Dolne and east of the Osława river and the Łupków pass, is now inhabited by Boyks, and the area west to the Poprad river and Krynica, as well as Slovakia and Transcarpathia south of the Carpathian watershed, by Łemks, perhaps 50,000 in all. Speaking a Ukrainian dialect and using Cyrillic script, they traditionally lived as shepherds and foresters.

These hills were a stronghold of the UPA or Ukrainian Resistance Army, fighting in 1945-47 for Ukrainian independence from Germany,

Poland and the Soviet Union, who assassinated the Polish Deputy Minister of Defence in 1947 at Jabłonki, in the Bieszczady. This led to Operation Wisła, a joint operation by the Polish, Soviet and Czechoslovak armies to drive out the UPA and deport many of the inhabitants of the area either to Ukraine or to the 'Recovered Territories', the former German areas of Poland. Many villages were razed, leaving only graveyards buried deep in nettles, but many survive, particularly in the Beskid Niski, and now some families are returning and Łemk and Boyk culture is reasserting itself. The Ukrainian Social-Cultural Association was in fact set up in 1956, and by 1978 had 171 branches and 6,000 members; more recently the Ukrainian Centre of Education and Culture has been set up at ul Kanonicza 15 in Kraków, showing exhibitions of Ukrainian art. The Kraków Ethnographic Museum has a wonderful collection of Łemk, Boyk and Hutul material, a Łemk music and dance group is based in the village of Bielanka, southwest of Gorlice, and a Hutul band can sometimes be seen at venues like the Jagiellonian University's Cultural Centre in Kraków. In July there is a festival of Łemk culture in Zdynia, south of Gorlice. There is a community museum of Łemk culture at Zyndranowa, right by the Dukla pass.

RELIGION

In the middle ages Poland was keen to receive Jews unwelcome in much of Europe, and then gained a reputation as 'the Paradise of Heretics', where any brand of protestantism was indulged — in 1773 only half the population was Catholic. It was only in the two centuries of partition and occupation that Polish nationalism aligned itself so closely with the Roman Catholic faith, and it was the post-Second World War border changes that turned Poland into a country 94% Catholic, just as it was being given an atheist government.

As described in the section on Polish History, the communists utterly failed to suppress the church, or the people's devotion to it. In 1937 (in a bigger but less Catholic Poland) there had been about 11,000 priests, in 1981 there were 20,676, and a Pope (Karol Wojtyła, who had been Cardinal-Archbishop of Kraków from 1965 to 1978, and then became Pope John Paul II), and by 1989 there were 24,678, with 14,335 churches.

In the communist period the church changed from a narrow-minded, reactionary and tacitly anti-semitic body, based in the countryside, to being the voice and conscience of the new urban working classes, and forging alliances with students, intellectuals and human rights activists. In particular the Catholic Intellectuals' Clubs (*Klub Inteligencji Katolickiej*) and the Catholic University of Lublin (KUL) had a pervasive influence, with figures such as Tadeusz Mazowiecki, the first Solidarity prime minister, being associated with the KIK.

As Tim Garton Ash has said, it was the Polish Pope's visits to his homeland that set off the Solidarity revolution and that may have blocked Soviet intervention. He focused his prayers for Poland's freedom on the Virgin Mary, already credited with repelling Muslim Turks and Tatars, Swedish Lutherans and, in 1920, Soviet Bolsheviks, and particularly on the icon of the Black Madonna at Częstochowa, firmly believing that she had saved his life when he was shot in St Peter's Square in Rome on May 13 1981, the anniversary of her first apparition at Fátima, in Portugal. Here she had both predicted the rise of communism, in 1917, and its collapse, once the Pope had as instructed consecrated Russia to her in 1984, the year before Mikhail Gorbachev came to power and set in motion the unwinding of the Soviet system. Make of this what you will.

Under martial law church attendance rose from 65% to 90-95% of the population, and pilgrimages to Częstochowa to 5m a year; this level of support has since declined. Increasingly the old Solidarity alliance has fragmented, with secular leftish intellectuals on one wing, and conservative nationalists on the other increasingly associating themselves with the Catholic church. There was a surprising amount of controversy when the church insisted on religious education being reintroduced in schools: most children were already receiving instruction in church, and parents liked this status quo, with a clear division of responsibility between church and state. Much the same applied in the more predictable debate over reforming the liberal communist abortion laws of 1956, with the church demanding a total ban and the bulk of the populace wanting reasonably free access to abortion to be retained. In the end a compromise came into effect in March 1993, allowing abortion when the mother's health was endangered or in cases of rape or incest, and providing for three years imprisonment for doctors in other cases. The church also wanted a ban on contraception, again resisted by the populace and rejected by pharmacists and doctors.

In October 1990 the church had achieved a 73% approval rating in a poll, but by early 1993 this was down to 41% approval and 45% disapproval, the first time that a majority had been against the church. It is clear that Poles do not accept all the church's teachings with equal fervour: although otherwise similar to the Irish in their boozy patriotism, families are much smaller in Poland. In addition, country people will still superstitiously put a red tassel on a horse's bridle against the evil eye, as in much of eastern Europe (and on Tibetan yaks).

Nevertheless, the church remains an absolutely central part of Polish life, with many people going to mass every day. On a Sunday evening it can be bewildering to see a town centre full of smartly dressed young people, all heading not for bars and clubs but for church, and to a secular Westerner it is this religious fervour, particularly the cult of mariolatry, that makes Poland seem still a rather strange and alien place, at a time when everything else in the country is moving rapidly towards assimilation with the West. Churches are always busy, though more so in towns, especially industrial suburbs, than in the country, and you will find many *Dewocjonalia* or religious knick-knacks shops.

Under the umbrella of the Catholic church are the 200,000 remaining

Uniates or Greco-Catholics (*Unicki* or *Greko-Katolicki*), largely following the Eastern Orthodox rites but accepting the authority of the Pope; these are mainly Lemks and Boyks, in the southeastern corner of Poland, and are more fully described in the sections on *Minorities* (in both Poland and Ukraine) and in the itinerary visiting the *Wooden Churches of the Beskid Niski*. The Uniate church is finding its feet again, on both sides of the border, and I was told that there are now Uniate students from Ukraine at the Catholic University of Lublin. The Polish Autocephalous Orthodox Church (the *Prawosławny*), in the east, has about 600,000 followers, and the Lutherans, in the west, number about 150,000. In addition there are about 2,500 Tatars, notably on the border with Belarus, with four or five mosques.

There are between 12m and 14m ethnic Poles living abroad, mostly descendents of partition-period emigrants from Galicia, but also the 150,000 who stayed abroad after the Second World War, and the 250,000 who emigrated (150,000 of them illegally) between 1981 and 1988. Most of them (8m-9m) are in the USA (with perhaps 5m in Chicago), and perhaps a million in Brazil and a million in Ukraine, Lithuania and Belarus. Since travel regulations were eased in 1987 these expatriates have been returning on visits, and it is calculated that 49% of all Western visitors to Poland are in fact ethnic Poles. In 1991 30.7m of a total 49m visits to Poland (up from a low of 4m in 1985) were by Germans, 25% of whom were of Polish origin; 80% of Berliners visit Poland at least four times a year, above all on shopping trips.

However almost a third of visitors to Poland (16.4 million in 1992) actually come from the East (including the Czech and Slovak Republics and Hungary), and only 5% of these are ethnic Poles; the rest come to trade. As many Poles leave the country, with about half a million each year going to work in Germany and Sweden, and many more travelling as 'trade tourists'.

Equally there are 2.5m Ukrainians abroad (30,000 in Britain, 1.5m in North America, particularly in the Canadian prairies), and they too are starting to return to visit their old haunts, particularly in Galicia.

Festivals

Public holidays in Poland have changed slightly since the end of communism, but as you would expect here most are religious in origin. There are 11 of them: January 1, Easter Sunday and Monday, but not Good Friday, May Day, May 3 (anniversary of the 1791 and 1973 Constitutions), Corpus Christi (a Thursday between May 30 and June 10), August 15 (the Assumption of the Virgin Mary, and the anniversary of the Miracle Battle of the Wisła in 1920, when the Virgin is supposed to have saved Poland from the Bolsheviks; this has replaced July 22, the communist Day of National Rebirth), November 1 (All Saints or All Souls Day), November 11 (Independence Day, 1918), and Christmas and Boxing Days.

Easter is the main religious festival of Poland, with the main church service late on Saturday night. Easter Sunday is spent feasting; in particular there must be a *pisanka* or Easter egg, either dyed brown by boiling with onion peel or painted in complex multicoloured designs, and *mazurek*, an Easter shortcake topped with dried fruit and nuts, jam or marzipan. Easter Monday is traditionally marked by young men splashing girls with water; nowadays it seems that men are equally vulnerable. Kalwaria Zebrzydowska is famous for its passion plays in Holy Week, and Częstochowa is particularly busy with pilgrimages to mark the Assumption.

Christmas celebrations begin on Christmas Eve with a family meal (with places set for dead members of the family), with fish rather than meat, followed by carols and midnight mass (*pasterka*). The next two days are a time for visiting and entertaining, with mummers and in Kraków the *szopka* cribs displayed.

There are any number of music festivals all over Poland, notably organ music in Kraków and Polish contemporary music in Poznań, both in late April, church music in Częstochowa in early May, chamber music in the Łańcut palace in the second week of May, choral music in Międzyzdroje (in the extreme northwest of the country) in the first fortnight of June, the Kraków Days in June, music by Wieniawski in Szczawno-Zdrój (southwest of Wrocław) sometime in June, the Moniuszko Competition in Warsaw in mid-June and a Moniuszko festival in Kudowa Zdrój in late June, old music in Stary Sącz at the end of June and early August, organ music in Koszalin in July, the Paderewski Music Meetings in Kasna Dolna, also in July, music by Szymanowski in Zakopane in early July, and by Chopin in Duszniki Zdrój in early August, the Kraków Old Music Festival in the second half of August, the *Vratislavia Cantans* choral festival in Wrocław in the first fortnight of September, and the Warsaw Autumn Festival of Contemporary Music in about the third week of September. There are also major competitions that are not held annually, such as the Chopin piano competition in Warsaw (October 1995, 2000 etc) and the Wieniawski violin competition in Poznań in November 1996, 2001 etc.

In addition jazz is wildly popular in Poland, with festivals in Wrocław in March, in Warsaw in June and late October, in Zamość in late August or September, in Kraków in September and November, and in Kalisz (piano) in November/December. There is also a country music festival in Mrągowo at the end of July and beginning of August.

Folk music and culture is served by festivals in Kazimierz Dolny in June, in Żywiec and Wisła, both in late July or early August, in Zakopane in late August (or September), and in Katowice and Zielona Góra in September, as well as the festival of Jewish Culture in Kraków in April/May. The World Festival of Polonia (expatriate) Folk Groups is held in Rzeszów every three years (1995, 1998 etc).

There are film festivals in Kraków in June (Short Films) and in Gdańsk in September, and theatre festivals in Wrocław in May/June, Jelenia Góra in August (Street Theatre), and Warsaw in October (Jewish Theatre) and December.

Orbis (see page 46) publishes a leaflet on 'Cultural Events in Poland', and information offices should be able to tell you more.

Chapter 5

In Poland

BEFORE YOU GO

Visas are no longer required for most Western visitors for a stay of up
to six months in Poland (your passport should in any case be valid for six
months), and the Poles themselves are now equally free to roam Europe
seeking work or cheap goods that they can sell elsewhere, continuing
the tradition whereby there were 'Polish markets' all over eastern
Europe. Nevertheless visitors are formally required to register within 48
hours of arrival; this can be satisfied by checking into any hotel, PTTK
hostel or official campsite.

If you wish to check, Polish consulates are at 73 New Cavendish St,
London W1N 7RB, UK (tel 071 580 3750), 2224 Wyoming Ave NW,
Washington DC 20008, USA (tel 202 234 2501), 7 Turrana St,
Yarralumla, ACT 2600, Australia (tel 06 273 1208), 443 Daly Avenue,
Ottawa, Ontario K1N 6H3, Canada (tel 613 236 0468) and vul
Yaroslavov 12, Kyiv, Ukraine (tel 224 8040), as well as Sydney,
Montréal, Toronto, Chicago, New York and elsewhere. In Warsaw the
British embassy is at aleja Róż 1 (tel 022 628 1001), with the consulate
at ul Wawelska 14 (tel 258 031), the American at al Ujazdowskie 29/31,
00-540 Warsaw (tel 628 3041), the Australian at ul Estońska 3/5, 03-
903 Warsaw (tel 176 081), the Canadian at ul Matejki 1/5, 00-481
Warsaw (tel 298 051), and the Ukrainian at al J.C. Schucha 7 (tel 296
449). Visa sections are generally only open for a few hours a few
mornings a week, and take only cash for visa fees. The British Council
is at al Jerozolimskie 59 (tel 287 401), near LOT at no 65 (tel 952 953),
and Polres (for rail reservations) at no 44 (tel 275 588).

Currency exchange is likewise no problem, with reasonably efficient
banks in most towns and private exchange counters (*kantors*) also
springing up just about everywhere. These deal only in cash, but at
competitive rates, so you have to decide how much folding cash to take
(US dollars and Deutschmarks *much* preferred to sterling, if you don't
mind), and how much to take in safer forms such as travellers cheques.
Certainly you should have some large Eurocheques or travellers cheques,
and some low-denomination banknotes for those petty frontier-hopping

expenses. It is now possible to buy and sell Bulgarian, Romanian, Russian and any other currencies across eastern Europe, which is a truly revolutionary change! The US dollar already operates as a parallel currency, as across eastern Europe. Credit cards are still not issued to Poles, so can only be used in tourist hotels, airports, and for car hire and so on. Personal cheques are also still rare.

Generally you have to pay 1% for travellers cheques, but some building societies will provide them free to account holders or buyers of travel insurance. Cash usually costs 0.5%, but some banks charge a flat fee which is better if you want large sums.

Theoretically there are 100 groszy to the złoty, but inflation means that you will never see any of these coins. (A small breadroll cost 50 groszy in the 1960s, and Z1,000 in mid-1992, ie 100,000 groszy.) Złoty are all in note form (celebrating the heroes of communism, and also Copernicus, Chopin and Curie), and all the same size, which makes life hard for the visually handicapped; it's wise to keep your six-figure notes separate from the smaller ones, lest you pay Z500,000 instead of Z5,000. In November 1992 a new 2m złoty note was introduced (and many were found to have the word 'constitutional' misspelt), but it is expected that in 1994 the currency will be reformed, with one new złoty replacing one thousand of the current złoty; the 50 and 100 złoty notes are to be replaced with coins. Note that the 200,000 złoty note has been withdrawn and is invalid. Some postage stamps are now overprinted with higher values, but this is not likely to happen to banknotes.

The złoty is now internally convertible, meaning in essence that Poland will risk its currency at world market rates, but the rest of the world is not interested in it, so it is not available outside the country. This is no problem, as you can change money easily on arrival, and can use dollars in the interim; in February 1994 US$1 was worth Z21,900, and £1 sterling Z32,300. There is also no problem changing złoty back into hard currency.

In May 1992, when the average monthly salary was about Z2m and the pound sterling was worth Z25,000, accommodation in youth hostels cost from Z20,000, and hotels from Z80,000; museums cost from Z2,000 to Z20,000, a kilo loaf of bread Z5,000, an omelette or a beer about Z8,000, a kilo of apples Z22,000, and a kilo of cheese about Z85,000. Bus fares were about Z250 per km. By May 1993 (when sterling was worth Z26,000) hotels cost from Z100,000, bread was up to Z8,000 and beer to a minimum of Z10,000, but apples were down to Z10,000/kg and cheap cheese to Z50,000/kg. Pasta and rice cost about Z12,000/kg, and plum jam the same for 500g, so an impecunious traveller could have a healthy diet of 3,000 Kcal a day for Z60,000 (£2.40); meat and cheese cost as much as in Britain, but other staples are about 40% of British prices.

General **Tourist Information** is available at the offices of the state tourist enterprise Orbis (also known as Polorbis), at 82 Mortimer St, London

W1N 7DE (tel 071 580 8028/637 4971), Suite 228, 333 N Michigan Ave, Chicago, IL 66601 (tel 236 9013), and 342 Madison Avenue, New York, NY 10173 (tel 867 501); in Australia information should be available from PeKaO Trading at 12 Fetherstone St, 2200 Bankstown NSW (tel 708 1320). In Poland itself there are Orbis offices in all major towns, whose primary concern is to hire cars and sell tours, ideally in hard currency, to foreign tourists, but whose staff do speak English and other languages and will often be able to help you if you are nice to them. There is no co-ordinated system of local tourist information, although Kraków, the country's main tourist centre, does have a good office near the station; elsewhere you will find offices that specialise in hiring out private rooms but also dish out a bit of information (particularly those bearing the COIT logo), and the local offices of the PTTK (the Polish Country-Lovers' Association, the organisation responsible for mountain huts, trail markings and all sorts of organised outdoor activities) and the PTSM (Scouts). You might think that there are lots of tourist offices, but on closer examination you will find that these are almost all concerned with outward tourism, ie booking Poles on to trips to Paris, Rome, Lourdes and such places.

However there are a few agencies which may be useful for booking sailing or riding trips, for instance; these include Almatur (the Polish Students Association Travel Bureau), at ul Ordynacka 9, 00-364 Warsaw (tel 022 268 404), Juventur (the Youth Tourism Bureau), at ul Gdańska 27/31, 01-633 Warsaw (tel 022 330 445), and Harctur (linked to the Scouts) at ul Niemcewicza 17, 00-973 Warsaw (tel 022 659 1415). Almatur in particular can also arrange accommodation in student hostels over the summer vacation.

GETTING TO POLAND

Although not a prime tourist or business destination in its own right, Poland is at the heart of Europe and is thus well linked to the rest of the continent; in addition there is a large expatriate community (*Polonia*) which keeps in close touch with the motherland, and in particular there are Polish travel agencies strategically placed in many countries to offer plenty of good advice as well as good fares. As in the communist period, most Polish tourism is group-based, but individual travel is increasingly catered for.

From Britain Poland can be reached by bus, rail, air and even by sea; in addition to the state tourism company Orbis (see above), there are two well-established Polish agencies in London, selling air and rail tickets and offering inclusive packages (see below), and also running coaches to Poland; these are **Fregata**, 100 Dean St, London W1V 6AQ (tel 071 734 5101), 117A Withington Rd, Manchester M16 7EU (tel 061 226 7227), pl Powstańców Warszawy 2, Warsaw (tel 022 274 304), Rynek Główny 33, 2nd floor, Kraków (tel 012 224 144), and also in New York and Chicago, and **Travelines**, 154 Cromwell Rd, London SW7 4EF (tel

071 370 6131), 18 Station Parade, Ealing Common, London W5 3LD (tel 081 993 1381), al Jerozolimskie 6, 00-375 Warsawa (tel 022 264 556), and also in San Francisco. You could also try **Tazab**, at 273 Old Brompton Rd, London SW5 9JB (tel 071 373 1186/370 6355), and **Bogdan Travel**, at 5 The Broadway, Gunnersbury Lane, London W3 8HR (tel 081 992 8866), whose brochures are virtually identical to those of Orbis, offering the same tours.

The Fregata **coach** (run in conjunction with Eurolines and the Polish state international road transport company PeKaEs) leaves London's Victoria Coach Station on Sundays (and Wednesdays and Fridays in summer) at 1330, returning on Fridays (and Mondays in summer), and costs (to March 1994) £90 return (£85 if under 25 or over 60) or £65/£60 single, to all destinations, far less than in 1991. The Travelines coach leaves Victoria on Thursdays at 1030 (returning on Saturdays), and costs £95 return in low season, or £115 in high season, or £65/£80 single, with student discounts of £5 in low season and £10 in high season. Both companies offer routes to Warsaw and to Wrocław, Katowice and Kraków, with Travelines claiming to reach Warsaw in 27 hours (2½ hours faster than Fregata) and Kraków in 28 hours, four hours faster. These should be faster via the Channel Tunnel. Fregata have a summer service to Gdańsk as well. Orbis and Tazab also offer inexpensive coach fares, using Eurolines, and White Eagle Lines (24A Earls Court Gardens, London SW5 0TA, tel 071 373 1088, and room 244 at the Grand Hotel, Krucza 28, Warsaw, tel 294 051) are even cheaper.

From Poland itself coaches can be booked through agencies such as Artus, Gromada, Harctur or Turysta, all found in most major towns, or DreamBus at the bus stations of Kraków (tel 012 214 444) and Katowice (tel 032 539 477); most of these run to Berlin and Köln, or to Italy (for pilgrimages), but Vitesse, at ul Snycersa 13, Kraków (tel 012 559 007), Trango, at Rynek Główny 28, Kraków (tel 012 214 645), and Victor, at ul Sobieskiego 4, Kraków (tel 012 339 219/331 262, or 071 733 1610 in London), charge Z1.6m for a through coach to London. Some of these can be a bit cowboy-esque, so try to find one that advertises double-deck air-conditioned Mercedes coaches, rather than keeping quiet about a clapped-out minibus. The PeKaEs office in Warsaw is at Żurawia 26 (tel 022 213 469/282 356).

Train travel is no longer any faster, taking 29 hours from London (via Ramsgate-Ostend) to Warsaw, against a possible 27 hours by coach, and it also costs more, although you can break your journey as often as you wish. Once the Channel Tunnel is open (and the new trains delivered) in late 1994 it will be possible to take a night train from London to Köln (Cologne) and, changing there and perhaps in Dresden or Berlin, reach Poland far more quickly than at present.

Full British Rail fares to Warsaw are £279 return or £140 single, to April 1994; EuroYouth fares (for those under 26, valid for two months with unlimited stop-overs) are £202 return or £104 single. Wasteels (tel

071 834 7066) and Eurotrain (tel 071 730 8518), both at Victoria station, charge £182 return or £100 single for those under 26, while Fregata and Travelines can offer reduced fares to all age-groups, as well as providing a couchette service with courier on summer Saturdays (£169 return to Warsaw). Internal Polish fares are far less than international rates, so it is cheaper to buy a ticket to, say, Poznań and rebook rather than buying a through ticket to eastern Poland.

For £247 (in 1994) you can buy an Inter-Rail pass, valid for one month's unlimited travel in 23 European countries, including Poland. A zonal system has now been introduced, so that you can pay only £165 for 15 days travel in eastern Europe alone, or £219 for a month's travel from the Channel ports to eastern Europe, excluding the Mediterranean and Scandinavian countries. If over 26 an Inter-Rail 26+ Pass costs £209 for 15 days unlimited travel or £269 for a month; this only covers 20 countries from the Netherlands eastwards to Poland and Turkey, although add-on tickets are available from London via Belgium.

Predictably the fastest (and with luck simplest) and most expensive way of travelling to Poland is by **air**. The main service from Britain is by the national airline LOT, in association with BA: LOT is in the process of transforming itself from a communist era cattle-truck airline with no airs and graces whatsoever into a more modern business with an eye to the market, and to privatisation. Having sold 17 Russian-made planes to Ukraine, it now operates Boeing 767s to North America and Asia, Boeing 737s to western Europe, and French ATR-72s to eastern and central Europe, with surviving Tupolevs on internal services and to Moscow. Other signs of the times are its TransAtlantic Frequent Flyer programme and smoking bans on shorter flights. Nevertheless I gather Polish passengers returning home still fill the aisles with TVs and stereos as hand baggage, service is off-hand and there is no vegetarian food.

LOT and BA each fly daily (in 2½ hours) from London Heathrow to Warsaw, with extra summer flights, as well as weekly flights from Heathrow to Gdańsk and Kraków, and in summer from Manchester to Warsaw. There may also be charter flights from Manchester and Glasgow to Gdańsk and Kraków. 1994 fares from Polorbis, Fregata and Travelines range from £172 return (low season short stay) to £254 (weekends in high season, ie summer and Christmas). It is also possible to fly to Warsaw with Swissair from Heathrow, Birmingham or Manchester via Zurich, or with Lufthansa via Frankfurt, which can prove cheaper options. LOT also flies as far afield as Bangkok/Singapore, Beijing, Cairo, Chicago, Edmonton, Montreal, New York, Tel Aviv, and Toronto, with onward connections on partner airlines. From April 1993 there has been an international departure tax of US$10 from Warsaw, or US$8 from Gdańsk or Kraków, paid when you buy your ticket, and from October 1994 there will be a UK departure tax of £10.

LOT offices are at 313 Regent St, London W1R 7PE (tel 071 580 5037); 500 Fifth Ave, Suite 408, New York, NY 10110, USA (tel 212 869 1074); Suite 2001, 388 George St, Sydney, NSW 2000, Australia (tel 02 232 8430); and Mutual Group Centre, 3300 Bloor St W, Suite 3080, Toronto, Ontario M8X 2X3, Canada (tel 416 236 4242). Other agents to try in Britain for cheap air tickets are Travel Cuts (tel 071 255 1944), Intra (071 323 3305), One Europe Travel (081 566 9424), Sunquest (081 749 9933), New Horizons (0756 798 066), Liftjet (0827 713 060), Bridge the World (071 911 0900), and Trailfinders, STA and Campus around Britain (London numbers respectively 071 937 5400/938 3232, 071 937 9921 and 071 730 3402).

Perhaps the best deal, despite BA's takeover of DanAir and the rises in eastern European rail fares, is to fly to Berlin (from £100 return) or (for Wrocław and southern Poland) Prague (from £129), and continue overland. There are also coaches to Prague: try Eurolines (tel 021 622 4373), Kingscourt Express (tel 081 769 9229), ADCO Travel (tel 071 372 0323) or Travellers Czech (tel 081 907 7049), all around £85 return. *Volan*, the Hungarian bus company, also runs from Budapest to Zakopane.

You can even get to Poland by **ship**, with Polish Ocean Lines (PLO) operating the *Inowrocław* on a regular weekly schedule, from Tilbury on Monday morning or Middlesbrough on Tuesday afternoon, reaching Gdynia on Friday morning and returning the same afternoon, reaching Tilbury early on Monday morning. It costs £108 full board from Middlesbrough to Gdynia or Gdynia to Tilbury, or £138 from Tilbury to Gdynia or Gdynia to Middlesbrough. PLO will also bring you by sea from North America and elsewhere, usually to the Netherlands or Germany rather than to Poland itself. In addition Polferries or Polish Baltic Lines (PŻB) operate ferries from Gdańsk and Świnoujście to Ystad and Oxelösund (Sweden), Helsinki and Copenhagen. Tickets for both companies can be obtained from Orbis, Travelines or Gdynia America Shipping Lines, 238 City Rd, London EC1V 2PR (tel 071 253 9561).

Equally it is possible to take the normal channel ferries and drive to Poland, usually either following the coach route via Dover, Calais, Brussels and Hanover, or by Scandinavian Seaways, taking 22 to 24 hours from Harwich or Newcastle to Hamburg, from where it is just 335km to the Polish border. Almost all the crossings (on all major roads) are open 24 hours a day, and insurance and information can be obtained there from the Polish Motoring Association (PZM). The eastern border crossings, very popular with 'trade tourists' from the former Soviet Union, can have delays of 24 hours or more (there are regular reports after the weather forecast on the radio), but the western and southern crossings are much better, with more crossing points being opened, less need to search vehicles, and no ex-Soviet border guards to hold things up on the other side. Rail crossings from the west are as smooth as silk, with EU passports barely being glanced at.

Inclusive tours are a very easy and worthwhile way of getting to Poland, as you will see from the many adverts on the travel pages of most broadsheet newspapers: in late 1993 the headline figure is £109 for 10 days half-board in Zakopane, travelling by coach, from Poland Tours (tel 0784 247 286), or £119 to £199 from New Millenium (tel 021 711 2232) or Inter-Poland (tel 081 332 2293). Fregata will take you to Zakopane for £238 for two weeks B&B in the Hotel Imperial, or from £13.50 per night; Orbis charge £278, including flights and six nights (sharing a twin room) in the Hotel Kasprowy, or £204 for coach travel and five nights half-board in the Hotel Giewont or seven nights in a pension. Orbis packages to Kraków start from £285 for seven nights bed and breakfast (by air) or £185 for five nights half-board (by coach), both in the Hotel Cracovia. Again, these prices are substantially less than in 1992.

Specialist tours are also very popular, although less good value: Orbis in particular runs general coach tours, Jewish heritage tours, riding, cycling and angling tours and stays in spas. Pegrotour (ul Grochowska 320, 03-823 Warsaw, tel 022 134 175, and Knesebeckstrasse 6/7, 1000 Berlin 12, tel 310 873) offers similar trips, as well as sailing and cycling tours. The PTTK runs many cheap hiking, cycling and canoeing trips, mainly for Poles, but they do also welcome foreigners; their foreign tourist office is at ul Świętokrzyska 36, Warsaw (tel 022 208 241).

GUIDE BOOKS

Two excellent general guides compete for the custom of independent travellers in Poland; these are *The Rough Guide to Poland* by Mark Salter and Gordon McLachlan (distributed by Penguin, second edition 1993) and *Poland, a Travel Survival Kit* by Krzysztof Dydyński (Lonely Planet 1993). The latter is far better than most of its stablemates and offers an insider's view, while the new Rough Guide is even more up to date. In addition the *Insight Guide* (APA 1992) gives a slightly glossier coverage, and the *Hippocrene Companion Guide* by Jill Stephenson and Alfred Bloch (published by Hippocrene in the USA and Thornton Cox in the UK, revised in 1993) has a good chatty approach but little practical detail.

Poland is also covered by the new wave of Inter-Railers' guides to Eastern Europe, of which the best are David Stanley's *Eastern Europe on a Shoestring* (Lonely Planet 1991) and *The Berkeley Guide to Eastern Europe 1993* (Fodor); less useful are *Fodor's Eastern Europe 1993* and *Frommer's Eastern Europe on $25 a Day* (Prentice Hall), and the French *Guide du Routard* (Hachette).

There are many books (and more appearing all the time) on Solidarity and the background to the events of 1989, of which the best are those by Timothy Garton Ash: *The Polish Revolution* (1983, revised 1991), *The Uses of Adversity* (1983, revised 1991) and *We the People* (1990), all from Granta/Penguin. Runners-up are Mark Frankland's *The Patriots' Revolution* (Sinclair-Stevenson 1990) and Misha Glenny's *The Rebirth of History, Eastern Europe in the Age of Democracy* (Penguin, new edition 1993), 'one of the first to sound serious and sadly accurate warnings about 1989 and all that'.

For Polish history before the modern period, the definitive account is Norman Davies' *Heart of Europe* (OUP) and the two-volume version *God's Playground* (OUP), while there are plenty of eye-witness accounts of resistance to the Nazis, such as Adina Blady Szwajger's *I Remember Nothing More*, Primo Levi's *If not now, when?* and others listed in the section on Auschwitz (page 169). The first half of Eva Hoffman's *Lost in Translation* (Heinemann 1989) is a luminous account of childhood in 1950s Kraków.

There has been a rash of books by travellers who headed east as soon as communism had collapsed, and these are mostly far better than one might have expected; those that cover Poland include *Stalin's Nose* by Rory MacLean (Flamingo 1993) and *Lambada Country* by Giles Whittell (Chapman 1992).

The major Polish writers are detailed on page 77; translations of most of Miłosz's books are published by Penguin, Schulz's by Picador, Mickiewicz's *Pan Tadeusz* by Hippocrene, and Witkiewicz's *Insatiability* by Quartet. *Young Poets of a New Poland* and *Ariadne's Thread, An Anthology of Contemporary Polish Women Poets* can be obtained from Forest Books, 20 Forest View, Chingford, London E4 7AY (tel 081 529 8470/0384) ('the window to eastern Europe'). Other books on eastern and central Europe can be found at Collets (40 Great Russell St, London WC1B 3PJ, tel 071 580 7358), Daunt Books (83 Marylebone High St, London W1M 4DE, tel 071 224 2295) and Zwemmer (28 Denmark St, London WC2H 8NJ, tel 071 379 6253).

THE POLISH LANGUAGE

In southwestern Poland a certain amount of German is still spoken, particularly in the Karkonosze resorts where more and more Germans are coming for cheap weekends, and here and elsewhere young people are rapidly learning English, but inevitably you will come up against a language barrier in rural Poland; this is such a monocultural country that very few people know how to listen to foreigners and pick out the few words they can recognize, or how to speak to foreigners in such a way that they can pick out a few obvious words. Therefore it is unfortunate that Polish is one of Europe's more incomprehensible languages. The reasons for its being so hard lie in history; for most of the Partition period the language was partly fossilised, with little normal evolution possible, while at the same time loyalty to the mother tongue became a key feature of the nationalist credo, further helping to set it immutably in stone.

However many of the problems lie in the initial appearance of the written language; once you get beyond this it does have its beauties. It is a phonetic language, intended to be pronounced exactly as it is written. How this results in Rome being spelt Rzym, and the beer known as Jihvets as Żywiec, is one of life's little mysteries. It is the clusters of consonants such as 'szcz' that are most off-putting, and there is a natural tendency to pronounce all these as something like 'shch..' (that well-known mixer), or to just ignore all 'z' compounds; however it pays to do a bit better than this if you can. In addition there are diacritical marks and accents on some letters; these are always listed after the basic letter in any alphabetical list.

Words are declined and can bear little relation to the root version in the dictionaries; as words are stressed on the penultimate syllable, pronunciation can be greatly modified by suffixes such as '-go'.

Pronunciation:

a	like 'u' in 'dud'
ą	'ong' or French 'on'
c	'ts'
ch	as in Scots 'loch'
ć	soft 'ch'
cz	hard 'ch'
e	as in 'heck'
ę	like French 'un'
g	hard, as in 'get'
h	also as in 'loch'
i	'ee', not 'eye'
j	like 'y'
ł	like 'w'
ń	'ny' as in 'canyon' ('ni' before vowels)
o	as in 'hot', not 'open' or 'moo'
ó	as in 'look'
r	rolled
sz	hard 'sh'
ś	softer 'sh' ('si' before vowels)
u	like 'oo' in 'book'
w	like 'v' in 'van'
y	like 'i' in 'fit'
ź	a softer 'z' as in 'jeans' ('zi' before vowels)
ż	like 'j' — or 's' in pleasure

Further information can be found in the *Polish Phrase Book* (Hugo), *Polish for Travellers* (Berlitz), *Teach Yourself Polish* (Hodder & Stoughton), *Colloquial Polish* (Routledge), and the *Penguin Polish Phrasebook*.

Vocabulary is mostly Slav, having much in common with the other Slav languages such as Russian, Czech and even Bulgarian; words such as *dobry* (good) and *woda* (water) will be understood across almost all of eastern Europe. However there are also many words in common with west European languages, such as (from one random page of my dictionary) *blok* (block), *blokada* (blockade), *blond* (blond), *bluza* (blouse), *boja* (buoy), *bojkot* (boycott), and *bojler* (boiler).

See also the sections on food and drink and on transport.

Basics

Good morning/Good day	Dzień dobry (jean dobry)
Good evening	Dobry wieczór
Good night	Dobranoc
Hi! (hikers' greeting)	Cześć! (Tcheush!)
Cheers!	Na Zdrowie!
Yes/No	Tak/Nie
Sir/Madam	Pan/Pani
Miss	Panna, Panienka
Thank you	Dziękuję (jean kuyen)
Please	Proszę
Goodbye	Do widzenia!
Bon voyage	Dobry podróż/Szerokiej drogii
What does it cost?	Ile to kosztuje?
Do you speak English?	Czy Pan(i) mówi po angielsku?
I do (not) understand	(Nie) rozumiem
I don't speak Polish	Nie mówię po polsku

Directions

Left/right	Lewy/prawy
North/south	Północ/południe
East/west	Wschód/zachód
Straight ahead	Prosto
Here	Tu, tutaj
There	Tam
This/that	Ten/tamten
How far is it to ..?	Jak daleko jest do..?
Where is/are..?	Gdzie jest/są..?
Is there..?	Czy jest..?
Hotel	Hotel
Campsite	Kemping, obozowanie
Tent	Namiot
Railway station	Stacja
Train	Pociąg
Bus station	Dworzec PKS
Bus	Autobus
Daily	Codziennie
Departure/Arrival	Odjazd/Przyjazd
Crossroad	Skrzyżowanie
Bridge	Most
Market square	Rynek
Church	Kościół (RC)/cerkiew (Orthodox)
Key (for church)	Klucz
Castle	Zamek
Hospital	Szpital
House	Dom
Museum	Muzeum

Car	Wóz, samochód
Tram	Tramwaj
Trolleybus	Trolejbus.

Link words

And	I
But	Ale, lecz
Or	Lub, albo
With	Z, przy, u
Without	Bez
If	Jeżeli, jeśli
Now	Obecenie, teraz
Today	Dziś
Yesterday/tomorrow	Wczoraj/jutro
To/from	Do/od, z
Via	Przez
For	Dla, za
What	Co
How/when	Jak/kiedy
Above/below	Nad/pod
Enough/after	Wystarczy/po
Big	Duży
Small	Mały
Very/many	Bardzo/dużo
More/less	Więcej/mniej
Good/bad	Dobry/zły
True	Prawdziwy
Fast	Szybki
Slow	Wolny
Open/shut	Otwarty/zamknięty
Strong	Mocny
Heavy	Ciężki
Difficult/easy	Trudny/łatwy
Light	Lekki
Beautiful/wonderful	Piękny/cudowny
Single, alone	Sam (jeden)
New/old	Nowy/stary

Verbs

Stop! Enough!	Zatrzymać (się), Stop!
To buy/sell	Kupować/sprzedawać
To exchange	Wymieniać
To want	Potrzebować, chcieć
To go (on foot)	Iść (piechotą/pieszo)
To depart	Odjeżdżać
To arrive	Przyjeżdżać
To wait	Czekać
To see	Widzieć

To sleep	Spać
To eat	Jeść
To work	Pracować
To have	Mieć
To be	Być
It is necessary	Jest rzeczą konieczną
It is possible	Jest możliwe, można

Living

Bed/room	Łóżko/pokój
Shower	Prysznic
Bath	Kąpiel
Water (hot/cold)	Woda (gorąca/zimna, chłodna)
(Too) expensive	(Za) drogi
Cheap	Tani
Money/bill	Pieniądze/rachunek
Shop/bottle	Sklep/butelka
Married/child	Żonaty/dziecko
Boy/girl	Chłopiec/dziewczynka
Man/woman	Człowiek/kobieta
Tired	Zmęczony
Ill	Chory

Hiking Terms

Cave	Jaskinia, pieczara
Cliff	Stroma ściana skalna, urwisko
Cloud	Chmura
Crag	Skała
Field	Pole
Fog	Mgła
Forest	Las
Frontier	Granica państwa
Gorge	Czeluść, parów
High	Wysoki
Hill	Wzgórze
Hut	Chata
Ice	Lód
Lake	Jezioro
Landscape	Krajobraz pejzaż
Ledge	Występ
Marsh	Bagno
Meadow	Łąka
Mouth	Usta
Pass	Przełęcz
Pasture	Pastwisko
Path	Droga
Peak	Szczyt
Precipice	Przepaść

Rain	Deszcz
Ravine	Wąwóz, parów
Ridge	Grzbiet, brzeg, skiba
River	Rzeka
Rock	Skała, kamień
Saddle	Siodło
Sheep fold	Szałas (owczarski), owczarnia
Side	Strona, bok, brzeg
Slope	Pochyłość
Snow	Śnieg
Spring	Źródlo
Steep	Stromy
Stream	Strumień, prąd
Summit	Szczyt
Valley	Dolina
Village	Wieś
Wandering	Wędrówka
Wood	Las

Numbers and dates

One/two	Jeden/dwa
Three/four	Trzy/cztery
Five/six	Pięć/sześć
Seven/eight	Siedem/osiem
Nine/ten	Dziewięć/Dziesięć
Eleven	Jednaście
Twelve	Dwanaście
Thirteen	Trzynaście
Twenty	Dwadzieścia
Twenty-one	Dwadzieścia jeden
One hundred	Sto
Two hundred	Dwieście
Three hundred	Trzysta
Four hundred	Czterysta
One thousand	Tysiąc
First	Pierwszy
Second	Drugi
Third	Trzeci
Half	Połowa
Quarter	Ćwierć

Monday/Tuesday	Poniedziałek/Wtorek
Wednesday/Thursday	Środa/Czwartek
Friday/Saturday	Piątek/Sobota
Sunday	Niedziela
January/February	Styczeń/Luty
March/April	Marzec/Kwiecień
May/June	Maj/Czerwiec

July/August	Lipiec/Sierpień
September/October	Wrzesień/Październik
November/December	Listopad/Grudzień

ACCOMMODATION

There is a broad choice of accommodation for visitors in Poland, with the standard falling somewhere between that in western Europe and that in the more Third World parts of eastern Europe; at the top end of the scale there are international hotels such as Forte's Hotel Bristol (described pre-refurbishment as 'fit only for a Graham Greene novel') and the new US$60m Hyatt and Marriott in Warsaw, costing up to £150 a night for a single room, and there are more and more new hotels opening in Kraków to cater for the hordes of Western tourists now rushing there. At the other end there are also plenty of basic bivouac sites which provide space for a few tents and virtually nothing else. In summer in all the tourist areas there is a sudden flowering of camp sites and youth hostels set up in village schools; outside the peak couple of months there is less available, but there are no problems camping wild, except in the National Parks, as long as you are sensible.

In the hills your mainstay, when not camping, will be the *schroniskos* or huts provided by the PTTK (Polish Country-Lovers' Association) and by other bodies such as the scouts or hiking clubs. Whereas these are usually on the main hiking routes, the PTTK also has rather posher *Dom Turisty* in resorts, and there are summer youth hostels in village schools; these will usually involve a detour from the hiking routes. The PTTK *Dom Turisty* (also known as *Dom Wycieczkowe* or excursionists' homes) in the towns are referred to in the text as hostels, as opposed to youth hostels which are **much** simpler; the PTTK *schroniskos* are referred to as huts.

Normally huts have basic dormitories with shared showers, with a *bufet* or snack bar generally open from 0800 to 2000; if you want the cheapest of ideal worlds, you can pay a minimal sum to camp at a *schronisko* and use the shower, *bufet* and electric light. The huts in the Tatras, in an attractive vernacular style with wide shingled eaves, are especially popular with students, who usually sleep in the corridors rather than paying extra for a bed; another tactic is for a couple to share a single bed, a surprisingly common practice in such a Catholic country. The largest huts, however, are those in the Karkonosze, developed for large-scale tourism in the days of German rule; but even these are dwarfed by those on the Czech side of the border, which have waitress-service restaurants and so on.

In 1993, when there were Z26,000 to the pound sterling, prices ranged from Z25,000 for camping or sleeping on the floor (*podłoga*), or Z30,000-40,000 in a dormitory (*sala sypialna*) of about twelve beds, to Z50,000-90,000 each in a 2-bed room, prices being highest in the Tatras and Karkonosze and lowest in the Bieszczady and Beskid Niski.

As so often in eastern Europe there is an assumption that Westerners want the best, so if you want a dormitory bed make it clear; but prices are low enough for you not to need to sleep on the floor. Food, in the Tatras, is not cheap, as it has to come by pony or by ropeway (which also affects the choice of vegetarian food), but here in particular you will find urns of free hot water for tea. One or two huts even sell beer, despite posters saying *Gory bez Alkoholu* (Mountains without Alcohol). Where there is a hikers' kitchen you will need your own stove. There is a map available showing the locations of all the huts, but they are always very clearly marked on the local hiking maps, and of course the PTTK's trail markings always direct you towards them.

The PTTK, an excellent organisation, also sets up tent-bases in summer, essentially huts under canvas, mainly in the Silesian Beskids, the Beskid Niski and Bieszczady, and also among the lakes of the north; these are intended for students but you are unlikely to be turned away. They are publicised in PTTK magazines and on hut noticeboards. The PTTK also operates some *Stacia Turystyca* or tourist stations (mainly in the Silesian Beskids), usually a farm with a basic dormitory and camping, with no food or hot water and dry privy toilets. There are up to 150 *bacówka* or huts owned by the scouts, mountain clubs and the like, usually kept locked, although you may find people there at weekends.

Youth hostels (*Schroniska młodzieżowe*) are run by a body called the PTSM, founded back in 1926; there are no less than 1,095 youth hostels in Poland, 965 of them only open from about July 1 to August 25 — note in particular the early end of the summer season, although the hostel signs are usually left up all year. These summer hostels are in village schools, with about 35 mattresses on the floor and no hot water. There is a guide published annually, most easily obtained at the Oleandry hostel in Kraków, or at PTSM regional offices; the information given here is based on the 1991-2 guide, but changes seem to be minor from year to year. Understandably, not all of these hostels are listed in the IYHF international handbook. Check-in ends at 2100, and lights-out could be as early as 2200; normally priority is given to those under 26, but foreigners are unlikely to be turned away, particularly if you have a tent. Pricing is complex, depending on age, nationality and membership category, but you should pay Z20-30,000, or Z50,000-plus in Kraków and Zakopane (in 1992).

Poland's 185-plus 'official' camp sites are mainly in the vicinity of towns and resorts and on lakes and the coast; they are open from May 15 to September 15, except for those in Warsaw and Kraków (May 1 to September 30) and those in the mountains in Zakopane and Szczyrk which are open all year. Category I sites should have 24-hour reception and hot water, while Category II have hot water only in the morning and evening; these are all listed on an excellent map (in English and German) available from Orbis, or the Polish Federation of Camping and Caravaning at ul Królewska 27, 00-060 Warsaw (272 408, 268 089), and places can be booked through *Camptur* at the same address. FICC members get 10% off, and as all over eastern Europe, you can also stay in a cabin on these campsites. However there are less than ten of these sites in the mountains, where you are far more likely to find student camping places or bivouac sites (*pole namiotowe*), which are generally little more than fields with a privy and perhaps a cooking shelter; someone may take a few thousand Złoty off you, but out of season they are just as likely not to. Water usually comes from a stream and should be boiled or purified. In addition you can camp at huts and youth hostels, and there are bivouac sites (*pole biwakowe* or *miejsca na biwaki*) provided free by the forestry administration, in an effort to control wild camping. There are about 50,000 places in the official campsites, and over 100,000 in the informal sites; prices in official sites in 1993 were generally around Z15,000 for a tent and Z10,000 to Z25,000 per person; a cabin cost about Z80,000 for two.

In towns the PTTK hostels offer a good range of accommodation, from Z28,000 for dormitories with as many as 28 beds, to Z90,000 each in a 2-bed room with bath, and may well be the ideal base; however prices may rise as they are likely to be privatised, as already in Kraków. Single rooms are rare, but you can normally just take a bed rather than a whole room. In the university towns of Warsaw, Białystock, Bydgoszcz, Częstochowa, Gdańsk, Katowice, Koszalin, Lublin, Łódź, Olsztyn, Opole, Poznań, Płock, Rzeszów, Szczecin, Toruń, Wrocław, and Zielona Góra there are *Miedzy-narodowy Hotel Studencki* or International Student Hostels, open in July and August in students' halls; in Kraków these cost a lot more, at up to Z100,000 each sharing a two- or three-bed room (although this may be 50% more than Poles pay), but are open well into September. To find out about these, ask at the offices of Almatur, the youth travel organisation; it is unlikely to be worth buying their accommodation vouchers, priced in dollars.

Most Polish hotels and motels are still run by Orbis or other state bodies, although private and joint-venture hotels are appearing fast, particularly in tourist centres such as Kraków. In small towns such as Nowy Sącz and Paczków hotels may charge perhaps Z80,000; elsewhere they can charge a lot more, particularly if you want a bath (by no means normal), up to £100 or so (hard-currency credit card prices), which will include Sky TV and other such dubious luxuries. Orbis, Fregata and Travelines can book hotels from the UK, from £17 or less for the most basic (sometimes a ZNP Teachers' Hotel or a sport hotel at a stadium) upwards. With exchange rate fluctuations these prices have actually dropped, from £106 to £85 for the Warsaw Marriott or from £63 to £56 for the Forum, for example. You can also book inclusive flight/hotel deals, or cottages in the lakes and other holiday areas.

In resorts and spas in the mountains or on the coast there are pensions and sanatoria, which always used to be booked through a trade union organisation, the FWP, but are now making themselves available to all comers. The decline, for various economic reasons, in the numbers of children from the main industrial centres coming to these rest-homes is likely to have serious health consequences, but it is opening up these resorts, formerly rather insular, to independent travellers; however, being

family-orientated, there are few single rooms. Nor are they keen on one-
or two-night stops, which put you in a bad bargaining position.
  Finally, both in these resorts and in many of the larger towns, you can
find private rooms without difficulty, and in a country which doesn't
actually rush to welcome foreigners this may be the best way to see
how people actually live. You may well get fed up with constantly
hearing the proverb 'A guest in the home is God in the home' without
ever being invited to visit a Polish home. The availability of private
accommodation is not a new phenomenom: in the early stages of the
development of tourism in Zakopane and the Podhale, all visitors stayed
in local houses, and until the government turned against it in the 1970s
it was still standard. You should look for a *Biuro Zakwaterowania* or
Biuro Kwater Prywatnych, often doubling as an information office near
a station, or signs for *noclegi* or *pokoje*. Prices range from about
Z30,000 for a Category III double outside Kraków, to Z130,000 for a
Category I double in Kraków.

TRANSPORT

As in much of eastern Europe, most travel is by public transport, and for
foreigners too this is likely to be the cheapest and easiest way of getting
around. Services are not as slow as in the countries further to the south
and the east, and remain cheap and comprehensive, at that happy point
between the introduction of some market awareness and the fare rises
and service cuts that will doubtless follow before long.

Planes

The national airline, LOT, operates internal flights from Warsaw to
Gdańsk, Katowice, Kraków, Poznań, Rzeszów, Szczecin and Wrocław;
these are organised to give connections at Warsaw from southern to
northern cities and *vice versa*, as well as with international flights. In
1992 all flights cost £32 (stand-by tickets may also be available) for
about an hour's flight, which seems fairly cheap until you realise that
nowhere is more than an overnight train journey from anywhere else, at
a much lower cost. In particular the improvements to the train services
from Warsaw to Katowice and Kraków have resulted in the air service
having little purpose other than as a connection with international flights.
  Airports (*lotnisko*) are usually close to city centres and linked by
municipal buses or a special connecting LOT service; in Warsaw you
need the Domestic or *Krajowe* terminal (No 2) at the Okęcie airport, off
al Krakowska 9km south of the city (bus 114). International flights (other
than those from the former socialist countries) use the newly rebuilt
terminal 1 at the south end of ul Żwirki i Wigury (bus 175); taxi drivers
here are rather shark-like, but there is no other easy way to get between
the terminals.

Trains

Under communism the PKP (*Polskie Koleje Państwowe* or Polish State Railways) became both a real people's railway, accounting for half of all passenger-kilometres in Poland, with the average Pole travelling 1,400km per year, the second highest figure in Europe, at fares about one-eightieth of those in Britain; and on the other hand a key part in the country's massive industrialisation programme, mainly by moving up to half a million tonnes of coal a day from the Silesian mines to the industrial centres and the Baltic ports, sometimes carrying 13% more than the theoretical maximum tonnage. The line via Wrocław to Szczecin was modernised, and between 1975 and 1984 the 224km *Centrala Magistrala Kolejowa* (CMK or Central Trunk Railway) was built from Zawiercie, northeast of Katowice, to Grodzisk, west of Warsaw, to feed coal traffic towards Gdańsk. This is both faster (160km/h, with 200km/h possible) and more direct than the two existing electrified lines between Katowice and Warsaw, so that almost all passenger traffic now takes this line. Additionally the *Linia Hutniczo Siarkowa* (LHS or Sulphur-Steel Line) has been built to the Soviet broad gauge (1,524mm) to carry iron ore from the then Soviet Union to the *Huta Katowice* steel plant, and sulphur in the other direction; this now allegedly carries three through trains a week from Moscow which terminate at Olkusz, east of Katowice (see page 164).

The PKP is one of the better-run Polish enterprises, and has now started to modernise its infrastructure and bring it into line with that of western Europe, with a US$145m World Bank loan for fibre optics, management information systems, and a computer reservation system. However there is a lot of leeway to be made up; it still employs over 400,000 staff, and thanks to mining subsidence and corrosion of the rails from atmospheric pollution trains have to creep along for most of the 50km from Kraków to Katowice, which should be a modern rapid transit *S-Bahn* service, as between Gdańsk and Gdynia. The track ballast needs cleaning every four years, as 1m tonnes of dust is shed every year from the 120m tonnes of coal carried; a leaky Romanian wagon was used under the centralised Comecon system, but the design was never changed, with more and more of the same type being ordered, in a classic example of the lack of feedback in the communist system.

Although passenger traffic has fallen with the country's economic decline, perhaps by as much as 25%, there has been a huge increase in international traffic, mainly from the West. In 1992 a EuroCity express service was introduced between Warsaw and Berlin, taking six hours rather than the previous seven, and InterCity services are being introduced on internal lines: Kraków can be reached in just 2 hours 35 minutes from Warsaw Centralna, and Katowice in 2 hours 45 minutes (at an average of 110km/h), and there are now 7 expresses a day to Kraków (at 5 minutes to the hour) and 10 to Katowice (at 35 past the hour), all via the CMK, and just one day and one night train by the old Częstochowa route to Katowice.

Fast (*pośpieszny*) trains run on all main lines, not just radiating from

Warsaw but also, usually overnight, from Szczecin, Gdynia and Białystok to southern towns such as Szklarska Poręba, Kraków, Zakopane and Krynica. Sometimes it can seem as if virtually every seat on these trains is reserved, so it may be worth forking out the extra for a *miejscówka* yourself, although over-crowding is not generally a great problem now: fares are 50% above those for slow trains, and they are marked in red on timetables. Express (*expresowy*) trains, marked in red with an R in a box on timetables, are all-reserved, with no standing, and stop only at the most important cities.

There are smoking and non-smoking compartments, but it is usual to go into the corridor to light up; there are two classes, second (*druga*) and first (*pierwsza*). Overnight trains are particularly useful for longer journeys, and sleepers (*miejsce sypialny*) or couchettes are inexpensive, and thus often not available.

Slow trains (*normalne* or *osobowe*) stop everywhere and manage an average of about 40km/h; these are often double-deck coaches of the standard eastern European design. Taking a bicycle on these trains is not a problem: just buy a half-price ticket and put it (the bike) in the vestibule; you can also take bikes on long-distance trains with a baggage/mail coach. Local tickets are only valid for *part* of that day, so don't buy them too long before you plan to travel. Alternatively you may find that you have to date-stamp your ticket yourself in a validation machine by the doors to the platforms. Major stations now have computerised ticket offices, but queueing can still be a problem.

The *Polrailpass* available from Orbis, or as an Explorer Pass from Campus, Wasteels etc offers a week's unlimited rail travel for £20 (in 1993) which sounds cheap enough but almost certainly would not be a bargain unless you wish to pay for the freedom never to speak to a Polish ticket clerk. In 1992 fares started at about Z180 per km, dropping to about Z120/km for journeys of c800km.

Departures (*odjazdy*) are listed on yellow posters, and arrivals (*przyjazdy*) on white; platform numbers are complex, with both a platform and a track number, and sometimes a sector as well.

Major stations (usually called *Główny* or Main) offer facilities such as waiting rooms, kiosks and *bufets*, and 24-hour post office and left luggage (very cheap but be prepared to calculate the value of your luggage and pay 1% of this as insurance; also check when they close for breaks). Station cafés are generally excellent for good fast food such as stews and soups; that at Nowy Sącz, for instance, only closes for cleaning 0030-0200 and 0800-0930.

The PKP is also responsible for running cablecars and funiculars, mainly around Zakopane, but also in Krynica, Karpacz and Bielsko-Biała. These are, of course, for tourists, not public transport, and are priced accordingly, charging double on Sundays and festivals, and in theory charging extra for baggage.

There were until recently 2,357km of narrow-gauge lines in Poland, but many of these have now closed; one line that is popular with tourists is that from Rzepedź to Maidan (Cisna) in the Bieszczady (see p 120).

Steam haulage was scheduled to end on all lines in May 1992, but there should still be some, particularly around Wolsztyn (west of Poznań), during the sugar beet harvest. Orbis and specialist operators such as TEFS (77 Frederick St, Loughborough, Leics LE11 3TL) and World Steam Tours (3 Shadwell Grove, Radcliffe on Trent, Nottingham NG12 2ET) have arranged tours with steam locomotives and depot visits. A rail museum is being set up at Jaworzyna (southwest of Wrocław), and a few Polish steam engines have made their way to Britain, to Pitsford (Northampton), South Tynedale and Scunthorpe.

Buses

Bus services are almost all run by the *Państwowa Komunikacja Samochodowa*, the State Motor Communications or PKS, although a few independent operators are appearing in holiday areas such as the Bieszczady and Karkonosze, as well as private *mikrobuses* around Zakopane. Buses are ideal for country travel, but for inter-city journeys you are best off sticking to the railways.

The infrastructure is remarkably well developed, with some computerised ticket offices, as in Kraków, and comprehensive information at every single bus stop (only occasionally vandalised) — too comprehensive, perhaps, as it is impossible to know, having waded through all the footnotes, whether a certain bus runs, for instance, on Saturdays and festivals *and* in July and August, or on Saturdays and festivals *in* July and August. A foreigner is unlikely to know which Saturdays are working days, and the symbol for working days varies by region, crossed pickaxes in the southwest, R (for *Robota*) in the central south, and A in the southeast. Some early-morning buses are marked as 'Priority to season-ticket holders and scholars', but Western travellers are unlikely to be turned off, I think. PKS buses are usually yellow and their stops are marked with a steering wheel logo, and in the country there is usually a shelter, often a substantial log cabin, in which you could even sleep in need.

Bus stations are generally close to main rail stations, and you should rely on the latter for snacks and left luggage. Buy your ticket from the window marked with the final destination of your bus; if you have no time, or if the bus is passing through from another town, you may be able to buy a ticket from the driver, as also when you join a bus at other stops, but you may not get a seat. There are also bus ticket offices at Wrocław and Katowice railway stations, for instance, and Orbis may also sell tickets for some international services. Timetables are on yellow for departures (usually inside the ticket hall) and white for arrivals (usually outside); fast buses (more expensive) are marked in red. Look carefully at the 'via' (*przez*) column, as towns listed here will have different word endings to the version of the same name in the main 'destination' column; you need to scan both columns to find all services going to your destination, as the main column will generally only show those buses terminating at that town and not those in transit. In addition to the international coaches (see page 48) there are increasing numbers of buses crossing borders, to cities such as Lviv and Košice and many smaller towns just over the border.

You may also find the driver charging you a few thousand złoty for baggage; he (rarely she) has to date-punch every ticket rather painstakingly two or three times, so it's not surprising that they are rather grumpy people as a rule. Only once outside a city did I have to buy a ticket and then at once cancel it myself; aisles are narrow, with standing passengers, so this can be a difficult manoeuvre. If you get on at an intermediate stop be sure to buy a ticket at once; fines are staggeringly high relative to fare levels (cUS$20) and the inspectors are also rather humourless. Be aware also that buses always try to get away a couple of minutes early.

Generally bus fares are marginally less than for local trains, with fast bus fares somewhat higher at about Z250/km.

City transport

The 13 major Polish cities wisely rely on trams as the backbone of their public transport system, with buses connecting with them at suburban terminals. These are generally rather antiquated Tatra vehicles made in Prague, although Kraków has now received trams made redundant in its twin city of Nürnberg by the extension of its U-Bahn (metro). Łódź and Warsaw are both building metros, but are not making great progress.

Tickets are cheap but should be bought in advance from newspaper kiosks marked *RUCH* (traffic), and then cancelled on boarding — a ticket with an arrow at either end must be cancelled at both ends, unless you happen to be a child or a pensioner, in which case you need only cancel one end. Checks are rare, but fines are again substantial. Intriguingly, you may see the odd route no 0.

Taxis are quite affordable, particularly for Western visitors, and there are now many freelance drivers in every city. Due to inflation you will never simply pay the price on the meter; try to discover the current multiplier, or how many noughts are being added, before travelling if possible. Keep clear of any driver wanting hard currency or reluctant to use his meter, unless you feel competent to agree a price in advance. Prices are 50 to 100% higher at night, on Sundays and festivals, and beyond the municipal limits. To call a radio taxi in Warsaw, dial 919, having first mastered the pronunciation of your address.

Cars

Although car ownership rose by 15% to 6.1m in the year 1990-91, double the 1980 level, use has fallen somewhat with the great rise in the price of fuel. In November 1992 the price was about 33p per litre (much less for diesel), and as a result many drivers coast downhill as far as possible in the countryside, where you also see many old motorcycles converted to haul flatbed trailers. In fact Poland has a more advanced car manufacturing industry than other eastern European countries, but the cars produced, mostly in conjunction with FIAT, were designed for local travel only, even though they were long a familiar sight, loaded to the roof, heading for the 'Polish markets' in all the neighbouring countries. Nowadays a wider range of cars is produced here (see page 37), but hire cars tend to be Peugeots, Renaults, Ford Sierras and the like: the main agency is Hertz, working through Orbis in Warsaw, Kraków, Katowice, Wrocław, and the main northern cities, and charging from £35 per day for a Renault Clio in 1994. In Warsaw there are other companies such as JUPOL-CAR (Avis with Juventur) and Budget, and cheaper but less reliable private firms are also appearing in some cities. Poland is also very easy to reach in your own car, with Warsaw just 850km from Hamburg; international driving licences are not required in practice, but you must of course have a green card for insurance abroad. This can be purchased at the border, from the PZMot (Polish Motorists' Union), which can also provide maps and further information.

There are 226,000km of surfaced roads, almost all good quality, well signed and often with broad shoulders, although mostly single-carriageway: there is unbroken dual-carriageway from Warsaw via Katowice to Ustroń, in the Beskid Śląski near the Czech border, and there are stretches of motorway along the corridor from the German border to Wrocław, Katowice and Kraków. There are plans to build 2,000km of toll motorway, with the Katowice-Kraków section to open by late 1994; tolls are also to be charged on ferries, hitherto free. The maximum speed is 90km/h, and 60km/h in towns; caravans are limited to 70km/h, and on the motorways cars only can travel at 110km/h. Seatbelts are obligatory outside towns, and no drinking and driving is allowed; the police can exact on-the-spot fines, and I was impressed by how considerate the driving was, with drivers taking care not to splash pedestrians.

There are not as many petrol stations as in the West, but many of them are open 24 hours a day; most are still owned by the state CPN company, with an inconspicuous orange sign that looks like an N on a square fan. Lead-free fuel is fairly common near the German border and in Kraków and Warsaw. Car crime is increasingly a problem, but guarded parking is available, especially near the major hotels.

Hitchhiking

Poland is unusual in that hitching has actually been institutionalised as a means of transport for young people: the PTTK through one of its many committees issues a set of vouchers, which are given to a driver to save up for prizes and to cover him or her against insurance claims. Officially the season runs from May to September and the minimum age is 17; these vouchers can be obtained from major PTTK offices, all-year youth hostels, and some Tourist Information centres. However there is no reason why you as a foreigner should have these; just take advantage of the general acceptability of hitching, and if the driver wants payment (as is usual in eastern Europe) just use cash.

Cars carry a two-letter code giving the voivodeship (province) of origin, but as so many in the south begin with K (Krosno, Kraków, Katowice) this may not be a great help. Most of the flash Western cars come from Warsaw.

FOOD AND DRINK

Poles claim to be the greatest gourmands (not gourmets) in Europe after the French and Italians, and the great summit meetings of 1000 and 1364 are remembered more for their banquets rather than for any diplomatic achievements. However while there is nowadays far more choice in Polish shops and restaurants than in Ukraine or Romania, Polish cuisine is not as varied as you might expect, largely due to the rather unenlightened tastes of the average Pole who insists on meat and potatoes at all times, preferably accompanied by vodka, and in good quantities, as exemplified in the saying 'A hungry Pole is an angry Pole'. However the diet was even more dull and repetitive until the mid-16th Century, when the Italian Bona Sforza, wife of King Sigismund I, introduced green vegetables, and the late 17th Century, when potatoes appeared. Nowadays in some ways the great national delicacy is the mushroom, gathered in the forests by the whole family and dried, boiled, baked, fried or in gravies, although it is in fact a major feature of most eastern European cuisines; Orbis will take you mushroom-hunting at Jodłówka Tuchowska, near Tarnów.

Naturally enough for a country at the centre of Europe, there are many foreign influences on Polish cuisine (and the reverse); the most notable import is *barszcz* or *barszcz czerwony*, the Ukrainian and Russian *borshch* or beetroot soup, together with the *kosher* Jewish vegetarian tradition of the milk bars (*bar mleczny*), a national treasure now almost eradicated by the flood of burger bars since the death of communism. In general the words to use if you want vegetarian food are *jarski* or *wegetariański*.

Most meals begin with soup, including *barszcz, barszcz klarowny* (clear or sweetened borshch), and *barszcz z uszkami* (borshch with meat dumplings). Other characteristic soups are *żur* (spicy thick sour soup), *żurek* (rye soup with sour cream, often with hard-boiled egg or sausage), *ogórkowa* (sour cucumber soup), *kapuśniak* (sauerkraut or cabbage soup), *flaki* (tripe soup, common in mountain huts now), *botwinka* (beet greens soup), *zacierka* (noodle soup), *grzybowa* (mushroom soup, often *z łazankami*, with noodles), *szczawiowa z jajkiem* (sorrel soup with hard-boiled egg), and *chłodnik* (Lithuanian beetroot and sour cream soup, served cold, often with hard-boiled egg and veal). At one time there were also many varieties of beer soup, served with curds for breakfast. *Krupnik*, a barley-based broth traditionally served after hunting, is 'a magnificent winter-warmer, thick and hearty, a meal in itself, the ultimate supper soup'. Soups are generally made with meat stock and often have chunks of meat floating around in them.

Main courses, other than in the few remaining milk bars, are based on meat, particularly pork (*wieprzowina*), with beef (*wołowina*), veal (*cielęcina*) and chicken (*kurczak*). The most ubiquitous is the pork cutlet in breadcrumbs (*kotlet schabowy*), but the most typically Polish dish is *bigos*, a hunters' stew, described as 'a sort of cabbagey mess in which floated minute, tasty sausages', or 'hot sauerkraut with meat and mushrooms'. Other characteristic dishes are *gołąbki* (literally little pigeons, but in fact cabbage leaves stuffed with mince or mushrooms and rice), *kaczka pieczona z jabłkami* (roast duck stuffed with apples), *maczanka beskidzka* (meat and bread casserole in wine sauce), *zrazy wołowe zawijane z kaszą gryczaną* (beef collops rolled in *kasza* or buckwheat), and other forms of *zraz* or collop. Steaks are variously known as *stek, befsztyk* or *bryzol*.

There are many types of dumplings, notably *pierogi* (found in most milk bars and cafés), like large boiled ravioli stuffed with meat (*z mięsem*), cottage cheese (*pierogi ruskie* or *z serem*), blueberries (*z jagodami*), or cabbage and mushroom (*z kapustą i grzybami*), and *pyzy*, steamed potato-flour dumplings. *Kulebiak* is a Lithuanian baked cabbage and mushroom dumpling or loaf.

Pancakes are also popular, particularly in the milk bars, such as *naleśniki*, served with cottage cheese (*z serem*), jam (*dżemem*), sour cream (*z śmietaną*) or just with sugar (*z cukrem*). *Placki ziemniaczane* or *kartoflane* are similar fried pancakes of grated potato. *Bliny* are also pancakes, of Russian/Jewish origin.

With your main dish you will usually have potatoes, and you can ask for other vegetables (usually charged separately), or in milk bars pick up a ready-made plate of salad (*sałata* or *surówka*), especially the ubiquitous *mizeria* (cucumber salad, often with sour cream) or *ćwikła* (beetroot salad, often with horseradish sauce). The quintessential eastern European herb is dill (*koper*), used for pickling cucumbers and the like, as well as in salads.

Desserts are rare in the cheaper restaurants and milkbars, although you may be able to find *lody* (ice cream), *kompot* (fruit compôte) or pancakes with jam or sugar. The best bet is usually to move on to a *kawiarna* (café), *cukiernia* (pastry shop) or *cocktail bar*. The latter specialise in milkshakes and fruit cocktails, rather than the alcoholic variety, while the others sell ice cream, pastries and hot and cold drinks. The best *cukiernie*, as in the Hotel Cracovia in Kraków, are indistinguishable from the best French *pâtisseries*.

Pastries and cakes include *sernik* (cheesecake), *keks* (fruitcake), *makowiec* (poppyseed cake), *racuchy* and *pączki* (doughnuts), *mazurek* (shortcake, essential at Easter) as well as éclairs and other buns.

Traditional soft drinks (*napoje*) are rapidly being supplanted by Coke and Pepsi, but where available are cheaper and better for you, being made with fruit juice and mineral water; *oranżada* and *lemoniada* are sickly syrups which would only aggravate dehydration. *Woda mineralna* (mineral water) is available nationwide, although most comes from the southern spas, and is of excellent quality. The Poles drink as much tea (*herbata*) as the British, although black and sweet, in a glass rather than a cup; as usual east of Calais you will probably be served with a teabag and a glass of water which may not even be hot enough to brew properly. Coffee (*kawa*) is also popular, usually made by pouring hot water on ground coffee, although *expressowa* can be found in good cafés, and *cappuccino* only in the best establishments.

As for street food, the most common takeaway is the *zapiekanka* or a half-baguette covered with tomato ketchup and molten cheese, and sometimes mushrooms. In cities and resorts such as Kraków and Zakopane burgers, hot dogs and pizza have more or less driven the traditional milk bars from the main streets, and chips (*frytki*) are available (in 100g units) from stalls and caravans in resorts and around rail and bus stations. Ice cream is also sold from street stalls just about everywhere.

In mountain huts and milk bars the staple dishes are *pierogi, kiełbasa* (sausage, especially in *fasolka po bretońsku* or beans British-style), *omlet* (more like a pancake than an omelette, and often served with jam), and *jajecznica* (scrambled egg). These are *samoobsługa* or self-service, meaning that you pay at the counter, collect your food from a hatch and return your dirty plates to another; as long as you buy a drink, it is generally acceptable to eat your own food here. I gather that you can also get a good midday meal in university refectories for about Z17,000 (Z10,000 for Polish students).

Shopping for food is easy enough, with good supermarkets in most major towns, with a good range of cans and jars, if not of frozen foods; see page 46 for an indication of prices. Fresh fruit and vegetables should be bought in markets or from trolleys and stalls at the stations if possible (take your own carrier bags); nowadays there is a great range of good exotic fruits just about everywhere, including bananas, oranges and pineapples. The Poles don't seem very interested in their own native fruits, with wild raspberries left unpicked even along the road up to Morskie Oko in the Tatras. As in most countries, strawberry jam is the people's jam, with some 1lb (454g) jars with English labels now available. *Marmolada* is a cheap mixed fruit jam, while *dżem pomarańczowy* (orange jam) is only found in major supermarkets. Cherry jam is still sometimes stirred into tea, following an old Russian custom.

Cheese (*ser*) can be found in most shops, nowadays sadly mostly in the form of processed German packets, although real cheese can also be found in markets and many shops. *Bryndza* is sheep's cheese, and in its smoked form, looking like a pork pie, is a Tatra speciality. Normally it is soft and creamy and can be found in butter-style packs. Softer cheeses include *ser topiony* and *twaróg* (curd cheese); *serem* (or *twarog*) is the cottage cheese used in pancakes, not to be confused with *sernik* (cheesecake) or *serek* (a mousse-like dessert). Yoghurt is also popular, but again pots of rather sweet and watery processed German yoghurt are now as common as the authentic version. *Kefir* or sour milk is a more characteristic taste of eastern Europe, although it can often be found in cartons or bottles; *zętyca* is similar but only available from the shepherds themselves or occasionally in markets. *Śmietana*, the sour cream used widely in cooking and salads, is available bottled in shops.

Bread (*chleb*) is a major staple, bought daily in supermarkets or largely private bakers' shops, and is made of wheat or rye flour, often with caraway seeds. Rolls (*bułka*) are also common, and filled rolls (*kanapka*) can be found at snack bars. You can also pick up good biscuits such as *herbatniki* to keep you going while hiking, and you may also find *Smakołyk Warszawski* (Warsaw Dainty), the best chocolate block I know for getting me up hills.

The main meal is *obiad*, something like a high tea, usually eaten after work, from 1500 onwards; Poles start the day with a light breakfast (*śniadanie*) of tea or coffee, bread and cheese, jam or cold meat, or eggs, and they may have a second breakfast (*drugie śniadanie*) of a sandwich or a snack in a milk bar by noon. Some more pretentious *kawiarnie* have what they call 'five' or 'five o'clock', afternoon tea, from 1600 to 1800; in the evening there is only a light supper or *kolacja*. Therefore restaurants are almost always shut by 2000, except for those *restauracje koncertowe* in resorts offering dancing until about 2300, and not even chips or *zapiekanka* may be found on the streets after about 2000, while in mountain huts the *bufet* tends to be closed by 1900; however station cafés are a good bet throughout the night for stews and soups. Restaurant menus are very detailed, listing the standard prices per 100g of a wide range of dishes that are probably not available; they are still often signed and counter-signed by the management, in a legacy of communist times. As for tipping, you need only round the bill up to the next thousand zloty.

Poles are even greater drinkers than eaters, with vodka (*wódka*) the national drink, of course. Its history dates back to the 8th Century, mainly as a medicinal drink, and it became established in its present rôle from the 15th Century, although it is still said to be drunk to keep body and soul together, and the standard toast is *na zdrowie!* or 'To your health!'. In one sense this is fair enough, as vodka is a pure drink and unlikely to give a serious hangover, but the other effects of Poland's massive alcohol consumption (specifically of spirits rather than beer) are mind-boggling, including high rates of absenteeism, industrial accidents and divorce, and widespread corruption, known as 'making a deal by drinking'. Alcohol has long been used as a political tool, under tsars, Nazis and communists, to keep the population docile, and 'liquid taxation' yields up to 20% of state revenue; but the government is belatedly beginning a campaign against alcoholism. The church is also taking a stand, asking for a week of sobriety in Lent, although this is difficult for a religion whose principal sacrament is alcoholic. Restaurants may have a alcohol-free (*bezalkoholowa*) room, or perhaps just a eating area behind a curtain, which is designed not so much to prevent diners from having a beer as to set them apart from the more hardened boozers. However drinking and alcoholism are seen as normal by society as a whole, so things will only change slowly; the Polish language apparently has a word for each stage of inebriation, just as the Inuit (Eskimos) have a word for every type of snow.

Vodka is usually made from rye, but also from other grains, potatoes and beet treacle. Although clear vodka (such as *Wyborowa, Polonez* and *Żytnia*) is the basic model, there are also flavoured and coloured varieties such as *Żubrówka* (bison vodka, with a blade of grass from Białowieża), *jarzębiak* (rowan vodka), *myśliwska* (juniper vodka), *pieprzówka* (pepper vodka), and *wiśniówka* (cherry vodka), as well as strawberry and blackcurrant flavours 'for the ladies'. The etiquette is to exhale before knocking it back it one, although it is safer and more practical to sip gently and ignore pressures to drink faster, and to follow it with snacks (*zakąski*) such as pickled gherkins and mushrooms, sausage, or herring with boiled potatoes. Vodka should be served chilled, although this is less important with the flavoured varieties.

Other liqueurs include *wisniak* (brandy), *krupnik* (a mead, made with herbs and honey), and *śliwowica* (plum brandy, found mainly in the southern highlands, and indeed through most of southeastern Europe).

Beer (*piwo*) is a part of the Germanic heritage that is widely spread but has not established itself as deeply as vodka, especially in the north; the PPPP or Polish Beerlovers' Party set itself to encourage beer drinking, not for its own sake but as a less harmful alternative to vodka, and Western beers, largely German and in cans, are now a prestige product, being more consistent and long-lasting than the bottled Polish beers. The best known Polish beers are *Okocim, Żywieckie, Tatra Pils, Leżajskie, Lwów*, and *Warka*. Historically Slavic beers were green and foamy, but you'll be glad to hear that today beers are in the standard German/Bohemian mould, although they will normally be served at room temperature. Beer soup (*gramatka*) with curds was once a breakfast dish, but again you'll be glad to hear that this is in the past.

Due to Hungarian influence, Tokay wine has long been used for Old Polish (*Staropolska*) style meals, and in communist times wine was of course imported from Hungary and Bulgaria, but it has never really caught on outside the better restaurants. There are also clones of Cinzano and the like, generally dismissed as 'womens' drinks'.

Small-town restaurants are often glorified beer halls, but these are reasonably decorous compared with the drinking bars, which are only patronised by men in search of oblivion — not a place for lone women! In larger towns hotel bars and new Western-style bars, patronised by the new middle classes, provide a more civilised environment for a drink.

Other vocabulary is listed below:

Bread	*Chleb*	Cucumber	*Ogórek*
Cake	*Ciasto*	Onion	*Cebula*
Pancake	*Naleśnik*	Mushrooms	*Grzyby,*
Jam	*Dżem, konfitura*		*pieczarki*
Honey	*Miód*	Beans	*Fasola*

Sugar	Cukier	Peas	Groch
Ice cream	Lody	Tomatoes	Pomidory
Sour cream	Śmietana	Lettuce	Sałata ogrodowa
Butter	Masło	Cabbage	Kapusta
Cheese	Ser	Aubergine	Baktażan
Eggs	Jajka	Fruit	Owoce
Omelette	Omlet	Apples	Jabłka
Scrambled		Pears	Gruszki
eggs	Jajęcznica	Peaches	Brzoskwinie
Boiled eggs	Jajka na twardo	Grapes	Winogrona
Fried eggs	Jajka sadzone	Cherries	Wiśnie,
Fish	Ryby		czereśnie
Pork	Wieprzowina	Drinks	Napoje
Beef	Wołowina	Milk	Mleko
Chicken	Kurczak	Tea	Herbata
Sausage	Kiełbasa	Coffee	Kawa
Salami	Salami	(Mineral/soda)	
Soup	Zupa	water	Woda (mineralna/ sodowa)
Vegetables	Warzywa		
Pepper	Pieprz	Beer	Piwo
Potato	Ziemniak, kartofel	(Red/white) wine	Wino (czerwone/białye)
Chips (French fries)	Frytki	Lemonade	Lemoniada
Rice	Ryż	Fruit juice	Sok

LIFE AND CULTURE

Poles can put up a fairly good façade of gruffness and even rudeness, but once this is penetrated they are immensely hospitable and generous. It is the old women (looking like Giles cartoon characters) who have suffered much this century and are least friendly and most likely to push you aside in queues, while schoolchildren are very forward with polite greetings, so there is hope for the future. I often get the impression that Poles are always talking of money, and certainly everything seems to have a price tag; I have never had a free bus ride (commonplace for foreigners in Romania, for instance), and I was pounced on when I smashed a jam jar in a supermarket. When there was a power cut at the museum in Karpacz I was not allowed in, whereas in Romania I would have been let in free, with apologies for the lack of light. The Poles are typically Slav, romantic and enthusiastic, and as quick to take offence as to laugh.

Attitudes are conservative, reinforced by the church, but they are also being affected by Western influences, most notably consumerism and greater social mobility, with less regard for those at the bottom of the pile. The influence of Catholicism in Poland, both in combating progress and in lessening social injustice, should not be underestimated.

Shops are now largely in the hands of the private sector, and in fact chains of shops such as pharmacies are now appearing, while the pavements and markets are also busy with people buying and selling just about anything. In particular there are now large numbers of 'trade tourists' from the former Soviet Union coming to Poland to sell tatty goods at very low prices.

Everywhere you go there are now private shops selling imported goods such as whisky, chocolate, cosmetics and electronic goods; these often double as kantors, changing hard currency. The Pewex chain, once described as 'the official black-market dealer of the People's Republic', no longer has a monopoly on imported Western goods, and no longer sells them only for hard currency; nowadays it is just another import shop, though found even in places as small as Jabłonka, west of Zakopane. It often seems as though the greatest desire of most Poles is to open a flower shop or hairdressers, as these seem to be sprouting up everywhere, and indeed if you are lucky enough to be invited to dinner you should be sure to take flowers for your hostess, as well as a bottle of vodka for himself.

In practical terms, you will buy most of your fresh food in markets, as the supermarkets, although otherwise well stocked, tend not to have fresh, or even bottled or tinned, fruit or vegetables. Take a carrier bag and you will have no problem; calculators and electronic scales are widespread, so that it is easier than elsewhere in eastern Europe to sell odd quantities and then to display the price to uncomprehending foreigners. Poland has even mastered the technology of making screw-top jars, unlike Romania, so that it is possible to travel with half-eaten pots of jam and the like. There are still deposits on bottles, although not on jars, but this admirable national system is sure to be further eroded by the flood of Western imports in throw-away packaging.

Handicrafts can be bought from the Cepelia chain, or increasingly from private shops and street traders, and art and antiques from the Desa chain: you can export anything bought here, but you should be very careful with anything else, and icons in particular, now flooding on to the black market, certainly should not be exported. In 1992 160 customs officers were sacked in a scandal involving the illegal export of works of art from Poland and the former Soviet Union. There are good photo books available of the Polish cities and countryside, and records, tapes, and, increasingly, CDs, of Polish music. Film is now widely available outside the Pewex shops and major hotels; stick to Western brands such as Kodak and Fuji, and avoid ORWO at all costs. Slide film and film of ASA400 and faster should be brought from home. One-hour photo labs are appearing but you might as well wait until you get home to develop films.

Opening hours for food shops are generally from 0800 to 1800 or 1900, and to 1300 on working Saturdays, although local corner shops and bakers may open as early as 0600. Department stores open from 0900 to 2000, and other shops generally from 1000 or even 1100 to 1800 or

1900. Having been promised a five-day working week back in 1971, this was again conceded to Solidarity in 1981, but the government then tried to insist on two Saturdays work a month, due to the country's economic collapse. The final agreement was for one Saturday's work a month, but of eight hours rather than the previous six, giving a total of 42 hours work per week. Now most shops open on the first and last Saturdays of each month, and some department stores open every Saturday. A very few delicatessens in Warsaw and Kraków are now open for nigh on 24 hours a day.

Museums (and offices) often shut by 1500, particularly in winter, and by about 1400 on Sundays; museums are closed on Mondays, and occasionally on Tuesdays as well. The *skansen* or open-air ethnographic museum, a species common in Scandinavia and eastern Europe, is particularly interesting as a display of local vernacular architecture, such as wooden houses, mills and churches, with equipment and furnishings.

Major **Post Offices** (*poczta*) open between 0800 and 2000 (or even 2100) Mondays to Fridays and the first and last Saturdays of the month, 0800 to 1400 on *Wolne Soboty* or free Saturdays, and 0900 to 1100 on Sundays, while either the central post office of each Voivodeship capital or one at the main rail station should be open 24 hours a day, and smaller offices may close by 1500. They can be hard to pick out, having the same red signs with white lettering as all other official buildings. Letters to be collected from *Poste Restante* at a town's main post office should be addressed to the *poczta główna nr 1*. Mail can also be collected from American Express offices in places such as Zakopane, Kraków, and Warsaw if you have an Amex card or travellers' cheques. Allow at least a week, if not two. A letter to Great Britain (*Wielka Brytania*) cost Z3,500 in 1992.

Telephone service is usually available at major post offices, often until 2100 or 2200, but unfortunately the system is archaic and overloaded and one of the major impediments to Polish economic advance. There are just 3.3m phones, but not even enough inter-urban lines for that number, so that any long-distance call involves long waits. There is direct dialling to major cities such as Kraków (code 012), Warsaw (02), Wrocław (071) and Zakopane (0165), and also to major countries such as the UK (0-044) and the USA (0-01), but this is still best done from the main offices. Not surprisingly, cellular phones, available since 1992, are proving popular, and you can rent one from the airport or hotels in Warsaw. Warsaw numbers are mostly seven digits now, but remaining six-digit numbers should be prefixed with a second 2 if calling from outside Warsaw. Local calls are more straightforward, with plenty of phones giving three minutes for one token (*żeton*), available from kiosks and hotel cloakrooms. Call 999 for an ambulance, 997 for the police, 981 for the PZMot breakdown service, 900 for the long-distance operator, and 901 for the international operator.

Addresses are straightforward, with *ulica* meaning street, *aleja* avenue, and *plac* place: ul Kopernika 4/12 means Copernicus Street no 4, flat 12.

Many street names are gradually being changed, with communists such as Lenin, Świerczewski and Dzierżyński, as well as Armii Czerwonej (Red Army), on the way out and the former names such as Piłsudki and Paderewski, and of course Jana Pawła II, taking over. Ulica 1 Maja is generally becoming ul (Konstytucja) 3 Maja.

There are about 75 daily **newspapers**, compared with 48 in 1989, and 164 weeklies, and the range of opinion and presentation is far wider than in the communist period, of course. The most important is *Gazeta Wyborcza* (Electoral Gazette), founded by Solidarity as its mouthpiece in the 1989 elections but now independent although still edited by Adam Michnik, which has a circulation of 550,000, or 850,000 for its weekend edition: it no longer has an English-language edition but many of its reports appear in the *Guardian* Europe pages. The main English-language paper is *The Warsaw Voice*, which gives a good insight into Polish politics, business and life, and lists cultural events: it costs Z7,000 or US$3, and can only be found in Warsaw and major hotels in Kraków and a few other cities. There are also many soft porn mags, openly sold on street stalls, as all over contemporary eastern Europe.

The state radio service broadcasts nationally on four channels, with local competition from private stations such as Radio Fun in Kraków; the news headlines are broadcast in (American) English in summer on some channels. There are two state TV channels, only one truly nationwide, and both now taking advertising, and the private TV Echo (in Wrocław) and Polonia-1 (not yet altogether legal), as well as Russian (rather than Ukrainian, Belarussian or Lithuanian), Slovak, Czech and German channels near the borders. The Astra and Sky satellite TV services are also well established, particularly in all major hotels, and I even saw a dish on a tram in Wrocław, purely for advertising, of course. There are TVs in 98% of homes, and 80% of Poles watch TV on any given night.

Folk **costume** is rarely worn these days, except possibly for church at Easter and Christmas in the remoter villages. In the southern hills some shepherds still wear the traditional round hat, and Dunajec raftsmen and Zakopane carriage drivers dress for the tourists, with embroidered waistcoats and long trousers flared over their shoes. Student hikers of both sexes have a virtual uniform of jeans, check shirts and headbands; as in the rest of eastern Europe, there are also plenty of military uniforms on the streets.

Music is one of Poland's chief glories, traced back as far as a Gregorian prayer of 986 and the *Bogurodzica* (Holy Mother) knights' song of 1300; the *polonaise*, a stately dance in 3/4 time, dates back to at least the 16th Century, while the *polka* (a mixture of the waltz and an Irish jig) was a Bohemian peasant dance until it caught the imagination of high society. Folk songs are now longer as omnipresent as in Romania and Bulgaria, partly due to the irrelevance of lyrics such as 'Where has Short Johnny gone with the hatchet?' or about how husbands should help mashing the poppy seeds; however classical composers such as Fryderyk Chopin (1810-49), Stanisław Moniuszko (1819-72), and Karol Szymanowski (1882-1937) all used folk melodies, although sometimes 'correcting' them. Chopin created both a national style and the concept of the virtuoso pianist, Moniuszko followed him in composing nationalist music, particularly operas, and Szymanowski (born in Ukraine) was at the heart of the intellectual ferment of Kraków and Zakopane in the first decades of this century, writing operas, three symphonies and two violin concertos. Additionally Henryk Wieniawski (1835-80) was one of the great violinists and composers for his instrument of the time. In the 20th Century Poland has produced more great pianists such as Ignacy Paderewski, Artur Rubinstein and Krystian Zimerman, as well as Polish-Americans such as the pianist Emanuel Ax and the conductor/arranger Leopold Stokowski.

Despite all their achievements, the golden period of Polish music has in fact been since the Second World War, with composers of the order of Lutosławski, Panufnik, Penderecki, and Gorecki. Witold Lutosławski (1913-94) and Andrzej Panufnik (1914-91) played piano duets together at underground concerts in Warsaw during the war, until Panufnik defected in 1954 to Britain, where he composed symphonies and folk song settings and was eventually knighted; Lutosławski remained, although he was condemned for 'formalism' in his first symphony and later refused to conduct under martial law. Krzysztof Penderecki and Henryk Gorecki were both born in 1933; Penderecki conducts the Kraków Philharmonic and has travelled worldwide to put on his large-scale dramatic pieces, mainly on religious themes, while Gorecki has led a quieter life, until forced to shuffle backwards into the limelight by the amazing success of his third symphony, the *Symphony of Sorrowful Songs*, written in 1976 but little known until 1993 when it sold over 8,000 CD copies a week in Britain, forcing itself high into the pop charts. Its success is surprising, as most of his work is fully accessible only to Polish Catholics; in 1979 he was forced to resign as director of the Katowice Music Academy due to his Catholic sympathies. The conductor Jerzy Maksymiuk and his Polish Chamber Orchestra have also had great international success.

In the 20th Century, Polish **theatre** has also been world-class, although it has recently been revealed that in the 17th Century Shakespeare's plays were often put on within weeks of their London premieres in Gdańsk, where there were up to 30,000 Britons fleeing plague and religious persecution. It is even said that Shakespeare himself might have visited Poland. Before the Second World War Stanisław Ignacy Witkiewicz (known as Witkacy, 1885-1939) and Witold Gombrowicz (1904-69) created the theatre of the absurd, and in the 1960s and 1970s the Laboratory Theatre of Jerzy Grotowski and the Cricot 2 Theatre of Tadeusz Kantor ('probably the most radical and influential director the world has seen this century') continued to break down barriers to theatrical expressivity. Under communism 2.5% of factories' budgets went to support cultural activities; this has now been slashed, and audiences are little more than half previous levels. Perhaps Poland's best-known film director, Andrzej Wajda, the chronicler of the Solidarity period, is also a theatre director; other Polish film makers are Roman Polański (although he made only one film, *Knife in the Water*, in Poland before defecting), Jerzy Skolimowski, Krzysztof Zanussi, Agnieszka Holland and Krzysztof Kieślowski.

In the field of **literature**, Poland has produced three Nobel Prize-winners, Henryk Sienkiewicz (1846-1916, the author of *Quo Vadis?*), Władysław Reymont (1867-1925, now little-known but a good novelist in the mould of Zola) and Czesław Miłosz (born 1911, one of the century's greatest poets and intellectuals). However, perhaps Poland's greatest poetry was written in the Romantic period, by Adam Mickiewicz (1798-1855), Juliusz Słowacki (1809-49) and Zygmunt Krasiński (1812-59), with another high period before the Second World War, with Witkacy, the Futurist poet Bruno Jasienski (1901-39), and Bruno Schulz (1892-1942), artist and writer of surreal stories. Since the war the main writers have been the poets Miłosz and Zbigniew Herbert, the foreign correspondent Ryszard Kapuściński, who is in fact one of our best travel writers, the science fiction writer Stanisław Lem, seen by some as Asimov's heir and by others as too philosophical to be readable, and novelists Tadeusz Konwicki and Jerzy Kosiński. Poles writing in other languages have included Joseph Conrad (in English), Isaac Bashevis Singer (in Yiddish) and Andrzej Kusniewicz (in French).

It is noticeable how many of these writers were born in Lithuania or Ukraine (Mickiewicz, Conrad, Miłosz, Kusniewicz, Konwicki, Lem, Schulz), and how many died violently (Witkacy, Schulz, Jasienski and the brilliant poet Krzysztof Baczyński, killed at 23 in the Warsaw Uprising). At the moment Poland is busy catching up with translations of all the books banned or unavailable in the communist period, from *Lolita* to Jilly Cooper.

The national **sport** is soccer, which peaked in the 1970s and has since gone downhill, although Poland have twice kept England out of the World Cup; the plague of corruption scandals sweeping European football has not spared Poland, with both the 1992-93 champions Legia Warsaw and the runners-up LKS Łódź being caught rigging matches. The other winter sport is skiing; while it is well known that the Pope is a demon skier, it is less well known that he has claimed to be a Fulham fan ever since he spent some time at a seminary in Roehampton.

Crime is of great concern to everyone at the moment, as Poland has experienced the same steady rise in crime since the end of communism as the rest of eastern Europe; however there is still less street crime than in most Western cities, and Warsaw is the only place you need worry about walking in at night. It is largely a question of adjusting from the authoritarian system of secret police and paramilitary thugs to a situation where the police themselves are unsure what is allowed and what their powers are; as the concept of a civil society managed to survive the communist period there is little organised crime or corruption, compared to the chaos in Russia.

Unfortunately much crime involves foreigners or their cars, which are very obvious targets, so that guarded parking, at most major hotels, is important; it is also estimated that 1% of Polish crime is committed by foreigners, usually Russian *mafiosi*, which has given rise to a degree of hysteria. There were 211 cases of highway robbery in 1992, mainly of Russians returning from trading trips to eastern Germany, and one case in which Polish gangsters mistakenly stopped three carloads of Russian soldiers heading home on leave; there was a gun fight which the soldiers won.

You should obviously not leave valuables in cars or in hotel rooms, and in markets and city buses watch out for pickpockets and carry your passport and money in a money belt. If you've heard that it is legal to hold drugs for personal use in Poland, think again; the law is being changed. It is thought that 20% of Europe's illegal amphetamines are now produced in Poland, and the main route for smuggling drugs from Asia to Europe is shifting north from the Balkans to Poland.

Most of any hassle you receive will be from the omnipresent drunks, who will insist on sharing a drink with you and are likely to find it incomprehensible if you prefer not to; it takes considerable tact and patience to disentangle yourself from them. In any case women travelling alone should avoid the seedier bars and even restaurants, where they may be taken for prostitutes.

Education is compulsory from 7 to 19, and is of course very Catholic, with the school year beginning with a trip to church. After this men must do military service (18 months in the army, two years in the navy or internal security forces, or three years in the missile and anti-aircraft forces); of 305,000 serving in the military, 191,000 are conscripts. University courses last five years and give a Masters degree. In addition there are now 50 new Foreign Language Teacher Training Colleges (NKJO) to produce teachers of Western languages and to retrain the large pool of Russian language teachers, now largely unwanted.

Health is a major problem in Poland, with all its environmental problems and just 2.17 doctors per 1,000 people. There is an infant mortality rate of 15.0 per 1,000 births, and life expectancy is 65 for men and 76 for women.

Heart disease rates are a third higher than in western Europe, as 45% of energy intake comes from fat, as against a WHO recommendation of 30%, and at least half the male population smokes, as against a third in western Europe. In 1991 the average Pole smoked 2,670 cigarettes (against 2,056 in the USA), and this is expected to rise by 3.3% by 2000. The American tobacco giant R.J. Reynolds opened a factory on the outskirts of Warsaw in 1993 to produce 8bn Camel cigarettes a year, and the other American giant Philip Morris plans to buy Poland's biggest cigarette factory in Kraków to produce Marlboros; already the country is awash with imported Camels and Marlboros, largely sold from street stalls, and many trams are painted in the Camel colours. There have also been reports of Polish gangsters giving tourists free coach trips to Belgium with packs of Russian Marlboros hidden in moonboots, flasks, loaves and seats, bought for the equivalent of BFr150 a carton and sold in street markets for BFr450-800.

Although the cold-eyed US tobacco barons have no interest in public health, there may be a silver lining to their invasion if their cigarettes replace the terrible Polish products which have twice the tar content. There is limited awareness of the health aspects of smoking, although smoking is banned in most public buildings and city transport; in October 1992 Kraków council banned new advertising on trams and buses.

Abortion is more of a live issue, with the church taking a very strong line against it. Under communism, abortion was effectively the main method of birth control, and most people still feel it is not the government's job to interfere, with only 10% of Poles in favour of a ban. However, in February 1992 the Christian Democrats, part of the governing coalition, sponsored a bill to ban abortion unless the mother's life was in danger, with no other exceptions; by January 1993 a compromise had been reached, allowing for abortion in cases of rape, incest, serious defects or threat to the mother's life or health. This could include mental health, leaving the door open for some kind of abortion on demand: the ZChN hoped for the more conservative Senate to limit the exemptions more closely. There has been an immediate increase in the number of babies being given up for abortion abroad, and reports of up to £10,000 being paid for male babies from Poland.

HIV is a major problem, with Catholic attitudes clouding the issues: houses for HIV-positive children were burnt down in July 1992 in Laski, west of Warsaw, as 'dens of sin and plague' and leaflets dropped by helicopter were burnt without being read by the hysterical villagers. The conservative Education Ministry has blocked the distribution of a translated British booklet on AIDS by the Health Ministry. Helplines can be found in major cities, but the subject is still hushed up as much as possible.

Homosexuality was never banned under communism, but it remains almost completely underground, with strong Catholic prejudices against it connecting with the Polish distrust of outsiders or strangers in any form. Most cities have Lambda groups of gay and lesbian activists (PO Box 249 in Kraków — phone numbers have to be kept secret), and in Warsaw there is a gay disco, Café Fiolka, as well as the Pink Service (ul Mickiewicza 60, tel 334 672), which publishes gay magazines and acts as an information and campaigning centre.

HIKING

It is hard to define the differences between trekking, hiking, backpacking and similar terms, and these definitions vary in different parts of the world. For me a trek is either an organised expedition with porters and guides, or simply a hike of a length that isn't usually necessary in the Carpathians, although of course if you wanted to carry the required weight of food you could link together enough routes to keep going for weeks on end. Rambling really just involves day walks which are, for me and in the Carpathians, not nearly enough to feel that I have got away from civilisation. Hiking seems to cover the area between these two extremes, and that is the name I have chosen for this book; backpacking is a mainly American umbrella term for all these activities, although it implies a degree of self-sufficiency.

Hiking in the Carpathians is not at all like hiking (or trekking) in the Himalayas or Andes. The distances are less and the altitudes lower, and you are almost always in a man-made landscape dominated by forestry at the lower altitudes and sheep above that. Yet in spite of this it is not the hiking from village to village, mainly along busy and obvious valley routes with occasional passes, that characterises trekking in Nepal or Peru; you are in fact on your own much of the time and can genuinely feel you are getting away from it all. Carpathian routes are mainly ridge routes in moorland or alpine scenery, with relatively few hard climbs to go up to a pass only in order to come down again; this makes them seem higher than they often are, although there are no glaciers or eternal snows. In fact the Polish Tatras peak at 2,499m, and the Slovak Tatras at 2,655m; to put this in context, Mont Blanc is 4,807m, Kilimanjaro, the highest peak in Africa, is 5,895m, Mera, the highest trekking peak in Nepal, is 6,476m and Everest is 8,863m. In practice you will spend most of your time here hiking at an altitude slightly higher than Ben Nevis (1,343m, or 4,406 ft) and Kathmandu (1,400m), although I do also describe a few routes at lower levels. One metre is 3.28ft, so 2,000m is 6,560 ft.

A lot of this hiking will be in forests, usually beech or spruce, and above this you will be in open moorland or downs country, with relatively few genuinely alpine zones. Almost all the paths are pretty good and well marked, although I occasionally try (and usually fail) to get away from the marked routes: quite simply, the best routes between almost anywhere you might want to get to are the marked routes. With the exception of the Karkonosze and the Góry Bystrzyckie, southwest of Kłodzko, there are none of the peat bogs that so bedevil walking in Scotland and the Peak District.

You are also likely to find yourself walking along the border with the Czech Republic or Slovakia: these paths are marked in the usual way, sometimes with both Polish and Czech or Slovak markings, as well as pillars rather like trig points to mark the border, while in the Karkonosze you will see the peculiar silhouette symbols for the various Czech huts. You are free to use these paths, although occasionally you will meet border guards (more often in the Tatras and Karkonosze) who may check your passport, though nowadays they show very little interest in Westerners.

Hiking is well established in Poland, as in the other former communist states, which encouraged it as a cheap and healthy outdoor activity for the masses, who were not normally able to travel much abroad; in fact the word *turyst* is more or less synonymous with hiker. There are marked paths in almost every mountain area, but the only ones that are at all heavily used are those in a few popular areas well-equipped with huts, hotels and even ski lifts (above all the Tatras). Here you will meet many Polish hikers in the summer months, particularly students from mid-July onwards. In other areas, particularly out of season, you will meet absolutely no-one other than a few shepherds, and will find fewer huts and facilities. There are very few Westerners in the mountains, although Kraków is now very much on the tourist trail.

EKO-Tourist (ul Radziwiłłowska 21/4, 31-206 Kraków, tel 12 228 863, or via ECOTOUR, Parsley Hay, Buxton SK17 0DG, tel 0298 84295) offer hiking itineraries in the Tatras, Pieniny, Beskid Sądecki and Bieszczady for US$310-390 for 8-15 days (excluding travel to Poland), while Orbis offer 13 day trips with 6 days hiking in the Tatras for £686, and Exodus Expeditions (9 Weir Rd, London SW12 0LT, tel 081 675 5550) offer 15 day trips with 11 days in the Tatras from £620 in 1994 (much less than in 1993). Sherpa Expeditions (131A Heston Rd, Hounslow TW5 0RD, tel 081 577 2717) combine the Polish and Slovak Tatras, charging £895 for 9 days walking, and also offer 10 days walking in the Beskid Żywiecki, Pieniny and Tatras for £695.

Trail markings, maps and hiking directions

Most outdoor activities in Poland are co-ordinated by the PTTK (*Polski Towarzystwo Turystyczno-Krajoznawcze* or Polish Country-Lovers' Association), which has committees running everything from canoeing to hitch-hiking, and which owns and runs mountain huts and marks hiking routes. Much of this tourism is still by groups of students on organised circuits; the huts have their own stamps to be collected in booklets, rather like youth hostels.

Routes are well marked by local PTTK volunteers, with stripes painted on stones and trees and sometimes on special poles; junctions may be unmarked or there may be a display of arrow signs giving hiking times, and a large circle as well as an arrow at the start of each route. Red stripes mark ridge routes, and in theory green marks lower routes parallel to the ridges, blue routes through the valleys, and black and yellow other connecting routes. There may also be markings for cross-country skiing routes, giving distances in kilometres rather than times. Nevertheless I feel it is worth giving fairly detailed instructions to save any problems, particularly if going in the other direction to that described. I must stress, though, that the timings given are generally the result of just one visit and are of course likely to vary with the weather, load, state of mind and of fitness and so on; they are net timings, excluding all stops of more than a couple of minutes but rounded up a bit, whereas the timings on signs include some margin for stops and delays. In addition, I was hiking alone and on business; anyone with company and on holiday is bound to take longer, and experience will tell you how much longer. The compass bearings given are uncorrected, ie just as they appear on the compass, which of course need correction before transferring to maps.

There are tourist maps of most areas, available in bookshops and tourist offices, which are amazingly detailed and show all hiking routes and sights of interest, as well as bus-stops, accommodation, museums, ruins, spas and so on; the legend is in Polish, English and German, but sadly the immensely detailed local information on the rear of most maps is only in Polish, although you should be able to decipher the lists of hotels and campsites. See page 282 for details of Hapsburg era maps.

Mountain rescue

Rescue is free, being funded mainly by the government, and operated by the GOPR (*Górskie Ochotnicze Pogotowie Ratunkowe*), which can be contacted through most mountain huts, or in Zakopane by phoning 34 44. They also have the odd outpost of their own, for instance below Tarnica in the Bieszczady.

RIDING AND OTHER SPORTS

Horses are big business in Poland, with famous studs producing Arab mares worth up to US$1.5m. *Vacations in the Saddle* are also something of an institution, with all-found horseback holidays available at eight major studs and plenty of lesser ones. The best of these are around Poznań, in Wielkopolska (Great Poland), and around Jelenia Góra, near the Karkonosze, and horses are mostly of Wielkopolski stock, as well as Silesians, Hannoverians and Arabs.

The main centres are:
   Sieraków, northwest of Poznań, which has ponies for children;
   Łobez, east of Szczecin, with accommodation in wooden bungalows;
   Racot, southwest of Poznań, one of the largest of Poland's studs, with a roofed manège and a neoclassical palace;
   Czerniejewo, east of Poznań, which also has an 18th Century palace;
   Łąck, south of Płock (west of Warsaw), which has a world-famous herd of Arab stallions, as well as English, Wielkopolski and Coldbloods;
   Wojcieszów, east of Jelenia Góra, with accommodation in an 'outhouse' of another 18th Century palace, and English thoroughbreds;
   Książ, east of Jelenia Góra, in the stables of the castle (see page 197), with accommodation in the hotel in a wing of the castle;
   Szczawno-Zdrój (Dworzysko), very close to Książ, with a covered manège and childrens' ponies; this offers mountain trips up to five days in length, winter sledging trips, and at the end of October the 'St Hubertus run' fox hunt.

These are state-owned and operate in conjunction with major tour companies such as Orbis and Pegrotours, but there are increasing numbers of private operations, such as one in a reclaimed manor house at Osiniec, near Poznań, used by Orbis, and others at Teleśnica and Polana in the Bieszczady. The Bieszczady National Park itself has plans to introduce pony trekking with Huṭul horses, the stocky mountain horses of the Carpathians that are said to see with their feet and need very little fancy feeding. Juventur has its own centre near Prudnik, near the border south of Opole, and the state Main Sports Centre (COS) at Drzonków, 7km east of Zielona Góra, specialises in equestrianism and the pentathlon. Auctions are held in Warsaw, Poznań, Książ, Łobez, and Janów Podlaski, on the eastern border north of Biała Podlaska; however in 1993 there are problems with the equine virus EVA that has now reached Britain in Polish breeding stock.

In 1992 Orbis offered eight-day inclusive packages for around £200 (with just ten hours riding and three hours in a carriage), but in 1994 they have moved to a daily rate, charging £31-39 per day for accommodation (in a double room, full board), while Pegrotours charge US$19-32 (double half-board); Orbis charge £6 per hour for riding, £9 for jumping lessons, and £14 for a ride in a two-horse carriage, plus £4 insurance, while Pegrotours charge US$4-9 for riding, US$25 for lessons, and US$8-22 for a carriage ride. However in most places you should be able to turn up on the spot and pay something more like local prices.

In addition there are the usual tourist *fiakers* offering tours of Kraków and Zakopane, and 'outside cars' to take visitors up to Morskie Oko in the Tatras.

Cycling

Poland is ideal country for cycling, as it is generally pretty flat, and the main roads have broad shoulders, although you should avoid the tram lines in cities, where there are no cycle lanes. Traffic is light except on the most important roads, and there are very few motorways from which cyclists are banned. A standard tourer is ideal, and a mountain bike will simply slow you down unless you do want to tackle some seriously rough stuff; however mountain bikes can be hired in Zakopane, even though they are not allowed in the Tatra National Park.

If you want to go in a group, Bike Tours Ltd (PO Box 75, Bath BA1 1BX) put on an annual 15-day tour from Kraków to Budapest, and Orbis, Pegrotours and the PTTK also promote cycling holidays: if you wanted to bring your own group, they would certainly be able to book accommodation and guides, especially in the Mazurian lakes.

Taking a bicycle by train is not a problem: just buy a half-price ticket and put the bike in the vestibule of a local train, or in the baggage/mail coach of some long-distance trains.

Caving

There is little karst in Poland, but nevertheless there are about 2000 caves of various kinds, totalling 125km in length. The most interesting are the 540 caves in the Tatra National Park, in both granite and limestone, which have been visited by tourists from at least the 17th Century, with the first guidebook published in 1887. The longest caves in Poland are here, Jaskinia Wysoka Za Siedmiu Progami (High Cave Behind Seven Thresholds, 10,050m) and Mietusia (9815m), and the deepest, Wielka Śnieżna (Great Snowy Cave, 776m), Śnieżna Studnia (730m) and Bandzioch Kominiarski (550m); most of the deepest caves are in Czerwone Wierchy (2122m), with their resurgence at Lodowe Źródło (Icy Spring) at 970m. Six caves in the Tatras are open to tourists, Mroźna, Mylna, Oblazkowa, Raptawicka and Smoczna Jama in the Kościeliska valley, and Dziura in the Ku Dziurze valley.

In the Pieniny there are 50 minor caves (up to 170m long), where a sort of Paleolithic boomerang has been found, as well as Neolithic remains from c23,000BC. In the Holy Cross mountains there are three groups of caves in limestone, of which the longest (2.5km) was found only recently during quarrying work. One cave here contained Paleolithic remains from c50,000BC, the most northerly in Europe. The largest area of karst in Poland is the Kraków-Wieluń plateau (including the Ojców National Park), where there are over one thousand caves up to 950m long and 68.5m deep, 50 of which contained remains up to 120,000 years old. In the 19th Century grand balls were held in some of these caves, and some were lit electrically by the early 20th Century; this is still the area where most Polish cavers learn their skills. The Sudeten mountains are mainly crystalline, but there is some metamorphic karst with 50 caves, some now destroyed by quarrying. Finally there are 120 caves in the Flysch of the Beskids, most caused by landslides; the longest (W Trzech Kopcach) is 826m, and the deepest (Diabla Dziura w Bukowcu) is 42m.

None are particularly spectacular for tourists, although the Kletno Bears' Cave (south of Kłodzko, page 205) and Wierzchowska Górna and Łokietka (in Ojców, page 167) are not bad. However there are interesting and rare bats and spiders living in many of the caves; in addition there are a couple of ice caves in the Tatras, such as Ciemniak, which are closed.

Caves are divided into three categories, firstly those open to all, either with fitted lights (such as Mrożna in the Tatras) or without, secondly about 100 caves open all to cavers, and the third closed to all. Permits for the second category (up to 100 or so per cave per year) are issued by the *Komisja Taternictwa Jaskiniowego* (Cave Climbing Commission) of the Polish Alpinists' Association (PZA), which in the absence of a separate caving association co-ordinates the 25 Polish caving clubs.

Climbing

For the last 10-20 years, Poland has been one of the more successful

climbing nations, with many successful Himalayan expeditions to its
credit, including the first winter ascent of Everest (by Leszek Cichy and
Krzysztof Wielicki, via the southeastern ridge in 1980) and the first
ascent of the South Buttress of Everest (by Jerzy Kukuczka and Andrzej
Czok); many of the peaks of the Mongolian Altai apparently have Polish
names. Other well-known climbers include Wanda Rutkiewicz, who died
near the summit of Kanchenjunga in 1992, having climbed Everest and
seven more of the world's 14 8,000m peaks, and Maciej Berbeka, who
has climbed six of them.

Not surprisingly, most of the initial training has been in the Tatras,
where the Polish Alpinists' Association (Polski Związek Alpinizmu, ul E
Ciolka 17, p.208, 01-445 Warsaw, tel 022 363 690) has a base on the
Hala Gąsienicowa and bivouac sites elsewhere. It is the granite rocks to
the east of the Polish Tatras that provide the most challenging climbing,
notably the east face of Mnich, the Monk, towering over Morskie Oko,
and Kazalnica, Żabi Mnich, Żabi Koń and Mięguszowiecki Szczyt, as well
as above the Hala Gąsienicowa. To climb here, or even to leave the
marked footpaths, you must have a permit and probably a guide, from
the PTTK, the Tatra Guides' Club (ul Krupówki 12, tel 2479), or the
Guiding Centre (ul Chałubińskiego 44, tel 3799). Piotr Konopka (of
Mountain Adventures, Droga do Bristolu 6, 34-500 Zakopane, tel 666
27) will also take you climbing or caving. Decent equipment is available
here, but you should bring as much as possible from home.

Additionally there are lots of climbing cliffs in the Kraków-Wieluń
plateau (the Jura), including the Prądnik, Karniowicka, Bolechowicka and
Minkowska valleys. EKO-Tourist (ul Radziwiłłowska 21/4, 31-206
Kraków, tel 12 228 863, or via ECOTOUR, Parsley Hay, Buxton SK17
0DG, tel 0298 84295) offers ten day climbing camps here and in the
Tatras for US$380, or US$330 for winter climbing, excluding travel to
Poland.

Paragliding

Paragliding is a young sport in Poland, having taken off in about 1991,
but there is plenty of potential given the great expanses of open hilltop
meadows. It is parachuting without the need to hire an aeroplane, or
even to cart around the clobber of a hang-glider. There is no room in the
National Parks, so the main centre for the sport is Bielsko-Biała, with the
Czaklen school at ul Sobieskiego 105, 43-300 Bielsko-Biała (tel 220 31).
I came across them flying from the top of Skrzyczne, above Szczyrk (see
page 184), where they had a clear take-off down the piste and an easy
return by the chair lift. The instructors speak some German, but if you
give them warning that you are coming it should be possible to find
some English speakers; when I was there, a British group was learning
to fly at the Bielsko Aviation Club. Unfortunately Polish paragliding
certificates are not accepted in the West, although Czech and Slovak
ones are.

It is also possible to paraglide near Zakopane, although not in the Tatra

National Park itself — ask at the gear shop at ul Kościuszki 15 (tel 3365), or the FlyCentre, ul Krupówki 12 (tel 3859). In 1991 it cost Z400,000 a day here, or Z970,000 for three days, against about Z700,000 (then about US$70) at Bielsko-Biała, or about five times as much in the Alps. Orbis in Jelenia Góra and the Karkonosze can organise hang-gliding for visitors.

Skiing

Skiing is very popular in Poland, with many people heading for the slopes of the Tatras, Silesian Beskids and Karkonosze, and many local hills, as well as skiing across country in many areas. Cross-country routes are marked by the PTTK in orange, often as a variant of a hiking trail, but showing distances in kilometres rather than time, while ski drags are shown on the standard tourist maps. Downhill runs are graded black, red, blue and green in descending order of difficulty, as standard. Many closed areas of the national parks are open to skiiers once safely under snow, but you should always take care to avoid avalanche (*lawina*) areas as shown on maps or signs, and enquire before leaving marked paths. Good equipment can be rented in Zakopane and other major resorts; the season should run from December to March, with most of the Tatra huts and cable cars closed for November, the chamois rutting season, but there has been little snow in recent winters.

In the Tatras the main centre for skiing is of course Zakopane; the most popular slopes (intermediate, but all more or less off-piste) are on Kasprowy Wierch, with two ancient chair lifts to the top as well as the main cable car, but there are many short ski drags on the hills around Zakopane itself, including some right next to the station and from the Gubałowka funicular, and in Bukowina Tatrzańska, to the east, which claims to be Poland's highest village, with great views to the Tatras. The main racing slopes are on Nosal, in Bystre (east of the Rondo roundabout, south of central Zakopane), reserved in the mornings for slalom practice. There are also ski jumps and a speed-skating rink here, near the main camp site, southwest of the Rondo.

The other main downhill skiing areas are the Silesian Beskids, with centres in Szczyrk (see page 184) and Wisła (page 186), the Beskid Sądecki, with centres in Krynica and Sucha Dolina (page 137), and the Karkonosze, with centres in Karpacz (page 213) and Szklarska Poręba (page 218), with the 'Piast Race' ski marathon, up to 50km, in Szklarska Poręba in March. None of these are comparable to the resorts of the Alps, with more easy runs for families, and accommodation in hostels and trade union rest homes rather than glitzy hotels and chalets.

Cross-country skiing is popular in the Bieszczady, around Suwałki and the Mazurian lakes, and in the Kashubian, Kraków-Częstochowa and Lublin Uplands. Orbis, the PTTK and Juventur all arrange one-week cross-country 'rallies' from hut to hut. New Millenium, Inter-Poland and Orbis also do skiing trips to Zakopane.

Boating

There is very little yachting on the Baltic coast, as very few private individuals have the funds for their own boats; but canoeing (or kayaking) is very popular indeed, particularly among the lakes and waterways of Mazuria. There are 3,200 lakes over one hectare in area in Poland, and the majority are in Mazuria, the two largest being the 113km² Lake Śniardwy and the 104km² Lake Mamry. These are connected by canals and rivers, and the area is ideal not just for boating but also for cycling and riding. Although the area is pretty flat, you should be prepared for portages around a few locks and power stations. The most obvious canoe route runs south from Węgorzewo to Giżycko, Mikołajki and Ruciane-Nida, linking the four main resorts of the area; they are also linked in season by steamers. Canoes can be hired in all four towns, but they are busy and polluted, so you should get away into the backwaters as fast as possible. You could continue all the way to Lake Zegrzyńskie just north of Warsaw.

Just to the west of Lake Śniardwy is the Krutynia canoe route, 90km long from Sorwity, just west of Mrągowo, southeast to Lake Bełdany and Ruciane-Nida; the PTTK organises daily groups on this route, staying in hostels only about 10km apart: this is really a very easy trip. You can do it yourself in five or six days, hiring a canoe in Sorkwity, and paying extra to have it returned to base; in summer you should be prepared to camp.

A similar route is to the east in the Suwalszczyna or area around Suwałki, where there are 200 more lakes, less visited and polluted than those of Mazuria proper. This route is 100km in length, following the Augustów Canal and the Czarna Hańcza river in a triangular route from Augustów to Lake Wigry; this is organised by the PTTK in Augustów (by the campsite on ul Sportowa), where you can also hire canoes. You can continue upstream on the Czarny Hańcza through Suwałki and a beaver reserve as far as Lake Hańcza; this is a wilder, faster stretch of river with little in the way of accommodation and services.

The Drawa river, from Czaplinek on Lake Drawsko west and then south through the Drawieński national park to Krzyż, and other lakes around Szczecinek, south of Koszalin, are perhaps less well-known but offer equally good canoeing.

Major canoe runs in the southeast of the country are from Żywiec north on the Soła river to Oświęcim, from Nowy Targ east and north on the Dunajec through the Pieniny gorge to Szczawnica, Nowy Sącz, Czchów and Tarnów, from Jasło north through Mielec on the Wisłoka to its junction with the Wisła, from Styżów through Rzeszów on the Wisłok to the river San, and on the San from Sanok to the Wisła, and on the Wieprz from Zwierzyniec (southwest of Zamość) north to Spiczyn (just northeast of Lublin). Many rivers, most notably the Wisła, are seriously polluted, and you should not venture off these routes without checking very carefully.

For competitive canoeing the place to go is Szczawnica, in the Pieniny (page 141), where there are slalom courses on both the Polish and

Slovak stretches of bank, and canoes can be hired on ul Pieninska, near the car park; the main Polish meet is in June, and the main one in Slovakia in September, at Červeny Klàštor. In addition there is the well-known raft-trip on the Dunajec river through the Pieniny gorge to Szczawnica, covered on page 143. If you want to go through the gorge by canoe, remember that it is a border zone and get permission first from the army at Czorsztyn, which should be a pure formality.

Sailing boats can be hired on the larger Mazurian lakes and on many reservoirs, notably Lake Solina in the Bieszczady and at Myślenice, south of Kraków, and Żywiec.

As well as the PTTK, Orbis, Juventur and Almatur, and the TRAMP Tourist Agency (ul Marszałkowska 66/24, 00-545 Warsaw, tel 214 447) will all arrange boat hire and canoe trips for you.

Part Three

Chapter 6

Hiking in Poland

WHERE TO HIKE

The hiking areas described in this book are all spread along the southern frontier of Poland, although there are isolated massifs further north, such as the Holy Cross Mountains (Góry Świetokrzyskie) just west of Kielce, as well as other interesting areas such as Białowieża (touched on on page 7) and the Mazurian lakes (likewise on page 87).

The mountains best known outside Poland are the Tatras, south of Kraków and Zakopane, the only genuinely alpine massif in Poland, which are spectacular but busy, with good infrastructure but many people using it. All the other mountain areas also have well marked hiking trails and good huts, and while the scenery is less impressive you will see more wildlife and fewer day-trippers. As you move from west to east the country seems less civilised and more eastern, from the Karkonosze, with its German hikers and foodstuffs, to the wooden Orthodox and Uniate churches of the Beskid Niski and finally the Bieszczady, very popular with students who stay in temporary tent bases in this largely undeveloped extremity of the country.

KRAKÓW

Kraków is by tradition Poland's most Catholic and conservative city, but it is changing fast, and will continue to do so as it becomes a prosperous city like any in western Europe. Nevertheless, in spite of the hordes of tourists now flooding in, Kraków is on UNESCO's World Cultural Heritage List and demands to be seen. It does not stand comparison with Prague for sheer beauty, but it does have a more compact and unspoilt historic centre, and as great a density of churches and art galleries. If anywhere in Poland is unmissable, it is Kraków. With Wrocław, it is the obvious base for the mountains, and I have never felt the need to go to Warsaw.

However it has many problems, above all the pollution from the Nowa Huta steelworks, in the eastern outskirts, which has been eating away the city's stonework and choking its inhabitants' lungs. Now the steelworks are only working at quarter capacity, but they are being replaced by road traffic, which rose by 20% in 1991. In addition there are now 3m tourists a year coming to this city of 800,000 people, which will increase as more accommodation is provided. Already by 1991 there were two groups of the ubiquitous Andean buskers, at either end of the main square, a biplane, horse carriages, and electric carts, as well as endless burger bars and even a topless bar, all aimed at separating tourists from their money.

Dominating trade routes along the northern side of the Carpathians, Kraków became the capital of the nascent kingdom of Poland from 1040 and developed with it until sacked by the Tatars in 1241-42 and 1259. However in 1257 it received a charter from Prince Bolesław the Bashful who rebuilt it on the present grid plan, and growth continued under King Kazimierz who established the Jagiellonian University in 1364 and the new quarter named after him. The city's Golden Age was from 1518 to 1572, under Sigismund I and his Italian wife Bona Sforza, when it became a centre of Renaissance learning, and had a population of 30,000 and 60 guilds.

However after the union of Poland and Lithuania in 1569 Kraków was on the fringe of the state, and power moved to Warsaw, although royal coronations and burials continued to be held in the Wawel cathedral in Kraków. The city stagnated for a while, but then with the Counter-Reformation the church took over the royal rôle as principal patron of architects and artists. At this time the city gained its present largely baroque look, with 50 churches and monasteries being built or substantially rebuilt. Nevertheless the city was again sacked by the Swedes in 1655, 1677 and 1702, and after the Partitions its population shrank to just 10,000. After the Napoleonic period Kraków was capital of a nominally independent republic from 1815 to 1846, but was then incorporated into the Austrian province of Galicia, which allowed industrial development and cultural freedom. Piłsudski and Lenin both had their bases here before the First World War, and it was also the centre of the *Młoda Polska* or Young Poland group of artists, and of the *Zielony Balonik* or Green Balloon cabaret in the Jama Michalikowa café, still at ul Floriańska 45.

In 1939 the Nazis arrived, and Kraków became capital of the General-Governorship, the German-occupied half of Poland, under the notorious Hans Frank. In November 1939 183 lecturers of the Jagiellonian University were sent to the Sachsenhausen concentration camp, and then the 68,000 Jews were herded into the Kazimierz ghetto and then shipped to the Płaszow camp (by the city's southern ring road) and Auschwitz by 1943. The events described in Thomas Keneally's Booker Prize-winning *Schindler's Ark* took place at Płaszow and the Unitra Telpod enamelware factory, where 1,200 Jews were saved from death. The city was liberated largely undamaged on January 18 1945, thanks to a cunning plan of the Red Army's Marshal Konev.

Under the communists the huge Nowa Huta (New Foundry) steelworks were built in an attempt to turn Kraków into a stronghold of the socialist proletariat, but in fact they became a bastion of Solidarity and Catholicism, despite not having a church for its 200,000 people until 1977, and also an environmental disaster. The church's triumph was reinforced in 1978 when the Archbishop of Kraków, Karol Wojtyła, became Pope.

Getting there

Kraków is very well connected, with through trains from all over Poland and indeed much of Europe (mostly overnight) and buses from a wide area of southern Poland. There are flights to Kraków from Britain (see *Getting to Poland*) and from Köln-Bonn, Frankfurt and Paris, and trains from Berlin, Frankfurt, Leipzig, Vienna, Budapest and Mangalia (on the Romanian coast), as well as private coaches from London, Italy and above all Germany. Orbis offers inclusive packages from £250 for a week's stay at the Cracovia Hotel or Holiday Inn, including the flight from Britain.

On arrival, you can find tourist information at ul Pawia 8, opposite the station (tel 226 091), or at Rynek Główny 1/3 (the Sukiennice, tel 217 706); in 1993 two useful publications, *Welcome to Cracow* and *Inside Kraków* started to appear monthly, in English.

Where to stay

It is true that there is a great shortage of accommodation in Kraków, but this is mainly at the top end of the market. In the summer season there is a reasonable amount of space in student halls and youth hostels, and more and more private rooms and mid-range hotels are becoming available.

There are four Orbis 3* and 4* hotels, the Forum, Holiday Inn, Cracovia, and Wanda, all relatively expensive and out of the way, and also the newly refurbished, private, Grand Hotel at ul Sławkowska 5 (tel 217 255). Orbis also runs the 3* Francuski, at ul Pijarska 13 (tel 225 122), also refurbished and probably the pick of the Orbis establishments. There are four fairly central 3* hotels, the Monopol, Pod Różą (busy since a casino opened here), Polski and Royal, and others further out, the Ibis, Korona, Piast and Demel, and the Pod Kopcem, which is in a class of its own, in an old hill-top fortress west of the city on al Waszyngtona, well worth it if you can get in (tel 222 055, bus 100).

Cheaper hotels include the Pollera (ul Szpitalna 30, tel 221 044), Warszawski (ul Pawia 6, opposite the station, tel 220 622), Polonia (ul Basztowa 25, on the corner of ul Pawia, tel 221 233), Europejski (ul Lubicz 5, also near the station, tel 220 911), Juventur's Saski (ul Sławkowska 3, tel 214 222), and the much larger Nauczycielski (Teachers') at ul Armii Krajowej 9 (tel 379 585).

Other possibilities are the Krak motel and campsite at ul Radzikowskiego 99 (tel 372 122), 4km to the northwest (take the airport

General Map of
KRAKÓW

to KATOWICE

J. GAGARINA

E40

Krak

BRONOWICKA (KROWODRZA)

E77
to
WARSAWA

Holiday
Inn

Wanda

CZARNOWIEJSKA

REYMONTA Zaczek

AL. 3 MAJA

Błonia

PUSZKINA

KOPIEC
KOŚCIUSKI

Cracovia

KOŚCIUSZKI

TYNIECKA

to AIRPORT
LAS WOLSKI
KOPIEC PIŁSUDSKIEGO

RYNEK
DĘBNICKI

DĘBNIKI

Forum

MICKIEWICZA KARMEL.

KRASIŃSKIEGO

P L A N T Y

RYNEK
GŁOWNY

WAWEL

DIETLA

KAZIMIERZ

to
NOWA HUTA

LUBICZ

B

(GRZEGÓRZKI

POKOJU

R. Wisła

PODGÓRZE

KAPELANKA

NOWOHUCKA

PŁASZÓW

E40
to
PRZEMYŚL

N

E77
to
ZAKOPANE

0   1   2

km

KEY   (N.B. some positions shown are approximate)

① Youth Hostel

② Nat. Gallery (new building)

③ Youth Hostel

④ Jubilat Dept. Store

⑤ St. Pauls Church

⑥ St. Catherines Church

⑦ Ethnographic Mus.

⑧ Remuh Synagogue

⑨ Corpus Christi Church

⑩ Old Synagogue

'93

bus 208 from the station, or numbers 118, 173, 218, 238 or 248), the PTTK Dom Turysty (ul Westerplatte 15, tel 229 566, with affordable dormitories if you can find a place, and a decent little bar upstairs), or private rooms from ul Pawia 8 (opposite the station, tel 221 921), or from people hanging around outside. The Wisła (ul Reymonta 22, tel 334 922) is one of the ubiquitous eastern European 'sports-hotels', usually linked to a stadium.

The summer-only student hostels include the Hotel Zaczek (at al 3 Maja 5, tel 345 477/331 914); take trams 15/18 (heading for Cichy Kącik) to the stop beyond the ring road and the National Gallery's New Building (the Museum of 20th Century Polish Art), opposite the Cracovia Hotel. In 1992 a single room cost Z100,000, a double Z160,000, and a triple Z180,000 (less for Poles); reception is staffed 24 hours a day by Jagiellonian University students who usually speak English and German, and there is a lively student jazz club and disco in the same building. Others are the Merkury (al 29 Listopada 48A, tel 118 244), the Letni (ul Jana Pawła II 82 2/3, tel 482 027, on the way to Nowa Huta by trams 4, 5, 10, 44 or fast bus A), or the Kapitol (ul Budryka 2, tel 375 989/377 491), all from Z90,000 in 1992. These are liable to change from year to year, but the Zaczek certainly seems pretty well established. Check at Almatur, Rynek Główny 7 (tel 226 352/226 708).

The main youth hostel is an ugly block just behind the Zaczek at ul Oleandry 4 (tel 338 822/338 920), charging from Z50,000 in 1992 for the dormitory. I prefer another in the Norbertine (or Premonstratensian) convent, by the river at ul Kościuszki 88 (tel 221 951), charging from Z37,500 for a bed in an eight-bed room. Take trams 1, 2, 6 or 21 to the Salvator terminus (or one stop before), and go to the left around the 17th Century church, to a door which a nun will open for you only between 1700 and 2300 hrs. You are unlikely to be turned away here, which is a comfort in high season. These two hostels are open all year; there is a third one at ul Szablowskiego 1 (tel 372 441), open from July 1 to August 25. Try also the PTTK hostel at ul Bulwarowa 37 (tel 440 863) and the Wawel hostel at ul Poselska 22 (tel 221 301).

There is camping at the Motel Krak (details above), the Krakowianka site (with cabins), ul Żywiecka Boczna (tel 664 191), near Borek Fałęcki station (on the Zakopane line), or by trams 8, 19, 22, 24 or bus 119 from the main station, the Ogrodowy site, ul Królowej Jadwigi 223 in Wola Justowska (tel 222 011), towards Kopiec Piłsudskiego by bus 134, (near a 16th Century wooden church moved here in 1947-49), and the Clepardia site, ul Mackiewicza 14 (tel 125 880).

Where to eat

Traditionally the best food in Kraków, and perhaps in Poland, has been found at the Wierzynek (Rynek Główny 15, tel 221 296/221 035), the site of a famous feast for Kazimir the Great in 1364. There are other restaurants aimed mainly at rich tourists, in the hotels, and in the heart of the Old Town, such as the Hawełka (Rynek Główny 34, tel 224 753),

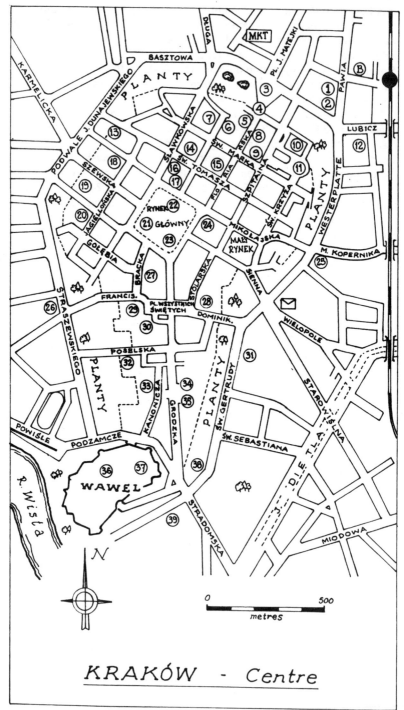

KRAKÓW - Centre

1. Hotel WARSZAWSKI + TOURIST INFORMATION
2. Hotel POLONIA
3. BARBAKAN
4. FLORIAŃSKA GATE
5. Hotel POLSKI
6. CZARTORY Museum
7. Hotel FRANCUSKI
8. MATEJKO Museum
9. Hotel POLLERA
10. SŁOWACKI Theatre
11. HOLY CROSS Church
12. Hotel EUROPEJSKI
13. PALACE of ART
14. HISTORICAL Museum
15. Hotel POD RÓZA
16. Hotels GRAND and SASKI
17. ORBIS
18. TEATR STARY
19. St. ANNE'S Church
20. COLLEGIUM MAIUS
21. TOWN HALL TOWER
22. SUKIENNICE
23. St. ADALBERT'S Church
24. MARIACKI Church + St. BARBARA'S
25. DOM TURYSTY
26. PHILHARMONIC
27. Museum of PHOTOGRAPHY
28. DOMINICAN Church
29. FRANCISCAN Church
30. TOWN HALL
31. Hotel MONOPOL
32. ARCHAEOLOGICAL and PHARMACEUTICAL Museums
33. WYSPIAŃSKI Museum
34. Church of Saints PETER and PAUL
35. Church of St. ANDREW
36. WAWEL CATHEDRAL
37. WAWEL CASTLE
38. Hotel ROYAL
39. BERNARDINE Church

KEY TO

  KRAKÓW - Centre

Kurza Stopka (pl Wszystich Świętych 10, tel 229 196), Balaton (ul Grodzka 37, tel 220 469), Cechowa (ul Jagiellońska 11, tel 210 936), Cyganeria (ul Szpitalna 38, tel 221 416) and the Staropolska (ul Sienna 4, tel 221 296/225 821), as well as the Pod Sokołom, a little further out on ul Piłsudskiego. You can get pizza at ul Jagiellońska 14, ul Mikołajska 16, ul Floriańska 38, ul Grodzka 29 and ul Szpitalna 38, and there is a salad bar in the courtyard of ul Św Anny 3. You can also find Chinese, Vietnamese, Mexican and Arab cuisine, but as yet no curry; a McDonald's opened at the end of 1993.

The milk bars formerly tucked away in odd corners all over the city have largely been swept away by the flood of new burger bars, leaving only a tiny one at ul Sienna 11, the Kuchik at Jagiellońska 12, and one of the most authentic remaining anywhere, opposite the Jubilat supermarket at the junction of ul Kościuszki and al Krasińskiego. Other cheap places to eat are dotted around the station, as well as what claims to be an Armenian restaurant. However when I descended from the mountains to refuel, I always preferred to graze at the *cukiernias*, of which my favourites are at the north end of ul Stolarska and at ul Krupnicza 6.

Of the cafés and bars, I noticed the Café Rio (ul Św Jana 2, the intellectuals and style victims' hangout), the Jagiellońska (in the cellar at ul Św Anny 6), the u Literatów (ul Kanonicza 7), and the famous Jama Michalika (ul Floriańska 45). There are jazz clubs at the Pod Baranami ('Under the sign of the Rams', at Rynek Główny 27), at no 8, and at the Zaczek (see above).

What to see

Kraków boasts 6,000 historic buildings (including 67 churches), and 2.3m works of art (1.6m in museums, the rest in churches or private ownership). You could spend several days doing nothing but visiting museums here, starting with the six branches of the National Gallery; however you should start by walking around the compact centre of the *Stare Miasto* (Old Town), defined by the ring of the Planty gardens, on the site of the city walls demolished in the early 19th Century. Why the Planty should be considered a tourist sight when it is really just the absence of a sight, I don't know, but it is a good place to read your mail.

The centre of Kraków is Rynek Główny, the Great Square, four hectares in area and lined by a superb unbroken array of Renaissance and baroque mansions. In the centre are three buildings, the small church of St Adalbert (Św Wojciech), with some 11th Century arches (a wonderful place to hide away briefly from the crowds), the Town Hall Tower, from the 14th Century (all that remains of the town hall, with a great view of the city), and, dividing the square in two, the Sukiennice or Cloth Hall, largely 16th Century, with 19th Century arcades by Jan Matejko. This is a covered market, now full of souvenir stalls, with upstairs the 19th Century Polish collection of the National Gallery. Also on the square are monuments to the poet Adam Mickiewicz and the patriot Tadeusz Kościuszko.

At the northeastern corner of the square is the Mariacki church (St Mary's), a fine 14th Century church and one of the best Gothic buildings in Poland. From the taller of its two towers, topped with multiple spires and a crown, a Fire Brigade bugler plays the haunting *hejnał* melody every hour on the hour (and on national radio at noon), cut short as it was by a Tatar arrow in 1241. Noon is also the time to see the opening of the Mariacki's greatest treasure, a gold-painted limewood altarpiece carved by Wit Stwosz (known to us as Weit Stoss of Nuremberg) in 1477-89, in a wonderfully over-the-top Gothic style, oblivious to developments south of the Alps. The interior is dark and atmospheric, like many Polish churches, but you will see clearly the stained-glass west window by Wyspiański and Mehoffer, and the Gothic east window, reminiscent of Sainte Chapelle in Paris, and with time you should make out the polychrome friezes by Matejko. Behind the Mariacki is the smaller church of St Barbara, with a 15th Century funerary chapel and a Christ in Gethsemane by the school of Weit Stoss.

From Rynek Główny you should head south along ul Grodzka, known as the Royal Way, to Kraków's other unmissable sight, the Wawel hill complex with the cathedral and castle. Where you cross the tram lines at Plac Wszystkich Świętych (previously Plac Wiosny Ludąw) you will find two monastic churches, that of the Franciscans to the right/west, and the Dominicans to the left/east. Of these the Franciscan church is the more interesting, built c1270 and rebuilt after the great fire of 1850, with rather pre-Raphaelite murals by Stanisław Wyspiański (1895), as well as his stained-glass windows over the main door; there are also 15th Century frescoes in the cloisters. The Dominican church was also built in a nice simple Gothic style in the 13th and 14th Centuries and rebuilt after the 1850 fire, with some pre-Raphaelite decoration. Next to the Franciscan church is the Renaissance *Rada* or town hall, with a newer extension behind on ul Poselska, where a plaque indicates the childhood home of the writer Joseph Conrad.

Continuing south down ul Grodzka you may spot a carved elephant and rhinoceros, which served as house signs before the introduction of numbers, before reaching the church of SS Peter and Paul, Kraków's first baroque church, built by Trevano for the Jesuits in 1596-1619, and next to it St Andrew's (also known as SS Klarycek or the Poor Clare's), which has a promising 11th Century Romanesque exterior but which was totally baroquified internally in the 18th Century.

Wawel Hill is the spiritual and historical heart of Poland, where its kings lived for many centuries, and returned to be crowned and buried long after the capital had moved to Warsaw. After climbing the ramp past souvenir sellers to another statue of Kościuszko you pass through a 16th Century gate and find the cathedral on the left. This is essentially 14th Century Gothic, but perhaps its best part is the row of side chapels along the south side, in particular the Zygmuntowska (Sigismund) chapel, a Renaissance jewel with its gilded cupola, built by Bartolomeo Berreci in 1519-33. The cathedral is full of magnificent tombs, with all but four of Poland's kings buried here, together with many bishops and in the crypts (dating from c1118) the poets Mickiewicz and Słowacki and the patriots Sikorski, Piłsudski, Kościuszko and Prince Józef Poniatowski. In the centre of the nave is the shrine of Stanisław Szczepanowski, Bishop of Kraków, murdered by King Bolesław the Bold in 1079, and canonised in 1253, a story with echoes of St Thomas Becket. In the first chapel to the right of the main west door is the tomb of King Kazimierz IV Jagiellon, by Weit Stoss, with Russo-Byzantine frescoes on the walls. Outside, opposite the west door, is a ticket office, for the cathedral treasury and tower.

Behind the cathedral is the castle and royal palace, rebuilt after a fire in 1499 by the Italians Berreci and Francesco Fiorentino, with an arcaded courtyard that always seems a bit out of proportion to me. In the royal apartments or *komnaty* are many treasures, mostly kept safely in Canada during the Second World War; the most notable are the remaining 136 16th Century Arras tapestries, of an original 360. In the Treasury and Armoury (closed Monday) is much more, such as the 13th Century *Szczerbiec Koronny* or 'Jagged' coronation sword, and appliqué tents captured from the Turks by Jan Sobieski in 1683. Most of the castle is free, if crowded, on Fridays, but it is rare for all parts to be open at the same time. Also on Wawel hill are the preserved foundations of buildings dating back to the 10th Century.

From here you can return by ul Kanonicza, a quiet and unspoilt street now being restored, with the Cricot 2 theatre archive at no 5, the Wyspiański museum at no 9, the gallery of Ukrainian Art at no 15, and a Renaissance portal and a fine courtyard by Santo Gucci at no 21, or continue south into Kazimierz. This was founded by the king of the same name in 1335, and became the Jewish quarter after 1495. This became one of the main cultural centres of the Polish Jews, but as can be seen by the many churches dotted around it was never an exclusively Jewish ghetto until the Nazis created one in March 1941, walling up a small area around the present Pl Bohaterów Getta (Heroes of the Ghetto Square), south of the river, until all its 68,000 Jewish inhabitants had been exterminated two years later. Now it is a pleasantly run-down area with arcaded streets such as ul Rabina Meiselsa (a good Jewish name), and a large market square, Plac Wolnica, with the Town Hall, now housing the large and important Ethnographic Museum.

There are still two functional synagogues here, the Remuh (ul Szeroka 40, built in 1557 and named after Rabbi Moses Isserles, also known as Remuh, a noted philosopher) and the reformed Tempel at ul Miodowa 24 (1862). The Remuh Cemetery was used from 1533 to 1799 and contains Rabbi Remuh's fine gravestone; the New Cemetery, in use since then, is at ul Miodowa 55. The Old Synagogue (*Stara Synagoga*) at ul Szeroka 24 was built in the 15th Century and since 1959 has been open as a Museum of Jewish History and Culture (closed Monday and Tuesday); the Bociana synagogue (ul Szeroka 16), built in 1620, is now an art centre, the High synagogue (ul Józefa 38), built in 1556-63, is now the Historical Monuments Restoration Workshop, the Kupa synagogue (ul Warsauera 8), built in 1643, is a storeroom, and the Ajzyk (Isaac) synagogue at ul Kopa 16, built in 1640-44, seems to be disused. In addition you can see the Jewish library at ul Skawinska 2, the hospital at ul Skawinska 8, the bath-house at ul Szeroka 6, and a fragment of the Nazi wall on ul Lwowska.

The Corpus Christi church on ul Bożego Ciała (Corpus Christi St) has some fascinating naïf paintings just inside the north door; the first ten metres above the ground are baroque but above that it's lovely plain 15th Century Gothic, stone for the nave walls and brick for the chancel and roof. At the corner of Augustynska and Skałeczna, to the west, is the church of St Catherine, also lovely 14th Century Gothic although with a huge gold baroque altar that must have taken quite a bit of erecting. Behind it on ul Paulinska is the church of St Paul, now baroque, with the graves of the artist Stanisław Wyspiański and the composer Karol Szymanowski.

Back in the heart of the Old Town, the area of ul Św Anny and ul Jagiellońska, west of Rynek Główny, was also Jewish until the university pushed them out; now it is the student quarter, with quiet streets lined with red-brick buildings, of which the most notable is the Collegium Maius (ul Jagiellońska 15), which now houses the University museum (only open 1200-1400, Monday-Saturday, with the wonderful Aula or Hall) and a shop where you can buy Jagiellonian T-shirts and mugs. The university church, by the Dutchman Tylman van Gamaren (who largely rebuilt Warsaw after the 17th Century Swedish wars), is Św Anny, 'one of the most beautiful baroque churches in Poland', if you like that sort of thing.

There are quite a few more attractive churches in the north of the Old Town, between Rynek Główny and the 14th Century Floriańska Gate, at the end of ul Floriańska, and the 15th Century Barbakan, all that remains of the city walls: the most attractive is Holy Cross, next to the Słowacki Theatre, a 14th Century chancel and a 15th Century tower and nave with one central pillar and Wyspiański-style paintings. St John's, at Św Jana and Solskiego, has 12th Century vaulting but is otherwise baroque, similar to St Mark's at Św Marka and Sławkowska, and St Joseph's at the east end of ul Poselska. Many of the churches in Kraków have English (and often French or German) information at the entrance, which you will not find elsewhere.

As for Kraków's treasure-house of **museums**, the best are the six branches of the National Museum (as distinct from the National Art Collection in the Wawel palace), all of which are closed for two days a week and free for one, in a complex rota which means that something is free most days; as I found to my cost this rota can literally change overnight.

The Sukiennice in Rynek Główny (closed Monday and Tuesday, free Thursday 1200-1730, other days 1000-1530) contains the 19th Century Polish Art collection, notably by Jan Matejko (1838-93, huge historical paintings) and Stanisław Witkiewicz (1850-1915), with early scenes of tourists at Morskie Oko and elsewhere in the Tatras.

The Czartory, at ul Św Jana 19, (closed Wednesday and Thursday, free Friday, hours as above) is Kraków's most famous collection, due largely to Leonardo's *Lady with an Ermine* (locally mistranslated as *Woman with a Weasel*) and a supposed Rembrandt, the *Landscape with the Good Samaritan*. There is a second-division Flemish collection, but some fascinating 14th Century Catalan and Sienese works, and lots of applied arts including turquoise-studded Turkish armour captured by the Ukrainian Hetman Mikołaj Hieronim Sienawski at Vienna in 1683.

The medieval collection, mostly of religious art, is in the Kamienica Szołayskich at Plac Szczepański 9, also closed Wednesday and Thursday, and free Tuesday.

The Matejko museum at ul Floriańska 41 (closed Wednesday and Thursday, free Friday) has a small display in the painter's home.

The Wyspiański museum at ul Kanonicza 9 (closed Monday and Tuesday, free Thursday) gives a good idea of this multi-talented pupil of Matejko whose work, in paint and stained glass, is seen in many of Kraków's churches; there is also an excellent collection of photographs of Kraków in 1869-1907. There is free loan of an English guide, but the exhibition has been moved around since it was produced.

The New or Main Building (*Nowy Gmach* or *Gmach Główny*, on the ring road at al 3 Maja 1, closed Monday and Tuesday, free Wednesday) contains the 20th Century collection (Wyspiański, Witkiewicz and their contemporaries), and temporary displays.

Of Kraków's other museums, the best is probably the Ethnographic Museum (open 1000-1400, closed Tuesday), at Plac Wolnica 1, in the old Kazimierz town hall, with an annexe nearby at ul Krakówska 46. This deals mainly with Polish folk traditions, although as noted elsewhere there is a superb collection of Łemk, Boyk and Huţul material (not always on display), and also much from other continents.

The Kraków Historical Museum's main branch is in the Krzysztofory Palace at Rynek Główny 35, as well as the Town Hall Tower, the Old Synagogue, the Theatre Museum at ul Szpitalna 21 and the former Gestapo HQ at ul Pomorska 2; all open 0900-1500 (to 1800 one night a week) except Monday, Tuesday and one weekend a month.

The Museum of Photography (closed Monday) is moving from Rynek Główny 17 and ul Bracka 4 (just south of Rynek Główny) to ul Józefitów 16; in addition there are the Archaeological Museum at ul Poselska 3 (closed Wednesday; the Geological Institute Museum here has shut), the Pharmaceutical Museum at ul Floriańska 25 (closed Wednesday), the Natural History Museum at ul Sławkowska 17 (closed Monday), the Polish Aviation Museum at al Jana Pawła II 39 (May-October, closed Monday), the Museum of the Struggle for Independence at al 3 Maja 7, the University Museum, mentioned above, and the 'Rydlówka' Museum of the Young Poland movement of artists at ul Tetmajera 28, Bronowice Małe, a manor house out west just beyond the Krak camp site (closed Sunday and Monday). There was also a Lenin museum at ul Topolowa 5 (behind the station to the east), and in his flat at ul Królowej Jadwigi

41, but these are now closed.

Art exhibitions are held in the Palace of Art at Pl Szczepański 4, the cultural centre at Rynek Główny 25, the Polish Art gallery at ul Floriańska 34, the Desa at ul Św Jana 3, and other private galleries sprouting up all over the Old Town. There is some amazing kitsch for sale on the streets, notably by the Barbakan, but also some good posters.

Practical information

Tourist information, at ul Pawia 8, near the station (tel 220 471/226 091), is remarkably helpful and well organised, and Orbis have their usual offices, which will sell you tours but not do a lot else, in the Cracovia, Holiday Inn and Forum Hotels, and at Rynek Główny 41 (223 044/224 035), where you can also buy rail tickets.

Consulates: there is still no British presence, but the Germans are at ul Stolarska 7, the USA at ul Stolarska 9, the French at ul Stolarska 15 (with the Institut Français at ul Św Jana 15, which has a lovely hallway), the Austrians at ul Św Jana 12, and the Russians at ul Westerplatte 11.

Shopping: there are excellent food stalls outside the station, open until 2100, and markets at Rynek Kleparski (near the station, with a deli open 0800-1900, and a good bread stall on ul Kurniki, on the way to the station), and Plac Nowy (in Kazimierz). There is also a small market on ul Senatorska, and a Jubilat supermarket (0900-2000, Saturday 0900-1500) at the junction of ul Zwierzyniecka and al Krasińskiego (the ring-road), both on the way out to the ul Kościuszki youth hostel. There are now half a dozen 24-hour shops in the centre. Crafts are best bought in the Sukiennice or Cloth Hall, in the centre of Rynek Główny.

The best shop for maps is at Rynek Główny 34, with others worth trying at ul Szewska 23, ul Floriańska 33 and ul Sławkowska 1, as well as the PTTK Mountain Tourism Centre at ul Jagiellońska 6/6A, which also has an excellent library, exhibition galleries and a bar; foreign-language newspapers can be bought at the Saski and Grand hotels and at any ORBIS hotel, and at ul Podwale 5; and foreign books at ul Szpitalna 19, ul Podwale 5, ul Bracka 6 and ul Sławkowska 1. The most detailed guide to Kraków is *An Illustrated Guide to Cracow* by Jan Adamczewski, published in Polish, English, French, German and Russian by Interpress Publishers, in Czechoslovakia, while the *Rough Guide* has 40 good pages on the city.

There is a hiking gear shop at ul Szewska 23, and sporting goods shops at ul Sienna 7 and ul Bracka 6.

The Central Post Office (for Poste Restante, clearly marked) is at ul Wielopole 2, on the corner of ul Westerplatte, open 0730-2030, Saturdays 0800-1400, Sundays 0900-1100; there is also a branch outside the rail station.

Transport: bicycles (*rowery*) including ATBs can be hired at ul Zacisze 14, and cars at the Hotel Cracovia (tel 371 120), ul Basztowa 15 (tel 211 066), the Motel Krak (tel 370 089) and the airport. There are now four or five lead-free petrol stations in Kraków, mostly open 24 hours a day. Bus and tram tickets should be bought in advance from RUCH kiosks and cancelled on entry, but they can be bought on the bus for an extra Z500; in 1993 they cost Z4,000 for a journey of any length on any one bus or tram, Z6,000 for an express bus, or Z12,000 for a night bus. The best **theatre** in Kraków is the Teatr Stary (Old Theatre) at ul Jagiellońska 1 (with a couple of studio theatres elsewhere — tickets from the main box office), although the largest theatre, staging Polish classics, opera and ballet, is the Słowacki Theatre, a reduced copy, splendidly restored for its centenary in 1993, of the Paris Opéra (**not** the new one at the Bastille), which you pass on the way to the main station. There are other theatres around town, and also lots of cabaret (even more subject to linguistic barriers), most notably at the *pod Baranami* (Rynek Główny 27), and the *Jama Michalika* (ul Floriańska 45). The Kraków Philharmonic orchestra, perhaps Poland's finest, is based at ul Zwierzyniecka 1 (now restored following a fire in 1991).

Festivals

Like many tourist towns with a busy peak summer season, Kraków has discovered the benefits of boosting off-season tourism with festivals. These start with the *Emaus* Easter church crafts fair, and festivals of Organ Music in April and Jewish Culture in late April/May, followed in mid or late-May by Juvenalia, the students' festival of misrule, then in May or June an International Festival of Short Films. One week after Corpus Christi comes the Lajkonik parade, when a Tatar chief in a glorious costume processes on a wooden horse from the Norbertine convent to collect tribute in Rynek Główny, and then in June Kraków Days, an umbrella for music, drama, arts and crafts.

   At the end of June and in early July the Kazimierz All-Poland Folk Music Festival is held, sometimes with a military band festival (featuring in recent years the bands of the Gordon Highlanders and the Belgian Navy, as well as those of the eastern European armies). In August comes Music in Old Kraków, involving top international musicians playing in churches and similar venues. In September there is a jazz festival and the All-Poland Fair of Folk Art. It is a Kraków tradition to display *szopki* or cribs in Rynek Główny and at ul Franciszkańska 4 a fortnight before Christmas, and subsequently in the Kraków Historical Museum.

Excursions

Together with the over-priced trips to Auschwitz (see page 169), the most advertised trip from Kraków is to Wieliczka (*Magnum Sal*), 15km southeast, which has joined Kraków on the UNESCO list of the world's most priceless monuments. This is a mine from which up to 25m tonnes of salt have been removed over 700 years; of the 300km of galleries, a 3km route is open through the oldest workings and 17th and 19th Century chapels, all wonderfully carved and ornamented. There is also a sanatorium 211m below ground for asthma treatment. It is easy to get here under your own steam, by train or bus from the main Kraków stations, and then join a group here, leaving every five minutes on a 2½ hour tour, costing Z70,000 (in 1993, including an underground museum). English-speaking guides are rare, but there is a good English booklet for Z20,000. However, in 1993 the mine was closed to visitors for a while, due to flooding and the damage done by human impact, and now only the upper 135m (of a total depth of 327m) are open.

Above ground, there is a private hotel, the Victoria, at ul Czarnochowska 15A (tel 782 690), camping at ul Kościuszki 36, a 16th Century wooden church, and the castle with one medieval tower and a mining museum (ul Zamkowa 1).

Other coach trips go to the Pieniny, to raft down the Dunajec gorge and visit the wooden church of Dębno, and to Ojców and Pieskowa Skała — all described below. Just southwest of Kraków is the Benedictine monastery of Tyniec, dating from the 11th Century but now largely baroque, where organ concerts are held on summer Sundays. This is a very pleasant excursion by bus 112, and can be busy at weekends; the setting is lovely, with the monastery on a limestone cliff above a small ferry. A few kilometres west of Tyniec are the mineral springs of Swoszowice, also a riding centre.

A little further southwest are the religious centres of Kalwaria Zebrzydowska and Wadowice; Kalwaria Zebrzydowska is second only to Częstochowa as a pilgrimage destination, particularly busy at Easter and on August 15, with 17th Century baroque churches dotted around on the sites of visions. Wadowice was the birthplace of Karol Wojtyła, now Pope John Paul II, and has now become a pilgrimage destination in its own right, with a museum in his home at ul Kościelna 7, and two hotels and a motel.

You might also wish to visit Nowa Huta, 10km east by trams 4, 5, 10 and 44, or fast bus A, to see the utterly featureless urban desert that 200,000 people, like so many others throughout the former communist bloc, have to live in. If you are really unlucky, you might end up in a private room here yourself. There are two old churches to the southeast on ul Klasztorna, and the church of our Lady (known as the Ark) north of the centre on ul Majakowskiego (named after Mayakovsky, the Soviet poet, so possibly due for renaming), and the church of St Maximilan Kolbe in the Mistrzejowice area.

On foot you could easily reach the Kościusko Mound (*Kopiec Kościuszki*), to the west along al Waszyngtona from the Cracovia hotel or following green trail markings along ul J Malczewskiego from the Salvator tram terminus (or by bus 100). Although only 326m high, it gives a good view of the area. The green markings continue westwards to the Las Wolski woods (popular on Sundays) and the 384m Kopiec Piłsudskiego, in memory of Poland's other great national hero; bus 134 terminates at a restaurant half-way up the hill. Just beyond this you reach the ring of fortresses built by the Austrians around Kraków; the two nearest are Fort Skala and Fort Olszanica, on the western spurs of

the Las Wolski; the most accessible is Fort Mydlniki, next to Kraków-
Mydlniki station (on the line to Katowice, not too far west of the Krak
campsite).

Moving On

From Kraków you can easily move to anywhere in Poland or, indeed,
central and eastern Europe, with overnight trains to Berlin, Budapest,
Vienna and Mangalia (on Romania's Black Sea coast), and day trains to
Leipzig and Frankfurt (change at Katowice for Prague and Budapest).
Kraków lies on the main east-west axis across southern Poland: 29 trains
a day go west to Katowice, with 10 continuing to Wrocław (2 going on
to Poznań, and 1 overnight to Szczecin and Świnoujście) and 7 east to
Przemyśl, 3 of these before 0600. There are also 11 trains a day to
Warsaw (at ten past the hour, some continuing to Gdynia), and others
to Lublin, Bielsko-Biała, Zielona Góra and Nowy Sącz, and night trains to
Warsaw, Bydgoszcz, Szczecin, Gdynia, and Krynica. Most trains to
Oswięcim (Auschwitz) go from Kraków-Płaszów rather than from the
main Kraków-Główny station (there are also 5 buses).

   Polish Railways (PKP) give information in English on 222 248, and you
can buy tickets from Orbis at Rynek Główny 41. Orbis will sell you air
and ferry tickets at ul Św Jana 2, and LOT has an office at ul Basztowa
15 (tel 225 076, 227 078). There is also a DELTA Airlines office at ul
Szpitalna 36. To reach the Kraków-Katowice airport at Balice, take bus
208 from the station, 209 from Salvator, or 152 from the Cracovia.

   To reach the mountains, you are generally better off going by bus,
both more direct and more frequent than the trains. There are 36 buses
a day to Zakopane, for the Tatras, as well as 15 to Rabka and 3 to
Nowy Targ for the Gorce, and 9 to Szczawnica for the Pieniny; and 8 to
Bielsko-Biała, 9 to Żywiec, and 7 to Cieszyn for the Beskid Śląski, as
well as the 1220 direct to Wisła. To the east there are 13 buses a day
to Krynica, for the Beskid Sądecki, 11 to Gorlice, for the Beskid Niski, 6
to Krosno and 4 to Sanok, for the Bieszczady, as well as a 1355 service
to Ustrzyki Dolne, which comes from Katowice and may already be full.

   To the west you can go by bus all the way to Jelenia Góra, in the
Karkonosze mountains, if you leave at 0645, or to Nysa at 1335;
however it's wiser to take a train to Wrocław and change there. To the
north there are 23 buses a day to Olkusz in the Ojców National Park and
7 to Kielce, for the Świętokrzyskie (Holy Cross) mountains. There are
also 3 buses a day to Warsaw, although the train is hugely preferable.

THE BIESZCZADY MOUNTAINS

For me the Bieszczady Mountains are the most special part of Poland; in
common with the adjoining area of Ukraine they are botanically unique,
and the social and historic aspects are also fascinating, due to the forced
removal of the indigenous Boyk population in 1947. Nowadays there is

an emptiness and spaciousness here that you do not often find in the more developed mountain areas of the Polish mountains, although in season there are many students hiking here. There are none of the big mountain huts found in the Tatras and the other Polish mountains, but rather a more diffuse network of small huts, youth hostels, student tent bases and bivouac sites (effectively little more than a field with a privy) mostly only functioning in the summer. There is a loop road through the area which now makes access much easier.

Rocks are sedimentary from the Cretaceous and late Tertiary periods, with limestone ridges and schist synclines. There is the standard submontane vegetation zone up to 550m and a lower montane zone to 1,170m, but no higher montane zone (spruce forest and dwarf pine): instead you pass directly into subalpine meadows, particularly the *połoninas* along the tops of long ridges, with East Carpathian grasses and flowers not found elsewhere in Poland. The montane forest is mainly (85%) *Fagetum carpaticum* or Carpathian beech forest, including some fir, spruce and sycamore, with grey alder by streams and green alder in the high mountain meadows. The remaining 14% of the forest, mainly in the newer, eastern areas of the National Park, is planted with spruce, pine and larch. Autumn colours are great!

The połoninas are mainly the long grass community *Poa chaixii-Deschampsietum caespitosae* (tufted hairgrass), with *Calamagrostetalia villosae* and the flowers *Trollius europaeus* and *Centaurea kotschyana*, and bushes of whortleberry and cowberry. Above them is the high mountain endemic sward *Nardetum carpaticum orientale*, composed mainly of *Nardus stricta* or matgrass. Three species (the spurge *Euphorbia carpatica*, the cow wheat *Melampyrum saxosum* and the fungus *Pleurotus wetlinianus*) are endemic to the Bieszczady, and 27 to the East Carpathians, including *Aconitum lasiocarpum, A tauricum ssp nanum* and *Dianthus carthusianus var saxigenus*, with other East Carpathian species such as *Aconitum paniculatum, Arnica montana, Carex dacica, C transsilvanica, Dianthus compactus, Laserpitium alpinum, Leucoium vernum var carpaticum, Symphytum cordatum, Telekia speciosa* and *Viola dacica*. We also find West Carpathian endemics such as *Aconitum variegatum ssp kotulae, Galium rotundifolium, Luzula luzulina, Potentilla pusilla, Senecio rivularis* and *Veratrum album ssp lobelianum*, as well as 80 other rare alpine species of plants. Although the border between East and West Carpathian flora lies at the Łupków pass, at the western end of the Bieszczady range, the połoninas are unique because of the balance of species from both ranges, although there are apparently also similarities with the Ardennes.

There are also some raised peat bogs in the San valley and below Wołosate, with *Sphagnum* and *Carex* sedge mires.

There are about 200 species of fauna here, notably more bears than anywhere else in Poland, perhaps 70 of them, as well as up to 100 bison, 30 wolves, between 3 and 12 lynx, 575 red deer and 100 roe deer, 120 boar and 13 elk, with 107 bird species (notably raptors such as the golden eagle, lesser spotted eagle, buzzard, eagle owl and Ural owl, as well as black storks, alpine accentors, water pipits and lots of dippers), 10 amphibia, 7 reptiles (particularly 200 Aesculapius snakes near Otryt in the San valley) and 20 fish.

Because of the inhospitable climate and terrain, the area was not colonised until the 14th to 17th Centuries; later it was depopulated due to industrialisation elsewhere and lack of work here. Before the Second World War there were perhaps 64 people per sq km in this area, mainly Boyks, Ukrainian-speaking highlanders who after the war were accused of feeding and supporting the UPA fighters, although most claimed to only want a quiet life. Already in 1945 there were major population movements, with Poles being deported from the new western territories of Ukraine and perhaps 750,000 supposed Ukrainians being deported to Ukraine, but in 1947 the UPA killed the Polish deputy minister of defence at Jabłonki, in the Bieszczady, and this spurred the Soviet, Czechoslovak and Polish armies to combine to eliminate the UPA once and for all. Virtually the entire populace of the Bieszczady villages was forcibly removed to the 'Recovered Territories' of western Poland; although almost no notice was given, this was not as traumatic as earlier deportations as there was no question of ending up in Stalin's Soviet Union.

Thus the population is now only 4 per sq km in the park area, and of the many abandoned villages generally only the nettle-swamped graveyards are still visible; prewar maps have been republished, showing all the vanished villages, and these are essential adjuncts to the more contemporary hiking maps, which as usual show every bivouac site and every category of church. Since the end of communist rule more Boyks have returned as tourists, including some from Ukraine, but only five families have moved back into the Park area.

The Bieszczady National Park (BPN) was created in 1973, initially to protect just 5,587ha of połonina, and has since grown to 27,064ha, to include the whole of the southeastern corner of Poland, mainly forest. As this area is now all state-owned land, setting the park's boundaries is just a matter of ajudicating between forestry and conservation interests. In 1991 the park was extended east to the Ukrainian border into a former military zone; this area, the San valley, is still undeveloped for tourism, and is thus particularly worth visiting. A UNESCO Biosphere Reserve is now being created in conjunction with Ukraine and Slovakia, to include the BPN and the Cisna-Wetlina (46,025ha) and San Valley (35,835ha) Landscape Parks in Poland, 40,601ha of landscape reserve in Slovakia, and 4,250ha in Ukraine. Up to 70% or 22,000ha of the BPN is to be strictly closed, with no human intervention, which may lead to some changes to the network of hiking paths.

There are other plans to better control human action in the park, with visitor centres to be built in 1993 and 1994 at its boundaries at Berezki and in an old farm east of Wetlina; these will provide bus parking, camping places, and much needed sewage plants. Hikers will have to get permits, at nominal cost, here or at various other outlets, to go beyond the road system. Permits will also be needed to cycle along side-roads

(Z10,000 from Tarnawa to Beniowa, Hulskie to Smerek, Zatwarnica to Suche Rzeki, and Z20,000 from Ustrzyki Górne to Rozsypaniec), with no cycling allowed elsewhere in the park. Although foreigners cannot always get away with pleading ignorance in Poland, this is probably an exception, but you should follow the system as far as possible.

To the north of the park area is Lake Solina (Jezioro Solińskie), a 25km² reservoir now much used for water sports, with various camp sites and other tourist accommodation along its shores, as well as equestrian centres at Teleśnica Oszwarowa and Polana. There are ski-drags at Cisna, Wielka Rawna, Komańcza, Solina (Jawor and Polańczyk), Ustrzyki Dolne, Lutowiska, Lesko and Zagórz, but undoubtedly the best skiing here is across country.

There is snow on the ground here for up to 140 days a year, until the end of March, usually about 80cm deep; however the maximum precipitation is between June and September, with an annual total of 800mm below 550m altitude, and 1,250mm at 1,000m. Temperatures average 16°C in July and –6.4°C in January. The połoninas are well known for the changeability of their climate, so don't go walking there without the right gear.

Getting There

The gateway to the Bieszczady is Ustrzyki Dolne, although it is also possible to approach from the west, from Sanok via Zagórz and Komańcza, or via Zagórz, Lesko and Baligród to Cisna and Wetlina; it is perhaps best to take a circular route, leaving via Cisna, perhaps by the forestry railway to Rzepedź, near Komańcza.

The main railway route from Kraków runs to Rzeszów and Przemyśl, north of the Bieszczady, with five trains a day from Wrocław and one overnight from Szczecin; from Przemyśl a train leaves at 1640 (with another at 1427 in summer, from Warsaw) and runs without stopping through Ukraine to Ustrzyki Dolne (making a good connection with the 1900 bus to Ustrzyki Górne) and Zagórz. There is no longer a military presence on the train, but a Ukrainian railwayman in a motorbike helmet checks all the doors from the outside. There are also trains to Zagórz via Nowy Sącz, Krosno and Sanok. However you may well be better off travelling by bus; from Przemyśl there are three buses a day to Ustrzyki Dolne, taking two hours, the same as the train, and costing less. Buses from Kraków run at 0800, 1320, 1625 and 1845 to Sanok, as well as at 0630 to Lesko; there is a through bus at 1355 to Ustrzyki Dolne, but as this starts in Katowice it may already be full.

Przemyśl is an ancient city which as for centuries still serves as the main crossing point between Poland and Ruthenia, now being just 10km from the Ukrainian border; the Austrians made this their main fortress in Galicia, and it suffered a major siege in 1914-15. There are traces of the fortifications still visible, and many churches, mainly a slightly heterodox baroque. From the rail station (with the bus station behind it through an

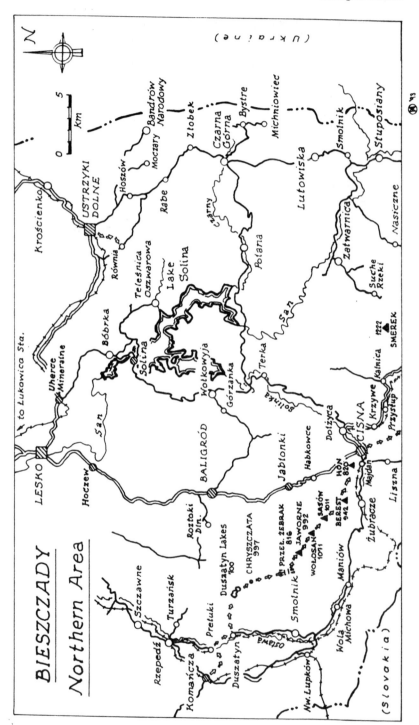

BIESZCZADY
Northern Area

underpass — both have frequent services to Lviv, and you can change Ukrainian, Russian and Lithuanian money here, as well as getting Ukrainian visas at the travel agencies around the stations) turn right along ul Mickiewicza and cross ul Jagiellońska by the Reformed Franciscan church (1645) to continue along ul Franciszkańska to the Rynek or market place, with its fine 16th Century arcades.

To the left/south here are the Franciscan church (1778), with the Jesuit church (1627), Diocesan and Regional museums behind it, and the Carmelite church (1630) above and behind them, with an amazing ship-shaped pulpit; this was the Uniate church between 1784 and 1945. To the west is the cathedral (originally from the 12th Century but now largely baroque) with a separate tower (1764) and school (1572), and beyond that the castle (1340), with a good view from the ramparts. From the PTTK office on the Rynek, a red stripe path leads via the castle to the Helicha fort two hours southwest, part of the Austrian defensive ring. Across the river to the north is the Benedictine church (1777), and along ul Grunwaldzka and right on ul PCK (Polish Red Cross St) the Salesian church of St Joseph, an interesting piece of 1920s Gothic.

If you are just passing through, the handiest place to stay is the Dom Wycieczkowy (or Hotel Przemyśław or Hotel Dworcowy) at ul Dworskiego 4, opposite the station (there is also tourist information here); the Hotel Sportowy (ul Mickiewicza 30), the Dom Nauczycielstwa (ul Chopina 1, north of the castle, run by the ZNP teachers' union), the PTTK's Podzamcze hostel nearby at ul Waygarta 5, and the youth hostel (open all year) at ul Lelewela 6 (across the river) are also cheap enough. In addition there is a summer-only hostel in a school at ul 3 Maja 38, and a campsite west along the river at ul Manifesto Lipcowego 8.

Sanok is a prosperous little town of 40,000, set on a 70m cliff above the river San, worth visiting for its wonderful collection of Uniate icons, and also its skansen of Boyk and Łemk buildings. The rail and bus stations are opposite the summer-only youth hostel at ul Lipińskiego 34, the main road southeast to Lesko. To go into town head west across the railway and a stream and up ul Jagiellońska to the Rynek; just before this the parish church is in Plac Św Michała to the left (not as shown in the *Rough Guide*). The Franciscan church, dating from 1384 and 1640, is on the Rynek, and opposite this, at the northeastern corner of the square, ul Zamkowa leads to the castle, on the right overlooking the San, which contains the Icon Museum, a superb collection, dating from the 14th to 19th Centuries, 'rescued' from the Uniate churches of the Bieszczady when the area was depopulated in 1947. The best are the earliest ones, superb images of Christ Pantocrater (Ruler of All) and St Nicholas. The same ticket also admits you to the Historical Museum at ul Zamkowa 2, by the castle gate, which in fact contains some interesting local art.

Continuing northwest on ul Zwirki i Wigury, turning right at the PTTK *Dom Turysty* and continuing on ul Mickiewicza and ul Białogorska, you will reach before too long a preserved tank by a footbridge across the river — you can also get here by bus 3 directly from the youth hostel, at three minutes before the hour, and then return on foot. Across the footbridge and a short distance to the right, at ul Traugutta 3, is the Museum of Folk Building or skansen, containing groups of buildings from the Boyks, Łemks and the 'People of the Foothills' and 'People of the Valley', including a smithy, windmills, watermills and churches from the 17th and 18th Centuries. Look at the map before entering, as you won't find another.

There is a camp site by the skansen footbridge and another (with sport hotel) on al Wojska Polskiego (Polish Army Avenue, the road east to Przemyśl — bus 1 from the Rynek); other than these, the youth hostel and the PTTK hostels at ul Mickiewicza 29, mentioned above, and also at ul Świerczewskiego 16, the only place to stay is the Turysta hotel on ul Jagiellonska, which in 1992 charged from Z160,000 for a single.

From here there are buses to Humenné (at 0650) and Medzilaborce (at 1540) in Slovakia, and others (many at about 0620) to Gliwice, Lublin, Katowice, Kraków, Nowy Sącz, Nowy Targ and Warsaw, and 22 a day to Rzeszów, as well as a complex network of local buses to the Lake Solina area, to Cisna via Komancza or Baligród, to Wetlina, and to Ustrzyki Górne via Cisna or Ustrzyki Dolne. There are 15 trains a day between Zagórz and Krosno, with one each continuing to Kraków and Katowice, to Łódź, and to Warsaw.

Fifteen kilometres north of Sanok is Ulucz, where you can find the largest wooden church in Poland, high on a hill over the San. Built in 1510 and painted internally in 1650, it is now part of the Regional Museum.

The next town, **Zagórz**, is basically unattractive but does have some *noclegi* (private rooms) and a summer-only youth hostel at ul Świerczewskiego 70. This is the junction for the branch to Komancza and Nowy Łupków, connecting with the forestry railway to Cisna; all buses from Sanok to the Bieszczady also stop here.

At **Lesko** you enter the tourist map of the Bieszczady, and find the start of a green stripe route to Połonina Wetlinska. Like Sanok the town sits on a cliff over the San; its main sight is a newly restored 18th Century synagogue on ul Stanisława Moniuszki, just northeast of the centre, now an art gallery and PTTK office (for private rooms), with an early 17th Century Jewish cemetery or *kirkut*, with about a thousand tombstones scattered among the trees, just northeast. Private rooms can also be booked at Rynek 1, and there is a camp site off the Wetlina road below a castle hidden in trees, a PTTK hostel at ul Bieszczadzka 4, a youth hostel (open all year) and motel on ul Świerczewskiego at the western town limits, and a place run by *Harctur*, the scouts' travel agency, by the ski-drag across the river in Huzele.

The Lesko-Łukawica station is 4km north, and buses stop on Plac Konstytucji 3 Maja, continuing to all Bieszczady villages as from Sanok, and to Katowice, Kraków, Przemyśl and Warsaw.

This area has a long tradition of peasant radicalism and was the heartland of Rural Solidarity; during the period of martial law many of its activists were interned in a basic camp at Uherce, just east of Lesko.

Ustrzyki Dolne is the place to stock up on supplies before heading into the hills, and is usually full of student hikers in the summer. The town centre is about five minutes left/west along the main road from the rail and bus stations; on ul Kopernica (to the right just before the Rynek) is a rather drab Uniate church built in 1847, used as a warehouse from 1952 to 1985 (now open for Sunday services at 1030), and at Rynek 6 a library incorporates the rear wall of the old synagogue. Just above the Rynek to the right/north, at ul Bełzka 7, is the National Park Museum (closed Sunday and Monday), which has a good display of the local wildlife (without English captions), and some good postcards. The Jewish cemetery, on the hill opposite the Rynek, across the railway line, is being restored, with the *matsevah* tombstones, which had been taken for road-building, being returned; however my favourite sight is the modern church of St Joseph the Worker, reached by ul Jana Pawła II (after the Pope, of course), one block west of the Rynek. Completed only in 1992, this has a stepped roof and soaring asymmetric towers somewhat in the style of Clifton cathedral in Bristol.

Accommodation can be in short supply here, with the Hotel Laworta now shut and for sale; the Hotel Bieszczadska at the west end of the Rynek and the Hotel Strwiąz at the junction of ul Sikorskiego and ul Szkolna, near the Uniate church, are both adequate, and private rooms can be obtained at Rynek 14, Rynek 4A and ul Sikorskiego 29. There are summer-only youth hostels in elementary schools 3km northeast in Brzegi Dolne and 3km southeast in Jasień, and a camp site on the Strwiążyk road, to the right at the west end of town, as well as a bivouac site in Jasień.

As for food, there is good draught beer and *pierogi* at a PTTK *kawiarna* at the bus station, a pizzeria at Rynek 3, and hotel restaurants; the market below the Rynek is especially popular with Ukrainians on Sundays.

From here trains and buses go to Sanok and Przemyśl, as detailed above, although the portakabin temporary rail station does not issue tickets beyond Przemyśl. Five buses a day go to Rzeszow, and one, at 0810, to Kraków and Katowice. There are a dozen buses to Ustrzyki Górne, the last at 1900.

The road south to Ustrzyki Górne passes through several villages with interesting Uniate churches, mostly wooden and in the Boyk style of a central dome and two equal smaller domes, rather than the Łemk style of three descending domes of the Beskid Niski. However the first, at Hoszów, built in 1898, is in the Huṭul style, squarer and with big eaves. From here you can turn west to Równia, one of the very best wooden churches, described in the box. Continuing down the main road there are simple churches with one dome at Rabe (1858), and at Żłobek (1835), at a 638m pass. The church of Czarna Górna, the next village south (with a summer youth hostel), was built in 1830-34 as a *cerkiew* or Uniate church, and although converted to Roman Catholicism in 1951 is one of the few internally unchanged, with its iconostasis intact, and an unusual colonnaded porch (get the key from the new priests' house opposite). From here you can take an occasional bus east to Bystre and Michniowiec, hard by the Ukrainian frontier, which both have wooden churches.

Lutowiska used to be the market centre of this area, with cattle brought up from Hungary to be fattened on the poloninas and sold on here. It still has a post office and restaurant, now serving the oilworkers from the barracks to the north, as well as a ski-drag, Jewish cemetery, and a church from 1898. Well south of Smolnik, the next village (not to be confused with the Smolnik near Nowy Łupków, to the west, which has an uninteresting church), is a fine example of a Boyk church, built in 1791 and now isolated in a beautiful hilltop setting. This is near the Smolnik skrzyżowanie (crossroads) bus stop, where some buses turn west to Zatwarnica; cyclists might wish to head south from Zatwarnica to the emptier north side of Połonina Wetlinska and the Suche Rzeki scouts' hut and camping place, or west to Lake Solina.

Just south of the crossroads is Stuposiany, where there is a summer-only youth hostel in the village school; from here to Ustrzyki Górne, as

---

One of the very best of the wooden Boyk churches is just south of Ustrzyki Dolne in Równia (Rivnya in Ukrainian). It is an easy 45 minutes walk over the hill, following blue stripes along ul Kolejowa, just east of the Rynek, and crossing over the stream and under the railway to climb up to the stadium. There should be a gate open to follow the path up the right-hand side of the stadium past some wooden loos (you could camp here or just above, but it is a bit of a lovers' lane). The path continues up into the trees, reaching the ridge in 8 minutes, and turning left there (not quite as on the map). Here the trees end and you can see Równia below in a patchwork of small fields; to the west is the Ustjanowa woodproducts factory, now thankfully closed, although many jobs have been lost.

The path follows the ridge southeast past the Gromadzyn TV tower, the Biathlon shooting range and the top of a ski-drag, and turns right after 12 minutes, zigging left and right and then going down with trees and a stream to the left, to cross the main stream by a footbridge and go up to the road. Go left for 100m and then left to the church, which was built in the 1750s. It is half-hidden in trees and well maintained, with three rounded domes and wide low shingled eaves with rounded cormers, supported by cantilevered brackets. Services are at 0930 on Sunday.

You can return by bus, with most buses going west to Ustrzyki Dolne from a stop near the church; a few also take an eastern route via Jasień from a layby 100m west. I returned over the hill and descended by the ski-drag, partly on a rather dodgy boardwalk, and then by ul Naftowa to ul 22 Lipca, the Ustrzyki Górne road. Ul Naftowa takes its name (meaning naphtha or oil) from the oil once brought north by pipeline from the wells to the south.

you enter the mountains, there are numerous bivouac sites along the banks of the Wołosaty river.

Ustrzyki Górne is the National Park's operational headquarters and the main centre for tourism, mainly hiking, in the Park; in fact other than the Park HQ and tourist accommodation there is nothing much here. At the northern end of the settlement is a new PTTK complex, completed in 1992 but awaiting sewage facilities; south of this are a post office, a PTTK museum (with good material on inter-war tourism in what are now the Ukrainian Carpathians), a large official camp site (which charged Z10,000 for a tent and Z7,000 per person in 1992), then a couple of bars and fish-and-chips stalls facing a food shop (open every day in season) by the junction left/east to the Park HQ, and then, beyond a bridge and the road junction left/southeast to Wołosate, the old 'Kremenaros' hostel, with a good cafeteria open to all comers and vaguely aware of vegetarian requirements, with an English menu. You can camp here, or in nearby bivouac camping places, but note that those shown on the tourist map as being by the bridge just north of the village are in fact a good kilometre further north, just before the BPN boundary.

In addition there is a tourist hostel with guarded camping 5km south at Wołosate, in what was clearly a state sheep farm until 1991. The *bufet* is not great here but the German-speaking manager is very positive and knowledgeable and promises improvements, including ponytrekking with 10 of the local Huṭul mountain horses. Camping here costs the same as in Ustrzyki Górne, and the hostel charges Z17,000 for a space on the floor, Z22,000 for a bed without sheets, and from Z42,000 for a normal single room. Before the Second World War this was a relatively large settlement on a cross-border trade route, with many Jewish merchants and a German wood factory; now Polish soldiers camp here in the summer to try to intercept Ukrainian smugglers who apparently try to blend in with the hikers.

There is an hourly bus (costing Z5,000) from Ustrzyki Górne to Wołosate, and a tourist 'Green Bus' service to Wetlina and Cisna, which claims to be 10% cheaper than the PKS buses but otherwise seems identical. The PKS buses to and from Ustrzyki Dolne often turn around at the bus stop 10 minutes walk north of the shop; only those continuing to Wetlina are sure to reach the centre of the settlement. In summer there are up to 12 buses a day heading north, some continuing as far as Krosno and Rzeszów, and 7 to Wetlina, some continuing to Sanok.

Hiking Directions

Route 1 is ideally a two-day hike east to the San valley, but it can equally well be a fine one-day circuit of the peaks east of Ustrzyki Górne; route 2 starts as a day walk to Wetlina through the best-known of the połoninas, but can be extended as far westwards as you want — I continued for two days to Cisna and Komańcza, and then onwards as in the Beskid Niski section to Dukla and Gorlice.

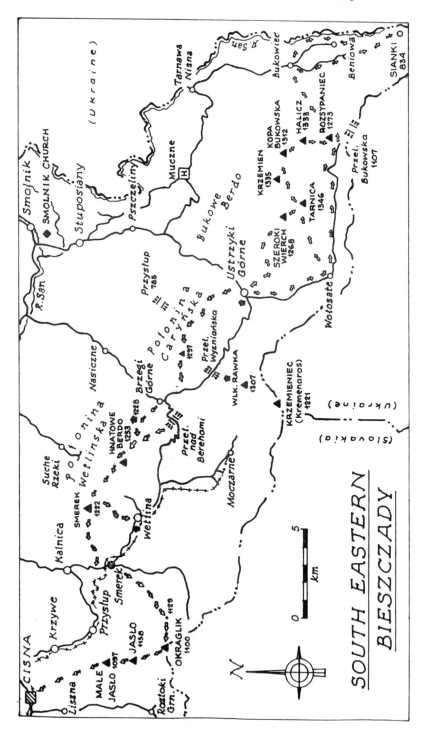

1: Tarnica and the San valley

The highest peak of the Bieszczady is Tarnica (1,346m), to the southeast between Ustrzyki Górne and the Ukrainian border, and beyond this is the emptiest and most recent addition to the park, the San valley. This can be reached over the hills from Ustrzyki Górne, or by minor roads starting on either side of Pszczeliny, north of Ustrzyki Górne. These meet at Muczne where there is now a hotel in what was a closed estate for high communist apparatchiks, where heads of state such as President Giscard d'Estaing of France were taken hunting. Beyond this is the equally tiny village of Tarnawa Niżna, with a bivouac site; beyond this there are only abandoned villages and overgrown cemeteries. To go into the San valley zone of the Park you should certainly have a permit from the Park headquarters, as the border police may check your papers: you must, of course, carry your passport.

From Ustrzyki Górne the most direct route to the San valley is by the road to Wołosate and on to the Bukowska pass, on the border below Rozsypaniec (1,273m), taking an hour to Wołosate and 1 ¾ hours more to the pass; however it is more interesting to head into the woods immediately from Ustrzyki Górne and then follow the ridge to Tarnica and onwards. Starting from the shop and road junction, this route, marked with red stripes, heads east past the Park headquarters along a former quarry road; after 10 minutes pass through a gateway and turn right to begin a good steady climb through a beech wood. Passing two *wiata* or shelters, it takes 50 minutes to reach the treeline, and then a steeper 15 minutes to reach the ridge of Szeroki Wierch. Heading east-southeast through the połonina, you pass a total of four peaks, each higher than the one before, before dropping after 45 minutes to the 1,275m pass under Tarnica. Here you meet a blue stripe route coming from the main road at Pszczeliny along the craggy Bukowe Berdo ridge and then dropping southwest to Wołosate (45 minutes away), and a yellow stripe route (not shown on the tourist map) up to the ironwork cross on top of Tarnica, reminiscent of that on Giewont above Zakopane, which took me 8 minutes up and 5 down. You are here just 2m higher than the summit of Ben Nevis, but in a far more hospitable setting, at least in summer. From here there are views, both east and south, deep into Ukraine, perhaps as far as the Gorgany massif.

From the Tarnica pass I headed northeast, following both red and blue stripe markings, passing a spring on the left (whatever the sign says, take your water from the spring itself, as the bushes below are used as a toilet) and a turning right to a summer-only GOPR mountain rescue post, before reaching the junction, at 1,160m, of the blue stripes to Bukowe Berdo. The red stripe path continues to the right, climbing gently along the steep hillside through low bushes. After 20 minutes you reach the ridge below Kopa Bukowska (1,312m): in the other direction you might be tempted to continue westwards along the ridge directly to Bukowe Berdo, but this is a strict reserve. Eastwards from here the path is easy for 15 minutes before climbing for 15 minutes to the summit of Halicz (1,333m); there is a smaller cross here, marking the site of a gallows used by the UPA for executions. Again it takes 15 minutes to drop past a mineral spring and climb to Rozsypaniec (1,273m) (not the peak of the same name further southeast on the Ukrainian border). There are some concrete pillars, similar to trig points, and some foxholes along this ridge, indicating that this was briefly the Polish border in the 1920s; there are many more of these border markings along the Ukrainian hiking routes.

The red markings continue just a little further south to the border (with a *wiata*) and down the road to Wołosate; the Połonina Bukowska continues southeast as a clearly defined ridge which would be a very tempting route were it not the Ukrainian border. The path into the San valley is not easy to find, marked with a white number 3 on some thin trees, about 200m from the southern edge of the trees. This is a so-called 'didactic route' rather than the tourist routes to this point, and you should meet almost nobody here. This is a beautiful silent wood of tall thin beech and fir trees with deer and bears; the berry patches are also virtually untouched on this side of the hill. After 30 minutes, mainly dropping eastwards along a minor ridge, the path, marked with the number 3 in white, crosses a stream where a 3 and a cross on a tree should prevent westbound hikers from going wrong. Eight minutes east of here be sure to keep to the left/north bank of the Halicz (or Potasznia) stream, and follow a track, rather overgrown in parts but clear enough, for 20 minutes to the start of a road (just before the park boundary), and on for 25 minutes to reach the road from Muczne. Where a road turns north 8 minutes before this main road you can ford the stream to the right/south and easily find the remains of the cemetery of Bukowiec.

Turning right onto the road, crossing the bridge and then turning right you re-enter the park and head south on a forestry road; however I turned left, through meadows and planted spruce, to swing right and follow the Ukrainian border, with an electrified railway just beyond the usual fence and watch-towers. After 25 minutes this road ends at a stream, in what used to be the village of Beniowa; in the trees ahead is the cemetery, still well-fenced and being tidied up, with Cyrillic gravestones, and behind a copse to the right is what is essentially a bothy, a hut left open for hikers to sleep in, with a supply of matches and candles. This is a lovely place.

From here you can cross the field to the west to rejoin the main road; 12 minutes south is a forestry house and a bridge, beyond which you should turn left, ignoring no-entry signs if on foot or bike. The forestry road continues south, passing to the west of Szczorb (818m) rather than as shown on the tourist map, and also passing an A-frame shelter which could be used as a bivouac; it takes just over 30 minutes to reach a curve to the right where a white number 2 is visible to the left. This whole area was planted with Austrian pine and spruce before the First World War and has since been clearfelled, so there are now far too many young trees. The Austrian seeds are not well adapted for this location and are now being replaced by beech as they sicken. Fir is also native to this area but may not survive, especially if the growing deer population is not culled.

This well-trodden path passes through meadows with chest-high grass and spruce woods, reaching an overgrown cemetery after 20 minutes; from here the path heads south, away from the stream, and goes up to the left into the wood beyond the marked tree. In about 10 minutes you reach a ridge in spruce which opens to show cows grazing in Ukrainian meadows; this is the southeasternmost extremity of Poland and the site of the forestry town of Sianki (pronounced Shanki), now vanished. To the northeast is the Ukrainian forestry town of Stary Sianki, with railway yards where trains are marshalled to cross the Uzhok pass (853m) just south. The San is here a small stream which you could easily cross but would be ill-advised to do so, although Ukrainian guards apparently come the other way to poach deer.

To return north, you must back-track to Bukowiec and then either take the road via Muczne or path 3 back to Rozsypaniec and the red stripe route.

2: West to Wetlina, Cisna and Komańcza

Having returned to Ustrzyki Górne, there are two routes west to Wetlina, one marked with blue stripes, via Wielki Rawka (1,307m) near the meeting point of the Polish, Ukrainian and Slovak borders, and another with red stripes, following the line of the połoninas to the north. I took this latter route, which starts behind the Ustrzyki Górne camp site at a footbridge across the Wołosaty river. Soon the path forks left and then climbs into the beech woods (a steep slog for 20 minutes, easier for 10 minutes, and steep for another 10) to the east end of Połonina Caryńska (pronounced Tsarinska), at a saddle at 1,107m. There is a steepish pull up to the first peak (at 1,234m), where a green stripe path joins from Przysłup to the right/north, where I gather the student hut has closed, although there may still be tented accommodation in summer. The green stripes turn left 25 minutes further west along the ridge, to the 'Pod Mała Rawka' PTTK hut (which boasts a ski-drag and a sauna!), and 5 minutes further on you reach the highest point of Połonina Caryńska, at 1,297m. This is a typically elongated mountain ridge, with great views of the longer but lower Połonina Wetlinska continuing its line to the west, and Tarnica and Halicz to the east.

After 5 minutes more the path turns left, passes above a spring, and enters the trees after 10 minutes; after 20 minutes in beech the path turns sharp left in a clearing, and continues dropping in more mature mixed wood for 15 minutes to emerge at the Brzegi Górne road junction, at about 740m altitude. A minor road turns north here to a bivouac site and the Zatwarnica road, but buses only run along the Ustrzyki Górne-Wetlina road.

The red stripe route continues to the right immediately after the bridge, climbing steadily, mainly in a broad clearing, and now passing to the left/south of an eroded stretch, to reach the Połonina Wetlinska PTTK hut in about 50 minutes; however if you are visiting only this połonina, the most interesting and scenic of those in Poland, the easiest way up is to take a bus or hitch to the Przełęcz nad Berehami or Berehami pass (872m) just west of Brzegi Górne, and follow the new yellow markings, not shown on the tourist map. The hut is visible from the pass, and it takes just 40 minutes to reach it: after 10 minutes fork right and follow a cart track up into a classic beech wood, forking left after 5 minutes more at a T-junction. Now the track climbs steadily along the hillside, reaching the treeline after 15 minutes and turning sharply right towards the hut. This is a small, friendly place without much in the way of facilities or supplies, in a beautiful windswept location at 1,228m.

The main ridge route carries on to the northwest, marked with red stripes as all ridge routes should be, passing above a good spring and through the typical long grass and flowers of the połoninas, with rowan and bilberries (always picked bare here, despite the notices forbidding it). After 30 minutes you will reach the rocky ridge of Hnatowe Berdo (1,253m), with at its far end a path down to Wetlina; although these unmarked routes are not open to hikers, they are nevertheless well used, and I have in fact come up this way myself, starting by the forestry house (with its radio mast) west of the Wetlina shops, forking left after 15 minutes by a shooting hide and then turning right in an overgrown clearing after 10 minutes more, before climbing steadily for another hour.

The main path swings a little to the right, to drop to a saddle between two beech woods (with a spring to the left), then climb and drop to another saddle (Przełęcz Orłowicza, 1,075m) after 30 minutes. Seven minutes further west is a junction with a yellow path left to the PTTK hut in Wetlina, and right to the Suche Rzeki scout hut, and a black path right to Cisna, linking to a green path to Lake Solina and Lesko. Smerek (1,222m), the westernmost peak of this połonina, is 17 minutes further, and from a nearby cross the path begins to drop steeply, entering the beech woods after about 15 minutes and emerging after 40 more minutes by a ford. There is now a bridge across the Wetlina (not on the map) 7 minutes to the right/west, leading to the road at the south end of Kalnica, by the timber yards of the narrow-gauge forestry railway.

Turning left or southeast for 1km you soon rejoin the red markings in Smerek village, where there is a small food kiosk. Just over 2km further east is the larger village of **Wetlina**, the second centre of tourist accommodation in the BPN: at the west end, by the Stare-Siolo bus stop, is a small camp site, and then, just beyond the yellow stripe path to the połonina, a large PTTK hut to the right and a summer-only youth hostel in the school to the left. The main bus stop and shops are 1km further east, with several houses offering rooms and the remains of the church destroyed as a reprisal against the UPA.

There are plenty of buses (both PKS and the private Green Line) towards Sanok, and three a day (six in July and August) to Ustrzyki Górne. Most people, having hiked through the połoninas, will continue by bus, at least as far as Cisna, from where there is a great trip on a forestry railway to Rzepedź; however you can continue on foot through the woods near the Slovak border to Cisna, and on via picturesque lakes to Komańcza, just south of Rzepedź. From Smerek this route, still marked with red stripes, is not as shown on the tourist map; it actually starts on the lowest track just west of the bridge near the food kiosk and turns left after 5 minutes to cross the stream and then head uphill to the right/southwest. After 22 minutes it reaches the treeline, just east of a radio tower, and after 5 minutes more turns left on to a forestry road, turning right again after 5 minutes up a steep but well-used path. The climb gets easier after another 5 minutes, reaching a 1,129m hilltop after 40 minutes, and then reaching the Slovak border, and a blue route from east of Wetlina, in another 20 minutes just before Okrąglik (1,100m).

The border with Slovakia is a total contrast to that with Ukraine: an open strip several metres wide with red and white posts, like milestones, every few hundred metres, and no barrier to crossing over. Indeed, in many places the border strip is used by both Polish and Slovak hiking trails. From Okrąglik the paths head almost due north; after 10 minutes the blue stripes turn left, rejoining the frontier and following it almost all the way to Krynica (see next section). After just 5 minutes the red path goes to the right around Jasło (1,158m) in a small połonina, and continues along a wooded ridge. After half an hour the path reaches Małe Jasło (1,097m) and turns left; after another hour on the ridge the path turns right and drops through beech, spruce and fir, crosses an asphalted forestry road and after 15 minutes reaches a stream. At the Solinka river, 5 minutes below, there is a log bridge to the right, and although the path theoretically fords the river you can cross by the railway bridge a bit further downstream into the village of **Cisna**: there are literally one or two trains a day, moving at little more than walking speed. To the left of the tracks is a camping field and to the right the rest of the village, with a monument at the main road junction to those killed by the UPA, and a new church to replace that destroyed after the UPA blew up the police station, killing six.

Also at the junction is a motel (charging from Z40,000), and at the southwestern end of the village (past the food shops and takeaways) a busy summer youth hostel in the school, opposite the 'Rest Centre' with cabins; there is a bus stop here on the road to Komańcza in addition to the main one on the road north to Baligród and Lesko, and it pays to check both, particularly if trying to get to Wetlina. Some buses deviate to Żubracze, 5km west, where there is the lively BEST Relax private hostel and camping place; these buses also pass Maidan, 2km west of Cisna, from where a narrow-gauge train heads west at 0630 (0930 weekends), also picking up at Zubracze — see box. There is no longer an open-air museum at Maidan; in any case it was only a few semi-preserved steam locomotives and carriages in a siding. There are various scout and student camp sites down the road which formerly ran south into Slovakia from Maidan. Back in Cisna, a turning opposite the bus stop and food shop on the Lesko road, marked with the red stripes, leads in 15 minutes to the excellent PTTK hut 'Pod Honem' at 663m, passing the Forestry Inspectorate Hotel on the way.

From the PTTK hut the red stripe route continues uphill in mixed woods, reaching a survey marker, hidden deep in the woods on the summit of Hon (820m) after 40 minutes; after twenty minutes there is a new path unofficially marked with green stripes down to Żubracze, to the left, and then over the next 30 minutes to Sasów (1,011m) three turnings right to the Habkowce camp site, at km34 on the Lesko road. From here the path, which had been following a wooded ridge, passes through more clearings, reaching Wołosan (1,071m) in 25 minutes and then dropping for 30 minutes to a pass at 920m where a path comes unmarked from Maniów on the Cisna-Komańcza road and continues to the right, marked with black stripes, to Jabłonki, where there is an all-year youth hostel. It was in Jabłonki in March 1947 that the UPA killed General Karol Świerczewski, Poland's Deputy Minister of Defence, precipitating their downfall in Operation Wisła (see page 233); the museum in his memory (at km27) is now closed, but might eventually reopen as a local natural history museum, and the hill to the east, formerly Woronikówka (828m), is now called Walter, after his *nom de guerre* in the Spanish Civil War. Baligród, 7km north of Jabłonki, has both a cemetery of soldiers killed by the UPA and a 17th Century Jewish cemetery; Balyhorod, as the Ukrainians called it, was the only stronghold left to the Poles in this area in 1946.

From here there is a 12 minute climb to Jaworne (992m), where the

---

The narrow-gauge railway from Rzepedź (and Nowy Łupków) east to Wetlina was built for military reasons, but is now a typical Carpathian logging railway, although now diesel-powered. It still carries logs, but is better known for the tourist train from Maidan (west of Cisna) to Rzepedź; this runs daily from June 1 to September 30, leaving Maidan at 0630 on weekdays and running via Nowy Łupków (0820-0920) to reach Rzepedź at about 1050. It returns at 1200, not taking the Nowy Łupków branch, and reaches Maidan at 1450. At weekends it starts at 0930 and runs direct to Rzepedź, arriving at 1215; it returns at 1245, calls at Nowy Łupków (1416-1426) and arrives at Maidan at 1600.

Even at 0630 there are plenty of young backpackers piling aboard, and the weekend trains can be packed with happy drinkers; the train averages under 10km/h, and although the scenery by the Slovak border, near the abandoned villages of Solinka and Balnica, is lovely, it is easy to see how its charms can pall, particularly if you have to sit around in Nowy Łupków. From here or Rzepedź there are mainline and bus connections to Zagórz and Sanok; from Maidan there are a few buses to Cisna, 2km east, where there are more buses, particularly in summer, between Sanok and Lesko and Ustrzyki Górne. Few forestry workers seem to travel on this train, but it may stop to shunt timber wagons along the way. Tickets are sold on the train, by a conductor who swings gymnastically between carriages on the move; fares are higher than equivalent bus fares, at Z20,000 from Maidan to Smolnik in 1992.

red stripe path turns 90° left and continues northwest along the ridge for 40 minutes to the Żebrak pass (816m) where it crosses a forestry track from the Komańcza road to Baligród, with a summer-only student camp site just 20 minutes to the right. The path climbs for half an hour and then heads north along the ridge for another half hour to Chryszczata (997m), where there is a wooden tower to look over the treetops, although there's not really a lot to see. This area, known to the Ukrainians as the Khreshchata forest, was the main UPA stronghold in the 1945-47 period, and there should still be traces of underground bunkers around here. After 8 minutes more the red stripe route turns right off a path heading west to some First World War cemeteries, and goes down, with some twists and turns, for 20 minutes to the two Duszatyn lakes at 700m, formed by a landslide blocking a stream. Here you begin to meet day-walkers coming up to this very attractive spot. The path passes to the right/north of the lakes and then follows the stream west for 45 minutes, crossing it twice on stepping stones.

This brings you to the logging station of Duszatyn, where you could pick up the train back to Maidan at 1149 (1320 at weekends); there is a camping place to the south, but the route onwards heads north along the road on the right/east bank of the Osława, rather than on the left bank as shown on the tourist map. After 30 minutes this crosses by a bridge to Preluki station, with another camping place 80m to the right. The hiking route continues west, turning right off the road to climb over the hill and down to Komańcza in 30 minutes, but as this is very boggy I would recommend the slightly longer route by the road, passing a student hostel and camping place.

Komańcza has a Uniate church, modern and active, opposite the station, and a long thin Roman Catholic church with four small spires. There is an Orthodox church, built in 1805, well hidden on the Dukla road, and, just 1km to the north, the convent where Cardinal Stefan Wyszyński was interned in the 1950s, up a lane to the left past a PTTK hostel. The village is not as touristy as Cisna, but does have a boozy restaurant and a *smażalnia* or beer and chips stall. Four kilometres north, along the road to Sanok, is Rzepedź (pronounced Jepezh), terminus of the forestry line from Maidan, which also has a fine wooden Uniate church (built in 1824) 1km west from the northern bus stop, and another (1803) in Turzańsk 1km east of the mainline station, and a summer-only youth hostel in the Rzepedź village school. Trains run on this line from Zagórz to the dreary logging town of Nowy Łupków (and potentially on into Slovakia); buses mostly run to Zagórz, Sanok, and points north, with a couple (at 1410 and 1834) to Cisna, and one at 1702 to Krosno via Dukla. Continuing north, the next village, Szczawne, also has a fine wooden church (1889) at the first bus stop, well south of the station.

From Komańcza the red stripe route runs northwest past the PTTK hut and the convent to the spas of Rymanów-Zdrój and Iwonicz-Zdrój, and then south of Dukla into the Beskid Niski, where I picked it up again. To reach Dukla, however, I went southwest from Komańcza following green and then blue stripes along the border, as described in the next section.

Czarnorzeki

KROSNO

to
GORLICE

BRZOZÓW

Haczów

Bóbrka

SKANSEN

IWONICZ-
ZDRÓJ

Czertez

Klimkówka

DUKLA

Rymanów-
Zdrój

SANOK

Jasionka   Baluciańka

Trzciana

Zawadka
- Rymanowska

Bukowsko

Tylawa

▲
471

ŁYSA GORA
557
▲

Wisłok

Barwinek   Jaśliska   Wola Niżna

Zyndranowa

Szczawne

Dukla
Pass
500

KAMIEN

578 ▲   ▲
      857

JAŁOWA
KICZERA

Jasiel

Rzepedź

Turzańsk

to KOŠICE

KANASIÓWKA
823
▲

Dołżyca

Komańcza

(Slovakia)

PASIKA
848
▲

BESKID NISKI

-Eastern Area

N

0   10

km

BESKID NISKI

The Beskid Niski (the Low Beskids) are, predictably, lower than the Bieszczady, without the hilltop połoninas, but they share much of the same historical and social background, with its mainly Łemk population largely removed in the late 1940s and only now beginning to return to their ancestral farms and villages. This section covers the eastern Beskid Niski, running through the empty country along the Slovak border and then largely bypassing the villages, although visiting some relics of the two world wars that raged in this area; the next section deals with the western Beskid Niski, continuing into the Beskid Sądecki (south of Nowy Sącz), focusing on the wooden churches still found in most villages there.

The hills are sedimentary, mostly parallel ridges covered in woods, mostly beech but also with some oak, sycamore, lime and hornbeam. The fauna includes deer (particularly along the border) and boar, but you are more likely to notice less exotic creatures such as tree frogs, newts and salamanders.

This route, which almost at once takes you from the 1:75,000 Bieszczady tourist map on to the less detailed 1:125,000 map of the *Beskid Niski i Pogórze*, starts from Komańcza (see previous section), reached via Sanok and Zagórz, and ends at Gorlice (see below). Between Gorlice and Sanok, strung along the main road from Nowy Sącz to Przemyśl, are the towns of Jasło and Krosno, both possible starting points for forays south by bus to link up with this hike.

Jasło can be reached by slow train and by direct buses from Zakopane, Krynica, Kraków, Rzeszów, Wrocław, Przemyśl, Lublin, Łódź, Warsaw, and Ustrzyki Dolne, and has local buses to Dukla and through the many villages south to Grab, on the border, where there is a summer-only youth hostel. There are two adjacent summer youth hostels in Jasło itself, in schools on ul Czackiego, a PTTK hostel at ul Puśzkina 4, and another at the stadium on ul Krasińskiego, as well as a regional museum at ul Świerczewskiego 1. To the west, halfway to Gorlice, is **Biecz**, a small town of just 5,000 inhabitants with a fine Old Town, with a 14-16th Century Town Hall, a Collegiate church of the 15th and 16th Centuries, a 17th Century Protestant church, and other Gothic and Renaissance buildings including a hospital and barbican, and a fine museum. The youth hostel here, at ul Parkowa 1, is open all year, and there is a PTTK hostel at ul Świerczewskiego 35. If you do stop here it is also worth noting the wooden church at Binarowa, 4km north, built c1500 and with 16th and 17th Century interior paintings.

Krosno, with a population of 47,000, is the capital of the whole of this southeastern corner of Poland, the second most rural voivodeship in Poland, but with the decline of the local oil industry it's not a particularly exciting place. However you can see the remains of 14-16th Century walls, the Bishop's Palace, parish church, and Franciscan church, all built in the 15th and 16th Centuries, and the 18th Century Capuchin church, just east of the centre. There is a Regional Museum at ul Piłsudskiego 16, and the birthplace of Gomułka at ul Mostowa 3 was a museum, but is doubtless now closed. However the best-known museum in this area is the skansen in the village of Bóbrka, 12km south (not to be confused with the Bóbrka by Lake Solina). Although the shingled towers of the wooden churches of this area often remind me of early oil rigs, these really are oil rigs here in the home village of Ignacy Łukasiewicz, inventor of the kerosene lamp and thus founder of the oil industry in 1854. There are local buses here, but think twice before taking the very roundabout green stripe path, which continues south to Dukla.

In Haczów, 11km east, also reached by local buses, is possibly the oldest wooden church in Poland, built in the last quarter of the 14th Century or the early 15th Century, with 17th Century arcades and polychrome wall paintings, and wooden village houses.

In Krosno there are hotels up to 3* standard, a summer-only tourist hostel at ul Czajkowskiego (Tchaikovsky) 43, and two summer youth hostels, at ul Konopnickiej 5 (2km northwest) and ul Karol Marksa (Karl Marx to you and me, so ripe for renaming), as well as an all-year youth hostel in Bóbrka, and a summer one and bivouac site in Czarnorzeki, 12km north by some anthropomorphic rocks called the Spinners (*Prządki*) and the ruins of Kamieniec Castle, also on the green stripe route. There is a motel and the area's only proper camp site at Moderówka, at the Szebnie rail station on the main road halfway between Krosno and Jasło.

Hiking Directions

1: From Komańcza to Dukla

This route, marked initially with green stripes, starts by turning right under the railway bridge south of the station in Komańcza, and then left after 15 minutes on to an asphalt road, following a stream for 40 minutes to Dołżyca, reached by two buses a day. Already the country seems more populated and pastoral than the Bieszczady to the east, with peasant farms, geese and haymaking. The road on is unmade, getting muddier after a fork to the right after 15 minutes; after 10 minutes the path again forks right, climbing to the border in 20 minutes. Here the blue stripe path comes in from the Bieszczady, and both continue together to the northwest, taking 40 minutes to reach Danawa (841m, border marker 113.1), 20 more to Pasika (848m, 115.1), and 15 more to Kanasiówka (823m). Here a yellow stripe path turns right to the bus stop at Wisłok Górne, and the green stripes continue north through a largely depopulated area of low hills; I kept left, along the border, following the blue stripes, and also Slovak red stripes.

After another easy half hour the blue path turns right away from the border, dropping easily for 20 minutes through beech trees and into the broad meadow of Jasiel, joining a road by a monument to soldiers killed here in an UPA ambush in 1946. The road continues north on the left/west bank of the stream (not as shown on the map), then crosses to the right before the path turns left after 25 minutes across stepping stones. It goes straight up through long grass and scattered trees to reach a 704m hilltop in 20 minutes, and then back to the border in another 5 minutes. The next stretch is slightly boggy, with a nature reserve on the Slovak side, but it soon dries out as you follow the border ridge in fine mixed woodland with lots of berries, and plenty of deer. It takes 40 minutes to reach marker 130.0 where the path and border turn 90° right, and another 45 to Kamień (a common name just meaning stone), the highest point on this route at 857m, and on the border, not as shown on the tourist map; after another quarter hour the blue stripe markings turn sharply right at the end of a field.

The path drops northwest for 10 minutes before running straight into a good road, turning left after 15 minutes on to the road from Jaśliska to the border, and right after 5 minutes across a ford on another unmade road. It goes straight up from the wide grassy valley into mixed woods, with beech, birch, pine and larch, and after 10 minutes in the woods turns sharp left across a field to markings visible on the trees opposite. After a couple of minutes the path turns into the woods to rejoin the border at marker 146.4; it takes 35 minutes in slightly muddy beechwood to reach Jałowa Kiczera (578m), the first of four hills called Kiczera. Here a new path marked with black stripes turns right to the village of Zyndranowa, where there is a Museum of Łemk culture by the church; this is in any case the best route to take, as the border path has been blocked by a new customs post, which looks as if it should incorporate a revolving restaurant — after 40 minutes, at marker 153.3, you now have to take a poxy little path to the right into slippery woods to emerge after a full half-hour at the bus stop below the border post at the Dukla pass (500m).

From here there are 10 buses, on weekdays, to Krosno, as well as buses to Košice, capital of eastern Slovakia. There is a bivouac site here, and a summer youth hostel in Barwinek, just north; here we meet the *Szlak EB*, the Friendship Path from Eisenach in eastern Germany to Budapest, which sounds fine but is often surprisingly overgrown. The Dukla pass has for centuries been one of the main crossing points from Poland to the south, and was the scene of much bloodshed in October 1944, as the Red Army passed the time while waiting for the Warsaw Insurrection to be crushed by breaking through the Germans' *Karpathenfestung*, or Carpathian Fortress, into Slovakia. There were 130,000 casualties (dead and wounded), and this is now known as The Valley of Death. The Moscow-Prague train (running through Slovakia, not Poland) is still named the *Dukla*. When I was in Dukla, 17km north, Soviet troops (as they then were) were touching up the inscriptions on the war graves before being withdrawn; the museum in Dukla gives a graphic account of the campaign.

Although it is possible to follow the *Szlak EB*, marked in green and then red, from the pass, I chose to take a bus to **Dukla** to refuel and begin hiking again from there, taking two days to Gorlice; along the road are various camping sites and a hotel in Tylawa, 7km north of the pass,

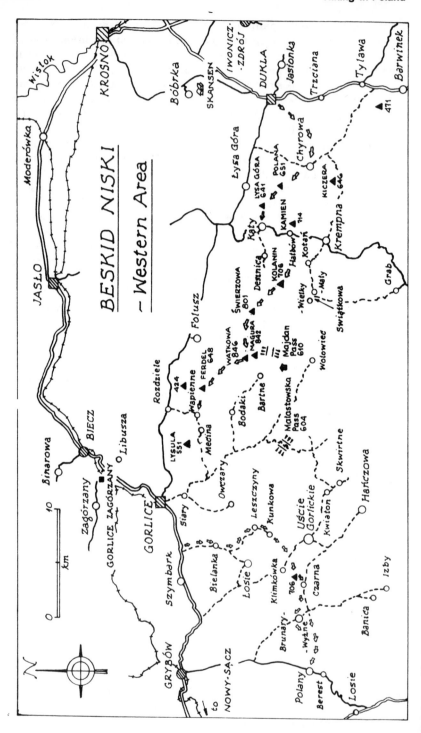

as well as historic churches in Tylawa, Trzciana and Zawadka Rymanowska, just east. Dukla is centred on its Rynek, a quiet square with the market hall in its middle now converted to hold a relatively stylish new food store; there are more basic supermarkets on the square and behind the PTTK hostel at Rynek 25. The only other accommodation is in private rooms, also via the PTTK, or summer-only youth hostels, on ul Kościuszki and at Trakt Węgierski (Hungarian Highway) 14, or in the small villages just east and west, Jasionka and Iwla. There is a Rococo parish church, with separate campanile, in the centre, and a similar Bernardine church to the north near the museum. Although I didn't see them, there should be a Jewish cemetery and ruined synagogue as well.

2: From Dukla to Gorlice

To rejoin the red stripe route, there is a branch of the *Szlak EB*, marked with yellow stripes, but its original route out of Dukla has been built on; it is now necessary to head south on the main road and turn right up ul Polna, an unmarked tree-lined lane at the town limits about 100m south of some blocks of flats. Fork left almost at once up a farm track, fork right after 7 minutes and go to the right around the second field to turn up a small path and after 7 more minutes pick up the yellow stripe markings. The path on remains badly marked: after 10 minutes take two turnings to the right, and then after 3 minutes turn left at a triangular junction and go up the edge of a field and on in beech and pine; fork right after 10 minutes to pass an attractive wooden farm cottage in 5 minutes. The cart track ends here and the path continues, largely overgrown by nettles, along the east side of Chyrowa, to meet the main red path after 30 minutes.

This path, also badly marked, crosses a stream after 5 minutes and heads across fields, forking left and following a hedge to the right down to the stream in Chyrowa; rather than heading straight for the road, as on the map, the path in fact turns right along this, right/east, bank, crossing the stream three times in 12 minutes to reach the 18th Century wooden church. In a few minutes you head up to the road and turn right and after 2 minutes left. There are quite a few buses to Dukla and Krosno, or south to interesting villages such as Krempna (see below).

This next stretch is chaotic but I shall describe it as well as I can: the path heads west up the right side of a hedge and into woods; 15 minutes from the road keep right in a clearing, then very soon take another hidden right turn. After 6 minutes turn right at a T-junction on to a disused forestry track, ignore two paths to the left before turning sharp left after 8 minutes, and going up briefly. Again ignore paths to the left, and after 6 minutes fork right to go up to a meadow and follow a narrow path towards the obvious hilltop of Polana (651m). There is a viewpoint on the summit but the path goes into trees and swings to the right around the hill before dropping into mature beechwood after 12 minutes. Keep right and after 10 minutes come up into a meadow; after crossing a cart track down into the valley to the north go left around a hilltop to arrive in 10 minutes in another meadow with a good view left. The narrow path continues, dipping and then climbing through meadow to reach a hilltop in 20 minutes, and the summit of Łysa-Góra (Bald Mountain, a common Slav name, as in Mussorgsky's *Night on the Bald/Bare Mountain*, 641m high) 6 minutes later.

The path drops at once into very mixed woodland, largely beech and fir, keeping left after 10 minutes to go down the left side of a field and then down a stoney cart track. Although the marked path in fact goes off to the left past some isolated larch and sycamore you might as well follow the track down to the village of Kąty (pronounced Conti as in Tom), just south of the bridge (nearer than shown on the map).

Once across the bridge you should take the road left, to Krempna, with some obvious short-cuts on the first steep section. (There is a summer youth hostel, and a historic church, in Desznica, a few kilometres to the right.) After 25 minutes, after some forestry huts on the left, the path disappears into woods to the left, but frankly I'd rather stick to the road: the climb over Kamien (714m) was navigationally awful, sweaty, overgrown and plagued by flies, particularly on top where there was no real view. At the pass on the far side a bus stop, cabin and A-frame foresters' hut are all that mark the site of the village of Hałbów. A little south on the road a track leads 250m right/west into the woods to the seven family graves of the populace of Hałbów, all Jews killed in July 1942. This small-scale tragedy affected me more deeply — and still does — than the museum of Auschwitz.

On this road, formerly the main route to Bardejov in Slovakia via the Beskid pass, you can catch buses from Jasło to a string of villages with lovely old Uniate churches: Krempna, just at the bottom of the hill (1841), Kotań (1841), Świątkowa (two churches, both from 1762), and Grab, of which all but Kotań have summer youth hostels. (An excellent route, particularly on mountain bike, would take you through Krempna, Kotań, Świątkowa-Wielki, Wołowiec, Bartne and on to Gorlice.) However, to continue just to the north on the ridge route of the *Szlak EB*, still marked with red stripes and frequently overrun by nettles and blackberries, you must find a tiny opening between the bus stop and the track to the graves. This path passes to the north of the hilltop and then follows the ridge west-northwest (with various forestry tracks on either side) for 50 minutes before turning left on to a major forestry track by a wooden cross. After 10 minutes, beyond a blocked stream and a shelter, the path turns right and climbs steeply in classic beechwood for 25 minutes to the top of Kolanin (706m), to drop steeply for 20 minutes, through silver birch and pine, to an asphalted road. Here there is another A-frame shelter, with the usual small table and two benches inside, and the path continues to its north side, forking right after 3 minutes. After 2 minutes more take the second right, slightly downhill, and after 5 minutes turn right again, on to a path blocked by foresters. This rises steadily up a muddy ride through mixed woods, and after 15 minutes a bigger track comes in from the right: this junction, like many others here, is unmarked, as the forestry industry has continued to develop since the route was marked. Keep right after 2 minutes, then left at a 'crossroads' to climb to a ridge for 7 minutes, then right for 20 minutes along a fast easy path to reach the summit of Świerzowa (801m).

The path drops, keeping left after quarter of an hour to come down to a forestry road with yet another shelter. Go about 300m up the road opposite and turn left into the woods just before the second, better, stream; the path is largely lost in bramble, but runs parallel to the road before turning left up on to a side ridge. After 20 minutes turn right on to a ridge track and then left after 3 minutes at a T-junction. It takes 3 minutes to reach the top of Magura (842m, a standard Slav word for hill), and a couple more to the junction of a green stripe route to the right. Continuing on the red stripe route you would drop to a 610m pass where you could turn right to reach Bartne, where there are two wooden churches, one now a museum and thus theoretically more accessible than others, and Bodaki, just down the valley road towards Gorlice, where there are two more historic churches and a summer youth hostel. Equally, continuing south from the pass you would soon reach the *pod Mareszką* PTTK hut, and continue along the red stripe route to Wołowiec, Hańczowa and, eventually, Krynica.

I took the green stripe route to the right, reaching Watkowa (846m) in 10 minutes and and continuing on an easy well-marked ridge route through beechwoods, passing a spring to the left after a quarter hour and reaching a junction in another quarter hour. From here a path marked with yellow stripes goes down to the right to Folusz, where there is a summer youth hostel and a PTTK hostel, and an unmarked path left down to Bartne. Continuing northwestwards, after 7 minutes you pass Kornuty (a barely noticeable summit of 830m) and continue along the ridge (partly in a nature reserve) for 40 minutes to a picnic shelter which has probably collapsed by now. After this the route was partly blocked by fallen trees, and after forking to the right after 10 minutes and crossing a cleared area is also unmarked for a while. Six minutes after this turn right off the forestry track on to a path which climbs slightly with a hill to the right before continuing along the ridge and then beginning to drop from Ferdel (648m); after 12 minutes a path marked in blue turns right to Biecz, passing through more villages with old churches.

Continuing on the green path, you'll need to turn left after 7 minutes onto a small unmarked path, climbing to the last hillock of the ridge and then dropping quickly. Keep left in a clearing, then turn right on to a track past a pumping station, reaching a bar on a dirt road after 15 minutes in all, and a food shop on the asphalt road in two more minutes; this is Wapienne, which sounds as if it should be in Flanders. This is entirely appropriate, as we are now in the area of the great Gorlice-Tarnów offensive of 1915, when Germany tried to knock Russia out of the war, with military cemeteries in almost every village. There are 170 in all, by three different architects, of which the most attractive, by the Slovak Dusan Jurkovic, is at the Małastowska pass, south of here, with a bivouac site and hut nearby. At the main road junction, 5 minutes to the right, the green stripes head left to the church of Męcina-Wielki, built

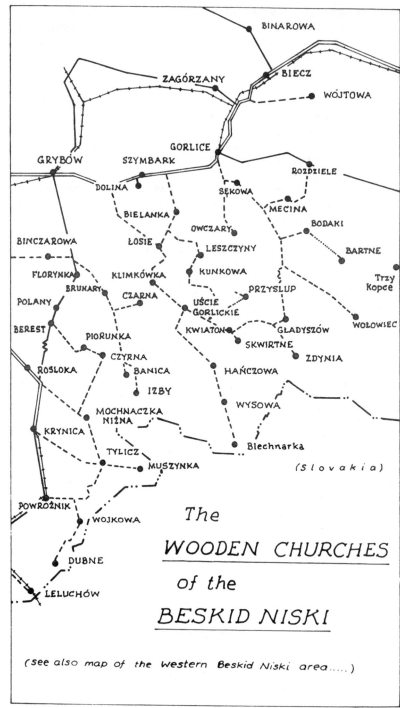

The

WOODEN CHURCHES

of the

BESKID NISKI

(see also map of the western Beskid Niski area.....)

in 1807 with two very Ottoman domes, and on to Gorlice, not far beyond the 551m hill of Lysula, while the cemetery and bus stop are to the right. I got off the bus at the early 16th Century wooden church of Sękowa (with a belfry actually lower than the nave), just a few kilometres south of Gorlice (ask for the key next door). There are many more buses to Gorlice from here.

Gorlice is an unattractive town, with not even a chip stall open after 2000. Nor is it ideally placed for moving on by rail, at the end of a 5km branch from Gorlice-Zagórzany (with nine trains a day); but there are plenty of buses, from the bus station next to the rail station north of the centre, including eight a day to Kraków (three continuing to Katowice), six to Zakopane, five to Rzeszów, two (1145 and 1405) to Ustrzyki Dolne, one (1905) to Bielsko-Biała, and many to the scattered villages to the south, including 24 to Uście Gorlickie, of which 16 carry on to Wysowa (see next section).

There is a PTTK museum at ul Wąska 7, just off the Rynek (mainly concerned with the oil industry), and the largest of the First World War cemeteries on Magdalenka hill, just southeast. It's not worth stopping, but if you choose to, there are the *Parkowa* and *Victoria* tourist hostels at ul Słowackiego (in the Municipal Park or *Park Miejski*) and ul 1 Maja 10, and a summer youth hostel in the elementary school at ul Michalusa 16.

THE WOODEN CHURCHES OF THE BESKID NISKI AND BESKID SĄDECKI

Of the 689 *tserkwy* or Uniate churches in the Przemyśl eparchy (the Uniate area now in Poland), it was calculated in 1987 that 346 were ruined (or being used as fertiliser stores and so on), 245 had been taken over by Roman Catholics, 28 were still being used by Orthodox congregations, 61 were in good condition but shut, and 9 were museums (some having been moved to skansens). Many of the icons and iconostases (or altarscreens) were in museums in Sanok, Nowy Sącz and elsewhere. With recent political changes, some of these churches are now being restored and reopened, but the scale of the loss can be easily comprehended. Not all were particularly historic or in the traditional wooden style, but most of those in the south were of interest. The best accounts of this subject are *Churches in Ruins/Tserkva v Ruini* by Oleg Wolodymyr Iwanusiv, published in 1987 by the Religious Association of Ukrainian Catholics in Canada, 85 Lakeshore Rd, St Catherine's, Ontario L2N 2T6 (volume 56 of the Shevchenko Scientific Society's Ukrainian Studies series), and the more scholarly *Wooden Churches of Eastern Europe* by David Buxton (CUP 1981).

Most of the remaining wooden churches are concentrated in the hills south and southwest of Gorlice; these are in the Łemk style, with a tower and two domes in a descending line (rather than the more Russian style of the Boyks, with its large central dome and two equal smaller ones on either side, found more in the Bieszczady); the belltower (sometimes separate) often resembles an early oil rig, with its plain shingled sides, and the roofs also are traditionally shingled, with eaves sweeping down almost to the ground, although many are now being replaced by tin roofs. They are all marked on the tourist maps, as either *kościoły* (Roman Catholic churches — the vast majority), *cerkwie* (Orthodox churches), and *kościoły w dawnych cerkwiach* ('churches in ancient orthodox churches', meaning Uniate churches). It may not be easy to find a key except where the priest's house is next to the church; visiting early on a Sunday morning is often the best solution.

It is hard to give precise dates for these churches, as the nature of wooden churches is that they are rebuilt and largely replaced over the years. Inscriptions on graves are usually in Łemk Cyrillic, not quite the same as Ukrainian or Russian script, but other notices are almost all in Polish, in Latin script, although it is noticeable that a few are once again in Cyrillic. You will also see traditional wooden houses, many in the *chyzá* (hizha) style with half the building for people, a quarter for the animals, and a quarter for hay. This area is also dotted with war cemeteries (maybe 170 in all, also marked on the maps), as there was hard fighting throughout this area in the First World War.

Hiking directions

I describe here a fairly simple route, suitable for walking or mountain-biking, linking some of the best remaining churches between Gorlice and Krynica; it is very rewarding to wander slightly further off the beaten track if possible, as almost every village is worth seeing. Alternatively it is possible to reach many of these villages by bus, although services are infrequent and hard to fathom. The most accurate map is the 1:125,000 PPWK *mapa turystyczna* of the *Beskid Niski i Pogórze*, but there is also an interesting 1991 reprint of the 1939 1:300,000 *Łemkowszczyzna* map of the Łemk country, as well as maps of the Beskid Sądecki which cover the western part of this area.

This route starts on the main Grybów to Gorlice road just east of Szymbark (where there is a hotel, bivouac site and museum) at the Bielanka-skrzyżowanie bus-stop and junction, just west of km155 and a few war graves. There are about two buses an hour along this road, as well as nine a day from Gorlice to Bielanka itself. Despite the sign, it is under 4km to Bielanka; 15 minutes down the road you meet a path marked with green stripes, coming from the new skansen and camp site at the east end of Szymbark, and after 10 more minutes you pass another camping field across the stream. Another 15 minutes brings you to Bielanka, where the church is a couple of minutes to the left, a classic Łemk edifice built in 1773 with an 'oil rig' tower and shingled roof sweeping almost to the ground. This village is a centre of Łemk cultural revival, with a song and dance ensemble based here, as well as a small museum (open intermittently) and a summer-only youth hostel. From here the main road continues to the right of the village, climbing for 12 minutes to a junction right to Łosie (where there is a small 19th Century church, partly of stone), and on to the left for 20 minutes more to a junction right to Leszczyny; the maps show this as the main route, but in fact the major route runs left towards Owczary. It takes under 20 minutes down the unsurfaced track to the church at Leszczyny, which dates from 1835 and has just been restored, with a new tin roof. From here it is 20 minutes down the valley road to the right to Kunkowa, where there is a long thin church built in 1868. I continued down the valley on what is now a virtually disused track; there is a dam now being built south of Łosie which will flood the village of Klimkówka, so the main road now takes a longer route around the hills to Uście Gorlickie (previously known as Uście Rus'ke, meaning Ruthenian), where the church (built in 1786) is supposed to have a particularly good iconostasis, and there is a summer-only youth hostel.

However it took me just over half an hour to the old road in the Ropa valley, and 5 minutes up to the new main road at the Kunkowa bus stop, with 14 buses a day from Gorlice to Wysowa, near the Slovak border. From here I followed the road north for 10 minutes and turned left/west after the second stream, just before the Klimkówka village limits. A forestry track climbs steeply up the left bank for ten minutes before crossing the stream and zigzagging up for 18 minutes to reach the main ridge of Sucha Homola at almost 700m. Here I met a blue stripe path running along ridges for almost all of its route from Grybów to Wysowa; 6 minutes to the right/north along this path there is a sharp turning back to the left in a dip, dropping down into pine and silver birch trees and taking 20 minutes to reach the road 2 minutes below Czarna church, reached by a new footbridge and lych gate; this is also well maintained, with a tin roof. There is a bus to Izby at 1238, returning to Gorlice at 1345, and also on workday mornings at 0658, returning at 0755.

Returning to the west down the valley it is only 1½km to the main road down the Biała valley; the most direct route on to Polany is by a track just south of these crossroads, but I turned right and followed this rather unattractive road for 15 minutes to reach Brunary-Wyżne church. There are two buses a day south to Banica and one to Izby, with interesting old churches in both villages, and several north to Grybów, Gorlice and even Nowy Sącz. Again this is a very attractive and well maintained church, with shingled domes and new vertically planked walls, in a nice setting looking towards the river.

From here, if you don't want to return south to the crossroads, you should continue north to cross the bridge and then turn sharp left along the river bank for 3 minutes before turning right up a farm track; this climbs steadily for 15 minutes to reach a coniferous wood. There is an obvious path about 50m to the left, running just south of west into the wood, forking right after a couple of minutes and then going left through bracken to reach in another 3 minutes a good dirt forestry track along the ridge. This leads down to the left and after VERY roughly 20 minutes reaches a junction from the right and after another 5 minutes a sharp turn to the right, about 10-15 minutes from the Czarna crossroads.

Coming from Czarna you should look for a minor forestry road to the left just above a small clearing to the right.

This track climbs westwards and after 15 minutes forks right (rather overgrown but well-trodden by deer at least); after 5 minutes more an active forestry track comes in from the left just before the main ridge. From here it drops to the west into a lovely landscape of hayfields, to cross a stream after a quarter of an hour and turn right. On reaching the main Mostysza stream the path crosses by a footbridge to the right and then climbs to the left through the village of Polany to reach the main Grybów-Krynica road (with buses almost hourly). The church (built in 1820, with a metal roof and shingled walls and tower) is just to the right; the village of Berest is 25 minutes to the left/south down the road. The church of SS Cosmos and Damian in Berest (to the left at the main junction) was built in 1842 in the standard Łemk style, with a particularly fine lych gate (with a shelf for mens' hats), and a good iconostasis with a 17th Century Russian icon; it is usually opened for a service at about 1800.

From here I went by bus to **Krynica**, perhaps Poland's most attractive spa (with a cocktail of 22 acidulous springs with a high content of trace elements, for disorders of the digestive system, the urinary tract and the circulatory system, and gynaecological problems), and the centre of quite a network of marked paths, from where you can continue to visit some more fine wooden churches in villages to the south and west. The rail and bus stations are both over 1km south of the centre, with trains to Warsaw, Gliwice and Gdynia as well as many more local destinations (for Slovakia change at Muszyna, just 11km west), and one bus a day to Kielce, Wrocław, Warsaw and Zakopane, with more to Grybów, Nowy Sącz, Kraków, and Katowice. There is also a regular local bus service along the main road through Krynica from the Huta pass to the north to Muszyna and Szczawnik to the southwest.

The centre of town is the very attractive pedestrian promenade, alija Nowotarskiego, lined with spa buildings and restaurants, with at its north end ul Piłsudskiego (formerly ul Bieruta) leading north towards Nowy Sącz, and ul Pułaskiego leading east towards Tylicz; at its lower, southern, end (on ul Kraszewskiego, near the stations) are major services such as the post office, PTTK (at the back of ul Zdrojowa 32, open Monday-Friday 0700-1500, Saturdays 0700-1100, and also at ul Kraszewskiego 8), and the supermarket (by ul Kraszewskiego 34). A funicular takes you just 142m up Góra Parkowa (741m) to the southeast from the top of al Nowotarskiego, operating from 0900 to 2000 in July and August. In winter there is skiing here and at skidrags to the north at Słotwiny and to the south at Powroźnik, as well as skating and sledging; the state Main Sport Centre (COS) is at ul Sportowa 1. There is also a song festival in September.

There is a summer-only youth hostel at ul Kraszewskiego 158 (well to the south), and the PTTK runs the rather drab-looking Hotel Rzymianka ('Roman') at ul Dąbrowskiego 15, to the left about 300m up ul Piłsudskiego; there is a camp site just over 1km west up the Czarny

Potok (Black Stream) valley, 2km (or a frequent bus ride) south of the centre. Other than these, there is a private rooms bureau at ul Pułaskiego 4/1, and many pensions previously block-booked but now entering the private sector and taking *ad hoc* guests, such as the Wisła (Bulwary Dietla 1, parallel to al Nowotarskiego, with an Orbis office to co-ordinate bookings), Kościuszka (ul Kościuszka 36, behind the post office), Belweder (ul Kraszewskiego 14), Mimosa (ul Świdzińskiego 2, off ul Pułaskiego), Stefania (ul Piłsudskiego 9), Stołówka (ul Sportowa 1, near the market and PTTK hotel) and Meran (ul Koscielna 9, to the right near the bottom of ul Piłsudskiego); you might also try the Patria Sanatorium for Foreigners at ul Pułaskiego 35. A new private hotel is the Kawiarnia at ul Świdzińskiego 12. There is a PTTK hut 5km west (and over 500m higher) at Jaworzyna Krynicka on the red and green marked routes, and plenty of private rooms to the east in Tylicz (see below).

There is no real milk bar in Krynica, although the Kryniczanka (on ul Dietla) is probably the simplest restaurant in town; others are large establishments, often with dancing for spa visitors, such as the Havana (ul Piłsudskiego 23), whose band could use tango lessons from David Byrne, the Koncertowa (in the Park Zdrojowy, at the top of ul Piłsudskiego), the Góra Parkowa at the top of the funicular, and others on the roads out of town, such as the Pod Kopcem and Roma out on the Tylicz road, and the U Marka and Czarny Kot on ul Stara Droga (the Old Road) on the road north.

An alternative route

An alternative to the route above would be to begin in Gorlice, where my Beskid Niski route ends, and head south, overlapping with the route outlined above, to Hańczowa. This takes you past the churches of Sękowa (early 16th Century, near the Siary bus stop), Owczary (1653, also known as Rychwald having been settled by Germans in the 13th Century), Leszczyny (1835), Kunkowa (1868), Uście Gorlickie (1786), Kwiaton (17th Century and particularly lovely), Skwirtne (1837, more in the Boyk style) and Hańczowa (1871).

There are summer-only youth hostels in Uście Gorlickie and Hańczowa, and buses back to Gorlice from Hańczowa, Uście Gorlickie and Kwiaton; alternatively you could continue west to Krynica on the *Szlak EB* path, marked with red stripes, passing close to the churches at Izby (1888), Banica (1798) and Mochnaczka Niżna (1887).

Moving on

The most obvious and convenient outing from Krynica is to the villages of Tylicz and Muszynka, to the southeast near the Slovak border; this can be done throughout by bus, but it is more interesting to walk one way at least. From the main road junction at the centre of town (at the top of the promenade) you should take ul Pułaskiego eastwards for 10 minutes (past the tourist office) and then turn left into the woods following red and green stripe markings. This is a good path rising steadily alongside a hill to the right and then a stream to the left, then after 15 minutes crossing the stream and swinging left to meet a yellow stripe path from the left after another 12 minutes. This is a circular route around Krynica from the rail station to the south of the town. It only takes a few more minutes to reach the top of Huzary (865m), just after the turning of the yellow stripe path to the right; the red route turns left (to continue near the border all the way to the Bieszczady, as part of the *Szlak EB* path from Eisenach in eastern Germany to Budapest), and the green and black routes turn half-left, dropping more steeply for 7 minutes (in mixed beech, fir and spruce) before the black stripes turn right. This climbs steadily and then drops to meadows and a cart track to arrive on the road at the west end of Tylicz half an hour later; the sign on Huzary that allows 1½ hours to Tylicz is plainly wrong.

This is a large village and resort, with shops, a restaurant, a ski-drag and lots of private accommodation (*Kwatera Privatna*) in ugly modern houses, as well as a camping site at its west end; nevertheless traditional country life does continue here, with lots of horse carts in evidence. It was founded in the 14th Century on the road to the Tylicz pass, on the present Slovak border, and apparently possessed a 'defensive wail' (*sic*) at this time, which must have driven away many attackers. In the 16th Century Vlachs and Łemks settled here, but the pass became less important after the opening of the railway via Muszyna and is now closed, and the population shrank to just 560. The church to the left above the main square is the Roman Catholic parish church of SS Peter and Paul, from 1612, rather shed-like with a strange neoclassical belfry from 1806, but with a fascinating lime tree with its trunk spilt wide open and its roots exposed. Continuing down the left-hand side of the Rynek (main square) to ul Krótka, turning left on to ul Pułaskiego and then right after the border police station and a bridge on to ul Konfederacji Barskich, you reach the former Uniate church of Saints Cosmos and Damian (1743), now the cemetery chapel and theoretically also maintained as a museum. This has an impressive tower, dwarfing the church, but is rather spoilt by a metal roof and domes.

Just beyond the cemetery there is a bridge to the right to two good mineral springs in a large summerhouse, where it is possible to camp, and then it takes just over half an hour on to Muszynka, up an easy road that doesn't really seem to be climbing to a pass. This church dates from 1689, also in the Łemk style, with interesting interior paintings; it is a bit too neat and tidy, with a garden-shed vestry, and if you wanted you could come by bus and happily see the church in the time the driver takes to do his paperwork before returning. There are seven buses a day to and from Krynica (the last via Mochnaczka at 2105), and more from Tylicz to Krynica; alternatively this is the start of a path marked with yellow stripes along the border to the southeast to the tiny villages, all with lovely wooden churches, of Wojkowa, Dubne and Leluchów, from where you can catch an occasional train or return to Powroźnik following blue stripe markings. About 2km along this path is a landscape reserve and monument to the rebels of the Bar Confederacy of 1770, which led to the First Partition of Poland.

To the west of Krynica is the main part of the Beskid Sądecki, divided into two parts, the Radziejowa massif (1,262m) to the west, and the Jaworzyna (1,114m) to the east, separated by the Poprad river. Although the botanical divide between the Western and Central Carpathians is at the Łupkow pass, at the eastern end of the Beskid Niski, the geological divide is at this western end, at the Tylicz pass. The highest areas, above 1,100m, show a largely coniferous Higher Montane Zone, with forest game birds such as capercaillie and hazelhen, as well as plentiful deer and boar, fox and badger and rarer lynx. These wild hills were the stamping ground of partisans of various persuasions, including from 1944 Soviets infiltrated to attack the Germans from the rear; nowadays this is a more popular hiking area than the Beskid Niski, with most following the red stripe *Szlak EB* Eisenach-Budapest path from Krynica to the Pieniny (or in reverse) along the main ridges and crossing the Poprad at Rytro. The main alternative is to loop south through the spa of Łomnica-Zdrój and the area's main centre, Piwniczna, and perhaps the ski resort of Sucha Dolina. Almost all of the area's hiking trails are also used for cross-country skiing in winter.

There is no shortage of budget accommodation, with PTTK huts strategically placed along the trails (although the Przehyba hut has burnt down and will be rebuilt), inns in Rytro and Piwniczna, and bivouac sites and summer youth hostels in many villages. The Beskid Sądecki *Mapa turystyczna* (1:75,000) is easily available in the area.

The main town of this area is, not surprisingly, **Nowy Sącz**, to the north of the confluence of the Dunajec and Poprad rivers, which is well worth visiting for its fine spacious Rynek, with a Second-Empire Town Hall in the middle, its churches, synagogue and ruined castle, and its museum with a superb collection of icons, as well as all usual services. The whole town has been repainted, pedestrianised, etc, to celebrate its 700th anniversary, with a visit by the Pope, in 1992.

Although the Nowy Sącz Miasto station is nearer the centre, on a minor branch to Rabka and Chabówka, north of Zakopane, the main (Główny) station is well south of the centre, down al Wolności (Freedom Avenue), past the bus station; there are through trains to Slovakia, Hungary and Romania from here, but if heading north you would, as a rule, be best off going by bus. There are 10 buses a day to Zakopane, 26 to Kraków, and no less than 56 to Krynica by various routes, if the timetable is to be believed, and also west as far as Nysa and Żywiec, east as far as Ustrzyki Dolne and Przemyśl, and north as far as Warsaw and Lublin. There are two buses, at 0630 and 1900, to the Slovak border at Mniszek, just south of Piwniczna. Arriving from the north or west you can get off at the underpass on Bulwary Obronców Narwiku (Defenders of Narvik Boulevard) to reach the Rynek by ul Lwowska.

From the station blue stripe trail markings lead right/northeast to the PTTK hut and campsite just across the river at ul Jamnicka 2; the excellent skansen is a few kilometres to the right/east from here at ul

Kasprzaka 83B, in Falkowa (bus 14/15). The main hotel is the Orbis Beskid (ul Limanowskiego 1, by the station); cheaper alternatives are the Panorama (ul Romanowskiego 4A, just west of the Rynek), and the summer-only youth hostel at ul Batorego 76. There are good restaurants in the hotels and at the northern end of ul Jagiellońska; the station has an excellent café open almost 24 hours a day. You can get tourist information at ul Długosza 21 and ul Jagiellońska 46A, and the PTTK office is at Rynek 9.

To reach the Rynek from the station take buses 7/25/27/28, or head north on ul Wolności, turn left and then right at its end and follow ul Jagiellońska past the park and through the pedestrianised section to reach the Rynek by the supermarket; just right at ul Lwowska 3 is the lovely *Dom Gotycki*, the Gothic or Canons' House, housing the museum. There are paintings of the 14-15th Century Kraków-Sądecki school, the first major Polish artists, and later popular religious art including two naïf scuptures of *Christus Frasobliwy*, the Man of Sorrows, elbow resting on a skull (the traditional *memento mori*) on his knee, and a collection of the work of Nikifor (1895-1968), a naïf Łemk painter from Krynica marginally more accurate than Alfred Wallis, although he had a good feel for architecture. Finally there are lots of icons dating back to the 16th Century, taken from the iconostases of the wooden Uniate churches of the region, such as Binczarowa, Berest and Szczawnik.

Just north is the parish church of St Margaret (Św Małgorzata), built in 1446 but with a strikingly clean modern interior, and just north of this, at the east end of ul Franciszkańska, the church of the Holy Spirit, a marvellous low Gothic church, built in 1410 with a tower from 1755. At the other end of ul Franciszkańska is the 17th Century library and the Evangelical or 'Swedish' church, built in 1771. Also northwest of the Rynek on ul Pijarski is the church of the Transfiguration (1663), further west in the cemetery across the Dunajec is the wooden church of St Helen (1686), and in the southern suburb of Dąbrówka the wooden church of St Roch (1595-1608).

Nowy Sącz (known as Zanz or Neu Sandez) was the base of the Hasidic dynasty of Rabbi Chaim Halbersztan, and from August 1941 to August 1942 the ghetto held 20,000 Jews until they were shipped to the camps. The synagogue (1700-46) on ul Berka Joselewicz has been converted to a lovely exhibition hall, and further north across the river Kamienica and left on ul Rybacka is a 19th Century Jewish cemetery with about 200 tombstones. North of the synagogue are the ruins of the castle of Kazimierz the Great (1350-60), with a view to the north.

Stary Sącz, 8km southwest, was the original settlement, existing before the foundation in 1280 of the convent of the Order of St Clare (the Poor Clares) by the princess St Kinga. The old town is pleasantly unspoilt, with two Gothic churches and a small museum at Rynek 6; there is a summer-only youth hostel at ul Kazimierza Wielkiego 14, and an inn, the *Szałas* and a camp site by the Poprad bridge, towards Nowy Sącz. There is a Festival of Old Music at the end of June and early July.

PIENINY

The Pieniny (meaning 'Foaming') is a small, remarkably well-defined area, an island of limestone in a sea of sandstone, notable above all for the gorge of the river Dunajec, along which tourists float in traditional rafts. The walking is very easy, on well-maintained and well-used paths, and makes an enjoyable day circuit combined with the raft trip. It can also be seen as an extension of the Gorce hike via the wooden church at Dębno, where all the coach trips from Kraków stop *en route* to the rafting.

The climate here is particularly mild (although the gorge has been known to freeze solid), and the flora includes many southern species. There is also an immense variety, due to the lack of glaciation, with over 1,000 vascular species found here, half of all those in Poland, of which 860 are natural, 146 naturalised, and 70 non-naturalised aliens. The meadows are particularly wonderful when the orchids are in flower, with up to 70 vascular species per 100 sq m.

There is one endemic species, the cress *Erysimum pieninicum* (or *E itananii*), and four endemic varieties, *Artemisia absinthium var calcigena* (a wormwood), *Centaurea triumfetti var pieninica* (cornflower), *Sedum acre var calcigenum* and *Minuartia setacea var pieninica* (sandwort), as well as the extinct endemic *Taraxacum pieninicum* (the Pieniny dandelion). *Dendrathema zawadzkii (Chrysanthemum sibiricum)* is found only here in central Europe, and *Juniperus sabina* only here in the western Carpathians. Otherwise, there is a conjunction of heat-loving species of the lowland grasslands (*Festuca pallens, Inula ensifolia, I salicina, Anthemis tinctoria, Potentilla recta, Melica transsilvanica*), and Tatran species (*Thesium alpinum, Dianthus praecox, Astragalus australis, Polygala brachyptera, Androsace lactea, Scabiosa lucida* and *Knautia kitaibelii*).

Although a small park of 2,708ha centred on the limestone cliffs, 72% of its area is in fact forest, of which 35% is strictly protected, and 62% is fir, with 25% spruce, introduced in the late 19th Century. Pines remain only on summits and ledges, as a relic of the early Holocene period. However the fir trees are now sick due to pollution and a decline in the water table, due to an increase in domestic water use, and are being naturally supplanted by deciduous species; ash, elm and sycamore are being planted in the western part of the park to replace spruce monoculture. A controversial dam is now being completed just upstream of the park at Czorsztyn, which will accentuate these problems.

There are 45 species of mammals (including a few lynx, wolf, wildcat, about 26 red deer and 30 roe deer, 5 boar, and bats including *Miniopterus schreibersi*, claimed to be the only animal native to both Poland and Australia, 95 birds (including the golden eagle and the eagle owl), 9 amphibians, 6 reptiles, and numberless insects, with 300 species of *Ichneumon* fly, and rare butterflies such as *Parnassias apollo* and *P mnemosyne*.

The Pieniny became a reserve in 1932, and a National Park in 1955, and now receives half a million visitors a year, of whom about 100,000

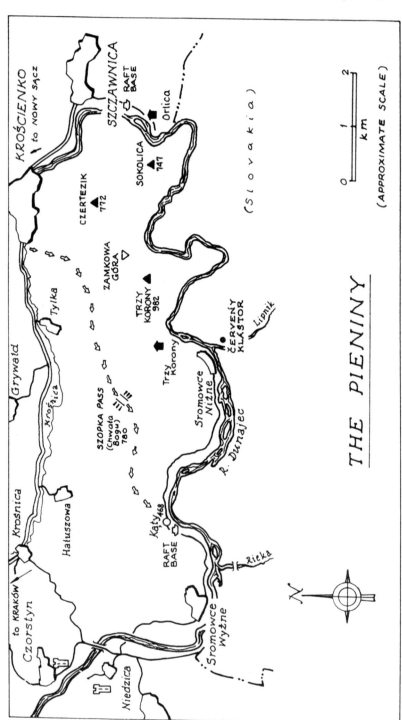

THE PIENINY

go rafting and probably don't walk far. Having visited Britain to see how we manage our National Parks, they now have plans to build visitor centres, first in Krościenko, next to the park headquarters at ul Jagiellońska 107, and at Kąty, the rafting base; the park museum is now out at Niedzica, on the right/south bank of the Dunajec west of the park itself. This is a 14th Century castle that was a rest home for art historians and now also houses the Spisz Land Regional Museum. A couple of kilometres upstream on the other side of the river are the ruins of the 13th Century Czorsztyn Castle.

Climbing is forbidden in the park, as the rock is very fragile; the park is just too small for hang-gliding or paragliding, and there is only between two weeks and two months of snow a year, although there is one ski-drag in the Park; however mountain-biking is not seen as a problem. The most popular sport here, however, is canoeing, with an International Canoeing Rally, 'the most important event of its kind in the world', held in June in Krościenko, and also a major Slovak competition in September. To canoe through the gorge, along the border, you need permission from the army base at Czorsztyn, which should be no problem: canoes can be hired in Szczawnica.

The most common map seems to be a 3-D moulded plastic souvenir; there should be a 1:22,500 tourist map, but when I was there the best available was a small panoramic map by Edward Moskała, which is adequate given the excellent trails and markings. The Gorce and Beskid Sądecki tourist maps, and the Slovak map no 24, *Spišská Magura Pieniny*, (widely available in Poland, like all the excellent Czechoslovak maps) all also cover parts of the area.

Getting there

The main local centre for tourist accommodation is the spa of Szczawnica, at the western end of the Beskid Sądecki, but the more obvious node point is Kroscienko, where the headquarters of the Pieniny National Park are located.

Szczawnica seems from the map to be rather a dead-end, but due to its pre-eminence as a spa (for asthma and respiratory problems) it is in fact very well-served by buses, with at least 15 a day to both Nowy Targ and Nowy Sącz, and others to Kraków, Katowice, Zakopane, Gorlice and Rzeszów. It is a long thin settlement along the Grajcarek stream, between the Beskid Sądecki to the north and the Małe Pieniny (Little Pieniny) to the south, with a bus station at the third stop along the main road, ul Manifestu Lipcowego, and the centre above that, to the east. The blue stripe path north to the Przehyba hut takes you through the main spa area and past the small ethnographic museum, while the alternative green stripe route continues the length of the town. There is also a yellow stripe path, almost invisible on most maps, passing through from the border path, via a PTTK hut on Rereśnik (843m) just over 1km to the north, to the main *Szlak EB* path. Other than this hut, and the Orlica hut at ul Pienińska 12 near the raft landing-place (see below), there is surprisingly little accommodation here other than pensions and sanatoria, and plentiful private rooms bookable via the PTTK at ul Manifestu Lipcowego 62A or Orbis at pl Dietla 7, or easily located by signs reading *noclegi* or *pokoje*.

Almost 5km east up the valley, reached by 20 buses a day, is the Łemk village of **Jaworki**, with traditional houses and a formerly Uniate church (still with its iconostasis) at the western entrance to the village, and a largely unspoilt lifestyle; there are three nature reserves to the south of the village, of which the best known is the Wąwóz Homole ravine, with splendid cliffs and outcrops, and eagle owls, kestrels and salamanders, reached by a green stripe path from the west end of the village to the border path along the Małe Pieniny ridge. This is also the start of a red stripe path east to Piwniczna.

Krościenko is smaller, more compact and unassuming, with buses stopping in a small Rynek just south of the main road. Again there are plenty of private rooms, from the PTTK at ul Jagiellońska 28, and camping on ul Zorodowa (across the bridge and to the left, on the right/east bank of the Dunajec). The red-marked *Szlak EB* crosses the river here, not quite taking the route shown on the maps, but close enough to find it without problem.

Hiking directions

The main route into the Pieniny starts at about 440m, up ul Trzech Koron, just before the park headquarters to the west of Krościenko. Go straight on where the cobbled road turns right, and follow yellow markings southwards up an unmade lane; after 20 minutes a green path turns left to Czertezik, where it meets the blue path that runs the length of the massif, continuing east to Sokolica (Falcon's Peak, 747m) and either by a ferry (which may cease operating by 1600) to the Orlica hut, or back by a green path along the river to Krościenko. The yellow route continues to climb steadily through woods and meadows for 10 minutes to meet the blue path at 678m, then drops to cross a stream and climbs on; after 7 minutes the blue path turns left for a scenic loop around the peaks of Zamkowa Góra (Castle Rock, with some ruins on it) and Trzy Korony (Three Crowns, the highest peak of the Pieniny at 982m, with views to the Tatras). Again it takes just seven minutes through hay meadows and mixed woods to reach the Szopka or Chwała Bogu (Praise God) pass at 771m. Everything in this part of the Pieniny is very close together, and there is a remarkable sense of compression in the scale of the landscape, with meadows, woods and peaks all jostling together.

This pass is the main crossroads of the Pieniny, with the main blue route going left to Trzy Korony, the easiest route to the summit, and right to the Snozka pass (653m) on the road to Nowy Targ. The yellow path drops down in under an hour to the PTTK hut and summer-only youth hostel at Sromowce Niżne, by the river but now without a raft harbour on this side of the river. Sromowce means 'shameful place', but its name was originally Schronowce or 'refuge' (as in schronisko), due to St Kinga having hidden there from the Tatars. She founded the convent of Stary Sącz in the 13th Century, and also has a chapel dedicated to her at the south end of Krościenko. There was a hermit here until the early part of this century, although as Violet Mason noted, 'the present hermit is rather tame, as he goes away for the winter and gets many visitors all summer'.

To reach the rafting base at Kąty, turn right along the blue route; although the path thus far has been wide and very well maintained, with lots of benches, but from here on it is back to business as usual with a narrower and less busy path. This crosses a sunken ride and climbs steeply up to a classic beechwood ridge (although the fir trees are only just below); after 15 minutes it turns right on to a track emerging from a meadow to the left, and after four minutes turns left off the track just as it enters another meadow. It takes 12 minutes, up and down through meadows and woods, to the start of the path left down to Kąty: this is marked with red stripes, although older maps show it in black. The path down is obvious at first, but after 13 minutes fork left across a field and then cross a stream to the right, to follow the left edge of a field and go into a wood. Almost at once you reach a road at a house and a spring, and follow it to the right for 5 minutes to the raft base, at 468m. This is 9km from the main road at Krośnica, served by buses to Sromowce (about five a day each from Nowy Targ and from Krościenko). The red stripe route continues westwards, initially on the road, to Niedzica Castle and Zakopane.

Rafting

There is a ticket office here, open 0900-1600 (tel 502 21), with a snackbar and kiosks; in high season there can be queues here, but you can buy tickets, and overpriced coach tours, from Orbis offices as far afield as Kraków and Zakopane.

The rafts are essentially five punts (taking ten passengers and two raftsmen) linked by a bar across the bow, a modular design that enables them to be taken apart and brought back upstream by lorry. The tradition of tourists rafting through the gorge dates back to at least 1830, and of course it derives from the custom of floating logs downstream to the mills and ports. Naturally, nowadays the raftsmen work full-time in the tourist trade, and their traditional round hat and blue waistcoat embroidered with flowers look rather out of place worn over everyday clothes and trainers. They rent the base from the park and pay it 2% of their takings, so they are now businessmen willing to haggle when business is slack to make up a fullish load. In 1991 the standard rate was Z50,000 each, and the season can run from April into mid-October if the weather is mild.

As the crow flies, the gorge is just 3km long, but as the river twists it is 9km; the Polish rafts actually travel 15km from Kąty to Szczawnica, in about two hours. You can also take a 10km trip on the Slovak side of the river, from Červeny Kláštor (Red Monastery), opposite Sromowce

Niżne, to a point just south of the border, south of Szczawnica; the great advantage of this is that you can then enjoy a very pleasant walk back along the Slovak bank (red markings), or via Lesnica (blue markings). In addition to the monastery, founded by German migrants in the 14th Century and now containing a regional museum, there is also a camp site here. There is no path along the Polish side, where the cliffs are much higher and steeper, and although in theory there should be buses to return people to their cars at Kąty, from the landing stage just south of the turning into Szczawnica, they are not very reliable other than at peak times. There is enough space to take your rucksack with you on the raft, if you don't want a circular trip.

The raft trip itself is not a white water ride, whatever you may be told; the point of it is the scenery, of multicoloured strip fields, forests, a superb tapestry of reds and golds in autumn, and then sheer limestone cliffs with eagles circling the crags. At its narrowest, the river is only 12m wide, at a point called Robber's Leap after the famous 18th Century Slovak outlaw Jánošík, but elsewhere it tends to be wide, shallow and slow outside the June period of high waters.

GORCE

The Gorce area, east of Rabka, is classic Beskid scenery, fine wooded hills giving good views (haze permitting) to the Tatras and providing a fine tonic if you become tired of the busy trails and huts of the Tatras. I describe an easy one-day traverse by the main route along the massif. The rocks are Cretaceous and Early Tertiary sandstones, shales and conglomerates, giving pleasantly rounded hills and relatively easy walking.

Typical of the Beskids, the fauna and flora are less diversified than the Tatra or Pieniny, with only one plant (*Botrychium lanceolatum*) which is found only here in Poland and in the Carpathians, and two endemic to the western Carpathians (*Soldanella carpatica* and *Cerastrium tatrae*). There are also seven Carpathian sub-endemics (*Aconitum moldavicum, Campanula napuligera, Campanula polymorpha, Dentaria glandulosa, Centaurea mollis, Chrysanthamum rotundifolium* and *Symphytum cordatum*). In the Submontane Zone, up to 600m, the forest is mainly oak, lime and beech, in the Lower Montane Zone, up to 1,150m, fir and beech, and above that spruce and fir. Due to planting, 53% of the forest area is spruce. The higher, central, part of the Gorce became a National Park relatively recently, in 1981, and has now expanded to cover 6,741ha; 95% of the original park area was forested, although there are plenty of clearings and meadows.

Getting There

The main bases for the area are Rabka and Nowy Targ, both on the railway and highway 95 from Kraków to Zakopane: **Rabka**, noted for its

Palm Sunday festival and also a festival of childrens' ensembles in June, is a pleasant spa (particularly for children) with saline springs, a church dating from 1606 by the river to the west, two hotels, the Sława and Janosik, at ul Zakopianska 2 and 16 (tel 76 120 and 76 980), and a PTTK hostel at ul Wąska 1 (tel 77 160), by the rail station.

Nowy Targ is a more compact town with more shops and services, the capital of the Podhale and best known for the 'New Market' after which it is named. This takes place on Thursdays, although things start to happen the previous evening, on an open space by the Biały Dunajec river east of the town centre, off ul Ogrodowa and Doroty. Although this was traditionally a farmers' market trading in livestock, farm produce, and agricultural equipment, this aspect has now been largely swamped by a massive car-boot sale of consumerist tat; however if you fight your way through to the far side you will still find local farmers trading piglets in sacks, bloody sheepskins, cows and saddlery. There is also a small museum of local crafts at the PTTK office (ul Sobieskiego 2, open 0900-1300), and two fine churches, St Catherine's just northwest of the Rynek (mostly from 1327 and 1601), and St Anne's in the cemetery (across the Czarny Dunajec bridge to the north and then to the left, originally from 1219). In the cemetery there are memorials to the Polish Legion, and the victims of Katyń and Auschwitz, as well as many graves of Red Army soldiers killed here in March 1945. The main hotel is the Janosik at ul Sokoła 8 (tel 28-76), one block west of the Rynek; there are also two fleapit hotels at Osiedle Bor, one stop west beyond the railway station (itself one stop west of the bus station) by buses 0/1/2 towards Ludźmierz, and a summer-only youth hostel at Niwa, on the main road northwest (bus 3 towards Obidowa). Nowy Targ is served by Kraków-Zakopane trains and by regular buses to Kraków, Katowice, Zakopane, Bielsko-Biała, and Nowy Sącz, as well as 25 to Szczawnica, and one a day as far as Krynica, Rzeszów, Przemyśl, and Lublin, in addition to several buses to Poprad, Dolný Kubín and Nižná in Slovakia, and to the borders at Łysa Polana and Chyżne.

Hiking Directions

There is a hiking map of the Gorce, at 1:75,000, available locally.

Starting from the rail station in Rabka, you should head east across the main street (ul Piłsudskiego) and up the traffic-calmed ul Orkana into the spa area, following red stripes (coming from Babia Góra); from the bus station you should turn left and take the first right to join this route. After almost 15 minutes, beyond the park, follow the road 90° right, and take ul Dietla, the fourth turning on the left, after 10 minutes; the route continues as a clear track beyond the end of the asphalt and forks left at the last house 15 minutes later. It takes just three quarters of an hour, climbing easily through hayfields, to reach the Maciejowa *bacówka* (815m), not very active out of season, by some ski-drags.

The path on continues to be well marked with red stripes, both for hiking and for cross-country skiing, passing through lovely hayfields and

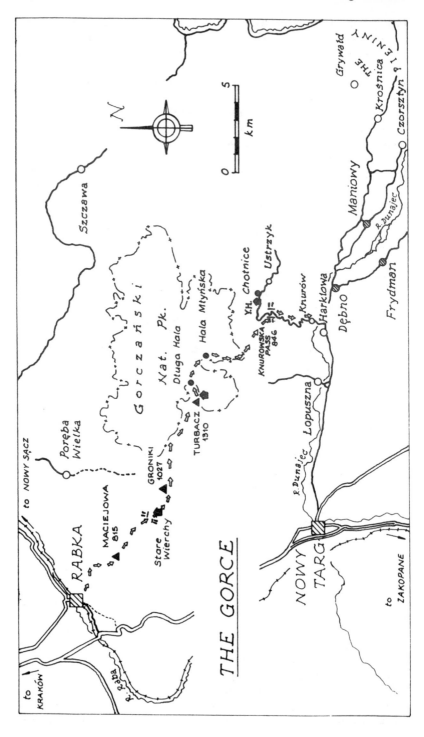

then spruce woods; after about 50 minutes it reaches the Stare Wierchy hut, just beyond the Pośrednia pass (918m), with a friendly snack bar, with a sadly limited menu. From here it is possible to follow green stripes south to Nowy Targ in a couple of hours, or blue stripes southwest to the main road and railway between Rabka and Nowy Targ; however you are here at barely 1,000m, and there are more and higher hills to the east.

The red stripes go on to the east, climbing easily to Groniki (1,027m), and then continuing along the ridge, mainly in spruce; after 30 minutes, just after the summit of Obidowiec (1,106m), green markings turn left, to join an occasional bus route through Poręba Wielka. Soon after a log cabin there is a memorial to the victims of a 1973 air crash. The main route gets steeper and rougher, climbing for one hour through spruce woods to the summit of Turbacz (1,310m), the highest point of the Gorce. This is almost as high as Ben Nevis (although it is possible to avoid it, going to the left/north), but in a far more mellow climate, in thick woods with views of meadows. Five minutes further on is the busy and deceptively large Turbacz hut. Here too there is a ski-drag, and routes south to Nowy Targ and to Łopuszna, on the road east to the Pieniny, and also two routes north to Poręba Wielka.

From here the main red stripe path, going all the way to Kroscienko and the Pieniny, crosses a large meadow, the Długa Hala, with a spring; after half an hour two more paths branch north (leading eventually to the park headquarters at Szczawa), while the main path swings south through another huge meadow, the Hala Młynska (1,282m), with great views to the east and south. After 50 minutes a black stripe path turns right for Łopuszna via the Pucołowski pond, and the red path drops through beech and spruce, and then follows a long ridge at about 900m for almost an hour. You pass a few houses as the track becomes a lane and in 10 minutes reaches an unmade road at the Knurowska pass (846m). There is a summer-only youth hostel in Ochotnica Ustrzyk, a little over 1km down the road to the north; the red path, now much quieter, follows the ridge all the way to Kroscienko, but I preferred to turn south (right) and follow the road down for 1¼ hours through Knurów to the main road (at 540m) from Nowy Targ to Kroscienko, with lots of buses from Nowy Targ to Szczawnica in particular, as well as to the Ochotnica valley and many minor villages.

Before catching the bus, though, you should walk east for 20 minutes to the lovely village of Dębno, which boasts one of Poland's more famous wooden churches, built of larch, without nails, in the 13th and 15th Centuries and visited by almost every group of tourists coming from Kraków for the raft trip through the Dunajec gorge. If there is no coach party, you should be able to get in between 0800 and 1200 and 1400 and 1700 by ringing a bell on the gate, and it is even possible, though unusual, to have electric light, which (without a torch) you will need to see the 15th Century wall paintings and altar triptych, and the 14th Century crucifix on the rood screen, the banner left by King Jan III Sobieski on his return from defeating the Turks outside Vienna, and other late-medieval knick-knacks.

There is another summer-only youth hostel here in the village school. When the Dunajec dam is completed, the reservoir will fill the valley as far as the eastern edge of Dębno; at the moment this is a lovely unspoilt village with geese patrolling the streets of wooden houses, milk churns cooling in the stream, and horse carts bringing in the hay, and with luck it will not change too radically. The next village east, Frydman, has a 13th Century stone church, and will also be just clear of the lake, but the village beyond, Maniowy, is being replaced by a new village on the hill to the north. Further east, just before Krościenko and the Pieniny region, Grywałd also has a lovely shingled 15th Century church with simple wall paintings from 1618 and a 16th Century altar triptych.

ZAKOPANE

Zakopane is now the undoubted winter sports capital of Poland, but as in many similar cases its origins were as a 19th Century summer resort, where the intellectuals and artists of Kraków rented rooms from the mountain people living here since the 16th or 17th Century. In 1873 the *Towarzystwo Tatrzanskie* (Tatra Society) was established, and in 1874 the Morskie Oko hut was opened at the prime beauty spot of the Polish Tatras (then of course ruled by Austria, in common with the Slovak part of the massif). However it was Dr Tytus Chałubinski (1820-89) who really established Zakopane itself when he set up a sanatorium for consumptives, 25 years after first discovering the mountains when fleeing the Hapsburg secret police after the revolutions of 1848-49. Skiing developed from 1894, and the railway arrived in 1899; it was in this pre-First World War period that the reputation of Zakopane was established, with figures such as the artist Stanisław Witkiewicz (1851-1915), of whom there is a bizarre photo in the Tatra museum, posing as a faun in a sheepskin and looking rather like G.B. Shaw or D.H. Lawrence, his more famous son Stanisław Ignacy Witkiewicz, known as Witkacy (1885-1939), the writer Henryk Sienkiewicz (1846-1916), the pianist and statesman Ignacy Jan Paderewski (1860-1941), and the composer Karol Szymanowski (1882-1937). In 1924 the whole 40km² estate was left to the new Polish state by Count Zamoyski, and it began to be more systematically developed; in 1946/47 there was armed resistance to communism by the stubbornly independent highlanders (*górale*) under the so-called 'Captain Fire', but after this the development continued apace.

Nowadays Zakopane is a prosperous town of 30,000, with both more BMWs and more gypsy beggars than the average. Podhale (the northern foothills of the Tatras) saw the highest rate of emigration to America, and many new houses are still being built with remittance money, in traditional local style with foundations of river boulders and three or more wooden storeys above. At the same time Podhale also has the liveliest folk culture and a fairly impenetrable accent.

The town lies at about 840m at the northern foot of the Tatras, overlooked above all by Giewont (1,894m), known as the Sleeping Knight for obvious reasons, with lower hills behind the town; of these, Gubałówka (1,120m) is particularly popular as a viewpoint towards the Tatras themselves, and can be reached by funicular.

Getting there

I must stress that the best route from Kraków to Zakopane is by bus, as the train takes a slow and roundabout route, generally taking over three hours against two by the more frequent buses. If you are travelling by Inter-Rail, of course, this won't be too much of a penalty. Through overnight trains from Gdańsk and Warsaw are also very useful. Although most tourists come via Kraków, Zakopane is also linked by bus to most towns in southern Poland, such as Katowice, Olkusz, Oświęcim, Krynica, Gorlice, Rzeszów, Przemyśl, Ustrzyki Dolne, Lublin, and also Warsaw, as well as to Budapest (contact Hungarotour, ul Łukaszowski 4/4, tel 5275).

Where to stay

As you would expect, Zakopane has a wide range of accommodation at all prices; at the top end Orbis's 4* Hotel Kasprowy, at Polana Szymoszkowa, well west of the centre (tel 4011) charges up to Z1m for passing trade, or £267-325 for a one-week Orbis package (£112-125 without flight; if you do fly a transfer is available from Kraków airport at no less than £40 each way!). This is the only place in town for foreign newspapers and books. Other major hotels are the Giewont (ul Kościuszki 1, tel 2011), the Gazda (ul Zaruskiego 2, tel 5011), and the Morskie Oko (ul Krupówki 30, tel 5076). Juventur, the youth travel agency, has its Hotel Słoneczny at ul Słoneczna 2A (tel 662 53), with rooms for five or fewer. There is also the Hotel Sport-Zakopane, completely refurbished in 1992, near the camp site and ski jumps (which look like border watch-towers) at ul Bronisława Czecha 2 (tel 5021), into which Fregata can book you for £15 twin or £9.50 single, and a new private motel, the Pawliwski, south of Poronin station.

In the mid-range the best deal is perhaps the PTTK Dom Turisty at ul Zaruskiego 5 (tel 3281), which in 1993 charged from Z40,000 in a 28-bed dormitory to Z140,000 each in a twin room with bath. There is a useful bookshop hidden away upstairs selling local guides and maps (open 1000-1800). There is another PTTK hostel up at the Kuźnice lower cablecar terminal, with marginally lower prices. The PTSM youth hostel, open all year and often overcrowded, is at ul Nowotarska 45 (tel 662 03), halfway between the centre and the station, and in 1992 charged from Z50,000 in a dorm of five bunks, including a breakfast of sausage or cheese and bread (there is a health food shop opposite as well). The old youth hostel on Al Przewodnikow Tatrzańskich 3 is closed.

Plentiful private rooms or places in pensions can be booked at ul Kościuski 7 (on the corner of Al 1 Maja, tel 4000), at ul Kropówki 12

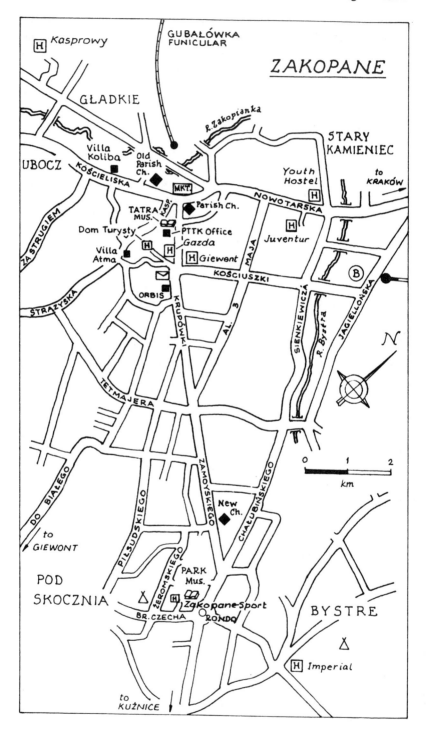

and 22, via Orbis at the Hotel Giewont and at the TRIP agency, ul Zamoyskiego 1 (tel 15947), and you may also find them for yourself on the roads south to Kuźnice. High season prices (mid December to end April and mid June to end September) were about Z80,000 each in a double in 1993. Orbis will bring you here by coach from Britain and put you up in a pension for seven nights for £189, and New Millenium for £119. Perhaps the best bargain I found in 1992 was at ul Za Strugiem 39, just beyond what looks like a new chapel on the left, with cabins at Z26,000 plus Z5,000 single night supplement; for this you get loo paper, hot water, and a residents' kitchen with stoves. I have also heard of people staying in the PKP hostel by the station.

At the bottom end of the market there has been a great growth in the number of camping sites: the official Pod Krokwią site is open all year at ul Żeromskiego (tel 2256), well on the way south to Kuźnice. Here they have a bar and snack bar (although the nearest shop is across the Rondo), they will look after your baggage while you hike, hire bikes, sell tickets for bus trips to Morskie Oko or the Pieniny, or arrange ski lessons. Billing is slightly inaccurate here (a pleasantly un-Polish trait), but in theory should in season (1992) be Z15,000 each and Z12,000 per tent. The other official site is just east at Droga do Olczy 12 in Bystre (tel 6250/2260), and simpler sites are just north of this at the 'U Daniela' in Oberconiówka (tel 612 96), and at the northern end of the Droga do Olczy in Ustup, on the main road north from Zakopane and Harenda (where there is an 18th Century larch church and the museum of the poet Jan Kasprowicz).

Where to eat

Stroll along the main drag of ul Krupówki and you will see a wider range of eating places closer to each other then anywhere else in southern Poland, mixed with all kinds of tourist shops and even the odd sex shop: you can find a crêperie, Chinese and Italian restaurants, as well as my favourite milk bar, for mammoth omelettes and pancakes, just to the right at its north end on ul Nowotarska. The best restaurants are the Jędruś (ul Świerczewskiego 5), the Watra (ul Zamoyskiego 2), the Wierchy (ul Tetmajera 2), and the Redykołka at the junction of ul Krupówki and ul Kościeliska. There is a vegetarian restaurant at ul Krupówki 40.

There are also hotel restaurants and many takeaways, some open till midnight, for *zapiekanka*, pizza, and the local speciality, waffles, and three excellent pastry shops (ideal if you descend from the mountains between meals) at ul Krupówki 22A, just above American Express (where you can change travellers cheques and collect mail), just to the left at the north end of ul Krupówki on ul Kościeliska, and behind the Hotel Giewont. In addition what look like pork pies with intricate stamped patterns, sold on the street and in the market, are in fact smoked cheeses or *brinza*, rather over-priced but worth tasting or taking home for that special present.

What to see

There are quite a few good museums commemorating the artists who came here around the turn of the century, but it is also worth wandering around the older parts of the town to see the particular 'Zakopane style' of architecture, a mixture of highland vernacular with elements of Secession or Art Nouveau imported from Vienna. Most of these houses are wooden, highly decorated, with a sort of bark rope filling the cracks between the logs. The best known example is the chapel at Jaszczurówka, just east of Bystre, built by the older Witkiewicz in 1908, as well as his Willa Koliba, (ul Kościeliska 19, 1893), which should by now have opened with a display of Zakopane-style antique furniture, and *Pod Jedlami* (Under the Firs) in Kuźnice (1897).

The Szymanowski museum is in his Willa Atma (ul Kasprusie 19), built in 1890 before the composer came to Zakopane; it is great to wallow here in his luscious late-Romantic music after a week or two of roughing it in the hills. The museum is free on Friday, and as usual closed on Monday.

Other memorial museums, which I haven't visited, include those to the poet Jan Kasprowicz at Harenda 10, the writer Kornel Makuszyński at ul Tetmajera 15, and the skiier/patriot Bronisław Czech at pl Zwycięstwa.

The Tatra National Park Museum (open 0900-1400, except Monday), at ul Chałubinskiego 42A, halfway from the town centre to the Kuźnice cablecar terminal, gives a good coverage of the park's geology and natural history. There is also a Park Information kiosk selling maps and magazines nearby on the roundabout at ul Chałubinski 44. In the town centre at ul Krupówki 10 is the *Tytus Chałubinski Muzeum Tatrzańskie* (Tatra Museum), which has a broader display of highlander culture. In Poronin, north of Zakopane, there might still be a museum where Lenin and Krupskaya spent their summers in 1913 and 1914. There are also a few minor art galleries at ul Krupówki 38 and 41, ul Jagiellońska 7, ul Bogdańskiego 16A and ul Piaseckiego 14.

The 19th Century church on ul Kościeliska is totally standard in its design, despite being made of wood, and has nothing in common with the Łemk wooden churches of the Beskid Niski, other than the curved edges of its shingled roof. The cemetery contains the graves of the pioneers of Zakopane such as Chałubinski, the older Witkiewicz, and other artists. The church on ul Krupówki is uninteresting, but the fine modern church of the Holy Cross is on the way to Kuźnice, on ul Zamoyskiego.

Practical information

There are various **information offices**, all playing different rôles: for hiking information go to the PTTK at ul Krupówki 12 (tel 5720/2429, open 0700-1600, ideal for that early-morning getaway, although they don't speak much English), for tickets go to Orbis at ul Krupówki 22 (tel

4151), and for more general information try the *Tatry* office near the station at ul Jagielloňska 7 (tel 4343/5410), the accommodation office at ul Kościuszki 7 (tel 4000), or another PTTK office at ul Krupówka 37 (tel 4707/2429, open 0700-2000, Sunday 0800-1300). The *Związek Podhalan* (Podhale Union) at ul Kościuszki 4 (tel 664 63) will give you information about *górale* folklore events. LOT have an office at ul Słoneczna 2A (tel 3635). As you've probably gathered already, Zakopane is a confusing place where almost every street name begins with K.

Shopping: the main supermarket is on ul Kościuszki just east of the Hotel Giewont, and the AlpinSport gear shop is just behind the same hotel. There is also an Adidas shop below the hotel Gazda on ul Krupówki, but this sells designer wear rather than practical gear. There is a market at the bottom (north end) of ul Krupówki, on the way to the Gubałówka funicular, and everywhere from here to the Kuznice cable car terminal you will find the local handicrafts for sale on the streets, notably the cheese mentioned above and the raw wool pullovers that seem indistinguishable from those found in Nepal, the Andes or British Columbia. You may also see the *ciupaga* or ceremonial alpenstocks carried by *górale* men at weddings, and the leather belts up to a foot wide now most often worn by the drivers of the tourist carriages.

Festivals: the *Jesien Tatrzánska* (Tatran Autumn) Mountain Folklore Festival should be held, in a tent in the Równi Krupowej valley, in late August or early September. Concerts of music by Szymanowski are held at his house, ul Kasprusie 19, in early July.

The excellent **Witkacy Theatre** (Teatr Witkacego) is at ul Chramcówki 15 just north of the station, and is very popular.

The Gubałówka **funicular** has run since 1938 from just north of the market and cemetery beyond the north end of ul Krupówka, to Polana Gobałówka, where there is a great view south to the Tatras, a restaurant and various souvenir stalls, as well as basic skiing in season. From here there are pleasant easy walking routes along the ridge, largely on back roads; you can also walk up this 300m hill in 40 minutes, following black markings from the old church on ul Kościeliska. In summer the funicular operates from 0730 to 2050.

There is also a chair-lift west of the Hotel Kasprowy, from Droga Junaków, the Zakopane-Kościelisko road, to Butarowy Wierch (1,158m) another viewpoint with a restaurant, just southwest of these easy paths.

Bicycles, including mountain bikes, can be hired at the main camp site, at ul Piłsudskiego 4A, ul Sienkiewicza 37, and at the 'Na Potoku' pension at ul Krzeptówki 1061.

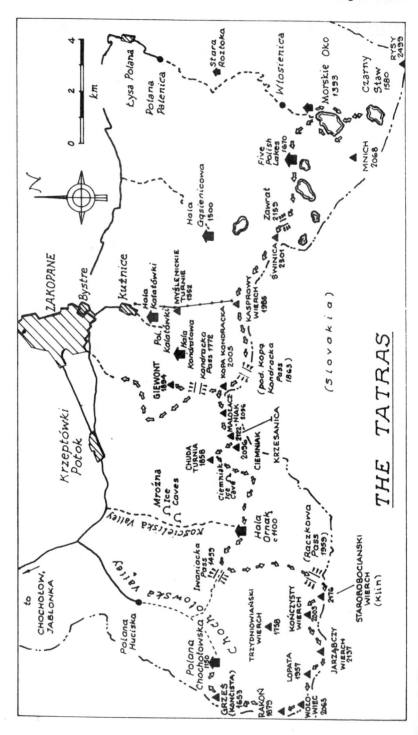

THE TATRAS

The Tatras are a relatively compact area of genuinely alpine peaks, with just 180km² of their total 750km² in Poland, very busy with perhaps a million Polish tourists in summer and more skiers in winter; however although some areas are crowded, the terrain is demanding enough for you to be able to get away from the bulk of the trippers, even though you are unlikely ever to have these mountains to yourself — I've been on top in a blizzard and still met several other hikers. According to a park ranger, the area was traditionally busy in spring with school groups, in summer with factory groups, who just rested and drank, and in September with students, 'true tourists' who get as far into the hills as they can and take a genuine interest in the environment. The general feeling is that the 'standard' of visitors is now higher, with more people who positively choose to come here rather than coming because their trade union sent them, and more foreigners. The quietest time of year is November, when cable cars and huts close to allow the chamois to be counted as they go about their rut.

The most crowded areas, above the lower paths, are of course at the top of the cable car at Kasprowy Wierch and at the classic tourist sight of Morskie Oko lake. However Morskie Oko is no longer as busy as it was, as the road has been blocked by washouts; in addition the hut, the oldest in the Tatras (founded in 1836, although the current hut dates from 1908), has been closed for several years for refurbishment, and may not yet be fully open. There are no plans to repeat the process elsewhere, due to the loss of the PTTK's government grant, the restrictions imposed by the Historic Buildings Board, and the difficulties of working for just four months a year due to the climate, with a building enterprise in the throes of privatisation.

The Tatras are both the highest and the youngest mountains in Poland, formed in the Paleozoic era 300m years ago, with later Mesozoic deposits, folded and glaciated in the Pleistocene. They are divided into three parts, the western Tatras, gentle domelike sedimentary peaks with some sharp dolomitic peaks and karst caves (highest peak Bystra, 2,248m, in Slovakia), the central Tatras, sharper crystalline peaks of Permian granite, gneiss and crystalline slates (highest peak Gerlach, 2,655m, also in Slovakia), and the limestone Bielskie Tatras to the east, entirely in Slovakia (highest peak Hawran, 2,154m). The central Tatras are intensely glaciated, with many lakes in classic alpine cirques; here you may also see debris flows, the remains of rapid slides of water-saturated debris from the steep rockwalls down onto scree slopes after intense summer rainfalls.

It's possible that tourist numbers would be even higher were it not for the 20 bears living in the Tatra National Park: perhaps we should have a few in the Lake District. Additionally there are around 160 chamois (the park symbol) here at the northern end of their range, and between 15 and 30 wolves (which can range overnight as far as the Gorce range), 10 to 15 lynx, 40 boar, 270 roe deer and 400 red deer, as well as marmots (in the cirque bottoms), wildcats, forest marten, bats and salamanders. Forest birds include the lesser spotted eagle, red kite, buzzard, hobby, capercaillie, hazel hen, black grouse and a few eagle owls. Above the trees are alpine accentors, water pipits, wall creepers and golden eagle. There are trout in Morskie Oko and a few other lakes.

The Submontane Zone of flora extends up to 700m, although oats and potatoes are farmed up to about 1,000m, and hay in manured meadows up to 1,300m; the forest here is largely the *Tilio-carpinetum* association (lime and hornbeam), with some pine and oak. Above this the Lower Mountain Zone extends to 1,250m, with Carpathian beech forest (*Dentario glandulosae-Fagetum*) on limestone slopes, and *Abieti-Picetum montanum* (largely planted spruce, with other conifers, beech, sycamore and rowan) on granite slopes. The Higher Mountain Zone continues to 1,550m, largely *Picetum tartricum*, Tatran primeval spruce forest, with fir and stone pine. Above this, to 1,800m, is the Subalpine Zone of dwarf pine (*Mughetum carpaticum* association) and herbaceous shrubs. In the Alpine Zone, up to 2,300m, are mountain pastures (*Seslerion Tatrae* on limestone, *Trifidio Distichetum* on granite). Above this is the Subnival Zone of bare rocks with lichens and a few vascular plants (*Distichetum subnivale*).

There is a greater variety of plants here than elsewhere, due to the range of altitude and geology, but there are few endemics left due to glaciation. These are *Erigeron hungaricus* (Hungarian fleabane), *Festuca aglochis* (a fescue grass), *Cochlearia tatrae* (Tatran scurvy-grass) and *Erysinum wahlenbergii* (a treacle mustard). Of the western Carpathian endemics the most important are the Tatra larkspur (*Delphinum oxysepalum*), *Saxifraga perdurans* and *Dianthus nitidus* (all pre-glacial relics). The flora is richer and more interesting on limestone, but many of the plants on limestone have an equivalent on granite: on limestone *Salix retusa* (willow), *Cerastium latifolium* (chickweed), *Gnaphalium hoppaneum* (cudweed), *Saxifraga cernua, Saxifraga moschata ssp Dominii* (saxifrages), *Draba tomentosa* (downy whitlow grass), *Silene acaulis ssp pannonica* (moss campion), *Hutchisensia alpina ssp alpina* and *Carex sempervirens ssp Tatrorum* or *Carex firma* (sedge), and on granite *Salix kitaibeliana, Cerastium uniflorum, Gnaphalium supinum, Saxifraga carpatica, Saxifraga moschata ssp Kotulae, Draba dubia, Silene acaulis ssp norica, Hutchensia alpina ssp brevicauli*, and the sedges *Carex sempervirens ssp sempervirens* and *Juncus trifidus*.

You may find edelweiss (known as 'cat's paws' to the *górale*, although the Latin name *Leontopodium alpinum* actually means alpine lions' feet) on the limestone peaks, and at least four varieties of aconites, four dianthus, nine gentians, four orchids, six lycopodia, and so on.

The climate of the Tatras is alpine, with a cold snowy winter but most precipitation in fact in the form of summer storms, 56% of the 1,610mm annual precipitation at the Hala Gąsienicowa weather station falling between June and September (particularly in June and August, it seems). Even here, down at 1,520m, it can snow in mid summer, and rapid changes of weather (usually for the worse, one assumes) are the usual causes of accidents in the Tatras. Remember that 30 to 40 people

die here each year, by no means exclusively in the ski season; there is
a risk of avalanches well into May. The emergency phone number for the
Tatra mountain rescue service (TOPR) is 3444.

In particular the *Hałny*, a warm mountain wind like the Alpine *Föhn*,
can be a hurricane-force wind from the south (caused by a difference in
pressure on the two sides of the range) and can melt all the snow
overnight and flatten up to 50,000m³ of timber (on one night in 1968
300,000m³ were laid low), as well as apparently aggravating circulatory
and nervous complaints. The seasons to avoid are March to May and
November/December. In fact the best weather comes at the end of
August and in September, when the colours are also fantastic.

At Kasprowy Wierch (1,985m) annual precipitation is 1,742mm on
average and the average temperature is –0.8°C; but up at 2,200m
altitude there is snow on the ground for up to 250 days a year and the
average temperature is –20°C.

The whole area of the Polish Tatras was created the Tatra National
Park (TPN) in 1954, covering 21,164ha (71% forest and 27% above the
tree line). In addition the Slovak side is mostly covered by their National
Park (TANAP) — see box. More than half the Polish park area, including
the entire area above the tree line, is a strict reserve, although there can
be inconsistencies where one side of the frontier is a strict reserve but
the other is not.

Both parks are to become a UNESCO biosphere reserve, which should
bring more consistency. In these core areas you should use only the
marked paths (260km of them), unless you have a climbing permit, and
you must not camp, fish, hunt, pick berries, herbs or mushrooms, or light
a fire. Nor is it possible to indulge in 'modern sports' such as mountain-
biking or hang-gliding. Considering how small and overloaded the park
is, these rules are the minimum required and are enforced with
remarkable leniency.

Outside the strict reserves, much of the forest is managed in the same
way as the rest of the Polish state forests, although in the western
Tatras eight villages still work their traditional forest within the park,
thinning out selected trees. In 1954 there were about 40,000 sheep and
other animals in the park, causing major degradation: these were
banished from the park, but a maximum of 1,000 were allowed in again
from 1981, to restore traditional management methods in a few
experimental areas. There is still tension on this issue between the *górale*
and the TPN; nowadays local sheep go to the Bieszczady for summer
grazing. Cheese is being made in the traditional way, notably in a
shepherds' hut below Kuźnice.

For the future, the TPN plans to improve sewage disposal and phase
out coal fuel from the huts (owned by the PTTK). Although state money
pays staff salaries, funds for improvements must come from sources
such as guide and carriage licences, wood sales and so on; in addition
the TPN has begun to levy an entry fee of Z5,000 a day, if you happen
to enter the park past a kiosk at a time when it is open. Groups of ten
or more must have an official guide.

There are seven huts in the Park, four large ones (unusually equipped with telephones) south and southwest of Zakopane, and three smaller ones to the east around Morskie Oko: all are in a distinctive style like overgrown log cabins with wide shingled eaves. They all have a *bufet*, usually open 0800-1900 and specialising in huge pancake-like omelettes and apple charlotte (*szarlotka*, not to be confused with *szarotka* or edelweiss), and a range of dormitories and rooms, although many students choose to save money by sleeping in the corridors. In 1993 prices ranged from Z40,000 in a dorm (or Z25,000 on the floor) to Z90,000 in a two-bed room. Meals are not cheap, due to the supply problems, at Z40-50,000, and the hikers' kitchens are just spaces for you to use your own stove, if you have one.

VYSOKÉ TATRY

The Slovak side of the Tatras is even busier than the Polish side, although the infrastructure is also better developed; currently prices here are about half those in Poland. The TANAP National Park was founded in 1949 to protect 76,763ha, with 46,116ha in buffer zones; its headquarters, with a good museum, are at Tatranská Lomnica, although the main resort is Starý Smokovec. The main ski centre is Štrbské Pleso at 1,355m. The resorts are linked to Poprad by the narrow-gauge Tatra Electric Railway, and by a rack railway to Štrbské Pleso from Štrba, also on the main rail line, and there are cable-cars or chair-lifts from all three resorts. There are 350km of marked paths, including the Liberty Road between the resorts and the 65km Tatra Magistral largely following the treeline along the length of the massif, through Štrbské Pleso and under Gerlach, the highest peak of the Tatras (and Carpathians) at 2,655m. As on the Polish side, visitors must stick to the marked paths unless they have a climbing permit or a guide. The limestone Belianske Tatry massif, to the northeast, has no marked paths, so you can't go there, although the Belianska jaskyna (cave) can be visited from the hamlet of Tatranská Kotlina, except on Mondays.

There are five large campsites, of which the best is the Eurocamp, south of Tatranská Lomnica, eight huts (*chata*), and no less than twenty mountain rescue (*Horská služba*) posts, with their HQ in Starý Smokovec (tel 0969 2820/2855). The best climbing is on Lomnický štít and Gerlach, but there are no less than 30 peaks over 2,500m, and 20 main glaciated valleys, of which the Bielovodská (White Water) valley, just east of Morskie Oko, is considered the most beautiful by many, and the Velká and Malá Studena (Great and Little Cold) valleys, north of Starý Smokovec, have most tarns.

For more information see Simon Hayman's *Guide to Czechoslovakia* (second edition 1991), also from Bradt Publications.

Hiking directions

The main hiking map is the excellent yellow 1:30,000 *Tatrzański Park Narodowy mapa turystyczna*; there is also a 1:75,000 map of *Tatry i Podhale* which covers the whole area as far north as Nowy Targ. Map no 21, *Vysoké Tatry*, in the excellent Czechoslovak series includes the Polish Tatras, and Freytag and Berndt (U Artaria, 1071 Wien, Austria) now publish three 1:50,000 maps of the Tatras.

The most obvious day-trip is to take the cable car from Kuźnice to Kasprowy Wierch, on the main ridge and border, and return by foot. Kuźnice, an easy 3km walk south from Zakopane, can also be reached by buses (every 20-30 minutes) from stop 7 at the bus station via Aleja 3 Maja; there are also lots of private mikrobuses (marked *Przewóz Osob*) to Kuźnice, costing Z2,500 from near the campsite.

The Kasprowy Wierch cable car, built in 1935, operates from 0730 (0800 from December to February) to between 1610 (December to February) and 2010 (July and August), and closes for 10 days in May and from late October to late November. It delivers more than 2,000 tourists a day the 900m up to the restaurant at the top terminal, and you may have to queue in season unless you can get there before 0750 for off-peak tickets, or buy in advance through Orbis. In 1991 tickets up cost Z30,000, plus Z10,000 for baggage, while tickets down were just Z10,000, plus Z5,000. Between December and May it is also possible to take chair-lifts to Kasprowy Wierch.

From here you can easily walk back down either direct, via Hala Gąsienicowa ('Caterpillar Meadow', with park and meteorological research stations and a climbing school, as well as the *Murowaniec* hut, the largest in the Polish Tatras with 200 beds) following yellow and then blue stripes, or via the cable car's half-way station at Myślenickie Turnie, following green stripes, or else west along the ridge and then via Giewont (1,894m, plus a 14m metal cross), the 'Sleeping Knight' that overlooks Zakopane.

1: From Kasprowy Wierch via Giewont

Seventy-five minutes west of Kasprowy Wierch (as below) most walkers turn right/north at Kopa Kondracka (2,005m) on to a yellow stripe path along a broad ridge. This drops more steeply (with some poor stone steps) to the Kondracka pass (1,772m) after 25 minutes; there are paths left and right here, both returning to Zakopane, and after 8 minutes more (now following blue markings) there is also a red stripe path left/west. To reach the top of Giewont (10 minutes above) you may have to queue to use the fixed chains in the one-way system: on the top of this limestone *turnia* there is always a crowd of picnickers around the cross, but there is plenty of room, with great views down to Zakopane.

To return to Kuźnice, you should take the blue stripe path east from the Kondracka pass down into the Kondratowa valley, with the Hala Kondratowa hut just below, and then the Kalatówki hut and some ski-drags, at the end of a better track. Less than 1km above Kuźnice is a

monastery and the memorial museum of the painter/insurgent/monk the
Blessed Brother Albert (Adam Chmielowski).

However I took a longer route back following the red markings west
from just below Giewont; after about 40 minutes this turns right on to
a good lower-level path (marked with black stripes) from the Kościeliska
valley to Kalatówki, and drops through spruce for 25 minutes to the
lovely Strażyska valley. To the right at the bridge here, where the black
stripes turn right, there is a GOPR (mountain rescue) kiosk; the red
stripes turn north and take 25 minutes along a 4WD track to reach the
park gate at the south end of ul Strażyska.

2: The main ridge

It is also possible to walk the length of the ridge in 2-3 days, passing via
Kasprowy Wierch. To start at the eastern end of the Polish section, at
Morskie Oko, you must now take a bus (at least 15 a day from
Zakopane, still claiming to go to Morskie Oko) to the Polana Palenica or
Palenica Białczańska car park, just 1km south of the Łysa Polana border
crossing, itself reached by frequent buses. Above the car park the road
is now closed to traffic due to washouts, and even bikes are banned
given the sheer volume of visitors, up to 4,000 a day; you can either
take a horse cart, or a walk of 1½ hours, with useful short-cuts marked
with red stripes. There are 40 horse-drawn 'outside cars' (half working
each day), each carrying 20 passengers for Z50,000 each in 1991,
although they seemed far more popular for the descent.

At a bridge half an hour up the old road a path marked with green
stripes leads left to the Stara Roztoka hut, or right to the Five Polish
Lakes (see below). Another 40 minutes up the road at the Włosienica
former bus terminal is a PTTK tourist centre and a Polish Alpine Club
(PZA) bivouac site, and the lake itself is 20 minutes above this at
1,393m. In a spectacular setting, this is the largest lake in the Polish
Tatras at 34.5ha in area (and 50m in depth), and its name means 'Eye
of the Sea': as in much of the Carpathians, and even in Spain, it used to
be believed that there was a link to the sea, and that wrecked ships
occasionally bobbed up here.

The red stripes continue around the left/east side of the lake, a classic
alpine lake behind a moraine dam, and climbs steeply to Czarny Staw
(one of the many Black Lakes in this area), half an hour from the hut at
1,580m. This is an even more impressive sight, tucked below the
overhanging 1,000m cliffs of Rysy, Poland's highest peak at 2,499m.
The red path (with fixed chains) continues over Rysy into Slovakia, and
although you will be told many times, even nowadays, that Lenin
climbed this way it is not to be tackled lightly.

However this is a side-trip: the main route heads west into the Valley
of the Five Polish Lakes (*Dolina Pięciu Stawów Polskich*), either by a path
marked with yellow stripes rising above the lake, under Mnich (The
Monk, 2,068m), one of Poland's best-known climbing rocks, and over
the 2,114m Szpiglasowa pass, or by a lower route marked with blue

stripes to the Five Polish Lakes hut.

I took the latter, a good stone-slabbed path, starting just below the Morskie Oko hut and climbing due north for an hour to 1,725m on the Opalone ridge and then dropping for 25 minutes to reach the hut at 1,670m, the highest and remotest of the Tatra huts, and thus in many ways the most pleasant to stay in. This valley is even more stunning than Morskie Oko, and many people spend a day or more just pottering around here. The blue stripes continue past the lakes (past Siklawa waterfall to the north, the highest in the Tatras at anything between 64m and 98m, depending on your source), joined after half an hour by the yellow stripe path from Morskie Oko, and climbing gradually to the west before swinging right and climbing more steeply to the Zawrat pass (2,159m, 1 hour 20 minutes from the hut).

Along the ridge east of Zawrat are some of the most demanding scrambling routes in Poland, returning by yellow or black paths to the Five Polish Lakes or Gąsienicowa huts. From Zawrat you could also drop north on the blue stripe route past another Czarny Staw and Hala Gąsienicowa to Kuźnice, but the through route turns left/west to follow the red stripe markings along the ridge.

However this can be hard work with a heavy backpack or in bad weather; the next stage, known as Orla Perc (the Eagles' Trail), is spectacular scrambling, with fixed chains (since 1906, though renewed since then) to haul yourself up. This short section, to Świnica (2,301m), took me 40 minutes; from here the path follows the Slovak border, moving from the crystalline High Tatras into the largely sedimentary western Tatras, much easier ridge walking with wide views. As you approach Kasprowy Wierch (an hour from Świnica) the path gets better and more crowded, with paths into the valleys on either side. With the increased numbers now visiting from the Slovak side there are now major erosion problems here, and large areas are being fenced off, so that the path may be diverted. From the cable car terminal (and weather station) you may have to head east in order to pick up the red stripe path westwards.

Seventy-five minutes beyond Kasprowy Wierch, after passing three minor peaks, you reach Kopa Kondracka and the path right to Giewont (as above, marked with yellow stripes along a high limestone ridge) and after another 30 minutes (at Małołączniak, 2,096m) a quieter blue stripe route (to the road west of Zakopane at Krzeptówki Potok). In 25 minutes, after a virtual staircase up Krzesanica (2,122m), the red stripe path turns north at Ciemniak, also 2,096m. This stretch from Kopa Kondracka is known as the Czerwone Wierchy or Red Peaks (due to the red hue of the grass in autumn), domed summits with 200m limestone cliffs below. The border runs due south from here, but you are obliged to follow the marked paths, dropping steadily in zigzags towards the lower Kościeliska valley. After 15 minutes, at the Chuda pass, there is an unmarked turning left on to something of a sheep track, soon marked with green stripes, which more or less follows the 1,900m contour south (100m above the Ciemniak ice cave) before dropping to the tree line after 45 minutes and then turning westwards into the Tomanowa valley; after another 45 minutes this reaches the Hala Ornak hut (just left on reaching the forestry road), a typical dark shingle-roofed Tatran hut at about 1,100m with a welcoming canteen.

From here you can leave the park by the road north up the Kościeliska valley, the loveliest and most interesting in the western Tatras; the road passes through limestone gorges with many caves, including the ice-coated Mroźna cave, which you can go right through (with a guide) by following black markings to the east, and others reached by following red and yellow markings. There is a rather Arthurian legend of King Bolesław the Brave and his knights sleeping in one of these caves, waiting to emerge to save Poland, although they seem to have missed every opportunity so far. The traffic-free road is 6km long and there is a Polish Alpine Club bivouac site 1km to the west from the road junction at Kiry, where there are also frequent buses back to Zakopane.

Alternatively you can continue west on a yellow stripe path crossing the stream by a good bridge, which climbs steadily for 40 minutes to reach the Iwaniacka pass at 1,459m; this path descends into the Chochołowska valley, but there is an superb day-walk to the Chochołowska hut following the border around the head of this valley. To take this route you should turn left at the pass on to a path marked with green stripes, which, after climbing out of thick dwarf pine in 5 minutes, continues steeply for half an hour to reach a minor ridge and on more easily for 45 minutes before climbing steeply for 15 minutes to regain the main ridge and border at 1,959m at the Raczkowa pass. The green stripe markings continue south into Slovakia, but you should turn right/west to follow red stripes up Starorobociański Wierch (Klin in Slovak, 2,176m, 25 minutes west), and on past the three lower peaks of Kończysty Wierch (2,003m), Jarząbczy Wierch (2,137m) and Łopata (1,957m) to reach Wołowiec (Volovec in Slovak, 2,063m) after 2 hours. There are fine open views all along this section, with many small alpine lakes in the deep valleys to the south. This is in fact a Slovak path with signs in Slovak, but you will have no problems as long as you keep to the main ridge, marked in red, and ignore yellow and green paths turning south. However if the weather turns nasty, there are green stripe paths north to Chochołowska from Kończysty Wierch and from border marker 249.5 just beyond Wołowiec.

At Wołowiec (border marker 249) the red stripes turn left into Slovakia and you should follow blue stripes north along the border, on an easier, wider path than before, passing below Rakoń (1,879m) after 20 minutes, then turning right/east after 40 minutes more on to a yellow stripe path, just after Grześ (Končista in Slovak, 1,653m). It takes 30 minutes from here, dropping down into dwarf pine and then spruce, to reach the Chochołowska hut (1,150m), scene of a secret meeting in 1983 between Wałęsa and the Pope, the site of which is now a virtual shrine. An easy 5-hour day-walk from here would take you up Trzydniowiański Wierch (1,758m), following green and then red stripes.

Starting in a picturesque meadow dotted with shepherds' huts, it takes another 50 minutes down a rough road to reach the Polana Huciska carpark and bus stop (with buses to Zakopane in theory at 0900, 1025, 1530 and 1645); it's another 4km to the main road, where there are plenty of buses from the Dolina Chochołowska bus stop, either back to Zakopane or north towards Jabłonka. The village of Chochołow, 10km north, is much-touted as an authentic Podhale village with unspoilt vernacular buildings; to my surprise it is not at all touristy, perhaps because it is not really very picturesque. The village houses, from the 18th and 19th Centuries, are mostly in plain wood, with a few nice carved details such as the fanlights, and are set at right angles to the road with ungated yards between them.

There is a very minor border crossing at Chochołow, still open only to Poles and Slovaks, so you should continue to Jabłonka to pick up the main E77 route from Kraków and Rabka, continuing through Chyżne to the Slovak border; buses go as far as Budapest from here.

OJCÓW

Stretching northwest from Kraków past the great pilgrimage centre of Częstochowa is the *Wyżyna Krakówsko-Częstochowska* (Kraków-Częstochowa Upland or Kraków-Wieluń plateau), more popularly known as the Jura, after its Jurassic limestone, offering good climbing and caving. After the cession of Silesia to Bohemia this became a natural line of defence and was fortified with a line of castles along the hilltops, of which only Pieskowa Skała now survives intact. However many of the spectacular ruins (notably at Ogrodzienic, near Zawiercie, and Olsztyn, near Częstochowa) can be visited by following the Trail of Eagles' Nests, a 160km hiking route (and interconnecting road route) marked with red stripes.

The best-known area of the Jura is the Ojców National Park (*Ojcowski Park Narodowy*), the smallest in Poland at 1,592ha, and one of the smallest in the world, just 20km from Kraków and easily reached either by bus or on foot following the red markings. In the 1960s there were up to 600,000 visitors a year to the park, and although there are now less than half as many it is still overloaded around June. When some English national park staff visited, the Poles were amazed to hear that we manage our parks for leisure and recreation as much as for conservation; here the priority is definitely conservation, although in fact only 21% of the park's area is a strict reserve.

The Jurassic limestone of this area was laid down 150 million years ago, covered with marl sediments in the Upper Cretaceous period and then glaciated (just once) before being covered in several metres of wind-borne loess. The combination of glaciation and karstitic weathering has produced a wonderful landscape of gorges and over 200 caves, with 200m cliffs above the Prądnik river, and up to 20 distinct microclimates, with rare Arctic and Mediterranean flora right next to each other. Up to 50 species of vascular plant have become extinct in the park in the last 30 years, due to atmospheric pollution from Upper Silesia, and pine and fir trees have also been suffering since about 1965 and are gradually being replaced by more resistant deciduous species. There are still at least 950 vascular species here, including 50 mountain species, as well as 1,200 fungi, 160 mosses and 73 liverworts.

Woods cover 79% of the park's area, mainly Carpathian beech forest in the shadowy and humid lower valleys, with various associations of pine, fir, sycamore, hornbeam and beech on the warmer drier slopes above, with the rare shrubby birch *Betula oycoviensis*, and also *Betula verrucosa*. Protected plants include *Aconitum gracile, A moldavicum, Anemone silvestris, Aquilegia vulgaris, Aruncus silvester, Carlina acaulis, Cerasus fruticosa, Daphne mezereum, Lilium martagon* (Turk's Cap lily), the clubmosses *Lycopodium annotinum, L clavatum* and *L selago*, the fern *Phyllitis scolopendrium* (under the sycamores), *Sempervivum soboliferum, Taxus baccata* (yew), *Trollius europaeus* (globe flower), and various gentians and orchids, such as *Cypripedium calceolus* and *Platanthera bifolia*, the lesser butterfly orchid.

There are something between 2,114 and 3,300 species of insects in the Park, including 600 butterflies (especially the European and scarce swallowtails *Papilio machaon* and *Papilio/Iphiclides podalirius*), and ground beetles such as *Carabus auronitens, C intricatus* and *C coriaceus*, and various types of true, burrowing and leaf-cutter bees.

In the Ice Ages there were mammoth, woolly rhino, cave bear, and reindeer here: nowadays there are 490 species of fauna (other than the insects), including 120 birds (of which 80 breed here), and between 10 and 17 (depending on the source) of Poland's 20 species of bat, especially the small horseshoe and large mouse-eared bats. The largest mammals, such as bears, red deer and wolves, are absent, but there are about 145 roe deer and 8 boar, with squirrels, badgers, raccoon dogs, polecats, muskrats and dormice, and possibly a herd of about 50 reintroduced bison.

Getting There

Most visitors will come from Kraków, either walking from its northern outskirts, following the red markings to Ojców, Pieskowa Skała and Częstochowa, or by buses 248 (via Zabierzów station, west of Kraków, to Zelków), 220 (to Giebułtów) and 277 (to Owczary) which all take you from the city to the beginning of the uplands.

I started with a bus from Olkusz, to the west on the Bytom-Kraków main road, to Pieskowa Skała, and after hiking through the Park to Rudawa continued by bus to Chrzanów and Oświęcim (for Auschwitz — see next section). There are hourly trains from Katowice to Olkusz (heading for Charsznica); there is a regional museum here, and it is also the jumping-off point for Europe's only desert, the Pustynia Blendowska, just to the northeast. From Olkusz three buses a day run to Kraków via Ojców, along the whole length of the park; another five run via Skała (and five more from Olkusz to Skała alone) which avoid Ojców village but can drop you at Pieskowa Skała, at the northern end of the park.

Hiking Directions

The area is covered by the 1:50,000 mapa turystyczna of the *Podkrakowskie Dolinki Jurajskie*, as well as a more detailed map (1:22,500) of the park itself.

The bus from Olkusz passes a very long series of stops in Sułoszowa before finally reaching the Pieskowa Skała (Dog's Rock) stop after about 25 minutes; this is at a T-junction to the left/northeast towards Częstochowa, and you should go left and up the steps to the right to reach the castle.

This was built in the 14th Century by Kazimierz III the Great, and from 1410, under four generations of the Szafraniec family, it was associated with tales of black magic, alchemy and banditry. After 1578 it was rebuilt as a Renaissance palace; after a fire in 1718 it was restored in baroque style, and again rebuilt after being damaged in the 1863 insurrection. It was used as a hotel and then after more restoration reopened as a branch of the Wawel museums of Kraków, with painting, furniture and a historical collection. The park and exterior courtyard are open free of charge 0700-2000, and the museum 1200-1730 (not free, two hours earlier from September to May, and closed as usual on Mondays); there is a good café here.

You should return to the road junction and follow the road south down the Prądnik ('little stream') valley; almost at once you see the *Maczuga Herkulesa* or Club of Hercules, a 20m limestone pillar seen in all the tourist leaflets. Soon after this a path marked with yellow stripes turns right up a forestry track, looping back down the Sąspówka valley to Ojców village; turning left where this reaches a road will bring you to Wola Kalinowska, where there may still be a summer-only youth hostel. The valley is lovely, just wide enough to fit in one field between more limestone outcrops, with the remains of some of the 60 watermills that used to line its banks.

After 40 minutes, although you can continue along the road, the marked path turns half left at a mill to go up a track to Grodzisko, once the site of an outlaws' hideout and the convent of the prioress the Blessed Salomea, where there are now only small cottages in apple trees. Ten minutes from the road the path turns right at a T-junction with another path, marked in blue, from Ogrodzieniec; the path drops past the baroque chapel, turning right again very soon and zigzagging down to the road in 5 minutes, at a relatively large farm just before a bus stop at the road junction left/east to Skała. Twenty minutes further down the valley a field opposite the Chapel on the Water (built in 1901 on a bridge over the stream to circumvent Tsar Nicolai II's ban on building a new Roman Catholic church on the land) is (or was) supposedly a bivouac site — I camped here but found not even the usual privy, although there is the spring of St John in an octagonal gloriette 150m north where the road and river curve around the Prałatki crag.

Here a road, used by some Olkusz-Kraków buses after passing through Pieskowa Skała and Skała (and in reverse), turns right/west to climb out

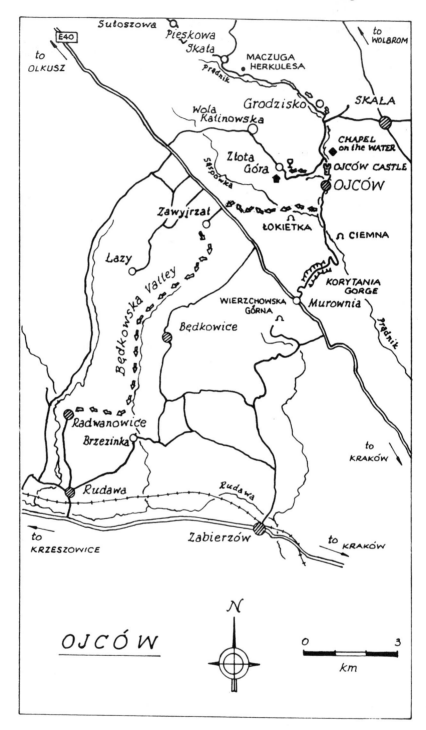

OJCÓW

N

0   3
km

of the valley. After 5 minutes this meets a new path, marked with black stripes, coming from the Ojców castle ruins to the left and continuing up the road, and by a short cut in beechwoods to the right, to reach the Złota Góra tourist complex, with a restaurant, shop and bivouac site; however if you take the path through the woods you will miss the PTTK's *Zosia* hostel, on the road to the left, and shut for the season by September. The road continues to Wola Kalinowska, just 1½ km further on.

From the bivouac site in the valley, the main road continues south around the castle rock to reach Ojców village in a couple of minutes. This is the only village in the park itself and was clearly built as a spa, with its wooden buildings elegantly scattered in parkland. The Park Museum, named after its founder Professor Szafer (presumably originally Schäfer) is in the *Łokietek* spa building of 1860, and a Regional Museum, with PTTK shop and post office, in the *Kazimierz* villa (1885) next to it. To the north a lane leads up to the ruins of the Ojców castle, also built by Kazimierz the Great, later rebuilt as a mansion but abandoned from 1826 and demolished except for the gateway and one octagonal tower. There are *noclegi* available here, and a youth hostel, closed for *remont*, at the south end of the village.

The road continues south on the left/east side of the stream, and the paths (marked in red, blue and black) on the right bank. After 10 minutes the red markings follow the stream south all the way to Kraków, and the blue and black markings cross the Sąspówka stream and swing west towards the Łokietka cave, one of the two caves in this area that are illuminated and can be visited with guides, although neither is particularly spectacular or interesting. The other is at Wierzchowska Górna, just outside the park to the southwest near the village of Murownia; this can be reached either by following a path marked in yellow, branching right off the red route to the south, or by following the road to Murownia through the Korytania gorge, a strict reserve with Asian cherry trees at the extreme northwestern end of their range. Another that is unlikely to be open is the Ciemna cave, on the left bank just south of these turnings west at a spot known as Krakowska Brama (Kraków Gate), which was inhabited at least 50,000 years ago, and again in the Second World War; but so many of these caves once sheltered a cave bear, or a hermit, or outlaws, or a fugitive king, that this loses its interest. When the valley formed the Russo-Austrian border, the caves were also used for gunrunning, with one cave reputedly having entrances on either side of the border.

However I took the former yellow path (now diverted to pass via the Złota Góra tourist complex) back towards Pieskowa Skała, turning right/west up the Sąspówka valley (ignoring a loop via a new private shop). This is a lovely quiet valley; after 15 minutes I turned left at forestry marker 23-28 into the beechwoods, and forked right after a few minutes to follow the main side valley, the Wąwóz Jamki. There are lots of rounded outcrops among the beech trees here, and to the left various small caves; don't poke around here, as this is a strict reserve. After 5 minutes negotiating the many fallen trees I turned left on a minor path up the second side valley, with the traffic noise of the Bytom-Kraków highway already audible; after 10 minutes, having climbed to the level of the surrounding farmland, I turned left on to a forestry track at a barrier and marker 20. It took 10 minutes to reach the edge of the wood and rejoin the blue path, which I should properly have followed via the Łokietka cave.

Turning right along the edge of the wood and continuing into it again, the markings turn 90° left after 10 minutes to cross the main road (with two motels on either side of Murownia, 3km to the southeast) and continue on an unmade road through the ugly village of Zawyjrzal, with odd limestone outcrops in copses to the right. After 15 minutes turn left in a dip on to a farm track, and then after 5 minutes right onto a similar largely unmarked track, dropping into very mixed deciduous woodland (with a couple more caves to the left). At this point you leave the area covered by the 1:22,500 map of the park itself. After 7 minutes keep left at a double fork to go along the right-hand side of some small fields and through a bit of wood to reach a very large spring at the head of the Będkówka valley. Just below this are some old greenhouses where you should turn left on to an unmade road down the valley, or go right to the youth hostel, open all year, at Łazy, on top of the hill.

Following the road down the valley, after 15 minutes the yellow path comes in from the right/west (not marked from the north, but down a very obvious side valley) and after 10 minutes turns left up a narrower side valley to go back to Murownia and Ojców. After another 20 minutes, after passing a largely silted-up artificial lake, turn right, following the blue markings up a track, keep left into a field and after 4 minutes turn up to the right (unmarked) at a gate. From the right-hand corner of the field you may have to go through nettles to join an overgrown little path which passes an old sluice and swings left in some trees to emerge right under the Cebulowa outcrop after 5 minutes.

From here the path is very hard to find (most walkers probably stick to the road down through Brzezinka to Rudawa), but if you follow the edge of the field due west and then head for the first house ahead, you will find yourself on a farm track dropping into the village of Radwanowice (marked in blue again) after about half an hour. Here there is a small shop, and about six buses a day to Krzeszowice; black markings head north up the Szklarka valley, and at the second bus stop, 5 minutes south along the road (where the church consisted of a wayside shrine and some benches under a plastic awning), green markings turn west to go up the lovely Raclawka valley. It took 30 minutes more down the road to reach the so-called Rynek of Rudawa, with just one shop, and 12 minutes more (across the railway bridge, with the station to the left/east) to reach the former Kraków-Katowice main road (now supplanted by a motorway); from the bus stop here there is one direct bus to Oświęcim (at 1821), as well as others west to Chrzanów (from where you can take either bus or train to Oświęcim) and Katowice, and east to Kraków.

AUSCHWITZ

It may seem somewhat beyond the remit of a book on hiking to describe a concentration camp, but Auschwitz is simply compulsory viewing for anyone visiting Kraków, especially now when, with communism barely out of the way, the older evils of racism are reappearing posthaste. In addition it is the start of a 51km marked route following the final exodus of the last 53,000 prisoners who were herded west by their guards as the Red Army drew near. There are plenty of overpriced coach tours from Kraków (usually at 0900 from Plac Szczepanski), but you can just as easily go by train; most trains (11 of them, taking 90-100 minutes) run to and from Kraków Płaszów rather than the main Główny station (two stops to the north), and once you have realised that the Poles call it Oświęcim you will have no further logistical problems. It is equally easy to get there from Katowice (13 trains taking 65 minutes).

For me, Auschwitz was something like the Taj Mahal, in that the external image is now so familiar that I initially found it almost banal and had to dig deep to understand, as far as I could, what it was really about. Indeed, with images of ethnic cleansing and urban terrorism rarely absent from our media, the banality of evil is a problem for all of us; luckily, even though Adorno said that poetry was impossible after Auschwitz, there are superb accounts from both participants and historians, most notably *The Drowned and the Saved* and *If This is a Man* by Primo Levi, the Italian chemist who spent the rest of his life in bearing witness to a world that wanted to forget until, probably, his own failing memory led to suicide in 1987, *Kommandant at Auschwitz*, written by the camp commandant Rudolf Höss before his execution in 1947, *Maus I* and *Maus II* by Art Spiegelman (Penguin/Pantheon), a superb cartoon account, and the film *Shoah* by Claude Lanzmann (a slightly inaccurate script was published by Pantheon (New York) in 1985). Other accounts of the camps include Thomas Keneally's *Schindler's Ark* (Sceptre 1986, now filmed by Spielberg as *Schindler's List* presumably because Americans (hi, guys) don't know what the ark was), *A Time to Speak* by Helen Lewis (Blackstaff 1991), *Wartime Lies* by Louis Begley, (Picador 1992), stories by Tadeusz Borowski in *This Way for the Gas, Ladies and Gentlemen* (Penguin 1976), more fictional interpretations of the whole Holocaust phenomenom such as *Time's Arrow* by Martin Amis and *Operation Shylock* by Philip Roth, and for historians' accounts, *The Destruction of the European Jews* by Raul Hilberg (Holmes & Meier rev 1985) or Martin Gilbert's *The Holocaust* (Fontana 1987) and *Auschwitz and the Allies* (Mandarin 1991). If you can read up on the subject before going, so much the better, but don't believe anything written by David Irving.

It was on April 27 1940 that Himmler ordered the setting up of a concentration camp in former army barracks at Oświęcim (Auschwitz in German); it was first occupied in June by 729 Polish political prisoners from Tarnów, and the first experimental gassings with Zyklon-B, of 600

Soviet POWs and 250 sick prisoners, were carried out in September 1941. In 1941 the much bigger satellite camp at Brzezinka (Birkenau) was opened, and in 1942 a third camp called Monowice (Monowitz) at a factory 6km away. In March 1942 the trainloads of Jews, gypsies and other 'undesirables' began to arrive; with four gas chambers and crematoria operating at Birkenau (operated by prisoners), it took just 20 minutes from the arrival of a train and the removal of those still fit for slave labour to sorting out the gold teeth from the ashes. The gas chambers could hold 2,000 and thus kill 60,000 a day, but with access to Nazi documents captured by the Red Army, historians now think that a maximum of two million were killed here, rather than the four million previously claimed by a joint Russian-Polish committee.

Auschwitz had three aspects; firstly this high-speed massacre, mainly at Birkenau, secondly as the centre of a network of sub-camps supplying labour to factories (men rarely survived longer than a year, and women just a month or two), and thirdly, as a centre of inhuman experiments by the evil Dr Mengele and his colleagues. It is also remembered for an uprising on October 7 1944, when crematorium IV (the third from the left in Birkenau) was burnt down.

On New Year's Day 1945 the camps were evacuated, and prisoners and guards set off, at a rate of 25km a day until April, along a route now marked with blue stripes as far as Wodzisław Śląski, 51km west. Not many of the prisoners survived this forced march. When Zhukov's army caught up there were only a few thousand survivors, a disproportionate number of whom have since been remarkably high achievers. Auschwitz also gained a saint in 1982 when Maksymilian Kolbe, a priest who took a Jew's place for execution, was canonised.

At once the camps, both in Poland and eastern Germany, were pressed into service by the NKVD (the KGB's forerunner) to imprison the non-communist opposition — another fact only officially revealed since the break up of the Soviet Union. The Auschwitz camp was opened as a museum and memorial in 1947, and throughout the communist era was busy with school parties learning of the evils of the pre-communist world, and parish outings (combining it with a visit to Częstochowa) and groups of Germans (mostly eastern) atoning for the same. This has now changed, with the great increase in Western tourists nowhere near making up for the shortfall in Eastern Bloc groups; in 1979, the year that the Pope said mass at Birkenau, there were 700,000 visitors, and just 400,000 in 1992.

In addition there have been great cuts in government funding for the museum (as entry is free, the number of visitors is irrelevant in this sense); an appeal was made to the people of Germany for funds, which raised £100,000, as well as a large quantity of hate mail; 'One man wrote that he would be happy to see Auschwitz repaired, provided Heinz Galinski, leader of Germany's Jewish community, was first into the renovated gas chamber. Another offered to pay for the first 50kg of Zyklon-B poison gas'. Guards are now needed at the Birkenau site to stop looters sifting through ashes for gold teeth. Nevertheless the priority of the museum administration is to change its emphasis from the anti-fascist approach of the communist era to a more humane approach appropriate to the world's greatest killing-field.

Auschwitz continues to be a source of controversy: in the mid-1980s Carmelite nuns moved into a former poison gas warehouse, with the best of motives, but after Jewish protests agreed to move to a new building some hundreds of metres away. In July 1989 American Jews led by the New York rabbi Avi Weiss tried to break in, and in a sermon in August Cardinal Glemp rebuked the Jews for preaching to the Poles and using their alleged power over the foreign mass media to foment 'anti-Polonism'. There was a great furore but Glemp was unrepentant, and undoubtedly had plenty of tacit support. The new convent opened in May 1993, and will welcome you on a retreat for US$25 per day (bed and all meals).

From the station it took me just 15 minutes to the Auschwitz museum (turn right and then take the second left, ul P Findera, or take any of buses 24-30); from Birkenau it took me 22 minutes to Auschwitz or just 17 minutes to the station, all considerably less than generally stated. Bus 17 runs very roughly every two hours from Plac Kosciuski in the town to Birkenau (heading for Harmęze).

The Auschwitz museum is open daily from 0800 to 1800, and Birkenau until dark: major captions are in English as well as Polish, and there are also many German documents. Children are allowed only into Birkenau, but there are lots of babes in arms in the Auschwitz museum. The main entrance block now contains a hotel (charging Z120,000 for a double back in 1991), with a left luggage service (for Z1,500) and bus and train timetables (in town there are also the Hotel Olimpijski at ul Chemików 2 and the Kamieniec inn at ul Zajazdowa 2, and Juventur's International Youth Meeting House at ul Legionów 1, 3km from the camp). In the museum reception there is a cinema with fairly frequent English-language showings of a 20-minute introductory film. I warn you now, so that you don't choke when you see it, of a horrible Freudian slip at the end: 'the Allied Powers will follow them *oven* to the ends of the world'.

From here the tour took me an hour and a half: passing through the archway cynically proclaiming *Arbeit Macht Frei* ('Work sets you free') continue to the third line of buildings to the exhibitions in blocks 4, 5, 6 and 7. Here there you will apparently see 2 tonnes of human hair, 3,300 umbrellas, 35,000 mugs and so on; however when these seemingly huge piles slip you can see that they are on angled shelves. In any case I found that more was less; the understatement of the six graves that are all that remains of an entire Jewish settlement deep in the Beskid Niski affected me far more deeply than this. However the rows and rows of photographs of the victims are more than poignant.

At the end of this row is the Death Block, with a wall for firing-squad executions (place your flowers here) and standing cells under a metre square in which up to four would-be escapers would be left to starve to death. From here you can visit other barracks blocks dedicated to victims from specific countries (which may be closed from October to April), and block 27 which remembers the Jews from all nations. The Jewish victims are now increasingly being given their due, having been lumped together with all the 'victims of Fascism' in the communist period. Passing the gallows outside the cookhouse, you leave the camp via the gas chamber and crematorium, much smaller than those at Birkenau.

To reach the Birkenau site, return towards the station, but turn left and cross the railway by a new bridge. This is where you really feel the scale of the Nazi undertaking; there are fewer visitors here, particularly at sunset when I visited, and you can just wander through row upon row of huts to soak it all in. The International Monument to the Victims of Fascism was erected here in 1967. From here you can return to the town, busy with its own life, and muse on the nature of time, memory, evil and so on. It is ironic that a 19th Century Jewish cemetery with about 300 tombstones still survives in Oświęcim.

Other camp museums are at Gross-Rosen (at Rogoźnica, west of Wrocław), Maidanek (just 3km from Lublin) and Stutthof (Sztutowo, east of Gdańsk), which are much less on the international tourist trail than Auschwitz. There were others, such as Sobibór (on the border east of Lublin) and Treblinka II (northeast of Warsaw), both flattened after uprisings and mass escape attempts.

BABIA GÓRA AND THE BESKID ŻYWIECKI

Babia Góra, although rather isolated and almost unknown to foreigners, is a unique habitat and very popular with the Poles, with perhaps the best view in Poland from the summit. There is also a great view *to* Babia Góra from the Kraków-Zakopane bus north of Rabka. It is the only alpine section of the Beskids, with primeval forests of fir and larch up to 350 years old and 40m high; however acid rain is having some effect here, at the eastern end of its range.

As part of the High Beskids (Beskid Wysoki) Babia Góra is a conical 'witches' mountain' of Magurian sandstone (with some schist below 1,000m altitude), very steep (up to 65°) on the north side, and marked by *maliniaki* or debris flows. Due to its isolation and exposure, flora zones are 100-160m lower on the northern slopes than they are in the Tatras, with a lower mountain forest zone of Carpathian beech forests (*Dentario glandulosae-Fagetum*) on acid-brown soils, and fir-spruce forest (*Abieti-Piceetum montanum*) on flat ridges with podzolic soils, with some sycamore and alder, up to 1,150m, upper mountain forest of spruce with rowan (*Piceetum excelsae carpaticum*) up to 1,390m, a subalpine dwarf pine zone (*Pinetum mughi carpaticum*), with some rowan, Silesian willow, bilberry and dwarf spruces and junipers up to 1,650m, and an alpine zone of *Luzuletum-Deschampsia caespitosa*, low grasses or turf (*Festuca versicolor*, an endemic association), mosses and lichen (*Umbilicaria cylindrica*), up to the summit of Diablak at 1,725m. Overall the forest is 67% spruce, with 8% beech and 5% fir. Average temperatures range from 6 to 4°C in the lower mountain zone to 0 to −2°C in the alpine zone; there is often fog, particularly at lower levels, and dawn is a popular time to climb to the top.

There are 700 species of vascular plants, 200 mosses, around 250 lichens, 120 algae, and 100-plus liverworts, with many rare species in all these categories. In the lower mountain zone flowers include the common speedwell and brooklime (*Veronica officinalis* and *V beccabunga*), and in the mown meadows *Gladiolus imbricatus, Crocus scepusiensis* and *Agrostis vulgaris*; in clearings in the higher mountain zone you can find the park's symbol, the rare laserwort *Laserpitum archangelicum (okrzyn jeleni)*, with ferns, bilberry (*Vaccinium myrtillus*), alpine sorrel (*Rumex alpinus*), and *Veratrum lobelianum*. The subalpine zone is very rich in flowers such as the rare cudweed *Gnaphalium norvegicum*, bedstraw *Galium anisophyllum*, ox-eye daisy *Chrysanthemum leucanthemum var saxicola, Alchemilla flabellate, Tozzia alpina ssp carpatica* (in only one place), with saxifrages, bilberry, crowberry (*Empetrium nigrum ssp hermaphroditum*, and standard Carpathian grasses such as *Deschampsia caespitosa* and *Nardus stricta*. Finally in the alpine zone you find more chickweeds *Gnaphalium supinum, Cerastium alpinum* (the alpine mouse-ear chickweed, found only here in Poland), *Lycopodium alpinum* (alpine clubmoss), and alpine sward with rushes such as *Juncus triffidus*.

In all there are 75 alpine plants and 34 protected species (of 124 in Poland), although no endemics, other than two *Alchemilla* sub-species; as for the fauna there are 2,500 species of insect, of which 900 are *Coleoptera* (beetles, notably *Sinodendron cylindricum*), and 115 birds (80 nesting here). These include the golden eagle, goshawk, sparrowhawk, buzzard, raven, long-eared and eagle owl, capercaillie, hazelhen, alpine accentor, and various woodpeckers, pipits, finches and tits. Of the mammals, there are roughly three lynx and three wolves in the park, with deer, boar, marten, badgers, squirrels, weasels, alpine shrews, and bats such as *Plecotus auritus, Myotis mystacinus, M nattereri*, and *Eptesicus nilssoni*. There are six species of amphibia (newts, salamanders, frogs and toads), five reptiles (snakes and lizards) and two fish.

The Babiogórski National Park (BgPN) was set up in 1954, covering 1,734ha (only 142 ha larger than the Ojców Park), 91% of it forest and 61% under strict protection; in 1977 it became a UNESCO Biosphere Reserve. There are plans to expand its area fivefold, but as the facilities serving the present park are very limited, this may be premature.

The Beskid Żywiecki is a rather more anonymous area, leading irresistibly towards the town of Żywiec (pronounced Jihvets), famed nationwide for its brewery, now privatised and perhaps concentrating more on exports than on its home market. This is the start of the holiday region of the Silesian Beskids, including the Beskid Maly (Little Beskids) to the north of Żywiec, and the Beskid Sląski (the Silesian Beskids proper) to the

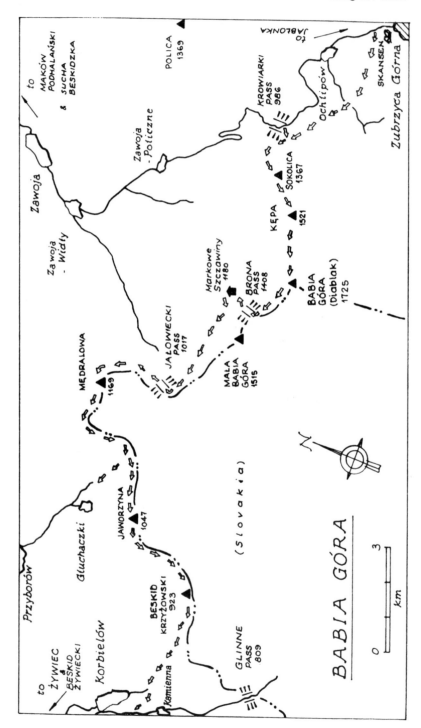

BABIA GÓRA

west — see the following section.

With a maximum altitude of 1,557m, the Beskid Żywiecki has no alpine level, but is similar in other respects to Babia Góra, with some peat bogs. It is popular with students, and surprisingly well provided with PTTK mountain huts, given the relatively undramatic scenery.

Getting There

The Przełęcz Krowiarki (Krowiarki pass, 986m) is the immediate jumping-off point for Babia Góra, but it is equally possible to walk in from Jordanów, near Rabka (see page 144) to the east, or Sucha Beskidzka to the north. From Jordanów you can follow red markings along the Beskid Wysoki (High Beskids), with Polica (1,369m) as the high point of this section; from Sucha Beskidzka you should also follow red markings to Zawoja, and then follow the road to the right to the Krowiarki pass.

In Sucha Beskidzka there is a tourist hostel at ul A Mickiewicza 127 (tel 427 31), and private rooms through the PTTK and 'Beskidy' offices at ul A Mickiewicza 38 (tel 427 57) and 65 (tel 427 53); there is a campsite 5km southeast in Maków Podhalański at ul Głowackiego 16 (tel 716 05). There is a regional museum in the castle of Sucha Beskidzka, just north of the centre, and a 17th Century monastery.

Zawoja, although a tiny village, is the park headquarters, with a small museum and youth hostel, open all year, and private rooms from the 'Beskidy' office in Zawoja-Widły, west of the centre. Buses, mostly from Sucha Beskidzka, run as far as Zawoja-Policzne, just short of the Krowiarki pass, but you will have to walk or hitch the last few kilometres. I started on the far side of the pass, in Jabłonka, reached by frequent buses from Nowy Targ and Rabka, and also by less frequent buses from Zakopane, Nowy Sącz, and Kraków. In Orawka, just to the north on the main road to Rabka, there is a wooden church from 1651, with polychrome murals from 1711, and a wooden chapel from 1728. From Jabłonka (where there is a *bufet* and food shop) there are 10 buses (on weekdays) to Zubryzca and Ochlipów, which after half an hour will drop you at the Orawski Ethnographic Park or Zubrycza skansen, an attractive park dotted with fine specimens of local architecture. Just to the south is a restaurant (of the beerhall tendency) and shop, and 15 minutes walk to the north the Ochlipów camp site with cabins and a shop open for two hours morning and evening. This is where the bus actually turns around, returning to Jabłonka, Nowy Targ or (at 1730) Kraków.

It is a two-day hike from the Przełęcz Krowiarki to Węgierska Gorka, south of Żywiec; the area from Rabka to Korbielów, including Babia Góra, is covered by the *Beskid Makowski* map, and from there to the west by the *Beskid Śląski i Żywiecki* map, both at 1:75,000.

Hiking Directions

1: Babia Góra

The pass is another 4km north of the camp site by road, although you can also follow green stripes west on a muddy track from just north of the skansen. From the layby at the pass (where there is the tomb of the chairman of the Kraków section of the Polish Academy, killed in an air crash in 1969) you should follow the red stripes to the left/west, up into spruce, turning left after 10 minutes and climbing steeply on a good path. The climb soon eases, and after 20 minutes you will emerge through dwarf pine on to the end of a ridge (Sokolica, 1,367m), to climb gently through bilberry bushes south-southwest, then west, for another 20 minutes to Kępa (1,521m), with cliffs to the right. The path swings left/southwest and then climbs gently west to another peak after 10 minutes; again the path swings left/southwest and then more steeply west on to more open moorland to a rocky peak after 15 minutes. It takes about 17 minutes more heading generally west-southwest across rougher ground to reach the rocky summit of Diablak (1,725m), where once again you find the Polish-Slovak border markers. From here there is a view deep into Slovakia and to the Tatras, often with spectacular cloud inversions.

Here you meet a path marked with green stripes following the border north to Mała Babia Góra (Little Babia Góra, or to the Slovaks Mala Babia Hora, 1,515m), and Hucisko rail station. Yellow stripes (brown on the map) mark a direct path to the Markowe Szczawiny hut, at the crossroads of almost all the paths to the north, but I continued to follow the red markings, starting westwards along the border with a steep descent on loose stones. Once on the level, after 10 minutes, the Slovak path to the left, marked in blue, is easier; after another 25 minutes, at the Brona pass (1,408m), the red markings turn right and drop on awkward stone steps, much worse than anything in the Tatras, to reach the Markowe Szczawiny hut (1,180m, a very pleasant lunch stop for me) in under 20 minutes.

From here paths marked in yellow, green and black head north to various points in Zawoja, and there's also a blue path directly back along the 1,100m contour to the Krowiarki pass. Continuing west, above the more obvious green route, the red path runs on the level along the side of a hill, with patches of trees killed by acid rain beginning to appear; after 35 minutes the red markings turn left as the yellow path continues towards Zawoja Widły, drops to a biggish stream after 5 minutes then climbs through a meadow to re-enter spruce and beech forest and after 12 minutes rejoin the green stripes (and Slovak blue stripes) from the left at border marker 87/3. It is unusual for a red striped path not to follow the main ridge throughout, which underlines the importance of the Markowe Szczawiny hut as a nodal point.

The paths drop and swing slightly to the right/north to leave the park after another 12 minutes, at the Jałowiecka pass (1,017m), with an A-frame shelter; they continue together for half an hour, rising and falling slightly in forest, to the point where the green stripes branch right/north towards Hucisko station and youth hostel (supposedly 3¾ hours away). The red stripes climb for 5 minutes and swing left, still following the very obvious border strip, with good views along it at times, and soon views to the right across a meadow. After 25 minutes of minor ups and downs (including Mędralowa, 1,169m), largely through spruce, the path and border turn sharp left, south of west, where a cart track continues ahead, and drop steeply for 3 minutes. Here they again turn left, while another path, not very well marked with green stripes, goes straight on to Przyborów (bus stop) and Jeleśnia (with a station, campsite and 'centre of folk art', apparently).

The path swings left to head southeast, again through beech and spruce, to turn right away from the border after 18 minutes, dropping southwest in spruce and then twice turning left on to forestry tracks, to rejoin the border in a meadow after 15 minutes; after a couple more minutes walking I turned right (at about 830m) to follow a muddy cart track down for 12 minutes to the Głuchaczki PTTK *Stacja Turystyca*, a farm with a very basic dormitory for hikers. A little further north you can find a parallel route, marked in black, passing through shepherds' settlements rather than the border forests, from Zawoja to Korbielów.

Returning to the border at the same point, the path continues steadily uphill through woods (with roe deer and capercaillie), reaching the summit of Jaworzyna (1,047m) in meadow after 25 minutes, then dropping for 20 minutes (with the border markers actually lost in the woods to the left) to meadows with scattered shepherds' huts. A Slovak path, marked in yellow, turns left into beechwood (to Sedlo Pod Beskydom, in fact meeting an old road in under 1km), while the red and blue markings continue ahead, climbing straight up and down (the drawback of following a border is that it goes over every hilltop) and after 15 minutes reaching Beskid Krzyżowski (923m) at border marker 98.

After dropping gently for 10 minutes you reach a junction where the red stripes continue along the border, past the former crossing point at the Glinne pass, south of Korbielów, and the Hala Miziowa hut to Węgierska Górka, continuing into the Beskid Śląski; I deviated to the right/north following yellow stripes to Korbielów. This crosses a meadow to a good log cabin and then winds through fields and down into mixed woods, following a path to the right of a sunken track (and ignoring an arrow to the right, which here means keep right on). After 30 minutes turn right on to a village lane, and at once left onto what soon turns into a tiny field path, going up to the right past two houses on the left, and then down to the main street of Korbielów in 15 minutes; the shops are not much good here, but there are 15 buses a day to Żywiec, with the 1629 continuing to Kraków.

2: The Beskid Żywiecki

Just to the right/north in Korbielów there is a map of local hiking routes

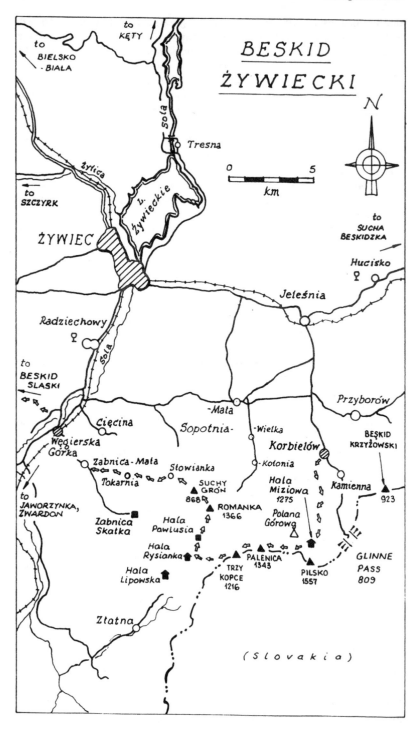

at a road junction; here I continued to follow the yellow stripes up the side road to the left/west, with blue stripes to the Przysłop pass (Prislop or the equivalent being a standard Slav name for any pass) forking right after 5 minutes at the end of the asphalt. Five minutes after this you pass a relatively good bivouac site with two A-frame shelters, fireplaces and a good stream, and after another 5 minutes you should turn left at an arrow and a no-smoking sign. After crossing the stream you have a good long steady slog uphill (into the Żywiecki Landscape Park) for 40 minutes, until the yellow stripes turn sharp left, with black stripes (not shown on the *Beskid Śląski i Żywiecki* map) continuing straight on to the Polana Górowa bivouac site. Five minutes after this the yellow path turns right on to a major forest ride, with a path marked with green stripes (also not marked on the map) coming in from Kamienna (south of Korbielów) at the upper terminal of a ropeway. The yellow stripes swing left into a meadow on a boardwalk, to reach the Hala Miziowa hut (at 1,275m) in a quarter of an hour.

From the hut, surrounded by ski-drags and protected peatbogs and with a good view back to Babia Góra, the green stripes (again not marked on the map) continue northwest via Polona Górowa to Sopotnia Wielka, about 1¾ hours away, where there are very infrequent buses; the yellow stripes continue south to Pilsko (1,557m) on the Slovak border. Continuing west on the red stripe path, it takes 10 minutes, only climbing slightly, to reach the border strip (and the blue Slovak path) again. The red Polish path deviates to the right around Munczolik (1,356m) after 13 minutes, but I stuck to the Slovak path, which although little-used is very good. There is a steep drop to the saddle of Hala Szczawina, and a steadier climb up to Palenica (border marker 112, 1,343m) after half an hour; just under 20 minutes further on, at Trzy Kopce (1,216m), the border and the Slovak path, together with a yellow path to Glinka, turn sharp left, while I continued ahead following the red stripes. These follow a more pleasant track, shadier than the border strip, dropping slightly for 15 minutes before climbing up the right-hand side of a meadow, joining a dirt road (and black markings from Złatna, under an hour to the southwest, with three buses a day) from the left, and climbing for another 15 minutes to the Hala Rysianka hut (1,290m), set high on the 1,322m hill of Rysianka with good views to the southeast. From here blue, green and yellow stripes continue to the Hala Lipowska hut, just 15 minutes west, and on to Złatna and Milówka, for buses to Żywiec.

The red stripes turn right and start off to the northeast under the end of a ski-drag, dropping down to go onto the grassy ridge of Hala Pawlusia (1,050m) where green stripes turn left to Skałka, for buses to Węgierska Górka; beyond this saddle (15 minutes from the hut) the red stripes continue along the left/west side of Romanka, but I deviated over the hill following yellow and blue stripes; this is a nature reserve, but has been badly affected (in small clearly-defined patches) by acid rain. In these patches there are now plentiful berries instead. The yellow path climbs steeply initially to a minor peak of 1,189m, and then more easily to the main peak of 1,366m some 30 minutes on. Here the yellow path ends, and I continued northwest following a blue path (from Sopotnia Mała, to the northeast); this actually starts by turning sharply to the left/southwest and dropping steeply for 7 minutes before turning northwards and continuing easily past a spring. After 13 minutes you should turn left on to a forestry road and then left again off this; again after a few minutes you join another forestry road, and keep right where it splits. After 5 minutes more the red route rejoins from the left, at the edge of a clearing just below Suchy Groń (868m).

Continuing on a cart track and heading into woods to the left of a power line, after 15 minutes the route reaches the Słowianka tourist station, with a small shop, where a black path drops southwestwards to the Zabnica Skałka bus stop (11 buses a day to Węgierska Górka or Żywiec). The cart track continues into woods, and after 5 minutes, at the foot of Skała (946m), the blue path heads on to the north to Bystra, while I turned left, still following the red stripes, climbing steeply but soon easing and then dropping gently; after 15 minutes turn right on to a farm track, and after 5 minutes left at a virtual T-junction to pass a new PTTK tourist hostel, the *Abrahamów*, in Tokarnia, a scattered settlement of delapidated houses and barns.

From here the route follows a cart track along the ridge to the northwest, with views to the Żywiec lake and the Beskid Śląski, dropping away to the left aiter 30 minutes, near a ski-drag above the village of Cięcina, and passing from meadows and hay fields into strip fields, with plenty of horse carts and ploughs. After 25 minutes go straight ahead at a junction with a rather confusingly marked tree in the middle, and then twice left to reach the road in Żabnica-Mała in 5 minutes: if starting here, you should take the lower track. It is another 25 minutes hiking along the road to the right/northwest to reach the main road and station in Węgierska Górka, by a war memorial at a pillbox where 11 died in 1939.

From the bus station, just to the right, there are 40 buses a day to Żywiec, and two (0617 and 0947) to Kraków; from the rail station, just behind, 16 trains a day run from Zwardoń (on the border) to Żywiec, with 10 continuing to Katowice. There is little accommodation here, other than basic camping places and trade union (FWP) rest homes — better to travel the 10km to **Żywiec**, which has an all-year youth hostel at ul Waryńskiego 4 and a PTTK hostel at ul Kościuszki 42, as well as a museum at ul Kościuszki 5, the 15th Century church of the Virgin, and a 19th Century Jewish cemetery. There is a Festival of Polish Mountain Folklore in early August, as well as a minor festival of wedding folklore in April. Jezioro Żywieckie (Lake Żywiec), just north of the town, is a reservoir with popular water sports facilities, mostly towards its other end, unfortunately, although easily reached by buses passing through Tresna; just a bit further north, also on the road to Kęty, are the smaller lakes of Porąbka-Kozubnik in the Beskid Maly, with similar facilities.

BESKID ŚLĄSKI

Although the Tatras are easily the most spectacular mountains in Poland, and Zakopane is the winter sports capital of the country, the Beskid Śląski or Silesian Beskids, southwest of Bielsko-Biała, are the most popular and developed mountain region, with in particular a great many trade union (FWP) rest homes and all-year youth hostels in the area. Szczyrk is Poland's second ski resort, with the country's most demanding run, and there are many cross-country routes in the hills around.

These are pleasant wooded sedimentary hills, typical of the Beskids, with many easy walks suitable for the city dwellers of Upper Silesia who flock here in the summer, as well as tougher longer hikes across the massif. They are divided into two main ranges, Barania Góra (1,220m), together with the higher Skrzyczne (1,257m), to the east of the Wisła (Vistula) valley, and Czantoria (995m) on the Moravian border to the west; the Barania Góra (Ram Mountain) is also divided northwest-southeast by the Żylica valley and a very scenic road linking Szczyrk to the Wisła valley via the Salmopolska pass.

Getting There

The main base for the area is **Bielsko-Biała**, a textile and car manufacturing town of 175,000, which still has the ruins of the 12th Century Old Bielsko castle and the 15th Century Sułkowski castle, with a district museum at ul Kosmonautów 16A, as well as 17th Century houses on ul Podcienie, an 18th Century market square, and a 19th Century Jewish cemetery. There is an International Puppet Theatre Festival here in May.

There are all categories of accommodation, from the 4* Orbis-Magura hotel at ul Greczki 93, the 3* Prezydent at ul Lenina 12, the 2* Pod Pocztą at ul 1 Maja 4A, and the Ondraszek inn on ul Armii Czerwonej, to the Pod Orlem PTTK hostel at ul Dzierżyńskiego 46c, the youth hostel (open all year) at ul Komorowicka 25, and the Pod Dębowcem camp site on ul Karbowa, on the main road east to Wadowice and Kraków. Tourist information is at ul Piastowska 2, one of the few street names not likely to have changed (tel 224 06). Bielsko-Biała can be reached by bus from most major towns in southern Poland, and by 30 trains a day from Katowice (to Zwardoń, on the Slovak border) and others on a minor east-west line from Wadowice to Cieszyn. There are various hiking routes from the suburbs into the hills, both the Beskid Śląski and the Beskid Mały to the east, but it is easier either to take a bus to Szczyrk (see below) or a chair-lift to Szyndzielnia from Olszówka-Górne (red stripe markings or municipal (MPK) buses 1/14/24), near the Dębowiec hut.

However most of the resorts are to the west in the Wisła valley, notably Ustron and Wisła, scattered settlements of rest homes and sanatoria, also with plenty of buses and trains from Katowice and Gliwice: see below for more details.

My route starts at Węgierska Górka, 10km south of Żywiec, as a

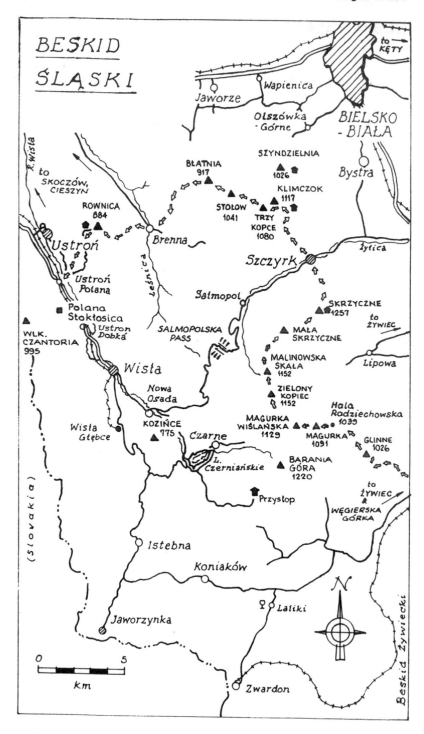

continuation of the hike from Babia Góra (previous section). The area is covered by the 1:75,000 tourist map of the *Beskid Śląski i Żywiecki*, available in most resorts and as far afield as Kraków. In addition there is a panoramic map of the *Beskid Śląski*, viewed from the north, by Edward Moskała, which is not good enough for hiking, and a 1:60,000 tourist map of the *Przedgórze Cieszyńskie*, only covering the area north of Szczyrk and Ustroń Polana.

Hiking Directions

1: Węgierska Górka to Szczyrk

From the bus station at Węgierska Górka you should follow the red stripes north along the road and turn left after the bridge over the Soła river, on to a lane past a small camping place, and then right on to a smaller lane which becomes a cart track. Fifteen minutes from the bridge you should again keep right and climb steadily in pine trees for 5 minutes to a meadow. From here the route, briefly unmarked, takes the first turning to the left, past small huts like allotment sheds, and (ignoring tracks up to the right) goes along a minor ridge and left up into woods, crossing a forestry track after 17 minutes and continuing to climb on a smaller stonier path. After 10 minutes this reaches another forestry track and climbs steadily past rather poor springs and into tall firs after another 17 minutes where it turns sharp left on to a track through a young mixed plantation with thick undergrowth.

After 5 minutes the route crosses another forestry track, forks right after another 5 minutes, and climbs to the Glinne ridge; after 15 minutes turn left on to an active forestry track and at once left again along a ridge with meadow and scattered spruce. After 10 minutes you reach the Hala Radziechowska meadow, with a junction with a path marked with blue stripes from the right, from Radziechowy, near Żywiec. The red stripes carry on in attractive mossy woodland to Magurka (1,091m) where green stripes come in from Twardorzeczka and Lipowa, also near Żywiec — a fairly unattractive route through a logging area.

The red stripes continue west along the ridge for 25 minutes, passing two sandstone outcrops (the second spoilt by a logging track past it); at Magurka Wiślańska (1,129m) it reaches a green stripe route from Istebna and Barania Góra to the left/southwest (with the Przysłop hut about 1½ hours away) to Szczyrk to the north. Here I turned right/north to follow the green stripes across a cleared area and soon into the woods again, going straight ahead where the main forestry track turns right; after 18 minutes yellow markings branch left to a tourist hostel at Nowa Osada, south of Wisła, and the path north then passes to the right of Zielony Kopiec (Green Mound, 1,152m) and crosses a forestry track at the next saddle. Twenty minutes from the junction of the last yellow path there is another, east to Lipowa, and also a blue path west as a short-cut to the red path to the Salmopolska pass. Another 10 minutes brings you to the summit of Malinowska Skała (Raspberry Rock, also 1,152m) and the start of the red path west.

From here the path continues north along a good ridge, passing ski-drags on Mała Skrzyczne after 35 minutes, and after another 10 minutes following an unmade road (from Hala Skrzyczeńska) for 8 minutes to the unlovely summit of Skrzyczne (1,257m), with a microwave tower, huts and a chair-lift. In addition to skiing, this is also a centre for paragliding (see page 85). Still following the green stripes, with a blue path from Lipowa, I continued north, going down to the right from the ski (and paragliding) piste across a cleared area, then zigging left to cross the piste and go under the chair-lift; after 13 minutes I turned right as the blue stripes went on ahead, and crossed the piste again. The path now follows a side ridge, turning right after 15 minutes and then turning left on to a forestry track; other tracks come in from the right, then the left, then the right again, before the path turns right on to an unmade road (ul Lesna) in Krupówka after 10 minutes. It takes 13 minutes to reach the main road to the Salmopolska pass, with the main junction of **Szczyrk** 50m below to the right/east.

This is a scattered resort, busiest in winter, which was graced with the title of town in 1974, although it hardly seems to deserve it. The bus station, tourist information, post office, youth hostel (at ul Sportowa 2, open all year), camp site (ul Kempingowa 4) and pizzeria are all further down ul Beskidzka, the road east to Bielsko-Biała and Żywiec; the best accommodation in town is at the PTTK *Dom Wycieczkowe* at ul Górska 7, the road northwest from the main junction. You could also try the pension Olimpija at ul Skosna 9, or private rooms from ul Mysliwska 13. No less than 38 buses a day run to Bielsko-Biała, just two to Żywiec, and 31 daily west to Salmopol, with five continuing to the Biały Krzyż (White Cross) stop, at the Salmopolska pass, although seemingly none continue west to Wisła. There are also buses more or less hourly (from Bielsko-Biała) to Szczyrk Biła, 2½km up ul Górska. The *Szlak Spacerowy*, marked with a diagonal green stripe, is a strolling route around town and should be ignored. There are rumours that Szczyrk will be rased if the area becomes a national park, but this will not happen soon.

2: Szczyrk to Ustroń

The green stripes follow ul Górska and continue past the Biła bus terminal and after 5 minutes the junction of a yellow path (barely visible on my map) left to the Karkoszczonka pass for the huts and ski areas above Szczyrk (there are cross-country ski markings on many of the paths in this area). The route continues as a forestry track, climbing northwards and and turning sharp left after 35 minutes at a crossroads where a blue path, from near the PTTK hostel, comes in from the right; it takes 8 minutes more to reach the ridge and emerge from the conifers, with the Klimczok hut (1,034m) visible about 300m to the left, although the sign tells you it's 10 minutes away. From here red, blue and green routes all go down to the east to Bystra Górne, for buses to Bielsko-Biała; the red route also continues past the hut and turns north to the

Szyndielnia hut and the chair-lift down to Bielsko-Biała, while, strangely, another red route runs southwest to the Salmopolska pass and Malinowska Skała.

From the hut I followed a short link marked in black down and then up by a ski-drag to the summit of Klimczok (1,117m), from where I followed yellow markings (from the Olszówka suburb of Bielsko-Biała) to the west, down into spruce and then beech, joined after 5 minutes by another short black link from Szyndelnia. It takes just 5 minutes more, either zigging right or taking a short-cut straight up, to the top of Trzy Kopce (1,080m), and then an easy 25 minutes in nice light wood, with a cross-country ski route, also marked in yellow, generally alongside, to Stołow (1,041m); from here the path drops in 15 minutes to a meadow with views of Brenna to the left, and 5 minutes later reaches an artificial mound on the summit of Błatnia (917m), just before the hut to the left. This is an interesting hut, with woodblock prints and pot plants, offering 17 varieties of tea, including Earl Grey, Ceylon and Assam, but the *bufet* closes at 1700, ridiculously early.

From here you can follow the yellow stripes north to Jaworze, or blue stripes to Wapienica, or red stripes to Nałęże and Meble, all for buses or trains to Bielsko-Biała or Cieszyn, or green stripes southwest to Brenna, for buses (mostly at 46 minutes after the hour) to Cieszyn, and a few to Bielsko-Biała. I took the green route to Brenna, forking right past the Wysoki Zamek (High Castle) student cabin, a very pleasant wooden hut, and (8 minutes from the PTTK hut) turning left at what seems to be a former war memorial (the High Castle), although this can be bypassed by a lower track to the left. The path goes down easily in woods, forking right after 15 minutes down a sunken track through a spruce plantation (largely unmarked), and after 10 minutes reaches a direct route to the centre of Brenna, with a tourist hostel and bivouac site as well as shops. The green markings continue steeply down in fields to the left of a sunken lane and then to the right of a wood, entering the village as ul Józefa Modzi, and after 15 minutes turn left and then right on to the main road just west of the centre of Brenna, a small village known for its traditional highlanders' huts.

To continue westwards to Ustroń, follow the green markings to the right across the bridge to the road junction up the Leśnica valley, at a war memorial and bus stop (at 390m). From here a path marked in black heads for the Salmopolska pass, and the green stripes follow the Leśnica road south for 10 minutes and then turn sharp right after a bridge, going through a no entry sign and a farmyard (like an English right of way rather than a typical Polish path), and turning sharp left in a farmyard after 10 minutes. The markings go straight up to the edge of the woods and straight on after 5 minutes where the lane turns left, turning right onto a forestry track after a couple of minutes, and after 5 minutes left on another track. The route twice forks right, reaching a minor ridge after 10 minutes and climbing more easily in beechwood to reach the main ridge in 15 minutes, with a blue route coming along the ridge from near Wisła to the south.

It takes 15 minutes walking northwest along the ridge to reach the Równica hut at 785m altitude; at Sunday lunchtime the car-park here was full of cars and the hut was full of trippers, and very few hikers — it might be more bearable overnight, but I doubt it. There is a road down to Ustroń, and a loop path marked in red; I followed this west along the road, turning left after 7 minutes, just after a trendy café, and went down into mixed deciduous woodland. The path crosses the road three times before following it and after 20 minutes passing a road right to the new resort complex of Jaszowiec. Again it takes a short cut to the left and crosses the road before rejoining it; after 15 minutes, beyond a camp site, you can turn right to cross the Wisła on a footbridge, or carry on to the ul Wczasowa (Holiday Rd) road bridge; the path becomes ul Popiernia, though hardly wide enough for a vehicle, ending up at the south end of Ustroń Polana station.

This lies between Ustroń to the north and Wisła to the south, and is the starting point for a red striped path (starting just to the north on ul Jodłowa or Firtree St) up Czantoria (995m) on the border to the southwest, and the chair-lift to Polana Stokłosica, half-way up Czantoria (starting by something called the *Maison de l'Europe*). Next to this is the only hotel proper in this valley, the Czantoria at ul 1 Maja 99 (tel 34 68). In addition to this there are a camp site, trade union rest homes and a motel on ul Baranowa (tel 25 46). In **Ustroń** there is an all-year youth hostel at Rynek 4 and a PTTK hostel at ul 22 Lipca 63 (tel 35 01). (The other Ustroń youth hostel (tel 22 40, also open all year!) is at Dobka, further south on the road along the right/east bank of the Wisła from the ul Wczasowa bridge, reached by 7 buses a day.)

The main road is very busy with buses, with 48 a day heading south to Wisła Uzdrowisko (by the rail station, just north of the centre), and as a rule two an hour (at 10 and 40 minutes past) to Cieszyn, and one an hour (at 10 past) to Skoczów, as well as eight a day to Katowice, three to Bielsko-Biała, and one a day to Gliwice (0838), Kraków (0858), Racibórz (1123), Częstochowa (1228) and Tychy (1918). From Wisła buses run south through Istebna (with the 19th Century house of Jana Kawulok open to visitors as a typical highlander's cottage) every hour both to Koniaków (with a display of its famous lace) and to Jaworzynka (a picturesque *górale* village right on the Moravian border, known for its old customs and dialect). There are also just two buses a day to Biały Krzyz (at the Salmopolska pass) for connections on to Szczyrk. Trains start at Wisła Głębce, well south of the centre, and run to many major towns on the far side of Poland.

Wisła itself is a small Protestant town surrounded by rest homes and ski-drags in the hills, with a pedestrianised promenade lined by waffle and *zapiekanka* stalls. The Beskid Regional Museum is at Plac B Hoffa, north of the centre, and tourist information is at ul Lipowa 4A. The main place to stay is the PTTK tourist hostel, at ul Czarne 3, and you may also be able to find rooms in rest homes such as those at ul 1 Maja 47 and 57; there is a good camp site 2½km south along ul Wyzwolenie, the road to Czarne and Szczyrk. Near a small reservoir at Czarne, quite a way further south, are a students' hostel, an all-year youth hostel, and trade union rest homes, reached by 12 buses a day. You can also find private rooms for yourself in most of these villages. In August there is a 'Week of Beskid Culture' here and in the villages to the south.

If heading towards Rybnik and Gliwice, to make your way towards Opole and Wrocław, you might choose to stop at what was the Hapsburg Teschen, a fine medieval town split by the River Olza and thus by Poland's border with the Czech Republic. The Polish half is now known as Cieszyn, and the Czech (or properly Moravian) half as Český Těšín; Cieszyn has a fine arcaded Rynek with 14th Century castle walls, a Gothic Catholic church and an 18th Century Protestant church, and the remains of an 11th Century rotunda on the Castle Hill above the town to the west. Accommodation can be found at the 2* Hotel Pod Jeleniem at Rynek 20 (tel 201 40), a 2* Motel at ul Bielska 200 (tel 226 41), and a 4* Orbis Motel, at ul Motelowa 93 (tel 204 51), with a camp site by the river at al Jana Łyska 12 (tel 208 33) and a summer youth hostel south of the centre at ul WOP 3 (tel 207 44). This is the major road crossing for traffic to Brno and Bratislava.

THE KATOWICE AREA

Katowice, the capital of Upper Silesia, has a population of 363,000, less than half that of Kraków, but it is just one of a cluster of only slightly smaller towns, such as Bytom (population 239,000), Gliwice (213,000), Tychy (182,000), and Rybnik (142,600), collectively known as the Upper Silesian Industrial District or GOP, with a total population of 2.5m. With 50 coal mines and many steel and other industrial plants, all totally out of date and uneconomic to run, it is still the industrial heart of Poland and its most polluted area. While Solidarity may have been born in the north, in 1981 it was most tenaciously defended in the south, with at least seven being killed at the Wujek colliery, and 1,300 miners occupying the Piast mine until December 27, two weeks after the declaration of martial law.

For the purposes of this book, the area is of most interest as a transit point between the eastern and western mountains, most typically the Tatras and the Karkonosze; by train you must go via Kraków to Wrocław, but you can avoid a return to Kraków by taking a bus from Zakopane, and many points further east, to Katowice or Gliwice and changing there. Equally, if you choose to visit Ojców or Oświęcim (Auschwitz) en route from Kraków to the west, you will have to change in Katowice for Wrocław.

Almost none of these towns are of any great interest or beauty, but they are well provided with parks, museums, concert halls; in particular the 600ha Silesian Park of Culture northwest of Katowice contains a skansen (the Upper Silesian Ethnographic Park), art gallery, botanical garden, zoo, planetarium, boating and swimming lakes, the 80,000-seat Silesia Stadium and an overhead railway through the park.

Katowice (briefly known as Stalinograd in the 1950s) itself houses the University of Silesia and the Silesian Philharmonic Orchestra, as well as the new Museum of Silesia at al Korfantego Wojciecha 2 (just northeast of the station), where there is also the local Orbis office (tel 597 881), while the Historical Museum of the City of Katowice is at ul Szafrańska 9 (southeast of the station). There is a 12,000-seat sports and entertainment hall in the shape of a flying saucer, and in September an International Students' Folklore Festival, which hardly bears thinking about — kebab-eating races and seminars on Australian soaps, perhaps.

The railway station is large and modern, with a PKS ticket office for buses, some of which stop outside and some 10 minutes to the north; many overnight trains pass through, so that even at three in the morning the station is pretty lively, while in the daytime long queues are normal for shops and ticket offices. Queue-barging is a highly developed art here. There are overnight trains to Prague, Vienna, Budapest, Leipzig and Berlin, and plenty of express trains from Warsaw and along the Szczecin-Wrocław-Kraków-Przemyśl line. More locally there are about 30 trains a day to Bielsko-Biała (18 going on to Żywiec), Częstochowa, Oświęcim, Kraków, and Tarnowskie Góry, and twice as many to Gliwice. There are a few trains direct to Zakopane, but generally for any destination in the mountains you should take a bus. The LOT office is at al Korfantego 36 (tel 580 684/585 891); although the airport at Balice is sometimes known as Kraków-Katowice International Airport (KRK), Katowice does in fact have its own airport (KTW) 33km north at Pyrzowice, with flights to Frankfurt as well as to Warsaw.

The local tourist information office is at ul Młyńska 11, on the north side of the station (tel 539 566/539 787), and the PTTK office at ul Dyrek Cyjna 10, northwest of the station (tel 539 352), for hiking information. There is a youth hostel, open all year, not too far east of the station at ul Graniczna 27A, and in summer you can get beds in a student hostel through Almatur at ul 3 Maja 7, just north of the station. In addition there are two 4* Orbis hotels, the Silesia at ul Piotra Skargi 2, and the Warsawa at al Roździeńskiego 16, as well as the 3* Katowice and Olimpijski, both on al Korfantego Wojciecha, and the 2* Centralny (ul Dworcowa 9), Sląski (ul Mariacka 15), all north of the station, the Polonia (ul Kochanowskiego, just south of the station leading towards the modern cathedral), Jantar (ul Nałkowskiej 10, out east in Katowice-Janów), and the Gościniec-Śląski Inn (a long way south on ul Kościuszki). There is also the camp site of Dolina Trzech Stawów (Valley of the Three Lakes) on ul Murckowska, to the southeast, and another at the *Stadion Śląski*, ul Dzierżyńskiego 10, Chorzów.

Gliwice, at the western end of the conurbation, may be a better transfer point between Zakopane or Wisła and the southwest, as the bus and train stations are immediately adjacent just north of the centre. This is a little-known city which houses the Silesian Polytechnic and Operetta and a regional museum, and just east in Zabrze a museum of coal mining at ul 3 Maja 19; a new steel-works was built here after the Second World War to double the national output, and the city now seems lively and prosperous. There is a surprisingly good bookshop, selling English magazines and Penguin books, on ul Zwycięstwa, the main road (lined with turn of the century architecture) from the station to the arcaded Rynek.

Gliwice is on the main line west from Katowice, and has eight trains a day (only three between 0700 and 2200, unfortunately) to Nysa, although as a rule it is best to go to Wrocław and change there for almost any destination in the southwest. There are six buses a day from Bielsko Biała, two from Kraków and one from Zakopane and as far east as Sanok, although it doesn't have the range of connections available at Katowice. Similarly LOT has an office at ul Zwycięstwa 56 (312 803), although the airport is at Katowice.

There is an all-year youth hostel here, at ul Belojanisa 60, and an Almatur student hostel at ul Wrocławska 8. The only hotel, the Myśliwski, is at ul Zwycięstwa 30.

Of the other towns, Bytom, between Katowice and Gliwice but away to the north, houses the Upper Silesian Museum (with historical, ethnographic and natural history collections) at Pl E Thaelmanna 2, and the Silesian Opera. There are two 2* hotels on ul 1 Maja, the Bristol at no 16, and the Pionier at no 19.

Tarnowskie Góry is north of Bytom and has a mining museum (just south at ul Jednosci Robotniczej 52) and boat trips through a drainage gallery, the *Sztolnia Czarnego Pstrąg* (Black Trout Adit), as well as a regional museum (Rynek 1) and 16th Century arcaded burghers' houses, including a wine cellar which claims to have entertained Goethe and three kings, although not together. In September there is a festival known as Miners' Days, with parades in pseudo-military costumes with brass bands.

Pszczyna, to the south beyond the industrial conurbation, just west of Oświęcim and only 20km short of Bielsko-Biała, has a largely 19th Century palace, now a magnificent Museum of Historical Interiors, with a splendid park behind. The town hall and Rynek (market place) are largely 18th Century; just south is the Goczałkowice-Zdrój resort at a reservoir, and to the northeast is the Jankowiecki Forest bison reserve. There is a summer-only youth hostel at ul S Batorego 26, towards the station, and the PTTK has an office on the Rynek and a hostel two blocks south.

WROCŁAW

Wrocław, the capital of Lower Silesia, is an interesting place: until the end of the Second World War it was the German city of Breslau, but when Poland was shifted bodily to the west it became Polish and absorbed the bulk of the Polish population of Lviv, which had been taken over by the Soviet Union. Seventy per cent of the city was destroyed in the last war, but it still boasts many churches, mostly Gothic brick hall churches, with baroque palaces and 80 bridges. Now it is Poland's fourth city, with a population of about 650,000, and the most attractive after Kraków. In addition to the ghosts of the Germans who used to live there, there are also those of the Jews who built Europe's largest synagogue here; before the Second World War there were 25,000 Jews here, and now there are virtually none.

It is thought that the first settlement here was founded in about the 6th Century AD, and the fortified Slav town of Wratislavia was established by the 10th Century in what is now Ostrów Tumski (Cathedral Island), with the Piast Duke Mieszko I establishing a bishopric there in 1000. Germans were increasingly moving into this area, settling on the opposite, southern, bank of the river Odra (Oder in German), and after its sacking by the Tatars building the new city of Breslau on a grid plan.

In 1335 the last Piast Duke died and Silesia was taken over by Bohemia; for two centuries the city grew in wealth until Bohemia was taken over by the Hapsburgs after the battle of Mohács in 1526; although the Catholic and Protestant religions had happily cohabited here after the Reformation, the city suffered terribly in the Thirty Years' War. In 1741 the city was captured by the army of Frederick II of Prussia and was increasingly Germanised, becoming the second city of Prussia and growing far more with the Industrial Revolution. In January 1945 as the Nazi armies retreated into Germany they declared the city a fortress, *Festung Breslau*, and held it until May 6, the eve of the final surrender of Germany.

The return of Wrocław to Poland, after six centuries under foreign rule, was traumatic for Germany, but three-quarters of its populace had already fled west, and the rest soon followed, to be replaced by displaced Poles from western Ukraine. The opera house reopened in September 1945, but it was to be many years before rebuilding was complete and the population reached its prewar level again. In 1990 the first commercial TV station in Poland opened here.

Getting There

Wrocław is the nodal point for all of southwestern Poland, in particular for the Karkonosze mountains. It lies on the main line from Świnoujście, Szczecin and Poznań to Katowice, Kraków and Przemyśl, and also on the line from Warsaw to Prague, Dresden, Munich and Frankfurt; as many trains travel overnight as by day, and towards Kraków trains leave at ten past the hour (Not every hour). There are daily through trains from Warsaw and Gdynia to the Karkonosze resorts, but you should take the opportunity to stop and see Wrocław. The main station is Wrocław Główny, a fine piece of Baronial architecture rather like Bristol Temple Meads station; this has all usual services, as well as an Orbis counter selling international bus tickets (which may be moved to the new bus station).

Buses do not travel very far afield, with none to Katowice or Kraków, a dozen to Jelenia Góra (for the Karkonosze), with just one (at 0840) continuing to Karpacz, and four (the last at 1310) to Szklarska Poręba, and about a dozen a day to Kłodzko (for the Góry Stołowe), with three (the last at 1320) to Paczkow and two to Złoty Stok. The bus station is now being moved from Plac Konstytucji 3 Maja, in front of the rail station, to ul Sucha, behind it.

There are also flights to Dusseldorf and Warsaw from the Strachowice airport, 10km west near the rail line to Legnica (bus 106): tickets from LOT at ul Piłsudskiego 36 (390 31/32).

Where to Stay

Wrocław has a full range of places to stay, from 4* Orbis hotels to hostels and camp sites. Of the Orbis hotels, the most expensive and luxurious is the Wrocław (ul Powstańców Śląskich 7, tel 614 641/9, 614 651/9), a large 12-storey block west of the station, but the 3* Monopol (ul Modrzejewskiej 2, tel 370 41), just south of the Rynek, is more attractive and atmospheric, and cheaper. The Panorama is ugly but convenient, at Plac Dominikański 8 (tel 443 681/9), not far east of the Rynek, while the Novotel, a long way south at ul Wyścigowa 35 (tel 675 051/9), is ugly and inconvenient except for drivers; Orbis also has a 3* motel, looking like a set of portakabins, way out west at ul Lotnicza (Airport Rd) 151 (tel 518 153). New and expensive private hotels include the Aspol (ul Mińska 38, tel 574 911), Savoy (Pl Kościuszki 19, tel 403 219), and Zaułek (ul Odrzańska 18A, tel 402 945).

Cheaper hotels can mostly be found near the station, such as the Grand (ul Piłsudskiego 100, tel 360 71) and, going west, the Piast at no 98 (probably the cheapest, tel 300 33), the Europejski at no 88 (tel 310 71), and the Polonia at no 66 (tel 310 21); the Odra is nearby at ul Stawowa 13. The sport hotel is the Śląsk on ul Oporowska, in Gajowice, 3km southwest (tel 611 611/612 061).

There is a summer student hostel at ul Drukarska 52 (south of the station), open from July 1 to September 15 in 1991 (tel 674 821): check with Almatur at ul Kościuszki 34 (tel 444 728) for current details. The PTTK has a Stacja Turystyczna at ul Szajnochy 11, southwest of Plac Solny, which is basically a very simple youth hostel (tel 443 073); official PTSM youth hostels (both open all year) are at ul Kołłątaja 20, close to the station, and at ul Kiełczowska 43, 1km from the Psie Pole suburban rail station to the northeast, reached by bus N from the main station. The Nauczycielski teachers' hostel is at ul Nauczycielska 2, east of the cathedral (tel 229 268). Private rooms can be booked at the Odra tourist office at ul Piłsudskiego 98 (tel 444 101).

The main camp site is at Al Paderewskiego 35 (tel 484 651), by the Olympic stadium to the northeast of town, reached by trams 9, 12, 16 and 17. There is another at ul Na Grobli 16 (tel 344 42), by the Odra east of the centre.

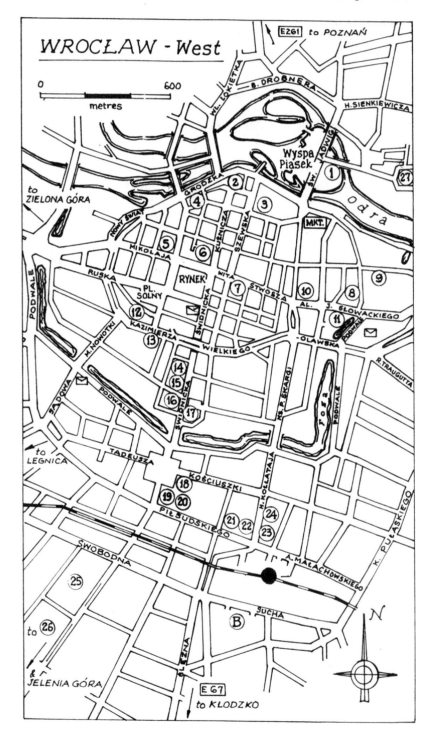

WROCŁAW - West

0   600

metres

to POZNAŃ

E261

WŁ. ŁOKIETKA

B. DROBNERA

H.SIENKIEWICZA

to
ZIELONA GÓRA

Wyspa
Piasek

ŚW. JADWIGI

Odra

27

GRODZKA

KUŹNICZA

SZEWSKA

MKT.

NOWY ŚWIAT

MIKOŁAJA

RUSKA

RYNEK

WITA STWOSZA

AL. J. SŁOWACKIEGO

PL.
SOLNY

PODWALE

M.NOWOTKI

KAZIMIERZA

ŚWIDNICKA

WIELKIEGO

OŁAWSKA

PODWALE

SĄDOWA

PODWALE

ŚWIDNICKA

KS. P. SKARGI

FOSA

PODWALE

R.TRAUGUTTA

to
LEGNICA

TADEUSZA

KOŚCIUSZKI

M.KOŁŁATAJA

PIŁSUDSKIEGO

SWOBODNA

A.MAŁACHOWSKIEGO

K. PUŁASKIEGO

ŚLĘZNA

SUCHA

to

JELENIA GÓRA

E 67

to KŁODZKO

N

WROCŁAW - Key

West

1. Church of St. MARY of the SANDS
2. COLLEGIUM MAXIMUM (University)
   and Church of the HOLY NAME of JESUS
3. Church of St. MATTHEW and OSSOLIŃSKI LIBRARY
4. Hotel **ZAVŁEK**
5. Church of St. ELIZABETH
6. TOURIST INFORMATION
7. Church of St. MARY MAGDALENE
8. ARCHITECTURAL MUSEUM
9. **RACŁAWICE PANORAMA**
10. Church of St. ADALBERT
11. Hotel PANORAMA
12. PTTK Tourist Station
13. ARCHAEOLOGY & ETHNOGRAPHIC MUSEUM
14. Church of St. DOROTHY
15. Hotel MONOPOL
16. OPERA
17. Church of CORPUS CHRISTI
18. Hotel SAVOY
19. ORBIS
20. Hotel POLONIA
21. Hotel EUROPEJSKI
22. Hotel PIAST
23. Hotel GRAND
24. YOUTH HOSTEL
25. Hotel WROCŁAW
26. NOVOTEL

East

27. Church of the HOLY CROSS
28. CATHEDRAL
29. NATIONAL MUSEUM
30. UNIVERSITY
31. TEACHERS' HOSTEL
32. Camping 'SLEŻA'
33. PEOPLE'S HALL
34. OLYMPIC STADIUM CAMPSITE

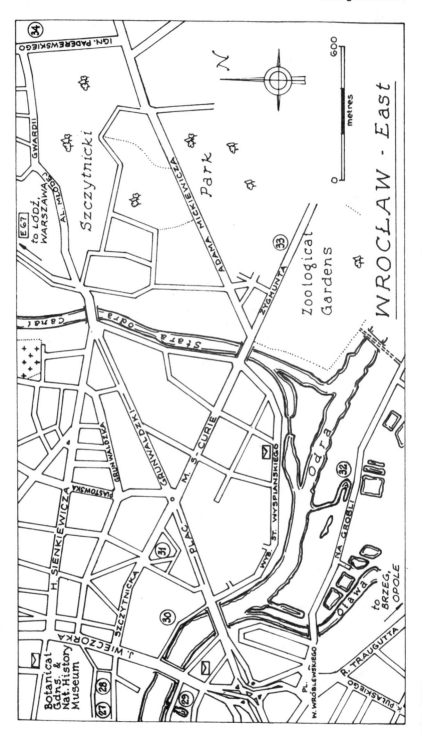

Where to Eat

There are not many good restaurants in Wrocław, outside the Orbis hotels, but more traditional milk bars survive here than in most other towns, particularly near the station on the corners of ul Gwarna and ul Stawowa with ul Piłsudskiego. Other bars and restaurants are around the Rynek, notably in the Dwór Wazów (Waza Court) at Rynek 5, and the Ratuszowa and Piwnica Świdnicka in the old town hall basement.

What to See

The core of the old town, centred on the Rynek, is an attractive mix of churches and baroque townhouses, with enough newer buildings (unattractive in themselves) to avoid the sterile museum feel of some towns that have been painstakingly reconstructed in their 19th Century state. As in cities like Dublin and Bath there is much pleasure to be had wandering around in the evening, looking through windows at fine interiors and ceilings. North of the river is Ostrów Tumski, an ecclesiastical enclave with parks and more churches.

Coming from the station up ul Świdnicka you pass through the very formal Plac Kościuszki to cross a backwater of the Odra and reach the Corpus Christi church (opposite the opera), with a good gabled brickwork exterior and simple Gothic vaulting. Just north of the opera is St Dorothy's (the church of SS Stanisław, Dorotea and Wacław), with an even plainer brick exterior, and a slightly more baroquified interior, also with a plain 14th Century Gothic vault.

Continuing north by the underpass under the inner ringroad (ul Kazimierza Wielkiego, with the Archeological and Ethnographic Museums to the left/west at no 34), the Rynek or market place is one of the biggest in Poland, with a mixture of Gothic, Renaissance and baroque buildings (with a great variety of gable ends), and a large block of buildings in the middle to break up its great expanse, notably the Ratusz or Town Hall. This features on the covers of all the tourist leaflets of Wrocław, and is a splendid blend of various styles, with Germanic brick Gothic (with an astronomical clock from 1580) on the eastern façade, highly decorated Renaissance stonework on the southern side, and simpler early Gothic to the north, while the west side, otherwise plain, has a baroque doorway, now the entrance to the town's Historical Museum (closed on Mondays and Tuesdays, free on Wednesdays), which has some superb interiors even if you can't understand the displays. Unfortunately the Gothic belfry has a very tinny chime. There is also a museum of medal making (Muzeum Sztuki Medalierskiej) at Rynek 6.

To the southwest of the Rynek is the smaller Plac Solny, once a salt market, as its name implies, and now a flower market, surrounded by largely 19th Century buildings such as the former Stock Exchange at no 16 (by Langhans, 1824). At the northwestern corner of the Rynek is a narrow gateway between two eccentric houses known as Jaś i Małgosia (usually translated as Hansel and Gretel), leading to the church of St

Elizabeth (Św Elżbiety), the former garrison church now being rebuilt
after a fire. Jaś and Małgosia are also the names of two restored historic
trams which rattle around the town in the summer.

A block east of the Rynek is the 14th Century church of St Mary
Magdalene, with a 12th Century Romanesque portal from the former
Benedictine abbey of Ołbin, to the north of the city. Further east along
ul Wita Stwosza on Plac Dominikański is the former Dominican church
of St Adalbert (Św Wojciecha), built in the 13th Century with later
chapels. A bit further east at ul Bernardyńska 5 is the former Bernardine
monastery, now housing the Museum of Architecture and
Reconstruction, actually a collection of sculptures and photos of the
buildings destroyed in the war.

Just to the northeast, at ul Purkyniego 11, is the Racławice Panorama,
immensely popular with Polish tourists but not quite as gripping for
foreigners, although it can cast some light on the Polish relationship with
the past. It is a 120m long painting of the battle of Racławice (northeast
of Kraków), where Kościuszko's peasant militia beat a Russian army in
1794, leading eventually to the final partition of Poland; the painting was
commissioned to mark the centenary of the battle, and was displayed in
Lviv until the Second World War. It was brought to Wrocław in 1946,
but until the Solidarity period it was deemed tactful not to brag about a
victory over Russia; it was finally put on show in 1985, in a purpose-
built rotunda. It is open 0800-1900 (except Mondays) with each
showing lasting about 45 minutes: ask to hear the English-language tape
of the commentary.

On the left/south bank of the Odra, a bit further east and ever closer
to the camp sites, is the National Museum (Muzeum Narodowe) at Plac
Powstańców Warszawy 5, covered by the same ticket as the Panorama,
with a great collection of medieval Silesian sculpture, in wood and stone,
and later Polish and European art. Following the river back to the west,
overlooking the next bridge (to Wyspa Piasek and Ostrów Tumski) is the
market hall (1908), with a clock tower like a Victorian railway station;
behind it at ul Krasińskiego 1 is the Post Office Museum, and opposite
it the brick church of St Vincent, closed for restoration. Behind it to the
west are the baroque buildings of the Franciscan monastery, now used
by the university, the Gothic church of St Matthew on ul Szewska, and
the Ossoliński Library, built as a hospital but now housing the books
collected by the Ossoliński family and brought from Lviv with the
Panorama. Immediately west is the Church of the Holy Name of Jesus,
built at the end of the 17th Century in typical Jesuit style, with *trompe
l'oeil* frescoes in the vault; abutting the church is the magnificent
Collegium Maximum, built for the Jesuit Academy in 1742 and now the
main building of the university. The main entrance and staircase lead to
the *Aula* or hall, a splendid baroque interior, open from 1000 to 1500
unless required for university ceremonies.

From here you should return east along the river to cross to Wyspa
Piasek (Sand Island), part park, part former Augustinian monastery: the
main sight here is the church of St Mary of the Sands (NMP na Piasku),

perhaps the finest in Wrocław. Although plain on the outside, it has superb soaring ribbed vaulting (1334-90) and, in the south aisle, a Romanesque tympanum from the original 12th Century church on this site. Opposite it to the west is the smaller late 17th Century church of St Anne, now used by the Orthodox believers from Lviv.

The small bridge next to St Mary of the Sands leads you to Ostrów Tumski, the ecclesiastical centre of Silesia, alive with priests and nuns: immediately on your left is the 15th Century church of SS Peter and Paul, with a fine vault with one central pillar. Next on the left is the massive church of the Holy Cross (Św Krzyża), in fact built on top of the church of St Bartholomew, built as the crypt of the Piast dynasty and now used by Uniates. Further east, down the peaceful ul Katedralna, is the cathedral of St John the Baptist, a large Gothic basilica with a grubby red brick exterior and two sawn-off towers. This was badly damaged in 1945 and rebuilt by 1951, but it remains a fairly gloomy building, although there are three fine chapels off the baptistery, behind the high altar (from the south side the baroque chapel of St Elizabeth, the Gothic Lady Chapel, and the baroque chapel of the Holy Sacrament by Fischer von Erlach) and a funerary monument from 1620 in the porch, with hermaphroditic figures in big skirts. On the north side of the cathedral is the tiny church of St Giles (Św Idziego), the only one in Wrocław to predate the 13th Century Tatar onslaught, with a fine Romanesque portal. Also here, at ul Kanonia 12, is the Archdiocesan Museum, which has much good Silesian religious art.

Immediately to the north are the Botanical Gardens (open daily), with the Natural History Museum to their north side on ul Sienkiewicza; about 2km to the east along ul Szczytnicka, beyond the Zwierzyniecki bridge (where you can take boat trips), are the Hala Ludowa (People's Hall, a huge domed hall built in 1913 by Max Berg to celebrate the centenary of Napoleon's defeat), and perhaps Poland's best zoo opposite on ul Zygmunta. North of the hall, along ul A Mickiewicza, is the Park Szczytnicki, a large area of woods with a Japanese garden and temple, and at its far end the Olympic stadium (not that it was ever used for the Olympics) and camp site.

On the other side of town, beyond the new bus station at ul Ślęzna 113, is the Jewish cemetery of 1856 (now the Museum of Funerary Art), containing about 1,200 tombstones, including two from 1177 and 1203, and that of Friedrich Lassalle (or Lasal), friend of Marx and Engels and founder of the first German workers' party.

To the east of Wrocław are two water pumping stations with superb 19th Century steam engines, which it is hoped to open soon as monuments of industrial archeology.

Practical information

Tourist information can be obtained at ul Kazimierza Wielkiego 39 (tel 443 111) and at the PTTK at Rynek 38 (tel 383 31), as well as at Orbis at Rynek 29 (tel 326 65/347 80), while the Orbis office at ul

Piłsudskiego 62 (tel 387 45) sells international tickets. Maps and guides can be found at the Księgarnia Turystyczna (Tourist Bookshop) at ul Świdnicka 19, just south of Rynek.

The main post office is at ul Z Krasińskiego 1, to the east behind Plac Dominikański, but more convenient offices are situated on Rynek and at the station.

Wrocław was for many years famous as the base of Jerzy Grotowski's Laboratory Theatre, but this has now mutated into a Theatrical Research Centre, not exactly dry as dust but less vital than its predecessor; this is in the centre of the Rynek, down an alley at Rynek Ratusz 27. Henryk Tomaszewski, who worked with Grotowski, later founded his own pantomine company, based (when in town) at the Teatr Polski, ul G Zapolskiej 3, west of the station; other theatres are the Współczesny, at ul Rzeźnicza 12, the Kameralny at ul Świdnicka 28, and the Kalambur, at ul Kuźnicza 29A. There is also a mime theatre, perhaps best for non-Polish speakers, at Al Dębowa 16.

The opera house (by Langhans, 1841) is at ul Świdnicka 35, and the Philharmonic concert hall at ul Piłsudskiego 19.

Festivals

Wrocław is known for three major festivals, Jazz on the Odra in March, a Festival of Polish Contemporary Drama in May/June, and *Wratislavia Cantans*, the International Oratorio-Cantata Festival in the first half of September.

Excursions

To the southwest, south of the road to Świdnica, is the isolated mountain of Ślęża (718m), topped by the remains of a pagan sanctaury, as well as one of eastern Europe's ubiquitous TV towers, and with various peculiar granite sculptures scattered over its slopes. The starting point is Sobótka, on the rail and bus routes to Świdnica, with various hostels and a hotel, and there are several marked hiking routes up the mountain, of which the most direct is marked in yellow and takes about an hour.

Thirteen kilometres beyond Świdnica (an attractive place itself, with a baroque Rynek and Gothic and baroque churches), heading for Jelenia Góra (and avoiding the ecological hell-hole of Wałbrzych), is Ksiąz, with a large and impressive castle, in fact a rather unco-ordinated mixture of styles from 13th Century to Nazi (a bunker built below the main courtyard), but with some fine interiors, notably the baroque Maximilian Hall. You can also visit the terraced gardens and a stud farm, as well as staying at a hotel in a wing of the complex.

Twenty-five kilometres north of Wrocław, on the main road to Poznań, is the small town of Trzebnica, known for its Cistercian convent founded in 1202 by Duke Henry the Bearded and his wife Saint Hedwig (Jadwiga in Polish): the exterior is early Gothic brickwork, with a fine carved portal, but the interior is largely baroque, apart from the superb Gothic chapel of Św Jadwiga, containing her tomb. There are a camp site and motel here, but most travellers will base themselves in Wrocław.

Forty kilometres southeast of Wrocław, on the main rail line to Katowice, is the town of Brzeg, with a largely Renaissance castle containing the museum of the Silesian Piast Dukes, whose effective capital this was. There are some attractive churches in the old town, mostly rebuilt after 1945, and one hotel and a summer youth hostel.

Finally, 50km south of Wrocław on a minor road to Paczków, and an even more minor rail line, there is Henryków, site of a Cistercian monastery, also founded in 1225 by Duke Henry the Bearded, famous as the origin of the *Liber Enricianus*, which contained the earliest surviving sentence written in Polish. The church is largely Gothic, although with baroque trappings, and is surrounded with the baroque buildings of the former monastery.

THE GÓRY ZŁOTE AND THE GÓRY STOŁOWE

This enclave in the Sudeten mountains south of Wrocław, surrounded on three sides by the frontier of the Czech Republic, is a pleasant region of low rocky mountains and small spas, very different to the flat plains of Upper Silesia, the industrial areas of both Upper and Lower Silesia, and the Karkonosze mountains, now dominated by tourism. The most interesting area is the Góry Stołowe (Table Mountains), in fact a table-like plateau with various smaller tables rising from it, the eroded remnants of higher sandstone mountains, which have now left all kinds of fantastic rock formations and erratic boulders hidden in the woods. This will soon be established as a national park, but it is already popular with student groups and other visitors. The fauna is fairly standard, although without bears or wolves, and the flora is a mix of beech, spruce, pine, rowan, sycamore and birchwood, with flowers such as *Colchium autumnale, Trollius europaeus, Dianthus praecox, Lilium martagon* and *Convallaria maialis*.

Getting There

The centre for the area is **Kłodzko**, strategically placed with two large fortresses dominating the Nysa Kłodzka river and the trade routes between Poland and Bohemia; it is still a very attractive town, with a fine Gothic bridge decorated with baroque statues in the manner of the Charles Bridge in Prague, a Gothic parish church and much Gothic and baroque architecture spread higgledy-piggledy on the slopes of the castle hill. You can also visit the castle and a network of defensive tunnels, both under the castle and under the town itself. However most holiday-makers head straight for the neighbouring spas, so that Kłodzko itself has a fairly low profile, with only a few hotels, notably the Astoria, by the rail (Kłodzko Miasto) and bus stations at Plac Jedności 1 (tel 3035),

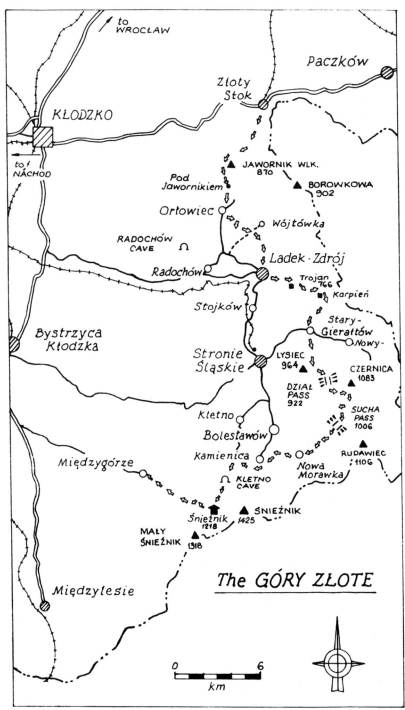

The GÓRY ZŁOTE

and the Nad Młynówka at ul Daszyńskiego 16 (tel 2563), and a summer-only youth hostel at ul Gagarina 5 (tel 3174). Orbis are at ul Grottgera 1 (tel 2775/3888). Although there are trains from Wrocław and elsewhere, this is one of the places that are most easily reached by bus, from Wrocław, Opole, Nysa or Jelenia Góra. From here there is a spider's-web of local buses and trains west to the spas such as Kudowa-Zdrój south of the Góry Stołowe, southeast to Lądek-Zdrój and Stronie-Śląskie, and east to Złoty Stok and Paczków.

Although most people will only be interested in the Góry Stołowe, I started with a two-day hike from Złoty Stok (Golden Slope), 19km east of Kłodzko, south to Międzygórze, and then took a bus to Duszniki-Zdrój for a separate long day's hike in the Góry Stołowe; although the easiest approach is by bus from Wrocław via Kłodzko, I in fact came from Nysa via **Paczków**, 10km east of Złoty Stok. This is a tiny town in a virtually complete ring of medieval walls, with the massively fortified 14th Century parish church of St John; there is a youth hostel, open all year, inside the walls at ul Kołłątaja 9 (tel 6441), one hotel, the Zacisze, just east at ul Wojska Polskiego 31 (tel 6277), and a camp site to the southwest by the stadium at ul Jagiellońska 8 (tel 6509). From the bus station (to the northeast by ul E Plater) there are nine buses a day to Kłodzko, at least 30 on weekdays to Nysa (by various routes), four to Opole (for main-line trains) and one or two to Częstochowa, Jelenia Góra, Katowice, Kraków and Wrocław, as well as 20 to Ząkowice (for buses from Kłodzko to Wrocław) — not bad for so tiny a place tucked away down by the border. There are a few trains daily between Nysa and Kłodzko, passing through the station several kilometres north (with a bus link very roughly hourly).

Hiking Directions

The whole area from Paczków to Kudowa-Zdrój is covered by a 1:90,000 tourist map of the *Ziemia Kłodzka*, which is quite good enough for hiking, although there are changes and inaccuracies, mentioned below; there are also 1:60,000 maps of the *Góry Bardzkie i Złote*, covering the area east of Kłodzko, and the *Góry Stołowe*, to the west.

1: The Góry Złote

This first route through the Góry Złote (Golden Mountains), the Góry Bialskie and the Snieżnika Massif is easy and pleasant, with the odd old church, spa and ruined castle along the way, and Poland's finest cave.

Złoty Stok has little to detain you, although it does have a youth hostel (unusually open from July 1 to August 31) in the school at ul Kościuszki 12, as well as a trade union rest home; from the bus-stop on Plac A Mickiewicza, the main crossroads, hiking routes marked in black, green and red all head south on ul 1 Maja to the Rynek where the black route turns right to go more or less directly across country to Bystrzyca Kłodzka, a good day's walk away. The other routes pass a Renaissance

church door, now part of a sport club, and head south up a paved path
and fork about 5 minutes from the main road. I took the red route left,
while the green markings carried straight on on a similar but higher route;
already there is a view over the Silesian plain, with the border just to the
east across a small valley.

Turning left off the road at once, the path soon joins another road from
the right, passing a quarry and a small mine; after about 15 minutes the
asphalt ends, continuing as gravel for 30 minutes (keeping right at two
junctions). Now the path climbs more steeply, crossing one forestry
track, then turning right on to another before arriving after 12 minutes
at an A-frame hut at a six-way junction (with the road just below to the
west): here the green markings reappear, and the red and green routes
continue south together in the usual mix of beech and spruce, around
Jawornik (870m) just to the east. Ignore the odd forestry markers, but
take advantage of the great raspberries along this stretch (in September).
After 30 minutes, you will drop on a more active forestry track to
another A-frame forester's shelter at Pod Jawornikiem, where the green
markings carry on ahead to the Radochów cave, bivouac site, and rail
station, just west of Lądek-Zdrój, and the red markings turn left and very
soon right on to a path along a side ridge.

This drops easily for 20 minutes to the attractive church of Orłowiec
(c1600, with the normal baroque overlay): here another path marked in
green goes left/northeast up the valley to turn south along the border,
but I headed right on the road, with a small shop but virtually no houses
(and three buses a day to Lądek-Zdrój), turning left (still following red
markings) after 15 minutes, just before the road to Złoty Stok. This is a
forestry track, rising gently and turning right on a left bend after 17
minutes to drop for 7 minutes through fields and newish houses (with
milk churns everywhere, like the West Country 30 years ago) to an
asphalt track: the baroque church of Wójtówka is just up to the left here.
The route turns right to cross the bridge, then left to take a path through
the woods for 5 minutes before turning right on to a forestry track,
climbing and forking right after 15 minutes.

After 5 minutes the route turns right onto a farm track through fields,
and then left on to asphalt on ul Wiosenna, leading to ul Widok, the road
to Złoty Stok, 17km north. **Lądek-Zdrój** is the oldest spa of the area,
dating from the 13th Century, and, as Bad Landeck, well known in the
19th Century: the old centre is just to the right/west over a fine 16th
Century bridge, with a baroque cross and a town hall (with an annoying
electronic chime) in an arcaded Rynek with Bohemian-style gables. The
spa area, a mixture of neoclassical and postwar buildings, is to the left,
with a PTTK office at ul Kościuszki 36 (tel 255) which may be able to
find you a room in one of the rest homes here; the only alternative is the
youth hostel (open all year) in Stojków, 3km south, or of course camping
wild. There is a minibus service to link the two halves of the town, and
buses run hourly between Stronie-Śląskie and Kłodzko; there are also
some trains on the same route, calling at a station 2km west of the old
town (on the red stripe route).

My route now follows blue stripes, part of the Eisenach to Budapest *Szlak EB*, along ul Pstrowskiego and ul Kościuszki, along the left bank of the Biała Lądecka; after 15 minutes it turns left past the spa buildings and up the dead-end of ul Lesna to the spa park, and again turns left after 8 minutes up a path into the woods. The ground becomes remarkably rocky, with the big outcrop of Trojan (766m) after half an hour, with a viewing platform and delapidated shelter; the path drops slightly, passing two more tall outcrops, and after 10 minutes an A-frame hut at a seven-way junction, with the green path along the border from Orłowiec. The route crosses straight across an asphalt track here, and goes up in 10 minutes to the overgrown medieval ruins of Karpień castle, covered in grass and nettles and largely lost in the trees.

Five minutes below the ruins the green route turns left on to a good forestry track, and the blue route turns right, turning left on to a path after 15 minutes and right immediately after, both unsigned, and then a few minutes later right on to an almost unused asphalt road. After 5 minutes the blue markings swing left on a track, and after 15 minutes you should turn right over a gate just before a farm, then left over a fence to the road in Stary Gierałtów. Five minutes to the left/east, after a bus stop (with six buses a day), turn right over the bridge and straight on up a track, rather than following the road east to the 18th Century church as shown on the map. A new bridge is being built to the east, so you may have to come back to the old route.

The path climbs for 10 minutes between fields and woods into the Góry Bialskie before going into woods and crossing a major gravel forestry road after 20 minutes more; it turns left on to a minor forestry track after a few minutes and climbs for 10 minutes to the ridge east of Lysiec (964m). It drops through a logged area for 5 minutes to turn right, rejoining the route as shown on the map, on another almost unused asphalt road; after climbing for 5 minutes this soon turns right, where an unmade track goes straight ahead, to an A-frame shelter at the Dział pass (922m), where brown markings come from Stronie Śląskie to the right/west. The blue markings keep left on the asphalt as another unmade track goes straight ahead, curving left after 5 minutes and climbing steadily for 20 minutes to the junction with a red path (shown as black on the map) from Nowy Gierałtów to the left. The road drops easily for 15 minutes to the central saddle of this massif, and turns left at a crossroads, to climb for 10 minutes to the Sucha pass (1,006m), just after an unmade road left down to Bielice, where there is a bivouac site.

Here, where the trees are cleared to provide a view, there are another A-frame shelter, a good map, and a fire tower; the blue markings continue ahead along an unmade road dropping down a valley for 30 minutes to a bivouac site and then turning left just beyond this at a T-junction by a bridge, where the right turn leads to another camping place in Nowa Morava and the bus stop in Bolesławów. The blue route soon turns right to continue west down the valley parallel to the road to Bolesławów (again not as on the map), and after 20 minutes turns left

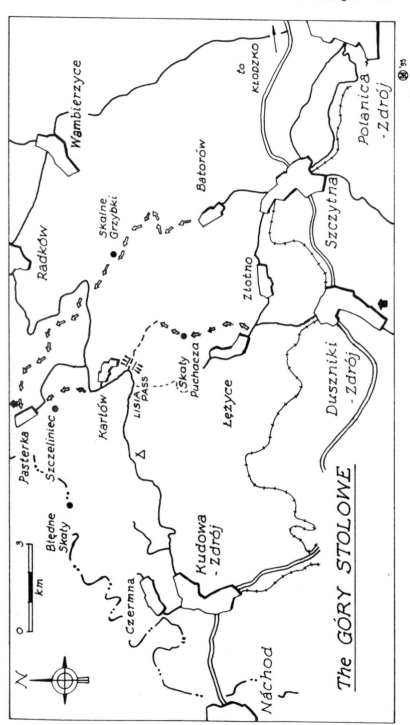

The GÓRY STOŁOWE

at a T-junction to climb steadily for 10 minutes before turning left up a path. This reaches a ridge in 5 minutes, crossing over a forestry track and going straight ahead on to another, turning 90° right at a stream after 5 minutes. It goes down a stoney track for 5 minutes more to an asphalt road, where it turns left and soon forks right up a lane after a few minutes to climb up behind the forestry headquarters south of Kamienica, with views north over the scattered houses of Kamienica, to fork left twice after 25 minutes on the saddle south of Młyńsko. After 4 minutes on this gravel track you reach another crossroads, where the blue markings turn left/south to head directly for the Snieznik hut; however to visit the Kletno cave you should turn right and after 1 minute left on to a lane, soon forking right and dropping easily for 12 minutes to join a route marked with yellow stripes (shown as brown on the map), just above a quarry. This follows a path on the right bank of the stream for 5 minutes to reach the cave entrance.

This is the most beautiful cave in Poland, another of the many Bear Caves (Jaskinia Niedźwiedzia) of eastern Europe, due to the bones of the now-extinct cave bear (*Ursus spelaeus*) found in it; it would be as appropriate to call it the bats' cave, as it is home to several rare species such as the grey long-eared bat *Plecotus austriacus*, the greater mouse-eared bat *Myotis myotis*, the whiskered bat *M mystacinus*, and Daubenton's bat *M daubentoni*, as well as spiders, moths and shrimps. It was discovered by chance in 1966, during marble quarrying operations, and the upper part opened in 1976 to tourists, who enter at Kletno III, with a big shelter incorporating a museum and café, and after 40 minutes emerge just upstream at Kletno IV, having passed through some fine displays of cave pearls, stalactites and stalagmites. There is a youth hostel, open all year, at the north end of the hamlet of Kletno, to the north almost in Bolesławów, and there are very rare buses to Kletno; in any case Stronie Śląskie is about 7km from the cave by the yellow path (slightly further by road), for more frequent buses and trains.

Continuing south, the path crosses to the left bank of the stream and heads south up a gravel road, twice taking a short-cut where the road takes a hairpin bend to the right, and then reaching the ridge in 40 minutes where a red route from Lądek-Zdrój comes in from the right on a forestry track, just before a crossroads where blue stripes turn west on another track to Międzygórze. From here the yellow path, and black and green ski routes, follow the road south for 10 minutes more to the Śnieżnik hut at 1,218m, just above the tree line close to the border between the peaks of Śnieżnik (1,425m) and Mały Śnieżnik (1,318m). Even though there is a wind generator, there was no electricity (or hot water) when I stopped here, but there was a good fire and a good atmosphere.

From here I followed the red stripes west, a well-used route high above a valley to the left, which turns sharp left after 30 minutes to drop downhill and turn right after 5 minutes at a picnic table, onto a very rocky path, initially more like a stream bed. After 8 minutes you should turn right onto a forestry track across a bridge, and then left at a T-junction to follow the right bank of the stream. After 15 minutes, just after a bivouac site, you reach the blue path from the right and the first houses of Międzygórze, and after 20 minutes more the bus terminus, with 20 buses a day to Bystrzyca Kłodzka, and six continuing to Kłodzko.

Międzygórze was a rather surreal place when I was there, pretending to be the small Canadian resort of Laurentine, with red phone boxes, English street names such as Hop St, Mix St, Car St, and Hovel St (!) and signs such as 'Robert and Stanley Duval — Confectioners Shop', as well as a Chinese restaurant. This seems to be an attempt to cash in on the autumn leaf colours; although there is cross-country skiing here, it is mainly a summer resort, with many sanatoria and trade union rest homes, private rooms, a youth hostel (ul Pocztowa 1, summer only), and a PTTK hostel at the western end of the village, by the 27m high Wilczki waterfall, which is a nature reserve.

From here you can take a bus via Bystrzyca Kłodzka, another attractive town strategically located above the river (hotel at ul Okrzei 26), to Kłodzko, and then either west to Duszniki-Zdrój, to visit the Góry Stołowe, or north to Wrocław, Opole or Jelenia Góra.

2: The Góry Stołowe

Heading west from Kłodzko, the first and least interesting of the three spas strung along the road west to the Czech town of Náchod (the main Warsaw-Prague road) is Polanica-Zdrój (south of the main road but served by all buses), with a camp site at ul Sportowa 7 (tel 210), to the east near the new bus station and PTTK hostel, as well as a hotel and rest homes in the centre; Orbis are at ul Zdrojowa 5 (tel 412), private rooms can be booked at ul Warsawska 14A (tel 608), and there is a summer youth hostel at ul Wojska Polskiego 23. Next comes Duszniki-Zdrój, and then to the west Kudowa-Zdrój, the largest and most attractive of the three, with an Orbis office at ul Zdrojowa 27 (tel 266), the Kosmos hotel at ul Buczka 8A (tel 511) and a sport hotel and camping at ul Łąkowa 12 (by the main road to the border, tel 627), as well as the usual rest homes, and a youth hostel in Jeleniów, near the railway station and the road to the border. There is a festival dedicated to Chopin's contemporary Moniuszko in June/July. Just to the northwest in Czermna (following green stripes) is the utterly weird *Kaplica Czaszek* (Chapel of Skulls), with walls and ceilings totally covered with skulls and crossed bones.

Duszniki-Zdrój itself is famous for the Chopin Festival held there every August (not the Chopin international piano competition, held in Warsaw every fifth October), and also for the *Muzeum Papiernictwa* or Museum of the Paper Industry, in an old paper mill dating from 1605, with a drying house from 1709, at ul Kłodzka 42.

There are about 45 buses a day from Kłodzko, with most continuing to Kudowa-Zdrój, as well as two to Legnica, three to Wałbrzych and eight to Wrocław, one (at 0722) to Bielsko-Biała, one (at 0833) via

Náchod to Hradec Králové in the Czech Republic, and seven (the last at 1509) south to Zieleniec, a ski centre with lots of hostels 12km south in the Góry Bystrzyckie, just west of the Pod Zieleńcem peatbog, noted for its tundra dwarf birch. Buses stop at a mini interchange at the main road junction, and just to the south (following red stripes past the SAM supermarket) is the attractive sloping Rynek, with a town hall from 1584, and the largely baroque old quarter; almost 2km further south is the spa quarter with the usual pleasant park. On a hill just east of the spa, following blue stripes, is the *Pod Mufflonem* PTTK hut; there is also a hotel at ul Świerczewskiego 2, a summer-only youth hostel at either ul Sawickiej 1 or ul Kłodzka 22, and private rooms from the PTTK at Rynek 14 (tel 549) or Orbis at ul Wojska Polskiego 6 (tel 349).

The campsite is just north of the main road at ul Dworcowa 6, on my hiking route; this initially follows the road to Łężyce and Karłów (as well as red markings that soon turn left to Kudowa-Zdrój, rather than starting west along the main road as shown on my map), passing the campsite on the left after 4 minutes and then the station on the right (with occasional slow trains). Turn right after 15 minutes to cross a level crossing and then follow blue markings (from the station) north up the road for 15 minutes to the Łężyce bus stop: there are 5 buses a day from Kłodzko and Duszniki-Zdrój to the centre of the village (where there is an all-year youth hostel) but only one, at 1514, from Duszniki-Zdrój to Karłów. To the right on the road to Szczytna (also with occasional buses) at Złotno are the rock outcrops known as *Grzybki* (The Mushrooms), not as interesting as the Rocky Mushrooms (see below).

In any case I followed the blue stripes to the right across a bridge 5 minutes further north; swing left after a couple of minutes beyond a farm to follow phone lines directly towards the obvious rocky outcrop of Skały Puchacza (Eagle Owl Rocks). The path goes into woods to the right and soon out again, then after crossing a stream turns right in mixed woods along the foot of the escarpment; after 5 minutes turn left at a T-junction on to a forestry track and after 7 minutes and two hairpins turn right up the very smooth steep pavement of what seems to be a former wagonway, with overgrown steps to the right. It took me 6 minutes to the top, under the outcrops, and another minute to the junction with a green route from Polanica-Zdrój and Batorów to Karłów, which I followed north through a young spruce plantation, turning right at a crossroads after 5 minutes and then left after 5 more at a junction with yellow stripes (again shown as brown on my map) from Batorów to the right.

The path continues across level sandy heathland for 10 minutes to Skalna Furta (Gate Rock) and the Białe Skały (White Rocks), very photogenic outcrops (with trees on top) and hollows through which the path winds with a bit of mild scrambling. The green and yellow routes continue parallel to each other, with the yellow path to the left slightly higher and perhaps more scenic until the Lisia pass, where it meets the road from Kudowa-Zdrój to Karłów and Radków, and the blue path from Skały Puchacza, and then detours via Góry Ptak (Bird Rock, 841m); the green path turns right after about 10 minutes on to a forestry track in

mixed wood and then left after 15 minutes on to asphalt from Radków
and Batorów, near the east end of Karłów (not as shown on the map).
After 5 minutes on the road you meet the main road just north of the
pass, and the yellow, blue and green routes all head north into the
village. Red stripes turn left after 5 minutes, leading to the Błędne Skały
or Erratic Rocks (850m), a fine reserve on the border, and Kudowa-Zdrój,
and then the green stripes turn left to follow the road to the Pasterka
hut.

Here at the 'centre' of Karłów you can find a shop, bar, post office and
a private hostel (tel 190), and a bus stop with eight buses a day
(summer weekdays) from Radków and Kłodzko, with four continuing to
Kudowa-Zdrój, one (at 1545) to Duszniki-Zdrój and three (one in winter)
to Pasterka; there is also a camping place to the east. The yellow stripes
carry on north straight towards the plateau of Szczeliniec, continuing
past a café where the road bends right, and after 10 minutes reaching
a kiosk, benches and an information board describing this 50ha reserve
(in Polish). From here it takes 10 minutes up small steps and then
following red arrows to the right to reach the Szczeliniec PTTK hut,
which is in fact only a daytime café, with some lovely photos for sale —
for overnight stays you must continue to Pasterka, or return to the
private hostel.

This massif is the heart of the Góry Stołowe, a kind of Dungeons and
Dragons scenery in which you pass through narrow clefts and windows
in the rocks, along square-cut 10m-deep canyons, suddenly emerge at
a viewpoint over the plains below and then plunge into a labyrinth of 5m-
square blocks of rock, often heading into seeming dead-ends. There is
a circuit from the hut, for which you will have to pay in season,
following red arrows outwards to a viewpoint on the far side of the
plateau and then white arrows for the *powrót* or return; this takes a
minimum of 25 minutes, but you should allow at least an hour to explore
a few dead ends and enjoy the views. If you can leave your baggage at
the hut, there is scope for a lot more exploration right across this
plateau.

Returning to the top of the steps (following white arrows again) I
pushed on to the north following the yellow arrows down a steepish
path, more roots than rock, reaching an asphalt road at a layby and then
winding down out of the woods (with a good short-cut at a hairpin to
the left), to reach Pasterka in 20 minutes, and 5 minutes later the turning
right/east (still following yellow stripes) to Radków, and the Pasterka
hut. The *bufet* here is only open from 0900 to 1900, but it is friendly,
with cheap beds. The asphalt ends here, with the route continuing as a
grassy path along the right-hand side of a wood, rising gently along the
left-hand side of a line of silver birch (not well marked, but straight
ahead), passing a large German milestone, and crossing a broad grassy
saddle.

After 20 minutes turn right across a streamlet by the remains of a
stone house and swing right (south of east) down a narrower strip
between thick spruce woods. The yellow stripes soon turn left to

Radków (past a camp site and hotel by an artificial lake), but I continued on the lower of two routes southeast, an unmarked grassy lane curving around the hillside and dropping slightly (shown as a red line on my map, supposedly equivalent to the bus route to Batorów). After just 5 minutes, at a hairpin at the head of a side valley, this meets again the red stripes from Karłów and follows them to the left. In 15 minutes you reach a German stone marking the turn left to *Magdalenens Lust* (Maiden's Desire, some rather unsuggestive outcrops and a viewpoint by a quarry, which rather spoils the view), 2 minutes walk into open beechwood. The route continues along this good forestry track, just below the 700m contour, crossing an asphalt road after 25 minutes and a track after 10 minutes before going straight on up a grassy track where the main track swings right. This passes through a young plantation to the genuinely mushroom-shaped Skalne Grzybki or Rocky Mushrooms; the very sandy path passes between two that virtually touch overhead, reaches a track after about 10 minutes and at once turns left to an A-frame shelter, again meeting the yellow stripes from the Lisia pass and turning left.

Again this is a nice little sandy path winding through the spruce trees and rock outcrops for 15 minutes to a junction with a blue route from Wambierzyce (a rather eccentric pilgrimage centre east of Radków); after 5 minutes more the blue stripes turn right for Polanica-Zdrój while I carried on following the yellow stripes on a slightly longer but more level loop through parallel reefs of outcrops, until the red stripes turned left after 5 minutes at an A-frame hut.

Near a tall thin rock like the Club of Hercules at Ojców, hidden in trees to the right, the yellow path turns left, then right, left, right, turning left on to a track and rejoining the blue route after about 12 minutes. Just after this is a bivouac site with two A-frame huts, and then a T-junction with an asphalt road at which the blue stripes turn left to Polanica-Zdrój; the yellow route turns right and after a minute turns left on to a cart track, rather than sticking to the road as shown on the map. After 10 minutes this rejoins the road in Batorów (near no 37), 5 minutes north of the shop and bus stop (with six buses a day); there is an all-year youth hostel here at ul Batorów 6. From here the yellow path turns right to Złotno and Duszniki-Zdrój, while the green route from Kudowa-Zdrój and Pasterka turns left at no 8; however I went straight down the road, turning left after 25 minutes and reaching the centre of Szczytna, on the main road east of Duszniki-Zdrój, in 10 more minutes.

There is a restaurant here, but no accommodation, although there is an all-year youth hostel a few kilometres southwest (reached following yellow stripes, or by four buses on weekdays) at Bobrowniki, on the edge of the Góry Bystrzyckie). The rail station and main bus stop are to the south of the main road, with 45 buses a day between Kłodzko and Duszniki-Zdrój, as well as early morning buses to Warsaw, Kraków, Bielsko-Biała, Łódź, Zielona Góra, and Hradec Králové, with more to Legnica, Wałbrzych, and Wrocław, as from Duszniki-Zdrój.

THE KARKONOSZE MOUNTAINS

The Karkonosze Mountains (in German Riesengebirge, in Czech Krkonoše) are, like the Góry Stołowe, part of the Sudeten system rather than the much younger Carpathians, and consequently are much more weathered and rounded in form. Having been folded and lifted, the metamorphic granite was glaciated and levelled; on the southern, Czech, side (two-thirds of the massif) there are long lateral ridges and deep valleys, but the Polish side slopes sharply along a fault line, with debris slopes, hanging valleys and lakes in glacial cirques, peat bogs reminiscent of semi-arctic tundra, and outcrops with names from old folk tales.

The weather is very changeable (especially in July, I'm told), with frequent fog, and you should always be prepared. Snow cover, at least a metre deep, can last up to seven months, and it can snow at any season. Annual precipitation ranges from 800mm at the foot of the hills to 1400mm on the summits.

They have always been largely unpopulated, with only gold miners venturing into the hills from the 13th Century, followed by woodcutters working for glass works, and then in the 15th and 16th Centuries Italian prospectors. From the 17th Century cattle grazing and the Thirty Years' War led to further depopulation, and from the late 18th Century the first tourists began to appear, staying in huts built for Protestant fugitives from Bohemia. The German Romantics, notably the painter Caspar David Friedrich, were inspired by the mist-shrouded peaks, and the railway arrived in 1867. They remain very popular with German hikers, sometimes still clad in *lederhosen*, and winter sports are also important; there are now 2.5m visitors each year (and 7m on the Czech side).

The *Karkonoski Park Narodowy* (Karkonosze National Park or KPN) was created in 1959, covering 5,563ha, and in 1963 the Czechs created their much larger park (KRNAP); they will soon form a UNESCO Biosphere Reserve. Two-thirds of the Polish park is forest, 98% of it spruce (largely planted in the 19th Century, although some beech forest remains below 1,000m) and almost every tree has been affected by acid rain. Trees killed by the eight-toothed bark beetle, which preys on the weakened trees, are not removed to avoid the soil being washed away, so you cannot avoid seeing stands of these eerie ghost trees.

The flora is rich, with more of a western European character than in the Carpathians: above the spruce level there is dwarf pine from about 1,250m to 1,450m, although most of the main ridge is in fact open wind-swept moorland with peat bogs, and a sub-alpine level to the top of Śnieżka at 1,602m. There are 900 vascular species of plant, including endemics such as *Saxifraga moschata ssp basaltica* (basalt saxifrage), *Sorbus sudetica* (Sudeten rowan) and *Campanula bohemica* (Karkonosze bellflower), glacial relics such as *Rubus chamaemorus* (cloudberry), *Salix lapponum* (Lapland willow, in the north-facing cirques), *Linnea borealis*, *Carex magellanica*, *Pedicularis sudetica* and *Saxifraga nivalis*, and other protected species including *Aconitum callibotryon, Arnica montana,*

Carlina acaulis, Daphne mezereum, Digitalis grandiflora, Gentiana ciliata, Lilium martagon, Pulsatilla alpina and *Trollius europaeus.* There are 150 species of fungi, 70 lichen, and 270 mosses and liverworts, including *Gymnomitrion obtusum, Tayloria acuminata, Bryum arcticum* and *Cynodontium fallax.* To the north of Szklarska Poręba is a separate 4ha crocus reserve.

The fauna includes 50 moufflon, introduced 80 years ago from France, and the usual forest animals such as red and roe deer, and 150 bird species, including the dotterel *Eudromias morinellus,* mainly found in Norway and Scotland, the redpoll *Carduelis flammea,* and standard forest birds such as alpine accentor, water pipit, capercaillie, black grouse and nutcracker. There are a few endemics, such as the butterfly *Torula quadrifaria* (in the dwarf pine zone), the snail *Cochlodina dubiosa corcontica,* and the dayfly *Rhithrogena corcontica.*

Getting there

The main base for the Karkonosze mountains is **Jelenia Góra** (Deer Mountain, or in German *Hirschberg*), now a voivodeship capital and industrial centre with 90,000 inhabitants, as well as a major staging post for visitors from Germany. The town was pretty well flattened in the war and the centre has been rebuilt as it was, with 16-18th Century arcaded houses all around the market square (known as the Plac Ratuszowy rather than the usual Rynek) with a town hall from 1747 in its centre; however from the rear these seemingly baroque buildings can be seen for what they are, modern flats. Nevertheless the effect is pleasant, with cafés and restaurants giving life to the otherwise gloomy arcades.

Just to the northeast is the 14th Century parish church of SS Erasmus and Pancras, with an octagonal tower and 16th Century German funerary monuments on the external wall, and good simple Gothic vaulting inside, and a lovely organ in a gallery above an older gallery with paintings of Christ and the Apostles. Just across ul 1 Maja, the main street east to the rail station, is the chapel of St Anne, originally built into the medieval fortifications, and further east along ul 1 Maja the baroque chapel of the Virgin (built in 1737 and now used by the Russian Orthodox community), and then the church of the Holy Cross, built for the Lutherans in the early 18th Century by the Swedish architect Frantz, with fine frescoes by artists from Prague and a superb organ. Apart from churches, you can visit the Regional Museum, at ul Matejki 28, southeast towards the camp site, which deals mainly with the local glass making industry, with some fine pieces on display.

There is a Festival of Street Theatre in early August, followed in September by a music festival and then a theatre festival, with a curio and antique fair in late September.

There is a wide range of accommodation, thanks to the floods of Germans passing through: at the top end is the 4* Orbis Hotel Jelenia Góra on the Karpacz road (ul Świerczewskiego 63, tel 240 81), built by an Austrian company in 1990 and offering all mod cons, in the middle

are the Hotel Europa (ul 1 Maja 16, tel 232 21; you can also get private
rooms here, tel 242 06), the Hotel Park-Sportowy and camp site (ul
Świerczewskiego 42, tel 269 42), Juventur's hotel Sudecki (ul Legnicka
1, tel 423 07) and the PTTK hostel (ul 1 Maja 88, tel 230 59), near the
rail station, and at the bottom are the youth hostels at ul Bartka
Zywciężcy 10, east of the centre (open all year, tel 257 46) and ul
Wiejska 86 (tel 241 55). Orbis are at ul 1 Maja 1, and the PTTK at Al
Wojska Polskiego 40, with tourist information also at ul 1 Maja 42.

To the south is the spa of Cieplice (or Cieplice Śląskie-Zdrój), now a
suburb of Jelenia Góra but retaining its own character, with a large spa
park (with a continuation to the south which contains an ornithological
museum at ul Wolności 268), two baroque churches and a massive
baroque palace. There are six hot sulphurous springs, with temperatures
between 20 and 44°C, and baths in mud from the Góry Izerskie to the
west. To the west of the park at ul Cervii 11 is the 3* Cieplice hotel (tel
510 41), and there is a hostel at Plac Piastowski 26, and camping on ul
Rataja, to the southwest.

A few kilometres further southwest (buses 7/9/15 or by train) is
Sobieszów, where the Chojnik hill (627m) forms an enclave of the
Karkonosze National Park and contains the Park headquarters and
museum at ul Chałubinskiego 23, with displays of natural history and
geology. There are two hostels here, linked by red stripe markings, one
(run by the PTTK) in the 14-16th Century castle on top of Chojnik hill
(tel 535 35) and one to the north of the centre at ul Cieplicka 188 (tel
536 27), and a camp site near the swimming pool on ul Łazienkowska.

A bit further south, at the end of the road, is Jagniątków, where you
can visit the home of the Nobel Prize-winning German writer Gerhart
Hauptmann, a large Secession mansion not to be confused with the
house of the Hauptmann brothers in Szklarska Poręba; there is a camp
site here too, in the centre of the village.

On the other side of Jelenia Góra are three former Red Army bases
that were to have been the main supply depots for any Soviet advance
into western Europe; covering 17,000ha, they are now utterly
devastated, burnt and churned up in exercises, and sterile where fuel
tanks were washed out and chemical waste dumped. It is estimated that
it will cost Z2.8 trillion to restore the area.

From Jelenia Góra most hikers will head south to the jumping-off
points of Szklarska Poręba or Karpacz, with a dozen buses and trains
daily to Szklarska Poręba, and up to 17 buses to Karpacz via Cieplice, as
well as a few via Mysłakowice or Kowary to the east, and three trains.
If you want to be more original, you can start the hike further to the east
by taking a bus (two a day to Kamienna Góra via Lubawka) to the
Kowarskie Rozdroże (Kowary crossroads) bus stop at 787m, from where
you can follow green stripes (or a road) to the Okraj pass hut (1,046m)
and then follow the Polish-Czech Friendship Path (marked in red) west
to Śnieżka. **Kowary** itself was an iron mining centre from the 15th
Century and is now known for weaving, with exhibitions in October, but
there is little to see beyond one Gothic church; there are easy hikes in

the hills to the northeast, with all-year youth hostels nearby in Bukowiec and Strużnica, and in Kowary itself the Kuźnica hotel, south of the centre, and a sports hotel and camp site on ul Findera, by a lake to the northwest, as well as private rooms from ul Podgórze 26 or the Kuźnica. Equally, you can start further to the west by taking any of 14 buses a day from Jelenia Góra to Świeradów-Zdrój and following red or blue markings east towards Szklarska Poręba.

Karpacz is a village of 5,000 strung out along one main road, ul Konstytucji 3 Maja, which runs from the railway station south past most of the places to eat and sleep, and then swings west to the Biały Jar (White Ravine) Hotel, where most buses turn around, and then to Karpacz Górny (Upper Karpacz, also known as Bierutowice) where there is a remarkable piece of architecture, the wooden Wang chapel, built in Norway around the end of the 13th Century and brought here by King Friedrich Wilhelm IV of Prussia in 1846. The only other sight in the town is the Regional Museum of Sport and Tourism at ul Kopernika 2.

The best hotel is Orbis' 4* Skalny at ul Obrońców (properly Obrońców Pokoju, 'Defenders of the Peace') 5 (tel 197 21), with more affordable alternatives being the Orlinek (ul Olimpijska 9, tel 195 48/67), the Biały Jar (ul Konstytucji 3 Maja 79, tel 193 19), Juventur's Zielone Wzgórze (ul Poznańska 5, tel 194 10), the Śnieżka (ul Konstytucji 3 Maja 67, tel 104 97), and the Mieszko (ul Mickiewicza 2, tel 195 92). The PTTK has two hostels, at ul Parkowa 6 (tel 195 13) and ul Obrońców 6 (tel 197 64), with a school for mountain guides at the latter, and there are two youth hostels, one open all year at ul Gimnazjalna 9 (tel 192 90), most easily reached by following green stripes downhill from the Biały Jar, and an overflow at ul Odrodzenia 17, at the second bus stop above the Biały Jar.

The Krkonoše mountains

The Czech Krkonoše mountains are naturally very busy with tourists from Prague and the industrial areas of Bohemia, and the huge *bouda* or mountain huts reflect the scale of the influx, usually seeming more like hotels with their waitress service restaurants.

The south-facing slopes receive a great deal of precipitation and thus a great deal of acid rain, with far more dead trees than on the Polish side. The higher part of the range is above the level of the acid rain and is flat and boggy, feeding many streams such as the Labe (Elbe), with fine waterfalls.

The first nature conservation area was established in 1904 by Count Harrach, and the KRNAP National Park was set up in 1963, covering a strip 39km long, and 5 to 15km wide. There are almost 1,000km of paths, marked with since 1932 with 'dumb signs', silhouettes such as an S to show the way to Špindlerova bouda, an L to Labská bouda and an M to Martinovka bouda.

There is a bivouac site at a swimming pool near the Skalny, and a proper campsite near the station at ul Konstytucji 3 Maja 8 (tel 193 16), where there is also an accommodation office for private rooms (tel 194 53). Orbis, at ul Konstytucji 3 Maja 50 (tel 195 47), or the tourist information centre at ul Konstytucji 3 Maja 25A (tel 19 716) should be able to find you a room in a pension.

Hiking directions

There is the usual tourist map of the *Karkonoski Park Narodowi*, at 1:30,000, but unusually it is spread on both sides of the paper, with a slight gap between the two halves. There are also the *Colour Marked Footpaths of Jelenia Góra Province* map (mostly at 1:100,000) and a *Panorama of the Karkonosze*, both in English, and a German guidebook to the *Riesengebirge* (Giant Mountains) by Maria Malarek, available locally for DM16 or Z40,000.

The obvious destination from Karpacz is Śnieżka or *Schneekoppe* (Snow Peak, which is indeed covered with snow for up to seven months a year); the easiest route is by the chair-lift which rises in 17 minutes from 795m above the Biały Jar to 1,332m, just below Kopa (1,375m), but there are also easy hiking routes. You can start at the Okraj pass, following red stripes (see above), near the museum (yellow stripes up the Łomniczka valley) or at the Wang chapel (blue stripes), but most people will probably start at the Biały Jar, following red and black stripes up the right bank of the Łomnica for 10 minutes to the lower terminal of the chair-lift. Here you can cut down to the yellow markings, following a toboggan run up to the Strzecha Akademicka (literally Academic Thatch) hut, or follow black stripes up the 'Silesian Road' via the Biały Jar proper to the upper terminal and the Pod Śnieżką hut. I stuck to the red stripes, turning sharp left along the road below the terminal, turning right after 3 minutes at the turn to the Orlinek hotel and the ski-jump and continuing on a good unmade road for 40 minutes. This passes one A-frame shelter and a couple of odd dugouts with roofs of branches, and then reaches the junction of the yellow stripes from the station and the museum, and the Nad Łomniczką hut, which in fact has no beds and merely serves as a place for older walkers to have a glass of *herbata* before turning back.

In fact the hike gets more interesting after this, as you emerge from the spruce into dwarf birch and then dwarf pine; the path follows the stream, then crosses it after 15 minutes below a waterfall and zigzags more steeply for 20 minutes to the Pod Śnieżką hut, at the Przełecz Pod Śnieżką (Pass Below Śnieżka, 1,394m), under 15 minutes above the Kopa chair-lift terminal following black stripes. Although very busy with hikers buying food and ices, this too has no beds, and in addition the Czech Obří bouda (hut) has also gone. From here it takes under 20 minutes by the direct path east, marked with red stripes, to the 1,602m summit of Śnieżka, with a weather station and *bufet* in flying saucer style, the 17th Century chapel of St Lawrence, and a Czech hut and chair-lift terminal. There is an easier alternative route, the 'Jubilee Way', marked with blue stripes, which bypasses the peak to the north and reaches the top from the east. During the martial law period the Solidarity activists Adam Michnik and Jacek Kuroń held secret meetings here with Václav Havel and Charter 77 activists from Czechoslovakia, and in 1990 Wałęsa and Havel met here for what was apparently a rather frosty summit meeting. Śnieżka is a fairly unattractive peak of broken rock with lichen and moss, and a view usually obscured by haze.

Returning to the pass, you can return to Karpacz, or take the obvious alternative along the ridge to the west, descending to the other resort of Szklarska Poręba; this can be done in a long day hike, but most people will spend a night in a hut. You should ignore the blue Czech path and head west following red stripes along a cobbled road, then a gravel track; after 20 minutes, at Spalona Strażnica (1,430m, meaning fire tower, although there is no tower now), blue stripes turn right to the Strzecha Akademicka and Samotnia huts and the Wang chapel. Straddling the border to the left is a large peat bog, up to 2.8m deep, feeding all the streams of the area. The red path continues, rather stonier, across a broad plateau with patches of dwarf pine, swinging right above the cirques of Mały Staw and Wielki Staw (Little and Great Ponds), with the two large huts and the smaller Scout hut of Domek Myśliwski (Hunter's Cottage) visible below. There are three viewpoints, with shelters at the third.

Thirty minutes from Spalona Strażnica green markings (shown in black on the map) turn right to link up with the blue path to the Wang chapel, and just 5 minutes further along the red route are the Słonecznik (Sunflower) outcrops at 1,423m. About 15 minutes to the right/north (following yellow stripes, also leading to the blue path) are the more striking Pielgrzymy (Pilgrims).

The path is much quieter from here on, but it has a real ankle-twisting surface; it is mostly level and then drops after 30 minutes to the Karkonoska pass (1,198m) and the border, with the Odrodzenie (Renaissance) hut to the right and the much larger Czech Špindlerovka hut to the left, with a road (built in 1928) and a dozen buses a day south to Špindlerův Mlyn, the main Czech resort in the Krkonoše. There is almost no traffic on the Polish road continuing north to Przesieka (summer youth hostel and rest homes) and Jelenia Góra, although it is marked with blue stripes. The red route continues as a broad track along the border, passing over the Bird Rock (Ptasi Kamień, 1,217m) amd then after 10 minutes joining an asphalt road from the left, dropping to the Dołek pass (1,178m) and after 10 minutes more reaching a green path left to the Czech Moravská hut, and 5 minutes later (at 1,268m) a blue path left to the Petrova hut, as well as a black route along a road north to Jagniątków.

These are typical of the Czech huts, big hotels up to four storeys high imposing themselves unsympathetically on the landscape; the Polish huts are larger and less attractive than those in the Tatras, but they are not too bad. The route continues as a rough stone path along the border,

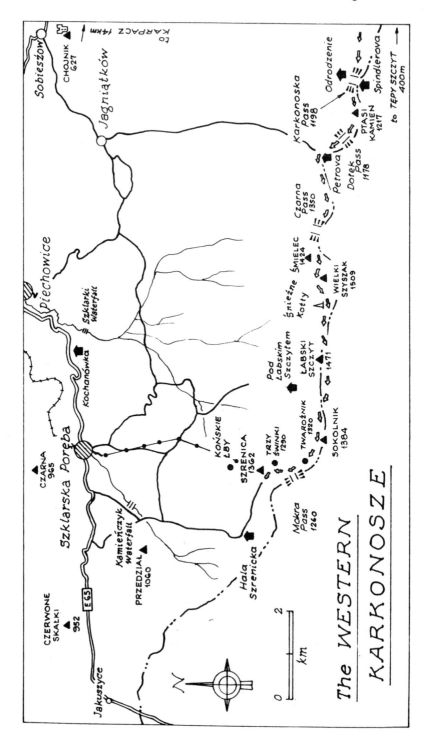

The WESTERN KARKONOSZE

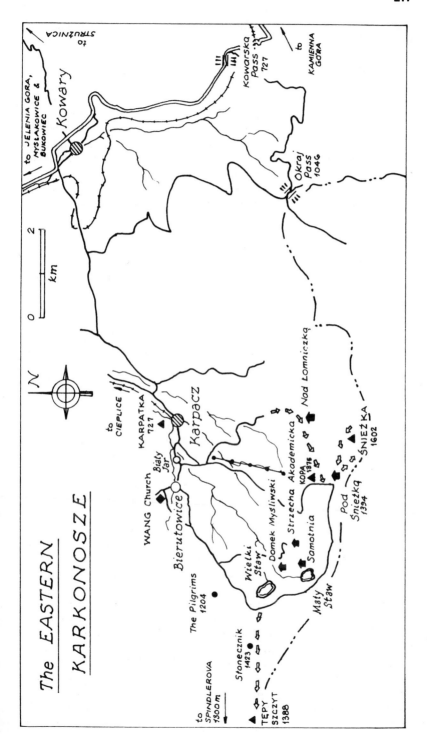

reaching various isolated outcrops at 1,416m after 15 minutes, and dropping past more rather neolithic rocks for 15 minutes to the Czarna Przełęcz (Black Pass, 1,350m) just south of the Black Cirque. Just beyond the pass the red route crosses one marked in blue, from Jagniątków to the Czech Martinova hut. The path continues westwards, passing to the south of Śmielec (1,424m), and then to the north of Wielki Szyszak (1,509m); now it climbs a bit more steeply, once again on what seems to be badly-preserved neolithic pavement, with Śnieżne Kotły (Snowy Cirque) to the right, and after 30 minutes swings right, at a turning left to the Czech Labská hut, to pass the TV tower on a spur called Grzęda (The Bed) between the two halves of the cirque, dwarfing otherwise impressive outcrops.

Five minutes further on there is a junction to the right, marked with yellow stripes, to the Pod Łabskim Szczytem hut and Szklarska Poręba, while the red path west soon switches to the Czech side of the border to bypass Łabski Szczyt (1,471m): this is the Polish-Czech Friendship Path, 28km long in all, created in socialist solidarity to allow citizens of Poland and Czechoslovakia to walk freely on either side of the border. Originally citizens of other countries were meant to use the parallel green routes on either side of the frontier, but now you are quite free to walk this route, and if you have Czech money you can spend it in the Czech huts; however you should not stay overnight or go any further south.

This is now a gravel track across an open moorland plateau, passing a delapidated shed at a junction left to the source of the Elbe (Labe) and the Vrbatova hut (and an unmarked track right to the Pod Łabskim Szczytem hut) after 15 minutes, before crossing back into Poland to pass to the north of Sokolnik (1,384m) and heading northwest along the border. After 20 minutes, just beyond Twarożnik (The Curds, 1,320m), it reaches the Mokra pass (1,260m) where the Friendship Path ends at another delapidated hut, with the Czech red stripes turning 90° left to the Vosecká hut. Polish red stripes continue briefly along the border, while green stripes come from Pod Łabskim Szczytem and then turn right below the Trzy Świnki (Three Swine, 1,290m) around the Szrenica cirque to the Końskie Łby (Horses' Heads). An unmarked path turns half-right here to the weather station, snack bar and the upper terminal of the chair-lift from Szklarska Poręba, on top of Szrenica (1,362m), less than 10 minutes away. This chairlift will bring you from an altitude of 706m (about 100m above central Szklarska Poręba) in about 25 minutes.

From here you should return to the red route on the border by following black markings to the left for 5 minutes; at once the red stripes turn right away from the border on a concrete road and drop to the Hala Szrenicka hut in 10 minutes. You can continue west following green stripes to the Szklarska pass and Świeradów-Zdrój, or follow the red stripes down the road to **Szklarska Poręba**; half an hour down this road, back in the spruce again, you reach the park boundary (at 846m) and turn right to see the 27m Kamieńczyk waterfall (perhaps the best in the Karkonosze), with a kiosk and a viewpoint over this attractive little canyon. The red path continues down this road, and in under 10 minutes reaches a crossroads at 755m, where a green path (not on the map) to the intermediate station of the chair-lift and the Pod Łabskim Szczytem hut, and a black path to the lower terminal of the chair-lift and the PTTK hostel both turn right. To find accommodation you should take the black route right, and to reach the *Julia* glassworks and rail station take the red route onwards; this latter forks left after 5 minutes and in 3 more minutes reaches the asphalt road (the E65) at a bridge and bus stop and the glassworks, which can be visited on weekday mornings.

From here it takes 10 minutes along the road to the right/east, with the Krucze Skały (Ravens' Rocks) above the trees to the south, to the centre of the resort: blue stripes up a lane to the left should lead to a campsite at ul Demokratów 6, and then the red stripes turn left to reach the railway station, although not quite as shown on the map. To reach the bus station, follow green stripes east along the main road, ul Jedności Narodowej (National Unity St), for about 5 minutes.

The only hotel is the Sudety at ul Krasickiego 10 (tel 172 736), but there are plenty of alternatives, such as the Motel Relax at ul Jeleniogórska 9A (tel 172 695/173 295), about 1km to the east on the main road (with an Almatur bivouac site opposite), the PTTK's Złota Jama (Golden Pit) hostel at ul 1 Maja 16 (tel 172 709), following green then black stripes from the bus station to the chairlift, and sport hotels at ul Turystyczna 27, by the chair-lift (tel 173 035/7), and at ul Sportowy 6 (tel 172 237). For private rooms try the *Biuro Zakwaterowania* near the bus station at ul 1 Maja 4 (tel 172 393), the tourist information centre at ul Turystyczna 26 (tel 172 939) or Orbis at ul Jedności Narodowej 16 (tel 172 347).

There is a youth hostel, open all year but well to the east of the centre at ul Piastowska 1 (tel 172 141). Just beyond the Relax is a reserve around the Szklarki waterfall, and the tiny Kochanówka PTTK hostel (tel 172 400), and beyond that the village of Piechowice, with a hotel at ul Turystyczna 8 (tel 172 911), hostels at ul Mickiewicza 9, near the station (tel 535 87), and ul Piastowska 5 (tel 536 31) and camping at ul Żeromskiego 119. Finally the Gospoda Graniczna hotel and camp site (tel 172 463) are at the Szklarska pass (886m, just north of the Jakuszyce border crossing).

Moving on

There are overnight trains to Warsaw and Gdynia, and ten local trains and a dozen buses to Jelenia Góra, with about six buses continuing to Wrocław and one each to Łódź (0730) and Lublin (1110). In the other direction there are six buses a day to the border at Jakuszyce, as well as three terminating at the Julia glassworks. Trains no longer cross the Czech border here, although there are plans to restore them.

There are also nine buses past the station to Świeradów-Zdrój, a spa and resort to the west in the Góry Izerskie, a similar range of granite and gneiss hills (maximum 1,126m), with a tourist hostel at ul Zdrojowa 8 (tel 231), a pension at ul Górska 14 (tel 248), and a bivouac site at ul

Zakopiańska, and a PTTK hut below Stóg Izerski (1,107m), at the start of the ridge route, marked with red stripes, back to Szklarska Poręba. This is covered by the 1:100,000 map of the *Góry i Pogórze Izerskie*.

From Jelenia Góra there are trains to Warsaw, Kraków and Zielona Góra, as well as buses to Kłodzko (0740, 0830), Szczecin (0825), Kraków and Łódź (0830), Brzeg (1400) and Poznań (1430), and virtually hourly to Legnica and Wrocław. There are also four buses a day via Szklarska Poręba to Jablonec in the Czech Republic, just short of Liberec, and weekly buses in summer to Prague and Berlin.

Part Four

Ukraine — The Land

and the People

After Poland, Ukraine may seem drab, but what makes it interesting is precisely the fact that it is so much further back on the road from primitive communism to the market economy. The Soviet Union was once described as 'Upper Volta with rockets': Ukraine was always less extreme, free of Asian peripheries, but it is still very run-down. Now, as Russia rushes towards capitalism or anarchy, Ukraine is a well preserved image of how it all used to be, with social conformity, state ownership, full 'employment', price controls and low crime.

Although corruption is endemic, both at the petty level of bribes with packs of cigarettes and at the level of international speculation, society remains fairly egalitarian in general, even if it is an equality of queueing — look as upmarket or as downmarket as you like, but (unless you're a gypsy) you'll all be treated the same. However it is one of the most sexually divided places I've seen. Women do many of the dirtiest jobs, on road gangs and sweeping bus stations, and also queue, shop and do all the housework, while men have a far more relaxed time. Women even wait to wash in the train until the men have finished.

However your main reason for going to Ukraine is likely to be to see the mountains, either the Carpathians or the Crimean mountains. These are remarkably undeveloped and unspoilt, although this also means that there is little infrastructure such as huts, camp sites or chair-lifts; the choice of food is limited and buses are erratic, although costs are very low indeed. Therefore this is a place for the more self-reliant traveller. Only one area of the mountains is alpine, but the less spectacular areas have many high open clearings like those in the Polish Bieszczady.

As there is so little published information on tourist facilities and hiking routes in Ukraine, and much of that is contradictory, and as I have not been able to spend as much time in Ukraine as in Poland, I have to apologise for any errors, and will welcome all feedback.

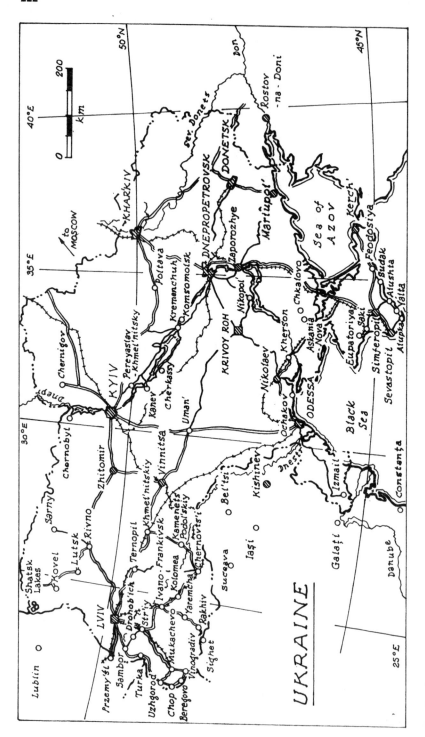

UKRAINE

Chapter 7

The Land

GEOGRAPHY

Originally Ukraine (which simply means 'borderland' — only *The Daily Telegraph* still refers to it as *the* Ukraine) was part of the vague confederation of Rus', which later evolved into Russia or Ruthenia; to the Russians Ukraine is still Malorossiya or Little Russia, Belarus or Byelorussia means White Russia (although the area south of its capital Minsk was known as Black Russia), and the Polish area around Lviv was known as Red Russia. Nowadays Ukraine is divided into 24 *oblasts* or provinces (as well as the cities of Kyiv and Sevastopil, and the Crimean Autonomous Republic), but people also still think in terms of older regions, such as Podolia (around Ternopil), Polessia (to the northwest, by the borders of Poland and Belarus), Volynia (south of Polessia, around Lutsk), and Precarpathia (the northern foothills of the Carpathians). Since 1945 there has also been the oblast of Zacarpatskaya (Transcarpathia) south of the Carpathian watershed: this is basically the area known in this century as Ruthenia, included in the new state of Czechoslovakia after the First World War, passed to Hungary by Hitler and then seized by Stalin. The watershed had long been the political but not the ethnic border of Ukraine, with a Ukrainian majority (including Łemks, Boyks and Huţuls) on the southern side, with a Hungarian majority further south. At least one of the various claimants for the title of geographical centre of Europe is in this area, at a monument near Rakhiv.

Ukraine as a whole covers 603,700km² (2.7% of the area of the former Soviet Union), with a population of 52m, 67% urbanised (18% of that of the former Soviet Union and producing 17% of its industrial output and about 20% of its national income). 8% of the present Ukraine is mountainous (6% of this being the Carpathians).

The Ukrainian Carpathians are young folded mountains, mainly thrown up in the Tertiary alpine orogeny (with some volcanism at that time), and glaciated in the Quarternary era. They now form three fairly clear ridges, running parallel from northwest to southeast, with deposits up to 5km deep in the geosynclines: first the outer (Middle, High and Huţul) Beskids, to the northeast, a broad area of folded sedimentary rocks corresponding to the outer anticline. Then comes the Mid-Carpathian Depression, with towns such as Volovets and Mizhgor'ya, and then the core zone of crystalline rocks, the Polonynian Beskid, formerly the main watershed, although now superseded by the outer Beskids (with passes between 839m and 974m altitude). Next, running east from Svalyava, is the Inner Carpathian Valley, which broadens into the Maramureş Basin and continues east to the Tisa and the Romanian border at Tyachev. Finally, passing just north of Uzhgorod, Mukachevo and Irshava, is a volcanic chain. Beyond the Tisa river, in the eastern Carpathians, lies the crystalline Chornohora massif, the highest in Ukraine, and to its south the much older Rakhiv and Chyvchyn mountains (also known as the Huţul Alps), part of the Maramureş-Bucovina massif which continues into Romania. Only the Huţul Alps and Chornohora have a glaciated high mountain landscape, with rockfields only here and in the Gorgany area — even the highest peaks are covered with clays and continuous vegetation.

Confronted with a map in Cyrillic script, it can be hard to make sense of this, so the main peaks are as follows: in the outer Beskids Parashka (Парашка, 1,271m), Magura (Магура, 1,368m), Grofa (Грофа, 1,748m), and Syvula (Сивула, 1,818m, in the Gorgany massif), and in the Polonynian Beskid Runa (Руна, 1,479m), Stoy (Стій, 1,679m, in the Borzhava polonina), Krasna (Красна, 1,568m), Menchul (Менчул, 1,501m) and Bliznitsya (Близниця, 1,881m). Hoverla (Говерла) in the Chornohora is 2,061m, and beyond it by the Romanian border Chyvchyn (Чивчин) is 1,766m high. The volcanic range, of which you will hear no more, consists of the Vyhorlat, Makovytsia, Syniak (1,018m), Velykyi Dil, Tupyi, and Hutyn massifs.

Much of the rest of Ukraine is part of the Chernozen or black earth belt, incredibly fertile soil stretching for 4,000km at about 50° latitude from south of Kyiv through Russia and Kazakhstan to Novosibirsk. Laurens van der Post said of it 'I have never seen more profoundly exciting earth, even its blackness was not the colour of negation but of the mystery of the great power with which it is charged. It is remarkable how old this earth looks, as if it were the original natural soil from which all other soils have been drawn'. This passes just north of the massive Donbas coal field (600km by 150km) on the Russian-Ukrainian border, which holds 60% of the former Soviet Union's coal reserves. With the nearby iron ore mines of Krivoy Roh, this became its leading industrial area, and its most polluted.

The Ukrainian **climate** is mainly temperate-continental, without the extremes of heat and cold found in Moscow and most of Russia; summers are often cloudy and winters sunny. Nevertheless, there can be strong cold winds sweeping from Siberia all the way to the Black Sea. On the southern and western slopes of the Carpathians there is a more Mediterranean climate, with up to 1,600mm of precipitation *per annum* on the peaks, and 600mm in the valleys. Average January temperatures are between −3°C and −10°; July temperatures range from 20° in southern Ukraine and Kiev and 18° in the North to 6° on the highest peaks, July being both the hottest and the wettest month. Flash floods are common in spring and summer. It is interesting that whereas Romanians speak of the 'Seventh Year' regularly producing bad weather, the Ukrainians speak of the 'Fourth Year' — more a measure of Romanian optimism, I think, than of significantly better weather to the south.

Green Issues

Those few remaining people within the former Soviet Union who look to Stalin as the man who, whatever his faults, made the USSR into an industrial world power are now at last being forced to realise that the dash for heavy industry was at the very least a poison pill, and probably one of his greatest crimes against his own people; 15-20% of the former Soviet Union is now classified as an environmental disaster area, with 35% deteriorating. Most of the dirtiest and most harmful industries were located in republics such as Ukraine; this is still strongly resented and seen as a key aspect of the colonial relationship with Russia.

In the aftermath of the Chornobyl disaster (see separate section) the environmental movement became in many ways the main opposition movement, and now a clean environment has been recognised as one of the key human rights of the new Ukraine. Equally though, it has been recognised that this will not be achieved for a long time, with parliament declaring the entire republic an environmental disaster area. By far the worst pollution is in the Donbas coalfield, on the eastern border with Russia, where the first foundry was founded in 1871 by 'the Welsh hermit' John Hughes; now morbidity here is 20-40% higher than in control areas elsewhere. In Krivoy Roj alone atmospheric emissions were 900,000t in 1991, 1.6t per resident. Only 14.3% of Ukraine's land area is forest (compared with a world average of 29%, or 37% for the former Soviet Union); 4.5m hectares have been planted since the Second World War (when this figure was just 11.4%), but this is not enough to counter Ukraine's atmospheric pollution, and there is some acid rain affecting forests in Transcarpathia. Additionally the Danube now carries 1.7m tonnes a year of fertiliser run-off into the Black Sea, so that it is now blanketed with phytoplankton, absorbing its oxygen. Of the 170 types of pesticides used (175,000t in total each year), 49 are known to be toxic, and underground water is now undrinkable over an area of 5,400km².

Radiation is a huge problem all over the former Soviet Union, with so many 'hot spots' that no-one knows where they all are, and 4.7m ha of land were affected by the fall-out from Chornobyl. There were 130 underground nuclear explosions for oil prospecting and quarrying, and in Moscow, for instance, there are 50 research reactors, all built in the 1950s and 1960s and now very leaky and unreliable.

As a result Ukrainian life expectancy has been falling since the 1970s, to 66 for men and 75 for women, 52nd in the world rankings. In 1991 there were 12.2 births per 1,000, the lowest rate since 1917, and mortality of infants in their first year of life is 1.5 times that in the west, at 13.6 per 1,000 in 1991. In 1991 deaths exceeded births and the population, which had been growing slightly until then, fell by 0.7 per 1,000.

Now ecological safety is seen as a fundamental human right, with a new Ministry of Environmental Protection set up to create a monitoring system and to extract realistic fines (instead of the former purely symbolic system) for pollution or the publication of false ecological information. The Green movement in fact dates from 1987, and can claim some successes, such as the abandonment of plans for a nuclear power station in the Crimea and a canal between the Black and Azov Seas. There are proposals for the 'AntiChornobyl XXI Ecopolis', a 'new type of living space' near Ochakov on the coast east of Odessa, where people will live in racial and environmental harmony.

In Ukraine there are three national parks, 15 state reserves, 1,608 wildlife reserves, 2,641 nature memorials (individual rocks and trees), and 1,196 other reserves, covering in all 1,211,000ha. This sounds impressive but is in fact only 2.1% of the land area, against 4.7% in Czechoslovakia and 7.8% in the USA. The parks are the Karpatskii (Carpathians), protecting 50,300ha, mostly on the north side of the Chornohora massif (page 340); the Shats'kii Lakes, a unique area of 32,500ha (including 22 lakes covering 6,400ha and the surrounding fir and pine forests, hiding place of many partisans in the last war), in the northwest-most corner of Ukraine; and Lake Sinevir, covering another 35,000ha of mountains to the west of Chornohora (page 353), and these will soon be joined by the Skole Beskid (page 360), linking with the Polish and Slovak Bieszczady parks. The state reserves are the *Chornomorskii* (Black Sea, 57,048ha southwest of Kherson, set up back in 1927), *Ukrainski Stepovii* (Ukrainian Steppes, 1,634ha), *Lugans'kii* (near the eastern frontier, 1,575ha), *Kanivs'kii* (southeast of Kyiv, 1,035ha), *Karpatski* (two areas on the south slope of the Chornohora massif, 18,500ha, as well as two areas of karst *klippen* near Zhihlove (east of Solotvino) and at Shirokiy-Luh (north of Teresva), basalt *klippen* (up to 1,501m) between Hust and the Terebla river, Europe's largest narcissus glade north of Hust — all in Transcarpathia), the *Yaltanskii Girs'ko-Lis* (14,584ha) and *Karadas'kii* (2,855ha) reserves in southern Crimea, 20,907ha in Polessia (*Polis'kii*), 14,851ha at the mouth of the Danube (*Dynayus'ki Plavni*), and last but definitely not least Askania Nova. This reserve of 11,054ha, near Chkalovo, just north of the isthmus to Crimea, was a sheep station where in 1889 its owner, Friedrich von Falz-Fein, set up a private zoo and breeding institute where the Askania soft-wool sheep was bred and the Ukrainian steppe pig improved, before it became a state nature reserve from 1919. Now it is still largely virgin steppe with rare grasses and prehistoric stone monuments known as *babas* or old women, populated by an amazing collection of yaks, American bison and Belorussian *żubr*, African water buffaloes, elk, llama, Przewalski horse, gayals, antelopes, zebra, sika deer, wild goats, sheep, storks, pheasants, guinea fowl, peacock, and ostriches. I don't guarantee that all these species are still there, but most should be. Trees include birch, plane, pine, spruce, catalpa, acacia and azalea. The Askania Nova and Black Sea reserves were created UNESCO Biosphere reserves in 1984, and two more are planned in Crimea and the Skole Beskid.

Chapter 8

The People

HISTORY

In the time of the Greek historian Herodotus, Scythian tribes ruled the northern shores of the Black Sea, from the Danube to the Don, trading with the Greeks, who established settlements in a few major ports. To the north, the steppes were roamed by tribes out of Central Asia such as the Pechenegs and the Slavs; what became the state of Kyivan Rus', and later Russia as we know it today, came into being when the Slav tribes supposedly invited three Varangian (Viking) brothers, Rurik, Sinyens, and Trevol, to rule them, in about 860AD.

In 965 the Kyivan Prince Svyatoslav defeated the Central Asian Khazar empire, and in 988 Prince Volodymyr married the daughter of the Emperor of Byzantium and led a mass baptism in the Dnepr, which is taken as the origin of Kyivan Rus' and of Russian and Ukrainian civilisation, and was widely celebrated a thousand years later; since then the church has always been subordinate to the state. Volodymyr's son Yaroslav the Wise was known as 'the father-in-law' of Europe (somewhat akin to Queen Victoria many centuries later) — his son married the daughter of the Emperor of Byzantium, his daughters the kings of Norway, Hungary and France, and his sister the King of Poland. Rus' developed into a loose federation of 11 city-states strung along the rivers that formed the trade routes from the Baltic to the Black Sea; but in 1240 Kyiv was devastated by the Tatars (or Mongols) and lived under their dominion for the next one and a half centuries. What is now Russia began to develop, as Muscovy, the northern part of Rus', was able gradually to free itself from the Tatars; many of the Slavs living to the south slowly migrated westwards into the realms of Poland and Lithuania (united from 1386) then expanding to their southeast, as far as the Black Sea, and began to call themselves Ukrainians.

After the fall of Constantinople to the Turks in 1453, Ivan the Great set up Moscow as the third Rome and formalised the laws and constitution in much the same manner as his Tudor near-contemporaries. Ivan IV the Terrible (1530-84) extended Russian rule to the Caspian and called himself Tsar or Czar (Caesar), but was unable to reach the more important Black Sea, as the Tatars were still firmly settled in Crimea and were even able to sack Moscow in 1571. In 1569 the southern Lithuanian lands and the *sich* of the Cossacks (mainly Russian freebooters living in the no-man's-land of the steppes around Zaporozhye) formally joined the Polish-Lithuanian Federation, but refused to be Catholicised despite the creation of the Uniate church (basically Orthodox rites combined with obedience to the Pope) in 1596; the Great Revolt of the Cossacks under *Hetman* Bogdan Khmelnytsky in 1648 drove out the Poles and Lithuanians and led to the union of Ukraine with Muscovy in 1654, which led to many optimistic assertions of fraternal solidarity and so on throughout the Soviet period, although in fact it was only due to Khmelnytsky's inability to fight off both the Poles and the Turks.

In fact, as Russia expanded to the Pacific under autocrats such as Ivan, Boris Godunov, Peter I the Great and Catherine II the Great, it became an empire in which Ukraine was a junior part; ever since this time Russian political thought has held that dictatorship, of the proletariat or otherwise, is necessary or inevitable, and that if Russia did not rule the Asians, then the Asians would rule it. Nevertheless what Ukrainians to this day distrust in the Russians is their Oriental blood and the Tatar influence.

There was resistance in Ukraine, although it is tempting to echo Lampedusa's comment on 19th-century Sicily, that they never struggled enough for independence to deserve it. Western Ukraine continued to be ruled by Poland and Austria, while outlaws such as Dolbush, a Huţul Robin Hood-figure, became folk heroes; in eastern Ukraine the *Hetman* Ivan Mazepa formed an alliance with Charles XII of Sweden against Peter the Great, who defeated them decisively in 1709 at the battle of Poltava. After this serfdom was extended to the previously semi-free Ukraine, although Catherine the Great knew perfectly well that serfdom was dragging Russia down and preventing it from becoming a mercantilist or proto-capitalist state like those of western Europe; its only justification was that it enabled Russia to produce an army capable of beating Napoleon, but in fact it was the weather that drove him back in 1812, and in any case Britain was able to put just as good and successful an army into the field. Three Russo-Turkish wars after 1768 pushed the southern frontiers of Ukraine back beyond Odessa and Izmail.

Ukrainian nationalism began to develop in the early 19th Century, with the great national poet Taras Shevchenko at the centre of a strong literary movement from 1840 — himself born a serf, he equated Ukraine's position under Russia with that of the serf under his master. This 'romantic nationalist' movement was suppressed, but from 1850 there was a greater tolerance, although in 1863 Ukrainian was declared a dialect of Russian, and in 1876 Ukrainian-language publications were banned. Nationalism was particularly strong in western Ukraine, where it was identified with the Uniate church, but Austria was equally opposed to its expression. There was mass emigration from these western areas, mainly to the USA, but in eastern Ukraine there was an influx of Russian peasants to the cities in the wake of industrialisation.

By the turn of the century it was possible to found nationalist societies and political parties in Galicia (the Austrian-ruled portion of western Ukraine, centred on Lviv), and in the years before the First World War Ukraine shared in the prerevolutionary turmoil of Russia, with strikes and peasant risings, although looking more to Germany for inspiration than to the Pan-Slavist movement. It was the collapse of the summer 1916 offensive by the Russian General Brusilov into Galicia that led to the abdication of the Tsar in March 1917 and the end of the Russian empire.

Not surprisingly, chaos ensued as Ukraine and Russia tried to evolve not just a new system of government but also a new relationship between them; in March 1917 Mykhailo Hrushevsky, former Professor of Ukrainian History in Lviv and leader of the Ukrainian Social-Revolutionary Party, was speaker of the Ukrainian Central Council or Rada in Kyiv, which gradually emerged as the strongest contender for authority against the Provisional Government in Petrograd. On October 29 1917 there was an armed uprising at the Kyiv Arsenal after the arrest of the leaders of the Russian Social Democratic Labour Party in the Mariinsky Palace; this was crushed and on November 20 the Rada declared a People's Republic, with the initial support of the Bolsheviks, who hoped in vain for a rôle in government. After winning just 12% of the vote in elections a week later, the Bolsheviks proclaimed their own 'Soviet government' in Kharkiv on December 25 (Christmas in the West, but not in the Orthodox calendar) and orchestrated another revolt at the Kyiv Arsenal in January 1918, sending in the Red Army, Cossacks and sailors of the Baltic Fleet in support. On January 22 1918 the government in Kyiv declared its independence from the Soviet Union, with Hrushevsky as President, and sought help from the Central Powers of Germany and Austria who drove the Red Army out of Kyiv. The Austrian territories of Galicia and Bucovina set up their own Western Ukrainian National Republic in November 1918, united with the rest of Ukraine in January 1919, but were soon mostly handed over to Poland and Romania.

At the Treaty of Brest-Litovsk in March 1918 the Bolsheviks renounced their claims to Ukraine, and the Central Powers were able to set up a puppet state under *Hetman* Pavel Skoropadsky; however the Russian Civil War was almost entirely fought on Ukrainian soil, with the White (monarchist) Armies of Generals Wrangel and Denikin, the Red Army, Poles, Romanians and bandit warlords all involved, until 1920. With the end of the World War, Ukraine was able to restore some degree of self-government under the former premier Volodymyr Vynnychenko and War Minister Simyon Petliura; this government was driven out of Kyiv by the Bolsheviks (who held the First Congress of the Ukrainian Communist Party in Moscow, set up a government under the Bulgarian Khristian Rakovsky, and as before took all 'surplus' grain to Moscow) before the Whites drove them out. In March 1920 the Soviets again took power, were driven out, this time by the Poles, in May, and finally seized power in November 1920, having at last succeeded in grafting an acceptably

Ukrainian facade on to their Bolshevism. It is nigh impossible to say how many millions died in this period, from typhoid, cholera and dysentry as well as in the fighting itself; but far worse was to come.

Lenin died on January 21 1924, and by 1930 Stalin had established himself as sole successor; purges of opponents began in Ukraine in 1929, together with a campaign of forcible collectivisation. The peasants chose to slaughter their livestock rather than surrender it to collective ownership, and refused to work the collective fields; by 1932 the harvest was just 51% of the plan quota, but Stalin continued to simply starve the peasantry into submission by setting impossible quotas and seizing every scrap of grain produced. Many of the peasants were labelled *kulaks* or village moneylenders and proto-capitalists (*kurkul* in Ukrainian), and deported to Siberia. Finally from 1933 the use of urban shock workers to bring in the harvest brought the Terror-Famine to an end: perhaps 6m died in Stalin's war against the peasants, although only one side was armed. Pasternak said of it, 'What I saw could not be expressed in words. There was such inhuman, unimaginable misery, such a terrible disaster, that it began to seem almost abstract, it would not fit within the bounds of consciousness. I fell ill. For an entire year I could not write'.

In September 1939 the Soviet Union occupied Galicia as the Nazis invaded Poland from the west, and most of the bourgeois and professional classes 'disappeared'. The suffering of the Terror-Famine was matched in the years after the Nazi invasion of June 22 1941, which launched what is known as the True, or Great, Patriotic War; at first the German armies were seen as liberators by many Ukrainians, but it soon became clear that all Slavs were to be treated as racially sub-human, as the Jews were. Initially the Organisation of Ukrainian Nationalists, which had begun a sabotage campaign against the Soviet regime in 1930, was prepared to work with the Germans for Ukrainian independence, but as soon as a Ukrainian state had been declared in Lviv on June 30 it was suppressed by the Nazis. By the end of 1942 the OUN forces, now fighting all over the western Ukraine, were reorganised as the *Ukrainska Povstancha Armia* (Ukrainian Insurgent Army or UPA): by March 1943 it was 10,000 strong and continued to grow (to at least 30,000) in reaction to appalling Nazi atrocities such as burning entire villages in their wooden churches and killing all the political prisoners in Rivne prison, as well as the deportation of perhaps 3m Ukrainians for slave labour. The Soviets had killed perhaps 10,000 Ukrainians at the time of the invasion, and the UPA was as keen to keep them out as it was to get the Nazis out, although this was always a vain hope.

Hitler himself was in Ukraine (at Vinnitsa) to direct operations from July to October 1942, in one of his few forays from the Wolf's Lair, his base in northern Poland, but it was to no avail, and the tide of the war turned in January 1943 at Stalingrad. It is only since the demise of the Soviet Union that we have learnt the full extent of the desparate measures taken to stop the German armies here, a place of largely symbolic importance; no less than 13,500 Soviet soldiers were shot by their own side, *pour encourager les autres*, and of the 91,000 German prisoners taken, only 6,000 survived to return home. In 1943 Red partisans were also infiltrated into the occupied areas to harry the Germans and the UPA, and from early 1944 the Red Army itself was reconquering western Ukraine; the UPA units had to pass through their lines as they advanced, relatively easy in the marshy forests of Polessia to the north and the Carpathian mountains to the south, but harder in Podolia, in between.

As detailed above, the borders of Poland moved far to the west at the end of the Second World War, so that almost all of the western Ukraine now became part of the Soviet Union, and the UPA struggle against the Soviet occupiers spread to this area, with attacks on recruiting centres and the killing of Marshal Vatutin in an ambush. For some reason this was one campaign against the Soviet Union that the CIA and so on declined to support with weapons, and so, as guerrilla fighting continued in the mountain areas of what were now Poland and Slovakia, in 1947 the Red Army and the armies of Poland and Czechoslovakia were able to conduct a joint operation to flush the fighters out and deport whole villages alleged to be supporting them to the 'Recovered Territories' of western Poland. The remnants of the UPA forces fought their way west to surrender to the Americans in 1947 and 1948, and their commanders, remaining to transform the guerrilla campaign into political warfare, were killed by 1952.

At the end of the Second World War 3m Ukrainians were in Germany and Austria, and although 90,000 Cossack former POWs were controversially returned by force, to go straight to the Gulag camps or indeed straight against a wall, most were able to stay in the free world; there are now 1½m in the USA, half a million in Canada, 120,000 in Argentina, 100,000 in Brazil, 25,000 in Britain, and 20,000 in Australia and Germany. Another 6m or so Ukrainians died in the Second World War.

Under Stalin the Ukrainian language was allowed to be used, even for *Pravda*, but this was only a superficial concession as the Soviet Union became more centralised; the Ukrainian Orthodox and Uniate churches were forcibly merged with the Moscow Patriarchate, and there was another collectivisation drive (and coincidental famine) from 1946, ending with 85% of peasant farms being collectivised. After Stalin's death in 1953 and the 20th Party Congress of 1956 there was a thaw under Khrushchev, leading to demands for civil rights and national self-determination; however in the Brezhnev years there was a clampdown and a rise in Russian chauvinism, while the economy stagnated as 15% of GNP was spent on defence and only Siberian oil and gas kept the Soviet economy afloat.

From 1973 to 1989 the First Secretary of the Ukrainian Communist Party and thus effective ruler of Ukraine was Brezhnev's ally Volodymyr Shcherbytsky, who was increasingly out of place in the Gorbachevite era of *glasnost i perestroika* (openness and restructuring). From 1988 Rukh (the Popular Movement of Ukraine for Restructuring) emerged as a focus for dissidence; additionally in 1989 there were 12 strikes in the coal mines of the Donbas (in Ukraine and Russia) finally leading to the creation of a free trade union, and five of the 25 *oblast* (regional) Party secretaries were forced to resign on grounds of corruption. In September 1989 Rukh held its first congress and the Central Committee of the Ukrainian Communist Party elected the Gorbachev nominee Volodymyr Ivashko First Secretary. His programme was to make government more Ukrainian and more accountable, and to close Chornobyl; in January 1990 Rukh showed its strength by forming a human chain along the 540km road from Lviv to Kyiv, and in February, after Gorbachev had accepted the principle of multi-party politics, the communist party renounced its monopoly of power, with elections being held in March for all 450 seats in the Ukrainian Supreme Soviet. This was too early for genuine multi-party elections, as Rukh was only able to register officially as a party in mid-February (and to produce a newspaper from the end of the month), so there was nothing like the clean-sweep by Solidarity in Poland; however the communist party and its allies won only 280 out of 450 seats, with the Democratic Bloc of Rukh, Green World (the environmental party) and other opposition parties winning 108 and the remaining seats going to independent candidates who could mostly be relied on to support the opposition.

The Ukrainian Insurgent Army

The UPA (Ukrainska Povstancha Armia or Ukrainian Insurgent Army) was created in 1942 to struggle for Ukrainian independence, initially hoping for support from the German occupiers against Soviet communism but soon fighting as much against the German security forces (although not against the *Wehrmacht*, which was generally left alone to fight the Red Army). The UPA stronghold was in the forests and marshes of Volhynia and Polisia, north of the Kovel-Sarny line, and particularly around the village of Antonivka; it then moved south to the equally thick forests around Kremenets. From these bases it launched many attacks on the SD or German security service and the Polish auxiliary police, capturing many weapons and being joined by many deserters, especially from the Ukrainian auxiliary police (further east) and the SS Galicia division of Ukrainians who volunteered to fight communism, as well as Azeris, Armenians, Jews and others. The Germans were never able to deploy sufficient resources to crush the insurgents (although they continued to try even when it was clear that this was undermining the fight against the Red Army) so under the notorious General von dem Bach and his successors they resorted to terror tactics such as dive-bombing villages and killing their inhabitants by burning them inside their wooden churches. (It must be admitted that Ukrainians to the east were not blameless in this period, wiping out some Polish villages.) This of course merely accelerated the flow of volunteers to the forests, so that by late 1943 the UPA was at least 30,000 strong, and very well organised. Its greatest coup was the killing of General Viktor Lutze, the chief of the SD in Ukraine, in an ambush near Rivno.

In February 1943 the first Soviet partisans were sent behind the German lines to harry the German supply lines and equally to attack the UPA; by April 1944 the Red Army had occupied most of eastern and central Ukraine, capturing Lviv in July and reaching the Carpathians by October. The UPA began to move its forces south into the Carpathian foothills, particularly the Chorny Lis (Black Forest) west of Stanislavisk (now Ivano-Frankivsk). One division of the Red Army was cut off by a German counter-attack in this area and fought as partisans against the UPA until June 1944 when the UPA finally eliminated it.

Again the struggle was between the UPA and the security forces of the NKVD, but now the pressure was on the UPA which took to spending the entire winter in hidden bunkers, only emerging for fresh air after dark. Its greatest coup in this stage of the campaign was the ambushing of Marshal Vatutin, commander of the First Ukrainian Front, who died of his wounds in Kyiv on April 15 1944: it is still not officially admitted that this was the work of the UPA. This led to the 'Cheka-Military Operation for the Liquidation of the German-Ukrainian Nationalist Bands'; Nikita Khrushchev was put in charge of the Soviet campaign to wipe out the UPA, and was able to bring far greater resources to the job than the Nazis had done. The UPA was largely on the run now, as the Soviets felled and burned the forests and even supposedly spread lice infected with typhus in villages supporting the UPA in the Chernovts'i region.

The UPA split into smaller cells to concentrate more on propaganda work, and then moved into *Zakerzonia*, the Łemk lands west of the new Polish border along the Curzon line, to oppose the large-scale resettlement of the local population. At first it had more success against the Polish forces than against the NKVD, controlling all the area around Baligród and establishing a great network of bunkers and defences, but again its greatest coup was its undoing: on 28 March 1947 the Polish Deputy Minister of Defence, General Karol Świerczewski, was killed in an ambush south of Baligród, and this led to Operation Vistula (*Akcja Wisła*), a joint Soviet-Polish-Czechoslovak operation to clear the population from the Łemk villages of the Bieszczady and Beskid Niski. About 65% of the Polish Ukrainian population (perhaps 150,000 in all) had already been deported to the Soviet Union in 1945-46; this second wave of deportations was not as brutal, as there was no question of being sent to the Soviet Union. Villages were given 24 hours to pack and then taken to the Jaworzno camp east of Katowice, before being transferred to the formerly German 'Recovered Territories' of northwestern Poland.

The UPA was now left with no local population to protect and no local support, and the survivors broke out in small groups to fight through to the American forces in Bohemia and Bavaria, to turn to a political and propaganda struggle in the West; as the Iron Curtain had not yet closed the UPA never received the CIA aid it might have expected a few years later. Most of the UPA commanders remained in Ukraine and Poland, and were all killed in ambushes between 1949 and 1952. The UPA's political leader Stepan Bandera was also assassinated in Munich in 1959.

This aspect of Ukrainian history was until recently hushed up in Poland and particularly in Ukraine, and most of the available information is in naturally partisan books published by the émigré community, such as *UPA Warfare in Ukraine* by Yuriy Tys-Krokhmaliuk (Society of Veterans of the Ukrainian Insurgent Army, New York 1972) and *The Ukrainian Insurgent Army in the Fight for Freedom* (United Committee of the Ukrainian American Organisations of New York, New York 1954). However in late 1993 a controversial law was introduced granting UPA fighters the same pension rights as Red Army veterans.

POLITICS

On July 16 1990 the Ukrainian Soviet declared sovereignty, following in the steps of the Baltic States, and in November up to 100,000 students demonstrated on the streets of Kyiv for more reforms, and some went on hunger strike, leading to the resignation of Vitaly Masol (Chair of the Council of Ministers) and his replacement by Viktor Fokhin.

On August 28 1991, after the attempted *putsch* against Gorbachev, the Ukrainian Soviet passed a declaration of independence, as the Soviet Union fell apart. This was ratified by a ratio of almost nine votes to one in a referendum on December 1; the *oblasts* west of Poltava all voted by more than 90% for independence, and only the four easternmost and most Russified *oblasts* and the Crimea were less enthusiastic, although even Crimea approved, with 54.19% in favour. At the same time Ukraine directly elected a president for the first time; he was the party's former ideology secretary and speaker of the Soviet, Leonid Kravchuk, who was (and is) not exactly popular but is seen as a good manager, providing stability and continuity. As a career *apparatchik* he is seen as a consummate power broker, who failed to condemn the *putsch* but otherwise judged perfectly when to change sides and play the nationalist card.

At once Ukraine was recognised by Russia, Poland and Canada (with Britain following in January), and the work of constructing a new state, the largest in area in Europe and the fifth most populous, had to be faced up to. The problems are far more complex than for the former satellite states of central Europe, which merely have to reorientate themselves towards already familiar concepts of democracy and free-market economics; in Ukraine and the other former Soviet republics it is necessary to create the state itself, with its currency and Central Bank, its army, frontiers and so on, and also to discover these alien concepts. In addition Ukrainian politics are bedevilled by the certainty that Russia, having grown so used to considering Ukraine as a natural part of its empire, cannot now think of it other than as a subservient province; as the rouble is still the only truly effective currency for the area, their economies are umbilically linked and it is impossible to take independent decisions.

On December 8 1991 the three Slav republics of Russia, Ukraine and Belarus signed an agreement to form a Commonwealth of Independent States; this finally did away with the Soviet Union, although President Mikhail Gorbachev did not finally resign until the end of the year, and it was even longer before 'the last Soviet citizen', a lone cosmonaut in the *Mir* space station, returned to a world he no longer recognised. The CIS was soon joined by all the Transcaucasian and Asian republics except Georgia, already plunged into civil war — the three Baltic republics had of course already gone their own way. There was never agreement as to the purpose of the CIS, or the form it should take; it was soon clear that Ukraine's view was that it should and could only be a temporary arrangement leading to total independence, whereas the Asian states wanted a continuing umbrella arrangement, and Russia was felt to be trying to recreate its empire, talking of its 'historical rights' over the area.

Disputes centred at first on the question of joint CIS armed forces, with Ukraine insisting on its own army and a fair share of the Black Sea Fleet (about 380 ships), based in the Crimean port of Sevastopil. Ukraine has traditionally supplied the sergeant class of the Soviet army, much like the Sikhs in India, and has now inherited the largest army in Europe, 700,000 strong, which will have to be cut by about half, although the state will find it hard to house the demobilised soldiers. Equally it is admitted that Ukraine cannot afford to maintain a deep sea fleet, but it is universally seen as necessary to stand up to Big Brother's bullying, so the dispute dragged on for a very long time and many summit meetings before a compromise could be arrived at. Eventually (in mid-1992) Russia also agreed with the other successor states to divide property abroad, so that they could at last start to open their own embassies.

The issue of the fleet was very closely linked to that of nuclear weapons: Ukraine, like Belarus and Kazakhstan, immediately declared an intention to become a non-nuclear state, but in March 1992 Kravchuk suspended the transfer of 2,500 tactical nuclear weapons to Russia to be dismantled under already concluded arms reduction agreements, claiming that Ukraine was not satisfied that Russia was indeed destroying them. This dispute was resolved (making the Black Sea Fleet non-nuclear), but there then arose the issue of the 176 intercontinental missiles (with 1,240 warheads) based in Ukraine, to be dismantled under the START-1 agreement, already signed by Russia, Belarus, Kazakhstan and the USA. These were theoretically under the strategic control of the CIS military headquarters in Moscow, but under Ukrainian operational control (so that Ukraine could prevent but not order their launch); Ukraine claimed to need US$1.5bn to dismantle them in Russia, the USA offered US$175m (said to be 'enough to blow them up, not enough to dismantle them'), while it was said that the warheads contained US$5 billion worth of plutonium, gold and other materials. Ukraine denied using nuclear weapons as bargaining chips, but demanded Western guarantees against Russian aggression before ratifying the START-1 treaty, let alone START-2, already signed by Russia and the USA. The West was reluctant to provide security guarantees or more money, but the USA eventually offered US$155m in additional aid, and Ukraine finally ratified START-1 in November 1993. Although the SS-19s have corrosive liquid fuel and are rapidly deteriorating, and must soon be dismantled, the 46 modern SS-24s, built in Ukraine, can more easily be maintained, and many deputies wanted to keep them. Nevertheless in January 1994 Kravchuk signed an agreement with Presidents Clinton and Yeltsin to dismantle these too, in return for further US aid. At least chemical weapons are not an issue for Ukraine, all being stored in Russia.

In January 1992 price controls were largely abolished, as also in Russia, and Ukraine introduced 'coupons' as a transitional measure to give some semblance of fiscal independence pending the (constantly

delayed) introduction of its own currency, the *hrivna*, long since printed
in Canada and now stored until the right moment. Basic foodstuffs rose
in price three or four times, without any obvious benefits to consumers;
it was soon clear that it was pointless freeing prices without first freeing
the retail system to allow some basic competition. At least, thank God,
Ukraine does not suffer from the degree of gangsterdom that has forced
prices up many times more in Russia. The coupon, initially equal to the
rouble in value, was briefly worth more than it on the black market, but
soon plunged to half the value of what had until then been the world's
least desirable currency. Renaming the 'transitional currency' the
karbovanets has done nothing to help; the term 'coupon' is generally
used in this book, although the abbreviations 'R' and 'K' appear.

In June 1992 that year's budget was passed at last, setting a deficit
of 2% of GDP (R54bn), but this limit was reached by mid-summer, partly
due to state revenue plunging as the huge rises in prices (28 times what
they had been a year earlier, although wages had risen only 10 times) led
to high tax-evasion. Industrial production also dived, largely due to
exports to other CIS states not being paid for, so that the coal mines in
particular were facing bankruptcy; unemployment rose from 31,000 in
June 1992 to about 500,000 by the end of the year. Food subsidies
were cut to counter the increase in the budget deficit, so that milk and
sugar rose 10 times in price, and vodka two and a half times, while
wages were frozen at about R3,000 a month, when the minimum
subsistence level was officially set at R4,000. Also in July Volodymyr
Lanovy, the vice-premier in charge of privatisation and a reformer from
the New Ukraine Party known as the 'Ukrainian Gaidar', was sacked
(though public pressure was blaming Fokhin for the sluggish pace of
reform), and was replaced by Valentyn Symonenko, a former communist,
which did not bode well for the reform programme. (In Russia the arch-
reformer Yegor Gaidar was himself voted out as Boris Yeltsin's acting
prime minister in December.)

In September a general strike was called by the Union of Free Trades
Unions of Ukraine (mainly miners and transport workers) and in October
Fokhin's government lost a vote of confidence by 295 votes to 6 (having
survived one in July) as those opposed to the austerity programme and
those in favour of more reforms united against it. Kravchuk appointed
Leonid Kuchma prime minister, and the opposition, unable to work
together, allowed his new government to rule by decree for six months
to forestall economic collapse.

Kuchma was supposedly in favour of the Chinese economic model for
controlled transition to a liberal market economy, but after visiting Poland
was apparently converted to the shock therapy approach; prices were
freed further in early 1993, most agricultural subsidies were abolished,
and a few small state industries were privatised. Western advisers were
made more welcome, and every state farm was instructed to yield 10%
of its land to the private sector (having previously given up just 1%),
although no bank credits were available to the private farmers. However
the Central Bank issued no less than K1.5 **trillion** in credits to state

farms, increasing the money supply by 25% and causing the currency to drop in value by a third. All this came just as Russia under its new prime minister Chornomyrdin was backpedalling on its reforms, reintroducing food subsidies, and there was great pressure for Ukraine to do likewise.

Meanwhile the debate over the future of the CIS continued, with Ukraine seeing it as needed only as long as the Rouble zone economies remained intertwined (and only signing 40% of CIS agreements), and the Asian republics and Russia (now claiming the right to keep the peace in all the former Soviet states) wanting a more permanent arrangement. In January 1993 Ukraine (with Moldova) refused to sign the CIS charter, feeling that as the Asian and Transcaucasian states had only a veneer of democracy the whole thing was bound to collapse anyway. Russia, now forced to trade at world prices, cut the amount of oil and gas it had contracted to supply at cheaper rates to Ukraine, so that petrol sales to private cars were suspended and Kravchuk flew to Moscow to negotiate; although Russia traditionally supplied 85% of Ukraine's oil and 70% of its gas, rather conveniently for Ukraine 93% of Russia's gas exports to the West flow through Ukraine, so that Ukraine had some room to negotiate.

The six-month period of rule by decree was largely wasted, so in May 1993 a power struggle developed between Kravchuk and Kuchma, with Kravchuk wanting executive power himself, including control of the Central Bank; parliament refused this but also refused to accept Kuchma's resignation. In June 1993 price rises led to miners' strikes closing half of Ukraine's pits; after nine days Kravchuk temporarily imposed presidential rule, although Kuchma remained prime minister until September when Kravchuk eliminated the post, supposedly to allow him to speed up reform, still proceeding at a snail's pace. The strikes were ended by huge new subsidies (estimated at K13 trillion, then US$2 billion) to the already highly paid miners; it was largely this that led to the karbovannets collapsing in value (from 3,300 to the dollar in June to 19,050 in August, and to 39,000 by January 1994, and thirty to the rouble) and finally pushed Ukraine into hyperinflation, combined with hypercorruption. The government continued to print money as fast as the presses could roll (K2.2 trillion (US$90 billion) between September and November 1993), and bank credits also soared by a third in the third quarter of 1993, to K16 trillion; the only good sign is that the 1993 harvest has been excellent.

Kravchuk has a parliamentary majority, but not the two thirds required to modify the constitution. Elections are due for parliament in March 1994 and for the presidency in June 1994, but there are some fears that they may be delayed, allowing a period of authoritarian rule.

While aid is being lavished on Russia to persuade the populace to stick with Yeltsin and his reform programme, little has reached Ukraine, which is resented, particularly as Ukraine has aligned itself with the West and sent soldiers to serve with the UN in Bosnia while Russia has maintained its historic pro-Serb alignment — Russia and Serbia (and to a lesser extent the Czechs) are seen as Big Brother nations, seeking to dominate their less powerful brothers, while Ukraine is on the side of the underdog. Nevertheless it has proved almost impossible to halt the flow of sanction-busting oil barges along the Danube to Serbia. Although still not wholeheartedly committed to Western ideals of democracy and the free market, Ukraine is nevertheless remarkably stable, free from the many border disputes of the rest of the CIS and the presidential-parliamentary tug-of-war (with an unholy alliance of conservatives and neo-communists with primitive nationalists) that came close to tearing Russia apart.

Late news

Presidential elections in Crimea in January 1994 were won by Yuri Meshkov, with 73% of the vote; although he looks reassuringly like Vaclav Havel, he is closer in his views to the Russian nationalist Zhirinovsky, and seeks closer ties with Russia. Although he claims to want economic and ethnic stability, it seems increasingly likely that Crimea will be the flash point of conflict between Ukraine and Russia. As the Ukrainian economy collapses, with GDP falling 20% in both 1992 and 1993, the eastern Ukraine is increasingly agitating for closer links with Russia and its more stable economy, leading possibly to secession and civil conflict.

So far Ukraine has barely begun to develop an effective political system; there are more than 30 small parties which disagree on most issues and are failing to build any consensus. All the parties are poor (the Democratic Party boasted 10,000 coupony in its account, the grand sum of US$10!) and regionally based, with the Republican Party having half, and the Democratic Party a third, of their membership in the traditionally more radical western Ukraine (which has only 10% of Ukraine's population), and the Green Party having a third of its members in just the one western *oblast* of Ternopil. This is largely due to public apathy; after the student demos and strikes of October 1990 the people rapidly became disillusioned, so that in a poll in June 1992 Rukh rated 17% in favour and 49% against, and New Ukraine 12% in favour and 31% against, while 42% claimed to be non- or anti-party. By-election turnouts rarely reach the 50% quorum, so that there are many vacant seats in parliament. Unlike in Russia, there is no state funding of parties, although this is likely to change.

Political parties began to form after the semi-democratic elections of March 1990, when the communist party prevented most opposition fronts and movements from standing, although the surrogate 'Democratic Bloc' was able to win about 25% of the seats. Now the political spectrum is coalescing into five main blocs: on the extreme right wing is the ultra-nationalist bloc, dominated by the Ukrainian National

Assembly (UNA, incorporating groups such as the Ukrainian Nationalist Union) and the Association for an Independent Ukraine (likely to either fade away or merge with the UNA); these groups are anti-Russian and seek a nuclear-armed Ukraine, and their paramilitary wing fought for the breakaway Transdniestrian Republic in Moldova. The UNA was originally set up by the émigrés of the OUN, but rapidly evolved away from their Stalinist-era timewarp.

The national-democratic bloc, equivalent to our conservative or Christian Democratic parties, was synonymous with Rukh, an umbrella for dissident groups, which at its 1992 congress elected a triumvirate of Mykhailo Horyn', Ivan Drach (the previous chairman), and Viacheslav Chornovil (a 1960s dissident) in an attempt to keep itself together. However this didn't last, with Chornovil's Wałęsa-esque anti-communist populism more acceptable to the membership (mostly in western Ukraine and the cultural intelligentsia) than Horyn' and Drach's pro-Kravchuk stance. The Republican Party (under Horyn'), the Democratic Party (under Drach and Yavorivskyi) and the more left of centre Party for the Democratic Revival of Ukraine have now split from it: the Republican Party, the best funded and organised of the Ukrainian parties (even having a few PCs), is seeking to transform itself into a 'natural party of government', although it is caught in the usual eastern European dilemma of trying to support both free enterprise and low taxation, and high defence and social spending. Chornovil's wing of Rukh leads the Congress of Democratic Forces, pressing for early elections and reform of the existing authoritarian system.

The liberal bloc is represented by another umbrella organisation, New Ukraine (led by Volodymyr Filenko), including business groups and social democratic parties, as well as elements of the Green Party, and standing for rapid reforms and a social market economy, and good relations with Russia, appealing to the Russophone technocrats but not the bulk of the population. This had the potential to become a strong centrist force, but so far seems to have failed to build up any momentum.

The state-bureaucratic bloc comprises the former communist *apparat* (the 'national-communists') and the leaders of the military-industrial complex, supporting Kravchuk, who is attempting to stay above any party allegiance and retain broad support. If there is no governing party, it is hard to have a concrete opposition party, but Kravchuk will need a party base before the next parliamentary elections.

The socialist bloc is likewise reluctant to form a party, as that would force the right wing to organise as well, but the Communist Party of Ukraine was reregistered in October 1993, seeking to emulate the former Polish Communist Party in bouncing back to power; it stands for traditional state control, appealing to those who see market reform as simply meaning higher prices.

In addition there are also small regional parties, speaking for the Romanians of Chernovts'i, the Russians of the Donbas, the Rusyn of Transcarpathia, and in Crimea the Mejlis of the Crimean Tatars and the Republican Party in Crimea.

In parliament the parties are loose and ill-disciplined (although they also tend to take a fairly Stalinist view of internal dissent); in theory there are 38 socialist members, 46 from Rukh, 42 from the Congress of National Democratic Forces (including 23 Democrats and 10 Republicans), and 52 from New Ukraine; however interest groups are stronger, such as the agricultural lobby (about 80 members, mostly state farm managers opposed to reform), and the industrial lobby (with up to 100 members, also against reform), and there are 200 members who vote on the whim of the moment. Deputies can belong to more than one faction and there is no whipping system, so that they frequently vote against the party line.

Few deputies now owe their careers to a party machine, so they take a light view of their party loyalties; this will change after the 1994 elections, when party identities will be more firmly established and deputies will owe their jobs to a specific party and interest group. Parties often splinter at their congresses, or potential dissenters are purged immediately beforehand; before September 1991 3,000 members were required for registration of a party (and 100,000 for the presidential elections), but this was then reduced to 300, leading to a boom in the number of parties. The threshold is likely to be raised again, to produce larger, more stable parties, and thus more stability. Parties are likely to differentiate themselves more clearly as social groups differentiate themselves; this depends on social and economic reform, which itself depends partly on the development of an effective political system.

(with thanks to Dr Andrew Wilson)

CHORNOBYL

If Ukraine is known for one thing, it is probably for the world's worst nuclear accident at the Chornobyl (Chernobyl) power station, 120km north of Kyiv, in the early hours of April 26 1986. The accident itself was tragic enough, but the saga continues to this day, with Ukraine so short of energy that it has been forced to reopen the Chornobyl station, and despite popular opposition to increase the nuclear share of the country's electricity production from a quarter to a third.

Although there was a notorious cover-up at the time, quite a lot has now been revealed about the background to the disaster, which not only helps explain its immediate causes but also gives a deeper understanding of the Soviet system, which it helped push towards its final disintegration.

Reactor 4 at Chornobyl was launched on December 20 1983, and entered commercial production from early 1984 — the usual six-month testing period was reduced, with the plant's director Viktor Bryukhanov signing the acceptance document on December 31 1983 to ensure bonuses for that year. Nevertheless, when criminal trials began in July and August 1987 it was two inexperienced operators who had died within two weeks of the accident who were made the scapegoats, with Anatoly Dyatlov, the plant's deputy chief engineer, who was sentenced to 10 years imprisonment and released after four. It is now clear that training and supervision were woefully inadequate and that safety equipment had never been properly installed; but it was a combination of these factors with design faults and an unlikely combination of events that led to melt-down.

In a Western pressurised water reactor the fuel rods are kept out of contact with the boiling water that drives the turbines, but in a Soviet RBMK (reactor high-power boiling channel) reactor it is the radioactive water cooling the rods that also drives the turbines; this requires an immensely complex system with thousands of welds, each one a potential failure point. Thus it is immensely important to keep the cooling pumps working in the event of a power failure, and on April 25 1986 a test was scheduled to see if it was possible to use the turbine's own momentum to drive the pumps for the 50 seconds between a power cut and the standby diesel generators coming on line. This was for some reason delayed until the unbriefed evening shift had come on duty and did not begin until 2310; although the plan was to keep the reactor ticking over at a level at which it could drive the pumps if need be, the operator mistakenly virtually closed it down, before then at 0100 raising the power too fast and increasing the flow of coolant; this reduced the steam pressure as its temperature rose due to voids or bubbles in the reactor core. The experiment should at once have been aborted and the reactor shut down, but this did not happen until 0123, by which time the temperature was rising uncontrollably fast; more cooling water was still being pumped in and at 0124 there was a massive steam explosion which lifted off the reactor's 1,000t top plate.

A second explosion followed at once, caused by steam reacting with zirconium or graphite, causing an immensely hot graphite fire in the core; zirconium-95 and ruthenium-103/106 were found in the fall-out, indicating that the temperature had exceeded their melting-point of 2,250°C and that there had been a total melt-down of the reactor. By 0635 fire crews had extinguished all the fires except for the graphite fire in the core itself; this was tackled by pumping liquid nitrogen into the basement to freeze the ground under the reactor and by dropping huge quantities of sand and lead on to the fire by helicopter until May 2. The fire was cooled but nuclear reactions continued, with between 2m and 8m curies of radioactive material being released daily until May 9 when the 5,000 tonnes of sand finally caused the remaining structures to collapse, blowing a last cloud of radioactive dust up to 60km. A total of 9 tonnes of radioactive material escaped, 90 times that released at Hiroshima.

It was later revealed that the local fire crews had never performed a fire drill at the power station and that they had no understanding of radioactivity; nevertheless the 186 fire crew and 16,500 Interior Ministry police who were soon involved performed heroically — two were killed almost at once by massive doses of radioactivity (and their bodies never recovered), and almost 5,000 others were taken ill. It is now thought that 5,000-8,000 of the 229,000 who worked on the site in 1986-87 have died (although the Soviet Union's official death toll was just 32), and 35,000 are ill, despite having been issued (seriously) with lead-lined pants and aprons and a cotton helmet with glass visor. By April 29 it was clear from Swedish monitoring and US satellite photographs that a massive disaster had occurred, but this was officially denied until May 1, when it was announced that the situation was stabilised (untrue, as we have seen) but that, the wind having changed, children would be evacuated from Kyiv on May 15. It was to be another three years before the long-term consequences of the accident began to be faced up to.

Glasnost' was in its early stages and this cover-up did nothing to improve its credibility, with another press conference on May 6 giving a very partial account of events and a broadcast by Gorbachev on May 14 mainly taken up with criticism of the Western media. Nevertheless in the long run the facts were so shocking, and the demand for them both in the West and in the Soviet Union so great, that they had to come out, and the revelations of incompetence and the way this was integral to the Soviet system fuelled the demand for openness and in the end contributed to the demise of that system. The disaster produced other changes: the Soviet Union's first charity rock concert was held in June 1986, and now one can frequently meet groups of 'Chornobyl kids' in Turbazas.

On April 27 the area within a 10km radius of Chornobyl was evacuated, and on May 2 this was extended to 30km; in all about 200,000 people were evacuated from 2,000 settlements, and 100,000 of these have been resettled elsewhere and compensated. Agriculture has been halted in a wider area, but pockets of dangerously high gamma radiation have been found as far away as Chernovts'i, near the Romanian border, as well as across the republics of Belarus, which bore the brunt of the early discharges, and Russia. About 5m people (2.8m in Ukraine) live in contaminated areas and perhaps 160,000 children received excess doses to the thyroid. Cancer increased 32% in Ukraine in the five years after 1986, with child cancers rising by 92% and cancer of the thyroid (which takes about six years to develop) by 82%. In addition to these cancers, there is also a syndrome known as 'Chernobyl AIDS', caused by massive damage to the immune system, and considerable numbers of deformed farm animals and perhaps babies. In all 600,000 people in Russia, 340,000 in Ukraine and 200,000 in Belarus are registered as suffering radiation-related illnesses. However all this is small beer compared to the effects on the Kazakhs living around the 'Polygon' nuclear test site near Semipalatinsk, only being disclosed in 1993; there were 500 test explosions here, a third of them above ground, and the resulting illnesses and deformities are truly awful, while the life expectancy in some villages is just 27.

One of the worst-affected areas is the 100,000km^2 of the Pripyat marshes, Europe's largest swamp; the water table at Chornobyl is only 4m below ground level, so that major pollution of water supplies was inevitable. The massive Kyiv reservoir, which stretches from Chornobyl to Kyiv, was drained in May 1987 to flush as much of the radiation as possible into the Black Sea, but the bed of the Dnestr in Kyiv still displays high radioactivity levels, so that swimming here is a risky activity, even if you don't touch the bottom. Although food in Kyiv may also be contaminated, all sources are unanimous that there is next to no health risk to short-term visitors.

In October 1986 the remains of Reactor 4 were sealed in concrete; it is now clear that this 'sarcophagus' was made on the cheap and is already crumbling, but it was seen as essential in order to keep the site's other three reactors working. After Ukrainian independence there was a consensus for a close down of the nuclear industry, but after massive cuts in the supplies of Russian oil, and rises in its price, the new republic was obliged to recommence nuclear generation. Reactor 2 was closed after a fire, but reactors 1 and 3 remain open; the station was shut down in 1990 but then reopened; parliament voted again in 1992 and 1993 for closure, but this was vetoed by President Kravchuk, and in October 1993 they voted, in the face of economic collapse and fuel shortage, to continue operation until 2003. As the Soviet nuclear industry was totally centred on Moscow, it is proving hard for independent Ukraine to run its industry alone; in particular only Russia has facilities for disposing of spent fuel rods.

There were various accidents at other Ukrainian nuclear power stations in 1992, two fires at Chornobyl in January 1993, a shutdown due to a turbine fault in April, and an explosion which killed one man at the Zaporozhye plant in May 1993, and some nuclear fuel has, it seems, been stolen from Chornobyl; although safety regulations have been tightened up, these are widely disregarded and there is still no effective culture of safety. Sixteen other RBMK reactors are still working in Russia, Ukraine and Lithuania, including Sosnovy Bor, near St Petersburg, where radioactive iodine was released from a cooling channel in March 1992, and Russia plans to recommence construction work on five new reactors frozen since the Chornobyl accident, and eventually to double its current 20,000MW nuclear generating capacity, despite the 'mini-Chornobyl' accident at the Tomsk-7 reprocessing plant in April 1993. The West is generally assumed to be assisting with safety improvements, but it seems that far more money is being invested in expanding the nuclear industry in eastern Europe, most notably at the Temelín power station in Bohemia, which it is hoped will be a prototype for a new generation of reactors. There is in fact massive scope for energy conservation in all of eastern Europe which would make new generating capacity irrelevant. Meanwhile 20% of Ukraine's state budget, and 17% of Belarus's, is being spent on the Chornobyl clean-up, and 340 Welsh hill farmers still cannot sell their sheep due to caesium fall-out.

One of the oddest stories to come out of Chornobyl recently has been a report from the UN's Drug Control programme that opium plantations

have been located within the evacuated zone. God knows what effect
that might have!

THE ECONOMY

The Ukrainian economy is in a worse state than those of Russia, Belarus
or the Baltic states, essentially because Ukraine is only in control of 5%
of its GNP, the rest still being under the control of the Union Ministries
and the Russian Central Bank. In 1992 Ukrainian production was 20%
less than in 1991 due to the collapse of the inter-republican trade
system, even though the Rouble was still being used for all transactions.
Ukrainian enterprises continued to export to Russia, as in former times,
although their customers stopped paying; eventually Ukrainian customs
began to insist on certificates promising payment before allowing
exports, but with such a long open border this is almost unenforceable.
For example, by the summer of 1992 the Hammer and Sickle tractor
factory in Kharkiv was owed R1bn (US$6m) by Russian customers, but
carried on producing without worrying about being paid, then turned to
the National Bank of Ukraine which as expected gave it R323m credit at
23% pa interest, a *very* soft loan with monthly inflation rising to 50%.
Even once the National Bank of Ukraine had been brought under control,
the Russian Central Bank continued to issue Rouble credits to non-
Russian enterprises in huge quantities, destroying all efforts at monetary
control; *apparatchiks* in both countries have failed to shake off their
belief in the production-led economy, producing goods even if no-one
wanted them, and issuing credits to bail out bankrupt enterprises in order
to keep workers in their jobs, leading to the brink of hyperinflation. It
was Gorbachev who first introduced the philosophy of *khozraschyot* or
standing on one's own financial feet without depending on state
handouts, but it is only catching on slowly.
  Hyperinflation is defined as the point at which barter takes over from
money (and economic systems break down), at about 50% inflation per
month. In Russia and Germany hyperinflation destroyed the old societies
in 1921-23 and allowed their replacement by communism and,
eventually, fascism. During 1921-23 the Russian money supply grew
1,700 times; in 1992 it grew 30 times, from around R200bn in January
to R6,200bn in December, as the Central Bank, under the control of the
economically illiterate parliament of Ruslan Khasbulatov, printed new
money to enable bankrupt state enterprises to pay staff. This brought
Russia, and Ukraine too, close to hyperinflation; to receive aid from the
IMF, inflation had first to be reduced to 5% per month, and the budget
deficit from 40% of GDP to 2%. Russia was able to improve its
situation, but Ukraine has remained stuck on the brink of hyperinflation.
Meanwhile in December 1993 Serbia reached an inflation rate of
50,000% per month, more than the maximum reached in Weimar
Germany. As Russia's economy has stabilised there have been increasing
calls in eastern Ukraine for economic reintegration with the Slav

republics of Russia and Belarus; the government, more concerned with holding the state together than with reforming the economy, has begun to move in this direction, infuriating the nationalists and western Ukrainians.

Ultimately to have control of its own economy Ukraine has to leave the Rouble zone, but any move in this direction is resisted by Russia, seeking to keep its economic dominance of the former Soviet Union, while charging world prices for its energy exports; this, and a dispute over the division of the former Soviet Union's US$80bn foreign debt, led to an alleged economic 'blockade' of Ukraine which led to there briefly being no fuel for private cars until grain and sugar could be bartered for oil from Iran. (In 1992 Russia exported 66m tonnes of oil, its main source of foreign currency, to Ukraine, and having promised 25m tonnes in 1993, of 40m tonnes requested, then allowed it only 15m tonnes, at world prices. However at least 15% of Russia's oil production, 40m tonnes pa, is lost through leakage from pipelines; this led to 600 being killed when a spark from a Trans-Siberian train ignited an oil spill.)

Back in 1989 the Ukrainian economy was still growing, by just 0.26%, but in 1991 it shrank by 11% and in 1992 by 20% to a GNP of US$226bn (US$4,340 per capita), although industrial output only fell by 10%, for the reasons noted above; in the third quarter of 1993 industrial output was 21% less than a year earlier (and just 2% of it came from privatised enterprises). As the industrial tax base collapsed, the budget deficit soared; income tax was introduced, at up to 50%, and VAT at 28%, and the turnover tax, which VAT has replaced elsewhere in eastern Europe, was not abolished. In 1992 inflation was 2,180%, rising to 8,500% in 1993; in human terms, this meant that by November 1993 the average monthly salary was K350,000, still only US$15, while a loaf of bread cost K1,000, a kilo of meat K8,770 (over half a day's wages), and a litre of sunflower oil K4,450. Unemployment was at 250,000, but was expected to rise to 1.5m by the end of the year. In 1992 a litre of Coke cost a dollar in both Ukraine and Britain, while a CD (US$8 in Hungary) cost US$30 in Ukraine. Nevertheless there are always long queues for prestige products such as Macburgers, Koka-Kola and Parmigiani ice-cream, as inflation makes it pointless to save. Under Soviet rule less than 5% of income went on rent and utilities, but this is climbing steeply.

Meanwhile there were reports that Western consultants, for the EU's £360m TACIS programme for aid to the former Soviet Union, were being paid £2,000 a day plus expenses, while the European Bank for Reconstruction and Development notoriously spent £55m on doing up its London offices.

MINORITIES

Ukraine is largely populated by Ukrainians, surprisingly enough, but you could be forgiven for suspecting that eastern and western Ukraine are inhabited by two separate groups; those to the west largely speak Ukrainian and those to the east largely speak Russian, and those in the formerly Polish areas of western Ukraine have a different culture, with a more developed sense of free enterprise and civil society, from those in the east who, having lived under Russian and communist rule for so long, are more communally minded. In addition there are real Russians in eastern Ukraine and all larger towns, various groups of Ruthenians in the Carpathians, Hungarians and Slovaks in Transcarpathia, Romanians and gypsies in northern Bucovina and Transcarpathia, Jews now mainly in Kyiv, and Tatars in Crimea. In 1990 the 52m population was 73% Ukrainian, 22% Russian, and 1% Jewish; while there are 12m Russians in Ukraine, there are also 5-8m Ukrainians in Russia, so that the two nations are inseparably bound.

Any **Russian** asked to define his national character will start by saying that all Russians are poets and dreamers; sadly they cannot all have the poetic sensibility of a Pushkin or an Akhmatova, and most are in fact excessively sentimental, egotistical and often irresponsible. They also talk of their bond with the land, hence the notion of 'Mother Russia', although they are not keen on mountains, needing a sense of *prostor* or not being hemmed in. Ukrainians put this, and their empire-building tendencies, down to the Mongol strand in the Russian make-up, while their passive acceptance of autocracy is blamed on the tradition of the Orthodox church. Russian religiosity also led them to accept communism as a sort of evangelical faith, with prophets such as Marx and Engels promising an earthly paradise, and still leads them to disregard the awfulness of their daily lives.

Where Russians always think in communal terms, Ukrainians are more individualist, not interested in collective farming or in being part of a Russian empire. Like the Poles, they look to the West, partly because of the Uniate church's allegiance to Rome, and see themselves as part of a common European home in a way that the Russians cannot.

In addition to the Ukrainians *per se*, there are three groups of **Ruthenians**, classed as Ukrainians by Poles and Slovaks, but seeing themselves as distinct from them, if part of the same Slav family, and speaking their own dialects. The name *Rusyn* comes from *Rus'*, the name of the original Slav state founded in Ukraine over a thousand years ago; after the rise of Russia, Ukraine became known as Little Russia or *Malorossiya*, but the name *Rusyn* or Ruthenian survived in eastern Europe as a term for the non-Catholic Slavs east of Poland. Ruthenia became the name for what is now *Zacarpats'ka oblast* or Transcarpathia, the corner of Ukraine to the southwest of the Carpathians, which has also been called Carpatho-Ukraine, Hungarian Ruthenia, Carpathian Russia, and Sub-Carpathian Rus'. It was Hungarian from the 10th Century until the end of the First World War, then Czechoslovak until 1939. Since the Second World War the heartland of the Rusyn has been part of Ukraine.

The Rusyn are divided into three groups, the Lemks, Boyks and Huţuls, with the Boyks in the area from the Bieszczady east (mainly north of the

Carpathians) to Kolochava and Ust-Chorna, Lemks south of the Carpathians through Transcarpathia and Slovakia, west of the Bieszczady in Poland and also some to the north of the Chornohora massif, around Deliatin, Kosiv and Vizhnitsa, and the Huṭuls around Chornohora, the headwaters of the Tisa and Prut and into Romania. The Boyks and Huṭuls traditionally have shingled houses with steep roofs to shed snow, while the Lemk *hizha* is thatched, with a less steep roof; the Huṭuls are pastoralists, living in scattered settlements near the high meadows, and also foresters and raftsmen, while the Boyks and Lemks are arable farmers living in elongated villages along the valleys and growing potatoes, oats, rye and wheat, with some corn on southern slopes. The Huṭuls have much in common with the people of Maramureṣ, in northern Romania, with icons on glass and embroidered sashes hung over them, while the Boyks and Lemks have some resemblances to the Górale of the Zakopane area, with their ornamental hatchets for weddings and festivals.

It's hard to say exactly how many Rusyn there are in Ukraine: in Transcarpathia 78.4% of the 1.25m population (in 1987) were listed as Ukrainian, which includes the Rusyn: 4-500,000 would seem a reasonable approximation, in addition to some north of the watershed.

There are museums of Huṭul ethnography in Kolomea and Kosmach, while the Kraków Ethnographic Museum has a wonderful collection of Łemk, Boyk and Huṭul material. In addition the Ukrainian Centre of Education and Culture has been set up at ul Kanonicza 15 in Kraków, showing exhibitions of Rusyn art, largely derived from their Uniate faith.

There are around 150,000 **Hungarians** in Transcarpathia, all along the border from Chop to Beregovo and south of Vinogradiv, and in the towns of Uzhgorod and Mukachevo, where many street names are in Latin script as well as Cyrillic, and a few Hungarian shop signs are reappearing. Draught beer is much more in evidence here, and it is easier to relax as a foreigner: people are used to the concept of multi-culturalism and to people not speaking their language. Many people in this area work to Central European Time; it may be stressed to you that the bus runs to 'Moscow Time'. In 1991 the Hungarians were granted cultural autonomy, with their own newspapers, holidays, schools and universities (many of the lecturers coming from Hungary).

The main **Romanian** enclaves are around Solotvino (in Transcarpathia) and in the Bucovina, around Chernovts'i; the latter was ruled by Austria and then Romania until Stalin annexed the northern Bucovina in 1944, so that now there are about 95,000 Romanians living on the Ukrainian side of the border and 30,000 Ukrainians on the Romanian side. The Romanians had a great reputation as smugglers in Hapsburg times, but now they are more settled, although they are agitating for more freedom to visit Romania and to have Romanian schools.

Bucovina was the epitome of the multi-cultural patchwork of the Hapsburg Empire, with a third of its population minorities of one kind or another, including Slovaks, Poles and even Italians, and some refugees from Russia and Bulgaria; Germans lived in this area from the 13th

Century at least, and before the First World War they made up about 2% of the population (including the family of the writer Gregor von Rezzori), although they have now returned to Germany. (There remain large numbers of Germans further east, on the Volga and in Kazakhstan, as well as those left in Romania.) There are still many **gypsies**, much less gaudy in costume than in Romania but still begging and sweeping out bus stations, having resisted communism's pressures to become useful productive units.

Eleven per cent of the population of Bucovina were **Jews**, some German-speaking such as the poet Paul Celan, and some Yiddish, but these have almost totally disappeared. Ukraine, Belarus and western Russia were the heartland of the Yiddish-speaking Ashkenazi Jews, and the Hasidic school was founded in the 18th Century by Israel ben Eliezier (Baal Shem Tow) of Podolia. The whole area was largely cleared of Jews by the Nazis, and they continued to feel threatened under Stalin, who was not above resorting to anti-semitism for political ends, so that the Jewish population, previously largely rural, is now almost entirely concentrated in Kyiv, as well as being very inter-bred with the rest of the population. In the mid-1980s about 1,000 Jews a year were able to emigrate to Israel, but this rose first to 1,000 a month, and then to about 100,000 a year, so that 16% of Israelis now speak Russian (or Ukrainian) — this is said to have raised the country's cultural tone.

There is one active synagogue in Kyiv, for a Jewish population of about 100,000, and there are now American rabbis and helpers working there to help Jews rediscover their heritage; there is a tension between Yiddish and Hebrew/Israeli focuses.

In Yalta and elsewhere in Crimea there are populations of Georgian and Azeri merchants and racketeers, as well as the native Tatars, expelled by Stalin but now returning (see page 324). There are also some remaining Karaite Jews or Krymchaks here, ethnically Turkic and perhaps descended from the Khazars, who once lived in cave villages but are now mainly in Bilohorska and Simferopil; in 1926 they numbered 6,400, but there are now less than half as many.

RELIGION

The 1000th anniversary of Christianity in Ukraine in 1988 was celebrated as the 1000th anniversary of the Ukrainian state; the Orthodox church and the state are intimately entwined, and the attitude of the church is conservative and authoritarian. The Russian Orthodox church, although semi-suppressed by the communists, allowed itself to be used by the KGB, and it now displays a patriotic triumphalism, reinforced by the Russian government's habit of seeking a blessing at all formal occasions. However in western Ukraine the Uniate church, although underground from 1946 to 1991, displayed a far more positive attitude to righting wrongs in this world, with most of the leaders of Rukh being firm Uniates.

The Uniate (Greek-Catholic or Eastern Rite Catholic) church was founded by the Poles from 1596 as a means of bringing the Orthodox peasantry under the sway of the Pope while allowing them to continue with Orthodox rites, with some doctrinal changes; being governed from Rome Stalin saw it as tainted with Western imperialism and forced its 4m adherents to merge with the Orthodox church. In September 1989 150,000 Uniates marched in Lviv demanding recognition and then in October reclaimed their Church of the Transfiguration; in December Gorbachev met the Pope and recognised the Uniate church, and in 1991 the Pope appointed 10 bishops and the Patriarch Myroslav Ivan Cardinal Lubachivskyi moved back into the Cathedral of St Yuri (St George) in Lviv. There is still much wrangling ahead about the redistribution of churches, but it is noticeable that outside western Ukraine and Transcarpathia there are now few churches left in the villages.

The Orthodox church in Ukraine is also fracturing: the Ukrainian Autocephalous Orthodox Church, founded in 1921, was incorporated into the Russian Orthodox church in 1930 but re-emerged in the 1980s, under Patriarch Mystislav I, and Metropolitan Filaret, head of the Ukrainian Orthodox Church of the Moscow Patriarchate, was defrocked in June 1992 for demanding full independence for the Ukrainian church rather than autonomy within the Russian Orthodox church. This led to the absurd situation of Filaret leading mass at St Vladimir's cathedral in Kyiv and his successor Metropolitan Vladimir leading mass at Pechersky Lavra.

There are 70,000 Hungarians of the Reformed (Calvinist) church in Transcarpathia, with Baptists, both Hungarian and Ukrainian, who share their church in Uzhgorod, and also Roman Catholics in western Ukraine, and Jews mostly in Kyiv. Canadian evangelists in particular are now flooding in, and it is seen as fashionable in western Ukraine to be religious and wear a crucifix; Orthodox theology holds that there should only be one church in one place, and wants the evangelists restrained. Most bizarrely, in November 1993 Marina Devi Kristos, leader of a cult known as the Great White Brotherhood, was arrested in St Sophia cathedral in Kyiv after urging her mostly teenaged followers to kill themselves to rise again three days later at the end of the world, which didn't happen.

The main festival of the Orthodox and Uniate churches is Easter (Pasha, **Паша**), the date of which is calculated by the Julian or Old Style calendar, 12 days behind our Gregorian or New Style calendar: in 1994 it is on May 1 (NS), in 1995 April 23, and in 1996 April 14. Trinity and Christmas are also major festivals, when many people return home; religious festivals are known as Green festivals, as opposed to Red or communist festivals, and a Christmas tree is known as a Green tree. *Krashenki* are beautifully painted Easter eggs, particularly in the Rusyn areas.

Pravoslavn'iy (**Православный**) means Orthodox, *Bogoroditsa* (**Богородица**) (or *Bogomater*) means Mother of God, *Pantocrater* (**Рантократор**) means Ruler of all, *Preobrazhensky* (**Преображенскі**) means Transfiguration, *Uspensky* (**Успенскй**) means Assumption or Dormition, and *Rozhdestva* (**Рождества**) means Nativity. The most typically Orthodox saints are St John Chrysostom, Patriarch of Constantinople in the early 5th Century, deposed for exposing the decadence of the Imperial court, SS Cyril and Methodius, the missionary brothers who introduced the Cyrillic alphabet, St Antony who spread the Orthodox religion on a flying millstone, and St Nicholas of Smyrna, our Santa Claus, identified by his checkered robes.

The iconostasis or altar screen (literally 'image-holder') is fundamental to an understanding of the Orthodox church: whereas the western churches tore down roodscreens for direct access to God, in the east access is through the mediation of a priest. The altar is in the space behind the iconostasis which symbolises heaven, which only the priest enters. Traditionally the iconostasis has three doors, the central one, used only by priests, being called the Royal or Holy Door and decorated with portraits of the four Evangelists and perhaps the Annunciation above them. The side doors show the Archangels or holy deacons acting as helpers in administering the sacrament. There are at least three tiers of small icons, with in the bottom row Christ Pantocrater and the patronal saint to the right, and the Virgin and Child and (usually) St Nicholas to the left, then above this the Deisis tier depicting Christ in Judgment, flanked by the Virgin, John the Baptist, the Archangels Michael and Gabriel, and the Apostles, and at the top the Church Feasts tier made up of icons of crucial events from the lives of Christ and the Virgin, with the Last Supper over the central door; in the 14th Century multi-tiered iconostases of this sort appeared in Russia, and then grew upwards in a familiar type of Russian gigantism until some had five tiers, with icons of the Patriarchs (from Adam to Moses) at the top, and the Prophets (from Moses to Christ) below. Above all is a crucifix, with Adam's skull at its foot.

The icons were painted in a largely symbolic manner, depicting the essence of their subjects, particularly through the ascription of spiritual meanings to light, with white signifying salvation, heavenly love and purity, gold divine light, red the fire of faith and martyrdom, green youth and hope. Along with blue, green also represented paradise and the celestial spheres, and black corresponded to the darkness of the underworld and death. Where Byzantine art remained very severe and formal, the Russian icon painters, notably Andrei Rublev in the early 15th Century, produced more human and emotional portraits, and in particular moved from painting the Virgin as an unearthly Queen of Heaven to showing her as a warm and tender mother: as Colin Thubron put it, 'This image of motherhood plucks a profound chord in the Russian soul. It pervades Soviet nationalism with its mystical invocation of the *Rodina*, the Motherland, and reaches back, it seems, to a time long before Christianity, when a primordial Great Mother ruled these pagan woods and plains'.

Orthodox and Uniate churches are recognisable externally by their cross with three crossbars, one for the board that proclaimed Christ as

Jesus of Nazareth, King of the Jews (INRI), one to hold His arms, and one for His feet; it also symbolises the Trinity, of course.

There are few remaining wooden Uniate or Orthodox churches, as found in southeastern Poland, and no wooden synagogues left at all. The basic style is that of the more conservative Boyks, with three sections, the *pronaos* or *narthex* (the porch, sometimes called the *babinets* or women's church), the *naos* or nave, and the sanctuary, with a cupola or dome above each section, and the *naos* slightly wider and with a higher dome than the others. The eaves project all round to form a gallery, either supported by cantilevered beams or on posts. The Huţul churches (always of spruce, though the Boyks and Łemks use ash and oak) are often on a cruciform ground plan, with an onion dome on each arm as well as above the *naos*; Boyks and Huţuls both usually build separate bell towers. The Łemks, more open to outside influences such as the Gothic style, built up the western cupola into a tall belfry, built not in the standard log cabin blockwork but with posts and rafters, and have no outside galleries.

Some interesting 16th Century Boyk churches can be visited in Drohob'ich, Botelka and Staryi Sambor, southwest of Lviv, and others are in the Uzhgorod and Lviv skansens. Łemk churches can be seen in Transcarpathian villages such as Kolochava and Maidan, and the best example of a Huţul church is perhaps the Strukovskaya church in Yasinya. There remain very few of the spectacularly tall wooden churches built east of the Dnepr, most notably at Novomoskovsk (northeast of Dnepropetrovsk) and at the Pereyaslav-Khmelnitsky (southeast of Kyiv) and Kyiv skansens. The Museums of Atheism set up in churches under communism have almost all closed as the churches have reopened, but the Museum of Religious History in Lviv is still open (see page 293).

COUNTRY LIFE

In the old Soviet Union, 20% of the workforce was in the agricultural sector (compared to about 25% in Poland, 12% in western Europe, and under 3% in the USA and UK). State farms were increasingly inefficient, with the subsidies paid to keep consumer prices down reaching R60,000 million in 1988, worth an extra month's salary for everyone, adult or child. Food subsidies are being done away with, but as yet there has been little effective reform of agriculture, although the number of private farms had risen to 10,000 by July 1992. In 1992 the harvest was better than in 1991 (unlike in Poland and Romania), and food was plentiful, with a grain harvest of 43m t, against a state requirement of 18.5m t. Russia is dependent on Ukraine for sugar (from beet) and grain, as well as for agricultural equipment and other machinery, while Ukraine depends on Russia for oil and timber.

In 1987 there were in Ukraine 2,466 state farms and 7,452 collectives, a total of 48.6m hectares cultivated. State farms had less independence than the collectives, not buying their own equipment or paying for their own welfare programmes, and were becoming increasingly important in the centralised state. The introduction of Gorbachev's *arenda* (leasehold) system in 1988 was a *de facto* decollectivisation, with families (which already had half a hectare each) working land on a private enterprise basis; after independence the collectives began to be broken up more completely, but there was a surprising amount of resistance in eastern Ukraine, as well as a lack of money for investment. In the less collectivist western Ukraine there was a better memory of how things had been before communism, and more of a drive to succeed through hard work. However the hinterland of Kyiv is crowded with *dachas*, which used to be very popular as holiday cottages but are now intensively worked as smallholdings, with weekend suburban trains crowded with people coming home with sacks of potatoes, as well as mushrooms from the forests.

In the Carpathians the economy is largely based on sheep grazing and forestry, much as it has been for centuries. Although the way of life has changed considerably in the communist era, you can still see one old woman tending one cow or a couple of geese, and soon families will again be putting their few sheep together to make up a collective village flock. Shepherds have tamer dogs than those in Romania, tending to use long leather whips instead, nor are they as inquisitive as in Romania.

Below the high meadows where the sheep graze in summer there are huge areas of forest in the Carpathians and their foothills, but overall in Ukraine 14.3% of the land area is forested, against a world average of 29%, or 0.2ha of forest per capita, against a world average of 1.4ha. The forests were over-exploited under the Soviet régime, but since 1945 a large area has been replanted, and 30% is now totally protected, being used mainly for the protection of water supplies. Traditionally logs were washed down mobile wooden flumes to the rivers where they were made into rafts, or to the narrow gauge forestry railways which ran up most valleys into the Carpathians. However nowadays it is more normal to use tractors and heavy lorries, although horse carts are still much used in the villages.

There is great potential for hydroelectric power in the Carpathians, still largely untapped, although in the steppes the Dnepr has been tamed with many huge dams and power stations. However you are likely to come across some of the pipelines carrying oil and gas into central Europe. The *Druzhba* (Friendship) line has been carrying oil from the Volga and Caspian fields since the 1960s, and in the 1980s this was followed by the *Soyuz* (Union) and *Bratstvo* (Brotherhood) gas pipelines, the *Mir* (Peace) electric powerline and others, all built in defiance of American sanctions to carry Siberian energy to western Europe. These were all routed through Ukraine and Czechoslovakia due to the instability of Poland, but now in 1993 I hear that Russia is planning to build new pipelines through Poland to avoid possible blockades by Ukraine. The *Soyuz* line runs between Lake Sinevir and Ust-Chorna to Hust and then west to Chop, while the others are further west, converging on Uzhgorod; the pipelines are buried but the landscape is massively scarred (see page 359) and the routes can easily be seen on aerial photos.

Chapter 9

In Ukraine

BEFORE YOU GO

There is no Ukrainian tourist information service; you will have to rely on the guide books listed on page 257, and on this book. You could also try the Association of Foreign Tourism at vul Yaroslav Val 36, Kyiv (tel 044 212 5570), or the State Committee for Tourism at vul Gospitalna 12, Kyiv (tel 044 225 3051/227 8624). Arrangements can still be made through Intourist, although this is not required; they are at 184 Marsh Wall, London E14 9FJ (tel 071 538 8600/5965) and offer a ten-day tour of Ukraine for £645-685. Intourist was created in 1929 by the communists, and can still only think in terms of regimented group travel where the customer is servant of the system, not king; in addition its focus is very Russian, and they have little interest in or knowledge of Ukraine and the other independent republics. Orbis, Fregata and other Polish organisations also organise tours to Lviv and the formerly Polish parts of Ukraine.

Visas can be obtained in 10 days for £15 (or in an hour for £25) from the Ukrainian embassies at 78 Kensington Park Rd, London W11 2PL (tel 071 727 6312/0891 515 919, visa section tel 071 229 2712, Monday-Friday 0930-1230) or Suite 711, 1828 L Street NW, Washington DC 20036 (202 296 6960), or in Przemyśl. You will need one passport photo and probably (from late 1993) either an invitation or hotel vouchers at US$1 for every night of your stay; booking through travel agencies such as Bob Sopel (see below) may allow you to get around this requirement. Visas can be obtained on arrival or in Moscow (US$50 for one month, or US$28 for a transit visa), but I have reports from lesser border crossings such as Uzhgorod of Westerners, especially on foot, only being issued three-day transit visas, extended only with an invitation from a Ukrainian organisation (not an individual) and US$30. As the land border with Russia is open (although this may change) it is possible to visit Ukraine with a Russian visa, although this is only worthwhile if you are in Russia anyway. Russian visas must be obtained in advance, with three photos and lots of paperwork, and are only valid for specific cities and dates.

In Kyiv, the British embassy is at vul Desiatynna 9 (tel 228 0504), the US embassy at vul Kotsyubinskoho 10 (tel 244 7344), the Canadian embassy at the Hotel Zhovtnevy, vul Rosa Luxemburg 5 (tel 291 8858), and the Polish embassy at vul Yaroslaviv Val 12 (tel 255 5114).

Ukrainian currency (coupons or *karbovantsi*) cannot legally be obtained outside the country (although they can be obtained at *kantors* near Polish border stations such as Przemyśl); you can change US dollars at the border when you pay for your visa. Once in Ukraine proper you can change money at the Bank for Foreign Exchange in major towns, or at Intourist hotels; US dollars in cash are always preferred, and the only travellers cheques accepted (and not everywhere) are American Express US dollar cheques. The black market dealers at Chop (instantly recognisable by their electronic calculators) will change cash in other currencies, such as Deutschmarks, forints and Czech/Slovak crowns, but those in other major rail stations and elsewhere will only know the rates for the Russian rouble and the US dollar. You may well be able to buy roubles elsewhere in eastern Europe, and then change these to coupons in Ukraine.

GETTING THERE

The Ukrainian Carpathians are less accessible from western Europe than the Polish mountains; there are some flights to Lviv and Ivano Frankivsk, but unless you are heading straight for Crimea it may actually be easier to travel via Poland, Hungary or Slovakia than via Kyiv.

For **flights**, the specialist agents are Bob Sopel Ukrainian Travel (27 Henshaw St, Oldham OL1 1NH, tel 061 652 5050/633 2232), and Eastern European Travel (66 Drake St, Rochdale OL16 1PA, tel 0706 868 765), closely followed by One Europe Travel (Research House, Fraser Rd, Perivale UB6 7AQ, tel 081 566 9424) and Fregata (see page 47). Ukraine International Airlines (Mizhnarodni Avialinie Ukraini, a joint venture with Guinness Peat Aviation, tel 0293 553 767 in the UK) fly new Boeing 737-400s from London Gatwick to Kyiv (Mondays, Wednesdays and Saturdays, costing from £289 return via Bob Sopel or £310-350 via Fregata, Intourist or Eastern European Travel, in 1993) and also on summer Saturdays from Manchester to Kyiv via Ivano Frankivsk, the most convenient route if you want to get straight into the mountains (there may also be a coach connection to Lviv, where the airport cannot take the 737s).

There are other fairly convenient routes involving connections. Bob Sopel use SAS, Swissair and Austrian Airlines. The cheapest, from £279, is with SAS from London Heathrow to Kyiv via Copenhagen four days a week (or from Manchester with a night in Copenhagen); Swissair fly from Manchester, Birmingham and Heathrow to Kyiv via Zurich three days a week, and Austrian Airlines fly daily but only from Heathrow to Kyiv via Vienna (both from £329); in 1994 Austrian will also fly to Odessa. Eastern European Travel charge £310 for flights with SAS, CSA or Ukraine International Airlines, and also organise their own charters from £279 return. Fregata (see page 47) use CSA (Czechoslovak Airlines), twice weekly from Heathrow or Manchester via Prague, charging £335 to Kyiv (£355 from June to September) or £345 to Lviv. In addition LOT fly weekly via Warsaw to Kyiv (with two hours in Warsaw) and Lviv (with one hour in Warsaw); Fregata will book you through to Kyiv or Lviv for £75 or £48 return respectively, on top of their fares to Warsaw (£169-249). One Europe Travel fares start at £272 to Kyiv; they and Fregata can also fly you to Poland and book you onwards by train.

An alternative is to fly to Moscow and then take an internal Aeroflot flight or a train to almost any major city; this is particularly handy as a route to Simferopil and Crimea, with two flights most days. Discount tickets to Moscow (and St Petersburg) are now available through many of the usual bucket shops (see page 50), although most will be unable to make the onward booking for you; a return ticket to Moscow costs from £200-230 upwards, plus about £90 for an air connection to Kyiv (note that while the daily Aeroflot flight to Kyiv uses Moscow's international Sheremetyevo airport, the three Ukraine International Airlines flights use the domestic Vnukovo and Bykovo airports).

Ukraine International Airlines also fly from New York to Kyiv, as well as charter flights from Toronto; internally there are flights from Kyiv, Lviv, Chernovts'i and Odessa to Simferopil and the Caucasian spas, and also to Tbilisi, Riga, Donetsk and Kharkiv. However the dominant airline is still Aeroflot (Russian International Airlines), which flies from everywhere to Moscow as in Soviet times; Lviv, for instance, still has, in theory, four flights a day to Moscow, and just four a week to Kyiv, which is as easily reached by train. Shannon airport in Ireland is still used by about 50 flights a week to the former Soviet Union.

Ukrainian airports are pretty basic, and you are likely to find them very confusing; in particular look out for the Cyrillic customs form which you may be required to fill in, and don't assume that a ticket automatically means a place on the plane.

There are now three **trains** a day taking about 19 hours from Warsaw to Kyiv via Brest (transiting through Belarus), one of which starts in Berlin and continues on some days to Kharkiv and Simferopil; the BR fare is £128 each way from London Victoria via Ostende (less from Liverpool St via Harwich). To reach Lviv you should go via Przemyśl, from where trains run via Lviv to Chernovts'i, Kyiv (from Wrocław and Kraków) and Odessa (from Warsaw on alternate days). There are also through trains from Prague and Budapest via the Chop border crossing (for Uzhgorod and Transcarpathia) to Lviv and Kyiv. There are rumours that the InterRail tickets may be extended to the CIS, but this will take time.

Eastern European Travel operate a **coach** from Manchester and London to Lviv every three weeks in summer, for £139 return; otherwise buses only make relatively short hops across the border, from Michalovce and Košice in Slovakia, and Miskolc in Hungary, to Uzhgorod, Nyíregyháza in Hungary to Chop, and from București, Radauți and Suceava in Romania to Chernivts'i (Cernăuți). In addition there are virtually hourly buses from Przemyśl in Poland to Lviv, with some continuing to Str'iy, Brody and Drohobych, as well as others direct to Trusskavets and to Khmelnitski via Ternopil; these bypass the queues of cars at the border, which can be over 24 hours long (with regular reports on Polish radio with the weather forecast) and easy pickings for bandits.

In addition to the companies listed above and on page 49-50, you may also wish to try Meridian East (tel 081 985 0844) or Regent Holidays (0272 211 711). Orbis do an eight-day trip to Lviv (via Warsaw) for between £490 and £520, and KL-Reisen GmbH (Raimundstrasse 157, D-6000 Frankfurt 1, tel (49) 69 563 047) offer a week in Kyiv for US$190-280, 11 days in Odessa and Crimea (US$475-654), two weeks in Galicia and Transcarpathia (US$408-653), and a cruise down the Dnepr from Kyiv to Crimea (US$670-790). Cruises from Odessa to Kyiv and Crimea are also offered by Unique Tours and Travel (tel 071 495 4848, with the German firm Reisebüro Mittelthurgau, £795-995) and the Odessa America Cruise Company (New York (516) 747 8880, US$599-1599). It is also possible to arrive by ferry across the Danube from Tulcea in Romania to Izmail in the far south of Ukraine, and by ship from Istanbul to Odessa and Yalta (see page 338).

Getting out

It is not possible to buy rail tickets out of Ukraine in Uzhgorod; you should try to book through Intourist in Lviv or Kyiv, rather than suffer the chaos of Chop. International trains stop here for between 1 hour 20 minutes and 2 hours, and there is time to buy tickets, as the international ticket windows (to the left) only open after the train's arrival; even so there is a mad scrum for tickets, mainly by trade tourists from central Asia when I was there, and it seems to take an age to write out the tickets. In theory Access, Visa and Diners cards are accepted here, but you should be sure to have enough hard currency (preferably dollars) to get you to Košice or Debrecen.

Customs and passport checks are fairly innocuous, although still very Soviet in character; I was asked emphatically if I had *Soviet* roubles, with no mention of coupons at all. Having stopped to change from Soviet broad gauge bogies to European standard gauge before the station, the train then stops again at the border for security checks. The line from Lviv to Chop is very busy and trains are frequently delayed, but most of the trains to Prague, Bratislava, Budapest and Belgrade depart in the late afternoon and evening. If you do get stuck here, there is a hotel in the square to the right/west of the station, and the station itself has rest rooms, costing from US$5 for 12 hours.

GUIDE BOOKS

There are few up-to-date guide books covering Ukraine, but at least there are many books published in and by the old Soviet Union which give a good outline of tourist sights without having anything relevant to say about travelling there today — these are easily found in public libraries. Many books calling themselves guides to 'Russia' also cover Kyiv and perhaps Yalta, but little else in Ukraine.

The Insight Guides to *Russia* (edited by Anna Benn, APA 1994) and *Eastern Europe* (by Rowlinson Carter, APA 1993) both cover Ukraine, and the *Insider's Guide to Russia* (by Gleb Uspensky, Moorland 1993) is a similar glossy guide to the cities of the Soviet Union, including Kyiv. The *Companion Guide to the Ukraine* by Lydle Brinkle was published by the American company Hippocrene (which has also published a Ukrainian dictionary) in 1991, just too soon to cover the new free Ukraine, but it is still very useful. *Ukraine: a Tourist Guide* is to be an annual publication from 1993 from Smoloskyp Publishers, PO Box 20620, Billings, MT 59104, USA.

The *Lonely Planet Guide* to the USSR, published just as the 1991 *putsch* was taking place, is the best general traveller's guide, but it treats the whole Soviet Union as still being bound by Russian/Intourist bureaucracy, which is not a great issue now in Ukraine. Books published just before this include the *Collet's Guide to Moscow, Leningrad & Kiev* (a very sketchy outline published in 1990), Martin Walker's *Independent Traveller's Guide to the Soviet Union* (Collins 1989) (not *Martin Walker's Russia*), and Simon Calder's *Traveller's Survival Kit, Soviet Union & Eastern Europe* (Vacation Work Publications 1989). Older books that are still of use are Victor and Jennifer Louis's *Complete Guide to the Soviet Union* (Michael Joseph 1976), easily the most detailed guide to the historical monuments of the former Soviet Union, and *USSR: from an original idea by Karl Marx* by Marc Polonsky and Russell Taylor (Faber 1986), an entertaining guide to the mentality of the system. The *Times Guide to Eastern Europe* (edited by Kenneth Sword, revised 1991) is good on the political context.

Soviet-published books include *Moscow, Leningrad, Kiev — a Guide* by Lydia Dubinskaya (Raduga 1981, revised 1988), *Kiev* by H Levitsky (Progress Publishing 1980), and *Greater Yalta, a Guide* by O Yolobuyev (Progress 1979).

The recent glut of travel books on eastern Europe has not yet reached Ukraine; one of the best accounts is still Robert Byron's *First Russia, then Tibet* (Macmillan 1933/Penguin 1985). Others include Nora Beloff's *No Travel Like Russian Travel* (Allen & Unwin 1979, notable only because it covers Transcarpathia), Laurens van der Post's *Journey into Russia* (Penguin 1965), Gerald and Lee Durrell's *Durrell in Russia* (Macdonald 1986, good on Askania Nova) and Fitzroy Maclean's *All the Russias* (Weidenfeld & Nicholson 1978/Viking 1992).

However there have been a few books on Soviet wildlife, thanks in part to TV programmes that did not deal specifically with Ukraine; these include *Realms of the Russian Bear* by John Sparks (BBC 1992), *The Nature of Russia* by JM Stewart (Boxtree 1993) and *The Natural History of the USSR* by Algirdis Kynstautas (Century Hutchinson 1987).

More academic books include *Ukraine: Perestroika to Independence* by

Taras Kuzio and Andrew Wilson (Macmillan 1993), *Ukraine: a History* by
Oleh Subteleny (University of Toronto Press 1989), *Ukraine: a Historical
Atlas* by PR Magosci and GJ Matthews (University of Toronto Press
1985) and both the two-volume *Ukraine: a Concise Encyclopedia*
(Toronto 1963) and the full *Encyclopedia of Ukraine* (two volumes in
1984 and three due in 1993). The most authoritative *History of the
Soviet Union* is by Geoffrey Hosking (Fontana/Collins 1990); in addition
his *Church, Nation and State in Russia and Ukraine* was published by
Macmillan in 1993. A cheap alternative is Mary McAuley's *Soviet Politics
1917-91* (Oxford Paperbacks 1993). Solomea Pavlychko's *Letters from
Kiev* (St Martin Press/Macmillan 1993) is a blow-by-blow account of the
changes of 1990-91.

See page 278 for Ukrainian writers and literature.

THE UKRAINIAN AND RUSSIAN LANGUAGES

It's said that ten years ago only peasants and intellectuals still spoke
Ukrainian; nowadays, while Russian is still the main language of the
towns and of eastern Ukraine, Ukrainian is far more widespread than it
was. Russian remains the lingua franca of the former Soviet Union, and
it will be understood everywhere. English is also being learnt everywhere
now, and most students will speak some.

It is often said, mainly by Russians, that Ukrainian is little more than
a dialect of Russian, but in many ways it is closer to Polish; in any case
there is much in common between all the Slav languages, so that words
for bread, water and so on are pretty much interchangeable. The
relationship between Ukrainian and Russian is more like that between
German and Dutch than that between English and Welsh.

The first hurdle is of course the Cyrillic script, in which letters can
have quite different sounds to those we are used to in our Latin script;
this was introduced in the 9th Century by the missionary brothers SS
Cyril and Methodius for their translations of the bible and liturgy, and
there are four systems of transliteration (which can be combined) and
also minor differences between the scripts used for Russian, Ukrainian
and other languages. In Ukrainian **И**, pronounced I in Russian, becomes
Y, and **Г**, pronounced G in Russian, becomes something like GH,
transliterated as H, so that Galicia is Halicia, Georgy is Heorhy and
Ukraine's highest peak is really Hoverla.

Nor does pronunciation always match the written form, so that the
Transcarpathian town of **Міжгір'я**, for instance, has two
pronunciations for the same spelling, contrary to the usual situation —
Mizh-horya is more common, but Mezh-hear-yay is also heard. **В** (v) can
often be pronounced u, so that I write *autovoksal* for bus-station, spelt
автовоксал, and Taurida for Tavrida, the old name for Crimea.

In upper case unly A, K, M, O and T are much the same in Cyrillic as
in Latin script; lower case letters are similar to upper case, but in
addition there is an informal hand-written script in which above all **д** is

written as g and т as m, so that the river Prut (**Ррут**) often seems to be the Prym, *karta* (**карта**) looks like *karma*, and and an *apteka* or pharmacy like *anmeka*. Generally **И** (I) is easily confused with N — remember LeNIN (**Ленин**); equally *kiosk* (**Kioск**) looks like *knock*. Finally **Ъ** (') is used (more in Russian than in Ukrainian) as a 'soft sign' for a momentary silence, and I have generally omitted it here; it should in any case be omitted before vowels.

Grammar is complex, and short-term visitors to the country need not bother themselves too much about it; suffice to say that there are six cases in Russian, seven in Ukrainian (and eight in Czech), which means that station names, bus destinations and so on do not always agree exactly with place names on the map. Pochtovaya is the station for Pochtovoe, and the genitive of Lviv is L'vovu, close to the Polish name of the city, L'vov. It is enough to add *..da?* to a sentence to turn it into a question, and *ne* to make it negative, as in *Eta ne Lviv* (This is not Lviv).

Vocabulary is largely Slav, but with strong Western, particularly French, influences, especially in Ukrainian; words you may recognise include *bagazh* (baggage), *bilet* (ticket), *byuro* (office), *dokument*, *dush* (shower), *etaj* (storey), *kava* (coffee), *kavaler* (boyfriend), *kombinatsia* (band), *passazh* (passage), *plyazh* (beach), *problema, trotyar* (pavement), and *turism*. A driver is a *shofeur, machinist*, or *kocher*, depending on whether he is driving an *omnibus* (also known as a *transport*), a *lokomotiv* or an *ekipazh* (carriage). A railway station is a *voksal*, either from a sign at Vauxhall station that mid-19th Century Russian engineers saw on a visit to London, or from *wagon-salle*. German borrowings are fewer, but include *platzkarte* (reservation), *sperkass* (savings bank), *butrybrot* (sandwich, also *sendvych*), and *landschaft* (landscape, also *peyzazh*).

I have not distinguished between Russian and Ukrainian above, because you won't be able to tell them apart in practice — I certainly can't. However I give Russian words where they differ below and in the food vocabulary on page 273.

There is a cheap paperback Ukrainian-English dictionary by Leonid Hrabovsky (Hippocrene 1991); this omits basic words like bus or hotel and is rather inconsistent. *Learn Ukrainian* by GI Makarova was published in 1975 by Vysticha Shkola Kyiv and is now found only in specialist libraries. There is a better choice for Russian, such as the Hugo Russian dictionary at £2.95 and Pan's *Traveller's Russian* at £3.50.

The Cyrillic script

А а	A		**Є є**	Ye	as in yes
Б б	B		**Ж ж**	Zh	similar to J
В в	V		**З з**	Z	
Г г	H	G in Russian	**И и**	I	short I, as in milk
Д д	D				
Е е	E	as in end	**Й й**	Y	as in pay
І і	I	long I, as in feel	**У у**	U	as in look

Ї ї	Yi	Ф ф	F	
К к	K	Х х	Kh	
Л л	L	Ц ц	Ts	
М м	M	Ч ч	Ch	
Н н	N	Ш ш	Sh	
О о	O	Щ щ	Shch	
П п	P	Ю ю	Yu	
Р р	R	Я я	Ya	
С с	S	Ъ ъ	'	
Т т	T			

	Ukrainian	Russian
Basics		
Good morning	*Dobroho ranky*	*Dobroe utro, Zdravstvuyte*
Good day/afternoon	*Dobri dyen*	*Dobryi den*
Good evening	*Dobrivechir*	*Dobryi vecher*
Good night	*Dobranich*	*Dobroi nochi*
Cheers!	*Na zdorov'e*	*Nazdravie*
Yes/No	*Tak/Ni*	*Da/Niet*
Sir/Madam	*Pan/Pani*	*Gospodim/gospozha*
Miss	*Panna*	*Devushka*
Thank you	*Dyakuyu*	*Spasiba*
Please	*Boud laska*	*Pazhalsta*
Goodbye	*Do pobachennya*	*Dasvidanye/Ciao*
Bon voyage!	*Shaslivoy dorohi!*	
What does it cost?	*Skilky koshtuye?*	*Skolko stoit?*
Do you speak English?	*Chy vy hovoryty po-Anglysky?*	*Vy gavaritye pa angliski?*
I don't understand	*Ya ne razumayu*	*Ya ne ponimayu*
I don't speak Ukrainian/Russian	*Ya ne hovoriyu po-Ukrainsky*	*Ya ne govoryu pa russki*
Directions		
Left/right	*Na lyeva/na prava*	*Lev'iy/prav'iy*
North/south	*Pivnich/pivden'*	*Sever/yug*
East/west	*Skhid/zakhid*	*Vostok/zapad*
Straight ahead	*Prosto*	*Pryamo*
Here/there	*Tut/tam*	*Tut/tam*
This/that	*Tsey/toy*	*Etot/tot*
(Is it) far?	*(Chy ye) Daleko?*	*Daleko*
Where is..?	*De/Kuda*	*Gd'e..?*
Is there..?	*Chy ye?*	
Hotel	*Hotel*	*Otel, gostinitsa*
Campsite/Tent	*Tabir/namet*	*Palatka* (tent)
Railway station	*Voksal, stantsiya*	
Train	*Poyizd*	*Poezd*

Bus station	*Avtovoksal*	*Aftobusnaya stantsya*
Bus/car	*Omnibus/avto*	*Omnibus/povozka*
Tram/trolleybus	*Tramvay/troleybus*	
Daily	*Shchodenniy*	*Ezhednevn'iy*
Departure/arrival	*Vidkhid/*	*Ot'ezd/prib'itie*
Crossroad	*Perekhrestya*	*Perekrostok*
Road junction	*Skreshchivanie dorog*	
Bridge	*Mist*	*Most*
Church	*Tserkva*	*Tserkov'*
Key (for church)	*Klyuch*	
Castle	*Zamok*	
Hospital	*Likarnya*	*Gospital', bolnitsa*
House	*Dim, khata*	*Dom*
Museum	*Muzei*	

Link words

And/but	*I/ale*	*I/no*
Or	*Abo, chy*	*Ili*
With/without	*Z/bez*	*S/bez*
If/now	*Chy/zaraz*	*Esli/teper'*
Today	*S'ohodni*	*Serodnya*
Yesterday	*Vchora*	*Vchera*
Tomorrow	*Zavtra*	
To/via	*Shcho/cherez*	*Do, k/cherez*
For		*Dlya*
What/how	*Shcho/yak*	*Chto/kak*
When	*Koli*	*Kogda*
Above/below	*Na/pid*	*Nad/pod*
Enough	*Dostatno, dosyt*	*Dovol'no*
After	*Pislya*	*Po, za*
Big/small	*Velikiy/maliy*	*Bol'shoi/mal'iy*
Very	*Duzhe*	*Ochen'*
Many	*Bahato*	*Mnogie*
More/less	*Bil'sh/mensh*	*Bol'she/men'she*
Good/bad	*Dobriy/pohaniy*	*Haroshchii/durnoy*
Fast	*Shvydko*	*B'istr'iy*
Slow	*Povil'niy*	*Medlenn'iy*
Open/shut	*Vidkritiy/zakritiy*	*Otkritiy/zakrity*
Strong	*Sil'niy*	
Heavy/difficult	*Tyazhkiy/trudniy*	*Tyazhyol'iy/trudn'iy*
Easy/light	*Lehkiy*	*Legkiy/lyogkiy*
Beautiful	*Krasiv'iy*	
Single/alone	*Odin*	*Edinstven'iy/odin*
New/old	*Noviy/stariy*	

Verbs

Stop!	*Stiy! Perestan*	
To buy/sell	*Kupuvati/prodavatisya*	*Pokupat'/prodavat'*
To exchange	*Minyatisya*	*Obmeniat'*
To want	*Khotiti*	*Khotit'*
To go	*Iti*	*Idti'*
To walk	*Khoditi*	
To depart	*Vidizhdzhati*	*Otb'ivat'*
To arrive	*Pribivati*	*Prikhodit'*
To wait	*Chekati*	*Zhdat'*
To see	*Bachiti*	*Videt'*
To sleep	*Spati*	
To eat	*Yisti*	*Est'*
To work	*Pratsyuvati*	*Rabotat'*
To have	*Mati*	*Imet'*
To be	*Buti*	*B'it'*
(It is) necessary	*Potribniy, (treba)*	*Neobkhodim'iy*
(It is) possible	*Mozhliviy, (mozhna)*	*Vozmozhn'iy*

Living

Bed	*Postil'*	*Postel'*
Room	*Kimnata*	*Komnata*
Bath	*Kupatisya*	*Banya, vanna*
Water (hot/cold)	*Voda (haryachiy/ kholod)*	*Voda (goryachaya/ kholodn'aya)*
(Too) expensive	*(Za) dorohiy*	*Dorogoy*
Cheap	*Deshevshe*	*Deshyov'iy*
Money	*Groshey*	*Den'gi*
Bill	*Rakhunok*	*Schyot*
Shop	*Kramnitsya*	*Lavka, magazin*
Bottle	*Plyashka*	*Butil'ka*
Married	*Odruzheniy*	*Zhenatyi (M)/ zamuzhenaya (F)*
Child	*Ditina*	*Rebyonok*
Boy/girl	*Khlopets'/divchina*	*Malchik/devyshka*
Man/woman	*Muzh/zhinka*	*Chelovek/zhenshchina*
Tired/ill	*Vtomleniy/khvoriy*	*Ustal'iy/bol'noy*

Hiking Terms

Cave	*Pechera*	*Peshchera*
Cliff/crag	*Krucha*	*Skala*
Cloud	*Khmara*	*Oblako*
Field	*Pole*	
Fog	*Mryaka*	*Tuman*
Forest	*Lis*	*Les*
Gorge	*Balka, yar*	*Ushchel'e*
High	*Visokiy*	
Hill	*Hor, kryazh*	*Kholm*

Ice	*Lid*	*Lyod*
Lake		*Ozero*
Ledge	*Vistup*	*Rif*
Meadow	*Luh*	*Lug*
Pass	*Pereval*	
Pasture	*Pasovisko*	*Pastbishche*
Path	*Doroha/shlyakh*	*Tropinka*
Peak	*Verkh*	*Vershina*
Precipice	*Provallya*	*Obr'iv, propast'*
Rain	*Doshch*	*Dozhd'*
Ravine	*Yar*	*Ushchel'e*
Ridge	*Hrebin'*	*Gorn'iy khrebet*
River	*Rika*	*Reka*
Rock	*Skelya/kamin'*	*Skala*
Saddle	*Sidlo*	*Sedlo*
Sheep fold, hut	*Hizha, koliba*	*Khizhina, saray*
Side	*Bik/storona*	*Sklon*
Slope	*Nakhil*	*Naklon, skat*
Snow	*Snih*	*Sneg*
Spring	*Dzherelo*	*Istochnik*
Steep	*Strimkiy*	*Krutoy*
Stream	*Potik/richka*	*Ruchey*
Summit	*Verkh*	*Vershina*
Valley	*Dolina*	
Village	*Selo*	
Wander	*Blukati*	*Brodit'*
Wood	*Derevo*	*Les*

Numbers and dates

One	*Odin, raz*	*Odin*
Two	*Dva*	*Dva*
Three	*Tri*	*Tri*
Four	*Chotiri*	*Chet'ire*
Five	*Pyat'*	*Pyat'*
Six	*Shist'*	*Shest'*
Seven	*Sim*	*Sem'*
Eight	*Visim*	*Vosem'*
Nine	*Devyat'*	*Deyvat'*
Ten	*Desyat'*	*Desyat'*
Eleven	*Odinadtsyat'*	*Odinnadtsat'*
Twelve	*Dvanadtsyat'*	*Dvenadtsat'*
Thirteen	*Trinadtsyat'*	*Trinadtsat'*
Twenty	*Dvadtsyat'*	*Dvadtsat'*
Twenty-one	*Dvadtsyat' odin*	*Dvadtsat' odin*
One/two hundred	*Sto/dvisti*	*Sto/dv'es'ti*
One thousand	*Tisyacha*	*T'isyacha*
First	*Pershyi*	*Sperva*
Second	*Druhiy*	*Vtoroy*

Third	*Tretiy*	*Tret'*
Half	*Polovina* (noun)/ *napolovinu* (adj)	*Polovina/ polovinn'iy*
Quarter	*Chvert'*	*Chetvert'*
January	*Sichen'*	*Janvar'*
February	*Lyutiy*	*Fevral'*
March	*Berezen'*	*Mart*
April	*Kviten'*	*Aprel'*
May	*Traven'*	*May*
June	*Cherven'*	*Iyun'*
July	*Lipen'*	*Iyul'*
August	*Serpen*	*Avgust*
September	*Veresen'*	*Sentyabr'*
October	*Zhovten'*	*Oktyabr'*
November	*Listopad*	*Noyabr'*
December	*Hruden'*	*Dekabr'*
Monday	*Ponedilok*	*Ponedel'nik*
Tuesday	*Vivtorok*	*Vtornik*
Wednesday	*Sreda*	*Sreda*
Thursday	*Chetreh*	*Chetverg*
Friday	*P'yatnitsa*	*Pyatnitsa*
Saturday	*Subota*	*Subbota*
Sunday	*Nedilya*	*Voskresen'e*

Wildlife

Animal	*Tvarina*	*Zhivotnoe*
Bear	*Vedmeed*	*Medved (mishka)*
Deer	*Olen'*	*Olin'*
Boar	*Dukiy kaban*	*Kaban*
Bat	*Kazhan, lilik*	*Letuchaya m'ish'*
Bird	*Ptak*	*Ptytsa*
Eagle	*Orel*	*Oryol*
Hawk	*Yastrub, sokil*	*Yastreb*
Owl	*Sova*	
Frog	*Zhaba*	*Lyagushka*
Trout	*Forel'*	
Sturgeon	*Oseter, nalim*	*Osyotr*
Tree		*Derevo*
Pine		*Sosna*
Spruce	*Yalina*	
Fir	*Smereka*	*El'*
Beech	*Buk*	
Birch	*Bereza*	*Beryoza*
Oak		*Dub*
Plant	*Roslina*	*Rastenie*
Flower	*Kvitka*	*Tsvetok*

ACCOMMODATION

In major Ukrainian towns travellers are still generally obliged to stay in one or two hotels authorised to receive Westerners, generally still run by Intourist; naturally these are the most expensive establishments, but they may have hot water and a receptionist who speaks a little English. The traditional floor manageress or *dezhurnaya* will certainly not speak any Western language, but despite external appearances may well turn out to be golden-hearted and not just a KGB stooge. However although the other hotels in town have to turn you away (and are likely to be fairly rough, with no hot water), you are permitted to rent a private room from a *babushka* hanging around outside; failing this, if expensive hotels are not to your taste, or within your budget, you will have to plan your itinerary to sleep on trains or in a nearby small town with just one basic hotel. This system may break down, and I have listed the major hotels taking foreigners in each town, and then some others which might be persuaded to let you in; this will depend on individual receptionists as much as anything else, and the dollar is as persuasive as a pretty face. At some major rail and bus stations you will also find rest rooms (*komnata otd'icha*) where you can rent a room by the hour.

It is possible to see the sights of Kyiv or Lviv between two overnight trains, but it's really not worth rushing them; these cities have camp sites, but at the moment these are also highly restrictive for Westerners; you are not allowed to use a tent but have to stay in a cabin which is not much cheaper than a hotel, and certainly far more expensive than a Ukrainian would pay to stay in a hotel. Camp sites are only open from June 1 to late September; most have restaurants and even discos, and can be good places to meet holidaying locals. It is possible to camp wild — I never really got over my amazement at being free to camp where I wanted in what was so recently the 'evil empire', the Soviet Union, and indeed it is a virtually unknown practice outside the mountains; no-one quite knows how to react to a tent in an unexpected place, particularly within sight of houses or a main road.

The Intourist hotels do however serve a useful function, in that they are often the only places to find basic tourist information and a town plan, either on the lobby wall or from the Tourist Services desk; you can also book train seats more easily (and as a rule no more expensively) at Intourist offices than at the stations. There is often a security man on the front door, who will not usually stop Westerners from going in; if there is a problem 'Intourist', 'Kashtan', or 'Beriozhka' usually work as passwords.

Outside the cities life is simpler; in towns where there is only one hotel you will be accepted without question and without paying hugely more than the going rate. The local equivalent of youth hostels are the 120 Turbazas, located mainly in small towns in the touristic areas; but whereas our youth hostels often impose a maximum stay of three days, Turbazas sometimes make this a minimum — it is still likely to be worth paying for three nights to stay one. Russian and central Asian Turbazas have a pretty awful reputation, but those in Ukraine are generally more acceptable; you will usually be in a two- or three-bed room, with basic toilets and cold showers down the corridor. Towels, curtains, and loo-paper are always pitifully thin, and there is never a bulb in the bedside light. There are no mountain huts other than these.

It seems that private room finding services are now appearing in the Crimean resorts, but I have no details as yet.

In 1992 Turbazas and private rooms could cost as little as K50 per night, and small town hotels K100-500; Intourist hotels charged between US$50 and US$183, or sometimes K1,000, and campsites from US$32 or, if I was lucky, K1,700. Travelines can book you into reasonable hotels in Lviv for £20-25 low season or £25-30 high season, and in Kyiv for £25-40 or £30-60. Bob Sopel, Fregata and Intourist use top grade hotels and quote more than twice as much, but One Europe Travel can arrange bed and breakfast in private rooms for £15 (minimum £60).

TRANSPORT

Virtually all travel in Ukraine beyond the most local journeys is by public transport, and for longer journeys almost everyone travels by train. **Air** travel is available but complicated and hardly reliable (not so much because of Aeroflot's sad accident record, but more because of its disregard of timetables and reservations); while it used to be possible to fly from Kyiv to Moscow for a couple of dollars worth of roubles, foreigners now have to pay far more realistic hard currency prices. Although there are Aeroflot timetables posted at many bus and rail stations, and often even an Aeroflot ticket booth, foreigners (ie Westerners) will usually have to find an Intourist office, usually in a major hotel (open 0900-1800, or even 0900-2100), and place themselves in their hands. In theory Aeroflot is being replaced by the airlines of the various republics, but this will probably not bring major immediate changes; both air and rail systems are still centred on Moscow.

The **railways** reflect the Soviet tendency to gigantism, with even basic local trains being made up of 12 heavy coaches, and stations built like cathedrals of the machine age, in the same spirit as those of Victorian Britain and India. As Laurens van der Post noted, 'the station at Kharkiv, one of the most important (in Ukraine) because eight trunk lines meet there, looks like a Greek temple from the outside whereas inside it is a marble palace. The booking hall is vast and domed, the walls covered with immense euphoric paintings, coloured mosaics and ceramics, and from the ceiling hangs a huge chandelier outshining anything in Versailles. Lavatories, waiting rooms, even restaurants can be inadequate ... but the outer shape of the railway and the main hall express the national faith in the machine in general and the immaculate conception of the railway in particular'. Most major towns are linked by trains, frequently running overnight; it's been said that all Soviet trains leave at 2300 and arrive at 0700, which means that some amble along and stop forever in stations (where the toilets are locked shut), while others try to go faster but generally arrive late.

Trains are long and heavy and, despite the huge locomotives used (often articulated units), never move very fast. Therefore, as in India, passengers settle in for a long haul, and train travel is easily the best way to meet Ukrainians in a relaxed and congenial atmosphere. As van der Post also noted, 'In Europe and America people travel in a train fully aware that it belongs either to a state or a company and that their ticket grants them only temporary occupation and certain restricted rights. In Russia people just take them over. They move in with their luggage, bundles and children as if for permanent occupation... Before long the train would resemble a second-rate boarding house or a whole village on wheels'. As with Indian trains and stations, all human life is here.

Ticket offices can be hard to cope with at first, and you may initially prefer to book your tickets at Intourist offices; there will usually be just one small door from the platform (rather than the street), and having found this you will find queues at various counters and people as confused as you moving from line to line to enquire what it is for. In bigger stations there will be specific windows for specific trains, fairly clearly marked, and at others there are separate queues for trains the same day and the next day, or for local and long-distance trains. In any case there is a lot of queue-barging. In a few major stations such as Simferopil foreigners are directed to special counters outside, by the Aeroflot booth; these are only open 0700-1700 and are still marked only in Cyrillic. Some ticket offices are now computerised, but calculations are always checked on an abacus, so that no time is saved; there are also some ancient push-button information machines in some stations, which are unlikely to be of use to you. Sleepers in particular should be booked a few days ahead if possible.

The 'general' or 'hard-class' seating is known as *obshe vagon*, and should only be used for local travel; for overnight trains, the most effective way of getting around Ukraine, you have the choice of *spal'n'iy vagon* (sleeping cars with nine two- or four-person cabins) or *platzkarte*, literally 'reservation' but meaning a couchette-style bunk converted from the day-time seating and luggage racks. It's usual to pay about R25 (in mid-1992) for sheets and something like a tea-towel, but a mattress and pillow are provided in any case, and if you have a sleeping bag or sheet bag you could use that; nobody bothers to undress, although Ukrainians generally change into a tracksuit on taking occupation of the train.

Other than on local trains, you will have a ticket assigning you to a specific coach and seat; each coach is an independent empire under the rule of its *provodnik* or *provodnika*, something more than a conductor, who takes your ticket at the door and controls access (and is notoriously corruptible), as well as selling tea and other services. They are used to Poles, Kazakhs and other nationalities, so they are quite blasé about foreigners who don't speak Russian or Ukrainian. Glasses for tea are usually provided, but the well-equipped traveller may well prefer to have his or her own. Hot water is free, from the boiler outside the *provodnik*'s cubby-hole at the end of the coach. The coaches are all non-smoking, with smokers congregating in the vestibules, which usually have such airtight doors that it can be hard to open them, and the combined smell of tobacco and toilets can be awful.

From Kyiv there are 18 trains a day to Moscow (Kyivski station), taking 15 hours, 8 to Lviv (6 from Moscow), 4 to Odessa and Kharkiv, 3 to Kishinev and Simferopil, and 2 to Ivano-Frankivsk, St Petersburg, Chernovts'i, Riga, Brest, Berlin, Budapest and Sofia. There is a daily train from Kyiv to just about everywhere else in Ukraine, and also between cities such as Lviv, Chernovts'i, Kharkiv, Odessa and Simferopil. Many relatively small towns such as Trusskavets, Zhitomir and Rivno have daily trains to Moscow, and often to St Petersburg and Riga as well; there are three a day from Moscow's Kurski station to Simferopil. Trains from Moscow and St Petersburg to eastern European cities such as Budapest, Bratislava and Prague all cross the Carpathians by the Lviv-Chop line, often very late due to the usual problems of passing from one state and one railway system to another. Between Chop and Mukachevo this route is lined with freight yards, a mark both of the scale of the traffic from the CIS to Hungary and Czechoslovakia, and of the inefficiency with which it is handled. Just east of Chop are the sidings where all coaches and wagons crossing the border have to change their bogies from the Soviet broad gauge to the European standard gauge; while it remains illegal to photograph strategic objects such as bridges and tunnels, you are now allowed to photograph the far less photogenic bogie-changing operation.

Bus travel is acceptable for local journeys, preferably into rather than out of major nodes; however bus stations in the larger cities can be absolute bedlam, with queues up to an hour long for tickets. There are no return tickets and no through tickets from small town A to small town B changing in city C — everyone has to buy a fresh ticket at C; then people start to panic about missing their bus home, so they start to queue-barge, so that the queue moves ever more slowly, so more people queue-barge and everyone gets more and more fed up. The staff also get fed up and take more and longer breaks; there is no single queueing system, so when the window you are queueing in front of shuts, you get stuck. Queues are also very slow, as calculations are made with both a cash register and an abacus, and then all details have to be copied on to the driver's manifest. Ticket holders in the know usually board the bus in the car park before it draws up to the departure platform, to be swamped by those who couldn't get tickets. Bus stations in smaller towns such as Kolomea and Hust are usually fine.

There is a semi-permanent fuel crisis, particularly bad in Transcarpathia for some reason, so that the bus timetables can be largely fiction, and those buses that do turn up are hugely overcrowded, more so than any I've used in Turkey, India or China, so much so that it takes five minutes to squeeze everyone in at intermediate stops. As Ukrainians are very reluctant to open windows this can be pretty stifling.

Otherwise buses are surprisingly civilised, with reserved seats as often as not, and inter-urban services operated by good Hungarian Ikarus vehicles (usually red, as opposed to the brown and white local buses) with two very cool drivers. Although they work a shift of about seven hours, there are hourly cigarette breaks, so that journeys are not as quick as they might be. Local buses will stop more or less anywhere, with people just throwing down a couple of rouble notes beside the driver, while the inter-urban buses are very reluctant to pick up any intermediate passengers at all, quizzing them about their destination before allowing them aboard. You may also have to pay five coupons for baggage as well.

A resort such as Yasinya will have buses to major centres about 200km distant, such as Lviv, Uzhgorod, Ivano-Frankivsk, Chernovts'i and Kamenets Podolsk, taking seven or eight hours to get there. Mukachevo has buses to towns such as Kolomea, Hust, Rachiv, Volovets, Trusskavets and Ust-Chorna, and 33 buses, both slow and express, to Uzhgorod, as well as six to Uzhgorod airport.

It is also possible to travel by **boat**, above all along the Dnepr river downstream from Kyiv to Kanev, Cherkassy (see page 315), Komsomol'sk, Dnepropetrovsk, Zaporozhye (page 320) and Kherson (page 319), 827km from Kyiv. There are both 'three-decker' ships and 'Meteor' hydrofoils, and in theory it is possible to change to a ship to continue to Odessa. This is no cheaper than travelling by train, but would be an enjoyable jaunt, particularly just as far as Cherkassy, 200km from Kyiv. There were also services upstream to Chernigov, Rechitsa and

---

Crossing the Frontier

Crossing by train from Slovakia I suspected initially that things had not changed at all and that this was still the frontier of the USSR, held in a timewarp ruled by Brezhnev: the train stopped under floodlights in no-man's-land, there were footsteps on the roof while our compartment was searched by Russian-speaking squaddies supervised by civilians in comically clichéed belted mackintoshes. After half an hour the train advanced to Chop station, packed with hordes of trade tourists or semi-legitimate smugglers. Here I was welcomed to Independent Ukraine and relieved of US$50 in exchange for an 'emergency visa' (having already had to pay $5 as a 'reservation fee' for the 5km journey across the border). Customs forms were in Russian, but in Roman rather than Cyrillic script as a limited concession to ignorant Westerners.

The train set off to change to broad gauge bogies and then departed for Moscow, while I was left to wait for a local train to Uzhgorod. First however I had business outside the station: I had seen a large statue of Lenin dominating the main square and the Hotel Ukraina, and I thought I had best photograph it while I had the chance, lest it turn out to be the only one left in the new free and post-communist Ukraine. I needn't have worried; I saw many more Lenins, as well as many statueless plinths.

Gomev in Russia, but these have been discontinued, due to Chornobyl and political changes. In addition there are boat and hydrofoil services (dependent on the state of health of the tourist industry) along the coast of Crimea and from Crimea to Odessa and to Sochi.

Ukrrechflot, which operates cargo and passenger ships on the Dnepr, the Danube and the Black Sea, was planned to be among the first state enterprises to be privatised in 1993. KL-Reisen, Reisebüro Mittelthurgau and Odessa America (see page 256) work with them to offer cruises from Kyiv to Odessa and Crimea in modern German-built ships.

Cars are not used for more than local travel, and there is not a lot to be gained by bringing your own car to Ukraine. Roads are poor (in 1989 there were 247,300km of roads, 201,900km of them surfaced, only 10 times the rail network) and petrol stations are only found every hundred or more kilometres on major routes; there is no lead-free fuel.

As in the rest of eastern Europe it is normal to freewheel downhill and to remove windscreen wipers overnight; speed limits are 70km/h on single-carriageways and 90km/h on dual-carriageways, and drink-driving is not allowed. The traffic police (GAI, literally State Automobile Inspectorate) pulls cars over for roadside checks on exhaust emissions; however they have little effect on terrible driving habits such as jumping red lights.

There is a considerable variety of Russian-made cars, with numberplates indicating their home *oblast* (**ЛВ** (LV) for Lviv, **KP** (KR) for Crimea and so on), as well as lots of old motorbikes and sidecars, and chunky six-wheel trucks, some of them fitted with portakabins to carry workers to farms, mines and forests. Hitch-hiking is not normal but it can work in remoter areas, with Ukrainians usually being expected to pay something equivalent to the bus fare. There are no self-drive hire cars, but Intourist can hire you a car with driver.

City transport is mainly by bus and trolleybus, running from 0600 to 0030, and normally you should buy tickets in advance from kiosks near the stops. However in Lviv, Uzhgorod and Yalta, for instance, there are unreliable ticket machines, which only take coins; in Yalta tickets for trolleybuses should be bought from machines but those for buses from conductresses. Equally there is no hard and fast rule for timetable information other than the ubiquitous word of mouth — in some areas there are timetables on every stop, and in Kyiv bus stops show the frequency of buses each hour. In Kyiv there is also a metro (see page 313), and also shared taxi minibuses (*Marshrutnoye taxi*) running from behind the Bassarab market. Taxis are common here but may try to charge you over the odds — have enough low denomination notes, as they won't have change; however almost any car will pick you up for a price (there have even been cases of fire engines moonlighting as taxis).

FOOD AND DRINK

Traditionally food in Ukraine is fairly similar to that in Poland, but with a stronger Russian influence; however at the moment supplies are limited and you will often have to make do with whatever you can find. Shops all have the same limited range of stewed plums and beans, and you will largely rely on the free markets for fresh fruit and vegetables, mainly cabbage in the spring but with much more variety in summer, when you see many peasant women with covered baskets of mushrooms, cherries, apricots and strawberries taking trains and buses to the towns. (Fruit should always be washed, especially in Kyiv.) Out of season, BBC Radio 4's *Food Programme* found the food 'horrid' even in Kyiv's best Intourist hotels.

As in Poland, soup is important, particularly *borshch*, based on beetroot with other vegetables and minced bacon; in summer this may be made with vegetable stock, but don't count on it — my promised meat-free *borshch* had a 4cm chunk of meat floating in it, so who knows what the carnivorous version would have contained. Other soups are *shchi*, a Russian cabbage soup, *okroshka*, a cold vegetable soup made with *kvass* and chopped spring onions, dill, parsley, radishes, roast beef, and a boiled egg, *rassolnik*, a kidney and cucumber soup, and *solyanka myasnaya* or *ribnaya*, a thick meat or fish soup.

Apart from Chicken Kiev (known here as *kutlyeta po Kiyevski*, and dangerously full of molten butter), the national dish is *vareniki* (in Russian *klushki*), ravioli-like dumplings stuffed with fruit (usually cherries) or sweet curd cheese and served with sour cream. A smaller version stuffed with meat is known as *Russki pelimeniye*, and the Kyiv version is stuffed with pork and apple. *Mlinets'* (*bliny* in Russian) are buckwheat pancakes, served with sour cream, cheese, jam, or, ideally, caviar. (Black or sturgeon caviar is known as *ikra chornaya* and the much cheaper red or salmon caviar is known as *ikra krasnaya*.) Buckwheat (*grechka*) is also used for *kasha*, a fine white porridge. With your meal you will probably have a salad, most often with cucumber (*salata z ohirok*), or pickled mushrooms (*marinovaniy hribi*), and almost always with dill. For the Russians and Ukrainians mushroom picking is perhaps more akin to the Japanese blossom-viewing ritual than food gathering, but dried mushrooms are vital as winter supplies.

There are usually no desserts other than ice cream (*morozhenoye*, sold rather slowly by weight) and perhaps *ryazhenka* or baked sour milk. Instead meals often end with tea and bread or biscuits with butter *or* a spot of jam, but not both. You may find pastries in cafés and on street stalls, sold with just a strip of paper to stop you getting grease everywhere. (In Odessa there were also a lot of surprisingly ungreasy potato pancakes for sale from street stalls.)

Basic cheese can be found in shops or markets, *kolbasa* is smoked sausage and *salo* is raw lard with garlic. Jam is rather bitter and jars once opened stay open: bring receptacles from home, and always take a bag with you to the market. To go with these, bread is still bought from state bakeries; brown bread is both cheaper and better where available. Both bread and cheese may have grit in them; as elsewhere in eastern Europe everyone wants to buy their bread at the same time, so that there can be long queues, with gypsies and old ladies ('But I only want one loaf') queue-barging.

Other possibilities are *kulinariya* shops, selling ready-cooked dishes, and *stolovayas* or cheap cafeterias. A *café* is often a cafeteria (especially in bus or rail stations), while a *cafeteria* often serves little more than coffee and alcohol. Long-distance buses sometimes stop at a *koliba* where drinks and *shashlik* (kebabs) are available. Odessa has always been more cosmopolitan, and even pineapples are available here, although few can afford them; Kyiv is catching up, as it thinks, with long queues for bananas, *KokaKola* and Parmigiani ice cream (with a hefty deposit on the bowls).

The main meal of the day is *obid*, usually eaten after work in mid-afternoon, preceded by breakfast (*snidanok*, or *zavtrak* in Russian) and a lunchtime snack known as *lehka perekuska* (literally a 'light snack'), and followed by supper (*vecher'*, or *uzhin* in Russian). Restaurants open around midday, with the main sittings at about 1400 and 1900, with an awful 'dancing band' playing from about 2000. In general people don't go to restaurants to eat, but rather to drink and dance; in Kyiv people are willing to pay twice the cost of a meal to get a table in the best restaurants. Thanks to Gorbachev's anti-alcohol campaign, there will probably only be mineral water to drink during the day.

Drink is every bit as important as food to Russian and Ukrainian men; alcoholism is a massive problem here, and has been from at least the 9th Century, when Islam was rejected as a potential religion because of its ban on alcohol. Stalin cut the price of vodka a little every year, as a bribe for the workers, and only Gorbachev had the courage to attempt to tackle this problem, although his sweeping attack on beer and wine as well as vodka drinking was an error, and of course there was a massive loss of revenue to the state. The 1991 *putsch* was partly ruined by drunkenness, and Yeltsin, the victor, also had a reputation as a mighty boozer at one time. Colin Thubron got it right when he wrote, 'vodka.. the curse and liberation of Russia, a self-obliterating escape from tedium and emptiness, from interminable winter nights, and the still longer, darker nights of the soul. It is drunk in furious catatonic debauches, with the full intention of rendering its drinkers virtually insensible'. You can learn more from William Pokhlebin's *A History of Vodka* (Verso 1992). If someone (invariably male) flicks his throat with a finger or makes a pouring motion with his thumb, he is inviting you to have a drink, and probably suggesting you treat him.

Ukrainian vodka is known as *horilka*, and *horilka z pertsem*, with a red pepper, is a speciality, particularly good for a Bloody Mary, I gather. Seagram (of Canada) is now producing three vodkas at the Lviv distillery, of which the best is Kievska Rus'; these can be bought at its own shop on vul Karla Marxa in Kyiv, where miniatures of its other products are also very popular, from US$1 each.

Beer is also available, although it is unpasteurised and thus does not keep long; the stand-up bars are not very customer-friendly. Local brands such as *Kolos* cost 10 coupons a half-litre in 1992, while imported beers in major cities cost five times as much for a smaller can.

Many vineyards were destroyed in the 1980s, but Ukraine still produces about a third of the CIS's wine, although as a rule the wines (and brandies) of Moldova and Georgia are better. Much of the Ukrainian wine is sparkling, and rather sweet for Western tastes; the best-known are *Krim* and *Sovetskaya Shampanska*, which sell for about 200 coupons. Crimea also produces Ruby and Madeira wines, which local drinkers tend to down in one, just like vodka; they can be found in handy 125ml bottles. Ukrainian wine can be bought in the UK through Ukraine Connect (tel 0726 61527).

As Joanna Simon has noted, major changes in attitude are needed in Ukraine and Georgia if they are to produce much better than the lowest common denominator; under the Soviet system grapes were picked too late because farms were paid by their sugar content, bad grapes were not picked out, machinery was not cleaned, and wine was kept standing for too long. Yet some managers would not believe that their wine was too bad to sell in the West. However in Moldova attitudes were more positive, and there are some excellent products, particularly from the Purkar and Krikova vineyards.

In summer you will see two-wheeled tanks on the streets selling *kvas*, a murky brown but very refreshing brew of dried black bread fermented with yeast, sugar and currants; it is very cheap and is popular with children as well as adults. You can either supply your own container or risk the glasses or jam jars provided. Soft drinks available in cafés and elsewhere include mineral waters such as *Lavtusa, Morschenka* and *Hutsulschina*, from the Carpathian spas, sometimes with fruit flavourings, and *kompot* or stewed fruit juice.

Tea is ubiquitous, but can be made in a variety of ways, either in a pot in the Western way, or stewed then diluted in a more Asian way, or as an infusion of green tea; it is traditional to stir in a spoonful of jam. Most comes from Georgia and is reckoned to be very poor quality, picked by machines. In the mountains you may be offered tea made from the leaves of the *chernika* or bilberry.

Kefir is drinking yoghurt, sold in American-style litre cartons; *keslay moloko* ('sour milk') is a similar product, only obtained directly from the farmer.

Russian words are given only where they differ from the Ukrainian.

	Ukrainian	Russian
Bread	*Khlib*	*Khleb*
Cake	*Torta*	*Tort*
Doughnuts	*Pampushka*	*Ponchik*
Jam	*Dzem*	*Varen'e*
Honey	*Med, lyuba*	*Myod*

Sugar	*Tsukor*	*Sakhar*
Yoghurt	*Yaourt*	*Yogurt*
Sour cream	*Smetana*	
Butter	*Maslo*	
Cheese	*Sir*	
Egg	*Yaytse*	
Omelette or	*Jajecznica*	*Yaichnitsa*
scrambled egg		
(Without) meat	*(Bez) m'yasa*	
Fish	*Riba*	
Pork	*Svinina*	
Beef	*Yalovichina*	*Govyadina*
Chicken	*Kurcha*	*Ts'iplyonok*
Sausage	*Kolbasa*	
Soup	*Borshch, sup*	*Sup*
Vegetables	*Ovochi*	*Ovoshchi*
Potato	*Kartoplya*	*Kartofel*
Rice	*Ris*	*Riz*
Cucumber	*Ohirok*	*Ogurets*
Onion	*Tsibulya*	*Luk*
Mushrooms	*Hryby*	*Gribi*
Beans	*Bibi, fasolye*	*Fasol'*
Peas	*Horokh*	*Gorokh*
Tomatoes	*Pomidor, tomat*	*Pomidor*
Lettuce	*Salata*	*Salat*
Cabbage	*Kapusta*	
Fruit	*Ovoch*	*Frukt*
Apple	*Yabliko*	*Yabloko*
Pear	*Grusha*	
Peach	*Persik*	
Grape	*Vinohrad*	*Vinograd*
Cherry	*Vishnya*	
Drinks	*Napiy*	*Napitok*
Milk	*Moloko*	
Tea	*Chay*	
Coffee	*Kava*	*Kofe*
Water (Mineral)	*Voda (mineralna)*	*(Mineralnaya) voda*
(soda)	*(sodova)*	*(sodovaya voda)*
Beer	*Pivo*	
(Red, white) wine	*Vino (chervoniy, biliy)*	*Vino (krasnayoe, beloe)*
Lemonade	*Limonad*	
Fruit juice	*Sik*	*Sok*

LIFE AND CULTURE

Ukraine is a conservative society, with the *babushkas* or grannies as its self-appointed moral guardians, letting you know if they disapprove of your style of dress or behaviour. There is a suspicion of politeness here and a routine artificial rudeness, so that people simply and bluntly demand a knife, a light, or the time, and playing cards *have* to be slammed down.

Almost all **shops** are still state-owned and receive stocks through the state system; little has changed, with shops frequently shut supposedly for stock-taking, and odd prices set by state committees such as 3 coupons 84 kopecks and so on. You will often have to take a chit to pay at a *kassa* and then go back to collect your goods; this means that having paid for half a kilo of cheese you have to be given neither more nor less, which is a time-consuming process. An approximation to a supermarket will usually be called a *Universam* (while a *Univermag* is a department store), a bakery is a *Bulochnaya*, and a smaller grocery shop a *Produkty* or *Prodovari*; they usually sell little beyond tinned or bottled vegetables, bread, ices and drinks. Fresh food will usually be sold in markets, now at free market prices, and with a bit more enthusiasm than in the state stores; take your own bags. Outside the markets can be seen those desperately trying to catch up with the new world rapidly passing them by: pensioners sitting by a set of bathroom scales, two dried fish or a box of German stock cubes.

Watch repair shops are omnipresent; I have an export-quality Sekonda which has never given any trouble but nevertheless caused great amusement, as all watches made for domestic use seem to need endless tinkering. Cheap Asian digital watches, cordless phones, make-up and cans of German beer and Coke are now available in *Kommissionarii* import shops and kiosks in resorts like Yalta. Some film is available, but to be safe you should bring all you need, especially slide film or ASA 200 and faster.

Opening hours of food shops are 0700-2000 or 0800-2100, on Saturdays to 1700 or 1800, and on Sundays to about midday, with lunchtime closing in smaller shops from 1300 to 1400, or 1400 to 1500 or even 1600. Other shops may not open until 1000 or 1100. Museums and galleries are shut on various days, most often Monday.

Post offices are open 0800-1800 on weekdays, and 0900-1600 on Saturdays and Sundays; stamps and envelopes are mostly marked *Poshta CCCP* (USSR Post) and priced in roubles. In 1992 postcards cost 4 kopecks and were put into 3 rouble envelopes to be sent to Britain, or 1 rouble envelopes within Ukraine. Letters can take up to seven weeks to get from Kyiv to the UK. Post offices are found in town centres and at major stations, due to historic links with the telegraph system.

Phones are in short supply, with just 7m in the whole republic; while there are plenty of public phones in the towns, these are usually out of order, and they are very rare in the countryside, indicated by signs at village post offices. Local calls still cost only 15 kopecks, but for long-distance calls you will have to go to a telephone office (open 0800-2400, usually next door to a main post office) or use a friend's phone to call the operator and then wait to be called back when a line is available. The wait is generally 15 to 20 minutes, but for international calls you might have to wait hours; however digital exchanges are now being installed in all major cities, which should improve matters. For political reasons calls out of Ukraine currently cost just 60 karbovantsi (2.1p) a minute to western Europe, or 150 karbovantsi (5.4p) to the USA and Africa, although Utel pays US$1.25 a minute to the American phone companies, making money only in the other direction. However if you call from a hard currency hotel you are likely to pay the full rate. In addition cellular phones are being introduced to the yuppies and racketeers of Kyiv in 1993.

Note that when calling Ukraine from abroad you should **not** drop the intial '0' of the code; thus to call Kyiv you should dial 0107 044 followed by the number. The code for Lviv is 0322, for Odessa 0482, for Sevastopil 0692, and for Yalta 060 or 0654. Dial 01 for fire, 02 for police, and 03 for an ambulance.

Addresses should ideally be written in Cyrillic, but if this is not possible, or indeed as a back-up, Latin script is sufficiently comprehensible for letters to reach their destinations. A street is a *vulitsa* in Ukrainian or *ulitsa* in Russian, an avenue a *doroha* or *prospekt*, a lane a *pereulok* and a square a *ploschad*. Every main street was of course named after Lenin, and in some cases I've had to use this name, although you will probably find it changed by now, like many other names. Most of the Lenin statues have also gone, although there are still plenty of Mounds of Glory, usually topped by a Second World War tank.

Names are in three parts, with a personal name, a patronymic, and a surname, as in Mikhail Sergeyevitch Gorbachev, or Mikhail, son of Sergei Gorbachev; female names end in –a, as in Gorbacheva. First names are usually abbreviated, to Vova, Misha or Sasha for Vladimir, Mikhail and Alexander, for instance.

The **media** are bursting out all over, often in unexpected ways; as in the rest of eastern Europe, one of the most popular products is soft porn. Most newspapers are in Russian, but these are often more nationalistic than those in the Ukrainian language. They sell for about 50 coupons each, when Solzhenitsyn's *One Day in the Life of Ivan Denisovitch*, Orwell, Harold Robbins and Jackie Collins sell for 10 coupons. In Transcarpathia I saw Hungarian magazines with headings such as 'Welcone Lady Di' (before a state visit), and titles like *Guten Tag* and *Amerika* in Russian and Cyrillic script.

Television is now very important in Ukrainian homes, although at first glance it still does not seem very watchable. The Russian Ostankino channel (which uses Beethoven's *Ode to Joy* as its theme, like the Olympics, the European Union and almost everyone else) seems always to have the best reception, and even on the two Ukrainian channels most films are still in Russian (other foreign films have all parts badly dubbed by one actor). There is up to two hours a day of stultifying parliamentary debate, lots of aerobics which I think is aimed mainly at a sedentary male audience, and a popular Mexican soap. I saw a sports announcer with a computer for the latest results, but there was no earphone or remote control to help when he forgot how to work it, and I swear I heard off-camera laughter instead! There is now advertising, mainly for Western products such as cars and chocolate bars (with tobacco and alcohol adverts only on Ostankino). In Lviv two Polish channels can also be received, and German satellite service can currently be received free, although it will be coded before too long. The BBC World Service now has a Ukrainian radio service.

In fact the grapevine is the most important medium, dominated of course by the *babushkas*, and you will see plenty of typed notices with tear-off phone numbers, offering wedding dresses, piglets or anything else. Don't be frightened to ask for help; everyone has to do it here as soon as they're off their own turf.

Everyday **costume** is now pretty anonymous, with most people wearing a shabbier version of Western clothes. Younger people wear jeans, tracksuits, trainers, and Chanel, Gucci, Hugo Boss, Yves St Laurent or Phuket T-shirts (all clearly churned out by the same factory), together with ridiculously short skirts and, in the southern towns, lurex leggings, baseball caps and shoulder pads. Although women can often be seen working in the fields in bikinis, men virtually never wear shorts; older women are always wrapped up with headscarves as well, while, outside Transcarpathia, men all seem to have gold teeth. In most homes you will be expected to change into slippers, but this is not a strict custom as in Islamic countries.

On Sundays and festivals you may still find folk costumes worn in Rusyn villages: white blouses and shirts are elaborately embroidered in red and blue, worn with red aprons, capes and even sometimes trousers, and sheepskin hats and jackets. Foresters and shepherds wear even wider leather belts than in the neighbouring areas of the Carpathians.

The Rusyn, especially the Huṭul, are responsible for the most interesting **music** in Ukraine; their main instruments are the accordion (*garmoska*), violin (*skrypka*), drum (*baraban*), jew's-harp (*drimba*), and cembalom. The *trembuta* or alpenhorn has its own music, while elsewhere in Ukraine *mandura* music has a very twangy Asian feel, often with a drone. The most characteristic Ukrainian song (also found in Poland) is the *kolomeyka*, after the town of Kolomea; this is a rhyming couplet of 14-syllable lines with a set rhythmic pattern, still being improvised to this day.

M.V. Lysenko (1842-1912) is seen as the founder of Ukrainian classical music, with operas such as *Taras Bulba* (from Gogol) and *Natalya Potavka*, and a collection of 240 popular Ukrainian folk songs. The best known Ukrainian folk tune is the *dumka* (as in Dvořák's *Dumky* trio), a wistful song with alternating fast and elegiac tempi, usually recalling some heroic exploit. The *Kassachok* (Cossack) is a dance, led by the women, who clap their hands when changing step, with the men having to follow. However the best known Ukrainian music is in Tchaikovsky's First Quartet and his Second Symphony, anachronistically known as the *Little Russian* because of the Ukrainian folk tunes in the first and fourth movements (his Third Symphony is known as the *Polish*, for the same reason). Music from a totally different tradition is that on a Pearl CD of *Eighteen Jewish Prayers* splendidly recorded in the 1920s by Kantor Salomo Pinkasovitch.

The best known Ukrainian **writers** are Taras Shevchenko (1814-61), Lesya Ukrainka (pseudonym of Larissa Kosach-Kvitka, 1871-1913) and Ivan Franko (1856-1916); their work has been published in translation by émigré publishers in Canada and the USA, but is hard to find in the UK. Nikolai Gogol (1809-52) and Mikhail Bulgakov (1891-1940) both chose to write in Russian, and their works (such as *The Government Inspector* and *The White Guard*) are well known in English. Mikhail Sholokhov (1905) wrote in Russian about the Cossacks, and his *Quiet Flows the Don* and *Virgin Soil Upturned* are easily available in English.

The notorious Leopold von Sacher-Masoch was born in Lviv in 1836, son of the Austrian police chief and a Ukrainian-Jewish mother; his best-known book is *Venus im Pelz* (Venus in Furs, 1870). There was controversy in Lviv in early 1993 over plans for a monument to him, which were rejected by the council.

Sport in Ukraine benefited from the same system of intensive coaching as in the rest of the Soviet Union, and in the Barcelona Olympics Ukrainian athletes won 40 of the Unified Team's 112 medals, and 17 of its 45 golds, mostly in gymnastics. The phenomenal pole-vaulter Sergey Bubka was beaten here, but soon raised his own world record for the 33rd and 34th times, to 6.15m. There are even Ukrainian yachts in the 1993 Round The World race. However football is the sport that catches the public imagination, and Kyiv Dinamo was for long the Soviet Union's foremost team. Now Ukrainians are looking forward eagerly to entering FIFA European competitions, and some Dinamo players are already playing for teams such as Manchester United. Tennis players such as Cherkassov are also making a big impression abroad.

Education begins at about 6½ years (after years of kindergarten from 0900 to 1800, provided by factories or trade unions), and matriculation is 10 years later; after years of russification, there is now a return to education in minority tongues, although it is proving hard to find enough Romanian-speaking teachers in particular. There are specialist schools for arts and music, commercial studies, and foreign languages, now very popular, and there is even talk of a return to the *Gymnazium* (grammar school) system. From 1992 students must pay for higher education, at about R30,000 annually for five years; there are 10 state universities as well as the historic Mohyla Academy in Kyiv, reopened as a private university. For some reason there are semi-derelict army personnel carriers in the courtyard of Lviv University, where the computer equipment is not too bad but lecturers have to go to the concierges' lodge to phone out.

Those men not going on to higher education have to do military service for 18 months (two years in the navy), cut in 1992 from two years or three in the navy. Ukraine has the largest army in Europe but intends to slim it down and create a more professional body; at the moment it is very egalitarian but probably wouldn't win a war. Some go on to join the OMON or special police, tough guys in blue and white striped T-shirts under blue fatigues, used against organised **crime**, which has arrived in Ukraine from Moscow (now largely run by so-called *mafia*) in 1992 and 1993. The regular police are equipped only with truncheons, contrary to what you might expect, and for most offences, including dabbling in marijuana and the black market, foreigners will usually only receive a good dressing-down after signing a confession or *protokol*. There are police checkpoints on most main roads, but buses get waved straight through.

As outlined on page 225, **healthcare** is a major concern in Ukraine, with life expectancy and the birth rate both falling. This is due in part to pollution, but also to stress, bad diet, the high level of industrial accidents (about 200,000 a year in the former Soviet Union) and the low priority formerly given to the medical industry, which produced just 192m syringes in 1989 (in the whole Soviet Union) against a planned total of 500m and a real need for several billion. Ukrainian doctors are as good as any in most ways, and medical treatment is free to visitors from those countries, such as Britain, with which the Soviet Union had reciprocal agreements, although there is a charge for prescribed medicines. Sanatoria in resorts such as Yalta were immensely popular when trade unions paid up to 70% of the cost, but now that individuals have to bear the whole cost themselves they are much less crowded. Private hospitals are also appearing, but without a health insurance system they are likely only to serve the richest, probably the same people who once benefitted from the hospitals restricted to the Party *apparat*.

Tick-borne encephalitis is a potential problem in warm forests, especially where there is heavy undergrowth, and some forests are theoretically closed around June; wear clothing that covers most of your skin and use insect repellants. A vaccine is available, but it is not free on the NHS. There is also now a short-term risk of diphtheria, as children are not being vaccinated after the usual kind of scare about side effects; in 1993 there were 1,300 cases in Kyiv, as well as some cholera near the Danube Delta.

Doctors all seem very aware of the risks of tobacco and alcohol, both major problems here as in all the neighbouring countries. Ukrainian cigarettes are very cheap indeed, at 10 coupons a pack, while Winstons cost 100 coupons; cigarettes are now coming in from Zimbabwe, largely on the black market, and from Russia, and the multinational BAT (British-American Tobacco) has invested US$20m in the Prilucky tobacco factory east of Kyiv, aiming to introduce better quality tipped cigarettes into a market dominated by high tar brands, while avoiding the 'brand imperialism' of Camel and Marlboro.

Homosexuality was legalised in December 1991, immediately after independence, but it is felt that this was an attempt by parliament to seem liberal and western, and not at all a reflection of popular demands. There is still a great deal of prejudice, but a gay and lesbian association, Ganymede, was founded in 1991, and a successful gay disco opened in Kyiv in 1993. HIV is not much discussed, although buses in the seaport of Odessa carry posters saying 'Stop AIDS'; there have been just over 100 cases of AIDS, mostly not homosexually transmitted.

Women in Ukraine

'Life for women is tough. They mostly work, out of economic necessity, but don't have the benefits of labour-saving devices in the home like washing machines. The hot water serving the complexes of flats comes from a central boiler house, but due to age and shortage of spare parts this often breaks down and the flats are without hot water for days, and sometimes weeks, at a time. Sometimes the cold water also dries up, but residents are warned beforehand so they can fill receptacles. In the villages water is drawn from a well, usually a communal one in the street. This is a chore in winter when temperatures can drop to -30°C.'

Women are in low-pay, low-status jobs, and they also have to queue, cook, clean and raise children in increasingly bad circumstances. Articles 35 and 53 of the Soviet Constitution guarantee equality, but not in the home. Nor is it common to see women driving private cars, although they often work as tram drivers.

It is common for unmarried couples to live together, with one family or the other, but an unmarried mother is a disgraceful thing, and pregnant schoolgirls are usually expelled. Family planning is based on conveyor-belt abortions, with an average of seven abortions per woman, and five to eight abortions per live birth (five times the US rate). In any case 'most women are married by the age of 22 as there really isn't anything else for them to do'. Often several generations live together, with grandmothers playing a crucial rôle in childcare. During pregnancy a woman sees her GP once a month, with no prenatal classes as such, and then goes into hospital alone; the husband is not allowed to be with her and doesn't see the baby until the mother returns home 10 days later. This is done on the grounds of hygiene ('grubby things, men' as my girlfriend commented). Maternity leave lasts for a year, with the option of six months unpaid after that. 'Babies are terribly well wrapped up with woollen leggings on in heat waves, and my daughter-in-law was scolded many times by outraged women who felt she was being a bad mother by leaving her son's legs bare.' Kindergartens, run by trades unions, take children from one to six, but fees are rising (and the kindergartens are seen as hotbeds of infection) so that some parents are dropping out, and staff are being made redundant.

It is still generally safe to go out alone at night, and hitchhiking is normal in the rural areas. You should bring all contraceptive and sanitary requirements with you, and even toilet paper is in short supply.

(with thanks to Linda Reynolds and Heather Anderson)

HIKING

Hiking is not as popular in Ukraine as in Poland, but there are marked routes in most of the mountain areas, and you will find Ukrainian mountain lovers either camping wild or staying in Turbazas in the mountain resorts. These are mostly in areas formerly ruled by the Hapsburgs and then the Poles, where the *Polskiego Towarzystwa Tatranskiego* was very active until the Second World War, although the main ridge of the Carpathians was a frontier and is still marked with concrete pillars and barbed wire. These border markers make it very easy to navigate along the ridge, which is handy in bad weather but may mean climbing over hilltops that a path would more naturally go around. In the Soviet period facilities became rather run-down, while the new border area became a military zone, even though all the surrounding states were supposedly allies. In general the mountains are less damaged than in Poland or Romania, with less logging, skiing, dam-building and acid rain, but nevertheless I saw less wildlife here than in those countries. There is a serious litter problem at camping sites and elsewhere in the mountains, as even those who most love the mountains are unwilling to carry empty tins and bottles down with them.

Trail markings and maps

Trail markings are not particularly good and are likely to deteriorate in the future, but they follow the same principles as in most eastern European countries, with horizontal stripes of red, green, blue and yellow sandwiched between two white stripes painted on rocks and trees.

Detailed maps (1:200,000) were classified secret by the First Directorate of the KGB, and have not all been released yet. Where they are available, thay can be bought from the Mountain Rescue Service (*Kontrol'no Spasatel'naya Sluzhba* or KSS, written **KCC**, a typically Soviet bureaucracy rather than being active mountaineers, unfit and fairly useless beyond the jeep tracks). They are expensive for Ukrainians, but Western visitors have no excuse for not buying them where available, although they do leave a lot to be desired. These do not show the marked routes, shown on the tourist leaflets available from kiosks in most resorts; these are of course in Russian or Ukrainian, but the basics are fairly comprehensible. Get into the habit of looking for these maps wherever you are, as they may only be obtainable outside the resort they refer to. By far the most useful is the booklet *Po Lesist'im Karpatam* (Through the Forest Carpathians), which shows in detail (1:50,000) a route from Yasinya to Volovets via Lake Sinevir, mainly following the former frontier.

Some kiosks will also stock the *oblast* atlases gradually being produced by universities and sold at the usual heavily subsidised prices; these give lots of detailed information on geology, crops, demographics and so on, but are also only in Russian or Ukrainian. You may even find the

Ukrainskiye Carpati atlas, published by the Principal Geodesic and Ordnance Survey of the USSR Council of Ministeries, in 1987. One address to try is Cartographia, vul Popudrenko 54, Kyiv.

You can also obtain pre-First World War Austro-Hungarian maps, still the most detailed, covering all Poland and Ukraine west of Kyiv and Odessa; these are obtainable at 1:200,000 and 1:75,000, over the counter or by mail from the BEV, Krotenthallergasse 3, 1080 Wien, Austria (tel 438 935, fax 439 992). Lascelles, Freytag & Berndt, and Bartholomew all publish maps at a scale of 1:2 million of Ukraine, Belarus and Western Russia.

Currently the only organised hiking trips that I know of are in Crimea, with Exodus Expeditions who offer 16 days from £1,150 (about twice what they charge in Poland), and Sherpa Expeditions (see page 81 for addresses), who offer 15 days for £930.

OTHER SPORTS

Skiing (*l'izhnyky*) is not highly developed in Ukraine; although there is plenty of snow, there is little infrastructure, with accommodation only in Turbazas and only basic ski-drags; nor do many people have the income for good equipment. The only exception is in Crimea, where there are good hotels an easy drive below the slopes on Ai-Petri and at the Angarsky pass; even so, the slopes are short and easy.

In the Carpathians, the best-known resort is at Tissovetz, an army Turbaza now open to all, with an Olympic-standard run from a maximum of 1,200m; it lies southwest of Skole, by a minor road west from Kozevo, in the eastern (*Vostochn'ie*) Beskids. However far more skiing actually happens just east, in the villages strung along the Lviv-Chop railway in the Opir valley, particularly in Slavskoe, where there are Turbazas, the Dinamo ski school, and ski-lifts on Trostyan (1,232m, see page 361).

The other main resort area is just to the north of Hoverla, in Krementsi, Vorokhta and Verkhovina; there are Turbazas and ski-drags in these villages, as well as at the Yablonitskiy pass, and a ski-jump (*tramplyn*) at the west end of Vorokhta. There is also skiing in isolated patches in Transcarpathia, for instance at Svalyava, Zhernava, Yasinya, and Ust-Chorna. These slopes would not be worth a journey, but cross-country skiing here must be an exciting possibility.

The former Soviet Union was a considerable force in the world of **climbing**, but this was largely focused on the Caucasus, Pamirs, Tien Shan and Altai in central Asia; in Ukraine climbing is mainly on the limestone cliffs of Crimea (all grades, with bolts on some shorter routes).

'The Crimean mountains boast limestone crags up to 500m high with generally sound rock, not polished despite the relative popularity of the area. Scattered trees characterise the easier climbs and provide convenient belays. The best times for climbing are May and September, as in high summer it is too hot. Popular locations include cliffs above the main Yalta-Sevastopil road (which has regular bus services) near Foros. Here the climbs are up to 440m in length, with numerous routes ranging from introductory grade up to very hard climbs, and convenient gullies for descent from the plateau above. Unintentional bivouacs are not uncommon at the higher grades. Camping is traditional near these cliffs, although there are only a few water sources and theft must be a potential problem for Western climbers.

The Russian grading system is used, ranging from 1 for the easiest to 6 for the hardest, and reflecting the overall difficulty rather than the hardest pitch. The long climbs are not bolted and have adequate natural protection; there are also numerous training areas where top-roping is used (notably cliffs below the main road at Kristovaya, near Livadia) and there are some hard bolted routes. Guidebooks are starting to appear, including *Rocks near the Sea* by A.N. Shcherbakov (incorporating Chelebi, Mshatka-Kaya-Si and Kush-Kaya areas, west of Foros, in both English and Russian). The clarity is, however, scarcely adequate and first-hand advice from climbers who know the area is invaluable. The guidebook's publishers Solaris (14-a/40 ul Gavena, Sevastopil, tel 247 781, fax 592 813) offer a guiding service. The local climbing techniques, equipment and traditions differ significantly from those in the West, and this should be borne in mind.' (Paul Knott)

As in the Pieniny in Poland, foresters have for many years taken tourists on **rafts** from Verkhovina down to Vizhnitsa on the Black (*Chern'iy*) Cheremosh river, east of Hoverla, and from Vorokhta to Deliatyn or Kolomea on the Prut, north of Hoverla. However this has largely died out now, although you could enquire at the Turbazas in Verchovina and Vorokhta. Hann Overland (tel 0833 744 705) has in the past operated a combined hiking and rafting trip, but this is not presently running due to the general unreliability of the system here. The best solution, if you are set on boating here, would be to bring your own kayak or inflatable dinghy, although this might require a car.

Cycling is common in country villages, with very basic machines that need pushing uphill and pedalling backwards to brake, but bikes are almost never used either as city transport (except in Mukachevo and the Hungarian towns, where they are mainly ridden on the pavement, it seems). However there are small touring and road racing clubs in the biggest cities, who have pretty good equipment and loads of enthusiasm. The Volgograd Cyclists' Touring Club, in southern Russia, is very keen to make contacts with western cyclists and will make arrangements for anyone planning to tour in the former Soviet Union; their contact (who speaks excellent English) is Pavel Protopopov, Prospekt Lenina 22/14, 400066 Volgograd, Russia (tel 8442 362 834).

Off-road riding is almost unheard of, and I have seen no mountain bikes in Ukraine, but there is a rather bizarre leaflet (*Velosipedn'iy Marshrut Po Karpatam*), with map, available from kiosks in some

Transcarpathian resorts, that describes a cycle touring route from Uzhgorod to Yaremcha via Uzhok, Volovets, Svalyava, Lake Sinevir, Ust-Chorna and Yasinya, and includes one stretch near Lake Sinevir that would be well-nigh impassable even with a mountain bike, and the Petros pass which would at least require a mountain bike — see pages 344 and 355.

It is quite straightforward to take a bike on a local train; note that it is probably worth staying in camp site cabins rather than hotels if possible, as it will be easier to bring your bike indoors with you — do not leave it out overnight.

'In 1993 we flew into Kyiv and cycled 1,000km west to Budapest. I advise you to carry lots of food since shops are well spaced in Ukraine. We saw no fresh produce in April. Likewise, bring your own coffee and tea. In the seven days of cycling we never saw a cycle shop.' (Bob Egan)

Horse riding is rare, although you will still see many horse carts in use. There are trotting races in Kyiv, but they are very drab and run-down, with the total bet on 12 races apparently only enough for 100 litres of petrol; most of the horses are still state-owned, some from the 14 state studs, but more from collective and state farms. Only the Huṭuls are accustomed to riding horses, and there is great potential for riding through the Carpathians if you can find a horse.

Some of the longest **caves** in Europe are to be found in Podolia, a huge area of 20,000km² of gypsum karst between Ternopil and Chernovts'i, including the 186km Optimisticheskaya system (near Korolivka), the 136km Ozernaya, the 87km Racoviṭa (in Bucovina, formerly known as Zoolushka), Ml'inki (23km) and Krystalnaja (22km) systems. In Crimea the Krasnaya-Kizil Koba system is 14km long. As the system is in transition, I do not have an address for a Ukrainian caving federation, and you will not be able to get into these major systems without their help; however there is still much exploration to be done.

Part Five

Ukraine Guide

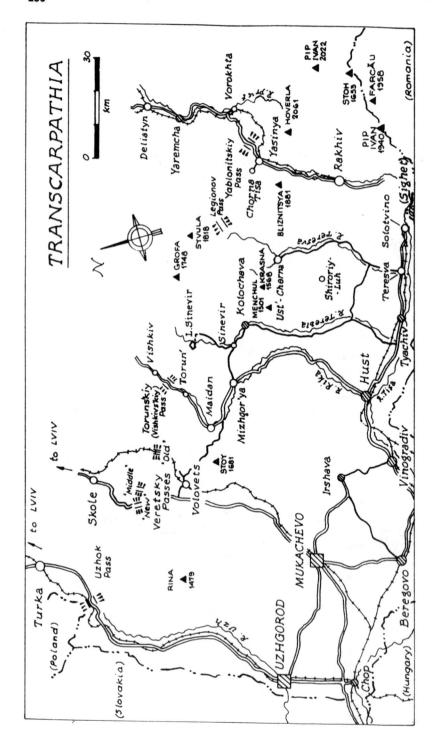

TRANSCARPATHIA

to LVIV

to LVIV

Turka
(Poland)
(Slovakia)

Uzhok
Pass

RINA
1479

R. Uzh

UZHGOROD

MUKACHEVO

Skole

'Middle'
'New'
Veretsky
Passes
'Old'

Volovets

STOY
1681

Torunskiy
(Vishkivskiy)
Pass

Vishkiv

Torun'

Maidan

Mizhgor'ya

Irshava

L.Sinevir

Sinevir

GROFA
1748

SYVULA
1818

Legionov
Pass

Kolochava

MENCHUL
1501

KRASNA
1566

Ust'-Chorna

Shiroriy-
Luh

R. Teresva

Teresva

R. Teresva

R. Rika

Hust

R. Tisa

Tyachiv

Solotvino

(Sighet)

Vinogradiv

Beregovo

(Hungary)

Chop

Deliatyn

Yaremcha

Vorokhta

R. Prut

Yablonitskiy
Pass

Chorna
Tisa

Yasinya

BLIZNITSYA
1881

Rakhiv

HOVERLA
2061

PIP
IVAN
2022

STOH
1653

FARCĂU
1958

PIP
IVAN
1940

(Romania)

0   km   30

Chapter 10

Orientation

TRANSCARPATHIA

Travelling overland, you are likely to arrive first in either Lviv or Chop; Lviv is described fully below, but Chop has nothing of interest beyond a hotel to the right of the station. However it is a jumping-off point for Transcarpathia, and particularly the towns of Uzhgorod and Mukachevo, before continuing to the mountains; it became a customs-free zone in March 1993.

The *oblast* of Zacarpatska (Transcarpathia, or Sub-Carpathian Ruthenia) can claim with some justification to be the crossroads of Europe — it contains one of the claimed geographical centres of the continent and is the only European region to be bordered by four states (Poland, Slovakia, Hungary and Romania, as well as Ukraine proper). It was ruled from the 10th Century by Hungary, Poland and the Hapsburgs, until the Austro-Hungarian Empire was dismembered after the First World War, when it became part of the new state of Czechoslovakia, although the eastern region seceded briefly as an independent Huţul Republic when Bela Kun's communists took over Hungary. The area south of Mukachevo was seized in November 1938 by Hungary under Hitler's ally Admiral Horthy, and the rest of Ruthenia followed in September 1939. It was only in 1944 that the Soviet Union pushed its frontiers beyond the Carpathian watershed; in November 1944 a Congress of People's Committees in Mukachevo voted for 'reunification' with their Slav brothers north of the Carpathians, but in truth Stalin had decided to go one up on the Tsars by establishing a Soviet presence in the Danube lands and central Europe.

When Nora Beloff visited in 1979, the region still seemed unassimilated, perhaps partly because there were still no proper roads to link it to the Soviet Union proper. The main links are still the railways, and it is noticeable that although the roads across the watershed are now good on the southern, Transcarpathian, side, their condition is far worse to the north, due not to the climate but to lack of interest in the neighbouring *oblasts*.

The population of 1.3m is officially 78% Ukrainian, but many of these are now redefining themselves as Ruthenian (or *Rusyn*), Huţul, Boyk or Łemk (see page 246). The Rusyn leader is the poet Volodimir Fedinishnets, who claims that the only place where they have been recognised as a distinct ethnic group was Yugoslavia (with 30,000 Rusyn in Vojvodina). The local dialect is largely Ukrainian-based, with elements of Slovak. The Hungarian minority is confined to the south-western border area; even towns such as Uzhgorod and Mukachevo are now largely Ukrainian. Nevertheless, the Hungarian influence remains widespread, with more beer and wine than vodka, and most people actually working to Central European Time, an hour behind Ukraine and Russia (it is stressed that buses and trains run to 'Moscow time'). As everywhere in the former Soviet Union, there is now a sizeable Russian minority in the cities, and there is a pocket of Romanians (who call the area western Bucovina) around Solotvino. There are also many gypsies, although no longer as colourful as their cousins in Romania. There is even a pocket of Germans just south of Mukachevo.

Before the last war up to half of the urban population was Jewish, but these have now vanished, with only a few, such as Robert Maxwell (born Jan Ludwig Hoch in Solotvino) escaping. In May 1944 the 13,000 Jews of Mukachevo, for example, were packed into trains bound for Auschwitz-Birkenau; during the five-day journey many went mad and many died. At one town the corpses were removed from the train, and those who had gone mad were shot. Most of the others were gassed immediately on arrival.

UZHGOROD

Uzhgorod (City on the Uzh) is the capital of Transcarpathia; known to the Hungarians as Ungvar, it is still largely Magyar in feel, with many street signs in both Roman and Cyrillic scripts. Dating from the 8th Century, it still has an attractive pedestrianised old town, mostly 17th and 18th Century, and 11th Century castle walls around a palace dating from 1598 (and tackily restored in 1990), although it is now a city of 80,000. As in much of this *oblast*, there is a relatively southern feel to the landscape, with orchards and, at least before Gorbachev's anti-alcohol campaign, vineyards surrounding the city. I've never before seen red squirrels and woodpeckers literally a couple of metres away in a city centre.

Getting there

Uzhgorod is on a minor rail line from Chop to Sambor via the Uzhok pass and Turka, but through trains from Lviv and elsewhere take the main line via Volovets and Mukachevo to Chop, and then turn north up this minor line to Uzhgorod. If stopping to visit Mukachevo, it is generally quicker and simpler to take one of the 24 slow or 9 express buses from there to Uzhgorod. From here buses run to all major towns of Transcarpathia, but not over the passes to the north. From the rail station, adjacent to the bus terminal, there are shared taxis or minibuses into town, route 1 passing to the north of the old town and route 2 through the new town, both terminating to the northwest on vul Sovetskaya, the road to Slovakia. Buses 5 and 8 also run from the station through the new town, and bus 6 past the old town; I gather buses are particularly badly affected by the fuel crisis here.

Where to stay
The two major hotels are on the main road from the station through the new town, Prospect Svobody (Freedom Avenue); the main Intourist hotel, to which you will probably be directed, is the Zakarpatye (tel 363 70/975 10; it has a satellite phone so you can call home) on Ploschad 50-Let CCCP (50 Years of the USSR Square), halfway to the river, and the Uzhgorod (tel 350 65) at Ploschad Khmelnitskogo 2, by the river, is smaller and more pleasant and might let you have a room for US$20, depending on the receptionist. The Druzhba, to the north on Ul Gen Petrova (or Tomyaniya) with a fine view, is a newer tourist hotel, with German satellite TV, which may have a room for R1,000. The Sport, to the west behind the Avangard stadium, was not interested in foreigners when I was there, but this could change. There are also two older hotels in the heart of the old town, the Korona (or Verchovina) at Pl Teatralna 5, and the Kyiv at Pl Koryatovicha 1. There are also two Turbazas on the north side of town, the Svitanok at vul Koshitskaya 30 and the Horizont at vul Sovetskaya 20, which are cheaper alternatives.

What to see
The main sights are all on vul Kremlevskaya (Kremlin St), running east from the old town centre; first the Uniate cathedral (built in 1646, with a large iconostasis and an over-decorated pulpit cover), next to the university library, built in 1644 for a Jesuit college, and then the castle, largely 16th Century, which contains the Regional Museum (strong on fauna and flora) and a private gallery of local artists, and opposite it a skansen or open-air museum of vernacular architecture (similar to that across the border in Romania, although with wood carvings more like those of the Tatras), with a Lemk church from 1777. On vul Ol'brakhta, the next road south, is a Hungarian Catholic church, also with a Baroque interior with fake marbling and a 'Wedgwoody' blue and white ceiling, as well as a concert hall in the huge former synagogue.

Next to a Hungarian Calvinist church on vul Sovetskaya is the Fine Arts Museum, in the Building of the Uzhansky Committee (1809), not particularly marvellous; just to the east, at vul Gor'kogo 74, is a museum dedicated to the local painter Fyodor Manailo. Across the Uzh river at Moskovskaya Naberezhnaya (Moscow Quay) 23 is St Paul's Orthodox church, built in 1930s Muscovite style as a memorial for Russians killed in the First World War and used as a Museum of Atheism until recently.

About 6km to the northeast in Nevitskoye, on the road to Turka and Sambor, are the 13-14th Century ruins of a castle, with an interesting wooden superstructure to a tower, reminiscent of the Saxon churches of Transylvania. Intourist (tel 109 504) will arrange excursions here.

Practical information

The main shops are opposite the two major hotels and in the old town; the main market is off vul Koryatovicha, in the old town; the most interesting dealings here are those in Slovak Crowns, openly traded for coupons and roubles.

Mukachevo

Mukachevo (Munkacs to the Hungarians), the second city of Transcarpathia, lies 35km east of Uzhgorod, and is very much over-shadowed by it. Dating from the 12th Century, its main monument is now the Palanok castle, built in the 14th, 15th and 17th Centuries on a volcanic plug about 3km from the city, but it also retains many Transylvanian-style houses, with two windows but no door opening on to the street, and some fine turn-of-the-century buildings in the centre. Mukachevo was also a great centre of Jewish learning, whose chief rabbi had almost princely status. It is now notable for its furniture and ski factory.

From the bus station you should turn left to reach the city centre by vul Mira, or from the railway station (served by Lviv-Chop trains, including those from Moscow to Prague, Budapest and so on) turn right or take buses 2 or 9. At vul Mira 28 is the 17th Century White Palace, built by the Rakoczi family and now a school, and at no 51 there is the small 15th Century Gothic chapel of St Martin hidden behind a Hungarian Roman Catholic church (built in 1904); just to the right/east on vul Dukhinovtsi is the Hungarian Reformed church, in railway station-cum-Scottish Baronial style, near the excellent indoor market. The main street, now pedestrianised, is still known as Ploschad Lenina, with the Hotel Zirka and the 'Electron' Technical Institute (with a fine Secession-style tower) at its top end.

Just to the left/west of here (towards the rail station) is vul Karl Marx (to be renamed?) which leads out to the Palanok castle; you can take bus 3, and from a bus stop by a café take the unmarked vul Tankistov to the left up to the castle. This is open 0900-1700, except Monday, although when I visited it was undergoing a total *remont* and was frankly best seen from the train; there is a museum of local history, an interesting treadmill well in the second courtyard, and a view of the dull surrounding plain.

LVIV

Lviv to Ukrainians, L'vov to Russians, Lvov to Poles, Lemburg to Germans, even Leopol in Latin, this is my favourite Ukrainian city, a place of trees, Gothic and Renaissance churches, cafés, and beer rather than vodka. It has a reputation for honesty and for water shortages, with water often only running for a few hours in the morning and evening, and hence dirty cars.

It was founded in 1256 by Prince Danilo, to protect Galicia against the Tatars, and named after his son Lev (lion); in 1349 it was captured by the Poles from Rus', and was taken over by the Hapsburgs in the Partition of 1772. Lviv prospered as capital of the Austrian province of Galicia, with its polytechnic institute founded in 1844 (in addition to a university dating back to 1661) and a conservatoire in 1904. After the First World War Galicia was handed to Poland, and in 1939 it went to the Soviet Union under the Molotov-Ribbentrop pact. Hitler, of course, reneged on this and the area was occupied by the Germans from 1941 to 1944; Stalin insisted at Yalta on keeping Lviv, although its prewar population was 63% Polish (with Germans and Jews), so almost 3m Poles were transferred to Poland, to fill the gaps left by Germans deported from Poland's new western territories, and the change was ratified by a non-secret plebiscite. The population of 800,000 is now about 80% Ukrainian (with Russians, Armenians, Belorussians, Hungarians and a few Jews) but they are still somewhat rootless; it's said that no-one really feels he belongs to Lviv, while there are still many in Wrocław who feel deep down that they belong to Lvov.

Getting there

International trains from Hungary, Slovakia and southern Poland all pass through Lviv, and it can also be reached by buses virtually hourly from Przemyśl, and by plane from Prague and Warsaw, making it a place you are very likely to pass through on your way to the mountains. It is also reached by buses from most towns in western Ukraine and Transcarpathia.

The railway station, with a proper European train shed, and the minor bus station next to it, are about 2km west of the centre by tram 1. There is an Intourist *kassa* on platform 1, but you would be better off going to the Intourist hotels for tickets, or just joining the regular queues. Tickets for local trains can be bought to the right, or from coin machines. The main bus station is further from the centre, south along vul Striys'ka.

The airport is at Snilow, 10km northwest; Intourist should be able to tell you about a bus, but if not ask at the *autostantsiya* no 4 on vul Kleparivs'ka, north of the centre by tram 6. There are just four planes a week to Kyiv, but it is only worth flying to more distant places such as Moscow, Baku, Kishinev, or Ashkabad, as well as Warsaw and Budapest.

Where to stay

As in Kyiv, there is a considerable range of hotels, only a few of which were officially admitting foreigners in 1992, but any of which might be persuaded. As in Kyiv there is some confusion about telephone numbers.

The four hotels open to foreigners are the Dnestr, between the station and the centre at vul Matejko 6 (tel 797 037), the George (formerly the Intourist, Pl Mickiewicz 1, tel 799 011/725 952), the Ukraina (Pl Mickiewicz 4, tel 799 921/726 646), and the Lviv (vul 700-letiya L'vova 3, tel 791 270/1).

The Dnestr is a modern block built for groups of wealthy foreigners, with 24-hour reception, a hard-currency 'night bar' open till 0400, an exchange desk open till 2000 and a travel desk open till 2100; it cost 1,500 coupons in 1992, then worth US$12, and in 1993 Travelines can book you in for £25-30, or Fregata for £59-70.

The Intourist was built in 1901 and still has some turn-of-the-century style, although there is not much to it apart from offices and another Intourist travel desk (open till 1800), and the money-changers in the lobby; in 1993 Travelines were quoting £20-25. The Ukraina seems to be little more than an overflow for the Intourist. The Lviv is a large post-war block, obviously past its best and relatively affordable.

Other hotels include the Pervomaiska/Pershotravnaya (Russian/Ukrainian for First of May) at Pros Svoboda 21 (tel 799 031/742 060), the Verkhovina (Pros Svoboda 13, tel 741 222), the Dnipr at vul Horodots'ka 45 (previously vul Pershotravnaya, tel 742 102), the Kyiv (vul Horodots'ka 15, in fact on vul Firmanska, the first left off vul Horodots'ka, tel 742 105), the Prikarpatskaya (vul Nalivaiko 6, also just south of vul Horodots'ka), the Arena (further west on vul Horodots'ka before the circus), the Kolkhoznaya (Pl Vossoedinennya 14), the Ul'yanovsk (vul Marchenka 6, further to the southeast, tel 728 512), the Dynamo out to the southwest on vul Str'iyiska, the Kommunalnaya just north of the Hotel Lviv, and finally the seedy-looking Hotel Narodni at vul Kosciuski 1.

There are two Turbazas, the Turist at vul Konoval'tsya 103 (3km southwest by tram 2 on what was vul Engel'sa, tel 351 065/575), and another on Pl I Franko. The camp site (tel 721 373/473) is 13km north on the Kyiv highway; take bus 127 (every 12-18 minutes, 0600-2400) from the Podzamche rail station (tram 6 or 7 along vul B Khmelnits'koho) and get off at the Agricultural College before Dubliany.

What to see

Lviv is a city of churches, above all, but there are also quite a few museums, and many fine Renaissance and baroque buildings. Coming from the station along vul Horodots'ka, you reach the centre with the opera house (1897-1900) on your right blocking the northern end of Prospekt Svoboda (formerly Lenina), where there is a Speakers' Corner on Sunday evenings. On its right/west side are hotels, the main bank and the Museum of Ethnographic and Applied Arts, with a good collection of clocks (closed Monday and Tuesday) at no 15, and on the left the former Lenin museum, a closed church built in 1610-35, and Pl Ivan Pidkov'i, named after a leader of the Ukrainian and Moldavian fight against the Turks. This leads east to Lviv's centrepiece, the Rynok or market square; this is a wonderful ensemble of four-storey houses, all from the 16th to 18th Centuries, with the Rathaus (Town Hall, 1835) in the centre and late 18th Century fountains. No 2, built in 1627, was the first post office of Lviv, and nos 4, 6 and 24 are parts of the History Museum (closed Wednesday); no 4 is the Black Stone House (1577-84), the palace of Jan Sobieski's secretary, no 6, the Kornyakt's house, was built by a Greek merchant in 1574-80 and bought by Sobieski himself (its arcaded court is now used for concerts), and no 24 dates from the 16th Century, with a 20th Century façade. No 18 dates from 1523, and no 28 from 1510 and the 17th Century; the north side of the square all dates from the second half of the 18th Century.

Southwest of the Rynok is Pl Katedral'na and the Roman Catholic cathedral, built from 1360 to 1471, with a late 16th Century tower; it is in Polish Gothic style but with remarkable baroque decoration all the way up the interior rather than just three metres or so above the ground. It is still very busy, and three new bishops were consecrated here in March 1991. Around the cathedral are small domed chapels in the style of those flanking the Wawel cathedral in Kraków; the chapel of the Kampians (1619) by the north wall has reliefs of the Evangelists, and the Boims' chapel (1609-17, open only on Tuesdays, Thursdays and Saturdays) is in German Renaissance style with a façade like an iconostasis. Just southwest of the cathedral is Pl Mickiewicz, at the southern end of Pl Svoboda, where there are four unconnected bookshops, cinemas and a statue of the Polish poet Adam Mickiewicz (1905).

East of the Rynok on vul Russkaya (at one time the only street the Orthodox were allowed to live on) is the attractive complex of the Orthodox church of the Dormition, built by Paolo Romano in 1590-1629 in classical style but with three typically Orthodox domes, with stained glass of the Baptism of Rus', the chapel of the Three Prelates (1578-91, with a Renaissance exterior but also with three domes), and the 66m Kornyakt tower (1572-78) on its east side. Across the road to the south is a good Secession block of flats, and beyond it at vul Pidval'na 5 the Town Arsenal (1554-74) and the remains of the city walls; to the north at vul Pidval'na 13 is the fine façade of the Royal Arsenal (1630-46), which now contains the town archives. Across vul Pidval'na (used by trams 1, 2, 4, 7, 9 and 12) is the Powder Tower (1554-56), a plain stone fortification with an eastern apse, now used as the Architects' Club, and on the hill beyond are the remains of the High Castle (13th-18th Centuries), where there is now a restaurant.

To the west of the arsenals on Pl Stavropogiskaya is the former Dominican church (built by Jan de Witt in 1748), which now houses a museum of religious history, which is not just the standard museum of atheism but also displays religious artefacts from aboriginal Australia, Tibet, the Islamic world and elsewhere; the church itself is a fine

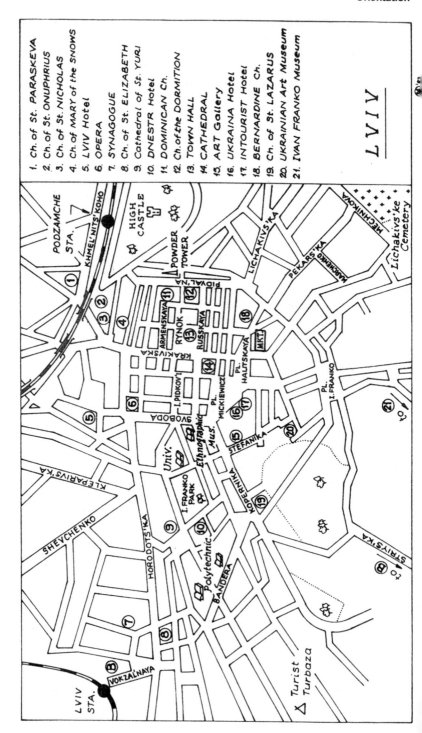

LVIV

1. Ch. of St. PARASKEVA
2. Ch. of St. ONUPHRIUS
3. Ch. of St. NICHOLAS
4. Ch. of MARY of the SNOWS
5. LVIV Hotel
6. OPERA
7. SYNAGOGUE
8. Ch. of St. ELIZABETH
9. Cathedral of St. YURI
10. DNESTR Hotel
11. DOMINICAN Ch.
12. Ch. of the DORMITION
13. TOWN HALL
14. CATHEDRAL
15. ART Gallery
16. UKRAINA Hotel
17. INTOURIST Hotel
18. BERNARDINE Ch.
19. Ch. of St. LAZARUS
20. UKRAINIAN Art Museum
21. IVAN FRANKO Museum

example of the baroque style. One block to the north is vul Armenskaya, with the Armenian cathedral dating back to 1363 (and a 16th Century bell tower and archbishop's residence), and just west on vul Krakivska (Kraków St) the baroque church of the Transfiguration, the first to be returned to the Uniates, in October 1989. On vul Teatralna, one block west, the Natural History Museum is at no 18, and the Jesuit church (1613) and monastery (1723-28) at no 11.

To the right at the northern end of vul Krakivska, on vul Honti, is the Roman Catholic church of Maria Snezhnaya (Mary of the Snows), built in the 14th-17th Centuries, and rebuilt at the end of the 19th Century, and now a museum of photography. Continuing north, there are three interesting churches nearby on vul Khmelnits'koho; at no 28 the Orthodox church of St Nicholas, built in the 18th Century, on late 13th Century foundations, with a cupola from 1880; at no 34 the 16th Century church of St Onuphrius, now the Ivan Feodorov Museum, after the first printer in Ukraine (in 1574), whose statue stands outside the Royal Arsenal and who is buried here; and at no 63 (beyond the railway) the Orthodox church of St Paraskeva (or St Piatnitsa, the Friday saint, in fact a fusion of four Orthodox saints), built in 1645 with a 16th-17th Century wooden iconostasis, with over 70 icons.

Heading west along vul Horodots'ka, the Uniate church to the right at the junction of vul Shevchenko and vul Kleparivs'ka is St Anna's, which was a builders' merchants store for many years; there is a studio theatre behind it, and a sports shop opposite. At the west end of vul Horodots'ka, near the station, is the 19th Century neo-Gothic Uniate church of St Elizabeth, but before that on a hill above Pl Khmelnits'koho, to the south of vul Horodots'ka, is the Uniate cathedral of St Yuri (St George). This was built by the Italian Merettini in 1744-70 (with a bell from 1341 and a two-tone green interior), part of a spectacular baroque complex with the Archbishop's palace of 1761. The first (illegal) congress of the Communist Party of Western Ukraine was held in the grounds in 1921, and the exiled Patriarch Josyf Slipyj was brought back here to be buried in August 1992. On the south side of the square, before the Dnestr hotel, are the museum houses of the minor artists E Kyl'chitskoy and A Novakoskogo. This is the student area, between the university and the polytechnic (there are up to 40,000 students in Lviv); to the west behind the polytechnic is the Roman Catholic church of St Mary Magdalene (1784) at vul Bandera (formerly Mira or Peace) 10, and south of this at vul Kopernika 27 the church of St Lazarus (also Roman Catholic, built in 1635-40).

The university is to the east of Franko Park, in what was from 1881 to 1918 the Galician Council building (with the University History Museum in room A221). Vul Slovatskoho leads southeast across vul Kopernika (with the 19th Century Potocki Palace, now used for weddings, and an 18th Century tower just west) into vul Stefanika, with the Art Gallery (including works by Titian, Rubens and Goya) at no 3 (opposite the domed classical temple of the Stefanik Library, 1826-49); the Ukrainian Art Museum is further on and to the right at vul

Dragomanova 42 (with icons from the 14th to 18th Centuries). Just east of vul Stefanika is Pl Mickiewicz, which leads to Pl Halitskaya (Galicia Square) and Pl Vossoedinennya (Reunification Square), with the main market and the Bernardine church (1600-30), now Uniate, with a very ornate 18th Century interior, an 18th Century plague column in front, and a well on its south side that a companion of Khmelnitsky was thrown into. Behind it are the remains of the city wall and an underpass under the tramlines to the early 18th Century nunnery of the Poor Clares at vul Lichakivs'ka 2, and an art exhibition hall.

Trams 2 and 7 (and buses 7, 10, 30 and 36) run east along vul Lichakivs'ka (formerly Lenina); get off at the church of SS Peter and Paul, a simple baroque (perhaps a contradiction in terms) church at the junction of vul Mechnikova, and turn left/north up vul Krupyars'ka and vul Strelts'iy to the Shevchenko Forest Park and the skansen or Museum of Ukrainian Architecture, where you can see Lemk, Boyk and Huţul houses and wooden Boyk churches from Krylki (near Turka, 1763) and Tissovitz (1863). There are also the remains of a 17th Century Cossack longship, an open-air theatre, and a small menagerie, with a bear in a tiny cage and a sad pair of elk with antlers like tree trunks.

Returning to the main road, vul Mechnikova will lead you south to the Lichakivs'ke cemetery (also a branch of the History Museum), with the graves of many musicians, writers and others, many with Polish or German names, and some good modern monuments, with the communist ones often defaced. From here you can return to town along vul Pekars'ka, past the Medical Institute and its botanical garden.

That completes a spiral tour of the main sights, but there are other odd things here and there; if you are interested in the writer Ivan Franko, his museum is south of Str'iyskiy Park at vul I Franko 152, and the synagogue, being reclaimed and restored in 1992, is at the south end of vul Mikhnovs'kikh, near the station.

Practical information

Hotel news stands may have the 1992 map of Lviv, which shows 230 changes to street names; even so there is still room for confusion, with both a Pl Mickiewicz and vul Mickiewicz and so on. Some of the Precarpathian tourist leaflets have older town plans, all in Russian, of course. There is a heavy coffee table book of superb photos of Lviv by Vasyl Pylypiuk (1990 Kyiv-Mistetsvo).

The City Festival is held on the penultimate Sunday of September.

The main post office is in a former Uniate seminary on vul Slovatskoho.

Excursions

Nestorov is a small town 16km north of Lviv, beyond Dubliany, just over the Main European Watershed, north of which rivers flow north to the Baltic; until 1951 it was known as Zhovka or Żółew, before being renamed after a First World War pilot who rammed a German plane. In the 17th and 18th Centuries it was very prosperous, and still has 16th-17th Century castle walls, 17th-18th Century houses, a synagogue built in 1692-1700, and various churches. The parish church, with its octagonal tower, was built in the 17th Century, the Dominican church is from the 17th and 18th Centuries, and the churches of the Nativity (1705) and the Trinity (1720, now a museum) are typical Boyk wooden churches with superb iconostases.

Nearby are the wooden church of the Holy Ghost in Potelych (built in the 1620s-40s, with fine wall paintings), and a 17th-18th Century Basilian monastery in Krekhiv.

On the main road west from Lviv to the Polish border, Horodok has a 15th Century Catholic church, a 16th Century Orthodox church, and the 17th Century Boyk wooden church of St John the Baptist.

If you don't want to wrestle with public transport, Intourist also offer day trips to the Carpathians.

IVANO-FRANKIVSK

The capital of the *oblast* of Ivano-Frankivsk, named after its favourite son, the writer Ivano Franko, was known as Stanislav until 1962; now locals just say Frankivsk. It lies between the Dnestr and the Carpathians; being served in summer by weekly flights from Manchester it may offer a useful route into the mountains (either via Dolina to Lake Sinevir, or via Yaremcha to Hoverla), but there is little reason to stay here, particularly as there is a cheaper hotel two hours to the west in Dolina.

The town was founded in 1662 and grew fast, with its Armenian population being granted their own charter in 1677; it was a rail junction from 1866, and capital of the West Ukrainian National Republic in 1918/19 before again being taken over by the Poles. In 1939 its population was 41% Jewish, 37% Polish, 19% Ukrainian and 3% German, and in 1959 67% Ukrainian, 25% Russian and 8% others.

The Chorny Lis (Black Forest) to the west of the city was a major base of the UPA: their camp between the villages of Zaviy, Posich and Maidan was attacked in November 1943 by the Germans, who were driven off. In 1944 first a Red Army division, cut off by the Germans and Hungarians, and then the Germans again tried to take the forest, but were both beaten off. The Soviets finally took the area in November 1944, and in the first six months of 1945 the Chorny Lis UPA group claimed to have killed 1,852, and lost just 101.

Getting there

Summer Saturday flights from Manchester to Kyiv stop at Ivano-Frankivsk airport, in the southern suburbs beyond the stadium. The town also lies on the railway line from Lviv to Chernovts'i, with trains from Kyiv and Moscow via Chernovts'i, and some from Lviv continuing south

to Rakhiv via Yaremcha and Yasinya. Buses run from Lviv, Ternopil,
Rivno, Yaremcha, Trusskavets, Vinnitsa, Kolomea and Rakhiv, to the bus
station by the rail station.

To move on to Lake Sinevir you should take a bus or train west to
Dolina and then a bus south towards Mizhgor'ya, and to reach Yasinya
and Hoverla you should take a train (or bus) towards Rakhiv.

Where to stay

The Hotel Ukraine (by the theatre, southwest down vul Lepkoho,
formerly Lenina, from the station) is the main establishment to which
foreigners are sent by the other state hotels; although far cheaper than
equivalent hotels in Kyiv, it is still far more expensive than the other
hotels in town, except for the Roxolana (vul Grunwaldska, west of the
station), a new joint venture private hotel which charges US$35, but
looks as if it is really making an effort. Others which may by now be
accepting foreigners include the Hotel Kyiv (built in 1912) and the Dnestr
(1913), which have a joint reception at the Kyiv opposite the post office
on the pedestrianised vul Radyanska (formerly Sovietskaya), due west
from the Ukraine and one block south of Bul Grushevskoho (formerly vul
Karla Marksa), which continues southwest towards the centre of town
from vul Grunwaldska.

The Prikarpati Turbaza is to the southwest of the old centre by the
Horodskoe lake, on vul Dzerzhinskoho, now doubtless renamed.

Probably the best restaurant outside the Hotel Ukraine is the Carpati,
two floors up above a ground-floor pastry shop at the far end of Bul
Grushevskoho, with a suave *Maitre d'* and live music, as well as a first-
floor café and terrace.

What to see

The city has a fine collection of 18th Century baroque churches, as well
as plenty of interesting *fin de siècle* buildings. There has been wholesale
renaming of streets, so that many addresses may have changed.

The Jesuit church and college (1729) are at the south end of the
pleasantly restored Pl Yuritskoho (also known as the Maidan), just north
of the Carpati restaurant; at the north end of the square is the former
cathedral (also baroque, 1672-1703), now an art gallery. To the west
along Bul Novhorodska is a brewery, with a building dating from 1767,
like a very plain Georgian pumping house or chapel; a terminal for local
buses lies just to the west, across the crossroads.

In the market square (Rynok) just east of Pl Yuritskoho is the Regional
Museum, in an odd little Stalinist-futurist building (1929-32), all angles
and tower. Beyond this to the east is the Uniate church (still marked on
maps as the Museum of Atheism), built in 1762 with a concave front
painted pale blue; inside there are a small iconostasis and a *trompe l'oeil*
ceiling. Northeast of here on vul Dnestrovska is the new market (open
0700-2200), in a flying saucer-like building like those built for circuses

all over the former Soviet Union. Beyond this and to the right on vul Panfilovtsiv, returning to the railway station (itself a typically Hapsburg pile from 1866, rebuilt 1906-8) is the fine former Teachers' College (1912-26), now a library.

KYIV

Although the Ukrainian capital is generally called Kiev (**Киев**) in the Russian style, Kyiv or Kiyiv (**Київ**) is perhaps a more accurate transliteration of its name as pronounced on the street. With a population of 2.6m (including at least 3,000 Westerners in 1993), it is the third city of the CIS and one of its major industrial centres, as well as the historic heart of ancient Rus'. It is older than Moscow and perhaps more beautiful, and it is certainly a more liveable city, with a southern warmth not found in Russia. Whereas in Moscow every private car is for hire, while every taxi sells vodka (Moscow taxi drivers being particularly crippled by hard currency protection payments), and you can't cross the road for pedlars, Kyiv is still a city that works as it is supposed to. It is said that Kyiv is the place to sample Soviet life as it used to be before capitalism and gangsterdom did their bit; most obviously everyone is too obsessed with economic survival to bother removing statues of Lenin. Although the Chornobyl disaster has blighted it somewhat for its residents, this will not affect the visitor. Parks cover 60% of the city's area, mostly on its northern fringes, and streets are lined with chestnut and lime trees.

The climate of Kyiv is temperate continental, more extreme than to the south but less so than in Russia, with a maximum average temperature in July of 20°C, and a minimum in January of –6°C. Autumn is warm and dry, and there is snow from November until late March, with annual precipitation of 615mm.

The city was founded in the late 5th or early 6th Century supposedly by the three Slav brothers (of the Polyani tribe) Kii, Shchek and Khoriv, with their sister Lybid, who is usually overlooked. By the 9th Century it was capital of Kievan Rus', ruling all the eastern Slav territories, and in 988 Prince Volodymyr adopted Christianity and married Anna, sister of the Byzantine emperor. The Golden Age of Kievan Rus' was from 988 to 1169, when Rus' split and Vladimir became the capital; in 1240 Kyiv was sacked by the Tatars, who ruled until 1320, when the Lithuanians and then the Poles took over. After Khmelnitsky's revolt, Ukraine united itself with Russia in 1654 and Kyiv became overshadowed by Moscow. Nevertheless this was a period of prosperity when many buildings were built in the characteristic Ukrainian baroque style; by the end of the 18th Century the population was 30,000. In the 19th Century industrialisation came to Kyiv, with telephones arriving in 1888, the first tramway in 'Russia' in 1892, and a funicular in 1905. Also in 1905 there was an armed revolt here, precursor of the revolution of 1917; in October 1917 the Central Rada (dominated by 'bourgeois-nationalists') declared

Ukrainian independence and crushed the workers in the first rising at the Kyiv Arsenal, while a communist soviet was set up in Kharkiv.

In January 1918 there came a second Arsenal uprising, with Soviet help, which succeeded in driving out the Rada; however the German-Austrian armies invaded and occupied Kyiv until November 1918. War continued afterwards between the communists, the Ukrainian nationalist government of Simyon Petliura, the Poles and the White monarchists, with Kyiv changing hands 15 times before the end of the Civil War in 1922 (and once three times in a single day, apparently). For a while Kharkiv remained capital of communist Ukraine, but in 1934 Kyiv took over again. In the Second World War the city was besieged for 83 days and then occupied by the Germans from September 1941 until November 1943; half of its housing was destroyed, and at least 200,000 killed, with at least 100,000 being taken for forced labour in Germany. Since then the city has been rebuilt, with wider streets, a mile-long welded bridge, named after Yevgeny Paton who developed mass-production welding techniques here for the T-34 tank, and a Metro, opened in 1960. Since 1965 the population has doubled, with huge suburbs being built on the left/east bank of the Dnepr; it is now 69% Ukrainian and 22% Russian.

Getting there

All Ukrainian rail lines lead to Kyiv, with overnight trains from all the further-flung towns of the republic, and to Moscow, St Petersburg, Minsk and Riga. The station is served by trams 10 and 35 and trolley bus 2, and by the Metro; trams 1, 3 and 9 also pass within about 400m. Flights take just 90 minutes from Moscow to Borispol airport about 30km southeast of Kyiv, with other flights using the Zhulyany airport by the railway just south of the city.

The main bus station is 3km south at Moskovskaya Pl, not too far south of the Dzerzhinskaya Metro terminal; in addition there are five smaller bus terminals in the suburbs, linked by local buses and trolley buses to the centre.

Where to stay

There are many hotels in Kyiv, of all standards, but although I have a list in English of 24 major hotels, only eight (the Intourist, Rus', Salyut, Dnipro, Lybid, Ukraina, Moscva and Bratislava, all expensive) were officially open to Western visitors in mid-1993; of these the Rus', Intourist and Bratislava have no single rooms. Others do now accept foreigners, although perhaps only in groups, and more probably will, so I list below all those I know of, and show most in brackets on the map. Phone numbers are even less sure than elsewhere in Ukraine; note that Kyiv numbers are now seven digits (usually starting with 2).

The Intourist (vul Gospital'naya 12, tel 220 4144/227 9553) is modern and luxurious, costing US$176 single/US$183 double for bed and breakfast in 1992. Next door is the Rus' (tel 220 4255/4461), a similar but tattier block, charging US$122/125.

The Salyut is to the north of the Pecherski Lavra, at ul Sichnevogo Povstannya 11A; it is shorter than planned due to defective foundations, but should be safe enough, although I gather it has mainly been used for trade delegations rather than independent travellers.

The Dnipro (vul Kreshchatik 1/2, tel 229 8287/8387/6569) was under *remont* in mid-1992 but looked very comfortable even so. In 1993 its rates were US$115/130.

The Lybid is another modern tower with all standard services at Pl Peremogi (Victory Square, Pl Pobeda in Russian, tel 274 0063/742 066/274 3206); this is handy for the rail station and the circus, but you will need to take bus 71 or trolley bus 8/9/17 to reach the city centre. It is cheaper at US$70/80, but not recommended.

The Ukraina, at Bul Shevchenko 5 (tel 229 2807), and the Moscva, at 4 vul Zhovtnevoi Revolyutsii (tel 228 2804), are older and probably slightly cheaper; the Ukraina offers good Ukrainian cuisine.

The Bratislava (Intourist's cheaper overflow) is at 1 vul Andrey Malysko (tel 559 6920/559 7280/576 866); this is near the Darnitsa metro station, east of the river and (NB) a long way north of the Darnitsa railway station.

Of the other major hotels, the Leningradskaya is in three parts; Block I is at Bul Shevchenko 4 (tel 217 101/257 101), Block II at vul Lenina 3 (tel 221 7080), and Block III at vul Volodymyrskaya 36 (tel 224 4226). The Kyiv is at vul Kirova 26/1 (tel 293 0155), and Block I of the Teatralnaya is at vul Lenina 17.

Other hotels include a group along the main road to the southwest, Prospekt Sorokaletiya (40-Let) Oktyabrya (40th Anniversary of the October Revolution Avenue, in Ukrainian Doroha Sorokrichchya (40-richchya) Zhovtnya), between the long-distance bus station and the Exhibition of Ukrainian Economic Achievements, by the Goloseyevsky Forest; from north to south, these are the Teatralnaya II (at vul Goloseyevska 7, tel 265 8988), the Mir (Prosp 40-Let Oktyabrya 70, tel 637 063), the Goloseyevskaya (Prosp 40-Let Oktyabrya 93, tel 261 4268), and the Zolotoi Kolos (Prosp 40-Let Oktyabrya 95, tel 679 001/614 001).

In addition to the Bratislava, there are a few others in the wilds east of the Dnepr, including the Slavutich (vul Entuziastov 1, tel 555 7926/0911), the Burevestnik on Truhanov island, the Desna (vul Milyutenko 46, tel 584 090) and Turist (vul R Okipnoi 2). Just north of the centre are the Spartak (a sports hotel) at vul Frunze 103 and the Avangard at vul P Karkotsa 27; the only one to the west is the Hotel of the Ukrainian Academy of Sciences at vul S Perovskoi 6. Other hotels in the centre but unlikely to take you in are the Sport, at vul Chervonoarmeiskaya 5, the Express at Bul Shevchenko 38, and an unmarked hotel at vul K Libknechta 39.

There are two Turbazas in Kyiv, the Druzhba (Bul Druzhby Narodiv 5, 3km south near the Dzerzhinskaya metro station, tel 268 3406/689

KYIV - Key to Maps

Central Kyiv:-

1. FLOROVSKY MONASTERY
2. CONTRACT SQUARE
3. FRATERNITY MONASTERY
4. STATE HISTORY MUSEUM
5. St. ANDREW'S CHURCH
6. St. SOPHIA'S CATHEDRAL
7. STATUE of VOLODYMYR
8. REUNIFICATION MONUMENT
9. PHILHARMONIC HALL
10. DNIPRO HOTEL
11. MOSKVA HOTEL
12. MUSEUM of UKRAINIAN ART
13. MARIINSKI PALACE
14. GOLDEN GATES
15. OPERA HOUSE
16. TEATRALNAYA HOTEL
17. St. VOLODYMYR'S CATHEDRAL
18. MUSEUM of ARCHAEOLOGY etc.
19. LYBID HOTEL
20. UNIVERSITY
21. SHEVCHENKO MUSEUM
22. LENINGRADSKAYA HOTEL I
23. MUSEUM of RUSSIAN ART
24. MUSEUM of WESTERN and ORIENTAL ART
25. UKRAINA HOTEL
26. PUPPET THEATRE (Synagogue)
27. St. NICHOLAS'S CHURCH
    (House of Organ and Chamber Music)
28. RUS' and INTOURIST HOTELS
29. ARSENAL

Kyiv - General; RAIL and METRO STATIONS:-

A. GEROEV DNEPRA
B. SVIATOSHINO
C. KYIV PASSAZHIRSKI (Main Station)
D. DZERZHINSKAYA
E. KYIV - MOSKOVSKI
F. DARNITSA (Metro)
G. PIONERSKAYA
H. DARNITSA (Rail)
J. ZHULYANY

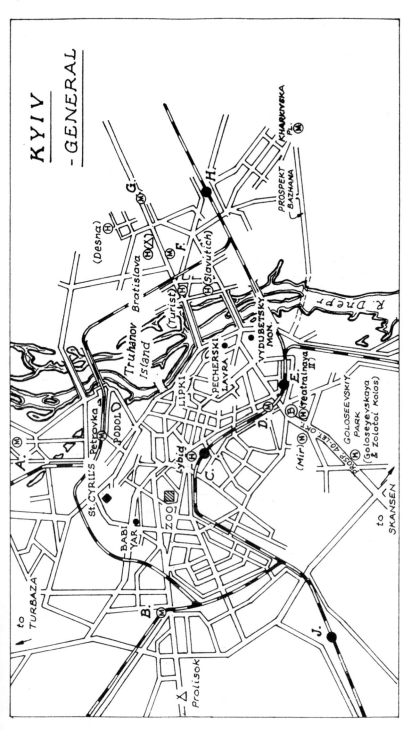

096), which declares 'Welcome to our Hotel' in English, but still turned me away, and the Pushcha-Voditsa, at vul N Junkerova 76, in the village of Pushcha-Voditsa, to the northwest.

The main camp site is the Prolisok (tel 440 093/441 293/444 9083, open from June 1 to September 30), 12km from the centre (1.5km beyond the ring road) on Prospekt Peremogi, the Brest-Litovsk and Zhitomir highway; to reach it you should take the Metro to Sviatoshino, then trolley bus 3 or 7, getting off where it turns right/north off the main road (after the Dachnaya bus terminal) onto vul Chernobylskaya, and walking a few hundred metres further west along the main road to the footbridge to the site on the south side. Buses 37, 259, 260, 262, 263, and 270 also pass the site but they are more erratic. The site will take foreigners in but ideally wants at least US$32 for a cabin (although they might settle for coupons); camping is not an option for foreigners, it seems, although wild camping is straightforward in the surrounding woods. This is quite a tourist complex, with a hard currency restaurant, lots of Spanish poker machines, a service station and a lorry park, where you might even be able to find a lift home.

There is another camp site on Prospekt 60-letiya Oktyabrya, just east of the Darnitsa metro station, but this is almost certainly closed to foreigners.

Where to eat

There are few reliable restaurants outside the main hotels, but the Gostiniy Dvir (Hospitable Court) on Andreevsky Izviz (tel 416 271) and the Lestnitsa on vul Boris Grinhenko (tel 229 8629) offer good Ukrainian food; you may also find something in the Hidropark and on Truhanov island, near the beaches. There are also places that sell western food for hard currency, such as the Apollo (Kreshchatik, tel 229 0437), the Ristorante Italia (vul Prorizna, tel 224 2054), and the Slavuta (tel 227 6484) and Slaviansky at the top and bottom of vul Gorkego, but you should perhaps avoid the Swiss Café (at the south end of Bul Shevchenko), which is mafia-run. Most cafés are in the Kreshchatik area, although others are appearing elsewhere.

What to see

The original site of Volodymyr's city by the Dnepr is what is now called Podol or the Lower Town, which later became the merchants' and artists' quarter. Yaroslav's later Upper Town lies above this to the southwest, around St Sophia's cathedral; south of this is Kreshchatik, the main street of the modern city, and beyond that is Lipki (Lime Trees), the smartest residential area.

The heart of **Podol** is Kontraktovaya Ploschad (Contract Square), site of a contract fair for hiring labour every spring from 1798 on; the Contract House (1817, now being restored) is on the north side of the square, while the building in the centre of the square is the 'Merchants'

Guesthouse' (1809-33). On the south side of the square, next to a *Univermag*, is the theatrical scenery store, like a turn-of-the-century art college but surprisingly not listed as of architectural merit although many less attractive buildings are.

Throughout this area are many merchants' houses built after the fire of 1811, as well as restored churches. To the east of the square at vul G Skovorody 2 is the Brats'kogo Monastererii (Fraternity monastery), now a hospital although you can look at the exterior of the plain 18th Century church, and beyond it at no 12 the churches of the Annunciation (1863) and St Nicholas Riverside (1782), about a foot apart, near some almost post-modern flats let down by the quality of their brickwork. Beyond these by the river is a former seminary (1778), now a marine academy, and south of this (vul Pochaininskaya 2) the church of St Ilya (1755), plain but simple and the nicest of this group of churches.

To the west of the square on vul Pritiska-Mykiltska, formerly ul Georgiya Livera (there is still a plaque to Livera who died in 1918 at the age of 14), is the Florovsky (St Flor's) monastery, still busy with old nuns in black with high headdresses and old women begging and helping themselves to free buns. The church (with a huge golden baroque ionostasis) dates from 1732, and the belfry gate tower from 1740-1821. In the square at the northern end of vul Pritiska-Mykiltska is the church of St Nicholas (1695-1707). Vul Academika Zelinskogo, just south, is now vul Pokrovs'ka; on its west side the church of the Intercession of the Virgin (1772) makes an attractive sight with St Andrew's on the hill behind it; opposite it is the Old Contract House (1801), now a school.

From here you should climb out of Podol up Andreevsky Izviz (St Andrew's Hill), a cobbled street lined with attractive two-storey wooden houses, something like 19th Century San Francisco, which is used for street festivals and as a film set; the British and US embassies are being established here, and it seems likely to become the most fashionable part of the city. The writer Bulgakov lived at no 13, now a museum, as did the Turbins in his *The White Guard*, and at no 15 is 'Richard the Lionheart's Castle' which Victor Nekrasov described as 'a place straight out of the Middle Ages, with vaulted Gothic arches, buttressed walls, stone staircases recessed into the thickness of the walls, suspended cast iron walkways, huge balconies, and crenellated parapets'. This is now being converted into a hotel in an American joint venture. The hill leads to **St Andrew's church**, one of the city's most beautiful monuments, now a state museum (closed on Thursdays), with concerts at 1600 on Saturdays and Sundays; it was built between 1747 and 1761, by the St Petersburg architect Bartolomeo Rastrelli, supposedly on the spot where St Andrew placed a cross and predicted the foundation of the city. It is in high baroque style, with one large central cupola, and four small onion-domed steeples to meet the five-dome rule of the Orthodox church; these are all bright green, with gold baubles that look like rows of light bulbs. Inside there are frescoes by Vrubel.

Opposite this is the State History Museum at vul Volodymyrskaya 2

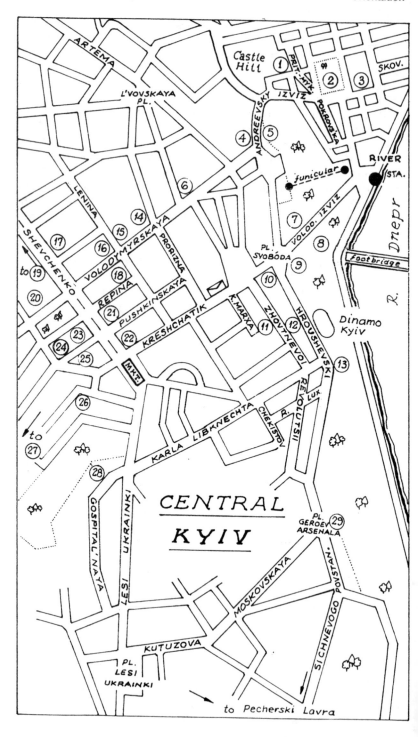

(closed Wednesdays), with the foundations of the church of the Mother of God, or the Tithe (Desyatinaya) church, the first stone church in Ukraine, built by Volodymyr between 989 and 996, and burnt by Batu Khan in 1240. Just south on vul Desyatinaya is St Michael's monastery (known as the 'Golden-Roofed'), dating from 1108 but demolished in 1934, leaving only the Refectory Church from 1713; this can be reached by funicular from the mid-19th Century post-horse relay station by the river station in Podol.

Heading southwest along vul Volodymyrskaya, you cross vul B Zhitomirskaya, lined with late 19th Century houses, and reach Pl Khmelnitsky, with a statue of Hetman Khmelnitsky (1888), and the cathedral of **St Sophia**, also now a state museum, shut on Thursdays. This was built in 1032 (to celebrate Yaroslav's victory over the Pechenegs) in Byzantine style, with 13 cupolas (one over the nave and three over each of four aisles); it was damaged by the Tatars in 1240 and rebuilt only in 1636, in the Muscovite style, so that it now has 19 pear-shaped domes, and from outside you would not know what a treasure is hidden inside. As you enter, the 11th Century mosaic of the Virgin Mary in 77 different tones of gold fills the apse in front of you, above the Double Eucharist, with separate Christs giving the bread to the left and the wine to the right, and the Annunciation on the columns, with the Archangel Gabriel to the left and the Virgin to the right.

Robert Byron calls this 'a masterpiece of Byzantine art in its highest epoch' and analyses its colours in detail: 'The colours of the Kiev Virgin are unique in Byzantine mosaic, and unique, therefore, in their effect, among all works of art... The mantle secretes its colour in a tone of unfathomable darkness, on which the highlights of each crease repeat, though with more glitter, the gold of the background. But the robe beneath the mantle, together with the sleeves that protrude from it, are invested with a tint whose radiant singularity no one that has seen it can ever forget. This tint is a porcelain blue, the blue of harebells or of a Siamese cat's eyes, an adamant, extrusive colour that stands clear from the aureate haze of the vault to proclaim its wearer's invincible personality. Below the robe, shoes of royal scarlet complete this proclamation. Round the waist is tied a cord of lilac pink, whose brightness exactly equals the brightness of the blue and which strikes a mean between that colour and the scarlet of the shoes, thus forming, despite its tiny area, the pivot of the entire composition. On the cord hangs negligently a little gold towel with a fringe. The sleeves have tight, patterned cuffs, also in gold.'

In addition he described frescoes of everyday life in Constantinople on the two spiral staircases on either side of the main west door, and the 6th Century sarcophagus of Yaroslav. To the southeast of the cathedral is the 76m belfry, built in 1752 with a fourth storey added one hundred years later, and to the south the refectory (containing an exhibition on 10th and 11th Century architecture in Kyiv), to the west the Metropolitan's residence and to the north the seminary (now the Ukrainian Literary and Artistic Archives), all built in Ukrainian baroque style in the early 18th Century, and surrounded by a wall in the 1740s.

One block west of St Sophia along vul Volodymyrskaya are the Golden Gates of Kyiv (known to us, thanks to Mussorgsky's *Pictures at an Exhibition*, as the Great Gates), which date from 1037 but are in fact a near total reconstruction of 1982. There is a museum here, shut on Thursdays. Just beyond the Golden Gates (Zolotye Vorota) metro station is the Opera House (1901, where the liberalising Russian prime minister Stolypin was assassinated in 1911) and two blocks further west, across vul Lenina (with the museums of archaeology, zoology, botany, geology and paleontology just south at no 15, and the Ukrainian Museum of Literature at no 11) and Bulvar Shevchenko, are the buildings of the Kyiv State University (founded in 1834 and known since 1939 as the Shevchenko University), built by Beretti between 1837 and 1843 in a heavy classical style and rebuilt in 1949; apparently the dark brick-red paintwork is authentically Greek. Behind the university are the Academician Fomin Botanical Gardens (1839), and opposite these across Bul Shevchenko is the cathedral of St Volodymyr, built by Beretti and others in 1863-86 in a Byzantine style; it has paintings by Vrubel and Nestorov, and a very good choir, but Fitzroy MacLean rightly called it 'a monstrous edifice'. To the north of the Botanical Gardens is vul Kominterna, leading to the station.

Opposite the university, across Shevchenko Park, are the Museums of Western and Oriental Art (ul Repina 15, closed Wednesdays) and Russian Art (ul Repina 9, closed Thursdays), with the Shevchenko Museum (closed Mondays) nearby at Bul Shevchenko 12 (Shevchenko's house-museum, closed Fridays, is at per Shevchenko 8A, south of St Sophia, where he lived in 1864, and the Shevchenko metro station is miles from either); these are all imposing 19th Century edifices. The Museum of Russian Art has ancient icons, then leaps to 18th Century court portraits and Grand Tour landscapes, and works by Savrasov, Repin and Shushkin (who all died in 1897 or 1898), with nothing later than 1917 other than some good 1920s ceramics. The Museum of Western and Oriental Art includes paintings by Bellini, Perugino, Boucher, Guardi, Jordaens, Goya, Rubens, and Velazquez. At the south end of Bul Shevchenko is the magnificent Bessarabsky Market (1910-12), and the main street of **Kreshchatik** runs east from here, lined with banks and office blocks, all rebuilt after the Second World War when the street was doubled in width to 54m; it is claimed that the Germans blew up all the major buildings along Kreshchatik, but it now seems clear that the Soviets in fact left bombs timed to explode after the arrival of the German army. The name comes from 'cross', probably referring to the streams that crossed it, in which Volodymyr and his people were baptised.

Its eastern end is not too far south of St Andrew's, at Pl Svoboda (or Pl Nezavisimosti, both meaning Independence; previously Pl Leninskogo Komsomola), where the former Lenin Museum is now an exhibition hall (while Lenin's statue was sold as scrap to Poland) and the Merchants' Assembly is now the Philharmonic concert hall. From here Volodymyrskii Izviz drops (past the 20m statue of Volodymyr to the north, dating from

1853 and repeatedly described by Bulgakov as 'the most beautiful spot on earth', then with an illuminated cross supposedly visible 50km away, and to the south the Steel Rainbow, raised in 1982 to commemorate the union of Ukraine with Russia) to the river station in Podol.

Vul Hroushevsky (formerly Kirova) heads south with parks and the Dnepr to its east; the Museum of Ukrainian Art is at no 6, opposite the Dinamo stadium (and open-air pool), where a monument commemorates the four footballers who were shot after daring to beat a *Luftwaffe* team. South of this is the Radyanskaya Park, with the Council of Ministers, built in 1935-38 in a futuristic style, and the Mariinski Palace built by Rastrelli in 1742-52 for Elizabeth, daughter of Peter the Great (a copy of his Razumovsky Palace in St Petersburg), and rebuilt after a fire for the Empress Maria, whence its name; the palace was used in 1917 by the revolutionary committee of the Russian Social Democratic Labour Party, who were arrested there and executed. Sadly, it is not open to visitors, but is worth seeing anyway. In the park to the south are monuments to those killed in 1917-18, and the grave of Marshal Vatutin, killed by the UPA in 1944.

Further south, now on vul Sichnevogo Povstaniya, is the Arsenal, still bearing the marks of the two uprisings of 1917 and 1918, with a cannon mounted as a memorial. Next comes the Park Vecnoi Slavy (Park of Eternal Glory) where the Eternal Flame used to be guarded by the Young Pioneers, and then Kyiv's other great sight, the **Pecherski Lavra** or Cave Monastery, about 4km south of the city centre by trolley bus 20, with the most convenient Metro stop at the Arsenal. The Lavras were the most venerated monasteries of Rus', which all believers should visit on foot at least once; in 1125 there were only four, in Kyiv, Moscow, Zagorsk and Ternopil. It was founded in 1051 by the monks SS Anthony and Theodosius, and the original catacombs have preserved the mummified remains of many of the monks.

The main entrance (closed Tuesdays, although you can still get in elsewhere and enjoy the tourist-free atmosphere) is at the Troitskaya (Trinity) Gate, with a church above, built in 1108 but rebuilt in baroque style after a fire in 1718; to the right inside the gate are cells containing gems, embroidery and engravings, and to the left are others containing an architectural exhibition, with the 17th Century baroque church of St Nicholas behind. In front of you is the Great Belltower, built by Gottfried Schedel in 1731-44 and rebuilt in 1895, the tallest in 'Russia' at 96.5m, with a great view from the top. Beyond this are the ruins of the Cathedral of the Assumption (1073-89), also destroyed by the NKVD when they abandoned Kyiv to the Nazis, and blamed on the Nazis ever since. Legend has it that 12 brothers were given an icon of the Assumption by the Virgin Mary and sent to build the cathedral, but each day's work sank into the ground overnight, only reappearing when the building was complete, so that the brothers died of shock. South of this are the 19th Century Metropolitan's palace, with the churches of the Annunciation, St Michael and the Refectory, housing a museum of Ukrainian folk art (and until recently a museum of atheism). East of the cathedral are the printing works (in use from 1615, now housing a museum of books and printing) and Kovnir's building, named after the serf-architect who built most of the baroque buildings of the Lavra; it contains a museum of historical treasures, including Scythian gold, and jewellery and coins from the 6th Century BC.

To the north is All Saints' church at the Economic (ie Traders') Gate, a fine example of Ukrainian baroque built by Mazeppa (1696-1701), and north of this is the Berestovo (Birchwood) annexe with the church of the Saviour, built in stone in the early 12th Century, with frescoes in the east end from 1640-43, and the grave of Yurii Dolgorukii, son of Volodymyr and founder of Moscow.

Behind the Refectory church (1893-95, in the Russian style) is a viewing platform, to look out from the Upper Monastery (Verkhnaya Lavra) over the green and gold domes of the Lower Monastery, rising above the trees (see rear cover); the Near Caves, the oldest part of the Lavra, are in the valley below, with the Far Caves on a hill beyond. The path down starts just north of the viewing platform, leading to a covered gallery down to a belfry amd the Near Caves (Blizhniye Pecheri), where you pay a few coupons for a taper rather than a ticket; heads should be covered and women should not wear short skirts. In Soviet times there was electric light here, but this has now been removed, and by November 1992 the caves were reported to be 'closed for repair'. A few hundred metres of caves are open, with the underground chapels of SS Theodosius and Balaam, and mummified monks under glass in open coffins (supposedly including Nestor the Chronicler, who wrote the first Russian history in 1113, and John the Long-suffering, who was buried up to his neck for 30 years); you emerge in the Church of the Elevation of the Cross (1700). Another covered gallery leads to the Far Caves (Dalniye Pecheri), surrounded by another fine belfry and the churches of the Nativity of the Virgin (1696, with an unusual arcade) and the Conception of St Anne (1679).

In the park to the south is the 72m-high Motherland Statue by Yevgeny Vuchetich, who also made the 'Swords into Ploughshares' statue outside the United Nations building in New York; this was produced in 1981 for a visit by Brezhnev but was not wanted by the people of Ukraine, who call it 'Brezhnev's Mother'. It contains a museum of the Great Patriotic War, with weapons outside.

Further south, across the highway leading to the Paton bridge, are the 180ha Academy of Science Botanical Gardens (vul Vydubetska 11) and the remains of the Vydubetsky monastery, with the superb church of St George (1696-1701), a refectory and belfry of 1730, and the church of St Michael (1070-88), of which only the west end and mosaics remain; Robert Byron thought the mosaics were by Russian artists (rather than Greeks) and 'remarkable mainly for their ineptitude'. However, 'more interesting proved two red granite plaques of mounted saints in low relief, which date from the 12th Century and have a Middle Eastern look. Each plaque depicts two riders affronted: one, SS Theodore Stratilates and Mercury, the other SS George and Demetrius. The first pair tramples a dragon; the second, a man in armour, who may represent Julian the Apostate'.

To complete the basic tour of Kyiv, you should also head north of the centre to **Babi Yar** and the church of St Cyril; from the Zavod Bolshevik metro station, take trolley bus 22 or 27 or walk north for 20 minutes on vul A Dovzhenko and vul Demyana Korotchenko to reach a park overshadowed by a TV tower. A fairly ugly monument stands over the filled-in ravine of Babi Yar, where the Germans killed about 100,000 residents of Kyiv, massacring about 30,000, largely Jews, on September 29 and 30 1941 alone, as reprisal for the time bombs left by the NKVD in Kreshchatik and elsewhere; happily, the inscription is now in Russian, Ukrainian and Hebrew, and it is still busy with visitors. From here it is a nice walk northeast down through the park to St Cyril's church (closed Fridays), in the grounds of a mental hospital at ul Frunze 103; this was built from 1146-94 and restored by Beretti in the 18th Century, and has 800m² of 12th-Century frescoes as well as paintings by Vrubel. Again Byron didn't think much of the frescoes, 'scarcely more than line drawings in red and white, and incompetent at that'. From here you can return to Pl Kontraktova by tram 11, from a stop near a preserved tram and the Spartak hotel.

There is little specific to see in Lipki other than the Museum of the History of Kyiv (in the Klovsky Palace at vul Chekistov 8, doubtless due for renaming, built in 1756 and closed on Fridays), but it worth taking a stroll there to see how the *apparatchiks* live; the main streets are vul Karla Libknechta (Vladimir Shcherbitsky, Party Secretary throughout the 1970s and 1980s, lived in a modern block of flats set back behind a metal fence on the north side, with a tunnel to the Council of Ministers), vul Karla Marxa (with various turn-of-the-century apartment blocks) and vul Zhovtnevoi Revolutsii (October Revolution St, with a Palace of Culture in Beretti's School for Young Ladies (1843) at no 5 and the State Bank (1905) at no 9).

Truhanov island was once a refuge from the Tatars and since the war, when all its buildings were destroyed, it has been a resort; although swimming is dangerous due to radiation, the park and restaurants are still very popular. There is also a hotel here, but it is not easy to reach without your own transport; there is a pedestrian suspension bridge from the west bank, just south of the river station. South of this are the Metro bridge (which also carries a dual carriageway road) and the Paton bridge, leading to the left-bank suburbs, which were only developed after the Second World War; the main one is Darnitsa, site of a German concentration camp where over 60,000 died.

Well south of the city is the skansen, or Museum of Folk Architecture and Rural Life, reached by taking trolley bus 11 or 24 to the Exhibition of Ukrainian Economic Achievements (VDNH), near the Yuzhnaya bus terminal, and then bus 24. This is open from May 1 to November 6 (1000 to 1800, except Wednesdays) and has 200 buildings on an 11km trail; in a roughly clockwise direction, they are from the Dnepr valley, Podolia, the Carpathians, Polesia, the Poltava area, southern Ukraine and

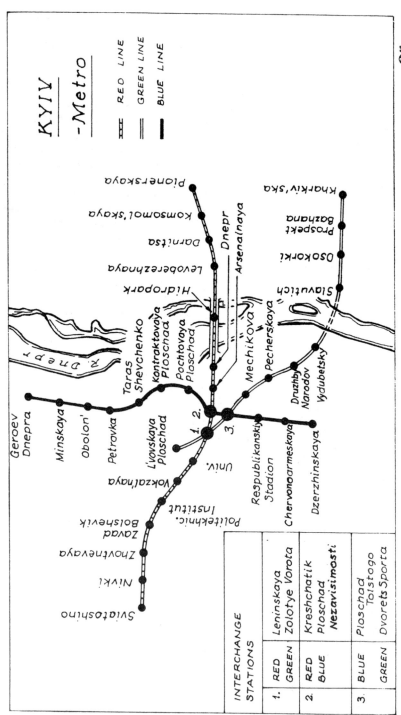

KYIV
-Metro

‖‖‖ RED LINE
≡ GREEN LINE
■■■ BLUE LINE

Pionerskaya
Komsomol'skaya
Darnitsa
Levoberezhnaya
Hidropark
Dnepr
Arsenalnaya
Kharkiv'ska
Prospekt Bazhana
Osokorki
Slavutich

Taras Shevchenko
Kontraktovaya Ploschad
Pochtovaya Ploschad
Mechnikova
Pecherskaya
Druzhby Narodov
Vydubetsky

Geroev Dnepra
Minskaya
Obolon'
Petrovka
L'vovskaya Ploschad
Univ.
Vokzalnaya
Politekhnic. Institut
Zavod Bolshevik
Zhovtnevaya
Nivki
Sviatoshino

Respublikanskiy Stadion
Chervonoarmeskaya
Dzerzhinskaya

INTERCHANGE STATIONS		
1.	RED	Leninskaya
	GREEN	Zolotye Vorota
2.	RED	Kreshchatik Ploschad
	BLUE	Nezavisimosti
3.	BLUE	Ploschad Tolstogo
	GREEN	Dvorets Sporta

the 'socialist village'. There is also a skansen at Pereyaslav-Khmelnitsky, 75km southeast of Kyiv, which has some of the wonderful tall wooden churches of eastern Ukraine.

A former synagogue at vul Shota Rustaveli 13 is now a puppet theatre, and the former Roman Catholic church of St Nicholas at vul Chervonoarmeskaya 75 is now the House of Organ and Chamber Music; this was built in 1900-09 by Leshek Horodotsky, the Kyiv equivalent of Barcelona's Gaudi, who also built the Museum of Ukrainian Art, a former synagogue at vul Yaroslavov Val 7, and his own house at vul Ordzhonikidze 10. Concerts are also given in St Andrew's and St Cyril's churches and at Pecherski Lavra, as well as in the Philharmonic hall. The theatrical box office is at vul Sverdlova 11. There is a zoo on the north side of Prospekt Peremogi, just beyond the Politekhnicheski Institut Metro stop, but as animals are being stolen, whether for sale or for eating, it may no longer be open.

Practical Information

The Metro is similar to those in Moscow, Prague and other Soviet bloc cities, with public address and route maps only in the trains, and station names hidden by the trains themselves. There are what can loosely be called interchanges between the three lines, but the stations have different names on the different lines and are separated by long tunnels with no signs. It costs 5 coupons for a ticket that you give up 10 metres on, allowing you to travel anywhere within the system (0600-0100); buy as many as you are likely to need to save queueing. The system is still heavily overmanned, with staff watching the escalators and trains running every 2½ minutes throughout the evening. By mid-1992 the new brown/green line was open as far as the river at Vydubetsky, although all its stations look half-finished on the surface. The two main lines connect with each other at Kreshchatik/Pl Nezavisimosti, and with the new line at Zolotye Vorota/Leninskaya and Pl Tolstogo/Dvorets Sporta.

Suburban trains run from the main Kyiv-Passazhirski station to Darnitsa both by the direct route and also by a loop via the Petrovka Metro interchange in the northern suburbs; there is a rail map opposite the Metro exit at the main rail station.

There are buses, trolley buses and trams to all areas, many running all night, and shared-taxi minibuses from behind the Bessarabsky Market. Chevrolets owned by BEST-Taxis tend to wait at the main Intourist hotels.

An excellent map (in Latin script and with an English, French and German key) can be bought for US$1 at the Intourist hotels; this was published in 1990 and is a product of the *glasnost'* era, with most names in Ukrainian rather than Russian. If anything it is too detailed to use in the street, but there is a simpler (and less accurate) free map in French.

Some foreign books can be bought at Kreshchatik 30, in the Ministry of Energy and Electrification building on the corner of vul Prorizna (also known as vul Sverdlova), and at Kreshchatik 44. The state hard currency tourist shops are known in Ukraine as *Kashtan* (Chestnut), rather than *Beriozhka* (Birch); the main branch is at Bul Lesi Ukrainki 24/26. The main department stores are at vul Lenina 2, Pl Peremogy, and Kreshchatik 15, and the *Tsentralny Gastronom* is opposite the Bessarabsky market. Selling art galleries are at Kreshchatik 2 and 26, and vul Lenina 3.

The best place for changing dollars and Deutschmarks (take care) is the subway at the bottom of vul Lenina, opposite the Druzhba Kino (Friendship Cinema), while the subway by the main Post Office (whose portal collapsed in 1989, killing 11) on Pl Zhovtnevei Revolutsii, now known as Central Square, is known as Speaker's Corner or 'Peoples' Culture Corner'. To change roubles for coupons, you should go to the main rail station.

The British Council has an office in Room 258 of the Kyiv Polytechnic Institute (37 Prospekt Peremogi, tel (441 1495/1428). The British embassy has a satellite phone (010 873 144 5256) if you *need* to call them from abroad. The tourist clinic is at ul K Libknechta 39 (tel 224 2022).

The city's main festival is the Spring Festival, held around the last weekend of May and even until June 3. The Shevchenko Days are in early May, with candlelit poetry readings at his statue in front of the university. There is also a Golden Autumn Festival in September.

Train tickets can be bought at Bul Shevchenko 38-40, in the Express building; foreigners should go to window 39 between 0800 and 1800, and be prepared to wait; it's marked only in Cyrillic, and staff don't speak English or French, as most of their clients are studying in the CIS. There are also boat timetables here, but tickets should be bought at the river station. Intourist have a booth to the left on the first floor of the railway station which should sell tickets 24 hours ahead, but is pretty useless. The Intourist service desks in the main hotels and at vul B Khmelnitsky 26 are likely to refer you to the Bul Shevchenko office, although they may be able to sell tickets.

Excursions

Chernigov (or Chernihiv) is 140km north of Kyiv on the Desna river, a city of 260,000 set in beautiful pine forests; founded in the 7th or 8th Century, it became a bishopric in 992 and was soon second only to Novgorod in importance. Its highpoint came between the 11th and 13th Centuries, when it was capital of the Chernigov principality and most of its great buildings were constructed. Chief among these is the Cathedral of the Transfiguration (Spasso-Preobrazhenski Sobor), built between 1017 and 1030 in stone, and rebuilt in 1792-98; it is closed on Thursdays. The churches of St Paraskeva (also known as the Good Friday or Pyatnitsky church), built in the late 12th Century and rebuilt in

1962, and SS Boris and Gleb (Borisoglebsky), built in 1123 and rebuilt in the 16th Century, are also central (just north of the port), while the Resurrection (Voskresenskaya) church is to the north near the market and the road west to the rail station, the Eletsky monastery (1069, with the 12th Century cathedral of the Assumption) just southwest, the Ekaterinskaya church (1715) to the south on the Kyiv road, and the Trinity (Troitski) monastery (with two late 17th Century churches and an 18th Century belfry and gate) is southwest on vul Tolstogo, near three underground churches on vul Uspensky. The History Museum is near the port on vul Revolutsii 16, and the house-museum of the writer Mikhail Kotsyubinsky at vul Kotsyubinsky 3. The Hotel Gradetskaya is at vul Lenina 68.

Another 120km east, close to the Russian border, is Novgorod-Severskii, where you can see the 11th Century monastery of the Transfiguration, the 17th Century church of St Peter, and an early 18th Century wooden church.

Kanev is the first major town you will meet on a Dnepr boat trip; it lies 150km to the southeast beyond the Kanev hills, and was founded in the 12th Century as a fort on the southern borders of Kyivan Rus'. The Cathedral of the Assumption (or St George's) dates from 1144, and 4km from the centre is Shevchenko's grave on Taras Hill, with a museum and hotel; although he died in St Petersburg in 1861, his body was returned here to his home town for burial.

Fifty kilometres further down the Dnepr is **Cherkassy**, another great city until it was sacked by the Tatars in 1239, and then by the Cossacks in the next century. You can still see the 11th Century church of the Transfiguration, the 12th Century Cathedral of the Annunciation (with a mosaic floor), the Eletsky and Troitsky monasteries and the 17th Century Military Chancellery. Shevchenko's birthplace-museum is to the west in Morintsy village. The Hotel Cherkassy is at vul Novaya 6.

OTHER UKRAINIAN TOWNS

The cities of Ternopil and Vinnitsa lie on the rail route from Lviv to Kyiv; **Ternopil**, the centre of Podolia, dates from the end of the 11th Century, and was the site of a Polish fort from 1540, before being taken over by Austria in 1772. In 1915 there was heavy fighting here as the Russian army halted the German advance, and the city was occupied by the Nazis between 1941 and 1944, when 23,000 were shot and 42,000 taken for slave labour; in 1944 there was a 40 day siege by the Red Army, and 85% of the city's buildings were destroyed, leaving some 19th Century houses on vul Lenina and the castle (now a palace) on vul Suvorova, as well as the 17th-18th Century Orthodox church of the Nativity, the 16th Vosnesenskaya church, and the Dominican church of SS Peter and Paul, built in 1749 and now the local museum. The main hotel is the Ternopil (or Ukraina) at vul Suvorova 12 (tel 79931).

Vinnitsa is twice as big, with a population of 280,000; it was founded

in 1363 as a Lithuanian fort, passing in 1569 to Poland, and then in
1793 to Russia. In the Second World War 40% of the city was
destroyed, but there are still many historic buildings, notably the 17th
Century Jesuit school on vul Lenina (renamed?), now the local museum,
the 17th Century Dominican monastery next door, now a sports club,
and the wooden church of St Nicholas (1745) across the river at vul
Mayakovskoho 2, now a museum of applied arts. There are also
memorial museums to the surgeon N.I. Pirogov, General Alexander
Suvorov, the designer of the first Russian plane Alexander Moshaiski,
and the writer M Kotsubinsky. Hitler's wartime headquarters are near the
Lastochka campsite (see below), and you can also visit a partisan camp
25km north at Kalinovka.

The main hotels are the Zhovtnevy (Oktyabrskaya in Russian) and the
Yuzhny Buh, both on Pl Gagarin (tel 24656/26540 and 24739/23876),
and the Ukraina on vul Lenina. The Lastochka camp site (tel 22906) is
in the village of Kolo-Mikhailovka, 10km south of the city.

The main road route from Lviv to Kyiv takes you through Brody (119km)
with a 16th Century Catholic church and a 17th Century castle, Dubno
(174km) with a 16th Century castle and a 17th Century monastery,
Rivno (219km) largely destroyed in 1921 and then a centre of the
partisan struggle in the Second World War, with a castle converted to a
rococo palace, an 18th Century wooden church and a late 19th Century
Orthodox cathedral, and Zhitomir (406km from Lviv and 131km from
Kyiv), which dates from the 9th Century; it was Lithuanian from 1320,
Polish from 1569, and Russian from 1793, before being caught in
fighting during 1918-21 and in the Second World War. There is little left
to see other than the 17th-18th Century Town Hall, and the largest linen
factory in the former Soviet Union. In Berdichev (43km south on the
main road to Vinnitsa), where the French novelist Balzac married the
local landowner Evelina Hanska in 1850, there is a 17th Century fortified
Carmelite monastery.

Kharkiv, 478km east of Kyiv and 700km south of Moscow, is the
second largest city in Ukraine, 'the classic Stalinist city, rebuilt in Brave
New World social-realist style after the Second World War'. It is indeed
an unattractive place, with 20% of Ukraine's industry; Robert Byron 'at
once conceived a dislike for the town, which is without feature except
for a good modernist post office'. The city was founded in 1655, when
land was granted to emigrants from Polish Ukraine, and was a major
industrial centre before the First World War; it was the capital of Soviet
Ukraine between 1918 and 1934, and changed hands six times in the
Second World War, when 30,000 were executed, 70,000 died of cold
and hunger and 120,000 were sent for slave labour. Now it is a city of
1.5m, with no less than 21 institutes of higher education and three
metro lines.

The centre of the city is Pl Dzerzhinskovo (doubtless renamed), a huge
circular plaza surrounded by the former Soviet Union's highest buildings,

such as the Palace of Industry (Gosprom); to the southwest on the banks of the river Lopan is the Pokrovsky (Protectress) cathedral, built in 1689 in the Russian style with three blue onion domes. On Universitetskaya Gorka (University Hill) are the Uspensky cathedral (1771) and a monument to the defeat of Napoleon in 1812; the Yekaterinsky Palace built by Catherine II is now part of the university, founded in 1805. Museums include the state history museum at ul Universitetskaya 10 and the art gallery on ul Pushkinskaya 11, just east of Pl Dzerzhinskovo.

The main hotels are the Natsional (or Intourist, tel 320 508/308 884/308 785) and Mir (tel 322 330/305 543), on Prospekt Lenina (doubtless renamed) just north of Pl Dzerzhinskovo, the Kharkiv at ul Trinklera 2, the Pervomayskaya at ul Sverdlova 11 and the Spartak at ul Sverdlova 4. There is a motel, the Druzhba, to the south at Prospekt Gagarin 185 (tel 522 091/507 905/520 142), and a camp site, the Lesnaya (tel 225 200), 16km south in Vysoky village on the Crimea road.

About 140km southwest of Kharkiv is **Poltava**, famous for the great battle of July 1709 (ending a three-month siege) when Peter the Great and the Cossacks routed Charles XII of Sweden and the Ukrainian *hetman* Mazeppa, killing 9,200 of 28,000 Swedes and ending the Northern wars. There is a museum (closed Monday) 7km west on the Dekanka road. The city dates from at least 1174, and has been a major industrial centre since the revolution, as well as a spa. The Poltava hotel is on ul Oktyabrskaya, and there is a motel at 32 ul Mickiewicz (formerly Sovnarkomovskaya); the local museum is at Pl Lenina 2, the art gallery al ul Dzerzhinskovo 11, and the Korolenko house-museum at ul Korolenko 1. The cathedral of the monastery of the Exaltation (Krestovozdvizhensky) is a fine example of Ukrainian baroque from 1650, with a belfry from 1786, and the Trinity church on ul Oktyabrskaya dates from 1750. You might also try to visit the church of the Transfiguration (1732) in Sorochinski (famous for its folk fair), and the church of the Assumption in Lyutenka (1686).

Odessa, Ukraine's main port, 490km south of Kyiv, is also a city of over 1m population, a free port until 1859 with a lively cosmopolitan populace, a blend of a score of nationalities (Germans, Jews, Armenians, Levantines, Greeks, Turks, Tatars and many more), with a dialect as distinctive as cockney. It is a city of trees, cafés, promenading and music: the violinists David Oistrakh and his son Igor, and the pianists Shura Cherkassy and Emil Gilels were all born here, as was Sidney Reilly, the 'Ace of Spies', born Rosenblum in 1874. It has always been the most enlightened and outward-looking 'Russian' town, remembered for its part in preparing the 1917 revolution.

It stands on the site of the medieval Kotsubievo, then the Tatar and Turkish fort of Hadjibey, captured in 1789 by the Neapolitan general de Ribas and refounded by General Alexander Suvorov in 1794. Its first governor was the émigré French Duc de Richelieu, who stamped his good taste permanently on the city, and a later governor was Prince

Vorontsov, whose *aide de camp* in 1823-24 was the poet Alexander
Pushkin, in love with Vorontsov's wife. The *Potemkin* mutiny of 1905
was followed by pogroms, and the city was only taken by the
communists in 1920; there was a two-month siege in 1941 before the
city was evacuated by sea to concentrate on the defence of Crimea;
fortunately it was occupied by the Romanian army which withdrew
quickly in 1944 and left it largely undamaged, despite a fierce partisan
campaign waged from limestone caves and tunnels under the city (which
can now be visited). Since most of the shipping moved to the new port
of Ilyichovsk, just south, the port has been less exotic, but sailors still
bring their stereos and stockings to the Sunday markets.

Odessa is six hours from Kyiv and 24 hours from Moscow by rail, and
it has daily trains from St Petersburg, Riga, Minsk, Kishinev, and all
major Ukrainian towns. Be warned that you may end up at the
Vostochnaya (East) station out in the marshalling yards, rather than the
main Glavna station, with no connection into the centre. The airport is
to the west, reached by bus 101 from the Aeroflot office on ul
Ekaterinskaya, or bus 129 from the rail station.

The best hotel is the Londonskaya (the Odessa under communism) at
Primorsky Bul'var 11 (tel 225 019/227 419), built in 1910 as 'a
reasonably accurate representation of a London club, dark and rather
grand with columns, stained glass windows and a wide and self-
important marble staircase', starting at US$100 for a double at the rear.
The Hotel Krasnaya (Red Hotel) at ul Pushkinskaya 15 (tel 227 220/225
328) was the Bristol, the best building in town (converted from a private
mansion in 1983, with lovely Art Nouveau caryatids and perhaps
Odessa's best restaurant), where you will find the main Intourist travel
bureau (tel 227 085), as well as the Londonskaya travel agency (tel 227
261) at the side. The Chernoye More (Black Sea) near the station at ul
Richelievska (formerly Lenina) 59 (tel 252 042/242 024/242 028) is 20
years old, charging US$65-85. Others which may now accept foreigners
are the Spartak (ul Deribasovskaya 25), Bolshaya Moskovskaya (Great
Moscow) at ul Deribasovskaya 29 (tel 224 016), Passazh (ul Sovetskoy
Armii 34, tel 212 290), Tsentralnaya (ul Sovetskoy Armii 40, tel 224
861), Sputnik (Bul Proletarsky 54, tel 224 610) and the Arkadia just
southeast at ul Genuzzskaya 24 (tel 250 085), near the Arkadia beach.
On the same street are two Turbazas and a tourist hostel, with another
tourist hostel across the park to the north. There are other Turbazas, as
well as sanatoria and rest homes, along the beaches north and south of
the city. The Delfin campsite on the coast road north (Doroga
Kotovskogo 298, near Odessa Sortirovochnaya station in Luzanovka
settlement, tel 343 00/362 12) is 'perhaps the best in the USSR', with
a bank and international telephone at a motel nearby; but any other site
you can get into is likely to cost you a lot less.

From the railway station ul Pushkinskaya leads ahead to the centre,
with ul Richelievska running parallel from the bus station just to the
left/west (with the Privoz flea market just beyond); at Pushkinskaya 72
is the Central department store (by a planetarium in a former church), at

no 17 is the Philharmonic, built as a stock exchange in 1899 in Florentine Gothic (opposite the Hotel Krasnaya), at no 13 is the Pushkin Museum, and at no 9 the Museum of Eastern and Western Art (the Potocky palace of 1856, closed Wednesdays, with works by Brueghel, Rubens and Caravaggio). One block further on it crosses ul Deribasovskaya, now largely pedestrianised to the left and the most popular shopping street, and one block further on ends at ul Lastochkina; the Naval Museum is just left at ul Lastochkina 6, and to the right are the Archaeological Museum at no 4 (with a statue of Laocoon outside) and the Literary Museum at no 2, opposite the Strawberry Hill Gothic Black Sea Shipping Company.

Ahead is Primorsky (Seafront) Bul'var, and following it to the left you pass the Londonskaya Hotel (with the Opera House, built by Fellner and Helmer in 1884-87 behind it) and soon reach the top of the Potemkin steps, built (as the Richelieu steps) in 1837-41, and dropping 30m from the Governor's Palace to the harbour; they are 142m long, and 21m wide at the bottom and only 12.5m wide at the top, so that they seem longer than they are. There is a funicular parallel to the 192 steps where 2,000 were shot in 1905, now crowded with courting couples. The area at the top of the stairs is alive with the sound of piano practice by students of the Nezhdanova conservatoire; ship bookings can be made here on the west side of the square. At the east end of Primorsky Bul'var is the Vorontsov palace (1826-27), now known as the Young People's Palace (Dvorets Detei). Returning inland from here the Pupils' House at ul Mendeleeva 4 (on the right before a bridge) is also by Helmer and Fellner and houses an art gallery, open only 1000-1300. Beyond this (ul Khalturina 5) is St Peter's Roman Catholic church, with a very simple baroque façade, and just beyond at no 4 a museum of history and ethnography, with natural history and geology nearby at ul Lastochkina 24.

The most popular beaches are at Arkadia, southeast of the station, where the Uspensky seminary was at one time one of the last three operating in the Soviet Union; other beaches, all linked by hydrofoil, are in Luzanovka, to the north, and Zolotoy Bereg (Golden Beach) and Chernomorka (once the German Lustdorf) to the south. The Kuyalnik sanatoria, on a mineral-rich lake (in fact a blocked estuary) just inland of Luzanovka, are famous for their curative muds which you can be coated with, or even have as a enema, for arthritic and respiratory complaints.

Kherson, on the Dnepr 182km east of Odessa, has a similar history to Odessa; it was a Russian fort from 1737, established as a town by Suvorov in 1778, on the site of a Greek colony (although its name comes from Hersones, a Greek colony near Sevastopil). In 1783 the first ship of the Black Sea Fleet was built here from Admiral Fyodor Ushakov, an event commemorated by a 1967 monument like an over-size Blue Peter badge. The city was occupied by the communists, then by the Austrians and Germans, and then by British, French and Greek forces and Denikin's Whites until 1920, and by the Germans and Romanians from August 1941 to March 1944, when 17,000 civilians and 40,000 POWs were killed. Now a major industrial city of 360,000 people and the main port at the mouth of the Dnepr, it also has good beaches, and a yacht club dating from 1907 on Quarantine Island.

There is a daily train to Kyiv, but you are more likely to stop here to change from bus to train between Simferopil and Odessa (the bus station is opposite the rail station), or to or from a Dnepr riverboat. The main hotels are the Kyiv (43 Prospekt Ushakova), the Fregat near the First Shipwright Monument, and the Pervomaiski (ul Lenina 26).

The main street is Prospekt Ushakova, leading south from the station to the port via the central Ploschad Svoboda and an 18th Century fire tower, and intersecting with the pedestrianised Suvorova. Just to the east on ul Perekopskaya (which continues for 12km along the Dnepr) are the remains of the fort, with the 18th century arsenal, mud ramparts, the Moscow and Ochakov gates, and a church built in 1781. There are also the Greek church of St Sophia from 1780 (by the river at ul Krasnoflotskaya 13), and the cathedrals of St Catherine (1786), the Holy Spirit (1835), and the Saviour (1806, with an iconostasis from Cyprus). The local history museum is at Ushakova 16 (with displays on shipbuilding, Suvorov and Ushakov), the natural history museum at ul Gorky 5, and the art gallery (formerly the Municipal Council) on ul Lenina, respectively one block north and south of Suvorova.

At Suvorova 14 is the house of John Howard, a British doctor who fought a typhus epidemic here in 1789, and in the steppe outside the city is 'The Legendary Machine-Gun Cart', a monument to the heroes of the Civil War which 'conveys revolutionary enthusiasm and a sense of irresistible advance'. Here too you can visit the catacombs, and other oddities are the Jubilee cinema on ul Perekopskaya, known as 'the German officer's cap' because of its shape, the Delphin children's cinema in the shape of a hydrofoil, and the Golden Key childrens' centre, a low-rent version of Disneyland.

Zaporozhye lies on the Dnepr just south of Dnepropetrovsk and the Donbas industrial area; most trains to Crimea pass through, as well as boats on the Dnepr, but it is only worth a stop if you want to visit the Cossacks' former headquarters (demolished in 1709 by Peter the Great) on Khortitsa Island, just southwest of the centre, where you can see a 700-year old oak and the city museum by the Sich gate at the north end of the island (bus 2B). There is also a local museum in the centre at Prospekt Lenina 59. The tourist hotels are the Zaporozhye and Dnipro at Lenina 135 and 202, and the Teatralnaya at ul Chekista 23; there is a camp site (tel 641 542) in Levshino village, on the Kharkiv-Simferopil highway, and the Zelyony Gai motel is 60km south on the 240km long Kakhovka reservoir (10km south of a nuclear power station).

The name Zaporozhye means 'beyond the rapids' (although the town was known as Fort Alexandrovsky until 1921), but the rapids were submerged by the massive Dneprogres dam from 1927, then the largest in Europe but only finally completed in 1937, and then 70% destroyed in 1941-43. It was rebuilt in 1947, with a second dam in the 1980s and a new town 10km north. Zaporozhye boasted the USSR's largest Lenin statue, as well as a lock 300m long with a 50m drop, and a main road (Prospekt Lenina, of course) 14km long, but it is now a sorry place with appalling pollution.

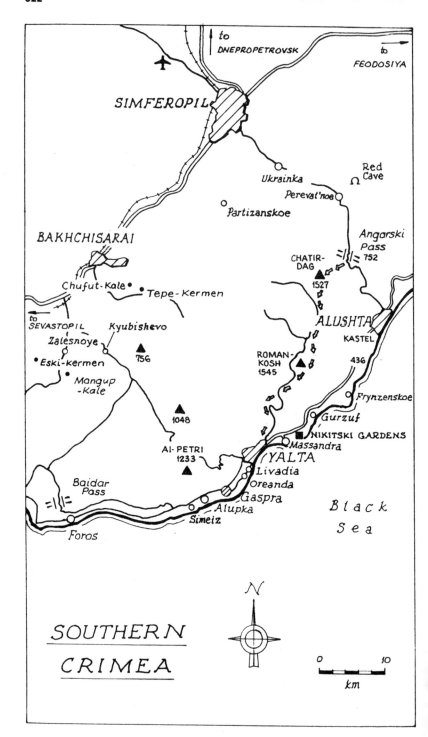

to
DNEPROPETROVSK

to
FEODOSIYA

SIMFEROPIL

Red
Cave

Ukrainka

Pereval'noe

Partizanskoe

Angarski
Pass
752

BAKHCHISARAI

CHATIR-
DAG
1527

Chufut-Kale

Tepe-Kermen

to
SEVASTOPIL

ALUSHTA

KASTEL

Kyubishevo

Zalesnoye
756

ROMAN-
KOSH
1545

436

Eski-kermen

Mangup
-Kale

Frynzenskoe

1048

Gurzuf

NIKITSKI GARDENS

AI-PETRI
1233

Massandra

YALTA

Livadia

Oreanda

Gaspra

Baidar
Pass

Black
Sea

Alupka

Simeiz

Foros

N

SOUTHERN

CRIMEA

0   10

km

Chapter 11

Hiking in Ukraine

CRIMEA

Crimea (Krim or **Крым**) is, with Sochi and Sukhumi to the east along the Black Sea shore, the holiday mecca of millions of Soviet citizens. Although most of the peninsula is hot dry steppe, the narrow strip south of the mountains has a very pleasant climate, hot but with a sea breeze for ventilation, and subtropical vegetation in places. Resorts such as Yalta were loved by Pushkin and Chekhov, the Russian aristocracy and successive Soviet leaders, as well as by up to a million ordinary people a year; even though the tourist trade is depressed at the moment, due to currency restrictions on Russian visitors, it is still fascinating to visit this 'Soviet Brighton' and see both the beaches of the people and the huge palaces of the aristocracy. Nowadays the resorts are young and unstuffy in spirit, and used to foreigners, even though the vast majority of visitors are Russian. It has often been noticed how happy Russians are to be crowded together in a small space: 'There was no room to sit, let alone to lie down. Yet people seemed not to mind; there were noisy sounds of merriment, guffaws of laughter, unexpected splashings, shrieks of joy'. There are open-air *stolovayas* or cafeterias, and *shashlik* kebab stalls; food is more varied here than elsewhere, but it is also expensive, with bread costing up to three times as much as elsewhere.

However there is far more to Crimea than the resorts, with Scythian, Taurian, Byzantine, Genoese and Tatar relics, including large cave villages with very early churches cut out of the rock. In addition there are the Crimean mountains rising from the sea to 1,545m and offering really delightful walking on a limestone plateau with great views along the coast, reminiscent of the Alpes Maritimes; in winter you can ski and be swimming an hour later. The mountains form a narrow chain 50km long, the western end of a system that extends through the Caucasus, the Pamir and the Tien Shan to the Altai mountains of Mongolia. In eastern Crimea they are volcanic, and to the west they are the remains of a Jurassic coral reef, now forming flat grassy plateaus called *yaily*, which are used for summer pasture.

The earliest recorded inhabitants of the area were the Scythians on the steppes north of the mountains and the Taurians in the coastal mountains; the Greeks came to trade and established colonies, which were taken over by the Roman and then the Byzantine empires. These were overrun by Goth, Alan and Polovtsian tribes, and then in the 13th Century the Genoese in turn established colonies. The Tatars first arrived in 1233, driving out the Genoese in 1475, and Crimea was their last stronghold, only falling to Catherine the Great's Russia in 1783; many Tatar names survive to this day. In the 19th Century the Russian aristocracy, led by the tsars, moved in to build great palaces along the coast, and the small villages with their white houses scattered along the hills were discovered by artists and writers. The so-called Crimean War of 1853-56 took place mainly around the naval port of Sevastopil, another in the long series of Russo-Turkish wars which Turkey for once won with the help of Britain and France; more Russian troops froze to death on the march to Crimea than died fighting the enemy, and more still died of disease (and the same applied to the Allied armies).

After the Bolshevik Revolution there were two attempts to set up socialist soviets in Crimea, but these were suppressed by the Whites (monarchists), who made their last stand here under Baron Wrangel in November 1920. At once Lenin issued his decree 'On the Use of Crimea for the Treatment of the Working People', nationalising villas and palaces as sanatoria; until the Second World War Crimea was an Autonomous Tatar Region, but having been occupied by the Germans from 1941 to 1944, Stalin then accused the Tatars of collaboration and deported them all (600,000 of them, a quarter of Crimea's population) to Uzbekistan, where two-thirds of them died. They were rehabilitated in 1967 (three years after the Volga and Crimean Germans themselves were rehabilitated), but still needed a permit to return to their homeland. Only since the break-up of the communist system have they begun to return *en masse*, and up to 70,000 Germans, Bulgarians, Armenians and Greeks are also able to return. Now you can see skull caps, Korans and maps of Istanbul for sale in Yalta, but the younger Tatars can also seem indistinguishable from their fellow ex-Soviet citizens, much like the Bosnian Muslims. Although there are now 250,000 Tatars in Crimea, 10% of the population, and they are guaranteed 14 of the 96 seats in the 1994 Crimean parliament, they live mainly in squatter camps and are marginalised by the Russian majority.

Meanwhile their homeland, with 2½m inhabitants, was transferred by Khrushchev to Ukraine in 1954, to commemorate the 300th anniversary of the 'fraternal union' of Russia and Ukraine. Russians make up 60% of the population, but there was nevertheless a slim majority in the 1991 referendum for Ukrainian independence, as the Tatars in particular feel safer under anyone but Russia. In May 1992 the Crimean *oblast* parliament voted for Crimean independence, but soon repealed this under pressure from Kyiv; instead it was agreed that Crimea should again become an Autonomous Region, this time within Ukraine. The Russian parliament voted to repeal the transfer of Crimea to Ukraine, but as so often Boris Yeltsin was happy to ignore his maverick parliament. Again in July 1993 the Russian parliament declared Sevastopil to be Russian territory, but Yeltsin quickly rejected this; this was seen as part of the internal power struggle rather than serious politics. The issue is not dead, however, with many Tatars still seeking autonomy and Russian nationalists seeking the return of Crimea to Russia, and increasing tension between the two groups.

Southern Crimea has upwards of 2,200 hours of sunshine per year and an average temperature of 13°C (4.1° in January and 24° in July); while the sea can be as warm as 27°C, and humidity is just 55-65%. Winters are wet, although it rarely freezes at sea level, and June weather can be unstable, but from July to mid-October it is hot and dry. There is enough of a breeze for one of the world's largest wind farms to be planned by an Anglo-American-Ukrainian joint venture.

North and east of the mountains the forests are mainly of downy, rock (Durmast) and common oak (*Quercus pubescens, petraea* and *robur*), with beech, hornbeam and thickets of dogwood, hawthorn, blackthorn and buckthorn; south of the mountains there is a Mediterranean flora with giant cypresses, palms, figs and magnolias growing in spectacular gardens, and downy oak, tall juniper (*Juniperus excelsa*) and *Arbutus andrachne* undergrowth. The Crimean *chir* pine (*Pinus pallasiana*) has longer needles and larger cones than the northern pine; the woods are very dry and smoking is forbidden in high summer.

There are 300 bird species, half of all those in the former Soviet Union, and many types of raptor, mainly in the mountains and coastal rocks, as well as on the steppes; these include the griffon and white-headed vultures, various harriers, buzzards, eagles, and kestrels, the peregrine and red-footed falcons, and the goshawk, sparrowhawk, merlin, hobby, and saker. Some of these are found nowhere else in Europe other than the Balkans, living mainly in Turkey and Egypt. There are also 40 species of mammal, including endemic sub-species such as the Crimean red deer and Crimean mountain fox, and the moufflon, introduced from Corsica in 1913 for shooting. There are also Crimean species of scorpion (*Euscarpius tauricus*), gecko (*Gymnodactylus kotschyi Danilevskii*), cicada (*Cicada taurica*) and mantis (*Ameles taurica*).

Getting there

You are most likely to arrive at **Simferopil** (Simferopol in Russian), the railhead and administrative centre for the whole Crimea. It was founded only in 1784, but stands on the site of the 16th-17th Century Tatar town of Ak-Mechet' (White Mosque), and near the site of the Scythian Neapolis, dating from the 2nd Century BC (the forum and other ruins are in the Petrovski valley, behind the bus station). Nowadays Simferopil (from the Greek for 'City of Unity') is a typically relaxed and prosperous southern town with many trees and parks, and houses built of a spongey-looking yellow stone. Even Lenin looks cool and relaxed on his plinth outside the rail station, itself rather interesting with its Moorish tower and colonnaded courtyard, and a good *bufet*.

There is no need to stop here, as buses and trolleys run from outside the station to the coastal resorts, part of a fascinating network of trolleybuses running from the airport, north of the city, over the mountains to Yalta, 86km away. In any case, there is not a lot to see; there is the Crimean Regional Museum at ul Pushkina 18 and an Art Gallery on ul Rosa Luxemburg, both near the Hotel Ukraina and the Centre trolleybus terminal. Unusually for Ukraine, there is a town plan in the station (by the post office) and a public transport map by the ticket kiosk on the north side of Bulvar Lenina, outside the station.

However the main hotels are the Ukraina at ul Rosa Luxemburg 9 (tel 755 73, a pleasantly shabby place with the Intourist travel office at the left-hand end of the unlit ground-floor corridor) and the Moskva at ul Bespalova 2 (tel 320 12, a more modern hotel near the main bus station). Non-Intourist establishments, which might or might not let you in, are the very cheap-looking Hotel Autovoksal at ul Kyivskaya 4, opposite the bus station, another at the airport, the Simferopil (ul Kirova 22), Sportivnaya (ul Zhelyabova 50), Kolos (ul Cyrkhi (Circus) 4), Yuzhnaya (ul Karl Marx 7), Dinamo (ul Franko 6), the Turbaza (ul Bespalova 21), and the Artek youth camp on ul Gagarina.

Most people move on fairly rapidly, usually to the coast; trolleybus 52 runs (every 10 minutes) from the rail station via the main *autovoksal* and Alushta to Yalta, and no 51 provides a more local service to Alushta, while nos 54 and 55 run from the airport to Alushta and Yalta. Buses take the same route and charge 20 coupons, instead of 15, but they are not much faster, taking almost two hours. There are buses to Sudak (four a day) and Evpatoria (nine a day) from the station forecourt, and others to Sudak, Kerch', Saky and 'mainland' destinations such as Odessa and Kherson from the *autovoksal* (south of the centre, reached by trolleybuses 2 and 6 from the rail station); in addition there are 'transit' buses here from Sevastopil to Novorossiysk (on the Russian coast of the Black Sea) and Nikolaev, beyond Kherson. To reach Bakhchiserai (see below), you should take a local train towards Sevastopil, or trolleybus 5 from the station to the Novoromanovka terminus for the *Stanitsa Zapadnaya* or Western Bus Station, for bus 145 (27 a day, with the last at 2021).

For longer journeys northwards you should take the train; there are up to five a day to Moscow (25 hours away), four to Kyiv, two to St Petersburg (31 hours) and Riga, and one a day to Lviv (at 0820, arriving at 1615 next day), Minsk, Kharkiv, Cherkassy, Lugansk, Kishinev and Warsaw, as well as distant Russian and Siberian cities such as Murmansk, Archangel, Vorkuta, Surgut, Ekaterinberg (formerly Sverdlovsk), Omsk and Novosibirsk: until recently Yalta was full of highly-paid workers from Siberia, all having as much fun as possible. To go straight to Moscow or St Petersburg, you might also consider flying from the airport north of the city, reached by trolleybuses 9, 54 and 55; you can also take a helicopter from Yalta in 25 minutes.

When I was there in 1992 foreigners were unable to buy tickets for trains or buses from Simferopil to Odessa, being expected to fly (US$56) or take a ship from Yalta (US$27); this may well have changed, but in any case I was able to take a bus to Kherson (five a day between 0620 and 1420, taking seven hours) and then go on by train — leaving Simferopil at 1420, I reached Odessa at 0829, on a train which had in fact left Simferopil at 1839. Buses leave at 0705 and 1020 and also take about 12 hours to Odessa. For those with cars, the Kherson-Odessa road was always shut to foreigners in communist days, forcing a long detour, but should now be open.

From Simferopil at 280m altitude the road climbs through rose plantations to the Angarski pass at 752m, where my hiking route starts — see below. Near Pereval'noe, the last village before the pass, are the Marmornoe (Marble) and Kizil-Koba (Red) Caves, which are open although being badly damaged by the visitors. On the south side are the Suuk-Koba (Cold Cave) and Binbas-Koba (Thousand-Headed Cave), with excellent stalactite formations. In the hairpins 5km south of the pass are a restaurant and the Kutuzov fountain, named after the general who lost an eye there fighting the Turks in 1774.

Fifty kilometres from Simferopil the road reaches the coast at **Alushta**; Aluston, the name of the Byzantine town, means 'Valley of the Winds' after the *miaky*, the wind that blows from the Angarski pass to cool the beaches, perhaps the best in Crimea. There are the remains of a 6th Century fort on ul 15 Aprelya and Genoese towers on ul Genueskaya, and a natural history museum at ul Partisanskaya 40. The bus station is at the main roundabout, just above the trolleybus terminal by the beach and the promenade, known as the Embankment (Naberezhnaya), and the Central Market is clearly marked on the hill above the bus station, with an older market at Pl Sovietskaya, to the east in the old town. There is a modern hotel across the roundabout from the bus station, and others on Naberezhnaya, as well as a Turbaza at ul Oktyabrskaya 11 and the Pansionat-Alushta Motel, possibly with camping space, 3km west.

From Alushta there are trolleybuses to both Simferopil and Yalta, nine buses a day to the airport, and one a day along the coast (much less built up) east to Sudak, as well as local buses. The best waterfall in Crimea is at Dzhur-Dzhur, 24km east, inland of Sornechnogorskoe. The main road west was built by the Russian army between 1824 and 1826, and totally rebuilt in 1961 when the trolley wires were installed; the villages along this stretch of the coast look like those along the Costa del Sol in the 1960s, with half-built tower blocks dwarfed by forests of cranes. The road passes to the north of Mount Kastel (436m) and Ayou-Dag/Gora Medved (Tatar and Russian for Bear Mountain, a smaller Gibraltar at 570m and subject of one of Mickiewicz's most famous sonnets) and then **Gurzuf**, perhaps the most picturesque village on the coast with Turkish streets built out onto the rocks. There is a museum in the house where the poet Pushkin stayed briefly in 1820; the singer Fyodor Chaliapin (1873-1938) and the landscape painter Konstantin Korovin (1861-1939) also stayed here, and Korovin House (1911) is now

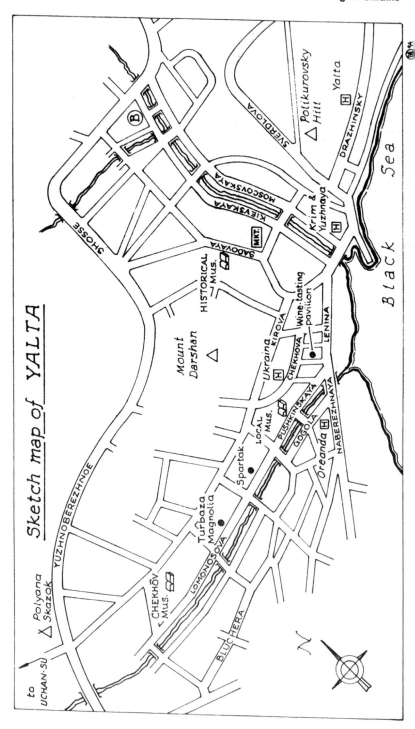

Sketch map of YALTA

an artists' holiday home. There is a Turbaza, and to the west of Pushkin Park (which now houses an army sanatorium with many fountains) an International Youth Tourism Centre. To the east is the massive Artek children's camp, with a 10,000-seat stadium, a cable-car to the beach and a 6th Century Byzantine fort on the cliff top.

To the west of Gurzuf are the Nikitski Botanic Gardens, created by the German botanist Kristian Steven in 1812 for Prince Mikhail Vorontsov (1782-1856), the Governor-General of Novorossiya; these magnificent gardens (not open on Thursdays and Fridays) contain 7,000 rare plants and trees, and 20,000 hybrids. Take bus 29 to the Upper Gate or bus 31 on the main Alushta road and then walk downhill. Above the gardens is the 30,000ha Zapovednik nature reserve, created in 1923 on the tsars' former hunting grounds; there are many species of animal here including Crimean deer, roe deer, and moufflon, as well as 135 bird species. Bus 33 will take you to Grushevskaya Polyana (Pear Glade) at 650m in the reserve, with a small museum. In November 1993 there was a huge forest fire in this area, but I have no information on the damage done.

The name of **Yalta** derives from the Greek *lalos* or shore, and it also was a Byzantine and then a Genoese colony; now it is a town of 90,000 twinned with Santa Barbara, Nice and Margate, and is relatively accustomed to foreigners, with some road signs in Latin script and 'Underground Crossing' signs in English at the bus station. Most of the foreigners are now Georgians, Armenians and Turks here for racketeering and black market dealing, and in 1992 there were outbreaks of fighting involving them, as well as between gangs of Russian and Tatar youths; Moscow prostitutes have long come here for working holidays, and there are also actresses hoping for work at the Yalta film studios. Although there are many ugly modern buildings, the Turkish street plan survives to the west of the centre, and there are many Turkish-style wooden balconies that allow you to scent the atmosphere that captivated Chekhov and his contemporaries. The setting is lovely, too, with a beautiful bay overlooked by the mountains.

The main highway now skirts Yalta to the north, with the bus station (and trolley terminus) just below the main interchange. From here you can follow the Bystraya (Dere Kouka) stream, between the two carriageways of ul Kievskaya and ul Moscovskaya, past markets on either side to a *Univermag* and cinema at Pl Sovietskaya, and then by an underpass to the pedestrianised promenade, named after Lenin but generally called the *Naberezhnaya* or Embankment. To the left/east is the port and old town with the Hotel Yuzhnaya (Southern) at ul Ruzvel'ta (Roosevelt) 12 (tel 973 12/258 60) and behind it at ul Moscovskaya 1 the Hotel Krim (tel 326 001/97 200); set in good gardens 20 minutes walk beyond these is the main Intourist hotel, the massive (17 storeys, and far longer than it is high) Hotel Yalta (ul Drazhinsky 50, tel 350 150). This has 1,200 rooms and all the usual tourist facilities such as currency exchange, a travel office, postal counter, hairdressers, restaurants and roof-top bars; it was built by a Yugoslav company, like many of the pleasure boats on this coast, and there is now alarming talk of an even bigger and better hotel for foreigners.

To the right along the promenade are the main post office and bank, and the Hotel Tavrida (the ancient name of Crimea), another Intourist place, in the oldest hotel building in Yalta, dating from 1875; this is at Naberezhnaya Lenina 13 (tel 327 784), behind the Sochi café and next to the Gurman restaurant, one of the first and best-known co-operatives in the Soviet Union. Just west, right up ul Chornomorski and left on ul Chekhova, is the Palas (1904-26, the first hotel in the Soviet Union to take foreigners), which is one of the cheaper respectable options in town. At the western end of the promenade is the Oreanda (Naberezhnaya Lenina 35, tel 325 794/322 034), a relatively small hotel with an Edwardian-style exterior and a more modern interior, refurbished and managed by a Finnish company to such good effect that Martin Walker of the *Guardian* judged it 'probably the best hotel in the Soviet Union'. As well as Finnish groups, it also once catered for Virgin Holidays, I believe. At the west end of ul Chekhova is the seedy Hotel Ukraina (ul Botskinskaya 13), and following trolley route 1 west from here to the Spartak cinema roundabout and right on to ul Lomonosova, you will reach the Turbaza Magnolia at no 25 (behind volleyball courts to the right: reception is at the top at ul Kornic 2), with accommodation mainly in cabins.

The camp site, with good cabins, is at Polyana Skazok (Fairytale Glade, with odd wooden carvings of ogres and also Vinni-Pukh (Winnie the Pooh), tel 395 249), open from 1 June to 30 September; this is 5km from the centre up ul Kirova and over the ring road, theoretically served by minibuses 6 and 30, but in practice you will usually need to take a bus to the stop on the ring road and then walk. If all else fails, and you draw the line at paying Intourist's prices, the bus station has *komnata otd'icha* or rest rooms available.

The best viewpoint over Yalta itself is Mount Darshan (140m), reached by a 'non-stopping cable-car' from the Tavrida; below this is the Orthodox Alexander Nevsky cathedral, opened in 1902, with a Byzantine/William Morris interior and a more Kremlinesque exterior with onion domes. On the other side of the town centre is Polikurovsky Hill, with another viewpoint in a park. The most interesting sight in town, other than the beachlife, is Chekhov's house at ul Kirova 112 (bus 8); he arrived in Yalta in 1898 and moved into the 'White Cottage' in 1899, where he wrote *Three Sisters* (1901) and *The Cherry Orchard* (1903), and lived until his death in 1904. His sister Maria (who painted the ground-floor pictures) opened it to visitors within a year of his death, living here until her death in 1957, and it became a state museum immediately after the revolution. It is open 1000-1715 except Mondays, Tuesdays and the last day of each month, and tourists pay double the standard rate, the huge sum of 15 coupons; you enter the gardens and visit first the museum (with a great collection of old postcards, photos of the great man, and posters for productions of his plays featuring all the great names such as Dench, Pryce, Redgrave and the Eglesfield Players, of Queen's College, Oxford) and then the pleasant simple house, well organised with English information, before leaving by the front door, with Chekhov's unpretentious nameplate.

In addition there are a Local Museum at ul Pushkinskaya 25 and a Historical Museum at ul Zagorodnaya 3 (in a former Armenian church, built 1903-17), both closed on Wednesdays. The Yalta Wine Tasting Pavilion is at ul Litkens 1 (1100-1830 except Mondays); the wine industry in Yalta dates from 1785, and soon supplanted French imports among the Russian aristocracy, although its products, mainly *Muskat* dessert wines, are rather sweet to western tastes. Its centre is the Magarach Institute of Viticulture in Massandra Park, beyond the Hotel Yalta, with 700 types of vine and several thousand hybrids. Its main cellar was dug in 1897, with seven 150m galleries, able to hold a million bottles, and 50,000 hectolitres in barrels. In addition the Imperial vineyards at Livadia were taken over as state vineyards in 1922; in 1993 one million bottles from the tsar's cellars were to be auctioned, with the best bottles of port (marked with the Romanov crest) expected to fetch about US$17,000.

The main excursion from Yalta, other than to the beaches, is to the Uchan-Su (Tatar for Flying Water) waterfall, 6km beyond Polyana Skazok, and Lake Karagol, 3km further on. There are restaurants at both the waterfall and the lake, which can be reached by bus 30, six times daily, on a road following the Vodopadnaya (Waterfall) stream, which runs from Lake Karagol down to the Hotel Oreanda, through hornbeams, pines and oaks. Unfortunately the waterfall is liable to dry up in summer.

The Yalta conference, which divided up Europe and left its eastern half to Stalin's tender care, was held in February 1945 in the **Livadia** Palace, built for the tsar in the 1860s, and rebuilt due to damp between 1909 and 1913 by N.P. Krasnov (1864-1939) in a neo-Renaissance style, in white Inkerman marble. It lies 3km west of Yalta, reached by bus 11 from the *autovoksal* or bus 5 from the *Spartak*. There are in fact three palaces, of which the Great Palace was the tsar's and the others for his suite. The conference was held in the White Hall of the Great Palace, and this is open to visitors; there is also a waxworks museum. The park, laid out in the 1830s and 1840s, also contains many statues, the Church of the Exaltation of the Cross (built in medieval Georgian/Byzantine style by Monigetti in 1862-66) and an arena where I saw open-air ballroom dancing to a truly awful band. Below this is Zolotoi Plyazh (Golden Beach), said to be the best in southern Crimea, where there is a Turbaza. Just to the west is Oreanda, where Tsar Nicholas I built a palace in a magnificent park in 1852; this burned down in 1882, and the remains were used in the Church of the Intercession of the Virgin.

The coastal corniche roads continue above rambling villages such as Gaspra and Koreiz, with the Golitsyn and Yusupov palaces, used for the foreign guests of the Soviet Union. The Ai-Todor cliff is topped by the Swallow's Nest (Lastochkino Gnezdo), a folly in the style of a Rhineland castle built in 1912 for the German oil magnate Baron Steingel, seen on every Crimean brochure and now housing a café; west of this are the remains of the Roman fort of Harax (or Kharaks), on the site of an older Taurian fort, and **Miskhor** (Greek 'Middle Town', 12km from Yalta), the warmest resort on the coast. Its park dates from 1790, and there are several large sanatoria in former palaces, such as the Red Flag (by Krasnov, 1897), and the Ukraina, the largest in Crimea, built in 1955.

In **Alupka** (16km west of Yalta) did Vorontsov his stately pleasure dome decree, between 1828 and 1846, employing the English architects Edward Blore (who also worked at Buckingham Palace and Windsor Castle) and Henry Hunt to build a palace in a mélange of Gothic, Jacobean and Oriental styles, blending the Brighton Pavilion and the Taj Mahal, with three pairs of life-size lions (copied from Canova) on the south terrace. This was the residence of Churchill and the British delegation in 1945, and it is now open (except Fridays) as a state fine arts museum; the art collection is missable, but the palace and the park under the peak of Ai-Petri (1,233m) are wonderful. There is also a kind of maze in the park, in the quarry used for some of the building stone, known as the Chaos. There may be a hotel at ul Letchikov 23, but in any case there is a Turbaza here, as in all these villages.

This is the end of the main tourist trail along the coast, with only the much quieter resorts of Simeiz and Foros (where Gorbachev was held during the *putsch*) to the west, and the main climbing cliffs. Koshka (The Cat), with an astrophysical observatory on top, is west of Foros. The main road to Sevastopil was constructed in 1848, over the Baidar pass (527m, 50km from Yalta), where an arch was built in commemoration; the modern highway takes a lower route, but tourists still come here.

The Yalta area has a complex bus network which is not easy to fathom, although individual bus stops have adequate information. Bus 27 is the main service west along the coast through Miskhor, running every 34 minutes and taking 50 minutes from the Yalta bus station to the east side of the palace at Alupka. Bus 26 runs every 34 or 40 minutes from Yalta to the Alupka bus station, west of the palace, and Simeiz, while nos 28 and 39 run from Yalta to Foros a few times daily, and no 42 from Yalta to Simeiz five times daily. These run from the main bus station, while more local services start near the markets and Pl Sovietskaya, or at Spartak. Trolleybus 1 runs every two minutes (but people still run to catch it) on a loop from the bus station to Spartak, with others to Gurzuf and Massandra; tickets (marked 5 kopecks) are two for a coupon (or from very unreliable machines) and must be cancelled on entry, unlike on the buses.

There are also water buses running at similar frequencies along the coast between Alushta, Yalta and Alupka, stopping at all major tourist sights such as the Botanical Gardens and the Swallow's Nest. There may also be hydrofoils, depending on the state of the tourist business, calling at major points between Foros, Yalta and Sudak.

Hiking directions

The standard map of Crimea is at a scale of 1:400,000, not nearly detailed enough for hiking, but there is nothing better; the town plan of Yalta is very poor.

The easiest access to the mountains is either at the Angarski pass, on the trolley route from Simferopil, or at Ai-Petri, where there is a weather station (3km from the viewpoint) and a monument to the anti-German partisans which can be reached by road from Yalta (13km beyond Lake Karagol, closed in winter) or by cable-car from Miskhor. There are a few buses from Alushta and Alupka to Bakhchiserai, but these go via Simferopil and Sevastopil rather than Ai-Petri; however in theory bus 41 runs five times a day from Yalta to Ai-Petri, and there are plenty of Intourist Toyota minibuses going up there. The cable-car starts at 86m near the Sanatorium Morskoyu stop on the no 27 bus route in Miskhor, above the circular *pensionat Druzhba*, and climbs to 1,153m, with a mid-station at Sosnov'iyu Bor (Pine Forest); there are various other minor cable-cars along the coast to the east, mostly to link a sanatorium to the beach. To the north of Ai-Petri is Sokolinoe, where there is a Turbaza at Orlin'iyu Zalet at the north end of the village.

As the cable-car was under repair, I started at the Angarski pass, at km 32½ on the trolleybus route from Simferopil to Yalta; there is a police checkpoint here, and mountain rescue (KSS) and weather stations, with skiing and a skating rink in winter; however the Turbaza (sometimes called a motel) has closed. The hills here are limestone, with cliffs, crags and rockfalls, and wild roses, vines, pine and cypress trees growing high on the slopes. To the east is the Demerdzhi ridge leading towards Sudak, and beyond that the Kara Dag (Black Mountain, 577m), Europe's oldest extinct volcano.

Heading west from the pass, it takes a couple of minutes up a track to the Turbaza site: from here a track goes up to the right, with a fork to the left to the Kutuzov lake. After a couple of minutes on this track I turned left at an unmarked fork and kept right (south of west), beginning to rise on a decent path in thick beechwood and crossing a stream after 15 minutes in all. Going up to the right, the path disappears at once, soon following the right bank of the stream; this was very slow going in humid weather, with lots of flies, but after 40 minutes I reached a minor ridge to the south. Just to the left I soon found a track marked with blue diamonds on white squares climbing steeply to the right; you might well find this earlier by keeping to the left lower down. The forest is now more mature open beech, with a few limestone rocks outcropping.

After 15 minutes this path enters a classical limestone meadow, with many wild flowers, and also lots of mosquitoes at first, and climbs easily to the west and then the northwest. You can follow it to the north, above cliffs to the right, and past the top of a ski-drag and a derelict polyhedral refuge, to reach a peak 30 minutes after entering the *yaila*, and then return southwest along a ridge, but there is a clear short-cut path to the left. The limestone ridges and crags are in very well defined parallel lines here, running southwest towards Chatir-Dag (1,527m), clearly marked with a tripod on the ridge to the left. It took me 50 minutes of very enjoyable walking to reach Chatir-Dag, and I then turned back east to take the obvious route down from this massif by a grassy spur, turning right after 7 minutes to go down the right side of a dry gully. There is a good clear view across to the main Roman-Kosh massif (a long thin ridge with no obvious summit from this angle), and the forested pass with a very odd squiggle-shaped field below.

After 30 minutes this path passes through a copse of beech and thorns, crosses another path and then drops south through classic mature limestone beechwood, turning right in a clearing to reach a picnic hut and fireplace in a meadow, with a very good spring just below along the path, after 10 minutes. The path turns right on to a cart track to cross a good stream flowing south towards Alushta, heading west and then south of southwest after another cart track comes in from the right. After 15 minutes it curves to the left (past a field and a breeze-block shed to the right) and heads south-southeast to enter the squiggle-shaped field, very bad stony ground which might as well have been left forested. From here I turned west into the woods and followed a clear ridge south, dropping to a cart track from the right after 15 minutes; as this turned too much to the east I turned right on to a minor cart track after 5 minutes to drop to a ford in 20 minutes. This is the Al'ma river, flowing north and west to north of Sevastopil, and beyond it is a metalled minor road from Yalta to Simferopil, which would be a fantastic cycling route southwards; 10 minutes to the left along the road are some forestry houses to the right, and two bridges across the river. If you wished to avoid the ford, it would be possible to keep to the east of the river to join the road at this point.

After 5 minutes I turned left, at forestry marker 136/137, on to a good unmade forestry track, and climbed for 5 minutes to a pass under a power line. Here I crossed a surfaced road from Alushta at marker 79/137, to go half-right/southeast up the track, which at once turned right to climb a ridge, marked with a few thin blue stripes. After 8 minutes this drops a bit to the left and then climbs, through beech and Cornelian cherry, to follow a ridge east of south. After 15 minutes there are great views from clifftops to the sea to the left, with interesting vertical strata and pines clinging to the slopes. The climb continues hard and steadily along the ridge for almost an hour (passing to the right of one hilltop) and then goes to the left around an attractive clearing in mature pines and to the right around a grassy hilltop, to reach a forestry marker at the foot of the main Roman-Kosh massif. The path zigzags to the right up this very steep grassy slope for over half an hour, to reach a meadow with some scattered dwarf pine; it continues just south of east along a limestone ridge and then to the right on to a karst plateau, with sinkholes and limestone reefs, and then a more tussocky basin. After 40 minutes the path turns right on to a cart track and climbs for 10 minutes to a pass of sorts; Roman-Kosh, the highest peak in Crimea at 1,545m, can be seen to the left with a tripod on the summit, while I kept more to the right, trying to keep heading west, or at least southwest, to avoid dropping down to Gurzuf. After crossing the heads of two dry dales and two ridges, I turned hard right after an hour to go around a gorge, turning left after 10 minutes on a cart track 5 minutes before a wellhead and a broad new track and a buried pipe; this goes southwest straight over the hill. From this cliff there is a great view of the back road to Yalta climbing from the right and the ridge above Yalta; the track drops to cross a high col westwards, crossing a good 4WD track after 15 minutes, and turning left on to the road after 20 more minutes. This climbs southwest for 7 minutes along the left side of a ridge, with great views to Ayou-Dag and out to sea, to reach a level grassy plateau with scattered stunted spruce trees, and on the clifftop to the left, a rotunda viewpoint perched above Gurzuf.

After a quarter of an hour the road swings right around an artificial pond and then left around the head of a rocky gorge, and after an easy half hour reaches the Nikitsky pass (1,443m); from here I followed this virtually unused road downhill for 19km to Yalta, but you could follow the ridge west to Ai-Petri and beyond if you preferred, presumably following the 'Partisans' Route' to the right 5 minutes after the pass. The road winds down into the pinewoods, with some viewpoints on to rather Japanese gorges, and after 1¾ hours (taking advantage of the many clear short-cuts) reaches the terminus of bus 33 at Zemlyanchnaya Polyana, although there are only five unreliable buses a day. It took me another hour to reach the main corniche road above the Yalta *autovoksal*, but you should take care after the bus stop not to take a path to the right into the village of Sovetskoe, from where you will have to take forestry tracks on down to the trolleybus depot. The hike from the Angarski pass is slightly too long to be done in one day, so unless you can get a lift down the road you will need to bivouac overnight.

The other main area of interest in this part of Crimea is **Bakhchiserai**, midway between Simferopil and Sevastopil, which was the capital of the Tatar Khans until the Russian annexation of 1783, and had 36 mosques before the Second World War; there are also four ancient cave villages in the hills to the south. You can reach Bakhchiserai by train or bus 145 from Simferopil (see above); buses terminate at the northern end of town, and to reach the centre you should continue on ul Lenina, take the second turning left at the Dom B'ita, just before the station, and then follow ul Rosa Luxemburg through the old town for about 20 minutes to the *Khan Serai* or Palace, just after the market and before the terminus of town buses 1 and 2 and a small mosque. The palace (open from 0900 to 1812, rather bizarrely, except Mondays and the last day of the month) was built in the 16th Century and restored after a fire in 1787; it has rows of minaret-style chimneys, a harem, a falcons' tower, and a courtyard with the 'Fountain of Tears', built around 1760 by an old khan unluckily in love with a virgin in his harem, and the subject of one of Pushkin's most famous poems, as well as one by Mickiewicz. There is also an exhibit about Suvorov, whose headquarters this was. To reach the Turbaza Pryval at ul Schmidt 43 you should continue for about 200m to the bus-stop, turn right down an alley and left up ul Proletarskaya, and follow stencilled signs up to the right for 10 minutes in all.

In this slightly Cappadocian scenery of limestone hills with a very thin covering of topsoil it is not surprising to see minarets, and also to see the cave villages and monasteries in this dry and rocky country; Genghiz Khan couldn't capture them, and it was only cannon that allowed the Turks to do so. They are still fairly inaccessible, and Intourist will bring groups in by helicopter (for US$20 an hour, from Simferopil airport or the heliport above ul Bluchera in Yalta). There is a walking map of the area south of Bakhchiserai, 'Po Peshchern'im Gorodam Kr'ima' (To the Cave Towns of Crimea), published by the Crimea Tourist Club, with which you could walk the whole way from Bakhchiserai to Eski-Kermen, although the routes marked with red dots on the map are not necessarily marked on the ground.

The nearest and the easiest to reach is Chufut-Kale (Jews' Castle), 5th to 6th Century caves inhabited by Karaite Jews (ethnically Turkic and Tatar-speaking, perhaps descended from the Khazars) from the 14th Century to the 1870s; this is half an hour beyond the Uspensky (Assumption) monastery at the eastern end of ul Rosa Luxemburg (or Rechnaya) in Bakhchiserai, with a cathedral and four churches all dug out of the rock, from the end of the 8th Century.

At the south end of this ridge is Tepe-Kermen, just north of Mashino (8km from Bakhchiserai), where there are up to 10,000 chambers, with churches dating from the 10th Century. Lining the north side of the minor road from Mashino back to Bakhchiserai is the 9th and 10th Century cave monastery of Katchi-Kalen.

Twenty kilometres south of Bakhchiserai, 7km south of Tankovoe on the Ai-Petri road, is Mangup-Kale; this is an 11th and 12th Century cave monastery which in the 14th Century was the capital of a Gothic principality, before being taken over by the Turks. There are pre-Byzantine frescoes here, and the remains of a church, a mosque and a Karaite synagogue.

A few kilometres west of Mangup-Kale, by a footpath from the village of Zalesnoye, is Eski-Kirmin, once known as the 'Cathedral in the Mountains', with 12th Century frescoes.

The other main city of Crimea is **Sevastopil**, west of Bakhchiserai and Foros; as the base of the Black Sea Fleet the area west of Mangup-Kale and Foros is still restricted, with even locals theoretically needing passes, and the port has been closed to commercial shipping since 1890. In 1992 Intourist did tours from Yalta for US$50, and cruise ships also visit; as a rule there should be no great problem now for individual travellers coming in on the many local buses or trains. I haven't been there, but it is said to be 'maybe the most beautiful town in the Crimean peninsula', set around its superb natural harbour.

It was founded in 1784 on the site of the Turkish Akhtiar, and became the main port of the Black Sea Fleet in 1804; it was the focus of the

Crimean War, being besieged throughout 1854-55 and being left with only 14 buildings standing (Tolstoy was there as a young artillery officer, dreaming of 'Girls, girls, girls' throughout). Again it was besieged for 250 days from October 1941, and when it at last fell to the Nazis, an active partisan campaign continued.

In the town itself the main sights are the museum of the Black Sea Fleet at ul Lenina 11, and the Sevastopil panorama on Bul Istorichesky, a 115m-long painting of the battle of June 6 1855, painted in 1905; in addition there are an art gallery at Prospekt Rakhimov 9 (with works by Raphael, Rubens, and Giordano, as well as Repin and Aivazovsky), the cathedral of SS Peter and Paul at ul Lunacharsky 34 (built in 1843, now a Palace of Culture) and the Vladimirsky cathedral on the town hill, disused since the Second World War, with a replica of the Tower of the Winds in Athens opposite. Four kilometres southwest of the city is Khersones, with Greek, Roman and Byzantine remains on a peninsula near the Feolent cliff and Georgievski monastery where Volodymyr is said to have been baptised.

There are many war memorials on Malakov hill, 4km from the centre by trolleybus, where in 1855 Sevastopil's defences were finally breached, and Sapun Gora (231m) 6km south on the Foros road, in addition to the church of St Nicholas in Severnaya Storona, on the north side of the harbour. The allied naval base of Balaclava is south of the Foros road, 15km from Sevastopil, and Inkerman is the eastern suburb of the city, half-way to Eski-Kermen.

The only hotel for foreigners is the Sevastopil, at Prospekt Nakhimov 8, and the bus station is at ul Vosstavshikh 7. There are Turbazas in Sevastopil and Severnaya Storona.

There are other interesting and attractive towns in Crimea which feel unjustly overshadowed by the Greater Yalta region; on the west coast these include the small spa of Saky, with curative muds, and Evpatoriya, known as a childrens' resort, with twisting alleys, 16th Century walls, a mosque (1552-57), and a cathedral (modelled on Haghia Sophia in 1898). Feodosia, the main town of eastern Crimea, has colder winter winds from the north but also a 16km beach with very clear water, some ancient fortifications, a partisan museum, a white Indo-Moorish palace described as the 'dacha' of the Sultan of Stamboul, and the house of the Turner-esque painter Ivan Aivazovsky. There are spectacular cliffs to the west, including the volcanic Kara-Dag, leading to Sudak (associated in legend with the Amazons) with a superb 14th Century castle 2km to the west. Like Feodosia and Sudak, Kerch', at the eastern extremity of Crimea, was a Greek colony 25 centuries ago, and now offers treatment with volcanic muds, and the ferry towards Krasnodar and the Caucasus; these resorts are more arty than those around Yalta, with buskers and painters. There are Turbazas on Tavrycheskoe Shosse and Pos Planerskoe in Sudak and Kerchenskoe Shosse (the Kerch' Highway) in Feodosia.

The water from Sudak to Kerch' is very clear, offering good snorkelling and scuba diving, but the Seas of Azov and Suvash to the north are salty and badly polluted, with unusable beaches; however the 120km spit between the two seas makes an interesting and unusual route for cycling ('velotourism').

Moving on

In addition to the buses, trains and 'planes from Simferopil (see above) there is also the possibility of travelling by boat or hydrofoil from Yalta and other ports on the south coast; however there is not much business at the moment due to the political and economic instability. In the summer of 1992 there was one ship passing through Yalta every 11 days from Batumi and Sochi to Odessa and Istanbul; the schedule gives you almost a whole day in each port, if you choose to take a cruise. There are also, in theory, hydrofoils from Odessa to Evpatoriya, Sevastopil, Yalta, Alushta, Novorossiysk, Ghelendijk, Tuapse and Sochi.

BUCOVINA

The Carpathian fringes east of the Chornohora massif and Hoverla are known as Bucovina, the name adopted by the Austrians in 1774 for the area recently vacated by the Turks. Now it is split between Ukraine and Romania, but it remains remote and undeveloped, and it is pretty hard to get into the hills without a long walk in. The famous painted monasteries of Bucovina are in the Romanian southern Bucovina. The northern Bucovina was described by Gregor von Rezzori, who grew up in Chernovts'i, in his (ironically-titled) *Memoirs of an Anti-Semite* as 'an almost astronomically remote province in southeastern Europe ... probably one of the most beautiful areas in the world ... rocky peaks loomed here and there from the green cones of the Forest Carpathians, and the poetic gentleness of the flowery slopes was all too deceptive in obscuring the wildness of the deep forests in which they were embedded ... these tremendous, windswept black forests had at least as much character as the glacier-crowned massifs of Styria'.

Chernovts'i (Czernowitz in German, Cernăuți in Romanian) was one of the most multi-ethnic cities in a highly mixed-up country; as capital of the northern Bucovina, ruled for many years by Austria, it had before the First World War a population that was one third Jewish and one third German, and there are still many Romanians living there. The city was founded in the 12th Century as part of the Kyivan Federation, ruled from the 14th Century by Moldavia, then by Hungary, until the Turks took over in the 16th Century; in 1768 it was taken by Russia, but very soon handed over to Austria, which ruled until the First World War. Romania ruled Bucovina until the Second World War, when the Soviet Union seized its northern half.

The railway from Lviv to Chernovts'i and Iași opened in 1867, and the line to Kyiv followed later; now Chernovts'i is linked by overnight trains to major cities such as Moscow, Kyiv, Odessa and Lviv, as well as international trains to Przemyśl, Bucureşti and Sofia (24 hours away). There are long-distance buses from towns in the Carpathian foothills such as Ivano-Frankivsk, Yasinya, Rakhiv, Trusskavets and Uzhgorod, as well as up to a dozen a day to Beltsi and Kishinev in the Republic of Moldova. Buses also cross the Romanian border to Rădăuţi, Suceava and Bucureşti. The rail station is near the Prut north of the centre, the bus station is southeast beyond the Hotel Bucovina, and the airport is to the left/east beyond this, near a minor rail station.

The best hotel is the Cheremosh, 4km south by trolleybus 6 at ul Komorova 13A (tel 48400), built in the late 1980s by Hungarians and costing just US$50 a night. Less remote are the Bucovina (ul Holovna 41, opposite the park and botanical gardens southeast of the centre by trolleybuses 3,5,7 and 8, tel 38249/38274), the Kyiv (nearer the centre at ul Holovna 48, tel 22483/26355), the Verkhovina (Pl Tsentralnaya 7, tel 22723), the Turist (ul Chervenoarminska (Red Army) 184, on the route of trolleybus 6 to the Cheremosh, tel 33911/43910), and the Voksal at the station. There is a campsite (not, in 1992, for foreigners) 3.5km east on ul Russkaya at ul Novoselitskaya 3 (tel 25496).

From the station, north of the centre, you can take trolleybus 3 or 5 to the city centre, or just walk to the left up ul Gagarin, turn half right and follow ul Holovna (formerly ul Lenina) to Pl Tsentralnaya and then Pl Padyans'ka (formerly Pl Sovietskaya), with a war memorial and the main trolleybus stops. This is a city of squares, parks, churches, and students; the central area is still largely Austrian in style, both in its architecture and in subtler things such as the relatively large number of public toilets. Many churches survive, built by the various ethnic groups of the district: the baroque Uniate cathedral (1825-30) is on ul Holovna, as is the Romanian Orthodox church (1844-64, in Byzantine style, now an art gallery, closed Monday), and the wooden Orthodox church of St Nicholas (1607) is on ul Volgogradskaya. Additionally there are wooden churches in the suburbs of Klokuchka (to the west, 1774) and Kalichanka (to the northeast, 1783), as well as the monastery of St George (1767, with frescoes) in Horecha, on the river Prut to the east.

The university, to the northwest (trolleybuses 2 and 4), was opened in 1875 in the former residence of the Metropolitan, built in an eccentric neo-Byzantine style in 1864. In the university park at ul Kotsubinsky 2 is a museum dedicated to the local writer Yuri Fedkovich (1834-88), and there is another (both closed Tuesday) at ul Dmitrov 5 dedicated to Olha Kobilyanskaya (1861-1942). The regional museum (and planetarium) is at ul Kobilyanskaya 28 (closed Wednesday), with an outdoor section (skansen) out in the suburbs by trolleybus 4. The Kobilyanska Theatre, at Pl Teatralnaya 1, just west of the centre, was built in 1904 by the ubiquitous Viennese architects Fellner and Helmer.

Following the River Cheremosh (the northern boundary of Bucovina) west for 65km you reach the logging town of Vizhnitsa, once a centre for rafting, where you can find the *Turbaza Cheremosh* (ul Chaikinoi 1) and the Verkhovina hotel (ul Gor'kogo 29), as well as a museum of woodwork and metalwork. On the north bank is Kut'y, obviously much less Austrian in style (best reached by the footbridge, a couple of kilometres downstream of the road bridge). There are buses from Vizhnitsa to Ivano-Frankivsk (0930), Putila, an old cattle raising centre in the hills to the south (five a day, with the last at 1115) and Kosiv, 8km north (eight a day). This is a small spa and resort, with a museum of Huţul crafts, a hotel, and a good market, and the *Turbaza Karpatskiye* just to the northwest by some ski-drags. There is a fairly new wooden church, and modern buildings such as the Town Hall in an interesting style with very steep pointed dormer windows. From here buses go via Verkhovina to Burkut at 1210 and 1845; there are frequent buses to Chernovts'i and Ivano-Frankivsk (with a few continuing to Lviv). For the western side of Hoverla (Deliatyn, Yaremcha and Yasinya) you will have to change at Kolomea. Marked paths from Vizhnitsa and Kosiv west to Verkhovina are shown in a leaflet *Po Kosivshchine*, available from local kiosks.

Heading north from Chernovts'i towards Kyiv, you cross the Dnestr after 50km at Khotin, where there is a fine 13-14th Century fort, rebuilt in the 15-16th Centuries (12 buses a day). Another 25km on is Kamenets-Podolsky, with another 14th Century fort restored by the Turks, with a historical museum in the grounds, a Turkish bridge, the 16th Century church of SS Peter and Paul, and a Gothic Dominican church with a Turkish minaret. One hundred kilometres further on is Khmelnitsky (originally Proskurov until it was named after the leader of the Cossack Revolt in 1954, the 300th anniversary of the Treaty of Pereyaslav); here there is a 16th Century fortress raised against the Turks. Although there are more direct routes to Kyiv via Starokonstantinov and Chmel'nik, the main road goes via Vinnitsa, 120km east down the River Bug (see page 315).

HOVERLA

The highest mountain in Ukraine at 2,061m (it was thought to be 2,058m, but has grown) is Hoverla, or in Russian Goverla, part of the Chornohora (Black Mountain) massif whose name it also often takes. This is the only alpine region in Ukraine, and thus the only area where you can be sure of getting above the trees, and as likely as not into the clouds; the second peak is Pip Ivan, meaning in the Huţul dialect 'Van can drink' (from the fog), and the rocky slopes can be dangerous in fog. Bernard Newman cycled through here and found it 'like the most picturesque part of the Pyrenees', although 'the mountains were friendly and never fierce'; it reminded Nick Crane of the Brecon Beacons, although to me it seems wilder than that.

The Chornohora massif is hard sandstone with soft schist strata, heavily glaciated, with flat-topped 'peneplain' ridges; in the Ice Age there was permanent snow above 1,300m and the Prut valley was filled with a 6.5km glacier at 1,000m altitude. The northern slopes are covered with beech to 1,300m and spruce to 1,600m, while the southern slopes are largely covered with beech right up to 1,600m, with alder and juniper brush up to 1,800m on both sides, with sub-alpine grass and flowers above. There are various areas of nature reservation, notably the southern slopes of Hoverla and the basin between Hoverla and Petros. The Huţul people live in this area, grazing sheep and cattle on the mountain pastures for up to five months a year, although they tend to bring them down to the village at dusk rather than spending all summer in the hills as in Romania. Nor do they compete with the Romanian shepherds in terms of friendliness, at least on the surface.

Tourism is important in the valleys around Chornohora, particularly the Prut to the north, the Cheremosh to the east and the Tisa to the west, with the main resorts in Kosiv, Verchovina, Yaremcha, Yasinya and Rakhiv; these are mainly climatic resorts where families spend time not doing a great deal, although some do get into the hills. There are Turbazas in these villages, and one in the Lazeshchyna valley below Hoverla, and even two 'tourist refuges' on Bliznitsya, west of Yasinya. Hiking is made easier by the fact that the main ridge was the Polish-Czechoslovak frontier in the 1920s and 1930s (and is now the frontier between the Transcarpathia and Ivano-Frankivsk oblasts) and so is marked with concrete pylons that make it hard to get lost. There are also lots of foxholes and trenches and stray scraps of barbed wire along the former frontier, and you have to pity the poor squaddies once condemned to guard these godforsaken hills.

Getting there

What was a main railway line from Hungary into Galicia still runs along the Tisa valley, but passenger trains no longer cross the Romanian border; trains run from Ivano-Frankivsk to Rakhiv, connecting at Deliatyn for Kolomea and Chernovts'i. Some of these are fairly modern diesel units that cope well with the gradients, but others are the standard huge Soviet trains that crawl uphill.

The biggest town in the immediate area is **Kolomea**, 70km west of Chernovts'i, which is notable mainly for its Museum of Huţul Ethnography at ul Teatralna 25 (closed Friday); there is also the wooden church of the Annunciation, built in 1587, which is signposted as a Museum of Architecture on the main road west. As the main city of Pokutia, Kolomea is not really in the Huţul country; in 1931 42% of the population was Jewish, but it is now 72% Ukrainian. The hills to the southwest, around the villages of Bereziv and Kosmach, were a stronghold of the UPA, who were attacked there both by the Germans and the Soviets.

The bus station is to the south of the centre, by the river Prut and the hotel Prekarpattia, which was quite happy to put me up for 400 coupons; buses run to Lviv, Ivano-Frankivsk, Kosiv, Hust, and more locally to Kosiv, Nadvorna and Yaremcha. From the bus station go to the

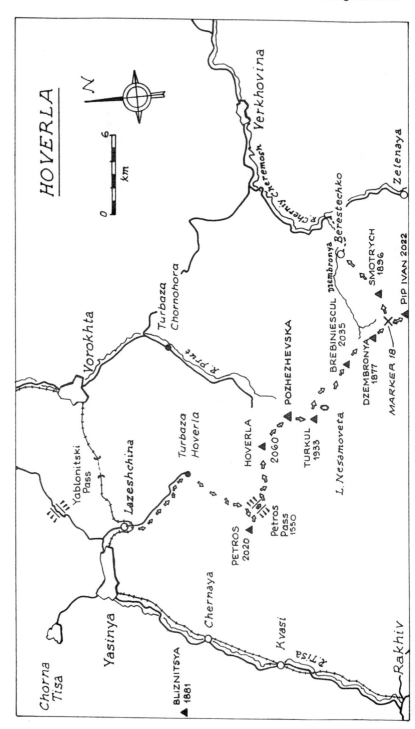

right to reach the centre, and left through a large T-shaped square (with a good food shop at the end) to ul Teatralna; the rail station is to the north of the centre, reached by bus 12 (four times an hour) from the bus station and the centre.

Coming either from here or from Lviv and Ivano-Frankivsk, you will probably want to stop in **Yaremcha**, south of Deliatyn at 523m, to pick up a hiking map and information from the KSS (Mountain Rescue). To the north of town (at km 166) is a small wooden church, being reshingled when I was there, and some excellent folded strata in the river cliffs opposite the bus station; the centre of town is to the south, along the main road (ul Svoboda) with a Partisan Museum (1000-1800 weekdays) in a modern building on the left, where the UPA is referred to only as bandits, if at all. The railway station is just to the south, with a Himalayan-style hotel opposite it and a market to the east of the line, south of the station. Further south there is a modern post office and then a bridge over the river Prut; just after this, where the road bends left, you should turn right and cross the railway line by some obvious steps to reach the rather unimpressive waterfalls that are Yaremcha's main tourist sight. The *Turbaza Hutsulschina* is across a footbridge, with big Tatra-style chalets, although they are tiled rather than shingled, and the KSS office is on the ground floor of the main block. In addition the Hotel Karpaty is south of the Turbaza, with rooms for 100 coupony, and there is a motel on the main road south, north of km 171. This was the first place I visited which really seemed like a resort, with obvious holiday-makers wandering around with hand-carved pipes.

There are two buses a day to Rakhiv and nine to Vorokhta, as well as others south to Mukachevo (0835), Hust (1140) and Uzhgorod (1200), and erratic local buses to Yasinya. Northbound, there are buses to Lviv, Ivano-Frankivsk and Chernovts'i. Trains run south to Rakhiv at 1020 and 1838, while four a day run north to Ivano-Frankivsk, with one (0405) continuing to Lviv and others to Chernovts'i (1800) and Kolomea (2237).

From here the railway south climbs steadily up the Prut valley through the villages of Mikulichyn and Vorokhta, and into spruce to cross into Transcarpathia by the Voronenka tunnel at 879m; the road swings right to cross by the Yablonitskiy pass (931m) and then drops to rejoin the rail line at Lazeshchina, just before Yasinya. Vorokhta (747m) and Krementsi (or Tatarow, just to the north at 681m) are one of Ukraine's main skiing areas, with the odd Sportbaza in Vorokhta and a camp site at the south end of Krementsi, and vernacular-style wooden houses up to four storeys in height; there is also camping and a Turbaza in Yablonitskiy, north of the pass.

Yasinya (meaning 'ash-tree' and also called Körösmezo or Zimir) is the Huţul capital and the nearest village to Hoverla itself, and a reasonable place to stock up before hiking, although it is basically just a dusty two-street place. The bus station is in the middle by the bridge, opposite a bread shop, bar and *kulinaria* or hot food shop, with a *gastronom* and Complex with a restaurant upstairs to the south. The *Turbaza Edelweiss* is a wooden chalet across a footbridge behind the bus station and KSS office, or to the left from the Chorna Tisa road (to the west north of the bridge), and there is also a modern six-storey Turbaza down a lane opposite no 8 on the road north, which is more likely to have space. There are walking routes from the Edelweiss down the west bank of the Tisa and southwest to Bliznitsya (1,881m) in the Svidovets massif; the 18th Century Strukovskaya wooden church, perhaps the best of the central-dome Huţul churches, with a separate belfry echoing its form, is several kilometres south by the river.

The rail station is a little way south of the village (not far east of the church), with just two trains each way per day. Buses run mainly to Rakhiv, Mukachevo and Uzhgorod, but there are also two buses a day to Kolomea, Kamenets Podolsky and Chernovts'i and one each to Ivano-Frankivsk and Lviv. There are also four or five a day to Chorna Tisa, 5km west along a road which is in any case busy with logging trucks.

Hiking directions

The 1:200,000 KSS map cost me 100 coupons, then enough for a night in a cheap hotel, but it is the only really detailed topographical map available; even this has only recently been de-classified by the military. The next best map that I have seen is a 1:300,000 map, available only in Poland, of the *Karpaty Wschodnie*; tourist leaflets available locally, such as *Zakarpatskie Marshrut'i* (Transcarpathian Routes), do show hiking routes but are not really adequate.

The nearest jumping-off point for Hoverla is Lazeshchina, where slow trains stop and a minor road turns southeast off the main road. From the station you should follow the railway almost 2km south (in fact the direction taken by northbound trains), then where it curves sharply north to cross the valley go down a farm track to the right to join the road up the valley by a roadside cross about 200m south of the viaduct. From here you have great views up the broad Lazeshchina valley to Hoverla, and the slightly lower Petros to the right. The road soon crosses to the right bank and passes a barrier 20 minutes from the viaduct; it continues as a rougher track, passing a good covered spring and a summerhouse and reaching a bridge and a junction in an hour. The *Turbaza Hoverla*, with various scattered cabins, is just to the right, and a path marked intermittently with green stripes goes from here to the top of Hoverla itself. The main track, now intermittently marked in red, continues to follow the stream, with lots of log weirs, passing a hut used as a bothy after 10 minutes. After half an hour the track crosses to the right bank of the stream at an active logging area; after 15 minutes it enters beech and spruce and soon continues as a sheep track, slightly to the left. After 10 minutes the track enters a meadow with a sheep shed ahead and a shepherds' hut to the left, behind some trees; the marked path follows the ridge behind the hut and soon fades. It climbs just to the left of a very minor stream, reaching the tree line in 20 minutes, and a T-junction at the Petros pass just 7 minutes later.

Turning right here, you can follow a track around Petros and then follow blue markings to the right to the spa of Kvasi, south of Yasinya, or green markings to the left down the Bogdan valley to reach the village of Bogdan, just east of Rakhiv in the Belaya (White) Tisa valley. There is no clear path up Petros itself, although the route is obvious above, starting up a moraine pyramid, following a spur and swinging right through dwarf trees; it's a steep climb from the pass at 1,550m to the summit at 2,020m, but can easily be done in 45 minutes. From the top you have, weather permitting, a good view along the main ridge beyond the pass, as well as west to the two peaks of Bliznitsya, and south towards Romania.

The track to the left is marked with red and blue stripes, almost at once passing good camping places in the trees and springs by the path, and swinging right after 20 minutes across an open ridge with views south into Romania. After 15 minutes the track turns left around a spur, with various forestry signs, and after 5 minutes more the track turns hard right where the path up Hoverla goes straight ahead. The path climbs steadily, leaving the dwarf bushes after 40 minutes and climbing steeply on to the left to reach a ridge to the right of a small crag; it then follows it to the right, climbs quite steeply past some false summits and reaches the cross on the summit of Hoverla in 25 minutes. Here you find the first border marker, no 39/12, and a trench full of empty cans that offers some shelter.

From here the path along the ridge of the Chornohora massif drops to the southeast for 15 minutes to a broad sheltered shelf, and then climbs more easily for 15 minutes to marker 38 on Breskul (1,911m); again it dips for 10 minutes to no 37.5, and climbs for less to no 37 on Pozhezhevska, with a weather station on a shoulder to the left/north and a Lviv University field station below the tree line, and a track north down the Prut valley to the Chornohora Turbaza and the road southeast of Vorokhta. To the right are moraine gullies and shelves with a good spring below. To the east the path swings right/south, passing no 36.1 in a dip after 15 minutes, passing to the left of no 36, heading just east of south across moorland, and climbing to no 35 on Dancer (really) at 1,850m after 20 minutes. From here it drops easily through dwarf bushes and then climbs to the south, with a trench to the left to protect you from falling over the edge; after 10 minutes you reach no 34, and continue southwest and then south, with some rocky outcrops on the moor.

After 15 minutes you reach marker 33, on Turkul (1,933m), with the remains of a border post near the top; from here the path swings slightly to the left, dropping fairly steeply east-southeast and meeting a pony track from the right after 10 minutes, just before marker 32. This dips among moraine ridges which offer some shelter, and continues to the east, passing below no 31 after 15 minutes; to the right is Lake Nesamoveta (or Brebiniescul), which is gradually becoming a bog but is still an attractive camping spot. The path climbs easily, reaching no 30 after 20 minutes, then dropping southeast and soon climbing steadily again to no 28.15, after 15 minutes more; again you are on moorland with avalanche slopes to the left. Marker 28.7, just a couple of minutes further on, is the summit of Rebra (2,001m, just north of the main ridge), but the hill is virtually level, with barbed wire scattered around. Hutin Tomnatyk (2,018m) is just to the right/southwest of the path along the ridge between markers 27 and 28; it takes almost half an hour to reach no 26.4 on an obvious outcrop. The path then passes to the right of no 26 (after 5 minutes) and after 10 more reaches Brebiniescul (2,035m) at no 25, where there are drystone walls and a poor spring.

From here a path drops down to the right, but you should keep to the left/east across a broad grassy slope to reach some better springs and then climb to no 24.1 just east of a crag; here there is barbed wire along the edge, and again one suspects it is there mainly to stop the guards from falling over the edge. Marker 23.5 is on another outcrop, 35 minutes from Brebiniescul, and no 20.5 an hour further; all along this stretch there is an easy pony track generally to the right/southwest of the ridge, and a sheep track along the ridge itself, passing Munchel (1,999m, at marker 23) and Dzembronya (1,877m, at no 21). Then the path swings left above a cliff to no 20 and drops briefly to no 19.5 after 10 minutes before climbing quite steeply to no 19 after 8 minutes. From here it follows the ridge down to the southeast and then climbs more gradually with a final scramble to marker 18 after 15 minutes.

Continuing east of south you will join a cart track from the left after no 17.8 and climb easily and then steeply, for 30 minutes in all, to reach the huge former Franco-Polish astronomical observatory that looms out of the mist like some medieval castle on Pip Ivan (2,022m, at marker 16). This was destroyed in the Second World War and there are plans to restore it, but these are unlikely ever to come to anything. Between the wars the Polish, Czechoslovak and Romanian borders met here, but now the border of the Transcarpathia and Ivano-Frankivsk oblasts meets the Romanian border 10km south at Stoh (1,653m); there is another Pip Ivan (1,940m) on the present border to the west.

Beyond here you run into the military zone along the Romanian border; you could easily find a way down the White Tisa valley to the west to Bogdan and Rakhiv, but a quicker way down is to return to marker 18 and follow the cart track to the north. After 10 minutes this drops away to the left from a saddle, to take a slightly roundabout route to the village of Berestechko in the Dzembronya valley; the more direct path carries on to Smotrych (1,896m) 15 minutes to the northeast, and then drops away to the left below the summit crag. It is intermittent at first but then clearer as it drops into dwarf pine; after 30 minutes it passes over a rocky outcrop with views into the steep-sided valley, and after 15 minutes more enters a brief belt of spruce. Below this are steep fields, with the first buildings after 10 minutes; there is a good track on along a ridge, reaching the village in the valley in 40 minutes. To start the hike from here, go through a gate with five post boxes opposite a wooden bridge to the north bank, just above a turning place with an odd square stone shrine, unusual in this area where everything is made of wood.

To hike this whole route you will have to camp or bivouac for one night; alternatively you could do a day-trip up Petros and Hoverla from Lazeshchina.

Moving on

From here it is 4km down the dirt road to the Cherniy (Black) Cheremosh valley, where there is a Polish-style bus shelter; at 0800 I caught a very full bus from Burkut and Zelenaya, to the south, to Kosiv. The nearest town is **Verkhovina** (known as Zhabie, from the Ukrainian for frog, until 1962), which dates back at least to 1424 and was the base of the legendary 18th Century *haiduc* (outlaw) Olexa Dolbuş, succeeded by Vasili Baiurak and Ivan Boichuk. In 1919 it was handed to Poland, but in 1920 there was a revolt for unification with Ukraine, which came in 1939. Ivan Franko came here most summers before the First World War, and there is a Franko museum, a bad Turbaza by the river and a couple of ski-drags. There are marked paths into the lower hills to the north and east, which are the main grazing grounds of the Huţul shepherds, and on to Kosiv and Vizhnitsa; these are shown on leaflets such as *Po Kosivshchina*, to be bought in kiosks here. When Bernard Newman cycled through this area, it reminded him of Wales and the Black Forest, with broad open valleys, forest, little gorges and 'stretches of real majesty'.

YASINYA TO UST-CHORNA

Continuing westwards from Yasinya (see previous section), there is a road, of which the central section is virtually impassable by cars, to the forestry town of Ust-Chorna in the Teresva valley. There is a route, strongly recommended by Nick Crane, westwards from Yasinya to Bliznitsya (1,881m) and along the Svidovets massif to Ust-Chorna; I describe a parallel route to the north of the road, following the former Polish border (now the border of Zacarpatskaya oblast) along the watershed. This is the first stage of the Yasinya-Volovets route described in the excellent *Po Lesist'im Karpatam* (Through the Forest Carpathians) booklet, with 1:50,000 maps, much the best you're ever likely to find here. You shouldn't try this hike without this, and even so navigation can be difficult. This is not an easy hike, particularly in bad weather, and you are unlikely to meet anyone else; it requires at least one night camping.

Hiking directions

This route starts at the Yablonitski pass, just north of Yasinya and Lazeshchina, on the road to Yaremcha; the railway loops around slightly to the east, but you could pick up the ridge route by heading west from the Voronenka halt, just north of the summit tunnel. At the pass is the Hotel Burkut (meaning mineral spring, and not to be confused with the

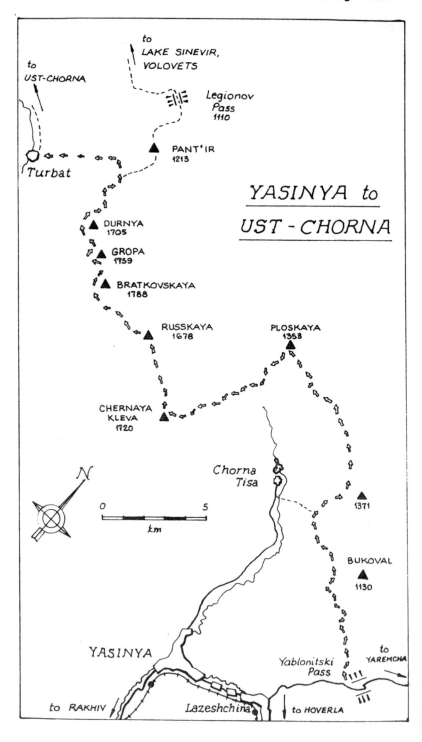

village of Burkut east of Hoverla), where I stayed in a suite without hot water, curtains or a light in the bedroom for 150 coupons (having initially been asked for US$5). Most vehicles stop here for a break, there are stalls selling painted eggs, carved wooden pipes and pipe racks, and a war memorial dated September 24 1944.

Go up the steps opposite the hotel and find the first border marker (number 12/2) opposite a statue hidden in the trees; from here on these concrete pillars are going to be your main guide, and to begin with even these are few and far between, although for the first hour or so your aim should be to keep the woods on your left and fields on your right. Pass a few wooden houses in something like the Zakopane vernacular style, and go up a dirt road, which degenerates into a farm track; after 15 minutes you should pass some chalets, amd then take the lower track below the summit of a hill to the right to reach a gate in 10 minutes. The track continues curving right around a small valley, past a good covered spring, and after 13 minutes turns left just before a farm yard, to climb through fields for 5 minutes to a stile. Continuing to the northwest you soon rejoin a track and in 5 minutes reach a better one and continue with beech and spruce on both sides, following the ridge mainly northwestwards. After about 12 minutes you round the head of a narrow valley to the right and start to climb to the right for 12 minutes to reach the summit marked in the booklet as 1063.8m, with forestry marker 33.

From here the path goes down steeply to the left/northwest and after about 10 minutes runs along a narrow ridge with views to the right before climbing very steeply for 15 minutes past a field. The path turns left from the summit (although the booklet shows a short-cut below to the left) and follows the ridge, with old trenches and foxholes, although it's hard not to stray off it. Again this swings to the right around the head of a valley and after roughly 40 minutes reaches a lookout at the hill marked as 1068m; continuing north of west, you should keep left at a junction after one minute, climbing briefly to the west then dropping and climbing (with a lot of fallen trees) to the north-northwest for 10 minutes to border marker 12/5, with foxholes below it. The overgrown path continues to the west for 5 minutes largely on the level to marker 13, just below a summit; it drops steeply just north of west, climbs after 5 minutes more to marker 13/5 and continues along a level ridge, passing to the right/north of a hilltop in a logged area, with views of mountains ahead and to the north. After 20 minutes there is a slight rise to a forestry marker before the path drops to the right/northwest past marker 15/1, climbs northwest for 10 minutes, then drops with the ridge past markers 16/4 and 16/5 for 10 minutes more before climbing steepish northwest for 5 minutes to marker 17.

From here a path runs back to the southwest, dropping down to the road just east of Chernaya Tisa, from where there are five buses a day back to Yasinya and Rakhiv. The main path follows the ridge north, level and a hellish climb through (or to the right of) fallen spruce to reach marker 18 (a junction with another path from the left) after half an hour. From here it is easier for 15 minutes until you leave the woods and climb steeply into a połonina or long thin hilltop meadow; there is no need to climb to the summit of 1,370.6m, as you can easily cut across to the left to pass a spring and join the ridge to the north, with spruce to the right and the połonina to the left, passing just to the right of the 1,354.9m peak after 15 minutes. Another 15 minutes brings you to marker 22 on top of another hill, and 17 minutes more to marker 22.7 where you re-enter the spruce and go down just north of west before climbing to marker 23 at 1,309.5m after 5 minutes.

The path follows the ridge and the border markers up and down and largely northwestwards without any problems, passing marker 25 in 35 minutes and reaching the Ploskaya połonina in five minutes more: *ploshcha* means level, which is the last thing this meadow is. Although the route shown in the booklet goes straight over this very steep 1,352.6m hill and then turns very sharply back to the south, I skirted around its south side on sheep tracks to use a good spring beyond the sheepfold, and camped at the far end, 25 minutes from leaving the trees and about 8 hours gross from the start. To the north you can see the eastern end of the Gorgany, the wildest and least accessible area of the Ukrainian Carpathians, hard sandstone peaks cut by valleys up to 1,000m deep and culminating in the peaks of Syvula (1,836m) and Grofa (1,748m).

The path continues steeply southwards down from marker 28 into beechwoods, perhaps the slipperiest surface known to man when muddy; however after less than 10 minutes you can climb in spruce to reach marker 29 at 1,133m in 5 minutes and swing left to follow an easy ridge southeast. You climb to marker 30 after 25 minutes and swing right to head southwest between young spruce on the left and older trees on the right, reaching marker 31 in 8 minutes. The path continues along the ridge, mostly climbing, reaching marker 32/4 (1,173m) after 25 minutes, continuing, still in the trees, on a narrow stony ridge, and turning right/just west of south at marker 33 after 20 minutes.

After this the path begins to slog more steadily upwards, reaching marker 34 in 40 minutes and turning left 10 minutes later on to an equally steep minor ridge; after marker 34/6 it swings left (east of south) as the slope eases and the spruce begins to open out, reaching the tree line in 25 minutes. A minor path continues to the southwest, rising very gradually, for 20 minutes to marker 35; this is Chernaya Kleva (1,719.5m), unfortunately not a połonina but a similarly shaped hill almost totally choked with dwarf pine. It is easy to get totally lost here, as the path can often only be followed at ground level; it took me about 45 minutes to reach marker 37, from where the path improves slightly as it heads west and then climbs slightly to the southwest past marker 39 (1,612.2m). The path soon swings northwest, still improving, and crosses a path about an hour from marker 37 before plunging back into dwarf pine; it climbs steeply, with a cliff to the right, to reach Russkaya (1,677.7m) at marker 42 after 40 minutes.

The path swings left along a level open ridge and climbs to marker 43 after 12 minutes, where it swings right to the right of dwarf pine and climbs on to reach marker 44 in 20 minutes. There is a pole here to prove that it is Bratkovskaya (1,788.1m), the highest point of this route. The path drops to the north and rises after 15 minutes to marker 45 (1,728.5m), where it turns very sharply to the left, continuing on the level before climbing over a bit of scree to marker 46 on Gropa (1,758.7m). Four minutes further on it crosses a path before stone walls at marker 46/4 and continues easily before rising to marker 49 on Durnya (The Fool, 1,704.6m) 35 minutes further on. From here it drops steadily through dwarf pine and then along a long grassy ridge between spruce woods, finally entering them after 40 minutes at marker 52, where there is a fireplace, although I don't think there is a spring nearby.

The path swings right and drops steeply north off the ridge (although another path continues along the ridge, which would take you more directly to Ust-Chorna) for 30 minutes; here the path to the right becomes a forestry track dropping east (with a good stream) to Bistritsa and Nadvornaya, while the path to Volovets turns left off these to continue northwards through 'primeval forests'. However I turned left around fallen spruce trees on to a very good path running along the west side of the ridge, crossing minor streams and after 30 minutes a bigger one as it curves away to the west around the head of the logging railway at 970.5m. It rises slightly to a spruce plantation and then a junction from the right after 8 minutes. A good path continues to the left, crossing a cleared pass and dropping southeast into young spruce, before zigging around streams and ravines and crossing a fire break after almost 40 minutes. The path continues to drop very easily, with steeper paths crossing it, and after 45 minutes emerges at a tree with a red cross by a house above a good footbridge.

Across the stream is the village of Turbat, a minor logging settlement on the track from Yasinya; just above the confluence you can cross the Brusturyanka river by the bridge of the forestry railway to reach the muddy track. This follows the left bank of the river northwest for 4km to Ust-Turbat where other forestry lines come in from valleys to the north, and then 10km southwest through the long village of Lopychov to **Ust-Chorna** (once Königsfeld) at 526m. The forestry railway is still active, with small diesel engines rather than steam.

This is the centre of the local tourist and forestry industries, first recorded in 1714; the Turbasa is a modern alpine-style block to the north of the village on the road northwest to Russkaya Mokraya and Komsomolsk, either a sharp left turn at the village limits sign, or by a track from a well before the curve in the road to a stile and a path up. When I was there in 1992 it was fine, although as expected there were no curtains or hot water, but by 1993 I gather it was in a much worse state. By the railway depot on the left bank is a small open air logging museum, with a few carvings and some old equipment, and a 303-year old spruce log. The village stretches a long way south along the Teresva valley, usually just one house deep; shops, a restaurant and a church are about 1km south, with a bus stop and timetable which seemed to be largely fictional; there should be a bus at 0600 to Uzhgorod, and a dozen from Komsomolsk to Tyachev, as well as a couple to Lopychov.

Moving on

The road from Yasinya to Ust-Chorna is almost impassable, but the road west from Ust-Chorna and Komsomolsk to Kolochava is worse; however you could walk the 10km fairly easily to move on to Lake Sinevir (next section).

The road south follows the Teresva valley for 50km (past the 18th Century wooden church of Neresnitsya) to the town of Teresva on the River Tisa, the Romanian border, and buses continue west to **Tyachev** (Tecsö to its many Hungarian inhabitants). Here the railway station is a block north of the bus station, both east of the centre; trains run from Solotvino to Chop and Lviv, and buses to Uzhgorod (up to 14 a day, by various routes), Yasinya, Kolomea, Chernivts'i, and Lviv.

Hust, 25km west of Tyachev and junction of the road to Mizhgor'ya and Lake Sinevir, was briefly capital of the autonomous Carpatho-Ukraine from November of 1938; it is not an especially attractive town, but is a useful transport node. In addition to the Chop-Solotvino trains, there are up to two dozen buses a day to Uzhgorod, as well as about eight to Mukachevo, Rakhiv, Ivano-Frankivsk and Svalyava, and a couple to Lviv, Volovets, Kolochava and Chernovts'i. In addition to the through buses to Lviv and Ivano-Frankivsk, there are eight others to Mizhgor'ya (from towns such as Rakhiv and Vinogradiv). As usual in Transcarpathia, long-distance buses on the main roads are more reliable; the few buses scheduled to run to Ust-Chorna and Lake Sinevir are less likely to actually turn up.

For accommodation you should head north for 10 minutes up vul Slivova, off the main road (vul Ivano Franko) by rail sidings 10 minutes east of the rail and bus stations; there is a basic hotel on the right before some industrial wasteland, with the modern Narcis Turbaza opposite it in front of a volcanic plug. The hotel will suggest that you stay at the Turbaza, but if this is full they charge R60 for a room, only lockable from the inside, with no hot water and horrible toilets.

From the stations buses 1 and 2 go west along the main road to cross a bridge into the horse cart-free zone of the town centre, where there is a restaurant, cafés, another hotel, and some unattractive churches (one with a 15th Century tower). However some of the surrounding villages, such as Sokirnitza, Krainikovo, Alexandrovka and Danilovo, boast superb wooden churches in the style of those to the south in Maramureş, with single tall thrusting spires, sometimes surrounded by four small 'witch's hats'.

LAKE SINEVIR

Lake Sinevir is somewhat tritely described as 'the pearl of the Carpathians' (hardly the only one!), but to tell the truth it's almost the only obvious beauty spot or tourist honeypot in the Ukrainian Carpathians (there are waterfalls elsewhere, but they are all disappointing), and it fails to live up to many of the claims made of it. It is close to the route following the old border markers along the watershed, and on the variant (a Yasinya-Volovets itinerary) described in the *Po Lesist'im Karpatam* (Through the Forest Carpathians) booklet, as well as on the rather optimistic cycling itinerary shown in another leaflet; only serious mountain-bikers should try this.

If you are not already on one of these routes, the easiest approach to Lake Sinevir is by bus, but as usual in Transcarpathia, this is in no way predictable or reliable. There should be buses direct from Hust, but these were not running when I was there in 1992. Even from Mizhgor'ya, served by buses from Hust to Lviv and Ivano-Frankivsk, you may have to take one of the 12 daily local buses for Kolochava (where there is an 18th Century wooden church with a massive belfry) as far as Sinevir.

Mizhgor'ya (Okörmezö to Hungarians) is a small village with three Turbazas (two to the south and one at the northern limits) as well as shops and cafés; the bus station is 200m east of the centre on vul Gorkego, opposite the market, and there are two churches, one behind the other, to the north opposite the post and telephone office.

Sinevir is an attractive linear village with wooden houses with verandahs in the style of Maramureş (to the south in Romania), fanned weatherboards, and crucifixes under semicircular covers of corrugated iron in the front gardens. From the junction to the lake (about 13km north) at the north end of the village it is over 2km south to the church, main bus stop and a few small shops. You may have to wait some considerable time to get a lift or a bus up towards the lake, but there are now some private rooms available at the start of this road. In Sinevir Polana, spread out along the valley road north, there are more great vernacular buildings, and in principle an old Uniate church and a museum of logging and rafting, up a side valley to the east. The bus stops in any case almost 3km short of the Turbaza, from where it is about 2km west to the lake itself, up a easy road.

Although the Turbaza has been kept a decent distance away, the lake itself is hardly untouched by human hands; there is a forestry hut, used by student groups, and well-made paths, railings and viewing platforms around the lake, as well as lots of large picnic shelters in which you could bivouac. On the far side is an unfinished natural history museum, behind big wooden statues of Sin and Vir, the couple after whom the lake is named. Vir was a shepherd who drowned, and Sin was so blue that she created the lake with her tears (*sini* means blue, though I don't think the pun works in Ukrainian); in boring fact the lake was formed (at 972m altitude) by a 'tongue landslide' about 10,000 years ago, blocking a stream which now makes its way through this natural dam.

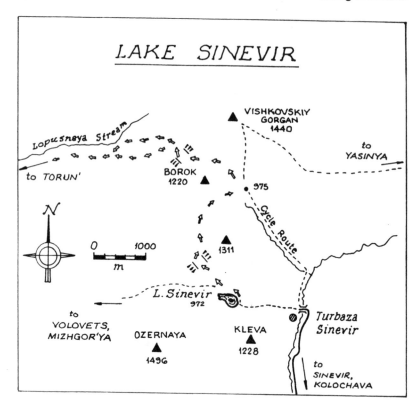

The surrounding area of sedimentary Flysch mountains was planted with monoculture spruce by the Austrians in the late 19th Century; much was cleared immediately after the Second World War to deny cover to the UPA fighters, but more recently 1,000ha of timber was destroyed in a great storm in 1989. Sinevir is now the centrepiece of a large National Park, otherwise almost unaffected by tourism, though not by logging.

Hiking directions

The Yasinya-Volovets route reaches the Turbaza from the north and then turns right/west up the road to the lake, continuing southwestwards from its far end towards Mizhgor'ya via the Kamenka polonina (1,579m). The route I took here, however, was a fairly unsuccessful attempt to rejoin the border markings northwest to Torun', on the main road north from Mizhgor'ya.

Appropriately the path from the Turbaza and past the forestry house is marked with blue stripes; this climbs above the lakeside path at a very steady easy gradient to reach a pass in 25 minutes. The path to the left leads to a meadow with fine views over the lake and a *hizha* or shepherd's hut, and then to the Yasinya-Volovets route; continuing up to the right the path climbs through young spruce, now following yellow stripe markings. After 5 minutes this drops to a very rough forestry road across a logged area, which is clearly no longer fit for cycles, whatever the leaflet says. Cyclists should return from the lake to the Turbaza and follow the next valley to the north. My path follows a streambed down for half an hour to meet (at a point marked as 975.4m in the Yasinya-Volovets booklet) the route east to Yasinya, and various other streams doubling as forestry tracks. It turns left and follows unorthodox blue markings northwest, up a rocky forestry track, forking left at a hut after 20 minutes. After 5 minutes turn right in a lovely meadow, briefly following yellow stripes again, and after 7 minutes dropping through spruce and fir, turn left down a **very** steep and rough forestry track (probably in fact the one that turned right at the hut). This was blocked at one point by a landslide when I came this way, but soon becomes less steep, and, as it descends into beech wood, less rough as well.

After 20 minutes a better track follows the Lopusnaya stream in from the right, and this may well be the correct route for cyclists to take; the yellow stripe route in fact continues across my steep track at the top and climbs through spruce for 10 minutes to meet the former border markers in a logged area where all painted route markings are now hopelessly lost; to reach the Torun' pass on foot you should follow the border markers west, and the cycle route to Torun' should follow a track down to the left.

Passing two foresters' shelters, the track extricates itself from the streambed, and after 35 minutes reaches the first fields, taking a bridge to the left bank after 15 minutes; it gradually becomes more built-up, although the houses are not as attractive as those at Sinevir Polana, and

after 45 minutes reaches the main road in Torun' (596m), just south of
two small churches.

   From here Mizhgor'ya is 17km south and Dolina 55km north, over the
Torun' (or Vishkivs'kiy) pass 9km north. There is a hotel in the small
village of Vishkiv, just beyond the pass and before another, lower, pass.
From Dolina (a centre of the oil and salt industries, with a better hotel)
you can continue by train or bus east to Ivano-Frankivsk or west to Lviv.

VOLOVETS TO MIZHGOR'YA

The highest peak in the Bieszczady is Stoy (1,679m), in the Borzhava
połonina just southeast of Volovets; it is in fact just off the main ridge
and crowned with military radomes, so the highest point on this route
(the final part of the *Po Lesist'im Karpatam* booklet, in reverse) is
1,598m, c1,120m above Volovets and 1,200m above Mizhgor'ya. This
is one of the very best połoninas, a long narrow ridge with wide views
above the forests. The flora is even richer than in the Polish Bieszczady
(see page 3), and the upper forest boundary is higher here at about
1,200m, with more conifers. Unless you come down to one of the
villages to the north, you will need to camp for one night.

   Volovets (Volócz in Hungarian) lies on the main rail line from Lviv to
Chop; trains from Moscow to Prague and Budapest stop there, as well
as those from Kyiv and Lviv to Uzhgorod and locals between Mukachevo
and Labochne. Buses run twice daily to Hust, and six times to
Mizhgor'ya, from just south of the station, across the tracks from a dull
church with Hungarian and Cyrillic gravestones. The Turbaza Plai is right
by the rail station, and the very simple Hotel Plai is at ul Pushkina 21, to
the right up the main street (past a reasonable restaurant), right at the
roundabout and right again by the *univermag*. Plai is a local word for a
mountain track, as well as the name of the peak south of the town.

Hiking directions

From the railway station in Volovets I walked south for 12 minutes on
the road and turned left (at a building marked PTU 117) on a path
between a stream and a playing field to pass under the railway. A decent
tractor track climbs into the spruce; after 10 minutes I turned right on to
a steeper path climbing just east of south. After about 10 minutes more
the path crosses a good path from the right, passes forestry marker
K/3/9 and then zigs right, left on to a forestry track, and then right on
to a packed stone path which continues around the hill to the left, up a
ridge to the south, and up a steep gully. After 20 minutes I turned right
on a good level path and then continued to climb without a clear path to
a small glade, where I turned slightly right/southwest up the ridge to
reach the tree line after 30 minutes; the route marked in the *Po Lesist'im
Karpatam* booklet is clearly to the west of my route, and there is a
shepherds' route to the east from the side valley southeast from

Volovets.

From here the route follows the ridge south-southeast past Plai with its weather station to Velikiy Verkh (High Peak), where it crosses the side ridge to Stoy with its radar station. It takes 10 minutes to reach the first hilltop of the połonina (1,219m), and then almost 20 minutes on sheep tracks through dwarf pine to pass Tomnatuk (1,347m). After 10 minutes I joined a track from the right which drops in 5 minutes to a saddle where it swings left to a two-storey block on the tree line; keeping to the ridge I reached the weather station on Plai (1,334m) in 20 minutes, although the route should in fact pass well to the west of the summit. From here a track descends northeast to Volovets or the village of Hukliv'iy, where there is an 18th Century wooden church.

Carrying on along the ridge, the path starts to climb steadily after 18 minutes, reaching the rocks marked as 1,330m on the map after 30 minutes and the survey marker on Velikiy Verkh (1,598m) after 15 more. The actual junction is 4 minutes further, just west of south: be sure to turn left/southeast here rather than heading into the military zone. After 10 minutes the path bends slightly left, then in 10 more bends right and soon starts to climb a bit, passing some muddy ponds after 20 minutes, just before Hemba (1,491m). This and two more minor tops are passed to the right/west before also passing on a good sheep track to the right of Magura-Zhude (1,517m) after 30 minutes. Zhude (Jew) is a small spur to the west with huts on it at about 1,200m, and there is also a good view down a steep valley to the north.

There is a good spring 5 minutes beyond the peak; continuing along the ridge for 10 minutes the path then joins a cart track from Zhude which passes to the right of two minor hilltops and then goes virtually to the top of Hrab (Hornbeam, 1,378m) after 17 minutes before turning right to some other huts. The hiking route turns left after a couple of minutes to continue south-southeast along a very faint path down and along the ridge or just to its right. Soon it climbs steadily through large areas of dwarf bushes, reaching Kuchera Kruhlaya (1,241m) 40 minutes from Hrab. The ridge turns right and drops for 8 minutes, swinging left again as it is joined from the right by a cart track just before a hilltop of 1,213m. The ridge is now very narrow and only just above the trees, and there are plenty of sheep, although both dogs and shepherds are far friendlier than further east.

The track forks left to the villages below just after Kruhlaya (1,209m, with another survey marker), 15 minutes from Kuchera Kruhlaya, while the hiking route continues southeast on the ridge, now just a narrow clearing between the woods, finally turning slightly right into beech trees after 15 minutes on top of Zvor (1,115m). It continues along the ridge passing through one or two clearings, forking right to reach another clearing on Opolonok (1,171m) in 15 minutes; the path goes along the left hand side of the clearing, drops southeast on a sheep track and then more steeply south just inside the beech wood, and then more easily in meadow to join a tractor track from the left. The path continues to the south east to reach the Prislop pass (938m) in 20 minutes (*prislop* being

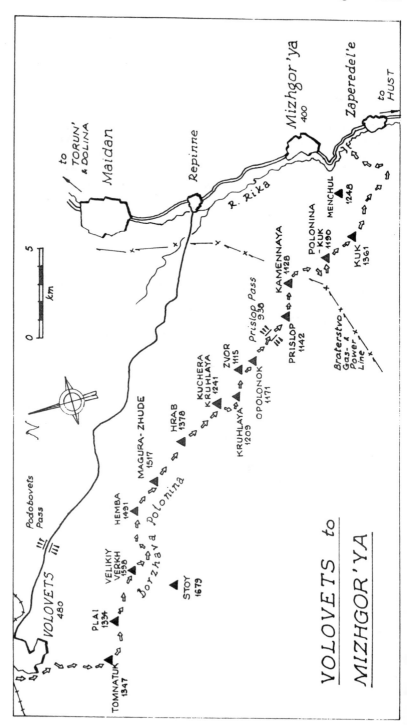

VOLOVETS to MIZHGOR'YA

a standard Slav word for any pass).

The track forks left to go down to a stream, while I continued to the right and up the left side of a clearing and into beech to reach the clearing on top of Prislop (1,142m) in 18 minutes. From here the path continues along the ridge of a small połonina for 20 minutes to Kamennaya (1,128m) where it turns right/south on to a major dirt road, above the *Braterstvo* (Fraternity) gas pipe, from the left (not marked in the booklet). After 5 minutes this passes under power lines and drops steeply for 10 minutes; there is also logging to the left, so this is a blighted area to get away from as fast as possible. The path climbs past a disused sheep fold to reach the ridge in 10 minutes and turn sharp left on to another large track where the gas pipe heads west to rejoin the power line.

It takes 10 minutes to reach the final połonina on this route at 1,190m; one track follows the left/east side of the clearing and then follows a side ridge left to Menchul (1,248m) and down to Mizhgor'ya; Nick Crane was taken this way and had no problems. The other track goes around the west side of the first hilltop via a spring, while the route in the booklet continues along the left side of the połonina, and then climbs, reaching the peak of 1,313m in 30 minutes and the summit of Kuk (1,361m) 10 minutes later.

Here the hiking route is supposed to turn sharp left and drop straight down into the woods, where there is no sign at all of a path; you should follow either the route via Menchul, or continue along the połonina (via the track on its west side) and on along the ridge before turning left down the valley between two hills 811m and 920m high. The route straight down through the trees is heavily overgrown, and following the stream is no better once you reach it; there were also lots of tiny non-biting midges. It took me half an hour to reach a stream coming in from the left and soon found an overgrown cart track, with amazing wild strawberries. After 15 minutes the track climbed to the right into beech to cut off a bend, crossing a forestry track and then following one down to the left and turning right just before the stream after 10 minutes.

Here I emerged into a meadow at a ford; after 5 minutes I reached the point marked as 514m in the booklet and then crossed to the right bank, and 7 minutes later back to the left. After 15 minutes more I reached a bridge (after a disused house) where the alternative route from the połonina comes in. Five minutes further on the track crosses to the right bank and then 15 minutes later reaches the confluence with the Rika river (at 398m); 2 minutes to the right/southeast, downstream, the route onwards to Sinevir and Yasinya continues along the right bank avoiding Mizhgor'ya, but I crossed a bridge to climb to the road. It takes 25 minutes along the road to the left/north to reach the limits of Mizhgor'ya, with shingle-roofed wooden houses. The first Turbaza, the Karpati, with the KSS office, is on the right after 10 minutes, and the next, the Mizhgor'ya, 50m up a track to the right after another 10 minutes, each with a bus stop just to the north. The town centre is another 15 minutes on — see page 353.

Moving on

There are regular buses back to Volovets along the road to the north of
the połonina (as well as on the Hust-Dolina road), but if you have time
there are (or were) interesting wooden Łemk churches in many of the
villages along the way. The first village is Soimy, with an early 20th
Century church, then at Repinne, the junction to Dolina, where a new
hotel or Turbaza is under construction, there is the 18th Century church
of St Demetrius, and in Maidan, a few kilometres up the Dolina road,
there is the 18th Century church of St Nicholas, with a huge arcaded
porch. Izki also has an 18th Century church, and just beyond in Pilipets
the church of the Nativity of the Virgin, also late 18th Century, certainly
survives, in the style of the Maramureş churches but with a shingled
onion dome instead of a spire. The road crosses the Podobovets pass to
return to Volovets *raion*, and 1.5km further on at about km 113.5 is the
Smerechik motel. Another 3.5km further the road meets the railway from
Lviv and soon reaches Volovets, 40km from Mizhgor'ya.

THE SKOLE BESKID

This area lies on the main Chop-Lviv rail line north of Volovets, in the
southern part of Lviv *oblast*, but there is as yet little tourist infrastructure
outside the small ski resorts of the Opir valley.

This has always been one of the main routes through the Carpathians;
in addition to the railway, built by the Hapsburgs in 1900, before the
other lines through the Ukrainian Carpathians, this was also the route of
the Tatars to Hungary, and the name Opir means resistance. In 1260 the
river was blocked and many Tatars drowned at Tuchlya, as narrated by
Ivan Franko and commemorated by a memorial on a hill to the west.
Later, in the Second World War, there was a slave labour camp at
Sviatoslav, south of Skole, whose prisoners were liberated by the UPA
in July 1943. In mid 1944 Red partisans moved into the Maidan forests,
between Skole and Turka, and the UPA moved from its training base on
Lopata (1,211m), west of the Opir river, to drive them out, while the
Hungarian regiment garrisoning the area kept clear by tacit agreement.

The Stuzhitsa reserve (2,542ha, with a 2,500ha buffer zone to be
added soon), to the west near the Polish border, is to be part of the
Bieszczady International Biosphere Reserve being created by Ukraine,
Poland and Slovakia. This includes primeval Carpathian beech forest,
mostly beech and fir, with mountain elm in places, and sycamore on
damp stony slopes and alder in the połoninas, and over 500 species of
vascular plants, notably orchids.

Skole is a ski resort with plenty of Turbazas and rest homes owned by
Lviv factories in which you will generally be able to stay without
problems. Further south up the Opir valley is Slavskoe ('Famous'), also
a skiing centre with Turbazas, cafés, and an old wooden belfry by a
newer church; the centre is to the left and then the right from the
station.

Hiking directions

As I was literally on the last day of my visa I was only able to take a half-day walk from Slavskoe (580m) west to Trostyan, a hill of 1,232m which offers superb views of the various parallel but very different ranges in this area.

From the station we crossed the foot bridge, climbed the bank and turned left on to a track beyond a house for about 10 minutes before turning right under the low and noisy *Mir* power lines. After a quarter hour or so we forked left and dropped (keeping right) and then climbed to a side ridge. From here you should keep right up the main track then left around the head of the valley for half an hour, rising to the Prislop pass (990m), on the north side of Trostyan, where a track comes in from a winter-only Turbaza and ski-drags to the left. The track continues westwards over the ridge, but you should turn left and climb steeply for 25 minutes through meadows with superb wild flowers.

The summit is disfigured with A-frame shelters and skiing installations, but the views are good, especially from the top of a ski-lift pylon. To the north are the Skibove Carpathians, long level parallel ridges, notably the Skibe Skole and the Skibe Parashka (1,271m), like the waves put up by a plough (the meaning of *skibe*), and beyond them the Bereh or Shore Carpathians, smaller hills up to about 800m on which the waves seem to break. East-northeast is Magura (1,362m), which simply means hill, at the western end of the Gorgany range, a long line of hills separated by deep valleys. Trostyan itself is part of a chain of hills that continues southeast along the *oblast* border and just north of Lake Sinevir. On the skyline to the south is the Borzhava połonina (1,679m, visible over the pass through the watershed of the Verchovina), the route east from Volovets described in the previous section, a typically high narrow ridge rising above the trees on its flanks.

Returning, you can go back to the Prislop pass and then follow the dirt road down to the southeast, past the Turbaza, and curving left to reach the railway a kilometre or so south of the station after about 50 minutes.

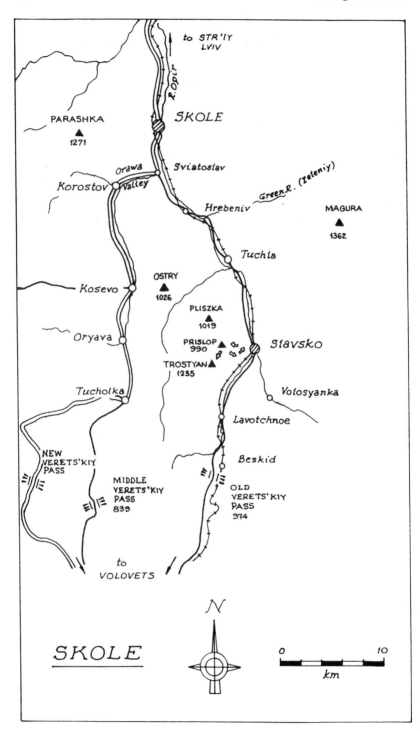

to STR'IY
LVIV

R. Opir

SKOLE

PARASHKA
▲
1271

Orawa
Valley

Korostov ○

Sviatoslav

Green R. (Zeleniy)

Hrebeniv

MAGURA
▲
1362

Tuchla

Kosevo ○

OSTRY
▲
1026

PLISZKA
▲
1019

PRISLOP ▲
990

Stavsko

TROSTYAN▲
1235

Oryava ○

Volosyanka

Tucholka ○

Lavotchnoe

NEW
VERETS'KIY
PASS

Beskid

MIDDLE
VERETS'KIY
PASS
839

OLD
VERETS'KIY
PASS
974

to
VOLOVETS

N

SKOLE

0   10
km

CYRILLIC VERSIONS OF PLACE NAMES

Zacarpatska	Закарпатська	Ust-Chorna	Усть-Чорна
Chop	Чоп	Yablonitski	перевал
Uzhgorod	Ужгород	pass	Яблоницкий
Mukachevo	Мукачеве	Lake Sinevir	Озеро
Hust	Хуст		Синевир
Tyachev	Тячів	Kolochava	Колочава
Rakhiv	Рахів	Borzhava	Полонина
Volovets	Воловецъ	polonina	Боржава
Mizhgor'ya	Міжгіръя	Ternopil	Тернопіл
Slavssko	Славсъко	Vinnitsa	Винница
Skole	Сколе	Rivno	Рівно
Lviv	Лъвів	Kyiv	Київ
Ivano-Frankivsk	Ивано-	Kharkhiv	Хархів
	Франковск	Zaporozhye	Запорожъе
Dolina	Доліна	Odessa	Одесса
Chernovts'i	Черновцъи	Kherson	Херсон
Kosiv	Косів	Krim (Crimea)	Крим
Verkhovina	Верховіна	Simferopil	Симферопіл
Kolomea	Коломъія	Angarski pass	перевал
Deliatyn	Делятин		Анѓарски
Yaremcha	Яремча	Alushta	Алушта
Yasinya	Ясіня	Gurzuf	Ѓурзуф
Lazeshchina	Лазещина	Yalta	Ялта
Hoverla	Говерла	Livadia	Ливадия
Petros	Петрос	Alupka	Алупка
Chornohora	Чорногора	Bakhchisarai	Бахчисараи
Pip Ivan	Піп Иван	Sevastopil	Севастопіл

364

Are you **suffering** from *Wanderlust* ?

then subscribe to the only
magazine that guarantees **no cure** !
Wanderlust is *the* magazine for the
independent-minded traveller, covering
destinations near and far, plus features on health,
news, food, horror tales and eco-tourism, as well
as offers, competitions and a hell of a lot more.

Phone or FAX Wanderlust Magazine for special
subscription deals on (0753) 620426, or write to
Wanderlust, PO Box 1832, Windsor, Berks. SL4 5YG, U.K.

Spas in Poland and Ukraine

The mineral springs of southern Poland were well known long before the theory of hydropathy was formalised by the Silesian Dr Vincenty Prysznic in the early 19th Century, but it was only in the last century that they became an institution of Central European life. Nowadays there are many spas (*Zdrój*), all over the country, which have been as popular under communism as they were under the Hapsburgs and Germans. Most are set in delightful countryside, usually with an attractive park, and in addition to the waters themselves they offer treatment with bilberry, sorrel, and salt baths for illnesses of the respiratory, circulatory and digestive systems, anaemia and nervous systems.

The most visitable spa is probably Krynica, and others mentioned in the text are Duszniki-Zdrój, Lądek-Zdrój, Rabka, Szczawnica, and Ustroń, while most of the resorts in the hills can also be counted as climatic resorts, where people go for fresh air and gentle exercise.

It is easy enough to get accommodation in the spas, as there is now space to spare and most spas have an office, often doubling as a tourist information office, to match visitors with rooms in sanatoria, pensions and private homes. All the main travel companies offer packages, with or without treatment, with prices ranging from £17 to £33 per day for a single room, full board, or £30 to £74 double, or about £200 for the full three-weeks recommended stay.

Saline springs include Rabka, Ciechocinek and Inowrocław, acidulous springs include Krynica, Kudowa, Polanica, Duszniki, and Nałęczów, and hot springs Antałówka hill in Zakopane, Cieplice-Zdrój, Ciechocinek and Lądek Zdrój.

Of those spas within easy reach of the hill areas described in this book, these are the most interesting:
Cieplice-Zdrój (a southern suburb of Jelenia-Góra, page 212) dates from 1281, and now deals with locomotive, rheumatic, urinary and paediatric ailments. In addition there is a 'radon inhalatorium' in a former uranium mine south of Kowary, treating respiratory ailments.
Duszniki-Zdrój (see page 206) deals with circulatory, digestive, respiratory and gynaecological complaints, while the neighbouring spas of Kudowa and Polanica deal respectively with circulatory, metabolic and internal secretory disorders, and with locomotive, rheumatic and gynaecological disorders.
Iwonicz-Zdrój (see page 121) is one of the bigger spas (for locomotive, rheumatic, digestive and respiratory complaints) and the 5km road from the Krosno-Sanok road is lined with wooden Łemk houses, giving way to a 16th Century wooden church, pensions and the 18th century park.
Krynica (page 134) is perhaps the most pleasant and interesting spa, handling digestive, urinary, circulatory and metabolic disorders, female ailments, and internal secretion problems. It is also a centre for tourism in the Beskid Sądecki and for winter sports, with some skiing, mainly cross-country, a sledge route, and an artificial ice ring.
Lądek-Zdrój (page 202) treats skin diseases, as well as the standard rheumatic, locomotive and circulatory problems.
Rabka (page 144) deals with rheumatic, respiratory, endocrine and metabolic disorders in children, and also with circulatory and respiratory disorders in adults.
Rymanów-Zdrój is similar to the neighbouring Iwonicz, but is quieter, with no accommodation other than private rooms. It was a centre of Hasidic Jewry and has an 18th Century Jewish cemetery, and a ruined synagogue.
Szczawnica (page 141) deals with respiratory diseases and asthma.

Świeradów-Zdrój (page 219) deals with locomotive, circulatory, rheumatic, gynaecological and nervous disorders.

Ustroń (page 186) treats orthopedic, rheumatic and respiratory problems.

Finally there is the *Klinga* sanatorium in the Wieliczka salt mine, near Kraków (page 102), treating respiratory ailments, bronchial asthma, and allergic catarrh.

More information can be obtained from the Department of Health Policy in the Ministry of Health and Social Welfare, ul Miodowa 15 in Warsaw (tel 6358 636).

There are about 500 mineral springs in Ukraine, mostly on the flanks of the Carpathians. The spas are, thanks to Hapsburg rule of Galicia, part of the same Germanic tradition, and the German word *Kurort* (**курорт**, literally cure place) is used for a spa in Ukrainian and Russian; they were equally part of the Soviet system for regulating workers' playtime. The one I know best is Morshin, just southeast of the military base of Str'iy, which was first recorded in 1482 as a salt mine and was opened as a spa in 1878 by its owner Boniface Stiller, booming in the 1920s and 1930s. Now there are seven sanatoria, used by 70,000 visitors a year in the Soviet era, most notably the Marble Palace built in 1930s Art Deco style, where Brezhnev apparently stayed in 1933 (when it was ruled by Poland) and a military sanatorium for senior officers. The buvette, where you can push buttons to get measured blends of water from the different springs, is known as the 'mushroom', and there is also treatment with peat muds from Morshin and from Obolonia (near Dolina). The various waters are analysed and prescribed in far more detail than in Poland, to give the familiar veneer of Soviet rationalism. There is one hotel-restaurant, and boating lakes with pedaloes and a closed menagerie. Life in the sanatoria is strictly timetabled from 0715 to 2300, and the entrances are all guarded by white-coated women to keep an eye on goings-on.

Other major spas in the Carpathians are Truskavets, near Borislav and Drohob'ich southwest of Str'iy (not to be confused with the skiing centre of Tissovets, further south), which is similar to Morshin but bigger, and Svalyava, source of one of the main bottled waters available in Ukraine. On the Black Sea, notably around Odessa, it is also common to coat oneself in healing muds in beachside sanatoria. However the main spas of the former Soviet Union are in the foothills of the Caucasus, above all the Mineralniye Vody (Mineral Waters) complex around Pyatigorsk, while the Black Sea resorts of Sochi and Sukhumi rival Yalta as seaside resorts.

Explore Eastern Europe with Bradt

If you enjoy hiking and want to explore the less crowded areas of eastern Europe we have three books for you:

Guide to Czechoslovakia by Simon Hayman
As can be seen from the title, this guide was published before the break up of Czechoslovakia, but it contains detailed hiking information on the mountains just over the border from Poland, and referred to in this guide. The emphasis here is on hiking, but other outdoor sports are covered: skiing, river-running, caving. There are also sight-seeing suggestions for the many towns and villages of historic interest, and information on accommodation, public transport, self-drive ... everything the adventurous traveller needs for a trouble-free stay.

Eastern Europe by Rail by Rob Dodson
Everything the rail traveller needs to know, from where to stay near the station to suggested itineraries making the most of your rail pass. Each major town has a plan showing station facilities such as luggage lockers, information desks and restaurants, to avoid unpleasant surprises.

* * *

We also publish a wide range of guides to other continents with the emphasis on natural history, hiking and backpacking. We also have an expanding rail guide series. Send for a catalogue:

Bradt Publications, 41 Nortoft Road, Chalfont St Peter, Bucks SL9 OLA. Tel: 0494 873478.

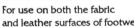

INDEX

Notes